BAHAMAS

MARIAH LAINE MOYLE

Grand Cay
Lake Okeechobee
Grand Bahama
Little Abaco Island
The Abacos
West End
West Palm Beach
UNITED STATES
Freeport
Marsh Harbor
Abacos
Moores Island
FLORIDA
Fort Lauderdale
Sandy Point
Great Harbour Cay
Bimini
Miami
Berry Islands
Gun Cay
North Cat Cay
Spanish Wells
Harbour Island
Gregory Town
New Providence
Nichols Town
NASSAU
Governor's Harbor
Eleuthera
Rock Sound
Straits of Florida
Andros
Exuma Cays
Congo Town
Staniel Cay
The Exumas
Great Bahama Bank
Santa Clara
CUBA
Camaguey
0
50 mi
0
50 km
1
95
75
41
1

BAHAMAS

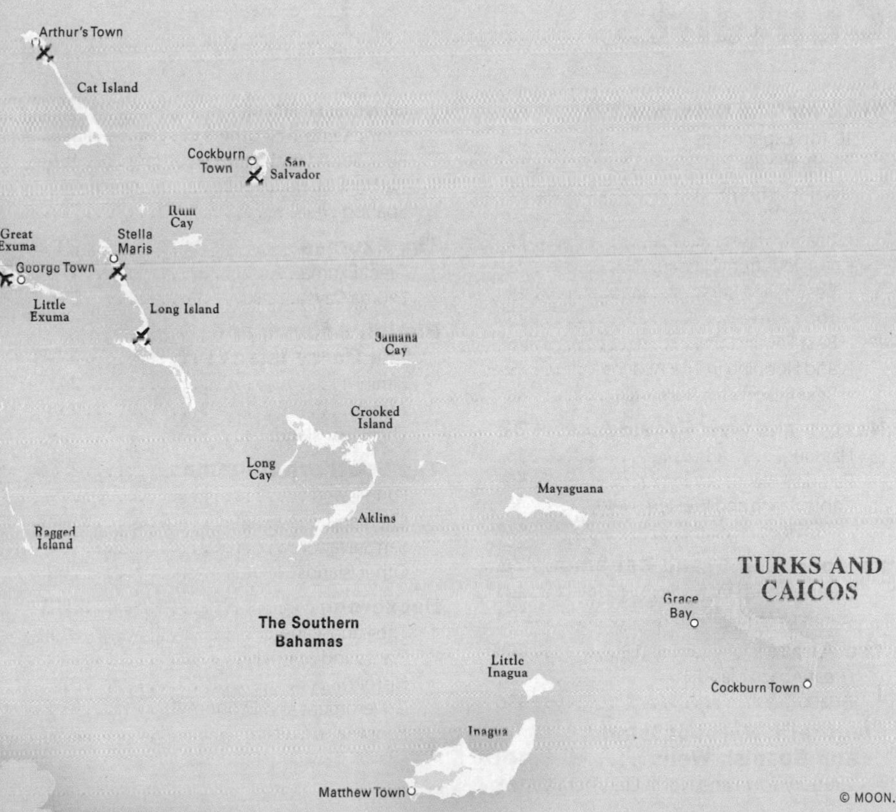
ATLANTIC
OCEAN
THE BAHAMAS
Arthur's Town
Cat Island
Cockburn Town
San Salvador
Rum Cay
Great Exuma
Stella Maris
George Town
Little Exuma
Long Island
Samana Cay
Crooked Island
Long Cay
Mayaguana
Acklins
Ragged Island
TURKS AND CAICOS
Grace Bay
The Southern Bahamas
Little Inagua
Cockburn Town
Inagua
Matthew Town
© MOON.COM

Contents

DISCOVER

The Bahamas

After spending a year on the International Space Station, astronaut Scott Kelly described The Bahamas as "the most beautiful place from space." Come down a little closer to earth and you will find these 700 islands do not disappoint. From hot-pink bougainvillea and chartreuse coco plum to the sea's vast ranges of turquoise, teal, and cobalt, it seems Mother Nature gave herself permission to express her wild artistic side in this corner of the world.

Immerse yourself even deeper and you will find that the islands' vibrancy extends far beyond the beauty of the landscape, expanding into the hearts of the people themselves. From the lively metropolis of Nassau to sleepy settlements throughout the Out Islands, you will be welcomed with genuine smiles and open arms. Whichever region you choose as your destination, be prepared to be captivated with friendly locals who are bursting with pride to show you their island and all its splendor.

Nassau and Paradise Island are by far the most visited, offering endless options: a balance of beaches, nightlife, casinos, shopping, and recreation. But you haven't experienced the "real" Bahamas until venturing into the Out Islands, each one with its own unique offerings.

Unwind and escape. Dive in and let loose. Immerse and explore. The deeper you venture into The Bahamas, the more rewarding your experience will be.

Clockwise from top left: the swimming pigs of The Exumas; a sailboat in The Abacos; yellow crowned night heron at the Rand Nature Center in Grand Bahama; pink flamingos at Ardastra Gardens, Nassau; reef shark.

10 TOP EXPERIENCES

1 **Blue Holes:** Explore the mysterious depths of The Bahamas' blue holes. **Dean's Blue Hole** (page 280) and those found in **Andros** (page 261) are some of the best.

2 Discover Atlantis: The world-famous ocean-themed resort, situated on the stunning Cabbage Beach, has endless entertainment for the whole family (page 60).

3 Cross the Glass Window Bridge: At Eleuthera's narrowest point, a single-lane bridge divides staggeringly contrasting bodies of water—the deep, dark blue Atlantic and pale turquoise of the Caribbean side (page 166).

4 Take in the Views at Elbow Cay Reef Lighthouse: This iconic candy cane striped lighthouse in The Abacos is one of the last manually operated lighthouses in the world (page 136).

<<<

5 Meet the Swimming Pigs: Visitors from all over the world come to the remote Exumas islands to see these national celebrities up close (page 226).

>>>

6 Diving & Snorkeling: Explore shipwrecks, sculptures, coral reefs—and dive with sharks (page 86 and page 261)!

<<<

7 **Junkanoo:** This boisterous cultural parade features intricate handmade costumes, music, and dancing (page 49).

8 Feast at the Fish Fry: A few simple huts serving traditional Bahamian food make for a tasty, authentic experience. Stop by **Arawak Cay** (page 52) and **Smith's Point** (page 94).

9 Hike to The Hermitage at Mt. Alvernia: At 206 feet, Mt. Alvernia on Cat Island is the highest point in The Bahamas. Climb all the stairs to the top and admire Father Jermone's work (page 292).

10 Fishing: The Bahamas are a dream for fishing enthusiasts. The Abacos (page 118) and Andros (page 260) are the most popular destinations.

Planning Your Trip

Where to Go

Nassau and New Providence

Visitors flock to the capital city of Nassau and neighboring Paradise Island for **nightlife, restaurants, beaches,** and **water sports.** Downtown Nassau offers a variety of options for the foodies and history buffs and hosts the largest celebration of **Junkanoo** in the country. **Atlantis** on **Paradise Island** draws families for its endless options of activities. The **Fish Fry at Arawak Cay** offers visitors a taste of Bahamian culture and cuisine. The quieter area of **Cable Beach** and **Western New Providence** have fantastic upscale dining options, boutique hotels, and less crowded beaches.

Freeport and Grand Bahama

Although **Freeport,** the capital city of **Grand Bahama,** may have seen the height of its glory in the 1960s when it was home to a booming financial sector and shipping ports, it still maintains a lively feel, with **shopping, nightlife,** and world-class **dining.** Where it differs from Nassau is the chance to escape into nature just outside the city. Visit **Lucayan National Park** and the **Rand Nature Centre** for brushes with wildlife, and **UNEXSO Dive Center** for spectacular snorkeling and diving.

The Abacos

A haven for **sailing** and **sportfishing,** The Abacos attract regular visitors from neighboring Florida for an easy **weekend getaway. Marsh Harbour,** the third-largest city in the country, offers all the amenities but with the trademark laid-back barefoot Abacos vibe. Use Marsh Harbour as a starting point to explore the many **islands**

Pineapple Air offers flights to select Out Islands from Nassau.

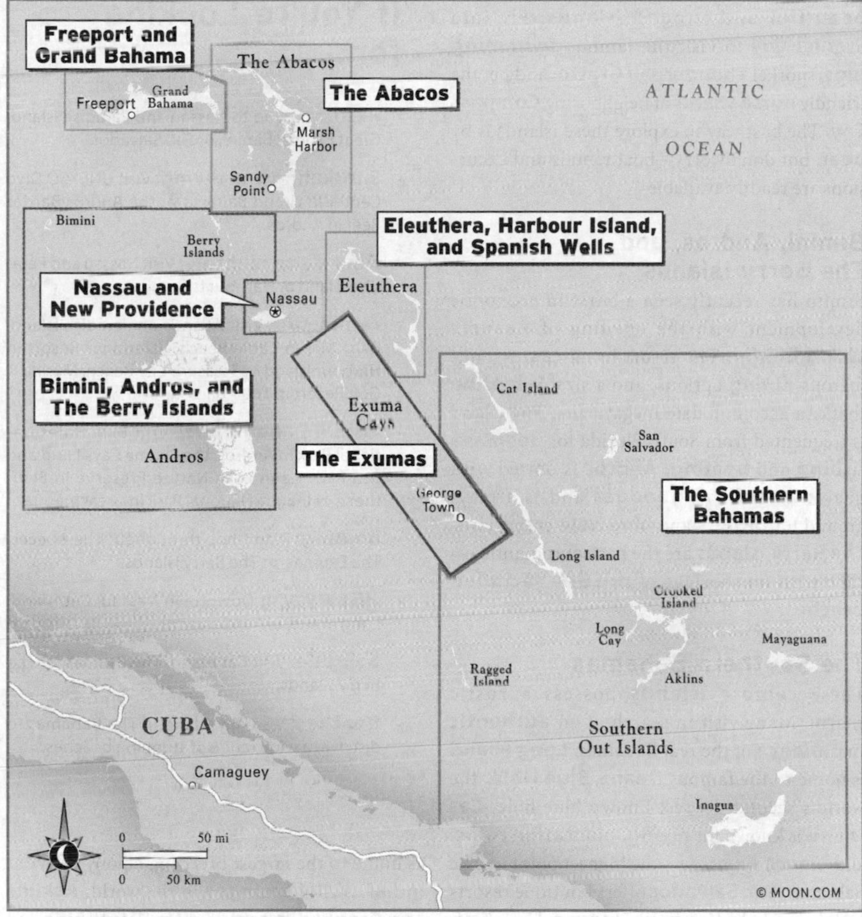

and **cays** throughout the Abacos, each with their own unique charm. Visit the **Elbow Cay Reef Lighthouse** in colonial **Hope Town**, or bask in the sunshine on **Treasure Cay Beach.**

Eleuthera, Harbour Island, and Spanish Wells

Eleuthera is one of the most accessible Out Islands, but feels a world away. The 110-mile-long island has **charming settlements, stunning rock formations,** and **remote beaches.** Skip over to **Harbour Island** by water taxi and cruise around in a golf cart while admiring the colorful **colonial cottages** along the picturesque harbor. Dine at some of the best restaurants in the country, overlooking the three-mile stretch of **Pink Sands Beach.** Traditionally a fishing village, **Spanish Wells** has seen major growth in recent years. New restaurants, bars, and boutique accommodations make Spanish Wells the new "in" place to vacation.

The Exumas

If you want to get lost in the beauty of The Bahamas, head to The Exumas. Use **George Town** as your starting point to explore these

beautiful and rugged islands. Fly into **Staniel Cay** to visit the famous **swimming pigs,** snorkel **Thunderball Grotto,** and pet the friendly **nurse sharks** at neighboring **Compass Cay.** The best way to explore these islands is by **boat,** but don't worry—boat rentals and excursions are readily available.

Bimini, Andros, and The Berry Islands

Bimini has recently seen a burst in economic development with the opening of **Resorts World Bimini.** The resort has a **casino,** numerous **dining** options, and a sizable **marina** that can accommodate megayachts. The island is frequented from South Florida for **deep-sea fishing** and **boating. Andros** is dotted with quaint **bonefishing lodges** and is a playground for **birders** and **blue hole** enthusiasts. **The Berry Islands** are the perfect romantic escape with no shortage of **pristine secluded beaches.**

The Southern Bahamas

These **remote islands** possess a rustic charm. Many visit in search of an **authentic experience** of the real Bahamas. **Long Island** is home to the famous **Dean's Blue Hole,** the world's second-deepest known blue hole. **Cat Island** is known for **diving, plantation ruins,** and **Mount Alvernia**—the highest point in The Bahamas. **San Salvador** offers boutique resorts and an untouched landscape. **Inagua** draws birders for its wide variety of birdlife, most notably as home to the largest breeding colony of **West Indian pink flamingos** in the world. **Acklins and Crooked Islands** are for flats fishing and those looking to get well off the tourist track.

If You're Looking for . . .

- **Resorts:** Head to Nassau and Paradise Island, Great Exuma, Bimini, or San Salvador.
- **Snorkeling and diving:** Visit UNEXSO Dive Center in Grand Bahama or the Andros Barrier Reef in Andros.
- **Dining and nightlife:** Visit Nassau and Paradise Island or Harbour Island.
- **Family fun:** Visit Atlantis on Paradise Island, Baha Mar in Cable Beach, Valentines Resort in Harbour Island or Treasure Cay Beach, Marina & Golf Resort in The Abacos.
- **Wildlife and nature:** Visit Blue Holes National Park in Andros, the Exuma Cays Land and Sea Park, Leon Levy Nature Preserve in Eleuthera, or Inagua National Park in Great Inagua.
- **Boating:** Island-hop throughout The Abacos, The Exumas, or The Berry Islands.
- **History:** Visit Downtown Nassau, Cat Island, Long Island, or San Salvador.
- **Solitude:** Visit Cat Island, The Exumas, or The Berry Islands.
- **Beaches:** Visit any island in The Bahamas to discover a wide range of stunning beaches.

Know Before You Go

When to Go

High Season kicks off around U.S. Thanksgiving at the end of November and winds down in May. The major spikes in visitors are at **Christmas** and **New Year's, Easter** weekend, and academic **spring breaks** throughout **March** and **April.** Hotels are at their peak rates during this time and are typically fully booked well in advance, especially in popular Out Island destinations, so advance planning is necessary for these times. If you plan on visiting an Out Island at any time of the year, pay attention to events such as regattas, Junkanoo, and long holiday weekends. It may be a challenge to book a domestic flight at the last minute, and room rates are at their peak.

Low Season starts in **August** when children head back to school. The heat intensifies, and the threat of hurricanes loom. Most **hotels** and **restaurants shut down** in the Out Islands from September until around U.S. Thanksgiving at the end of November. Rates are at their lowest during this time, if you can find a hotel that's open. Nassau doesn't see much of a change in rates, however, since travelers continue visiting year-round. It's an extremely quiet time of year in the islands, so be prepared for relaxation. If you seek diversions, this may not be the best time to visit.

The **winter** months can be cool, as there are regularly passing cold fronts pushing down from the northeast, but it's still warmer than most northern locales, so most visitors don't mind. Keep in mind the farther north you are, such as The Abacos, the cooler it may be. Farther south is significantly less affected by northern weather and can be much warmer, as in The Exumas and Long Island.

The **summer** months bring heat, stifling humidity, and the wet season, with daily afternoon **thunderstorms,** but if you prefer beaches all to yourself and warmer ocean temperatures, you'll enjoy a trip during the summer, when you can find the most discounted rates at hotels, if they are open.

Peak **hurricane season** is **August-September,** and in recent years there have also been several major hurricanes as late as October. When planning your vacation and looking for diversions, be aware that many resorts, restaurants, and gift shops in the Out Islands shut down August-November. You may find a resort or two open, but not a lot of restaurant options except for local cuisine.

As with most subtropical island locales, come prepared for coastal weather. Full rain regalia may not be necessary, but a long-sleeved shirt or shawl is helpful year round.

Passports and Visas

A valid **passport** and a **return ticket** are required. If you arrive commercially but plan on departing the country via boat or private flight, you may need to provide written documentation, a flight plan, or a cruising permit upon airport check-in or Bahamas immigration; otherwise you may be required to book a return ticket on the spot.

Visas are not required for U.S. and Canadian passport holders. If visiting for any purpose other than tourism, you must contact the Department of Immigration prior to your visit.

Vaccinations

There are no vaccination requirements when traveling from the United States or Canada; however, if you are traveling from or have visited a country with a risk of yellow fever, you need to present a vaccination certificate. This includes a long list of countries in Africa and South America. Check with the Department of Immigration or at www.bahamas.gov.bs for an updated list.

Transportation

Lynden Pindling International Airport (NAS) in Nassau is easily accessible by direct flights from major cities in the United States and Canada, as well as London, several Caribbean islands, and Central America. Visitors fly into the international airport or by charter to one of the two private airports in Nassau.

For **interisland travel,** each island region has one or more airports with daily commercial flights from Nassau on Bahamasair and other domestic airlines. A number of the Out Islands can be accessed by direct flights from Miami and Fort Lauderdale as well. Locals often travel by **Mail Boat** (freight boats serving all of the Out Islands), and some islands also have the **Bahamas Fast Ferry** from downtown Nassau.

Nassau is easily navigated by catching a **taxi** or **jitney** (bus). The jitney is by far the most economical mode of transit, and many locals use these buses for their daily commutes. I wouldn't recommend using them if you are in any hurry, but it's a great option for seeing a bit of scenery. Jitneys are privately owned and don't operate on a fixed schedule.

There are international **rental car** companies in Nassau, but be prepared to drive on the left side of the road. Many Out Islands have **golf-cart rentals,** which is a fun way to explore smaller communities like Harbour Island, Hope Town, and Treasure Cay. To explore the larger islands, organize a car rental prior to your visit.

Finding Your Way Without Addresses

The Bahamas has never officially set up a street address system, which makes it impossible to put an address into a GPS system to navigate quickly and painlessly. As with many things in the islands, this instills a sense of a challenge; some are willing to tackle it, others, not so much. Most addresses are simply a street name, unless it is within a shopping center or a newer development where building numbers were established by the developer. If it's a long street, like West Bay Street, which runs for miles along the northern perimeter of New Providence, you may have trouble finding places without reference points, and it typically comes down to using known geographical features. It's much easier for residents who are familiar with local landmarks.

To establish reference points, it is customary to call a retail store. If you are looking for a particular hardware store on Shirley Street, for example, you could call them and be directed to go past a specific gas station on the left, and the store will be three buildings down on the right, next to the laundromat. But this means you have to also know where the gas station and the laundromat are. If you are looking for a residential address and are asking a local, you may end up with directions like, "Drive past the fig tree, go up the hill until you see a Potcake in the yard, and turn left there. Then you'll see some men playing dominoes in the shade. The house is on the left." To avoid this confusion, you may be best suited to just grab a taxi. If you're adventurous and willing to take the time to explore, this may make for a tale to tell.

If you decide to venture out on the open roads, a great free app for international travel is Maps.me. Download the Bahamas map while you are still on Wi-Fi. The app uses your phone's GPS, giving you the ability to track your movements while you are on the road, offline, and without using cellular data.

Nassau Getaway

If you decide to stay in Nassau, there is plenty to keep you entertained. Most of the resorts are on loungeable beaches, but this itinerary will keep you busy.

Day 1

Plan for a mid-morning arrival at Lynden Pindling International Airport in Nassau and head downtown. You'll be weary from travel, so grab a cold beverage and a bite at the **Fish Fry at Arawak Cay** and settle in for a warm Bahamian welcome. After lunch, head to **The British Colonial Hilton Nassau** hotel to drop off your bags and get your bearings. Take a stroll along the **wharf** at **Woodes Rodgers Walk** and **Bay Street,** stopping along the way to pick up souvenirs. Make your way down to **Junkanoo Beach** and saddle up to the **Tiki Bikini** bar, watching the tourists play beach volleyball. For dinner, head over to **Lukka Kairi** for upscale Bahamian flavors and live music.

Day 2

Rise early and grab a coffee at **Biggity.** Make your way to **Christ Church Cathedral** to meet up for the three-hour **Tru Bahamian Food Tour,** where you'll sample Bahamian cuisine at a local restaurant. You'll get a great overview of the history of downtown Nassau and its prominent historical buildings. After your tour, make your way to **Queen's Staircase,** walking up the impressive hand-carved stairs through limestone rock up to **Fort Fincastle.** If you're getting weary of the heat, pop into the **Pirates of Nassau Museum** as a cool reprieve and learn about the history of pirates in Nassau. Make dinner reservations at **Graycliff Restaurant** if you're feeling like splurging for formal dining. After dinner, catch live music at **Pirate Republic Brewing Company** and sample draft beer at the country's only craft brewery.

Day 3

There's still more to discover downtown, so visit

Cable Beach

Sweet Retreats

There are gorgeous boutique hotels and resorts throughout the islands that may take a little longer to get to but are worth it. Enjoy top-notch service, fresh seafood, and locally sourced fruits and vegetables. These are a few top picks off the beaten path.

- **Highbourne Cay, Exumas:** In the Northern Exumas is an island that attracts yachters to its first-class marina, and is only accessible by boat, seaplane, or helicopter. On land you'll find breezy, nautically inspired cottages and cabanas.
- **Lumina Point, Exumas:** This eco-friendly off-the-grid resort on Stocking Island sits on a gorgeous crescent stretch of beach tucked among native vegetation. All of its nature-inspired cottage rooms overlook calm Elizabeth Harbour.
- **Kamalame Cay, North Andros:** This barrier island just off mainland Andros is a luxurious private retreat among coconut palms, with a three-mile stretch of white-sand beach.
- **Tiamo, South Andros:** Only accessible by boat or seaplane, this resort offers activities to keep you occupied.
- **Carriearl, Berry Islands:** On less visited Great Harbour Cay in the Berry Islands is a tiny four room boutique hotel, run by a wonderful British couple and fondly known as the "Britz Ritz."
- **Fernandez Bay, Cat Island:** The clubhouse and guest suites are built of stone and thatch roofing, giving a sense of the rich history of Cat Island. Enjoy sunsets from your veranda overlooking one of the top beaches in The Bahamas.

the pathway leading up to Carriearl

- **Cape Eleuthera Resort, Eleuthera:** On the southern end of Eleuthera, far removed from anywhere, this resort offers modern accommodations and is a top destination for offshore fishing.
- **Club Med, San Salvador:** Getting here is relatively painless, but getting away from it all is even easier. Club Med offers all of the activities and dining options you could possibly want, and visitors can be as social or as solitary as they'd like.

a few more cultural sights. Spend the morning lounging on the beach and then get to **Fort Charlotte** by 11:30am to watch the firing of the cannons, or take a guided tour. Make your way to nearby **Ardastra Gardens, Zoo & Conservation Centre** to watch the **Marching Flamingos** for the afternoon show. Don't miss the **National Art Gallery of The Bahamas.** Then walk next door for a tour of **John Watling's Distillery,** with artisanal rum and vodka. After your tour, hang out for a few drinks at the **Red Turtle Tavern.**

Day 4

Cool off at **Atlantis**'s 141-acre **Aquaventure** waterslide park. Cross the bridge from downtown Nassau onto **Paradise Island** to explore this

cannons at Fort Charlotte

vacation wonderland. Purchase an Atlantis day pass or check in to one of the Atlantis hotels for full access. The water park alone can entertain, but there's plenty more to explore. Cruise around **The Dig,** and the many **outdoor lagoons.** Settle under the shade of a lounger on the gorgeous stretch of **Cabbage Beach.** There are plenty of options for lunch and dinner throughout Atlantis and the Marina Village. Consider booking a table at **Bahamian Club.** If you'd like to venture a few minutes away, make reservations at **Dune** at **The Ocean Club.**

With More Time

DAY 5

For the adventure seekers head out with **Stuart Cove** for an exhilarating **shark dive, reef dive, or wreck dive.** Alternately, book a day trip with **Powerboat Adventures** and head out to **The Exumas** to safely watch a shark feed from the beach, pet stingrays, and feed iguanas. When you return to the dock, grab drinks and a casual dinner at nearby **Green Parrot Hurricane Hole.**

DAY 6

Make your way toward **Cable Beach** and check into the **Baha Mar** resort. Settle into one of the seven **tropical pools,** or make your way to the **BEACH Sanctuary,** where you can get into the water with nurse sharks, rays, and turtles. Check into the luxurious **ESPA** for a signature spa treatment, or book a round at the **Royal Blue** golf course and meet at the **Royal Blue Tavern** for happy hour. For evening diversions, try your luck at the **Casino,** or keep an eye out for events at the Current, where you can view works by local artists. Reservations are recommended at most restaurants, so plan ahead.

DAY 7

Hire a taxi or rent a car for the day to explore **Western New Providence.** Start out by grabbing a coffee with a view at **Louis and Steen's New Orleans Coffeehouse,** and dine on one of their pastries or a Cajun breakfast wrap. Head to **Clifton Heritage Park** and take a tour of the plantation ruins, rent snorkel gear and dive the **underwater sculpture garden.** Afterward, follow interpretative trails which lead to the beautiful bay at **Jaws Beach.** Later, head over to catch the sunset at nearby **Compass Point** and snack on wings and nachos, chased with a cold beer.

DAY 8

You're close to the airport, so plan this as your departure day.

Best Beaches

Every beach you come across in The Bahamas is the most beautiful beach you've ever seen. Here are a few favorites.

NASSAU AND PARADISE ISLAND

- **Cabbage Beach, Paradise Island:** One of the country's top beaches can be found right in front of bustling Atlantis resort on Paradise Island. For the quieter side, check into The Ocean Club.

THE ABACOS

- **Treasure Cay Beach:** Regularly winning awards as a top Caribbean beach destination, this sandy-bottom shoreline is a perfect family destination.
- **Tahiti Beach:** Best accessed by boat, Tahiti Beach on Elbow Cay is reminiscent of the South Pacific. At low tide it's truly spectacular.
- **Guana Cay Beach:** A slight bluff edged with colorful vegetation lines this spectacular beach on the ocean side of Guana Cay.

THE EXUMAS

- **Chat 'N' Chill Beach:** On Stocking Island is a curved sandbar beach marking the entrance to a protected creek, within already protected Elizabeth Harbour. Its namesake bar and restaurant is one of the top hangouts in The Exumas.
- **Tropic of Cancer Beach:** A popular stop-off signifying your entrance into the tropics.

ELEUTHERA, HARBOUR ISLAND, AND SPANISH WELLS

- **Pink Sands Beach, Harbour Island:** Three miles of pale pink sand are dotted with colorful beach umbrellas and edged by boutique hotels and restaurants.

ANDROS, BIMINI, AND THE BERRY ISLANDS

- **Shelling Beach, Berry Islands:** This beach on Great Harbour Cay gets the gold medal for solitude. Lined with seagrass, at low tide the beach turns into a picturesque sandbar.

Cape Santa Maria Beach

SOUTHERN BAHAMAS

- **Cape Santa Maria Beach, Long Island:** Lined with vibrant coconut palms, the lake-calm water glows in tropical blues and greens.
- **Fernandez Bay, Cat Island:** Watch the sunset from a beachside cottage. Sailboats anchor in this protected harbor, and powdery soft white sand slopes into this inviting place for a swim.
- **Guanahani Beach, San Salvador:** On one of the farthest reaches of one of the farthest removed islands in The Bahamas, Guanahani Beach is a top kiting destination due to its protected waters and outlying islands, which provide a gorgeous backdrop.

Excursions from Nassau

The Out Islands of The Bahamas are considered the "real Bahamas." I recommend making an effort to get to the islands, most of which have two flights per day **from Nassau,** making it relatively easy to hop over for a **day trip** or for a quick **overnight.** If you can't decide which Out Islands to explore, consider a sampler of one or several.

A Romantic Escape to The Berry Islands

OVERNIGHT

Spend some alone time with a loved one on beautiful empty beaches. From Nassau, catch the early flight into **Great Harbour Cay.** Pick up a rental car and head north to **Sugar Beach** to explore the **caves** and do some hiking. Stop and pick up fresh conch salad to-go at **Hubo's** on the dock. While you're in town, arrange a boating excursion for the following day at the dock master's office at the **Great Harbour Cay Marina.** Drive to the south end of the island to **Shelling Beach** and **Shark Creek Beach.** Set up camp for the afternoon with a picnic. Check in at **Carriearl Boutique Hotel** and settle in for European hospitality and five-star treatment.

In the morning, meet with your prearranged guide to explore the islands by boat, perhaps to **Hoffmann's Cay Blue Hole.** Plan on doing some **snorkeling,** to look for a wide variety of sealife. Head back to the dock in order to catch your afternoon flight back to Nassau. While you wait for your flight, walk across the street and grab lunch and a cold beverage at the nearby **Beach Club,** right on **Great Harbour Beach.**

Andros for Nature Lovers

OVERNIGHT

Catch the early flight from Nassau into **Fresh Creek (Andros Town).** Get an airport pickup and head to **Small Hope Bay** to arrange your explorations. Start with a **Blue Hole tour,** do an orchid walk, or go birding with a guide. Arrange a guide for a half-day of **bonefishing.** Return to the lodge in the evening for family-style dining.

Shark Creek Beach in Great Harbour Cay

Best Beach Bars

Beach bars are gathering place for locals, seasonal homeowners, boaters, and visitors. From lean-tos to high-end cuisine, these are the ones that serve tasty food and offer that laid-back flip-flop vibe and lively happy hours. Swim attire is acceptable, and there's an option for a cooling dip as needed.

- **Tippy's, Eleuthera:** Just on the outskirts of Governor's Harbour is an open-air bar and restaurant serving fresh, seasonal island cuisine and live music on weekends.
- **Chat 'N' Chill, Exumas:** On a gorgeous sandbar beach, this is a gathering spot for a lively sailboat crowd. Expect a party most days of the week, but Sundays are best, with roasted pig and Bahamian specialties.
- **Tiny's Hurricane Hole, Long Island:** Fitting to its name, it can fit only a few people under the shade of its thatch roof, but you can spread out on the beach under a cabana or in a nearby hammock.
- **Nipper's, Abacos:** Drawing a crowd of salty boaters, Nipper's is a nonstop party every day of the year. It overlooks one of The Bahamas's best beaches.
- **Nirvana, New Providence:** One of Nassau's only true beach bars, Nirvana is right on Love Beach, a great spot to feel as though you're in the Out Islands.
- **The Sand Bar, Spanish Wells:** Newly emerging from being a dry island, Spanish Wells knows how to create a laid-back beach-bar vibe. Overlooking a small bay, sit in the shade of umbrellas while you sip on a signature frozen cocktail.

Nirvana beach bar in New Providence

- **Pete's Pub, Abacos:** Most visitors arrive by sea, and this sandy open-air bar serves tasty fresh fish and cold beer.
- **Banana Bay, Grand Bahama:** On Fortune Beach, a shallow sandbar at low tide provides views for patrons sitting at picnic tables on the shady porch.
- **On Da Beach, Abacos:** On Elbow Cay's stretch of Ocean Beach is an open-air beach bar serving up healthy and fresh seafood delights.

The next morning, don your snorkel and head out to the **Andros Barrier Reef,** the third largest in the world. Take a **scuba course** to get a taste of the underwater world. In the afternoon, take a tour of nearby **Androsia batik factory,** where hand-designed fabrics are made. Get ready for your afternoon flight back to Nassau.

TWO NIGHTS

If you decide to extend your stay, organize an all-day safari to the remote **west side of Andros.** Here you'll see the famous West Indian pink flamingos and a variety of other wildlife. For a cultural tour, visit the Seminole village of **Red Bays** to witness the thriving **basket-weaving** and **woodcarving** traditions. Support the

Top Festivals

- **Junkanoo** (Dec.-Jan.): This positively Bahamian festival pulsates with the rhythm of the people and is the top cultural festival of the year. It is celebrated throughout the islands, but the largest parade is in Nassau.
- **National Family Islands Regatta** (Apr.): The biggest sailing event in the country is hosted in George Town, Exuma, and draws domestic and international crowds.
- **Long Island Regatta** (May-June): Sloops made in Long Island and race against sailboats from around the country at this three-day festival.
- **Eleuthera All That Jazz** (Mar.-Apr.): Attracting international jazz musicians, this festival in Governor's Harbour is the event of the year.
- **Eleuthera Pineapple Festival** (May-June): Celebrating the rich heritage of pineapple agriculture in North Eleuthera, this festival embraces all things pineapple.
- **All Andros Crab Festival** (June): This festival celebrates and honors the importance of the local land crab with crab cuisine and informational booths.

Junkanoo in downtown Nassau

- **Spanish Wells Fishermen's Festival** (July): Recognizes fishing and its contribution to the community of Spanish Wells with a send-off celebration.

community by purchasing their hand made goods as souvenirs.

If you want to splurge for star treatment, book a night at **Kamalame Cay.** Take the short ferry ride from Staniard Creek to this private island just off Andros. Here you can arrange **diving, snorkeling,** and **day trips to a remote cay.** Relax at their **spa** and enjoy dining at the **Great House.** You may be tempted to stay even longer. When you're ready to head back to civilization, arrange with Kamalame Cay to hop a **seaplane** back to Nassau or direct to Fort Lauderdale.

Explore North Eleuthera

DAY 1

Catch the *Bohengy III* from the Bahamas Fast Ferry dock at Potter's Cay and hop off at your first stop, the colonial fishing settlement of **Spanish Wells.** Grab a golf cart for a few hours and explore the community and its beautiful beaches. For lunch, stop in at **The Sand Bar,** also a great spot to take a refreshing swim. Hop on the water taxi and head over to mainland Eleuthera. Organize a taxi or a rental car and head to **Preacher's Cave** to see where the first settlers arrived in The Bahamas and took shelter. Head south on Queen's Highway and stop at the **Glass Window Bridge** to photograph this natural wonder. Check into **The Cove Eleuthera** for the night and enjoy a welcome cocktail at the **Point Bar** overlooking the cliffs and crescent beach and dinner

horses on Pink Sands Beach

in the elegant dining room of the **Freedom Restaurant.**

DAY 2

In the morning head to the restaurant for a smoothie. When you're ready, hop on the road and head south. If you're looking to get in the ocean, stop into **Rebecca's Beach Shop** in Gregory Town and rent surfboards to hit the break at **Surfer's Beach.** If surfing isn't your thing, drive toward **Hatchet Bay** and explore the **grain silos** that line Queen's Highway.

Turn around to head back north to Three Island Dock, where you'll catch a water taxi to **Harbour Island.** When you arrive, rent a golf cart from the dock. Have lunch at the popular **Sip Sip** and get your first glimpse of **Pink Sands Beach.** Hop in your golf cart to explore this colorful colonial town. Check for low tide and stop at **Girl's Bank** to take a photo of the **Lone Tree.** Check into a hotel or rent a storybook cottage in town. For dinner, don your resort wear and feel fabulous at **The Dunmore.** To watch the sunset in a more relaxed environment, make a reservation at **Acquapazza Italian Ristorante** on the harbor. If you're into nightlife, mix a cocktail and cruise around on your golf cart until you find some action. **Gusty's, Beyond the Reef,** and **Daddy D's** will have something going.

In the morning, grab coffee at **Bahamas Coffee Roasters.** Check out boutique shopping and explore art by local artists. For lunch, head over to **Queen Conch** for a fresh conch salad, and enjoy outdoor dining on the harbor. Savor a few more moments on the beach before catching the *Bohengy III* from Harbour Island's Government Dock in the afternoon, and arriving back in Nassau in the evening.

THREE NIGHTS

To extend your stay, head back to mainland Eleuthera and rent a car. Make your way down to **Governor's Harbour** in Central Eleuthera. Check into **Pineapple Fields** and head next door to the **Leon Levy Nature Preserve,** 25 acres of protected forests and mangroves. If you're here on a Friday, plan to head down to **Cupid's Cay** for the **Friday Night Fish Fry** to mingle with locals and seasonal homeowners.

The next day, stop into the **Haynes Library,** the oldest government complex on the island. Stop into **Eleuthera Island Farm** for in-season produce, fresh bread, and local jams and sauces. Plan on lunch at **Tippy's Restaurant** on a gorgeous stretch of Eleuthera beach. Take the afternoon flight from Governor's Harbour back to Nassau.

Escape to The Exumas

FOUR NIGHTS

DAY 1

Depart Nassau on the morning flight to George Town, Great Exuma. Grab a rental car from the airport and make your way south to **Little Exuma,** watching for signs for **Tropic of Cancer Beach** to set out your beach towel and relax. For lunch, head south to **Santanna's,** an open-air bar and restaurant wedged between Queen's Highway and the ocean. On your way back north, stop at the **Rolle Town Tombs,** dating to the 1790s. Settle into your hotel in George Town and then head to the **Fish Fry** in the evening to mingle with the locals.

DAY 2

The next day, make your way into town for breakfast at the **Driftwood Café** and then stop into **Sandpiper Arts & Crafts** for locally made souvenirs. Arrange your transportation over to **Lumina Point,** an off-the-grid eco-resort on **Stocking Island.** Spend the afternoon hiking and exploring the gorgeous **beaches.** Head over to **Chat 'N' Chill** for an afternoon cocktail and swim on the beach, where you'll fit right in with the laid-back boater crowd. If it's a Sunday, the place will be packed for their famous **pig roast.** For a quiet sunset over the harbor, head back to Lumina Point for dinner at **The Beacon.**

DAY 3

Awake for a beach walk in solitude. Arrange with a local charter company for a full-day exploration to **Staniel Cay.** Along the way you'll **snorkel with stingrays** among shallow **coral gardens** and stop at breathtaking **sandbars.** Get dropped off in Staniel Cay and check into the waterfront cottages at the **Staniel Cay Yacht Club.** Grab a tropical drink and dinner at the bar at the Yacht

an organized snorkel excursion in The Exumas

Best Family Fun

Spot wildlife throughout the islands and in the sea. Each island offers boating excursions and day trips to the local sights, with options for fishing and snorkeling. With so many beaches, building sand castles with your little ones is a perfect way to while away the afternoon.

- **Atlantis, Paradise Island:** Swimming pools and waterslides for all ages, aquariums and marine habitat exploration, and an interactive kids adventure club make Atlantis is a top destination for families.
- **Baha Mar, Western New Providence:** Newly opened Baha Mar caters to adults but hasn't forgotten about kids. It offers the Explorer's Club for ages 3-12 with marine encounters, Bahamian art experiences, games, movies, and dancing.
- **Blue Lagoon Island, New Providence area:** Kids and adults alike will enjoy spending the day swimming with dolphins and interacting with the other sea animals.
- **Ardastra Gardens, Nassau:** Wander the gardens and see a variety of plants, birds, and animals. Make sure you're there to watch the Marching Flamingos, and grab a family photo with them. Children will love feeding apples to the colorful lory parrots.
- **Harbour Island:** A great place for families, Harbour Island sees an influx of people with children throughout December, spring break, and Easter holidays. Spend your days on the beach, rent a paddleboard or tandem kayak for the calm harbor, and, for older children, let them explore on their own.
- **Treasure Cay, Abacos:** For beach lovers, check into Treasure Cay Resort, or into a beachfront vacation rental where your little ones can play in the calm water.

a family enjoying a quiet paddle on Harbour Island

Club while you mingle with the boat owners and crews from the marina.

DAY 4

Rise with the sun and rent a small skiff to explore on your own, or opt for a guided tour. Snorkel nearby **Thunderball Grotto** and feed the infamous **swimming pigs at Big Major's Cay.** Stop in for lunch at **Compass Cay** and pet the resident **nurse sharks.** Enjoy one more night in Staniel Cay and fly out directly to Fort Lauderdale or back to Nassau.

WITH MORE TIME

Extend your stay with a night at the private island **Fowl Cay Resort,** with private beaches striking hilltop views. Arrange an adventure into the **Exuma Cays Land and Sea Park** and discover endless miles of undeveloped hiking and diverse sealife. Fly out from nearby Staniel Cay.

Island Hopping in The Abacos

The Abacos has many islands to choose from. Use Marsh Harbour or Treasure Cay as a base, or pick your favorite island and stay a while. Here's an itinerary for those who like to stay on the move.

Day 1

Take the morning flight from Nassau to Marsh Harbour and then hop the mid-morning ferry to **Great Guana Cay.** Rent a golf cart or explore by foot. Book a dive trip with **Dive Guana** to nearby wrecks and reefs. Spend the afternoon at the pool at **Grabbers Bar and Grill,** sip on some cocktails and watch the sunset over the harbor.

Day 2

The next morning, head down to **Guana Cay Beach** and walk its two miles. If it's Sunday, don't miss the famous **Pig Roast at Nipper's,** but plan for lunch here any day, overlooking Guana Cay Beach. Catch the afternoon ferry back to Marsh Harbour and stop for happy hour drinks at **Snappas** and then make your way over to the **Abaco Beach Resort.** Enjoy dinner and live music at the **Pool Bar,** or opt to dress up a bit for dinner and get a table at **Angler's Restaurant.**

Day 3

In the morning, grab coffee at **Bliss Coffee Shop,** people-watch from their street-side porch, and maybe pick up some local artwork before catching the ferry to **Hope Town** on **Elbow Cay** for a wide array of restaurants and boutique shopping. Make your way down to **On Da Beach,** a great spot to soak in views of the ocean and enjoy a tasty fresh fish sandwich. Watch the sunset overlooking the harbor at **Firefly Sunset Resort Bar and Grill.** Check into the **Abaco Inn** and cozy up in a bungalow overlooking the ocean where you can stay close to your room and dine at the **Abaco Inn Restaurant.**

Tahiti Beach on Elbow Cay

Best Resorts for Romance

Swaying palm trees, deserted beaches at sunset, room service, elegant cuisine from international chefs, and luxurious spa treatments are what these resorts offer.

- **Tiamo, Andros:** Feel as though you are getting away from it all as you arrive by boat or seaplane. Watch the sunset from the private beach in front of the Star Light Villa, which also has its own private veranda and private pool.
- **The Cove Eleuthera:** Plan your dream wedding on the beach, or escape for an easily accessible getaway for two. Luxurious suites and villas offer privacy and views.
- **French Leave Resort, Eleuthera:** Enjoy the activity and diversity of Governor's Harbour, and the quiet of your oceanfront room overlooking the sunset side of the island.
- **Cape Santa Maria Resort, Long Island:** Wake up each morning overlooking one of the best beaches in The Bahamas from your private villa or bungalow.
- **Abaco Inn, Abacos:** Cottages overlooking the ocean side on Elbow Cay are private and cozy. Away from town, all the activities of Hope Town are just a short golf-cart ride away.
- **The Ocean Club, Paradise Island:** Dine overlooking Cabbage Beach, say your vows at Versailles Gardens, or head to the spa and indulge in a couple's massage.
- **Kamalame Cay, Andros:** Escape the crowds and choose whether you come into contact with other guests or not. Opt for room service, hide out under your beach cabana, enjoy spa services, or spend a day on a private cay just off Kamalame. For complete exclusivity, arrive and depart via seaplane.
- **The Other Side, Eleuthera:** Glamping at its finest, this eco-chic property offers seven "tents" and "shacks" within close proximity of Harbour Island.

Arrive by seaplane to Tiamo in South Andros.

Day 4

Head to the morning social gathering place at **Hope Town Coffee Shop** and enjoy a coffee and a pastry overlooking the harbor. Wander down the street to the **Wyannie Malone Historical Museum** to learn about local history. Catch a water taxi across the harbor to the **Elbow Cay Reef Lighthouse** and climb to the top. Rent paddleboards from **Abaco Paddleboard** and explore the calm White Sound, or opt for a **surf lesson** on the ocean side. In the afternoon head to **Tahiti Beach,** and grab a snack and drinks from **Thirsty Cuda Bar & Grill,** a boat that's regularly anchored just off the beach. When you're ready for dinner, head back into town and relax into the lively scene at **Cap'n Jacks** on the harbor.

Day 5

Catch the ferry back to the mainland and make your way up to the ferry terminal at Treasure Cay to get to **Green Turtle Cay.** In New Plymouth you'll want to stop into the **Albert Lowe Museum,** in an 1825 Loyalist cottage. Wander down the street and venture into the **Loyalist Memorial Sculpture Garden.** Make your way back north, stopping at beautiful beaches along the way. Grab lunch at **The Tranquil Turtle Beach Bar** at **Bluff House.** After lunch, stop by **Coco Bay** and look for the population of resident turtles. Follow a dirt road along Coco Bay toward usually deserted **North Beach.** Walk around the corner to witness a giant cross stuck in the rocks, erected as a tribute to a life-saving expedition. Have dinner at the **Green Turtle Club Restaurant** and stay for drinks and live music at the **Dollar Bar.** For the best Goombay Smash, head into town and stop at **Miss Emily's Blue Bee Bar.**

Day 6

Catch the ferry back to the mainland and make your way up to **Treasure Cay.** Check into the **Treasure Cay Beach, Marina & Golf Resort** and head down to **Treasure Cay Beach** to stroll its 3.5 breathtaking miles. Grab a bite at **Coco Beach Bar** and spend the afternoon cruising around by golf cart or bicycle. Make reservations at **Treasure Sands Club,** with a farm-to-table experience overlooking Treasure Cay Beach.

Day 7

As you depart Treasure Cay, head north about 10 minutes to **Treasure Cay Blue Hole,** down a long dirt road. Head back to Marsh Harbour to catch the ferry to **Man-O-War Cay,** where you'll discover the rich boatbuilding history at the **Heritage Museum.** Make sure you stop at **Albury's Sail Shop** and watch the women handcraft high-quality canvas creations. You can easily walk the island, and have dinner at **Dock & Dine** and overnight at **Schooner's Landing Ocean Club.**

Day 8

Make your way back to Marsh Harbour and make your way into **Little Harbour,** stopping at **Pete's Pub** for lunch and visiting **Pete Johnston's Art Gallery and Foundry.** Head to the nearby **Abaco Club on Winding Bay** and check in for the evening. Golf on the elevated headlands at the **Abaco Club Golf Course.** Enjoy dinner at **The Cliff House,** an impressive restaurant overlooking Winding Bay.

Day 9

Explore the south end of the island by organizing a tour into **Abaco National Park,** nesting grounds of the **Bahama parrot.** Spend your last night in the quiet community of Schooner Bay at the charming, chic **Sandpiper Inn.** Call ahead to make sure the **Cabana Bar and Grill** on the beach is open, as it will be a highlight of your stay.

Day 10

Make your way up to Marsh Harbour and fly back to Nassau, or take a direct flight to the United States.

Nassau and New Providence

If The Bahamas had an astrological sign, it would most likely be a Gemini. Geminis are depicted as twins, with dual personalities. In the same way, The Bahamas offers two sides: on one hand is the quiet splendor of untouched islands.

On the other is the bustling metropolitan city island of New Providence.

The capital city, Nassau, is the seat of government and center of commerce. Though it's one of the smaller islands, at 21 miles long by 7 miles wide, New Providence is home to 70 percent of the population of this island nation. It's not quite a "city that never sleeps," but compared to the country's sleepy Out Islands, it's fast-paced, lively, boisterous, and expressive. The arts, a thriving culinary scene, and rich history contribute to an overall vibrancy. Festivals litter the calendar, and in any given month you might experience a rum festival, a wine and arts festival, farmers markets, and, if you plan for it, the largest Junkanoo celebration in the country.

New Providence's centralized location within the archipelago plays two roles: protection from the elements of the Gulf Stream and the Atlantic, which envelop either side of the surrounding islands and cays; and ease of accessibility to the remainder of the country. Visitors inevitably pass through Nassau when transiting within the islands.

Historically, downtown Nassau and Paradise Island have been the center of the action. Atlantis is a destination in itself. Many visitors head over the bridge to Paradise Island and stay there for the duration of their trip. Cruise ships dock in Nassau Harbour and funnel thousands of visitors each week into the shopping district of Bay Street. The majority of government, banking, and medical services are also located in downtown Nassau, so on weekdays you will often witness business professionals walking side by side with crowds of tourists. A mix of fine dining, local favorites, cafés, and pubs are dispersed throughout this highly trafficked area.

Head west on Bay Street and you'll ease into Cable Beach, dotted with all-inclusive resort hotels and the newly opened Baha Mar. Continue on and you'll find yourself slowing

Previous: cruise ships docked in Nassau; colorful historic buildings in Graycliff Heritage Village. **Above:** traditional Bahamian architecture.

Look for ★ to find recommended sights, activities, dining, and lodging.

Highlights

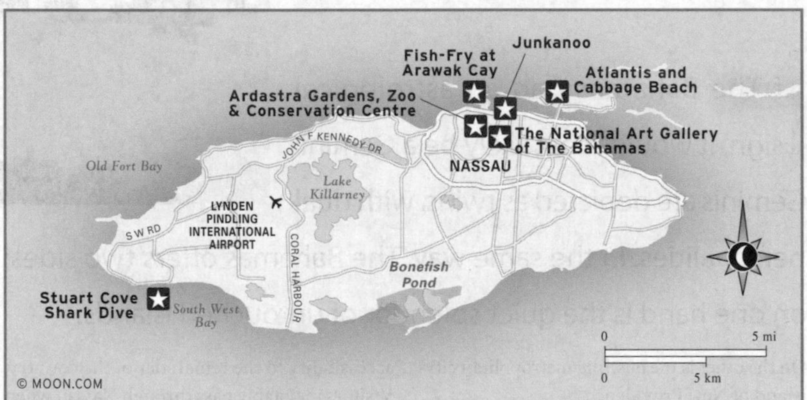

★ **The National Art Gallery of The Bahamas:** It's home to some of the country's most revered fine art, including permanent and rotating collections as well as project space (page 40).

★ **Ardastra Gardens, Zoo & Conservation Centre:** Get up close and personal with the national bird of The Bahamas with the famous daily Marching Flamingos show (page 42).

★ **Stuart Cove Shark Dive:** For certified scuba divers and thrill seekers, the Shark Dive is one of the most exhilarating dives in the world. A two-tank dive gets you alongside these magnificent creatures in their natural environment (page 44).

★ **Junkanoo:** The heartbeat of Bahamian culture is this annual festival and parade held on December 26 and New Year's Day. Enjoy intricate handmade costumes, music, and dancing (page 49).

★ **Fish Fry at Arawak Cay:** This bustling, colorful patchwork of eclectic restaurants offers visitors a true taste of Bahamian flavors and island hospitality (page 52).

★ **Atlantis and Cabbage Beach:** The world-famous ocean-themed Atlantis resort has something for everyone—and it's perched on Cabbage Beach, one of the most beautiful stretches of sands in The Bahamas (page 60).

down and unwinding as you run parallel to the ocean and its accompanying uncrowded white-sand beaches. Colorful bougainvillea cascades over brightly colored stucco walls and towering palm trees. Poinciana and lush tropical vegetation create a canopy over the meandering ocean road, evidence that you are on the more verdant side of the island. Gated canal-oriented communities attract affluent homeowners, and you'll find a diverse restaurant scene suitable for distinguished tastes. Don't be surprised if you find yourself dining next to a celebrity at one of the more upscale establishments.

PLANNING YOUR TIME

New Providence is by far the most visited island in The Bahamas, and for good reason. Not only is it a fantastic place to use as a home base, and as a jumping-off point for accessing the other islands, it is also almost a requirement, since many of the islands are only accessible via Nassau's domestic airport. Unlike other areas of the country that shut down completely during peak hurricane season (Sept.-Oct.), most of the resorts, hotels, and restaurants in New Providence remain open year-round.

Downtown Nassau offers shopping, nightlife, and both historical and modern architecture. It's also a prime place to explore all ranges of Bahamian-influenced cuisine, from the casual Fish Fry at Arawak Cay to contemporary dining at Lukka Kairi on the historic wharf of Woodes Rodgers Walk. Spend a night at the historic Graycliff Hotel and start your trip with a walking tour of downtown Nassau to get your bearings. Along the way you'll uncover hidden gems tucked away on side streets. You can spend one or two additional days exploring the Pirates of Nassau museum and the historic forts in the area to get a sense of the island's rich history.

If you are looking for a variety of resort hotels and a quieter pace, staying on Cable Beach is a great centralized location. You can easily spend your entire vacation in Cable Beach and use it as a home base for day trips. There are plenty of beaches and dining options nearby, and historic downtown Nassau is only a 10-minute drive. It's also close to the airport, so you can be off the plane and into the sand within a matter of minutes.

Paradise Island is probably the least representative of Bahamian culture, and you may feel as though you could be at any tropical getaway resort anywhere in the world—but it is safe, clean, and has all the amenities you might be looking for on vacation. Water parks, shopping, and a range of dining options are available, but you'll be paying top dollar. Most visitors spend a few days at Atlantis before they are ready to head to the Out Islands.

Getting around is easy by rental car, jitney bus, or taxi. Most of the sights are along the scenic Bay Street corridor that runs east-west along the northern side of the island. It takes about 30 minutes by vehicle from one end of the island to the other, so seeing the entire island's scenic areas will take you less than one day. Although many will say that you aren't experiencing the real Bahamas until you get away from Nassau, as with most capital cities, it's still a noteworthy stopover in order to get an overall feel for architecture, art, history, and culture. The top attractions can be fully experienced in one or two days, then trade your walking shoes for flip-flops and head to one of the other treasured islands that make The Bahamas so unique.

ORIENTATION

Everything of interest can be found along New Providence's Bay Street corridor. Departing the airport, you'll find yourself on JFK highway, which leads east into the commercial center of the island, with shopping malls and services for residents. Most visitors will have no interest in traveling to this area, so the best option is to take West Bay Street from JFK. Heading east will lead you through Cable Beach and eventually into downtown, where the road turns into East Bay Street. Past the downtown area is a residential neighborhood

Nassau and New Providence

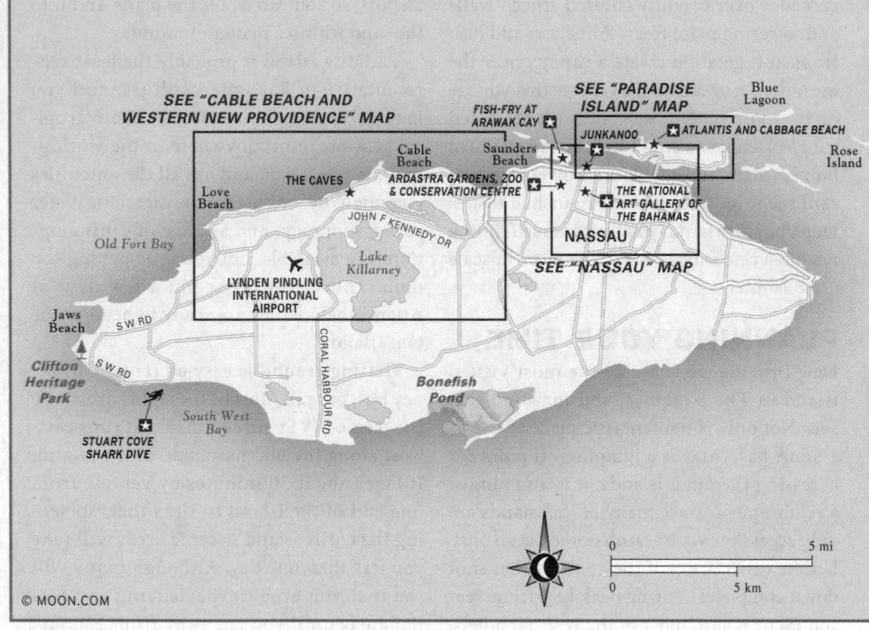

known as Eastern Road. From downtown Nassau, there is a bridge that leads over Nassau Harbour onto Paradise Island.

Navigating in Nassau is straightforward on Bay Street, but it can prove difficult if you are looking for a specific address. Except in developments and gated communities, homes and businesses do not have numbered addresses. Smaller islands are easy to navigate along one main highway, but due to New Providence's size and density, visitors can easily become overwhelmed. If you are unsure about navigating the island, consider utilizing a taxi for a few days in order to get your bearings.

Nassau

The bustling downtown scene has been the epicenter of the country's commerce for hundreds of years. From fishing and straw markets to bootlegging and rum running, it seems as though there was never a dull moment in the history of downtown Nassau and its harbor. The city was ravaged by invasions and fires in its early years, so although the settlement was founded in the late 1600s, the oldest surviving buildings date to the mid-1700s. You'll feel a sense of the city's rich history as you wander through the streets. Some of the buildings have been elegantly restored, while others are waiting for their turn.

SIGHTS

Many of Nassau's historical sights are centralized in the downtown area and can be seen on foot in a few hours. Depending on the day of the week and the number of cruise ships in port, the downtown area can be packed with tourists or fairly quiet. Ask your hotel about the cruise-ship schedule if you prefer to enjoy the sights without too much company.

Historic Downtown Nassau

Nassau was originally named Charles Towne in 1656 by the King of England, Charles II, prior to being renamed Nassau in 1695. The original city was built within the boundaries of Olde Nassau, also known as the Historic Charles Towne District (www.historiccharlestowne.com), which extends along the harbor between Nassau Street and Elizabeth Avenue and up to Meeting Street. Take a stroll through streets lined with shady poinciana trees and colorful bougainvillea, and view a mix of traditional British and Bahamian-influenced architecture.

The pastel pink and white **Government House** (Duke St. and George St., Marching Band tel. 242/322-2020, Ministry of Tourism tel. 242/356-0435, free) is the current home of the Governor General and sits on the top of Mount Fitzwilliam, overlooking Shirley Street and Nassau Harbour. Join the Royal Bahamas Police Force Marching Band and the Royal Bahamas Defense Force Guards every other Friday 11am-11:30am for a changing-of-the-guard ceremony, or sample local bush teas and live music at the public tea party the last Friday of the month 4pm-5pm January-May and October-November.

In front of Government House is a statue of Christopher Columbus, imported from London in 1830 as a tribute to Columbus's 1492 landfall in San Salvador. A short walk to the west is **Graycliff Heritage Village** (West Hill St.), a collection of brightly-colored revitalized historical buildings.

The Heritage Museum of The Bahamas (tel. 242/302-9150, Mon.-Sat. 9am-5pm, $12.50 self-guided tour, $18.50 guided tour), located within the Mountbatten House, was built in the 1850's and features artifacts dating back to prehistoric times. Book the **Heritage and History of the Bahamas Tour** (tel. 242/302-9150, experiences@graycliff.com, Mon.-Sat. 10am and 2pm, $45 adults, $40 children), which takes you through the museum, the historic Graycliff property, and the cigar and chocolate factories. Head toward Bay Street and stop at **Balcony House** (Market St. and Trinity Place, tel. 242/302-2621, Mon.-Wed. and Fri. 9:30am-4:30pm, Thurs. 9:30am-1pm, donation), the oldest surviving wooden residential structure in Nassau, which has been fully restored as a museum.

Historic Forts

In the days of pirates and threats of invasion from Spain, France, and the United States, forts were an essential line of defense for this vulnerable island capital. On the eastern edge of downtown sits **Fort Montagu** (Bay St. and Eastern Rd., free), which marks the east entrance into Nassau Harbour. This is the oldest of the three forts, built of limestone in 1742. **Fort Fincastle** (top of Elizabeth Ave., daily 8am-4pm, $5) is the newest fort, built in 1793. It's located on top of Bennet's Hill and is one of the highest points in the city at 125 feet above sea level.

Further west is **Fort Charlotte** (W. Bay St. and Chippingham Rd., tel. 242/326-4872, daily, $5), built in 1789, and is the largest and most impressive fort in Nassau sitting on 100 acres overlooking Paradise Island and the shipping port. The fort has a dry moat, dungeons, underground passageways, and 42 cannons, which have never been fired in warfare. Watch the Royal Bahamas Defense Force Rangers as they do a reenactment of military drills and fire the cannons each Wednesday and Friday at 11:30am. Tours are available upon request; tips are appreciated.

Pirates of Nassau Museum

Known as the Pirate Republic, Nassau was the center of the action during the golden age of piracy. **Pirates of Nassau** (King St. and George St., tel. 242/356-3759, www.piratesofnassau.com, Mon.-Sat. 9am-6pm, Sun. 9am-12:30pm, $13 adults, $6.50 ages 4-17) takes you into those days. Upon entry you will be transported to the Nassau wharf

Nassau

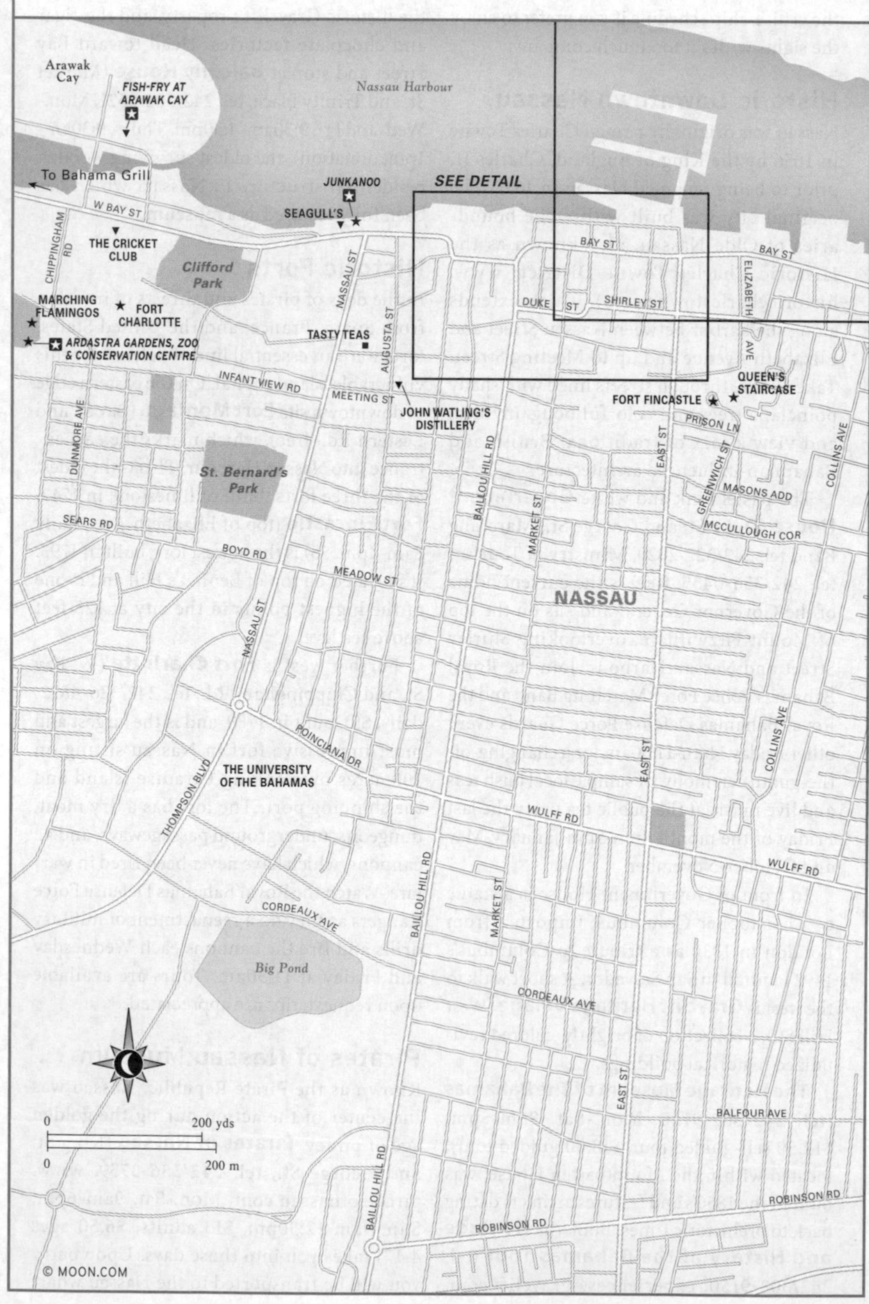
Arawak Cay
FISH-FRY AT ARAWAK CAY
Nassau Harbour
To Bahama Grill
JUNKANOO
SEE DETAIL
SEAGULL'S
W BAY ST
THE CRICKET CLUB
CHIPPINGHAM RD
Clifford Park
NASSAU ST
MARCHING FLAMINGOS
FORT CHARLOTTE
ARDASTRA GARDENS, ZOO & CONSERVATION CENTRE
TASTY TEAS
AUGUSTA ST
INFANT VIEW RD
MEETING ST
JOHN WATLING'S DISTILLERY
BAY ST
DUKE ST
SHIRLEY ST
ELIZABETH AVE
QUEEN'S STAIRCASE
FORT FINCASTLE
PRISON LN
DUNMORE AVE
St. Bernard's Park
BAILLOU HILL RD
MARKET ST
EAST ST
GREENWICH ST
COLLINS AVE
MASONS ADD
MCCULLOUGH COR
SEARS RD
BOYD RD
MEADOW ST
NASSAU
POINCIANA DR
THOMPSON BLVD
THE UNIVERSITY OF THE BAHAMAS
WULFF RD
CORDEAUX AVE
Big Pond
BALFOUR AVE
0
200 yds
200 m
ROBINSON RD
© MOON.COM

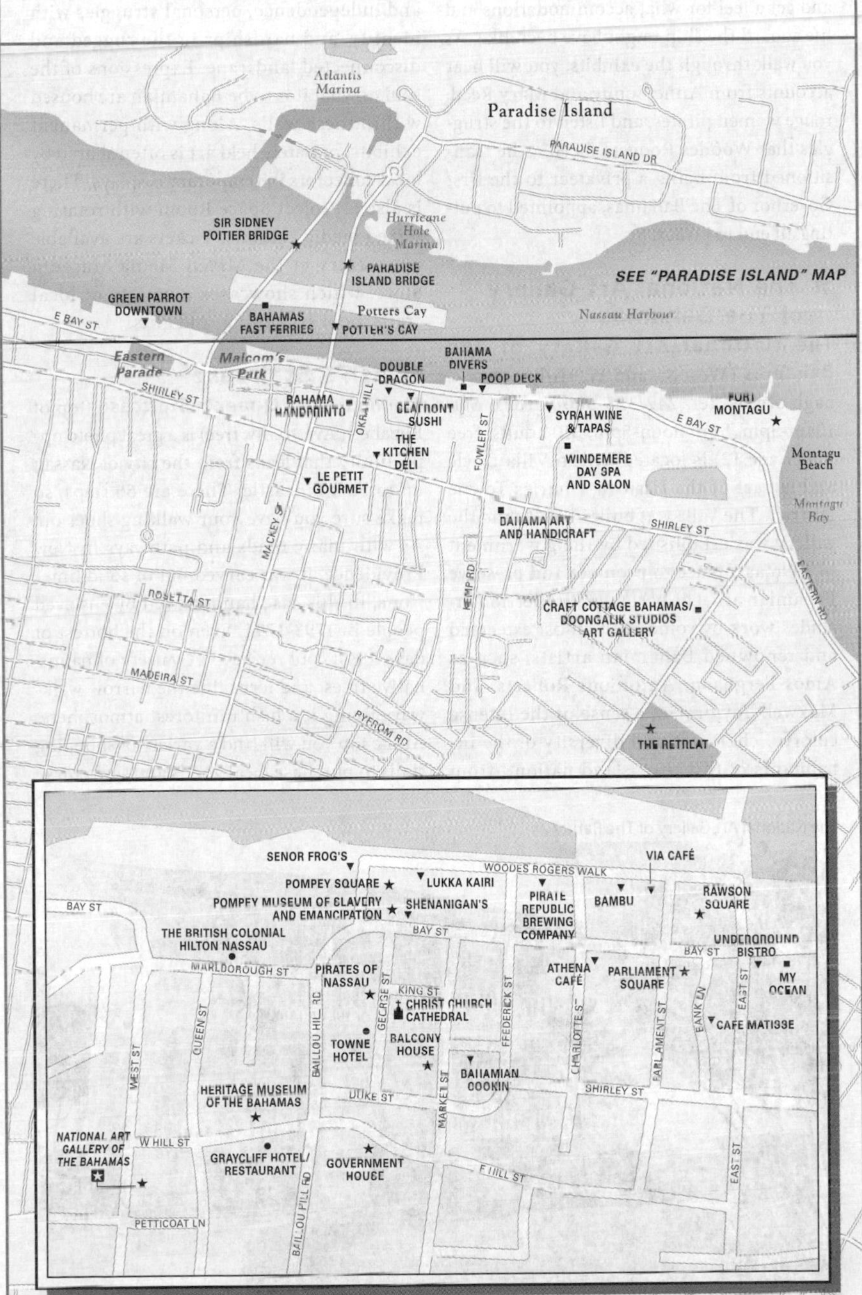
Atlantis Marina
Paradise Island
PARADISE ISLAND DR
Hurricane Hole Marina
SIR SIDNEY POITIER BRIDGE
PARADISE ISLAND BRIDGE
SEE "PARADISE ISLAND" MAP
GREEN PARROT DOWNTOWN
BAHAMAS FAST FERRIES
Potters Cay
POTTER'S CAY
Nassau Harbour
E BAY ST
Eastern Parade
Malcom's Park
SHIRLEY ST
BAHAMA HANDPRINTS
OKRA HILL
DOUBLE DRAGON
SEAFRONT SUSHI
BAHAMA DIVERS
POOP DECK
SYRAH WINE & TAPAS
FORT MONTAGU
E BAY ST
THE KITCHEN DELI
WINDEMERE DAY SPA AND SALON
Montagu Beach
LE PETIT GOURMET
MACKEY ST
FOWLER ST
BAHAMA ART AND HANDICRAFT
Montagu Bay
SHIRLEY ST
EASTERN RD
KEMP RD
ROSETTA ST
CRAFT COTTAGE BAHAMAS/ DOONGALIK STUDIOS ART GALLERY
MADEIRA ST
PYFROM RD
THE RETREAT
SENOR FROG'S
WOODES ROGERS WALK
VIA CAFÉ
POMPEY SQUARE
LUKKA KAIRI
PIRATE REPUBLIC BREWING COMPANY
BAMBU
RAWSON SQUARE
BAY ST
POMPEY MUSEUM OF SLAVERY AND EMANCIPATION
SHENANIGAN'S
BAY ST
THE BRITISH COLONIAL HILTON NASSAU
UNDERGROUND BISTRO
BAY ST
MARLBOROUGH ST
PIRATES OF NASSAU
ATHENA CAFÉ
PARLIAMENT SQUARE
MY OCEAN
KING ST
GEORGE ST
CHRIST CHURCH CATHEDRAL
FREDERICK ST
CHARLOTTE ST
EAST ST
BANK LN
QUEEN ST
BAILLOU HILL RD
TOWNE HOTEL
BALCONY HOUSE
PARLIAMENT ST
CAFE MATISSE
WEST ST
BAHAMIAN COOKIN'
HERITAGE MUSEUM OF THE BAHAMAS
DUKE ST
MARKET ST
SHIRLEY ST
NATIONAL ART GALLERY OF THE BAHAMAS
W HILL ST
GRAYCLIFF HOTEL/ RESTAURANT
GOVERNMENT HOUSE
E HILL ST
EAST ST
PETTICOAT LN
BAILLOU HILL RD

at night. Step aboard the pirate ship *Revenge* and get a feel for what accommodations and life aboard the ship might have been like. As you walk through the exhibits, you will hear accounts from Anne Bonny and Mary Read, rouge women pirates, and listen to the struggles that Woodes Rodgers faced as he transitioned from being a privateer to the first Governor of The Bahamas, appointed to putting an end to piracy.

★ The National Art Gallery of The Bahamas

The National Art Gallery of The Bahamas (West St. and W. Hill St., www.nagb.org.bs, tel. 242/328-5800, Tues.-Sat. 10am-5pm, Sun. noon-5pm, $10 adults, free under age 12) is located within Villa Doyle and is part of the Historic Charles Towne District. The Villa was built in 1860, and the gallery was established by the government in 1996 as a place to promote and preserve Bahamian art. The permanent collection includes work by some of the most esteemed and renowned Bahamian artists, such as Amos Ferguson, Antonious Roberts, and Maxwell Taylor. Get a sense of the intense colorful character and diversity of the inhabitants of this tiny island nation—from colonialism, upheaval, foreign influences and independence, personal struggles with identity, and hardships in the rugged and disconnected landscape. Expressions of the soul of what it is to be Bahamian are housed within these walls. Along with permanent exhibits, privately held art is often shared by local collectors in temporary displays. There is also a Project Space Room with rotating mixed media exhibits. Tickets are available upon entry at the Mixed Media Museum Store, which showcases a variety of local crafts, books, clothing, and gifts.

Queen's Staircase

The impressive **Queen's Staircase** (top of Elizabeth Ave., daily, free) is a great photo opportunity that leads from the city of Nassau up to Fort Fincastle. There are 66 steps, so make sure you have your walking shoes on. As with many roads and pathways in New Providence, it was carved out of solid limestone, in this case hand-carved by enslaved people in 1793-1794. Even on the hottest of days it is a cool reprieve. A variety of palms, native trees, and ferns line the narrow walkway, giving it a lush rainforest atmosphere. At the top you will find a variety of shopping stalls to purchase local goods and souvenirs.

The National Art Gallery of The Bahamas

Rawson Square and Parliament Square

Divided by Bay Street, these squares have prominent statues facing each other from opposing playing fields. To the north, **Rawson Square,** with a statue of Sir Milo Butler, the first Governor General of the independent Bahamas, is the welcoming arena for visitors arriving via cruise ship and a common meeting area for tours. Shady and inviting, lined with mature Bismarck palms and silk cotton trees, the square was named for Sir Rawson W. Rawson, Governor of The Bahamas in the 1860s.

Parliament Square has a statue of Queen Elizabeth, a tribute to the days under the British crown, and includes the Senate Building, the Supreme Court, the House of Assembly, and the House of the Opposition. The buildings in Parliament Square are the epitome of British architecture with a West Indies flair—paradise pink in color, lined with contrasting white quoins (stone blocks traditionally used on the corners of buildings for reinforcement or aesthetically to give a sense of permanence and strength), stately columns, and emerald green board-and-batten shutters. The Coat of Arms stands brightly over the square, using a marlin and a flamingo to further instill a sense of allegiance to the tropics.

Pompey Square and Pompey Museum

Pompey Museum of Slavery and Emancipation (Bay St. and George St., tel. 242/326-0495, Mon.-Wed. and Fri.-Sat. 9:30am-4:30pm, Thurs. 9:30am-1pm, $3 adults, $2 seniors, $1 ages 6-12, free under age 6) is located within Vendue House, which served as a slave and commodities marketplace throughout the mid-1700s. The building has been twice destroyed by fire and was restored to its original architectural style in 2011. The museum takes visitors through the history of slavery as it relates to the British Empire, the United States, and other Caribbean islands. Plaques of reading material provide a sobering account of the unimaginable hardships of the recent ancestors of modern-day Bahamians. Staff are knowledgeable and ready to answer any questions.

Pompey Square (Bay St. and George St.) is the epicenter of events and festivals in the downtown area. Peruse craft stalls at the Authentically Bahamian Marketplace (tel. 242/302-2067, Sat.-Sun. 8am-6pm). Local vendors sell straw crafts, shell and sea-glass products, ceramics, aromatherapy, and spa products. It is a peaceful spot to sit by the water fountain and people-watch. Call to confirm the market hours, as it varies based on the weather and other events. Security and public restrooms are available.

Christ Church Cathedral

The original Parish of Christ Church was built between 1670 and 1684 and was destroyed by the Spanish, along with a subsequent church. The third building was made of wood but was later replaced by the present-day structure, made of locally quarried limestone, in 1754. Another building was added in 1861 to accommodate a choir, at which time Christ Church was designated a cathedral. At that time, a British settlement was not considered a city without a cathedral, so Nassau officially became a city with the establishment of **Christ Church Cathedral** (George St. and King St., tel. 242/322-4186, daily 9am-4:30pm, services: Sunday 7:30am, 9am, 11:15am and 6pm, Mon. and Wed. 1pm, Tues.-Thurs. 7am). Enter the quiet sanctuary and admire the beautiful stained-glass windows encompassing the perimeter of the congressional.

The Retreat

The first property to be designated as a national park in New Providence, **The Retreat** (Village Rd., tel. 242/601-7432, www.bnt.bs, Mon.-Fri. 9am 5pm, $10 adults, $3 children ages 5-12, $5 ages 13-18) was the private residence of Arthur Langlois and his Bahamian wife, Margaret, prior its acquisition by the Bahamas National Trust in 1977. Once considered out of town, economic growth over

Food Tasting Tour

walking tour of Nassau with the Tru Bahamian Food Tour

If you are looking for a quick way to discover the food and sights of Nassau, try the three-hour **Tru Bahamian Food Tour** (tel. 242/601-1725, www.trubahamianfoodtours.com, $69). The friendly and entertaining guide will lead you down the back streets to discover Nassau in a way you might not find on your own. Starting at Christ Church Cathedral, a short walk will find you sitting down to a traditional Bahamian meal at Bahamian Cookin'. Next, you head over to the Talking Stick Bar and Restaurant for a specialty Bahamian cocktail. Visit Graycliff's Chocolate Shop and sample handcrafted chocolates, and then step into the Drawbridge Patisserie & Gelateria to try sorbets flavored with local Bahamian fruits. A final stop at the Tortuga Rum Cake Company lets you try one of their six cakes and pick up a few to take home. Throughout the tour you'll stop at prominent buildings and sights and get details on the city's rich history, along with a few interesting stories and local lore.

the last century has established it as a peaceful escape within the city. The Langloises purchased the property in 1925 and had a passion for palm horticulture. After years of seed collection and cultivating 11 acres of land into a dense rainforest-like setting, the Langloises went on to become world famous for their private collection of mature exotic palms and tropical plants, including over 200 species of palms. The property is now the primary headquarters and educational center for the National Trust, a nonprofit organization that manages 29 designated parks throughout The Bahamas. Regular events at the Retreat include Jollification and the Wine and Art Festival. A gift shop and a reference library are on premises, and guided tours are available.

★ Ardastra Gardens, Zoo & Conservation Centre

Ardastra Gardens (Chippingham Rd., tel. 242/323-5806, www.ardastra.com, daily 9am-5pm, $18 adults, $9 ages 4-12, free under age 4) opened in 1939 as a conservation and educational center for interaction with the national bird of The Bahamas—the West Indian pink flamingo, also known as the Caribbean flamingo. The Bahamas is home to the largest population of these flamingos in the world, with around 50,000 nesting at Inagua

National Park. Enter the gardens and wander past chatty parrots, exotic birds, raccoons, and other small mammals. The grounds are filled with lush trees and labeled vegetation, so you can learn about foliage that grows here as well.

Every day at 10:30am, 2:15pm, and 4pm, the **Marching Flamingos** put on a show. Arrive early and mingle with them as they wander around the gardens, preening, prancing, and interacting with each other, and then grab a front-row seat at the Flamingo Stage when showtime draws near. The Drill Sergeant (their trainer and handler) leads them into the circular pen and gives commands. The excitement is watching as they follow his directions, acting together as a flock. The pink exhibitionists strut in front of the audience and make their way around the arena, providing a great opportunity for photos. Once they have completed their circuit, audience members can enter the ring and have their photo taken as they congregate around each guest. Along with the flamingos, another exciting experience is hand-feeding the friendly lory parrots. Enter their aviary with fruit in your hand and in an instant you'll have several colorful birds perched on your arms and shoulders. Parrot feeding times are daily at 11am, 1:30pm, and 3:30pm.

Beaches

Located just a few minutes' walk west of the cruise-ship docks on West Bay Street is **Junkanoo Beach,** a small, beautiful strip of white sand with plenty going on. Visit one of the many daiquiri shacks, get your hair braided, or enjoy a quick massage. The Tiki Bikini hut offers four shots and four beers for $10, the best deal on the island. Free parking is available in the Western Esplanade on the west side of the beach.

Montagu Beach isn't necessarily the most picturesque beach on the island, but it's less touristy and has a great local vibe, making an interesting cultural experience, especially on weekends during the summer. Regattas and events are regularly held on this beach, and you'll often find vendors selling fresh seafood, seasonal fruits and vegetables, and tasty barbecue dishes. There are parking and public restroom facilities. It's located to the east of Fort Montagu on East Bay Street and Village Road.

the Marching Flamingos of Ardastra Gardens

Local Experience: People-to-People Program

The Bahamas is known for beautiful beaches, turquoise water, and ever-present sunshine. But what makes The Bahamas genuinely special is the warm and inviting nature of its people. Launched in 1975, the **People-to-People Program** (tel. 242/356-0435, www.bahamas.com/people-to-people) is a free service offered by the Ministry of Tourism that connects visitors with Bahamians to experience this remarkable country from a local's perspective. The program hosts around 5,000 visitors each year, and many participants create lifelong friendships. Prior to your visit, complete a registration form to let the Ministry of Tourism know which islands you are planning to visit, and what your interests are. Ideally, fill out the form at least a week prior to arrival. You are then connected with the ambassador directly so you can arrange activities—typically a meal with the host family, trips to the beach or a local hot spot, or a tour of the island. Not only do visitors enjoy this interaction, but the Bahamian volunteers are equally enthusiastic to show off their homeland with pride and learn about another culture in return. Both parties have interesting and enriching interactions they wouldn't otherwise have. Visit their website for more information.

SPORTS AND RECREATION

Snorkeling and Diving

If the Bahamas is known for anything other than pristine beaches, it is activities in and on the water. Many of these water-oriented companies are based downtown, but often you can arrange a pickup from your hotel anywhere on the island.

★ STUART COVE SHARK DIVE

If you are a scuba diver, the **Stuart Cove Shark Dive** (tel. 242/362-4171, www.stuartcove.com, $182) may be the most exciting dive you'll ever do. This two-tank dive gets you up close with wild sharks in their natural habitat. Feel the exhilaration as you anxiously boat out to the dive spot, one of four locations where the sharks are regularly fed. The first dive is just a free swim to get to know the sharks, who mingle around but are merely curious—they know that food is coming, so be prepared for them to be fairly active as they swim around you. The second dive is where the sharks get their dinner. You won't be doing a lot of moving on the second dive, instead in a safe kneeling position on the bottom of the boat while you observe the feeding. Once the food is gone, the sharks move on, and your heart can resume its normal pace. This dive is available every afternoon at 1pm. Stuart Cove's has been in operation for 30 years and is known as the number-one dive center in New Providence. Pickup from major hotels is included. Other services include scuba certification courses, multiday packages, night dives, and snorkeling. Specialty activities include snuba, a great way to experience being underwater without having to be dive-certified, and you'll be safely connected to a breathing apparatus in shallow water. You can also try your hand at SUBs, a seahorse-shaped mini submarine that takes you down around reefs no deeper than 15 feet.

BAHAMA DIVERS

Bahama Divers (Nassau Yacht Haven, E. Bay St., tel. 242/393-5644, www.bahamadivers.com) is the largest retail and full-service dive shop in The Bahamas, selling scuba and snorkel gear, spears, slings, and boating accessories. They offer several dives not found elsewhere, such as interesting ship and plane wrecks and the Lost Blue Hole, a 200-foot-wide opening in the sea floor that descends 200 feet from its 30-foot depth below the surface. Certification courses, snorkeling trips, and customizable charters are also available.

Stuart Cove Shark Dive

Fishing

Nassau is a great spot to use as a base for fishing expeditions. Depending on the time of year, you'll be after marlin, sailfish, wahoo, tuna, or mahimahi. Nassau's proximity just off the Tongue of the Ocean makes it one of the most accessible places for some of the best fishing in the world.

Experienced and professional captains at **Born Free Charters** (tel. 242/698-1770, www.bornfreefishing.com) will assure that you have a memorable day on the water. They offer deep-sea fishing, trolling, spinning-rod, and bottom fishing, or you can charter a snorkeling or beach picnic excursion to a nearby island.

With four boats ranging 27 to 38 feet, **Reel Dreams** (tel. 242/364-6641, www.reeldreamsbahamas.com) regularly assists clients with the big catch.

Specializing in fishing, snorkeling, and Exuma day trips, family-owned and operated **Chubasco Charters** (tel. 242/324-3474, www.chubascocharters.com) guarantees you will catch a fish, or your fishing trip is free.

Boating

Flying Cloud (tel. 242/394-5067, www.flyingcloud.info) is a 57-foot catamaran offering half-day, full-day, and dinner cruise excursions. Day trips go to the beautiful beaches at Rose Island for snorkeling and beach activities. Dinner cruises are within the proximity of the Nassau Harbour area. Enjoy simple tasty fare and tropical drinks at the full-service bar, and be prepared to be wowed by a beautiful Bahamian sunset.

Island Yachts (tel. 242/322-6901, www.islandyachts.co) offer a range of yacht charters from a 50-foot Leopard Catamaran to a 160-foot Bilgin accommodating up to 12 people with 5 cabins, deep sea fishing charters on 31-foot Bertram to a 55-foot Hattaras and a range of center consoles. Opt for a helicopter tour or even a private island rental for large bookings. Mention Moon Bahamas when booking.

Spas

If you are staying in the downtown area and are looking for a bit of pampering while you are on holiday, **Windemere Day Spa and Salon** (Harbour Bay, tel. 242/393-8788, Caves Village tel. 242/327-6136, www.windermeredayspa.com, Mon.-Tues. 8am-5pm, Wed.-Sat. 7am-6pm) offers face, skin, and body services at a reasonable price. They have a second location in Western New Providence at Caves Village Plaza.

ENTERTAINMENT AND EVENTS

Nassau is bustling with events. On any given weekend you are guaranteed to find something going on, and you may find yourself overwhelmed with options, but it can take some research as there is no centralized calendar of events. A good place to start is Facebook—although many establishments don't have websites, they normally have a Facebook page. Go to the Events page and

Day Trips to the Out Islands

Nassau is a great place to use as a home base, but getting to the other islands can be a challenge if you have time constraints. Luckily there are several easily accessible islands and cays a short distance from downtown Nassau. Get out to these islands and you'll feel like you're in another world—a world where time slows down and waves languorously lap against the quiet shoreline. If you have a free day, definitely look into one of these day trips. It's what being in The Bahamas is all about.

ROSE ISLAND

Located on Rose Island are two establishments that are only accessible by boat. **Footprints** (tel. 242/427-2485, www.footprintsroseisland.com, $30 transportation only) has a true Out Island vibe. Opened in August 2016, owner Ronnie Thompson plays only Bahamian music and calypso, and serves Bahamian food and barbecue. He is originally from an Out Island himself and wants his guests to experience true island hospitality. The welcoming open-air bar is decorated with T-shirts and dollar bills and overlooks a breathtaking stretch of beach with a volleyball court for the active types. Rental cottages are available for overnight guests. Day trip departures from Nassau are daily at 10am and 11am and return at 4pm or 6pm.

Sandy Toes (tel. 242/363-8637, www.sandytoesbahamas.com, day trips from $89) attracts a lively party crowd but also offers plenty of room to escape for peace and quiet. The day trip departs daily at 10am and gets you back to the dock at 5pm. The full-day package includes transportation to and from the island, a Bahamian lunch buffet and nonalcoholic beverages, and add-ons such as drink packages. Snorkeling and massages are also available. Overnight in the luxury beach villa for a true island getaway.

BLUE LAGOON ISLAND

Perfect for a family getaway, you will find plenty to keep you occupied on picturesque **Blue Lagoon Island** (tel. 242/363-1003, www.bahamasbluelagoon.com, day trips from $69). Your day starts by riding to the island on a high-speed double-decker cruiser, enjoying views of downtown Nassau. The day trip includes lunch of grilled burgers with fresh fruit and sides. Relax in a hammock or on an inflatable water toy, or explore beautiful beaches and natural lagoons. For additional cost you may purchase alcoholic beverages; rent paddleboats, kayaks, or snorkeling gear; and book a Segway safari tour or an eco-nature walking tour. Their animal encounters include swimming with the dolphins and interactions with the loveable sea lions.

PEARL ISLAND

Just a short boat ride from downtown Nassau, this charming barrier island is marked with a pastel and white lighthouse, alerting mariners of the upcoming treacherous entrance to Nassau Harbour. **Pearl Island** (tel. 242/422-2211, www.pearlislandbahamas.com, day trips from $65) staff will meet you at your cruise ship or on East Bay Street at Harbour View Marina to carry you over to the island. Receive a souvenir photograph and a welcome rum drink or fruit punch when you arrive on the island. There are ample spots throughout this slender island to find a secluded place to lounge the day away, or stay cool by drifting in the water on one of their floats or kayaks. A tasty

Located just a short boat trip from downtown Nassau is beautiful Pearl Island

Bahamian lunch is included in your day trip. For an additional fee you can do the snorkel tour, feed the fish and explore the reef just off the shore, or visit the bar for one of their specialty cocktails.

SHIP CHANNEL CAY

A one-hour high-speed boat ride allows you to discover an entirely different island chain—the beautiful, rugged, and remote Exumas. **Powerboat Adventures** (tel. 242/363-2265 or 242/323-8888 for charters and groups, www.powerboatadventures.com, $213 adults, $150 children) was the pioneer of fast boats to The Exumas, starting in 1990, and is one of the top-rated tours in The Bahamas. Your first stop is to feed the iguanas at Allen's Cay, then spend the remainder of the day on the private island of Ship Channel Cay while you pet stingrays, meet swimming pigs, watch a shark feeding, and experience a drift snorkel. Lunch and all beverages are included. Book tickets online or at their office at Margaritaville on Paradise Island. Boats depart daily, weather depending, at 9:15am from Margaritaville and arrives back in Nassau at 5pm. The fares are definitely worth the splurge.

HARBOUR ISLAND

The ***Bohengy III* ferry** (tel. 242/323-2166, www.bahamasferries.com, Wed.-Mon., $225 adults, $154 children) runs to Harbour Island, a colorful colonial town and the original capital of The Bahamas. Take a stroll on the three-mile Pink Sands Beach, one of the most beautiful in The Bahamas; peruse boutiques; and enjoy lunch at one of the many top restaurants. The ferry departs from Potter's Cay in downtown Nassau daily at 8am and returns at 6:30pm. Your day package includes round-trip ferry service, a guided tour, all-day golf-cart use, a $20 lunch voucher, and hotel pickup and drop off. The ferry does not run for several weeks during low season in September and October.

click "Discover," search for "Nassau," and see what pops up.

Nightlife

A friend once said, "In The Bahamas, every night is like Friday, and every Friday is like New Year's Eve." This is a fairly accurate description of the amount of partying going on at any given time. And, with more bars and drinking establishments than anywhere else in The Bahamas, New Providence is party central. A great place to start if you are staying downtown is on Woodes Rodgers Walk. Keep an ear out for music and a crowd—that's where the party will be. Between Woodes Rodgers Walk and Bay Street is where all of the downtown action happens. You are almost guaranteed to stumble across a party any night of the week.

Bambu (Woodes Rodgers Walk, tel. 242/326-6627, Thurs.-Sat. 9pm-5am) offers a variety of music, including dance, hip-hop, club, and live music. They have reasonably priced drinks and attract a lively crowd; just don't plan on going early as it doesn't pick up until after midnight. Located upstairs from Harley Davidson, expect a cover charge of $10 or higher. **Pirate Republic Brewing Company's Tap Room** (Woodes Rodgers Walk, www.piraterepublicbahamas.com, daily 10am-2am) has regular live music and events and serves up a selection of their craft beers made on the premises.

For the spring-break crowd, **Señor Frog's** (Woodes Rodgers Walk and Navy Lion Rd., www.senorfrogs.com/bahamas, daily 11am-late) will keep the party going until the early hours. Open-air and right on the harbor, the staff is friendly and animated and will even assure that children have a great time if you plan on going early. Order their 28-ounce signature Yard Drink in a souvenir cup to get your party started. **Via Café** (Woodes Rodgers Walk and Parliament St., tel. 242/322-7210, Mon. 8am-6pm, Tues.-Thurs. and Sun. 8am-1am, Fri.-Sat. 8am-3am) is a restaurant and café by day and lounge by night. Happy-hour specials and late-night snacks are available. Visit on Thursdays for salsa night. Head onto Bay Street and check out the **Underground Bistro** (tel. 242/468-7543, daily 10am-1am) which features local artists and open mike nights, and is the only place in town with hookah and vaportinis.

Festivals and Events

The summer months are typically quiet because most people are on vacation, traveling or hitting the beaches, and it's entirely too hot to be outside. Once October arrives, get ready for nonstop festivals and events. Many smaller events are going on as well, but the following are the big events worth a visit.

PARADISE PLATES

The first event of the season is **Paradise Plates** (Grand Ballroom, Atlantis Resort, www.handsforhunger.org, early Oct.). Organized by the local nonprofit Hands for Hunger, Paradise Plates features gourmet food, beer, and wine from the island's top restaurants.

INTERNATIONAL CULTURAL FESTIVAL

The **International Cultural Festival** (Botanical Gardens, Chippingham Rd., www.culturalfestbahamas.com, mid-Oct.) originated from the recognition of United Nations Day by the Bahamas Ministry of Foreign Affairs. Its aim is to showcase the diversity of the international community in The Bahamas. The festival is divided into national villages representing countries throughout the Caribbean, North and South America, Europe, Asia, and Africa. Sample food, listen to performances, and shop for arts and crafts from every continent. You'll be amazed by the diversity that contributes to the population of The Bahamas.

WINE AND ART FESTIVAL

The Bahamas National Trust hosts the **Wine and Art Festival** (The Retreat, Village Rd., www.bnt.bs, end of Oct.) nestled within the lush foliage of the Retreat. Enjoy a sampling of wines from local distributors and then wander through the grounds discovering the incredible talent of top local artists. Artistic work includes paintings, carvings, woodwork, jewelry, clothing, candles, and other handmade products.

JOLLIFICATION

Residents of Nassau will agree that **Jollification** (The Retreat, www.bnt.bs, mid-Nov.) represents the official kickoff of the holiday season. There are local crafts of all varieties, but the focus is on Christmas decorations and ornaments. Children can visit the kids' center and make their own crafty creations, and an adult's beer garden is the center of entertainment after an afternoon of shopping.

THE BAHAMAS INTERNATIONAL FILM FESTIVAL

The Bahamas International Film Festival (multiple venues, Nassau and Harbour Island, www.bintlfilmfest.com, mid-Dec.) draws filmmakers and actors from all over the world for this weeklong event. The focus is on independent films that might not otherwise be available in The Bahamas, as well as providing an environment for education and expansion for local filmmakers.

TOP EXPERIENCE

★ JUNKANOO

Junkanoo (Bay St., downtown Nassau, Dec. 26 and Jan. 1) is an authentically Bahamian parade rivaling any Carnival or Mardi Gras celebration in the world. It is the pulse of the islands, and Bahamians are positively passionate about their Junkanoo celebration. Intricate and intensely colorful costumes are handmade of papier-mâché, crepe paper, ribbon, and beads, and large floats are constructed using Styrofoam and plywood. Each of the six major groups, with nearly 1,000 people, has a different theme each year. The excitement builds throughout the evening, and the parade can last into the early hours of the morning. The energy that flows as you witness this spectacle is contagious. Marching bands with horns, goatskin drums, whistles, and cowbells ensure that every spectator is in nonstop motion. Choreographed dancers spin cartwheels and flip batons, enlivening the setting. Judges vote on best music, costumes, and best overall presentation. Local businesses sponsor the groups.

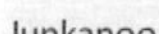

Junkanoo

There are Junkanoo celebrations in Grand Bahama, Harbour Island, Bimini, Exuma, and Abaco, but the largest celebration by far is the Nassau festival. Visit the **Educulture Junkanoo Museum** (West St., Mon.-Fri. 9am-5pm) to learn more about the festival, its tradition, and its heritage, and to view retired costume pieces. If you aren't in The Bahamas during the holidays, Atlantis does a small weekly Junkanoo parade at the **Marina Village** (tel. 242/363-2000 for schedule, www.atlantisbahamas.com).

MARATHON BAHAMAS

Celebrating its 9th year in 2018, **Marathon Bahamas** (starts at Junkanoo beach, ends at Arawak Cay, www.marathonbahamas.com, mid-Jan.) is a top destination event for running enthusiasts and a Boston Marathon qualifier. The course is flat and scenic, providing entertainment along the way. It's a popular wintertime event because of the mild temperatures. Afterward, enjoy a postrace party and a Junkanoo band. The event includes a full marathon, a half marathon, a relay, and a 5K.

SHOPPING

Nassau has always been a hub for shopping because of high-end name brands at duty-free prices. Often you can find jewelry and accessories for cheaper than in the United States. In recent years, businesses have found it difficult to compete with the shopping available on the cruise ships, but there's still a lively scene on Bay Street. Get off the beaten path and you'll come across some fantastic art galleries showcasing the best of Bahamian arts, crafts, and home goods.

Bay Street is a good starting point, where you will find a variety of clothing, souvenirs, and high-end apparel such as Cartier, David Yurman, Fendi, Gucci, John Bull, and Coach. Most stores operate Monday-Saturday 9am-around 5:30pm, and on Sunday have shorter hours or close completely.

The Bahamas has a strong heritage for straw markets. The largest, although maybe not the most authentic, is the **Straw Market** (Mon.-Sat. 7am-7pm), on the west end of Bay Street. Hundreds of vendors in an enclosed pavilion hustle for your business. If you love bargaining, this is a great place, because Bahamians don't typically barter in other situations. Find straw crafts, cheap T-shirts, handbags, and souvenirs. There are

Public Holidays

The Bahamas shuts down on public holidays. By law, liquor stores are not allowed to open on public holidays and Sundays; marinas' ship stores are an exception. Often, especially in the Out Islands, grocery stores and shops close as well. On national voting days, no establishment is allowed to serve alcohol until 6pm. You may also find general shop closures for parades, regattas, and community weddings and funerals in smaller settlements. Easter Weekend is a classic example, as stores typically shut from Good Friday until Easter Monday, maybe opening on Saturday if it is part of their regular hours. If a holiday falls on a weekend, keep an eye out for an observance day the following Monday. Generally, be prepared not to have all amenities available.

- New Year's Day—January 1
- Majority Rule Day—January 10
- Good Friday—March or April
- Easter Sunday—March or April
- Easter Monday—March or April
- Labour Day—1st Friday in June
- Whit Monday—7th Monday after Easter
- Independence Day—July 10
- Emancipation Day—1st Monday in August
- National Heroes Day—2nd Monday in October
- Christmas Day—December 25
- Boxing Day—December 26

Straw Crafts

Straw crafts are an integral part of Bahamian heritage that is still alive and flourishing today. It is a traditional, creative, and sustainable practice that allows communities throughout the islands to maintain entrepreneurial integrity and independence. It has been told that for generations, families in communities such as Cat Island, Long Island, Eleuthera, and Exuma often plaited straw late into the night by lantern and candlelight, telling traditional stories and thereby preserving the folklore of Bahamian heritage. There are close to 200 Bahamian straw weave patterns named with common words in everyday Bahamian vocabulary, such as fish pot, peas-and-rice, hole in the wall, and soursop. Straw crafts are typically made from the dried fronds of the silver thatch palm, coconut palm, and sisal plant and are used to create floor coverings, placemats, serving trays, baskets, hats, handbags, shoes, and even clothing.

Traditionally straw products were used by Bahamians in a purely utilitarian sense. It wasn't until Eunice Albertha Brown of Fox Hill, Nassau, began selling straw goods to visitors in 1936 that a link between Bahamas tourism and the Bahamian straw industry was established. By the 1950s, an entrepreneurial network that connected New Providence to the Out Islands was developed, allowing trade between the islands and promoting much needed trade income in even the smallest settlements. Although you can find many straw crafts in the capital, you will also find locals selling their wares throughout The Bahamas.

also smaller markets on Paradise Island and Cable Beach.

Bahama Handprints (Ernest St., off E. Bay St. and Mackey St., tel. 242/394-4111, www.bahamahandprints.com, Mon.-Fri. 10am-4pm, Sat. 10am-2pm) has been silk screening fabrics in true island style since 1966. Visit their shop and printing factory and view the printers at work as the fabrics come to life in the form of linens, handbags, and clothing. You can pop in the back for a look, or request to book an informative tour for $10 pp. All of their ocean-inspired fabrics are printed by hand. Some of the designs still in production today are original vintage prints from the 1960s and 1970s, while other patterns change seasonally.

My Ocean (tel. 242/325-2141, www.myocean.com, Mon.-Sat. 9:30am-5pm) offers a variety of locally made soaps, candles, ceramics, spa products, textiles, and jewelry at three locations: Prince George Plaza, Festival Place, and LPIA Airport. **Tasty Teas** (21 Delancy St., tel. 242/698-1101, www.tastyteasbahamas.com, daily 9am-4:30pm) has a wide selection of whole tea leaves, filtered tea bags, ice teas, and tropical juices, all made with local plants, herbs, fruit, and spices.

Head inland to visit **Bahama Art & Handicraft** (E. Shirley St., tel. 242/394-7892, Mon.-Fri. 9am-4:30pm, Sat. 9am-4pm) with a selection of gifts, paintings, mosaics, wood and straw work, and interesting jewelry—such as earrings and pendants—using the quills of the invasive lionfish.

Creative Nassau, located on Village Road, is a beautiful property tucked in between commercial businesses and residences. Within the compound are two establishments worth a visit: **Craft Cottage Bahamas** (20 Village Rd., tel. 242/446-7373, Mon.-Fri. 10am-4pm, Sat. 9am-1pm) has straw bags, jewelry, hand-painted glass, bath and body products, artwork, and clothing. You will be greeted warmly by the store owners, and they will be happy to give you the story behind their many artisanal products. On the same property is **Doongalik Studios Art Gallery** (20 Village Rd., tel. 242/394-1886, www.doongalik.com, Mon.-Wed. 10am-4pm, Sat. 9am-1pm), originally formed in the 1970s to promote the artistic talent of Bahamians. The studio now showcases work by dozens of local artists, including paintings, sculptures, and ceramics. A Saturday farmers market also operates throughout the winter months.

FOOD

The restaurant scene in New Providence has exploded in recent years, offering a plethora of options for all palates. Traditional Bahamian food is something every visitor should try at least once. Food trucks are everywhere, but they aren't always in the same place. Bahamians, from laborers to professionals, eat at food trucks for breakfast and lunch daily. But the international and high-end dining offerings around the island should not be overlooked.

Bahamian

TOP EXPERIENCE

★ FISH FRY AT ARAWAK CAY

One of the most iconic areas of Nassau, **Arawak Cay** (W. Bay St. and Chippingham Rd., daily, $10-15) was formed as a result of dredging the port area in 1969. Leave it to industrious Bahamians to capitalize on the new land: Over the years, the mound of dredged soil has become a hodgepodge of restaurants known as the Fish Fry. It is known by both locals and visitors as the go-to spot for traditional Bahamian fare and whiling away the afternoon under the shade of a lofty umbrella. Colorful wooden buildings dot the shipping portside, although most don't offer waterside dining.

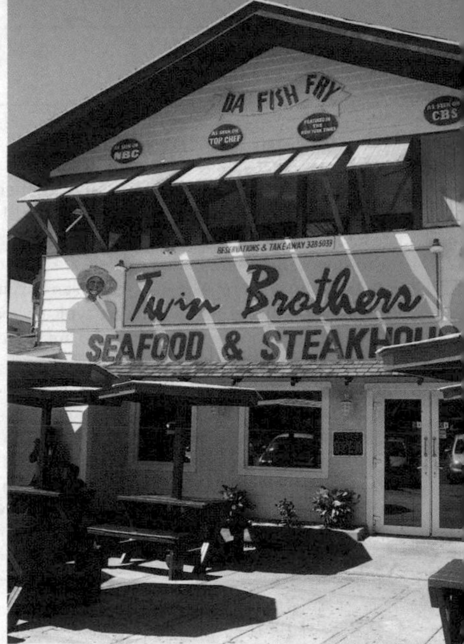

Twin Brothers at the Arawak Cay Fish Fry

Sample fried snapper, or restaurant-hop to find your favorite version of conch fritters. It's a popular hangout on a Sunday afternoon for cold Kaliks, and each establishment puts their own spin on drink specialties, including Sky Juice (gin, coconut water, sweetened condensed milk), Goombay Smashes (gold rum, coconut rum, pineapple juice, orange juice) and Bahama Mama (white rum, dark rum, coconut rum, orange juice, pineapple juice, grenadine). Local favorites are Twin Brothers, Goldie's, Oh Andros, Curlie's, Trudy's, and Frankie's Gone Bananas.

Located under the bridge on the way to Paradise Island is **Potter's Cay** (under the southbound Paradise Island Bridge, daily, $10-15), a mishmash of colorful lean-to shacks serving up fresh Bahamian food and cold drinks. Don't be surprised to hear rake-and-scrape (a traditional form of music using a carpenter's saw and a knife, drum, and accordion) as you watch the Mail Boats and inter-island cargo boats come and go. The place is rough around the edges, but you'll be greeted with a smile, and it's the best place to get fresh conch salad. The vendors may even show you the special way to crack the hard conch shell, a tricky technique. A great place to visit during the day, it can attract some shady characters late at night.

Tucked in on a side street is a Nassau staple, **Bahamian Cookin'** (Trinity Place, tel. 242/328-0334, www.bahamiancookin.com, daily 7:30am-4pm, $12-20). Opened in 1986, this restaurant is now operated by its third generation of women owners and serves up Bahamian specials such as steamed chicken, pork chops and mutton (goat), broiled grouper, and minced lobster.

In the heavily touristed areas of any given

city, you may find the restaurants overpriced and mediocre, and you may be well advised to get off the beaten path to find something authentic. Not so with ★ **Lukka Kairi** (Woodes Rodgers Walk, tel. 242/326-5254, www.lukkakairi.com, Sun.-Thurs. 11am-10pm, Fri.-Sat. noon-10:30pm, $20-30). Front and center at the cruise-ship docks of Woodes Rodgers Walk, Lukka Kairi is a stunning example of upscale Bahamian cuisine. Located on the second floor, this open-air restaurant is a great spot to watch the foot traffic and cruise ships coming and going, or listen to live music on weekends. They also have their own locally made house brew on tap. Free parking is available for customers.

For mariners and yachties, **The Poop Deck** (Nassau Yacht Haven, E. Bay St., tel. 242/393-8175, www.thepoopdeck.com, daily 11:30am-10:30pm, $20-30) is the spot. Located at the Nassau Yacht Haven (the name sounds fancier than it is), you'll be hanging out with sailboat cruisers, charter boat captains, and fisherfolk. The food is simple and tasty, but most people are there for the social scene. There are happy hour specials daily 4pm-7pm. A second location is at Delaporte in Western New Providence. **Bahama Grill** (W. Bay St., just west of Arawak Cay, tel. 242/356-4745, www.bahamagrill.com, Mon.-Tues. 11am-10pm, Wed.-Sat. 11am-11pm, Sun. 11am-9pm, $10-20) is a local's favorite known for slow-cooked barbecue ribs and rotisserie chicken. Dine in or take out.

Fine Dining

★ **Café Matisse** (Bank Lane, off Bay St., tel. 242/356-7012, www.cafe-matisse.com, Tues.-Sat. lunch noon-3pm, dinner 6pm-11pm, $25-50) is a longtime favorite for upper crust Nassauvians living out east. Owner Greg Curry floats around the room, checking that patrons are enjoying themselves. Tucked between Bay Street and Shirley Street, it is marked only by a tiny yellow sign. In good weather, request a table outside in the beautiful courtyard shaded by bamboo, palms, and native trees. The staple favorites remain, but certain menu items change every six months, keeping things fresh.

Graycliff Restaurant (W. Hill St., tel. 242/302-9150, www.graycliff.com, Mon.-Fri. noon-2:45pm, 6:30-9:30pm, $40-60) has a reputation the world over for being the top choice in fine dining. Their wine cellar is one of the most extensive and cherished in the world, winning awards from *Wine Spectator* and the *World of Fine Wines* magazines. There

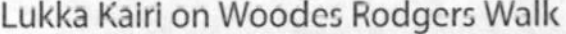

Lukka Kairi on Woodes Rodgers Walk

Artisanal Food and Drinks

Nassau may not spring to mind as a foodie destination, but **Graycliff** has been paving the way for decades. In 1988, Graycliff started consistently wining the *Wine Spectator* magazine Grand Award. It touts one of the largest and most expensive wine cellars in the world, with 275,000 bottles in the cellar, including an 1865 Château Lafite, and the world's oldest bottle of wine, a Rüdesheimer Apostelwein from 1727, priced at $200,000. The in-house five-star restaurant offers an opportunity to pair exceptional food with one of the many wines. In 1996 Grayfliff began hand-rolling cigars. The late master cigar roller, or *torcedore,* Avelino Lara, at one-time Fidel Castro's personal roller, created the original Graycliff blend. Since its inception, the boutique **Cigar Company** has won multiple awards and sells its seven blends worldwide.

In 2011, **Graycliff Chocolatier** was established, producing hand-crafted chocolate with the highest standards. Try their Hennessey and caramelized onion chocolate spheres, or the white chocolate and curry bar. The combinations may sound odd, but the flavors will dance in your mouth with surprising integration. Opened in late 2017 is **Bahama Barrels,** where you can sample wine produced at Graycliff from Italian and Argentinian grapes. Graycliff produces their wines on-site and gives guests an opportunity to blend their own wines. If you would like to try one of Graycliff's many experiences, including a wine luncheon and a tour of the wine cellar, a cigar rolling lesson and rum tasting, or a chocolate factory tour and demonstration, call tel. 242/302-9150 or email experiences@graycliff.com.

Located on the historic Buena Vista Estate, **John Watling's Distillery** (17 Delancy St., www.johnwatlings.com, tel. 242/322-2811) produces local artisanal rum and vodka. Dating to 1789, the beautiful estate is perched on a hill under a canopy of mature trees. **The Red Turtle Tavern** is a great place to go for Friday happy hour. Get a tour of the colonial estate home and working distillery, and sample the rums. Smell the more than 1,000 aging barrels as you walk through the aging cellar and learn how rum at the distillery is made the old-fashioned way.

After years of domination by the mega-beer companies of Commonwealth Brewery (producers of Kalik) and the Bahamian Brewery (Sands products), the craft beer scene has finally made an appearance in The Bahamas. Founded in 2012, **Pirate Republic Brewing Company** (Woodes Rodgers Walk, tel. 242/328-0612, www.piraterepublicbahamas.com) is the first and only craft brewery in The Bahamas, with distribution throughout the islands and the Tap Room in downtown Nassau featuring regular events. Take a tour of the brewery, or sample a flight of their flagship and seasonal brews in the Tap Room.

are four air-conditioned dining rooms and an outdoor patio. Reservations are required, and a dress code is enforced.

International

Forget that you're in The Bahamas: **Double Dragon** (E. Bay St., tel. 242/393-5718, www.doubledragonbahamas.com, Sun.-Thurs. noon-10pm, Fri.-Sat. 12:30pm-10pm, $10-20) is arguably the best Chinese food ever. Double Dragon is run by a Chinese Bahamian family and is a relaxed dining experience. The restaurant attracts Chinese patrons (a true sign of authenticity). There are plenty of options to satisfy your hunger: Try their crispy chow mein noodles, pan-fried wontons with oyster sauce, or the shrimp honey walnut special. Everything is homemade from scratch, and they never use MSG.

In the last few years, sushi has become increasingly popular in Nassau, but **Seafront Sushi** (E. Bay St., tel. 242/394-1706, www.seafrontsushibahamas.com, Mon.-Fri. lunch noon-4pm, dinner 6pm-10pm, Sat.-Sun. 6pm-11pm, $15-25) paved the way back in 2001, making sushi accessible to the average Bahamian not yet familiar with Japanese cuisine. On Friday and Saturday night it will be packed, and they don't take reservations. If service gets backed up, order another round of the tasty sake's and a large Sapporo beer.

The island's oldest Greek restaurant,

Bahamian Cuisine

Bahamian food is influenced by locally available resources, other Caribbean islands, and flavors from the days of British rule. If you order from a food truck or a to-go lunch establishment, your meal is usually served in a Styrofoam container (many restaurants in Nassau have switched to compostable containers in recent years; a complete ban on plastic bags and Styrofoam containers is due to be implemented by 2020) and you'll be surprised by the large portions of food you will receive, often enough for two meals for a modest eater. Your meal will consist of protein (lamb, pork, mutton, beef, chicken, fish, shrimp, or conch) and two sides. When they say "two sides" it means peas and rice plus two additional sides—typically homemade baked mac and cheese, coleslaw, potato salad, or sweet plantain.

Conch: Conch is a Bahamian staple, considered the national dish of The Bahamas. A common way to serve it is as conch salad. Similar to ceviche, conch salad is made with fresh raw conch, "cooked" in lime juice and mixed with bell peppers, onion, tomatoes, and hot peppers. The tropical version often has mango, papaya, or pineapple mixed in. Other conch dishes include conch fritters, cracked conch (battered and fried), conch chowder, stewed conch, steamed conch, and scorched conch.

Peas-and-rice: Peas-and-rice is a side dish that always accompanies fish, chicken, or meat. Pigeon peas are traditionally used for proper Bahamian peas-and-rice, but due to influences from other Caribbean islands, kidney beans are sometimes used instead. Along with beans or peas, ingredients include white rice, onion, tomatoes or tomato paste, fresh thyme, browning sauce (for color), salt pork or bacon, and occasionally hot peppers.

Boiled fish and souse: Boiled fish and souse are both served at breakfast. Bahamian souse is an adaptation from British cuisine, a light broth with potatoes and onion seasoned with lime, allspice, and goat pepper (an extremely hot Bahamian pepper). The most common souse is made with bone-in chicken wings and drumsticks, but you can be more adventurous and try mutton (goat), sheep's tongue, pig's feet, and chicken's feet souse. Boiled fish uses a very similar broth to souse and is typically prepared using grouper, but mahimahi, snapper, and hogfish are substituted when grouper is out of season.

Athena Café (Bay St., tel. 242/326-1296, Mon.-Sat. 9am-6pm, $15-30) is a great spot to get souvlaki and gyros and also for Bahamian dishes such as conch fritters and conch chowder. On display are photos and plaques so that diners can learn about the important influence of Greek people in Nassau when they first arrived for sponge trading in the 1860s. Today there is a sizeable Greek Bahamian population with numerous restaurants throughout town, but Athena is still the original.

Bars and Pubs

Green Parrot Downtown (E. Bay St., tel. 242/328-8382, www.greenparrotbar.com, daily 11:30am-midnight, $12-20) is the sister restaurant to the Green Parrot Hurricane Hole on Paradise Island. Opened in 2006, they have a lively crowd and some of the best burgers in town. Newly opened in 2017, **Shenanigans** (Bay St., tel. 242/676-8628, Sun.-Tues. 11am-7pm, Wed.-Sat. 11am-midnight) is the only authentic Irish pub in Nassau, serving up real draft Guinness, not found elsewhere on the island. It is a great spot to watch sports. It's small and intimate, but breathing space is available on the outdoor balcony.

The Bahamas Cricket Association, also known as the **Cricket Club** (W. Bay St., across from Arawak Cay, tel. 242/326-4720, www.bahamascricket.com, Sun.-Wed. 8am-10pm, Thurs.-Sat. 8am-10:30pm, $15-20) is a no-frills pub serving British and Bahamian food. It's another great spot to watch sporting events and has a breezy porch overlooking the port. Their homemade meat and pot pies are dynamite. **Seagulls** (Junkanoo Beach, W. Bay St., tel. 242/322 7080, daily 9am-9pm,

$7-14) is a popular spot for cruise-ship passengers and people staying downtown. A true beach bar, right on Junkanoo Beach, it serves up tasty cocktails, cold beer, appetizers, and sandwiches at affordable prices.

Cafés and Light Bites

Biggity (329 Bay St., tel. 242/322-4576, Mon.-Thurs. 8am-4pm, Fri. 8am-5pm, Sat. brunch 9am-4pm, $10-15) is an adorable and highly Instagrammable café filled with art and locally made products such as hot sauces, candles, and repurposed wine and rum bottle pendant lights. Biggity serves healthy salads, sandwiches, espresso, fresh coconut water, and bush teas. **Le Petit Gourmet** (Shirley St. Plaza, tel. 242/393-4022, Mon.-Fri. 8am-3pm, Sat. 8am-2pm, $8-12) serves a different menu each day for a fresh healthy breakfast or lunch with an international twist. **The Kitchen Deli** (E. Shirley St., tel. 242/394-5202, Mon.-Fri. 7:30am-3:30pm, $10-15) features homemade soups, deli sandwiches, salads, a mix of traditional Bahamian food, and dishes such as lasagna, roti, and quiche. **Syrah Wine & Tapas** (E. Bay St., tel. 242/676-0962, www.syrahvino.com, Tues.-Sat. noon-10pm, $10-20) offers tasty light dishes such as beer-battered hogfish with smudder slaw, sweet-chili Mongolian beef, and minced mushroom and herb fritters. Although offering a full bar, Syrah is known for its wine selection, with so many available that the list is in a Rolodex. There's live music on weekends.

ACCOMMODATIONS

There are very few accommodations options in downtown Nassau, apart from a few chain hotels. Prices reflect high season (Nov.-Apr.) double-occupancy rates. Expect lower rates throughout the summertime and non-holidays. Rates listed are not inclusive of 12 percent VAT (sales tax) and any additional resort fees.

$100-150

Towne Hotel (40 George St., tel. 242/322-8450, www.townehotel.com, $125-150) is quirky and modest. You'll be greeted by Max, the hotel's resident blue macaw. The Talking Stick Bar and Restaurant serves breakfast, lunch, and dinner. Make sure to try their famous planter's punch cocktail when you arrive. Bahamian artwork adorns the lobby and is scattered throughout the building. A beautiful courtyard with a pool is surrounded by 46 fully-equipped exterior-entry rooms, and if you're looking for sunshine, you can relax on the sun deck on the top floor. It's tucked away on a quiet street, but you're in the heart of downtown.

Over $250

★ **The British Colonial Hilton Nassau** (1 Bay St., tel. 242/302-9000, www.hilton.com, $300-350) is located front and center in downtown Nassau between Junkanoo Beach and Pompey Square on Bay Street, a great location for accessing all that downtown has to offer. There is a small beach in front of the hotel with lounge chairs and thatched umbrella shades, and the use of kayaks and paddleboards is complimentary for guests. The original hotel was built in 1899 by Henry Flagler but burned in 1921. A new hotel was built, and the stately entry lobby emits a classic old-time setting. Tastefully decorated modern rooms offer striking views of the harbor or downtown Nassau. Upgrade to an executive room or suite and get access to the Executive Lounge business and meeting spaces.

It is not often you can say you've slept in the same room as royalty. With a registrar of guests such as Winston Churchill, the Duke and Duchess of Windsor, and Lord Mountbatten, ★ **Graycliff Hotel** (W. Hill St., tel. 242/302-9150, www.graycliff.com, $435-495) has regularly hosted royals and celebrities since its beginning. The building was built by a former pirate in the 1720s as his private residence. In 1844 it was advertised as Nassau's first inn, offering guests comfortable accommodations, meals, and use of a carriage. The property was purchased in 1973 by the Garzaroli family. The rooms are spacious and stately with attention to historic detail.

The Royal Bahamian Potcake: Beloved Island Mutt

Bahamian Potcakes roaming the streets

The Royal Bahamian Potcake is the mixed-breed island dog of The Bahamas and the Turks and Caicos. Although it isn't officially a recognized breed, it is considered more of a breed than a common mutt, as it tends to have specific characteristics and traits, depending on the island. Potcakes got their name because they were typically fed the crusty bottom of a pot of rice, called pot cake. They are descendants from dogs that arrived during colonialization, a mix of terriers that hunted rats on sailing ships and those that came from the Carolinas during the Loyalist period. They have gotten larger overtime due to breeding with labs, shepherds, pit bulls, and Dobermans, common breeds in the islands as guard dogs. Potcakes are very loyal, have a mellow demeanor, and are protective of their families. Usually they weigh around 45 pounds but can range from 30 to 70 pounds. In recent years, Potcakes have become more desirable; some celebrities (like Shania Twain) own Potcakes and promote their adoption in the United States and Canada. Local organizations such as the Humane Society and BAARK have helped with spay and neuter programs for street dogs. You will still see Potcakes wandering the streets, but their population is much more under control than in the past.

Four-poster beds, antique furniture, and an expansive colonial-style balcony overlooks West Hill Street with glimpses of the harbor.

INFORMATION AND SERVICES

Visitor Information

The Bahamas Ministry of Tourism (tel. 242/356-0435, U.S. tel. 800/224 2627, www.bahamas.com) is an excellent source for information on the island, activities, and travel information. They will be happy to help you plan your time and discover local events. Once you have arrived on the island, pick up the ***What to Do*** guide for up to date information. You can find it at the airport and hotels, or visit www.bahamasnet.com to read the digital version.

Banks

There are a number of banks with full services throughout the island. **Scotiabank** (tel. 242/356-1697, www.scotiabank.com/bs) has locations in downtown Nassau and a prominent location on Paradise Island. **Royal Bank** (tel. 242/356-8500, www.rbcroyalbank.com/caribbean/bahamas) has locations in western New Providence on Cable Beach, Old Fort Bay Towne Center, and an ATM at Caves Village. **Commonwealth Bank** (tel. 242/502-6200, www.combankltd.com) and **First Caribbean International Bank** (tel. 242/502-6834, www.cibc.com) are also available. There are no U.S. banks on the island, but you will be able to do banking in both Bahamian and U.S. dollars. Make sure to bring multiple forms of ID, including your passport, if you plan to utilize any services. Most banking hours are Monday-Friday from 9am or 9:30am until 3pm or 4:30pm, depending on the bank.

Health and Emergencies

Emergency and medical services are located downtown. **Princess Margaret Hospital** (Shirley St., tel. 242/322-2861, www.pmh.phabahamas.org, 24-hour emergency services), **Doctor's Hospital** (Shirley St., tel. 242/302-4600, www.doctorshosp.com, 24-hour emergency services), and the **Walk-In Clinic** (Collins Ave., tel. 242/328-0783, Mon.-Sat. 7am-10pm, Sun. 7am-3pm, holidays 8am-3pm) are recommended.

For police, dial 911, 919, or tel. 242/322-4444; for **fire,** dial 919; for **ambulance,** dial 242/322-2861; **air ambulance,** dial 242/327-7077; **Bahamas Air Sea Rescue Association (BASRA)**, if you run into issues at sea, such as breaking down, dial 242/646-6395.

Media and Communications

If you have an unlocked or GSM cell phone you can go into any **Bahamas Telecommunications Company** (tel. 242/302-7827, www.btcbahamas.com) or **Aliv** (tel. 242/300-2548, www.bealiv.com) location and purchase a local SIM card for about $10. If your phone is locked by your provider, you can buy a local cell phone for around $50. You can either sign up for a prepaid plan starting at $20 for 500 local minutes, data, and additional minutes to call the United States and Canada, or you can put $5, $10, or $20 increments on your phone and use your minutes as needed. You can use BTC Top Up to add funds to your account at grocery stores and other retailers by providing them with your local phone number.

You would be hard pressed to find accommodations that don't offer internet on the island, and most restaurants and retail establishments have free Wi-Fi available, so there is no need to visit a specialized internet café. If you don't get a local phone or SIM, you can often get away with using a service like WhatsApp or Skype and communicate through Wi-Fi. Internet service is speedy almost everywhere.

GETTING THERE

Air

The proximity of The Bahamas to the mainland United States makes it an easy destination to get to. From Miami, the flight is about 30 minutes in the air. **Lynden Pindling International Airport** (NAS) has daily direct flights from major cities such as Dallas, Washington DC, New York, Toronto, London's Heathrow, and many others. Airlines such as American, Delta, JetBlue, Southwest, British Airways, Air Canada, and the national carrier, Bahamasair, provide service. Travelers preclear U.S. immigration and customs at the airport in The Bahamas, meaning you don't have to go through that process upon arrival in the United States, allowing you to arrive as though you were on a domestic flight. There are two terminals at LPIA, the U.S. departures and the International and Domestic departures. The U.S. terminal is strictly for flights to the United States. International and Domestic terminal flights run throughout The Bahamas as well as to Canada, Britain, and other Caribbean islands. The international airport is in western New Providence, and there is no public transportation available—you have to take a taxi or rent a car to get where you need to go.

There are two other airports in Nassau that

host charter and private aircraft. These share the same runway as the main airport. **Jet Aviation** (tel. 242/377-3355, www.jetaviation.com/nassau), formally known as Executive Flight Support, and **Odyssey Aviation** (tel. 242/702-0200, www.odysseyaviation.com) both have port-of-entry immigration and customs services and a courtesy shuttle.

Boat

The Bahamas attracts boaters from Florida and other parts of the United States, either for the weekend or through the winter months, as well as those transiting to islands farther south. There are plenty of full-service marinas in Nassau that allow you to get your bearings and stock up on supplies before heading to the Out Islands.

MARINAS

Bay St. Marina (tel. 242/676-7000, www.baystreetmarina.com) has 89 slips capable of accommodating vessels up to 150 feet and a 12-foot draft; it is located near the Green Parrot Downtown. Located on the eastern side of downtown, **Brown's Boat Basin** (tel. 242/393-3331) has haul-out facilities and a marine store. The **Nassau Yacht Haven** (tel. 242/393-8173, www.nassauyachthaven.com) is a popular marina with reasonable rates. The Poop Deck restaurant and bar, Bahama Divers, and a convenience store are located on the property. **Palm Cay Marina** (tel. 242/324-5132, www.palmcay.com) is located on the southern side of the island and is a great staging point for heading off to The Exumas. They have 194 slips, a café, a restaurant, and fuel services.

GETTING AROUND

Taxis

Taxis are readily available from the airport or from the major hotels. If you need service and there are no taxis around, call the **Bahamas Taxi Union** (tel. 242/323-5818) for a pickup, or download **The Bahamas Ride app** (similar to Uber and Lyft) (www.bahamasride.com). For limousines and special services, try **First Choice Limo and Taxi Dispatch Service** (tel. 242/328-5555, www.tchoicelimo.com). You can choose to use taxi services as needed, but many taxi drivers will give you their business card, so you can call them directly to arrange travel during your stay.

Jitney Buses

Buses in The Bahamas are known as jitneys. The fare is $1.25 to get anywhere on the island, whether you are going one block or across the entire island. Make sure you carry exact change with you, as they don't provide change. The jitney is by far the most economical mode of transit, and many locals use these buses for their daily commutes. I wouldn't recommend using them if you are in any sort of hurry, but it's a great option for seeing a bit of scenery. Jitneys are privately owned and don't operate on a fixed schedule, so don't plan on trying to catch one late at night and or on a Sunday afternoon.

Rental Cars

There are international rental car companies in Nassau, but be prepared to drive on the left side of the road. **Avis** (tel. 242/377-7121, www.avis.com.bs) has locations at Lynden Pindling International Airport, Nassau Cruise Ship Dock, downtown, and Paradise Island. **Budget** (tel. 242/325-8154, www.budget-rentacar-nassaubahamas.com) has locations at the airport and downtown. **Hertz** (tel. 242/377-8684, www.hertz.com) has locations at the main airport, Jet Aviation, and Odyssey Aviation. **Dollar/Thrifty** (tel. 242/377-8300, www.dollar.com) is at the airport. Local car rental company **Virgo** (tel. 242/793-7900, www.virgocarrental.com) may not have the classiest vehicles, but they offer great daily rates as well as free pickup and drop-off anywhere on the island. Locations are downtown on Kemp Road, on East West Highway near Marathon, and at the Airport Industrial Park near the airport.

Paradise Island

There is never a dull moment on Paradise Island. The impressive Atlantis resort towers over the low-lying barrier island, glowing fiery flamingo pink in the afternoon, noticeable from nearly everywhere in Nassau. Once you head over the bridge, you might stay for the duration of your trip, since you will never have to look far to be entertained with nightlife, dining options, beach activities, and water parks.

SIGHTS

TOP EXPERIENCE

★ Atlantis

Atlantis is probably the most iconic attraction this nation has ever introduced. The arch of the Royal Towers and the bursting sunset pink of this massive structure are known worldwide. Originally opened in 1998, the resort offers six different hotels, each with their own amenities, surrounding the 141-acre Aquaventure water park.

Inside the largest hotel, the Royal Towers, is an expansive lobby with cavernous arched ceilings and "The Dig," a series of aquariums filled with exotic sealife, giant manta rays, and sharks that gracefully glide through re-creations of the ruins of the Lost City of Atlantis. Farther inside is the animated casino and a maze of shopping, restaurants, bars, and lounges. Watch for events at the Atlantis LIVE concert series, which features world-famous top musicians, and the Joker's Wild comedy club. If you stay at Atlantis, a wrist band will give you access to all of the amenities of the property.

Shopping, restaurants, and events and the casino are open to the public, but the water park, beach facilities, and marine habitats and aquariums are only available to Atlantis guests. Bahamian residents and the guests of some hotel and cruise-line partners can purchase day passes. Visit www.atlantisbahamas.com/daybooking for more information on these affiliations.

Versailles Garden

Stretching 0.25 miles from The Ocean Club to Nassau Harbour is **Versailles Garden,** an impressive work of Old World elegance. Terraced steps lead up to **The Cloisters,** the remains of a 13th-century French monastery that was brought to New Providence by Huntington Hartford and rebuilt in 1968. Fountains and statues intermingle with Bermuda grass and bougainvillea. It's a popular place for elegant weddings and private events. It can be seen from Paradise Island Drive, but it's easiest to valet park at The Ocean Club and stroll the length of it. It sprawls southward toward the harbor from The Ocean Club's south pool deck.

Hog Island Lighthouse

Hog Island Lighthouse is located at the western tip of Paradise Island, marking the northwest entrance to New Providence and the Port of Nassau. Built in 1817, it is the oldest lighthouse in The Bahamas, and the oldest remaining lighthouse in the West Indies. Paradise Island was originally known as Hog Island until it was renamed by developers in 1959, but the lighthouse kept its original name. You can't access the lighthouse from Paradise Island, but you can view it from many areas in Nassau, including Fort Fincastle and Fort Charlotte.

BEACHES

★ Cabbage Beach

Cabbage Beach rivals any beach in the Bahamas for breathtaking beauty. The beach stretches almost the entire length of the northern edge of Paradise Island and can be accessed through one of the many hotels along the beach, including Atlantis, Sunrise Beach Club, The Ocean Club, and a few public access

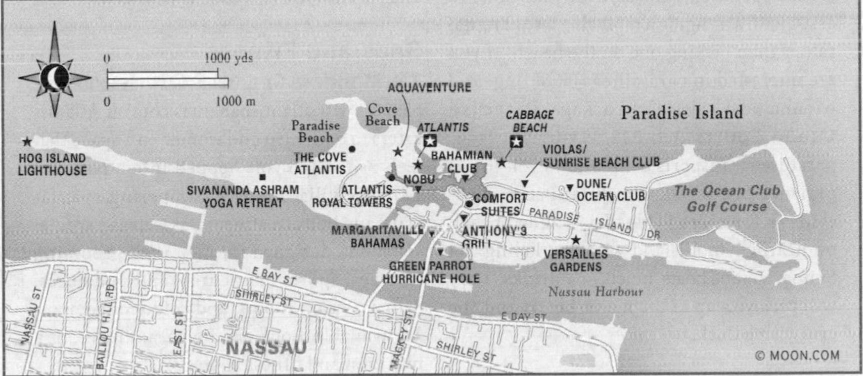

points. If you are closer to Atlantis, you will be caught in the middle of Jet Ski operators, crowds of people, and vendors trying to sell their wares. The beach becomes quieter farther east, closer to The Ocean Club.

Beaches in The Bahamas are not private property, but don't expect to be able to unpack your personal beach paraphernalia directly in front of one of the hotels unless you are a guest; find a spot closer to one of the public access points. Beaches are especially crowded with locals on summer weekends.

Cove Beach

Cove Beach is directly in front of The Cove Atlantis and is protected by a whale's tail-looking rock feature. The Cove tends to draw a quieter and more refined crowd, so its beaches feel like a bit of a sanctuary on an otherwise busy island.

Paradise Beach

Farther west, in front of the Reef Atlantis, is **Paradise Beach.** Guests of the Reef can use the beach chairs, umbrellas, and facilities provided by the resort. This is one of the quieter areas of the beach, not frequented by water-sports operators. West of the Reef are private residences, but the beach can also be enjoyed if you are visiting the Sivananda Yoga Retreat.

SPORTS AND RECREATION

Water Parks

Spanning 141 acres, **Aquaventure** is the highlight of anyone's stay at Atlantis. The 11 swimming pools are designed for all ages, with fresh- and saltwater lagoons, water slides, and river rides. Splashers is a Mayan-themed water playground for small children. The mile-long rapid river called the Current will keep you hanging on to your float with waves, tidal surges, and rapids threatening to spill you overboard, or you can drift through relaxing tropical landscape on the gentler Lazy River.

The six-story Mayan Temple includes the terrifying Leap of Faith, a 60-foot nearly straight-down slide that shoots you through a clear tunnel within a shark lagoon. On the same tower is the dual Challenger Slide, where you can race a friend. If you aren't into so much activity, find a spot at one of the 20 swimming and lounging areas under a shady umbrella and enjoy poolside service. Aquaventure is available to Atlantis guests. Some guests of partnered Paradise Island and Nassau hotels and cruise lines may purchase day passes. Visit www.atlantisbahamas.com/daybooking for more information on these affiliations.

Water Sports

On Cabbage beach you'll notice a plethora of Jet Ski operations. Check with your hotel to assist with arranging a reputable Jet Ski rental rather than picking one on the beach. If you are interested in parasailing, Jet Skiing, and banana boat rides as a package, **Paradise Ocean Sports** (tel. 242/393-0998, www.paradiseoceansports.com) allows you to experience one or all. The Total Package includes a catamaran ride to a secluded beach on nearby Athol Island with snorkeling, Jet Skiing, banana boats, lunch, and drinks. They will pick you up at the major hotels and the cruise ship dock.

Golf

The Ocean Club boasts a stunning 18-hole, 72-par championship **Golf Course** (Ocean Club, Paradise Island Dr., tel. 242/363-6682, www.fourseasons.com/oceanclub) designed by Tom Weiskopf. The course is surrounded by ocean on three sides, making for breathtaking scenery, but due to a lack of protection from the elements, it can be technical, with challenging conditions when it's windy. Expect beautiful year-round golfing weather. Greens fees vary but range from $230 in the July-October low season to $295 in the January-April high season. The course is available only to guests of The Ocean Club and Atlantis; a dress code is enforced.

Spas and Fitness

The **Mandara Spa** (tel. 242/363-3000, ext. 65900, www.atlantisbahamas.com) at Atlantis caters to both men and women in a space that feels as though you stepped into a peaceful Balinese villa. Enjoy a pampering spa, facials, and body treatments, as well as a special spa menu designed for men with grooming services, sports manicures, and pedicures. Saunas, steam rooms, and cold plunge pools are available. Book private yoga, Pilates, or a nutrition and fitness analysis.

Sivananda Yoga Retreat (Paradise Island, tel. 242/363-2902, www.sivanandabahamas.org, $10 per class, $10 per meal, $45 day pass, garden rooms from $113) is a working ashram that has been providing yoga development, spiritual education, and a healthy lifestyle for over 50 years. Yoga classes are held on platforms overlooking the water daily 8am-10am and 4pm-6pm. The lush five-acre compound spans harbor to ocean on a beautiful, peaceful stretch of beach west of Atlantis. A day pass includes two yoga classes, two meals, two *satsangs*, and

Cabbage Beach

Sivananda Yoga Retreat

any talk or program on their schedule. A delicious vegetarian and vegan buffet is offered daily at 10am and 6pm. There are tent sites as well as shared and private villas for overnight guests and those participating in a yoga vacation program. The retreat is accessible via water taxi from downtown Nassau at the dock at Bay Marketplace on Elizabeth Street.

ENTERTAINMENT

Nightlife

If you are looking for late-night action comparable to that of South Beach or Las Vegas, head to **Aura** (tel. 242/363-2000, ext. 65734, Thurs.-Sun. from 10pm), between the Royal Towers and the Coral Towers, upstairs from the Atlantis Casino. Dancers on podiums keep the crowds entertained, and DJs spin the latest dance music. There are two bars, two VIP sections, and a private VIP parlor. There's typically a steep cover charge ranging $25-75. No shorts, flip-flops, or athletic wear are permitted.

Sea Glass Lounge (tel. 242/363-2000, daily 11am-1am) at the Cove Atlantis is a more sophisticated scene, with gaming tables, views of the ocean, and tasty appetizers served daily until 11pm. **Moon Bar** (tel. 242/363 2000, daily 6pm-3am) overlooks the casino floor at Atlantis. A popular spot for a pre- or postdinner drink, it offers a wide variety of wines, draft beers, and specialty cocktails. The **Atlantis Casino** features 90 gaming tables and 850 slot machines. World Poker Tour tournaments are held periodically. High ceilings, glass sculptures, and bright lights can't help but excite gambling enthusiasts. The casino is open 24 hours daily.

If you aren't in The Bahamas during the big celebratory parades of December 26 and New Year's Day, **Junkanoo at Atlantis** is the next best thing. A smaller version of the parade, you can at least get a taste for what Junkanoo is all about. Plus you don't have to stay up all night to watch, like the main event requires. Call tel. 242/363-2000, ext. 66639, for the current schedule and to book tickets.

SHOPPING

Paradise Island offers a range of shopping options, from high-end apparel to beach wear and local crafts. Small shops can be found throughout Atlantis, featuring Atlantis and Bahamas logo apparel and souvenirs, as well various sundries. The **Crystal Court Shops** are located between the Royal Towers and the Coral Towers near the Atlantis Casino. Shop a full selection of international designer stores such as Versace, Amici, Gucci, Rolex, and Cartier. The **Marina Village** (www.atlantisbahamas.com, daily) is an open-air plaza at the marina. Find a bench to sit on while you eat an ice cream and watch the marina traffic, or cruise through retail outlets such as Paradise Blue Surf Shop or Piranha Joe, and Bahamian crafts at the Plait Lady. The **Bahamas Craft Center** (daily 9am-6pm) is located across the street from the Marina Village and features Bahamian handicrafts, conch shell jewelry, Junkanoo art, and straw crafts. Local artisans are often creating their crafts at their stalls.

FOOD

Fine Dining

The majority of restaurants on Paradise Island are within Atlantis. Enter **Bahamian Club** (Atlantis, tel. 242/363-2000, ext. 66508, daily 6pm-10pm, $40-60) and you may feel as though you should be sitting next to Ernest Hemingway in this tropical version of a big-game hunting lodge. The elegance and refinement with hints of a seafaring romanticism (and cozy forest-green leather booth seating) will invite you in; a diverse menu with escargots, chana masala, and lobster waldorf will please your palate.

At The Ocean Club is **Dune** (Paradise Island Dr., tel. 242/363-2501, www.fourseasons.com/oceanclub, daily breakfast 7am-11am, lunch noon-3pm, dinner 6pm-10:30pm, $45-60) with its colonial and coastal-inspired decor giving this top restaurant an inviting feel. Enjoy breathtaking views of the ocean in their indoor dining room, or sit on their shady and breezy outdoor balcony perched over Cabbage Beach. French, Asian, and Bahamian-inspired cuisine includes dishes like Peking duck with shallot confit and lotus root stir-fry, and yellowfin tuna tartare with spicy radish and ginger marmalade.

International

Nobu (tel. 242/363-3000, Sun.-Thurs. 5:30pm-10pm, Fri.-Sat. 5:30pm-11pm, $20-40) is the world-renowned restaurant of celebrity chef Nobu Matsuhisa. Although you can find this restaurant elsewhere in the world, here they take advantage of fresh Bahamian seafood such as lobster, conch, yellowtail, and bluefin tuna. Enjoy a predinner cocktail at their neoteric fluorescent-lit bar with backless leather ottoman seating. The ambience is lively and fast-paced yet refined. Sit at the bar and watch the master sushi rollers crank out specialty sushi and sashimi, or sit in one of their two smaller dining rooms for a more reserved atmosphere.

Casual

Located just across from the Marina Village in the heart of Paradise Island, **Anthony's Grill** (Paradise Village Shopping Plaza, tel. 242/363-3152, www.anthonyparadiseisland.com, daily 8am-10:30pm, $15-30) is a popular spot for American and Bahamian breakfast, lunch, and dinner. Get take-out or dine-in on seafood, pizza, and pasta dishes, or try their specialty slow-cooked ribs with homemade barbecue sauce.

Just down the road on the east side

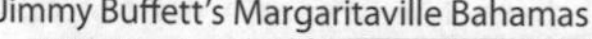
Jimmy Buffett's Margaritaville Bahamas

of the Paradise Island bridge is **Jimmy Buffett's Margaritaville Bahamas** (1 Marina Dr., tel. 242/363-0400, www.margaritavillebahamas.com, Sun.-Thurs. 11am-midnight, Fri.-Sat. 11am-1am, $15-25), a great spot to enjoy a view of the harbor, take a dip in the pool, and enjoy a laid-back open-air tropical atmosphere. Check the calendar for live music, dancing, and events, and pop into their retail shop for your Bahamas Parrothead gear. Next door to Margaritaville, perched on the edge of the Hurricane Hole marina, is ★ **Green Parrot Hurricane Hole** (Marina Dr., tel. 242/328-8382, www.greenparrotbar.com, daily 11:30am-midnight, $15-30). This open-air bar attracts yachties and boaters. Bring a spare T-shirt and add it to the collection of signed shirts hanging from the ceiling. If you're looking for a relaxed atmosphere within a short walking distance of Atlantis, hit up **Violas Bar & Grill** (Casino Dr., tel. 242/363-2234, www.violasbarsunrisebeach.com, daily 7am-10:30pm, $10-20). It's at the Sunrise Beach Club on the north side of the island on Cabbage Beach and serves breakfast, lunch, and dinner. They tend to keep it simple with menu items such as burgers, wings, pizzas, and quesadillas. Stop in on Friday nights for karaoke starting at 8pm.

ACCOMMODATIONS

$150-250

The **Atlantis Coral Towers** (Paradise Beach Dr., tel. 242/363-3000, www.atlantisbahamas.com, $250) are fully family-oriented and situated closest to the Marina Village. The rooms are newly renovated in ocean and coral hues, providing a beachy ambience. Private cabanas with a swim-up bars allow for the adult members of the family to relax.

The **Atlantis Beach Tower** (Paradise Beach Dr., tel. 242/363-3000, www.atlantisbahamas.com, $230) sits farther east and is all about the beach. It is removed from all the action, a quiet escape from the rest of Atlantis, with fewer crowds at the beach and pool. It's the oldest part of the property and has the fewest frills, but if you don't mind walking a bit to access the water parks, it's a great value. Located between the Coral and Beach Towers is the Atlantis movie theater, for those days of inclement weather, or just a few hours out of the sunshine.

Over $250

Nearly 20 years after its opening debut, the ★ **Atlantis Royal Towers** (Paradise Beach Dr., tel. 242/363-3000, www.atlantisbahamas.com, $285) still do not cease to awe. High domed ceilings with marble flooring and an impressive aquarium welcome you as you enter the lobby. Royal Towers is the place to take full advantage of all that Atlantis has to offer. It's centrally located within close proximity of Aquaventure, the casino, shopping, and restaurants. The rooms are the largest and most spacious of all the towers, and it is home to the famous Towers Bridge Suite, the adjoining open air section. The Bridge Suite features 10 rooms, a 1,250-square-foot living room with a grand piano, and the absolute best views in Nassau.

Comfort Suites Paradise Island (Paradise Island Dr., tel. 242/363-3680, www.comfortsuitespi.com, $314) is the only off-site hotel with an agreement with Atlantis for guests to have use of their facilities at no extra charge. It's actually closer to Aquaventure than the Beach Towers, plus they offer complimentary breakfast. Due to the cost of meals on Paradise Island, this makes it a great deal for a family getaway. The **Sunrise Beach Club & Hotel** (Casino Dr., tel. 242/363-2234, www.sunrisebeachclub.com, $382) is a family-run hotel with lush rainforest like grounds, mature landscaping, and two beautiful pools. One-bedroom villas, up to five-bedroom suites with full kitchens or kitchenettes can accommodate couples, families, and groups. Violas is the on-site bar and restaurant, but it's only a short walk to the restaurants and shops at Atlantis.

★ **The Cove Atlantis** (Paradise Beach Dr., tel. 242/363-3000, www.atlantisbahamas.

com, $540) is the most sophisticated of the Atlantis properties, modern and elegant with ocean-view rooms, expansive lush pool decks, a poolside concierge, and gaming. Relax on one of their dreamy daybeds in the center of the pool, or opt for the privacy of one of 20 cabanas with full concierge service. Two white-sand beaches are separated by a protective "whale tail" rock formation. The Cain Pool is an adults-only area, but there is also a family-friendly pool, although most people with children opt to stay at one of the Atlantis towers, closer to Aquaventure.

Amid towering coconut palms and expansive lawns is ★ **The Ocean Club** (Paradise Island Dr., tel. 242/363-2501, www.fourseasons.com/oceanclub, from $1,160), newly acquired by Four Seasons Resorts and a true island destination of luxury. The decor is a mix of traditional Bahamian functionality, British colonial grandeur, and contemporary elegance. The oceanfront rooms and suites are chic and inviting. The Garden Cottage offers a spacious parlor, a dining area, and a private courtyard, and the three- or four-bedroom Villa Residences offer room for families to spread out in style.

GETTING THERE AND AROUND

Paradise Island is about a 35-minute trip from the airport by taxi. The fare is about $45, which includes the $2 bridge toll. Once you are on the island, most places are walkable within the Atlantis area, but if you are staying at Atlantis and dining at Dune, grab one of the many taxis standing by.

Marinas

Arriving by boat, you have two choices for marinas on the Paradise Island side. **Atlantis Marina** (tel. 242/363-6068, www.atlantisbahamas.com, VHF channel 16) services yachts up to 240 feet, and included in your dockage fee is access to all of the Atlantis facilities, water parks, and beaches. Access is easy for sailboats and large yachts via the 100-foot entrance channel, and it's situated in the heart of Marina Village. **Hurricane Hole Marina** (tel. 242/363-3600, VHF channel 16, www.hurricaneholemarina.com) has great access to amenities and services in Paradise Island's downtown area, and it is located adjacent to Green Parrot, with Margaritaville just a short walk away.

The Cove Atlantis

Cable Beach and Western New Providence

Cable Beach is a 2.5-mile stretch along the north central side of the island. There are all-inclusive and resort hotels, but there's not much in the way of sights or shopping within walking distance. If you're happy lounging by the pool or on the beach, you'll be all set. Outside Cable Beach, the remainder of western New Providence is residential, with an upscale island vibe. Although it may seem fairly rural at first glance, there are actually a large number of restaurants, allowing local residents to avoid traveling to bustling downtown.

SIGHTS

The Caves

Located between the Caves Heights development and the Caves Village shopping center are **The Caves** (W. Bay St., near Caves Village, free). It's easily visible from Bay Street, and there is ample parking. It's a popular quick stop for those touring the island, but it's a fairly unexciting natural rock formation. You'll see tiny bats flitting about within the dark interior. Watch your step and wear proper shoes, as it's slippery and can be dangerous.

Clifton Heritage Park

Follow West Bay Street onto Western Road and drive until you reach the very western point of the island and **Clifton Heritage National Park** (S. West Rd., tel. 242/362-5121, www.cliftonheritagepark.com, daily 9am-5pm, $10). There is evidence that it was once a settlement for the indigenous Lucayan people between AD 1000 and 1500. You can explore the more recent ruins of 18th-century plantation home and slave quarters. Follow interpretative trails to walk along a variety of landscapes, including cliffs, coastal wetlands, ancient dunes, and sandy beaches. Listen to marsh birds and songbirds, and view native flora. Bahamian artist Antonious Roberts recently created *Sacred Space*, female figures carved from unwanted casuarina tree stumps still rooted in the ground.

BEACHES

Driving west from downtown Nassau, just a few minutes past Arawak Cay, is **Saunders Beach.** It's a lovely stretch of white-sand beach with jetties that provide calm water for swimming, but it's right alongside the road, so there's some traffic noise. The beach itself is pretty and clean, and there will be no vendors hassling you. Across the street is a Shell gas station where you can pick up snacks and water. Parking, showers, and restrooms are available.

Farther west is **Goodman's Bay Park.** It's empty with plenty of parking during the week, but it will be packed with locals on nice weekends in summer. Families barbecue under the shade of casuarina trees, and vendors sell hot dogs and soda. It's a long stretch of beach with shallow water just east of the resort hotels of Cable Beach. Keep an eye out for turtles in the bay.

Cable Beach refers to the 2.5-mile stretch where the hotels and resorts are. The beach itself is inclusive of Goodman's Bay, but it also includes the beach in front of Baha Mar and Melia. Past Blake Road is **Orange Hill Beach.** You'll see a sign for the Orange Hill hotel on your left when you are heading west. Pull off onto the side of the road wherever you can; there isn't designated parking. It's protected from the road by beautiful bright green *Scaevola* plants, coconut palms, and sea grapes. It's a popular spot for locals to set up wedding ceremonies and beach receptions, and it's typically uncrowded; there are no amenities.

Love Beach is located near the west

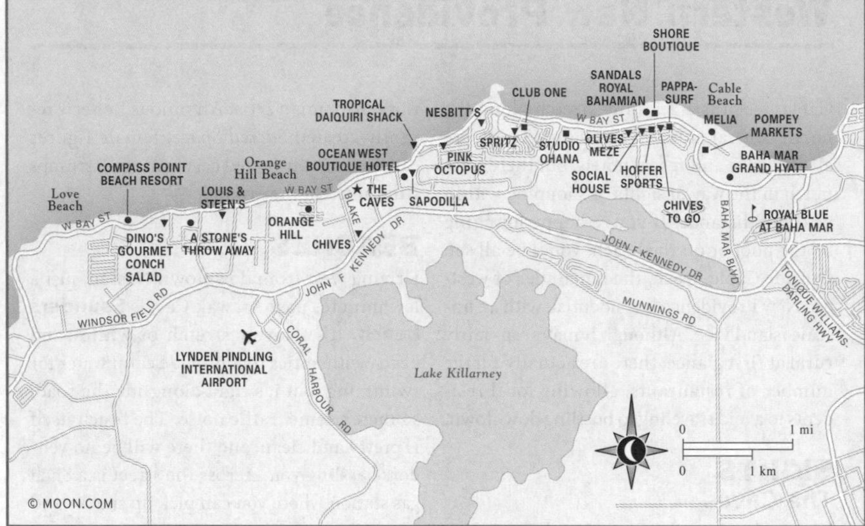

end of West Bay Street before it turns into the gated communities of Old Fort Bay and Lyford Cay. The beach stretches for about 0.5 miles from Compass Point to the west. Condos line the beach, and it's a social scene for residents and their dogs. Walk around the rocky point on the western end of the beach to find a secluded beach; you might have it all to yourself. Swim in front of Nirvana Beach Bar in a natural sandy pool protected by rocks at low tide. Food, restrooms, showers, and parking are available for patrons of Nirvana.

Calm and protected **Jaws Beach** is on the western side of the island. Technically it is within Clifton Heritage National Park, but there is an entrance to the beach on the northern side before you reach park headquarters, so if you just want to visit the beach, you can avoid the park entrance fee. Scenes from *Jaws: The Revenge* were filmed at this beach, providing its name. Alongside the beach are coastal wetlands, mangroves, and marsh. The beach is rarely frequented by tourists, so expect to have it mostly to yourself, but be aware of your surroundings: Don't plan on going solo or staying late for safety reasons. There are no services at the beach.

SPORTS AND RECREATION

Paddleboarding

Get out on the water and explore the island from a different vantage point with **PappaSurf** (Henrea Carlette Bldg., Cable Beach, tel. 242/327-3853, www.pappasurf.com, daily 9:30am-5:30pm), offering tours, lessons, rentals, and special paddleboarding events. Paddleboard yoga will challenge your balance, and the monthly full-moon paddle provides serenity under the stars. If you're traveling with your dog, Pup & SUP is a great activity to share with your four-legged friend. Check the website for rates and a calendar of events.

Snorkeling and Diving

Grab your snorkeling gear and swim out from any of the beaches on the northern side of the island to get a look at the diverse reef life. See turtles at Goodman's Bay and coral reefs off Cable Beach and Love Beach. The most interesting snorkeling is at two sites: 17 feet underwater is a statue of a Bahamian girl constructed by sculptor Jason deCaires Taylor. Named ***Ocean Atlas,*** it's the world's largest underwater sculpture and reaches from the seafloor to the surface. A dive flag marks the spot. **Coral Reef Sculpture Garden** ($10 park entrance fee, $10 snorkel rental), commissioned by the Bahamas Reef Environment Educational Foundation (BREEF), is easily accessed from the beach at Clifton Heritage National Park. In the surrounding area are reef balls to assist with promoting reef growth, a sunken plane from a James Bond movie, and a variety of fish and coral reefs.

Golf

Royal Blue at Baha Mar (Baha Mar Blvd., Cable Beach, tel. 242/788-8000, www.bahamar.com) is a Jack Nicklaus Signature golf course, one of 290 in the world designed by Nicklaus himself and the only course in The Bahamas with significant elevation, making it technical and challenging but enjoyable for all levels. This 18-hole, par-72 course offers a mix of ocean views, white-sand dunes, brackish ponds, limestone moonscapes, and rainforest. The Royal Blue Tavern, located at the clubhouse, is stylish and colonial-inspired, with high ceilings, dark wood floors, and golf matches playing on large monitors. Breakfast and lunch are served daily, and there is a happy hour on Friday. Greens fees range $295-395, with discounted rates for Baha Mar guests.

Spas and Fitness

For those looking to stay active on vacation, there are a few opportunities outside of the resorts. **Club One** (Sandyport Plaza, tel. 242/327-2685, www.clubonebahamas.com, Mon.-Thurs. 4am-10pm, Fri. 4am-8pm, Sat. 6am-6pm, Sun. 8am-6pm) is a full-service fitness center at Sandyport Plaza offering weights, treadmills, ellipticals, and stationary bikes. Televisions with headphone connections are mounted at some machines. Classes include spinning, Pilates, yoga, strength training, and dance. Day passes ($16) include all fitness classes, or ask about purchasing a 10-pack for a discounted rate. Day-care and personal training and also available.

Studio Ohana (Shoppes of Cable Beach, 2nd fl., above Liquid Courage, tel. 242/327-0802, www.studioohanabahamas.com) is a yoga studio offering a variety of classes throughout the week. Their vinyasa flow classes are focused on strength and alignment. They also offer yin yoga, aerial yoga, and barre classes at the studio and at several resorts in the area. Check the website for a schedule and rates.

Pamper yourself at the exclusive **ESPA at Baha Mar** (Baha Mar Blvd., Cable Beach, tel. 242/788-8000, www.bahamar.com). The first ESPA in the Caribbean, this 30,000-square-foot space features 24 private treatment rooms, saunas, steam rooms, and relaxation zones. The spa is an experience in itself: Enter the lobby and immediately begin to decompress with their minimalist decor and calming music. Arrive early and enjoy the steam room and sauna, the outdoor chill zone, or the gym. A multitude of signature and advanced body treatments range 60 minutes to two hours, including massages, facials, manicures, and pedicures. Even men have an exciting option for grooming with a Barefoot and Beer treatment. Receive a hand and foot treatment in a relaxed lounge environment while watching sports and enjoying a cold beer. Private and group yoga sessions are also available.

ENTERTAINMENT

The **Baha Mar Casino** (Baha Mar Blvd., Cable Beach, tel. 242/788-8000, www.bahamar.com) is the Caribbean's largest casino at 100,000 square feet. The decor is ornate, with domed ceiling and picture windows looking onto the terraces, pool decks, and ocean. At night the walkways and fountains are lit with a kaleidoscope of colors. The casino offers all aspects of gaming, from slot machines to video poker to table games. Visit the Book sports bar and wager on sporting events. The casino offers butler service in the high-end gaming areas, high-limit betting, and private gaming salons.

An intimate 48-seat theater, **The Island House Cinema** (Mahogany Hill, Western Rd., tel. 242/698-6300, www.the-island-house.com) is a truly opulent experience. Opt for a couch for four, individual reclining chairs, or cushy bean bags. Order from the wine and cocktail menu and receive full service through the show. Both blockbusters and independent films are shown at two nightly screenings, 6pm and 8:30pm.

SHOPPING

Located on Cable Beach east of Sandals resort is locally owned **Shore Boutique** (Cable Beach, tel. 242/327-1006, Mon.-Thurs. 10am-6pm, Fri.-Sat. 10am-6:30pm), which focuses on upscale resort wear; much of it can be worn at the beach or as evening attire. **Hoffer Sports** (W. Bay St. Shopping Center, tel. 242/327-6622, www.hoffersport.com, Mon.-Thurs. 9am-5:30pm, Fri. 9am-6pm, Sat. 9am-6:30pm) focuses on active and sportswear, sunglasses, sandals and flip-flops, and board shorts. There is a wide variety of men's clothing but a very small selection of women's clothing.

Shopping at Baha Mar includes a selection of designer stores such as Rolex, John Bull, and Tiffany. **Uniquely Bahamian** (Baha Mar Blvd., Cable Beach, tel. 242/788-8000, Mon.-Sat. 9am-5pm, Sun. noon-8pm) is a family-run store featuring Bahamas-made gifts. **Forget-Me-Nots** (Baha Mar Blvd., Cable Beach, tel. 242/788-8000, www.bahamar.com, daily 10am-6pm) has all of the accessories you might need for a day at the pool or the beach.

Across the street from Melia on Cable Beach is the **Pompey Market** (W. Bay St., Cable Beach, daily 8am-6pm), a small straw market where you can buy T-shirts, handbags, and souvenirs. Within the marketplace is the **Daiquiri Shack** (daily 8am-11pm), serving alcoholic and nonalcoholic blended and mixed drinks with fresh fruit.

FOOD

Fine Dining

Hidden among mature native trees on the Island House property, ★ **Mahogany House** (Mahogany Hill, Western Rd., tel. 242/698-6300, www.the-island-house.com, lunch Mon.-Fri. 11:30am-3pm, dinner daily 6pm-10pm, $35-50) attracts an affluent crowd from Lyford Cay and Old Fort Bay. Sit at the bar and sip on specialty cocktails, a diverse range of bottled and draft craft beers, or an extensive wine list. Get there early, as bar seating tends to fill up quickly on Friday and Saturday evenings. Other dining options include outside seating on comfortable couches and chairs, and seats in the dining room. The menu changes periodically, but expect to see pizzas, homemade pastas, charcuterie platters, and meat and seafood entrées. Visit the wine shop, and watch for occasional wine tastings. Dinner reservations are advised.

Pink Octopus (627 W. Bay St., tel. 242/676-5377, Tues.-Sat. lunch noon-3pm, dinner 5pm-10:30pm, $7-15 small plates) was opened in 2017 by Israel-born chef Gal Kotzer, who worked previously at One & Only Ocean Club and Atlantis. Don't let the dated looking exterior fool you; inside is an adorable space decked out with local art and a welcoming seating area. The menu focuses on small shared plates using local ingredients. Popular menu items include stone crab claws, sheep tongue tacos, and cauliflower steak. **Sapodilla** (W. Bay St., tel. 242/327-2161, www.sapodillabahamas.com, Tues.-Sat. 6pm-midnight, $30-60) is an experience. The winding driveway sets a stately mood as you weave through the tropical grounds within this lovely estate. Enjoy a predinner cocktail in the elegant lounge while you listen to live piano music. Once you are seated, the chef makes a point of visiting every table. Try the caesar salad made table-side, or Bahamian flamed dessert coffee. The food is decent, but most go for the ambience and the service. Indoor and outdoor dining is available.

International

Shima (Mahogany Hill, Western Rd., tel. 242/698-6300, www.the-island-house.com, Tues.-Sat. 5:30pm-10pm, brunch Sat.-Sun. 11am-3pm, $20-35) is Southeast Asian with an emphasis on Thai curries and Vietnamese cuisine. The crispy soft-boiled eggs are a perfect balance of savory and sweet. Dine at the casual outdoor bar seating overlooking the pool deck, or inside among the firecracker decor and tall ceilings. The building that houses ★ **Social House** (1 Skyline Dr., Cable Beach, next to Starbucks, tel. 242/327-2098, www.socialhousebahamas.com, lunch Mon.-Fri. 11:30am-3pm, Sat. 11:30am-4pm, dinner Mon.-Thurs. 6pm-10pm, Fri.-Sat. 6pm-10:30pm, $15-25) has changed owners and restaurants many times over the years, but it seems as though Social House is here to stay, having become very popular among local residents and guests of the nearby hotels of Cable Beach. Asian fusion favorites are spicy rock shrimp, conch crispy rice, and tempura black cod guindara lettuce wraps with guacamole and jalapeno aioli. If you are shy of spicy food, make sure to double-check with your server, because a lot of the menu items have a kick. The best bet is to share plates so you can sample a little of everything.

Meze Grill (Shops of Cable Beach plaza, tel. 242/327-6393, Mon.-Sat. 10am-10pm, Sun. 10am-4pm, $15-20) is a Mediterranean-inspired restaurant on Cable Beach with an emphasis on meat and seafood. Meat eaters will also vote for the Flaming Saganaki, a firm Greek cheese called kefalograviera, flambéed at your table with brandy and put out with a douse of lemon. This is a popular spot on a Friday evening for middle- and upper-class Bahamians and politicians, and brunch with bottomless mimosas is served on Sunday.

Contemporary

Spritz (Sandyport plaza, tel. 242/327-0762, www.spritzbahamas.com, Tues.-Sun. 11am-midnight, $20-30) is a family-friendly restaurant located in Sandyport, overlooking the canal. It's a popular spot on a Friday night for resident and expat families with young children. The road is often blocked off so children can ride their bikes and skateboards. Known for excellent thin-crust pizzas, Spritz also offers pastas, seafood, and salads.

Open for breakfast, lunch, and dinner, **Compass Point** (W. Bay St. near Love Beach, tel. 242/327-4500, www.compasspointbeachresort.com, Sun.-Thurs. 8am-10pm, Fri.-Sat. 8am-11pm, bar menu

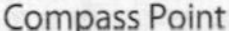

Compass Point

until midnight, $15-25) is one of the few restaurants in New Providence that has sweeping views overlooking the ocean. The high-top bar tables overlooking the ocean are the coveted spots. Cocktails include specialty margaritas and mojitos, which can be enjoyed with tasty bar food like loaded nachos and crispy chicken wings. A full dinner menu is also available, and there is occasional live reggae music on weekends.

Philosophy Smokehouse (Serenity Dr., between Old Fort Bay and Lyford Cay, tel. 242/814-7901, Thurs.-Sat. 6pm-late, $10-20) is a casual outdoor venue serving Texas-style barbecue, including ribs, chicken, brisket, and burgers, at picnic tables. They also have a fantastic fried and stuffed portabella mushroom burger for veggie lovers. Thursday night is more adult-oriented, and Friday has kids' karaoke.

Bars and Pubs

The Swimming Pig (Baha Mar Blvd., Cable Beach, tel. 242/788-8000, www.bahamar.com, daily 24 hours, $25-40) is in Baha Mar and is owned by a local restaurateur. It's one of the only places on the island open 24 hours, that serves breakfast, lunch, and dinner and a late-night menu 11pm-7am. A selection of international draft beers and tasty gastro pub food is available.

Nestled across from the beach near Delaporte are a collection of modest restaurants serving up tasty Bahamian food. **Nesbitt's** (W. Bay St., Delaporte, tel. 242/327-6036, daily 8am-midnight, $10-15) has been a staple local's bar for 40-plus years. It's a popular spot on Friday afternoon for the after-work crowd, and serves traditional Bahamian fare for breakfast, lunch, and dinner.

The Tropical Daiquiri Shack (no phone) is an essential stop to get you from one bar to the next. Past Delaporte heading west, it stands out as a tropical pink plywood box with sunbeam yellow shutters on the side of the road. They are open when they are open, and have been known to pick up and move, so you might find the building in another location. However, they've been near Delaporte on the bend in the road for several years. Wear your swimsuit and go for a dip in the ocean between cocktails.

Nirvana Beach Bar (tel. 242/327-4392, daily 10am-10pm, $10-15, cash only) is located right next to Love Beach. It's been around for many years and they welcome guests with open arms. Nirvana Beach Bar is a popular spot for families in the neighboring condo developments on Friday afternoons, and any day of the week taxis arrive from 10am carrying cruise-ship passengers from downtown looking to escape the bustle of Junkanoo Beach. The bar and restaurant is open-air and very casual. They have fantastic conch fritters, a fresh conch salad bar, and friendly staff. Beach lounge chairs are available, and the staff will be happy to assist you with setting them up.

Cafés and Light Bites

Emmanuel's Food Truck (W. Bay St., across from Saunders Beach, tel. 242/477-7227, Mon.-Sat. 7am-3:30pm, $10-12) is closer to downtown and serves up fantastic Bahamian food. If you're looking to try boiled fish or souse for breakfast, definitely stop here. Arrive early as they sell out of souse quickly. Portions are large, so you are likely to be satisfied if you split a dish between two people. **Chives** (New Providence Community Center, Blake Rd., tel. 242/698-3090) and **Chives To Go** (Henrea Carlette Plaza, Cable Beach, tel. 242/698-0560, both Mon.-Fri. 11am-3pm, $15-20) serve up healthy quick lunches with vegetarians and vegans in mind. The Blake Road location has a lovely outdoor covered seating area overlooking a pond.

Newly opened in 2016 is **Louis and Steen's New Orleans Coffeehouse** (Tropical Gardens area, tel. 242/601-9907, Mon.-Fri. 7am-6pm, Sat. 8am-6pm, Sun. 10am-6pm), which roasts its own coffee blends and serves up Cajun and Creole food and French pastries overlooking the ocean at the breezy open-air outdoor deck. Almond and coconut milk options are available. **The Island House Coffee Bar** (Mahogany Hill, Western Rd., tel. 242/698-6300, www.the-island-house.com, daily breakfast 7am-11am, lunch 11:30am-3pm, bar until 10pm, $10-15) is a relaxing spot to grab coffee. Sit inside the comfortable air-conditioned coffee bar or on the patio overlooking the pool. A breakfast buffet of pastries, fruit, and granola is available.

Dino's Gourmet Conch Salad (W. Bay St., Gambier, tel. 242/377-7798, daily noon-10pm, $10-15) is a relaxed hangout across from the busy boat launch at Gambier Village, near Compass Point. This simple open-air stand with comfy bar stools attracts both visitors and locals, so it's a great spot to mingle. The conch salad is made to order, and there can be a long lineup, so be prepared to settle in with a cold beer and wait a while.

ACCOMMODATIONS

While the majority of the resort hotels are located on Cable Beach, surrounded by restaurants and a few shopping options, there are quite a few smaller hotels along West Bay Street heading west. These are farther from the restaurants, but most have a quiet beach nearby with few crowds. Prices reflect high-season double-occupancy rates; low season should be less. Rates are not inclusive of 12 percent VAT (sales tax) and any additional resort fees.

$150-250

Ocean West Boutique Hotel (W. Bay St., tel. 242/698-6744, www.oceanwestbahamas.com, $225) is up the hill from West Bay Street just before Caves Village, with views of the ocean to the north and Lake Killarney to the south. Ten elegantly decorated rooms have partial or full ocean views; some have French doors that open onto private balconies. Breakfast is available on-site, and Sapodilla restaurant is on the same property.

Orange Hill (W. Bay St., tel. 242/327-7157, www.orangehill.com, $158) is a no-frills hotel, popular with those transiting through on their way from Nassau to the Out Islands due to its proximity to the airport. There is a restaurant on-site serving breakfast, lunch, and dinner, and on any evening there's a fun scene at the bar, which is run on the honor system.

Over $250

Melia Nassau Beach Resort (Cable Beach, tel. 242/327-6000, www.melia.com, $360) is a family-friendly all-inclusive resort situated on a beautiful stretch of beach, featuring three pools, seven restaurants, four bars, a fitness center, and a kids' club. A complimentary shuttle runs to Baha Mar to take advantage of the casino and dining. **Sandals Royal Bahamian** (Cable Beach, tel. 242/327-6400, www.sandals.com, $670) is an adults-only luxury all-inclusive resort with its own private island. The resort is on 15 acres and has seven pools, a fitness club, a full service spa, 10 restaurants, and nightly entertainment. The all-inclusive package includes unlimited scuba diving and water sports. Hop on the ferry to the island, which has two beaches and the Beach Bar. There are private cabanas and hammocks to truly relax. The average rate for a double room with all-inclusive amenities in peak season is $670 with a minimum three-night stay.

★ **Baha Mar** (1 Baha Mar Blvd., Cable Beach, tel. 242/788-8000, www.bahamar.com, $275) is a sensational display of a destination resort, with three hotels onsite to choose from. Arrive at a towering radial fountain, and be prepared to be dazzled by an impressive waterfall show choreographed to music, film, and lights. The resort is situated on a beautiful stretch of beach, with an 18-hole Jack Nicklaus Championship golf course and golf club, a convention center, resident art studios, Peter Burwash International tennis courts and facilities, and the luxurious ESPA spa and fitness center. The Grand Hyatt has 1,800 rooms, including 230 one- to three bedroom suites.

Each room offers crisp contemporary design with its own balcony. Five expansive pools include the Blue Hole, inspired by the natural saltwater pools of The Bahamas. Various dining options are available, including cocktail bars, a piano bar, international restaurants, and casual pool-side dining.

The resort also established the educational Baha Mar Ecological Conservation Habitat (BEACH) Sanctuary, which allows guests to immerse themselves in the natural habitat of The Bahamas, with a turtle nesting sanctuary, an aviary, and a flamingo habitat. The SLS Baha Mar has 300 rooms and 107 residences, and the Rosewood Baha Mar offers 185 ocean-view rooms and suites with private balconies as well as five beachfront villas. Additional dining and shopping options are slated to open over the coming years.

A Stone's Throw Away (Tropical Gardens Rd., just off W. Bay St., tel. 242/327-7030, www.astonesthrowaway.com, $260) is a charming hotel with only eight rooms and two suites on one of the few elevated spots on the island. The balcony boasts panoramic views of the ocean, and the hotel is walking distance to a coffee shop and several restaurants. The brightly colored cottages and a lush landscape at **Compass Point Beach Resort** (W. Bay St., tel. 242/327-4500, www.compasspointbeachresort.com, $315) will make you feel like you're on vacation in a tropical paradise. Eighteen well-equipped oceanfront and ocean-view bungalows have air-conditioning and Wi-Fi. Watch the sun set from the resort's restaurant, which serves breakfast, lunch, and dinner daily. Within walking distance are several other restaurants, a coffee shop, and beautiful Love Beach.

The Island House (Mahogany Hill, Western Rd., tel. 242/698-6300, www.the-island-house.com, $650) is a newly constructed boutique hotel. There are two restaurants, a coffee bar, and a cinema. Guests have access to the pool, workout facilities, and the Bamford spa. The grounds are nestled within a lush tropical setting, but it is far removed from the beaches or the activities of Cable Beach. In addition to the services available at the hotel, a few shops are within walking distance at the Lyford Village shopping plaza.

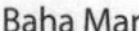

Baha Mar

GETTING THERE AND AROUND

Lynden Pindling International Airport is located in western New Providence, so all of the hotels and restaurants are within a 10-minute drive. A taxi is the easiest form of transportation. Walking and biking are not recommended, as there aren't many sidewalks, and everything is spread out. The slower paced number 10 and number 12 jitney buses run along West Bay Street to downtown and are popular with tourists.

Freeport and Grand Bahama

Grand Bahama truly is the best of both worlds: a harmonic balance between city life and nature. Located only 56 miles from Florida, this northernmost island in the Bahamian archipelago

is home to Freeport and the neighboring resort town of Lucaya, the second-largest populated region in the country. Despite this designation, it only houses approximately one-sixth of the population of Nassau. Grand Bahama has enough going on to keep you entertained, and you can expect smaller crowds and the genuine small-town feel of the islands.

Whereas Freeport has historically been the center of commerce, banking, and government offices, Lucaya is where the tourists frolic. Port Lucaya is the pulse of the island, a vibrant area that draws the majority of visitors due to the opportunity for shopping and dining as well as a first-class marina and boating scene. Over 50 miles of white-sand beaches stretch along the southern shore, and there are numerous beautiful beaches right in the Lucaya area. The Smith Point's Fish Fry on stunning Taino Beach gives visitors the opportunity to mingle with locals on Wednesday nights.

Step outside the Freeport-Lucaya area and you will be surrounded by towering native pine trees and palmetto forests as you drive endless miles of undeveloped natural landscape on the eastern side of the island. Small settlements dot the way as you head into bonefishing territory, home to a smattering of remote mangrove cays and secluded beaches. Head about 40 minutes east of Freeport and hang out at Bishop's Beach Bar to find true island hospitality.

The western side of the island, by sharp contrast, is low-lying and rugged. West End is a quaint fishing village with Old Bahama Bay Resort and Marina as the only hub of action on the western tip of the island. Paradise Cove offers amazing snorkeling just off the beach.

Grand Bahama offers several parks and nature reserves perfect for bird-watching and admiring the diverse array of native flora and fauna. Under the sea you will find spectacular diving. Book a trip with UNEXSO Dive

Previous: Port Lucaya Marina, towering native pines grow all over Grand Bahama Island. **Above:** Grand Lucayan—Lighthouse Point.

Look for ★ to find recommended sights, activities, dining, and lodging.

Highlights

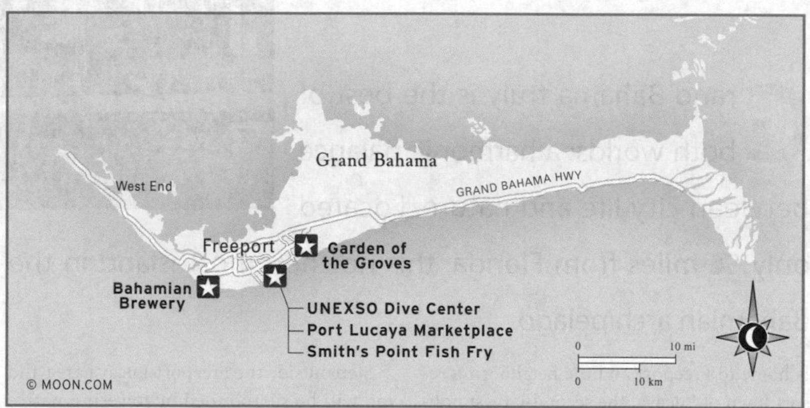

★ **Garden of the Groves:** Meander around peaceful ponds or find solace in the spiritual labyrinth in this tranquil sanctuary (page 80).

★ **Bahamian Brewery:** Learn about the five flagship beers at this 100-percent Bahamian-owned brewery through one of the daily tours and tastings (page 82).

★ **UNEXSO Dive Center:** Grand Bahama is known for the breathtaking snorkeling and diving, and UNEXSO offers plenty of excursions for all ages and abilities (page 86).

★ **Port Lucaya Marketplace:** Home to a variety of restaurants, shops, tour operations, and weekly entertainment, this marketplace is the center of the action (page 92).

★ **Smith's Point Fish Fry:** Every Wednesday evening, locals come out to the Fish Fry at Taino Beach to enjoy Bahamian fare, live music, and entertainment (page 94).

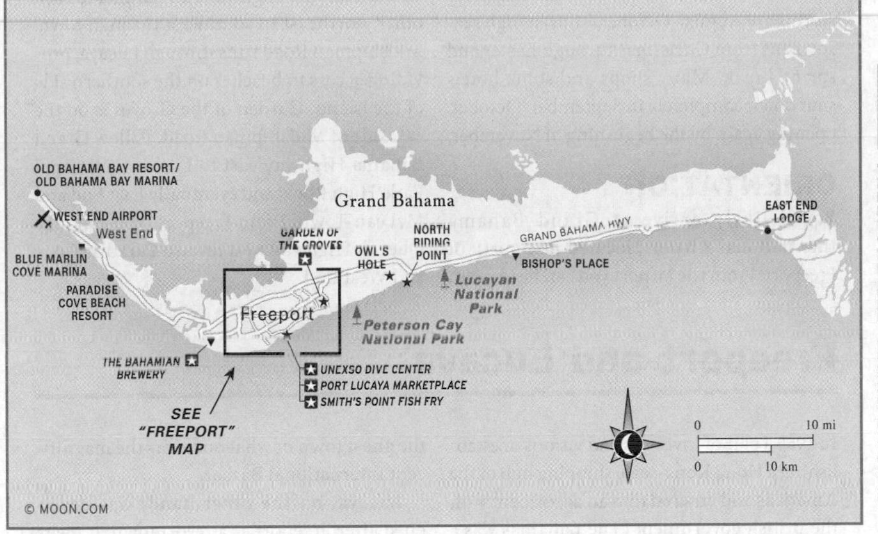

Center to explore shipwrecks, blue holes, coral reefs, abundant marinelife, and even swim with the dolphins. Whether you are looking for a family-friendly holiday, an escape to nature, or a bit of action without the crowds, Grand Bahama won't disappoint.

PLANNING YOUR TIME

If you are looking for restaurants, shopping, and nightlife options, using Port Lucaya as your base is a no-brainer. Two of the island's most popular hotels—the Grand Lucayan and Pelican Bay—are located in Port Lucaya, and most of the dive operators and nature tours are met from the Lucaya area. If you are looking for the all-inclusive experience removed from the bustle of the city, the Viva Wyndam Fortuna Beach is about 10 minutes east of Lucaya on a beautiful stretch of white-sand beach. To really get away from it all, head out to Old Bahama Bay on the very western side of the island within the aptly named settlement of West End, where you'll still have all of the first-class amenities but with the feeling of the Out Islands.

Once you get outside Freeport and Lucaya, you'll find yourself among trees in nature, with the occasional small settlement here and there. Because it's so close to the United States, many folks opt to arrive by boat or hop on a short flight for a long weekend. But if you are traveling from afar, you'll want to spend at least four or five days to really experience the top sights. If you are staying in the Freeport-Lucaya area, a full day can be spent exploring both East and West Grand Bahama, including Lucayan National Park, Ol' Freetown Farm, and Bishop's Place in High Rock to the east. Heading west will lead you to Deadman's Reef at Paradise Cove, where you can snorkel off the beach in crystal-clear shallow water. Plan for at least one full day if you want to scuba dive, enjoy the Dolphin Experience, or take one of the many nature tours available. If you really want to relax and unwind, seven days will allow you to see the sights, with a few beach days in the mix.

Due to its northern location, winter can be cool, dropping into the 60s with average temperatures in the 70s. Summer is hot and humid, but it's a fantastic time for a dive trip or to spend time in the water, and you'll enjoy lower room rates and smaller crowds. Keep in mind that hurricane season runs June-November, but the most active months for storms are August-October. Tourist high season runs from Christmas through Easter and spring break. Many shops and some hotels shut down completely in September-October, opening again by the beginning of November.

ORIENTATION

You'll likely arrive at Grand Bahama International Airport, located just north of Freeport. From the airport you can head south on either East Mall into Freeport, or Coral Road into Lucaya. East Sunrise Highway and Grand Bahama Highway run parallel to each other, northeast to southwest through town. Midshipman Road runs through Lucaya, providing access to beaches on the southern side of the island. Garden of the Groves is on the east side of Midshipman Road. Follow Grand Bahama Highway east to Lucayan National Park, High Rock, and eventually East End and McLean Town. From Freeport, you can take Queen's Highway west toward Paradise Cove and West End.

Freeport and Lucaya

In 1955 a pair of investors had visions of establishing a Hong Kong-scale shipping hub of the Americas and entered into an agreement with the British government (The Bahamas was a British colony at the time). The treaty created a territory within The Bahamas that benefited from various tax concessions and independent governance. From this agreement, the Bahamas Port Authority established the city of Freeport. Around this time, offshore banking was becoming a popular vehicle for wealthy people around the world to minimize income tax payments, and soon after its establishment, Freeport became one of the fastest-growing cities in the world, with a new population of expat bankers, shipping merchants, lawyers, and accountants. Developers invested heavily in canals, highways, and infrastructure. By the mid-1960s it was a very desirable place to live and work.

With the establishment of Bahamian independence in the 1970s and changes to government bureaucracy, the economy of Freeport eventually declined. Recently, three major hurricanes in 12 years and a stagnant world economy has hindered Freeport's effort at reestablishing a thriving community. Freeport is still a name that rings familiar to world travelers; these days, however, Freeport's downtown looks a little worse for wear, including the ghost town of what once was the magnificent International Bazaar.

Lucaya, on the other hand, was developed after Freeport as a resort town. It melts into Freeport on the ocean and harbor. Port Lucaya is alive and vibrant and attracts cruise-ship passengers, yachties, and tourists, and is known for duty-free shopping, straw markets, top restaurants, bars, and nightlife. You can still feel the impact of a slow economy, but the Freeport and Lucaya area is the perfect place to station yourself, with top tours, great hotel options, affordable prices, and nature within close proximity.

SIGHTS

★ Garden of the Groves

Nestled on the outskirts of Freeport is **Garden of the Groves** (Midshipman Rd. and Magellan Dr., Freeport, tel. 242/374-7778, www.thegardenofthegroves.com, daily 9am-4pm, $16.50 adults, $11 under age 13), named for Wallace Groves, a financer from Virginia who helped to establish the city of Freeport in the 1950s. The garden originally opened in 1973 on 12 acres of gardens and wildlife habitat that is home to a variety of flora, indigenous and migratory birds, and butterflies. It can be explored on your own or on guided tours, available daily at 10am. Nature-specific

Four Days in Grand Bahama

DAY 1

Arrive on a Wednesday and head out to take a look around **Port Lucaya Marketplace,** where you'll discover art galleries and the straw market. When evening rolls around, head to **Smith's Point Fish Fry** and settle into your new surroundings by mingling with the locals.

DAY 2

Morning

On Thursday morning, wake up early and go for a walk on one of the beautiful beaches, such as **Lucayan Beach** or **Coral Beach.** Hit up the **Rand Nature Centre** and spend an hour or so walking the nature trails and looking at the interpretative displays. Then, consider lunch at one of the laid-back beach bars on one of three stunning beaches:

- **Manta Ray Bay** at Silver Point Beach
- **Banana Bay** at Fortune Beach
- **Margarita Villa Sand Bar** at Churchill Beach

Afternoon

After lunch, be sure to take a dip in the sea. Head to the **Bahamian Brewery** for their afternoon tour, and then hit **Agave Lucaya's Tza Tza Mojito Bar** for happy hour.

DAY 3

Morning

Friday morning, grab coffee at **Bootlegger's Coffee and Chocolates,** and then get on the road to West End.

Afternoon

Enjoy lunch at **Teasers Tiki Bar at Old Bahama Bay.** On your way back, stop at **Paradise Cove** for snorkeling at **Deadman's Reef.** Rest for a few hours before heading to **Garden of the Groves** for dinner.

DAY 4

Morning

Saturday morning, rise early and head east to **Lucayan National Park** for the **Grand Bahama Nature Tours,** with lunch on a private beach included.

Afternoon

On your way back, stop at **Ol' Freetown Farm** for some souvenir hot sauces and jams, and to see the animals.

DAY 5 AND WITH MORE TIME

If you decide you are having so much fun that you need to stay for a few extra days, make sure that you fit in **The Dolphin Experience with UNEXSO,** head out to lunch at **Bishop's Place** in High Rock, book a motorized bike tour of the island with **CocoNutz Cruisers,** or simply relax on one of the many beautiful Grand Bahamian beaches.

Freeport

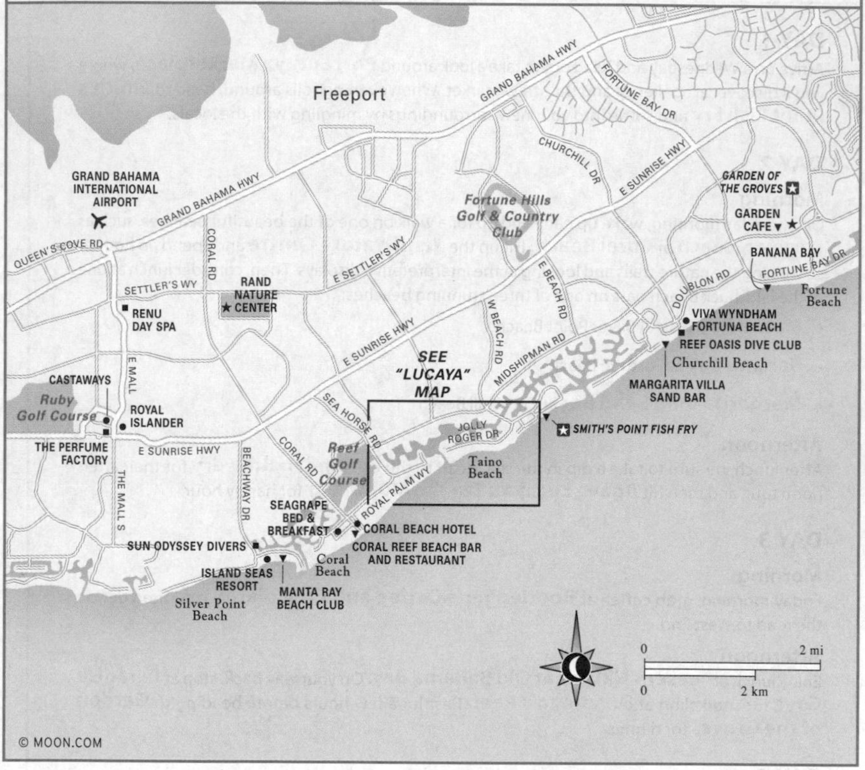

tours, such as birding tours, are also available with Grand Bahama Nature Tours.

Within Garden of the Groves is a walking **labyrinth.** The spiritual labyrinth was built in 2008 as an exact replica of the circa-1220 Christian path at the Cathedral of Notre Dame de Chartres in France. It is a metaphor for life, encouraging introspection. There are no dead ends and it is not a maze, rather a calming walk for the mind and body. Also within the gardens is a children's playground with a playset for little ones, and a chapel, a favorite place for weddings, prayer, and meditation.

Visit the **Garden Café** (Mon.-Thurs. 9:30am-4pm, Fri. 9:30am-9:30pm, $15-25) for daily lunch or Friday dinner. Expect delicious specials like prime rib, lobster tail, steak, and grilled tuna for dinner. Lunch has a fantastic selection of healthy options, such as veggies with hummus, feta flatbread and salad, and a smoked salmon plate. The café is on the edge of a pond filled with waterbirds, fish, turtles, and a calming waterfall. At the Garden Shop, you can stock up on Bahamian handmade items such as Androsia handmade batik and hand-dyed apparel, native coconut shell soy candles made by Bahama Sol, Pasión bush teas, and Abaco ceramics. Other crafts, jewelry, and books are available, as well as vests and caps embroidered with Garden of the Grove signature hummingbird.

★ Bahamian Brewery

Established in 2007, the mission of the **Bahamian Brewery** (Queens Hwy. and

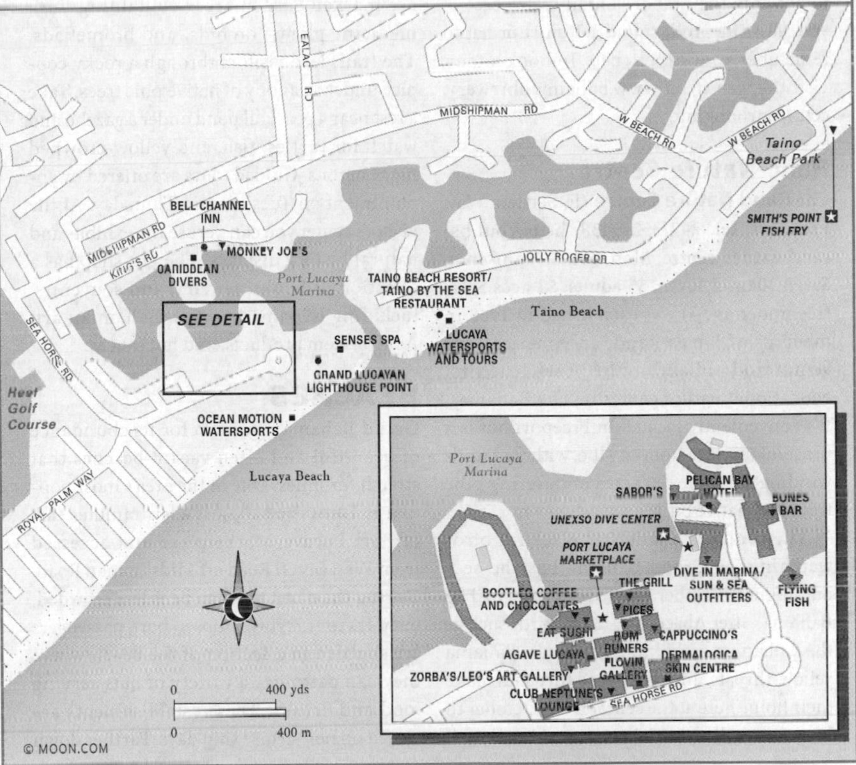

Grand Bahama Way, tel. 242/352-4070, www.bahamianbrewery.com, Mon.-Sat. 9am-6pm, Tour $10) was to create a "truly Bahamian beer." The company hires only Bahamians and is proud to be 100-percent Bahamian owned. Their flagship beer Sands was named for Jimmy Sands, founder of the brewery, and High Rock is named for a town in Grand Bahama.

The brewery offers several different varieties: Sands is a flavorful, easy drinking beer with the hot tropical climate in mind. Sands Light is a lower-alcohol version. Bush Crack is a higher-octane canned beer with party crowds in mind. Strong Back Stout is dark and flavorful, with chocolate and coffee notes, but still enjoyable in the warm climate. The special Amber Ale was originally made exclusively for Atlantis resort, but is now served in selected locations in Nassau and Grand Bahama. Bahamian Brewery also brews a nonalcoholic Triple B Malt. It's rich in vitamins and considered a health drink by locals. The newest product is the Sands Pink Radler, a low-alcohol fruity beer made using real grapefruit juice. All of these products can be found at liquor stores, bars, and restaurants throughout The Bahamas, but it tastes the freshest on tap at the brewery.

Stop into the brewery for one of their tours, so you can learn about the brewery and sample all of the products. The tour takes you through the brewing process, viewing the mash kettle, the *lauter* tun, and the wort kettle. View the bottling line, then peek into the fermentation room to see the shiny tanks. Wrap things up in the tasting room to sample all of the beers on draft. Don't forget to pop into their retail shop to grab a case of your favorite product and a T-shirt or hat to remember your experience. To book a tour, visit the website at www.bahamianbrewery.com/tourbooking.

Rand Nature Centre

The **Rand Nature Centre** (E. Settlers Way, Freeport, tel. 242/352-5438, http://bnt.bs/rand-nature-centre, Mon.-Fri. 8:30am-4pm, Sat. 8:30am-2:30pm, $5 adults, $3 ages 5-12, free under age 5) was established in 1968 in memory of James Rand, an American inventor and philanthropist. It was the first educational nature center in The Bahamas. It's conveniently located in Freeport but is a peaceful reprieve from city life, with foot trails winding through 100 acres of towering pine trees and native bush.

The center is a fantastic place for bird-watching, as Grand Bahama has the second highest number of native species in The Bahamas after Abaco. Migratory birds such as the Cuban emerald hummingbirds, Bahama yellow-throats, and red-legged thrushes make their home here at the center from October to May. You will also find year-round curly tail lizards, butterflies, raccoons, and 130 species of native plants. Tucked into the underbrush are marked garden areas containing bush medicine plants, orchids, and bromeliads. The trails lead visitors through a rocky coppice under a canopy of native pine trees. Take a rest near a peaceful pond under a gazebo and watch for turtles, fish, and yellow-crowned night herons. Guided tours are offered by appointment on Tuesday and Thursday. At the visitors center you can peruse the exhibits and natural history displays. The gift shop has a selection of books, jewelry, and souvenirs, including handmade soaps, Bahamian art, Abaco Neem products, and hot sauces.

BEACHES

Grand Bahama is known for its abundance of beautiful and often vacant beaches that stretch for miles. One of the area's most popular is **Taino Beach,** just a few minutes east of Port Lucaya Marketplace and accessed from West Beach Road off Midshipman Road. During the day it tends to be is less crowded, but if there are cruise ships in port, passengers are shuttled to a section of the beach where they can patronize a variety of huts serving food and drinks. These establishments are closed on non-cruise ship days. Farther down

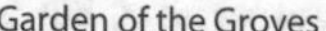
Garden of the Groves

the beach at Smith's Point is the venue for the weekly Fish Fry, a collection of open-air food stands serving local Bahamian food. Often there is live music and always the chatter of locals easing into the evening after the workday. Parking, restrooms, and a grassy park with a children's play area are available.

Lucaya Beach is in front of the Grand Lucayan Resort. The stunning stretch of beach is perfect for soaking up rays and people-watching. Hammocks, lounge chairs, and umbrellas are available to guests of the resort. Nonguests can purchase a day pass to access the beach facilities, pool, and nonmotorized water equipment. The two-mile stretch of Lucaya Beach and **Coral Beach** are technically the same. If you want to escape the crowds of the Grand Lucayan, the Coral Beach end, to the west, is publicly accessible by driving down Coral Road. Parking is available along the street, and there is marked beach access between the Coral Beach Hotel and surrounding condos.

Farther west is **Silver Point Beach**, which stretches in front of Island Seas Resort and Manta Ray Village. Street parking is available off Beachway Drive or by turning down Silver Point Drive. Amenities are available to guests of Island Seas Resort. Rental of beach chairs, umbrellas, kayaks, paddleboards, and other water activities are available at Manta Ray Village, which also has a restaurant and bar, restrooms, and a small selection of souvenir shops.

To the east of Taino Beach, divided by a canal, is **Churchill Beach.** From Midshipman, take Doubloon Road and Spanish Main Drive. You will find estate homes along the western side, and a few beach bars, including Margarita Villa Sand Bar, on the eastern side. At low tide, **Fortune Beach** is a shallow sandbar, perfect for little ones, who can safely splash in the warm sea. You will be able to find a quiet stretch anywhere along the beach, but for a little more action, stop in at Banana Bay for lunch and a specialty cocktail. From Midshipman Road, take Fortune Bay Drive. There is ample parking along the quiet stretch of beach road. Restrooms are available to patrons of Banana Bay.

SPORTS AND RECREATION

Snorkeling and Diving

Along with its beautiful beaches, Grand Bahama is known for wonders below the surface. A reef system runs from West End

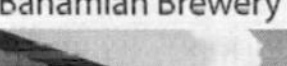
Bahamian Brewery

to Freeport, and there are a variety of options for all levels of divers in depths from 10 to 100 feet. Each outfit has a variety of dive spots along the southern edge of the island. This slender cusp of reef borders the shallow Bahama Bank and abruptly drops off into thousands of feet just one mile off shore. Along the ledge is a variety of sea life, coral reefs, and specialty shark dives. All dive operations offer snorkeling trips, and you'll be able to book training sessions or refresh courses if you need to brush up on your scuba certification.

TOP EXPERIENCE

★ UNEXSO DIVE CENTER

Explore Grand Bahama's diverse and enchanting underwater world with **UNEXSO Dive Center** (UNEXSO Bldg., Royal Palm Way, Port Lucaya Marina, tel. 242/373-1244, U.S. tel. 800/992-3483, www.unexso.com, 8am-6pm daily). The acronym stands for Underwater Explorers Society. They offer 30 different ocean dive sites, including eight wrecks and three inland caverns, but the highlight is the Dolphin Experience, featuring friendly Atlantic bottlenose dolphins.

Established in 1987, the organization initially trained and socialized five dolphins, and eventually worked with them to swim out alongside the boats so divers and snorkelers can interact with them at the open reef. Now they have 14 dolphins in a nine-acre protected sanctuary. Choose from several different program options for all ages. The Dolphin Close Encounter is the introductory program. Take a 20-minute boat ride from the UNEXSO facility to a mangrove cove called Sanctuary Bay and interact with dolphins while standing in the water on a shallow wading platform. If you're ready to get into the water with the dolphins, you can dive in and swim with them at Sanctuary Bay, or opt for the Open Ocean Dolphin Swim. The dolphins will then be released from the sanctuary in order to follow the boat to a location not too far offshore so guests can swim with them in their natural ocean environment.

Fortune Beach

Other popular dives with UNEXSO include shark feeding at Shark Junction, Blair House, which boasts an impressive array of marinelife, night dives, and numerous wreck dives, including Theo's Wreck. They offer guided tours of three caverns that feature interesting geological formations. The cavern dives are for experienced divers and are accessible only with an authorized dive instructor due to hazardous conditions. Reservations must be made well in advance for all dives. Dive courses include Discover Scuba, open-water certifications, and advanced and specialty courses. Snorkeling trips are offered several days per week. All programs leave from UNEXSO at Port Lucaya Marketplace.

OTHER DIVE OPERATIONS

Other dive operations include **Sunn Odyssey Divers** (30 Beach Way Dr., tel. 242/373-4014, www.sunnodysseydivers.com), located near Island Seas Resort, an owner-operated outfit catering to smaller groups for more than 20 years. Morning two-tank dives depart at 8:30am, and afternoon dives depart Monday-Saturday at 2pm. Dive certification courses are typically held in the afternoons.

Reef Oasis Dive Club (Viva Wyndam Fortuna Beach, Churchill Dr., Freeport, tel. 242/350-2923, www.reefoasisdiveclub.com, daily 8am-5pm) offers daily snorkeling and diving trips to reefs and wrecks with up to 21 divers. It is located at the Viva Wyndam and open to nonguests. **Caribbean Divers** (Bell Channel Inn, Lucaya, tel. 242/373-9111, www.bellchannelinn.com) is family-owned, operated, and offers smaller groups and more personalized trips to wrecks, caverns, and coral reefs. They rent equipment and offer instruction. Lodging and diving packages are available with Bell Channel Inn.

DIVE SIGHTS

Theo's Wreck is located 1.5 miles off Grand Bahama. The MS *Logona* is a 230-foot-long cement freighter that was decommissioned and sunk in 1982. Instead of sinking it into the depths of the ocean, UNEXSO towed the boat into shallower water to use it as a dive site and create an artificial reef. It's about 100 feet down and rests at the edge of the continental shelf. There are two places where divers can enter the wreck. It was the sight for the 1993 IMAX film *Flight of the Aquanaut*.

Pygmy Caves is geared toward more advanced divers due to the complexity and depths of 60 to 80 feet. Overgrown ledges cut into the reef, and the coral forms small caves, but they are too small for any human to enter, hence the term "pygmy." Keep an eye out for beautiful brown and white striped Nassau grouper and Caribbean spiny lobster hiding among the crevices.

Shark Junction is one of the highlighted dive sights in regular use by UNEXSO for the shark-feeding dive. It's a 45-foot dive to visit the local reef sharks. You'll also run into stingrays, nurse sharks, and moray eels hovering around waiting for food handouts.

Cavern Dives: Grand Bahama has the second-largest underwater cavern system in the world, with over 32,000 feet of mapped tunnels. There are several options for the less advanced diver, but if you are fully certified for cave diving, Grand Bahama is a top destination. **Ben's Cave** is located at Lucayan National Park and extends for nine miles underwater. Nondivers can view it along the trail system by navigating down a flight of stairs that enter the cave. Experienced divers

UNEXSO Dive Center and marina

can explore this with UNEXSO or Calabash Tours. The dive site has a freshwater "lens" from rainwater runoff. Salt adds mass to water, making it heavier than freshwater, meaning the freshwater sits on the surface. As you descend, the water gradually becomes saltier where the ocean water seeps in through the porous limestone cave system. In contrast to the wide array of coral and marinelife you'll experience on reef dives, on this dive you'll be admiring stalactites, stalagmites, and ancient fossils in a peaceful dark setting. **Owl's Hole** is a 30-foot opening in the earth when part of this cave system collapsed during the Pleistocene. This particular part of the cavern system is about 90 feet deep. Fresh water sits on top of salt water until 30 feet deep, and the dive is known for the evident contrast when traversing this lens, known as a halocline, between the two different water densities.

Water Sports

Ocean Motion Watersports (Lucayan Beach, Lucaya, tel. 242/373-9603, www.oceanmotionwatersportsbahamas.com) is one of the largest water-sports operations in Grand Bahama and has been in operation since 1990. They provide all of the water-sport services at the Grand Lucayan Resort. You can rent equipment or opt for waterskiing, windsurfing, or sailboating instruction. Other activities include parasailing, Wave Runners, snorkeling, banana boat rides, paddleboarding, and kayaking. **Lucaya Watersports and Tours** (Seahorse Rd., Port Lucaya; Taino Beach Resort, Jolly Roger Dr., tel. 242/373-6375 or 242/727-0968, www.lucayawatersports.com) has two locations that offer a variety of options, including glass-bottom boat tours, Waver Runner island tours, sunset cruises, scooter and bicycle rentals, and bonfire beach parties at Taino Beach Resort.

Biking

As with most islands of The Bahamas, Grand Bahama lacks hilly terrain, making for easy biking, especially for those not in prime biking shape. Many hotels and vacation rentals have bikes available to guests, including Viva Wyndham Fortuna Beach. When you go off on your own, make sure you bring a map of the island with you and bring plenty of drinking water. Keep a close eye on the traffic on narrow roads. Bahamians aren't as used to sharing the road as in other parts of the world, but for the most part drivers will give you space.

Grand Bahama Nature Tours (Freeport, tel. 242/373-2485, www.grandbahamanaturetours.com) offers a five-hour 12-mile biking, sightseeing, shopping, and beach trip on either mountain bikes or cruisers. Learn the history of Freeport and stop at Bell Channel Bay Bridge, Garden of the Groves for a tour and lunch, and a swim at Taino Beach. **CocoNutz Cruisers** (Port Lucaya, tel. 242/808-7292, www.coconutzcruisers.com) is owned by Freeport native Alfredo Bridgewater and offers tours on electric bicycles, so it's more like riding a scooter, which can be a blessing in the heat. On this tour you'll hear local lore and history, and you'll stop along the way to see interesting sights and beautiful beaches. Lunch and bottled water is included on this 5.5-hour tour.

Fishing

An angler's perfect escape, **North Riding Point** (Burnside Cove, tel. 242/727-4250, U.S. tel. 864/248-6113, www.nrpcbonefishing.com) is a luxury bonefishing camp located just before Lucayan National Park on the south side of the island. Five seaside guest cottages and a two-bedroom house are for rent, and dining is first-class. The outfit uses nine different launch sites on the north, south, and east flats, depending on the wind and tide. Regular trophy-size bonefish and permit fish are caught with their experienced guides. Average bonefish are 4 to 7 pounds, but bonefish over 10 pounds are encountered daily. The permit in the area average between 25 and 45 pounds. You'll also come across the occasional tarpon, snapper, and muttonfish. Rates are inclusive of fishing, accommodations, and meals for three to seven nights; half- and full-day fishing trips are also available.

H2O Bonefishing (Lucaya, tel. 242/359-4958, U.S. tel. 954/364-7590, www.h2obonefishing.com) is a package service that will arrange accommodations and guided fishing excursions for a headache-free experience. Three- to seven-night packages are available. Fishing options include either fly-fishing the flats or deep-sea fishing for tuna, mahimahi, and wahoo, depending on the season. After a day out, saddle up to Bones Bar to tell fish tales and enjoy the comfortable accommodations at Pelican Bay Hotel in the heart of Port Lucaya.

Lil B Fishing (Freeport, tel. 242/351-6917, U.S. tel. 519/957-1534, www.lilbfishingbahamas.com) focuses on light-tackle reef fishing, which is fantastic for young children as you're almost guaranteed consistent action. The four-hour charters depart at 9am and 2pm for two to six passengers. Bait, equipment, and fish cleaning are included. Private charters are available.

Captain Phil's Guide Service (McLean's Town, East End, tel. 242/353-3086, www.bahamasbonefishing.net) is located in East Grand Bahama and caters to both beginners and experienced fishing enthusiasts. Captain Phil will show you the splendor of bonefishing in his own backyard of the Little Bahama Bank. Transportation from Freeport can be arranged.

Golf

Fortune Hills Golf & Country Club (E. Sunrise Hwy., Freeport, tel. 242/373-2222 or 242/373-4500, 9 holes $40, 18 holes $60) is a 3,453-yard, nine-hole, par-36 course, a par-72 when played twice from different tees. It has the longest par-5 in The Bahamas and is known for its challenging hole 3. As the name implies, the course is located on some of the hillier and higher ground of Grand Bahama. Services include club and cart rentals, a snack bar, a pro shop with a golf pro on hand, a putting green, and a driving range.

Reef Club Golf Course (Seahorse Lane, Lucaya, tel. 242/352-5466, U.S. tel. 855/350-4653, www.grandlucayan.com, Dec.-Apr. daily 7am-6pm, May-Nov. daily 7am-7pm, 9 holes $59, 18 holes $90) is a Robert Trent Jones Jr.-designed links-style course at the Grand Lucayan. It's known for its wide lush greens and varied features, such as water hazards and bunkers. It's great for players of all abilities. There's a snack bar, a pro shop, a golf pro on hand, and putting and chipping practice greens. Ranked in the Top 100 Golf Resorts in the World by *The Golfer* magazine, the 18-hole course is a 6,930-yard par-72.

Ruby Golf Course (W. Sunrise Hwy. and Wentworth Ave., tel. 242/352-1851, $50) is a favorite with locals. This par-72 course was designed by Jim Fazio and Joe Lea, who added plenty of bunkers along the fairway to provide a challenge. It was built in 1964, and there is a pro on hand to brush up on your skills. A snack bar and a driving range are also on-site.

Nature Tours

Run by Grand Bahama native Shamie Rolle, **Calabash Eco Adventures** (tel. 242/727-1974, www.calabashecoadventures.com) provides professional and educational tours for all ages. Rolle has experience working for numerous other operations on the island, including UNEXSO, before he started Calabash in 2007. Tours include pickup and drop-off from your hotel. Favorite tours include the Peterson Cay Kayak and Snorkel Adventure; the Inland Blue Hole Snorkel Adventure, which takes you into Ben's Cave and Owl's Hole; or, if you are certified, the scuba version of the cave dive.

Grand Bahama Nature Tours (Freeport, tel. 242/373-2485, U.S. tel. 866/440-4542, www.grandbahamanaturetours.com) is one of the top ecotourism operations on the island and has been running a variety of excursions for over 20 years, operated by informative and entertaining trained guides who are island residents. You'll learn interesting local facts about history, ecology, and local plants and animals. Most tours include lunch and beverages, park admission fees, and equipment. Kayaking through Lucayan National Park is one of the top tours, as is snorkeling around Peterson Cay. They also offer Jeep safaris, off-road ATV tours, bike tours, and birding tours at Garden of the Groves.

Since 1969, **Reef Tours** (Port Lucaya Marketplace, tel. 242/373-5880 or 242/373-5891, www.reeftoursfreeport.com) has been opening the doors for visitors to experience the wonders of Grand Bahama with a variety of tours and activities for people of all ages. Get your feet wet with one of their many water-based adventures, including snorkeling, sailing, or a glass-bottom boat tour. Captain your own vessel for a half day or a full day of boating, join one of the reef fishing or deep-sea fishing charters, or end the day with a relaxing and enchanting twilight wine-and-cheese evening sail along the coast. To discover Grand Bahama by land, try the Segway tour, 4WD tour, or Harley tour. For a bird's-eye view, soar 400 feet above the clear waters on a parasailing tour. Pickup and drop-off are included on all tours.

West End Ecology Tours (West End, tel. 242/727-1156, www.westendecologytours.com) is located on the western side of the island, which is an environmental playground for nature enthusiasts. It is the top outfit for those staying at Old Bahama Bay. West Grand Bahama is filled with mangroves, estuaries, and a variety of marinelife and migratory birds, and the tours provide educational experiences and delve into conservation and preservation. Visit Stingray Cay, one of the most popular tours in Grand Bahama, limited to six people for an intimate interaction with the rays. Swim in the shallow clear water with these gentle creatures and enjoy the unforgettable experience of petting and hand-feeding them. Other tours include a variety of fishing expeditions and birding.

Spas

Renu Day Spa (Millennium House, Level II, E. Mall Dr., Freeport, tel. 242/352-7368, www.renudayspabahamas.com, Tues.-Sat. 9am-5pm, after-hours appointments on request) is located in the center of Freeport and is run by a team of experienced therapists, stylists, and technicians, with a full offering of nail services, hair removal, facials, and body wraps, along with a variety of massage options, including deep tissue, aromatherapy, prenatal, and hot stone. Organic products are available, as well as a soothing selection of locally made teas and refreshments. It's a popular spot for wedding and bridal parties. They also offer workshops such as Reiki certification.

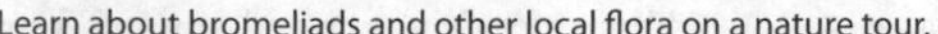
Learn about bromeliads and other local flora on a nature tour.

Senses Spa at Grand Lucayan (Seahorse Lane, Lucaya, tel. 242/350-5280, ext. 5281 or 5282, U.S. tel. 855/350-4653, www.grandlucayan.com) is a top-rated, 25,000 square-foot, three-story oceanfront facility with a full-service spa (Mon.-Fri. 8am-6pm, Sat.-Sun. 9am-6pm), a fitness center (Mon.-Fri. 6am 8pm, Sat.-Sun. 7am-8pm), and a salon. Fragrant body wraps and essential oil facial treatments will relax and rejuvenate you, or try the ocean-view couples massage for a truly blissful experience. The fitness center has weights, treadmills, bicycles, and steppers. They offer personal training sessions and fitness assessments as well as weekly classes open to nonguests; classes include circuit training, Pilates, aqua aerobics, yoga, and meditation.

Dermalogica Skin Centre (Port Lucaya Marketplace, tel. 242/373-7546, www.dermalogicaskincentre.com, daily 9am-7pm) is conveniently located in the Port Lucaya Marketplace and offers free skin mapping consultations. You'll receive a skin fitness plan, product recommendations, and samples. Other services include face and body treatments, massage, waxing, and tinting.

ENTERTAINMENT AND EVENTS

Nightlife

Club Neptune's Lounge and Nightclub (Seahorse Rd., Lucaya, tel. 242/374-1221, Tues.-Sat. 7pm-2am) is the happening place for both visitors and locals, especially on weekends. Nightly happy hour is 7pm-9pm. They also offer regular live music and karaoke. Comfortable couch seating and a dance floor are located downstairs, and there is a small lounge upstairs with a mellower ambience.

An island beach party around a bonfire at **Taino by the Sea Restaurant and Beach Bonfire** (Jolly Roger Dr., Freeport, tel. 242/350-2200, U.S. tel. 888/311-7945, www.tainobeach.com, Oct.-Apr. Sun. and Thurs. 5pm-8pm, May-Sept. Sun. and Thurs. 6pm-8pm) is the highlight of any trip to the island. The bonfire experience includes a Bahamian dinner buffet and all-you can drink Bahama mamas, kamikazes, or nonalcoholic fruit punch. DJs spin music, and there are exciting fire dancers and crowd-inclusive games.

Home to regular live music and events, **Marketplace Square** (Port Lucaya Marketplace, tel. 242/373-8446, www.portlucaya.com) is located at the center of the Port Lucaya Marketplace on the harbor. Watch the action from one of the many bars surrounding the square, or get right in the mix by standing in the crowd. Live music is Friday-Sunday 8pm-11pm, weather permitting. Regular Bahamian bands include the Ultra Vibes Band, the Inagua Boys, and Wilfred Solomon and the Magnetics. There are seasonal concerts, special guest appearances, and holiday fireworks on New Year's Eve and Bahamian Independence, July 10th.

Festivals and Events

Grand Bahama hosts the second-largest celebration of Junkanoo in the country after Nassau, celebrated during three main events in Freeport. The main celebration is late at night and early in the morning on New Year's, when the downtown area comes to life with the full regalia, spirit, and energy of a top-notch **Junkanoo Parade.** Later in January, the children demonstrate their talents at the annual **Junior Junkanoo** parade. Students from schools across the island compete for the best costumes, music, and dancing. At the end of April is the **Grand Bahama Junkanoo Carnival,** features a series of music competitions and rush-outs (costumed people engaging in choreographed dances and parades) at Taino Beach.

Pelican Point Coconut Festival (Pelican Point, East Grand Bahama, Easter Mon. 11am-8pm) is a homecoming festival for the community of Pelican Point in East Grand Bahama. The festival attracts hundreds of visitors. All the many ways to eat and drink coconuts are showcased, including jams, jellies, coconut tarts, and, of course, Gully Wash (a concoction of gin, coconut water, sweetened condensed milk and nutmeg, elsewhere called Sky Juice). There are also coconut crafts and coconut contests.

Extreme Kayak Fishing Tournament (Taino Beach, www.extremekayakfishingtournament.org/bahamas, last weekend in Apr. Thurs.-Sun.) is a challenging international event where competitors utilize kayaks instead of powerboats to bring in the biggest catch. Afterward, stick around for the beach bonfire, live music, entertainment, and awards dinner. International transportation and accommodations packages are available for participants.

Ol' Freetown Cultural Festival (Freetown, tel. 242/350-8600, esmith@bahamas.com, Whit Monday in mid-May) offers visitors a chance to experience the culinary skills, hospitality, and heritage of the residents of Freetown in East Grand Bahama. There are also traditional games such as cane peeling and live rake-and-scrape music.

Regattas are huge events in The Bahamas, and the **Grand Bahama Regatta and Heritage Festival** (Taino Beach, end of July Fri.-Sun. 10am-midnight) is no exception. This regatta attracts class A, B and C sloops from all over the country and includes three days of sailing races and sculling competitions. Festivities take place at Taino Beach, with live music, dancing, food, and drinks.

The year 2018 marks the 48th annual **BASRA Bernie Butler Swim Race and Beach Party** (Coral Beach, www.basragrandbahama.com, mid-Aug., 10am-6pm) charity swim marathon and beach festival, open to all ages.

Celebrating their 32nd year in 2018, the **GBPA Conchman Triathlon** (Taino Beach, www.conchmantriathlon.com, 1st Sat. in Nov.) hosts the Sprint, Olympic, Team, and Iron Kids races. The Sprint is a 750-meter swim, a 25-kilometer bike ride, and a 5-kilometer run; the Olympic is a 1,500-meter swim, a 50-kilometer bike ride, and a 10-kilometer run.

McLean Town Conch Cracking Festival (McLean Town, East Grand Bahama, tel. 242/350-8600, esmith@bahamas.com, National's Heroes Day, 1st Mon. in Oct.) is a homecoming event in the eastern settlement of McLean Town. This annual event started in 1972 and attracts both locals and visitors to see who will be awarded the coveted trophy for being the best conch cracker in the country.

Festival Noel (Rand Nature Centre, Freeport, tel. 242/352-5438, 1st Fri. in Dec. 7pm-10pm) kicks off the holiday season annually with music, crafts, and wine-tasting in the natural beauty of the Rand Nature Centre. All proceeds go to the Bahamas National Trust for park development and conservation.

SHOPPING

There is plenty of opportunity for shopping between Freeport and Lucaya, from high-end luxury accessories and apparel to fantastic bargains. There is 12 percent VAT (sales tax) on all goods and services in The Bahamas, but the tax is waived for visitors on Grand Bahama, as long as the invoice is more than $25. Most items are also duty-free, which makes for additional savings over U.S. prices. When shopping, make sure you carry proof that you are not a resident of the Bahamas. Look for "Authorized Tax and Duty-Free Goods" certificates in store windows. Most stores are open Monday-Saturday 9am or 10am to 5pm or 6pm, and many stores in Port Lucaya Marketplace are also open Sunday. Supermarkets, wholesale clubs, and building supply stores close at noon on Sunday.

★ Port Lucaya Marketplace

There are 40 stores and boutiques and more than 20 bars and restaurants at **Port Lucaya Marketplace,** perched on the picturesque edge of the Port Lucaya harbor and marina and within easy walking distance of the Grand Lucayan and Pelican Bay Hotel. The marketplace is open and spacious, with fountains, tropical landscaping, and cobbled walkways. In the center, on the waterfront, is Marketplace Square, which showcases live Bahamian bands on weekends. Bars and

Bahamian Fish Fry

Bahamians are serious about their local fish fry. In even the smallest settlements throughout the country, a collection of open-air lean-to establishments huddle on the waterfront near the docks, where the catch comes in to be cleaned in the shade of a wooden roof. Stacks of empty conch shells are usually piled high. It's not always the prettiest of locations, since it's unofficially the "commercial waterfront," but the seafood is always fresh and the atmosphere is always inviting. The fish fry is typically the social pulse of the community, with regular gatherings on specific days of the week. The community comes out in force to catch up on local "sip sip" (gossip), throw back a few beers, and let loose with energetic rake-and-scrape music.

As with most Bahamian food, it's neither light nor heart-healthy, but it is tasty, and every shack has its own version of native dishes, each with a loyal following. The "fish" can refer to any number of varieties, including whole fried lane snapper, in which the tail and head are attached; the eyes and brain are coveted, and picking the bones is a leisurely task, not to be rushed. Grouper, jack, hogfish and barracuda (I don't advise eating barracuda, as it is subject to ciguatera, a fish toxin that can cause illness) are also served, as well as conch salad and conch fritters, lobster (also called crawfish), and meat dishes. The menus depends on whatever fish were brought in that day. If you want to experience hanging out with locals in a friendly environment, a local fish fry is the spot.

restaurants such as Rum Runners and Pier One surround the square and are a great place to enjoy a cocktail while viewing the entertainment. This is the spot to be for fireworks on New Year's Eve, Bahamian Independence Day (July 10), and U.S. Independence Day (July 4).

Leo's Art Gallery (Port Lucaya Marketplace, tel. 242/373-1758) doubles as a studio and gallery for local artist Leo Brown. His attention to detail is expressed through vivid and exotic wildlife scenes and religious themes, and his work is popular among locals and visiting art collectors. The tiny space is intimate and showcases his impressionistic style. **Flovin Gallery** (Port Lucaya Marketplace, tel. 242/352-7564) is located toward the east side of the marketplace and features a collection of original paintings and sculptures by some of Grand Bahama's top artists. There are also a wide range of prints available. **Sun & Sea Outfitters** (Port Lucaya Marketplace at UNEXSO, tel. 242/373-1244, www.unexso.com) is the largest shopping establishment in Lucaya, with 4,500 square feet of floor space, featuring swimwear, resort wear, boutique clothing, dive and snorkel gear, T-shirts, artwork, and Bahamian-made souvenirs.

Port Lucaya Straw Market is one of Freeport's most popular, and stalls can be found at both the eastern and western end of Port Lucaya Marketplace. Up to 120 vendors sell artisanal crafts and Bahamian souvenirs such as handmade straw handbags, hats, dolls, baskets, and ornaments as well as soaps, jams, jellies, hot sauces, and T-shirts. You'll also find artisans at work on items such as wooden handicrafts and jewelry, which can be personalized for you. Other shopping includes popular duty-free items such as fashion and accessories, jewelry, watches, and perfumes.

Located in a replica 19th-century Bahamian mansion, **The Perfume Factory** (W. Sunrise Hwy. and E. Mall Dr., Freeport, tel. 242/352-9391, www.perfumefactory.com, daily 9am-6pm) is an opulent experience, complete with an elegant tea parlor sitting room. Discover a wide variety of locally made fragrances for men and women with Bahamian-saturated names such as Sand, Goombay, Island Promises, Paradise, and Pink Pearl, which is rumored to contain conch pearls. The newest fragrances in their line include Bahama Mama, Bahama Papa, and Freeport and Bahama Blue for men and women. Participate in a short complimentary factory tour and see how the perfume is made, and create your own fragrance by blending from any of the 35 scents into perfume or body lotion.

FOOD AND DRINK

Grand Bahama features a wide array of selections for every palate and budget. Local Bahamian fare not found elsewhere in the islands make Grand Bahama a top pick for a foodie traveler. A 15 percent gratuity is often added to your bill. Be sure to ask if you don't see it spelled out. The 12 percent VAT (sales tax) is also added to your bill. Prices listed here reflect average entrées, excluding tax and gratuity.

TOP EXPERIENCE

★ Smith's Point Fish Fry

The **Smith's Point Fish Fry** (Smith Point, Lucaya, Wed. 6pm-late, $10-12, cash only) is a local's spot that visitors have gravitated toward. On Taino Beach, the fish fry is half a dozen or so open-air establishments serving Bahamian food and barbecue on open-air grills or half oil drum cookers. Outriggers Beach Club is a family-run establishment right on the beach and is the most popular spot due to the location and view, but the line is always long. If you don't mind waiting, you'll have a nice view of the ocean while waiting. The beach is stunning at sunset, and often there is seating available over the sand, if you get there early enough.

Farther back from the beach are other places bunched together mostly under one roof, but they are decidedly independent, with their own separate kitchens and staff. Da Bus Stop and Penny's are popular dining choices, but all of them have a similar menu. Locals are loyal to their favorite establishments, never venturing next door. The evening gets going around 6pm-7pm, but the real excitement happens later, with music, dancing, and sometimes a bonfire, depending on the weather.

It's no-frills and greasy but the cuisine is a tasty, and you'll dine at a picnic table with plastic cutlery. Go with the mindset that this is a local hangout and not generally catering to tourists. You are on Bahamian turf, so enjoy it as a cultural experience. Mix and mingle with the locals; for many, this is the highlight of their week. Expect traditional Bahamian dishes like conch salad, cracked conch, barbecue chicken, steamed pork chop, and whole fried snapper served with peas-and-rice, fried plantain, coleslaw, baked macaroni, or potato salad. Smith's Point is located off West Beach

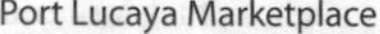

Port Lucaya Marketplace

Road, and parking is available as long as you get there relatively early.

Bahamian

★ **Banana Bay** (Fortune Bay Dr., Lucaya, tel. 242/373-2960, daily 10am-5pm, $10-15) is a hot spot for locals and tourists alike. Perched front and center on Fortune Beach, this is arguably the best casual oceanfront dining in Grand Bahama, with both outdoor and indoor dining, but sit outside and enjoy breathtaking views of Fortune Beach. There are daily specials as well as longtime favorites like Indian Summer Curry Chicken Salad, grouper sandwich, crab cakes, and mahimahi tacos. If you have a sweet tooth, don't miss their delectable homemade banana bread. Cocktail specialties include the Frozen Wacky Banana, Guava Duff (a dessert-inspired rum drink), and the Frozen Tango Mango Daiquiri. Bring your swimsuit and go for a dip in the sea after lunch.

The rustic and charming **Margarita Villa Sand Bar** (off Spanish Main Dr., Mather Town, tel. 242/373-4525, www.sandbarbahamas.com, daily 11:30am until late, $10-15) is tucked amid a sand dune on Churchill Beach. Choose outdoor seating on picnic tables under the shade of the thatched roof, or on the elevated platform deck overlooking the ocean. Indoors is air-conditioned, with a sandy floor and a few bar-top tables. The interior is eclectically decorated with fun photos and is the perfect spot for American football fans to watch a game, especially when the Miami Dolphins are playing. Mixed drinks are made from scratch, they host regular live music, and bar favorites include burgers, Philly cheesesteak, onion rings, and chicken wings. It's located a five-minute walk from the Viva Wyndam and a five-minute drive from Port Lucaya.

Manta Ray Beach Club (Silver Point Dr., Lucaya, tel. 242/822-5002 or 242/823-5004, daily 11am-late, $10-20) is located on a beautiful stretch of beach just east of Island Seas Resort. This open-air beach bar has a lovely view of the ocean. They host jazz on the beach every Sunday 6pm-8pm and have recently built colorful wooden huts that resemble bath houses that sell local souvenirs and crafts. Menu items include nachos, wings, burgers sections, wraps, and sandwiches.

Fine Dining

Husband-and-wife team chef Tim Tibbitts and sommelier Rebecca Tibbitts opened

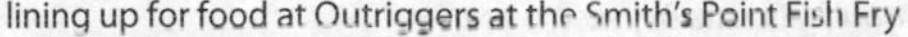
lining up for food at Outriggers at the Smith's Point Fish Fry

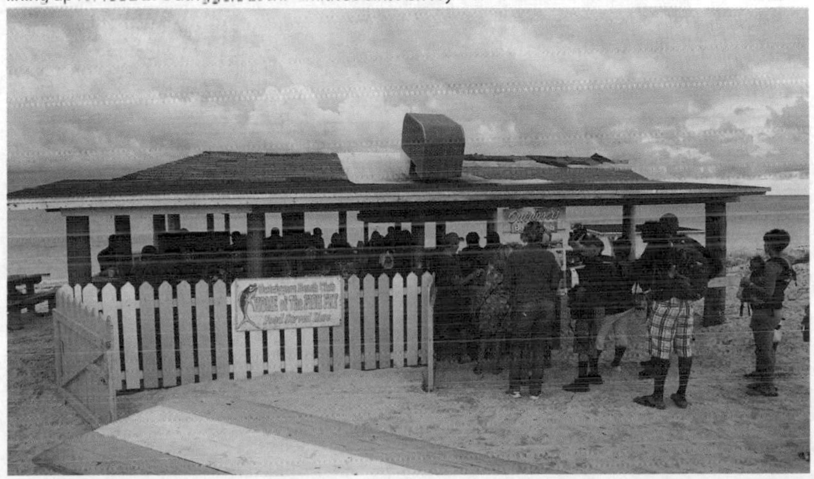

★ **Flying Fish** (1 Seahorse Rd., Lucaya, tel. 242/373-4363, www.flyingfishbahamas.com, Mon. 5pm-9pm, Wed.-Sun. lunch 11:30am-2:30pm, dinner 5pm-9pm, $30-50) in February 2012 and have since been blasting their way through awards and prominence, both locally and internationally. Established as "Freeport meets New York City," the elegant and refined eatery has an emphasis on island hospitality. The menu is ever-changing to reflect seasonal products, but items may include conch ceviche, *sous vide* beef short ribs, and warmed Brussels-sprout caesar salad. On weekend nights, the outdoor patio is the spot to be, serving gourmet pub fare. Happy hour on the patio is daily 5pm-7pm, weather permitting.

International

East Sushi at Pier One (Port Lucaya Marketplace, tel. 242/352-6674, www.pieroneandeast.com, Mon.-Fri. 11am-10pm, Sat.-Sun. 4pm-10pm, $15-35) is along the harbor at Port Lucaya in a two-story building, boasting beautiful marina views and stunning sunsets. There are two menus to choose from: the traditional Bahamian menu; and the highly-recommended East's menu, with Japanese favorites and specialties such as seaweed salad, miso soup, tuna *tataki, gyoza,* and spring rolls. They also serve a selection of Indian and Thai curries and Mongolian and Cantonese dishes. Eat indoors or out, but if the weather is decent, opt for outdoor seating to view the sharks.

Cappuccino's Italian Restaurant (Port Lucaya Marketplace, tel. 242/373-1584, daily 5-10pm $15-30) is a wonderful choice for an intimate and romantic evening out. This family-run restaurant has comfort Italian food favorites such as penne pomodoro and *gnocchi al pesto,* seafood specials like grouper with lemon wine sauce and shrimp diavolo over linguine, as well as chicken, veal, and filet mignon.

Pisces Seafood Restaurant and Pizzeria (Port Lucaya Marketplace, tel. 242/373-5192, www.piscesportlucaya.com, Mon.-Sat. 5pm-2am, $20-30) is a Port Lucaya staple known as one of the best pizza joints on the island. It's run by the same owners of nearby Neptune's Cocktail Lounge. There is outdoor seating to watch the foot traffic in the marketplace, and indoors is a cozy air-conditioned dining room.

Adjacent to the Market Square, **Agave Lucaya** (Port Lucaya Marketplace, tel. 242/374-4887, Sun.-Thurs. 11am-10:30pm,

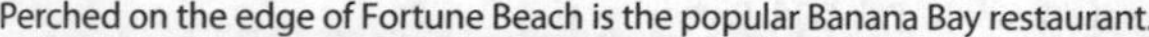

Perched on the edge of Fortune Beach is the popular Banana Bay restaurant.

Fri.-Sat. 11am-midnight, $12-20) combines a wonderful fusion of Caribbean and Latin flavors with dishes such as coconut curry chicken tacos, "cracked" lobster tail, ahi tuna nachos, and Caribbean jerk shrimp burritos. They serve authentic mojitos at the Zsa Zsa Mojito Bar, along with homemade sangria and margaritas. Half-price drinks during lunch and dinner (daily 11am-2pm and 4pm-7pm) and $2 Tuesdays makes it a popular local favorite.

Contemporary

Sabor's (Pelican Bay Hotel, Port Lucaya, tel. 242/373-5588, www.sabor bahamas.com, daily lunch 10am-4pm, dinner 5:15pm-9:30pm, $15-30) Bahamian fusion menu includes burgers, pasta, and pad thai along with plenty of red-meat specialties. Enjoy a relaxing view over Port Lucaya Marina and the pool at Pelican Bay Hotel, with twinkling hanging lights, Christmas palms, and slow-moving oversize ceiling fans. If you are an avid angler, try the Hook and Cook experience: a half-day fishing trip that includes a sunset dinner where whatever you catch will be prepared and served.

Open for breakfast, lunch, and dinner, **Dive in Marina Bar and Restaurant** (Port Lucaya Marketplace at UNEXSO, tel. 242/373-1244, www.unexso.com, Sun.-Thurs. 8am-8pm, Fri.-Sat. 8am-10pm, $15-20) is on the edge of the Port Lucaya Marina and the UNEXSO pool. The menu has plenty of options for a calorie splurge, like the Guilty Pleasure Burger and loaded nachos, or lighter fare like grilled shrimp with watermelon and feta, or a grilled veggie wrap.

The Grill Restaurant & Bar (Port Lucaya Marketplace, tel. 242/602-7750, Tues.-Sun. 3pm-10pm, $20-35) is a steak house featuring prime cuts of rib-eye, New York strip, and porterhouse, and offering fantastic views of the Port Lucaya Marina. A variety of seafood specialties include Bahamian lobster, tuna, salmon, and shrimp. The outdoor patio overlooks the marina, or dine in the air-conditioned dining room.

Bars and Pubs

At **Bones Bar** (Pelican Bay Hotel, Seahorse Dr., tel. 242/374-4899, www.bones-bar.com, daily 3pm-late), enjoy freshly squeezed cocktails, draft beer, and a wide selection of rum while perched alongside the harbor. A perfect hangout spot after a day in the sun or fishing, it's the clubhouse for H2O Bonefishing, so you'll likely be among the company of fishing enthusiasts finished with an exciting day. Bones offers a wide array of specialty cocktails with bins of fresh limes, oranges, and lemons behind the bar, ready to be squeezed. A relaxed yet classy vibe with island decor, amusing signs, walls made with reclaimed wood, and brightly painted louvered shutters, the barn doors open onto the dock overlooking the harbor. There's also a swim-up bar from the pool with underwater stools. Happy hour is daily 3pm-7pm.

Coral Reef Beach Bar and Restaurant (Coral Rd., Lucaya, tel. 242/373-2468, www.coralbeachonline.com, Sun.-Thurs. noon-8pm, Fri.-Sat. noon-9:30pm) is a popular spot for guests of the Coral Beach Hotel and also attracts a local crowd. Settled poolside and just a few steps off Coral Beach, the inviting colorful and curvy concrete bar is decorated with tropical reef fish and serves breakfast, lunch, and dinner. Expect local fare such as tuna and grits, a popular breakfast dish, and typical American breakfast and lunch options. Shrimp, conch, and fish feature on the lunch and dinner menus.

Rum Runners (Port Lucaya Marketplace, tel. 242/373-7233, 9am-1am daily) is on the edge of Marketplace Square, a is great spot to watch live music or just people-watch. It's a laid-back flip-flops and T-shirt kind of a place. Frozen tropical drinks are served in coconuts, providing a true island feel.

A pub and restaurant on the canal in Lucaya, **Monkey Joe's** (Kings Rd., off Midshipman Rd., Lucaya, tel. 242/373-6331, Mon.-Thurs. 4pm-11pm, Fri.-Sat. 4pm-2am, Sun. 11am-11pm) is a British-style pub with a cozy dark interior and wooden booth seating. They serve pub favorites like shepherd's pie and beer-battered fish-and-chips, and host live music on weekends on the outdoor patio. Happy hour is Monday-Friday 5pm-7pm.

Cafés and Light Bites

Zorba's (Port Lucaya Marketplace, tel. 242/373-6137 or 242/373-6141, www.zorbasbahamas.com, daily 7am-10:45pm, $10-15) is the only authentic Greek restaurant in Freeport. Order your meal at the counter to stay or take out. They offer typical Greek favorites as well as Bahamian breakfast and lunch specials each day. They also serve espresso and have delectable pastries.

★ **Bootleg Chocolates** (Port Lucaya Marketplace, tel. 242/373-6303, www.bootlegchocolates.com) is a family-run chocolatier and coffee shop. The family can trace their Bahamian roots back to the 1600s. Their grandmother lived in West End during the heyday of bootlegging and rum running and used to tell exciting tales of life during that time, reflected in the business's name. The flavors are island-inspired, such as Gully Wash (a local name for a gin and coconut water drink, elsewhere known as Sky Juice), Guava Duff (a traditional Bahamian dessert), and Vanilla Bean with Rum. Another favorite is Bahamian Sea Salt and Hibiscus Caramel. Adventurous chocolate enthusiasts can try Goat Pepper and Balsamic Caramel. Chocolates are available singly and in 6- and 12-piece gift boxes.

The tranquil setting of the **Garden Café and Bar** (Garden of the Groves, Midshipman Rd. and Magellan Dr., tel. 242/374-7778, www.thegardenofthegroves.com, Sat.-Thurs. 9:30am-5pm, Fri. 9:30am-9:30pm, $10-20) is situated on the edge of a peaceful pond. Watch ducks, birds, and fish feature with the gentle soothing sounds of the waterfall in the distance. Dining is available next to the pond, under the three-tiered deck under a mature fig tree, and in an indoor air-conditioned space on the enclosed upper deck. The menu offers salads, sandwiches, and plated salmon, steak, and shrimp. The full bar includes draft beer.

ACCOMMODATIONS

Grand Bahama has some of the most affordable resort hotels in the country. Prices reflect peak-season double-occupancy rates. Rates may be lower at other times of the year and are not inclusive of tax or any added resort fees. Apartments, vacation rentals, and beach cottages are popular options for extended stays.

$100-150

Seagrape Bed & Breakfast (Royal Palm

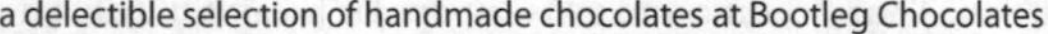
a delectible selection of handmade chocolates at Bootleg Chocolates

Way, Lucaya, tel. 242/373-1769, U.S. tel. 954/234-2387, www.seagrapehouse.com, $95, 2-night minimum) is a two-bedroom guest house run by Freeport resident Katybel Taylor. Both rooms have private entrances and their own en suite bath, a microwave, a mini fridge, air-conditioning, and internet. Enjoy the tropically landscaped backyard patio for breakfast or happy hour. Seagrape is located just a few steps to the beautiful Lucayan Beach and a short walk to Port Lucaya Marketplace in a quiet residential neighborhood. Continental breakfast is included in the rates.

Royal Islander (E. Mall Dr., Freeport, tel. 242/351-6000, www.royalislanderhotel.com, $102) is located in downtown Freeport and is a decent budget option for those who don't need to be directly on the beach. It's a popular spot for those passing through on business or for travelers who intend to be out exploring the island. Built in the height of the booming Freeport days, today the hotel looks dated, but the modest rooms are clean, and there is a lovely landscaped outdoor pool, hot tub, and pool bar. An on-site restaurant serves breakfast, lunch, and dinner, and a tour desk will assist with transportation and arranging activities around the island.

Run by three generations of a Danish family who emigrated to The Bahamas in the 1980s, **Bell Channel Inn** (Kings Rd., Lucaya, tel. 242/373-1053, www.bellchannelinn.com, $109) will make you feel at home with their warm welcoming hospitality. All 32 of the clean and comfortable no-frills rooms have views of the harbor and Port Lucaya plus a balcony or direct access to the pool. Caribbean Divers is located on-site to book dive trips and rent gear. Dive and stay packages are available. The restaurant and bar, Upstairs on the Bay, is open for breakfast, lunch, and dinner and serves American and Bahamian dishes overlooking the harbor. It's a popular spot for the nightly happy hour and live music on the weekends. Next door is Monkey Joe's Bar and Restaurant, and the inn is within walking distance of the restaurants and shops at Port Lucaya.

Coral Beach Hotel (Coral Rd., Lucaya, tel. 242/373-2468, www.coralbeachonline.com, $110) is on a breathtaking quiet stretch of beach just a few minutes west of Port Lucaya. This hotel-condo facility rents basic hotel rooms, or you can visit the website VRBO to book condos that are fully equipped with kitchens and furniture. There is a pool onsite, and the Coral Beach Bar and Restaurant serves breakfast, lunch, and dinner on a beautiful shady patio overlooking the beach.

Taino Beach Resort (Jolly Roger Dr., tel. 242/350-2200, U.S. tel. 888/311-7945, www.tainobeach.com, $136) is on one of the best beaches in the area, a few minutes from Port Lucaya which is far enough for a sense of privacy. A ferry runs from Port Lucaya Marketplace to Taino Beach, and the weekly Fish Fry is a located a few blocks away on the beach. Taino on the Beach is the on-site restaurant that serves breakfast, lunch, and dinner daily with breathtaking views. A lagoon-style pool is surrounded by lush tropical landscaping and a waterslide, a waterfall, caves, a lazy river, a jetted tub, and a kids' area. The swim-up Grotto Bar is within an impressive cave. Swim from the poolside or sit on the dry side and enjoy a tropical cocktail out of the sun. The on-site activities director will do his best to keep you entertained throughout your stay. Activities include a weekly beach bonfire, bingo, pool games, beach volleyball, and kids' camps. There is a fitness center, a gift shop, and even grocery service.

Castaways (East Mall Dr., Freeport, tel. 242/352-6682, U.S. tel. 866/410-9676, www.castawaysresort.net, $147) is located in downtown Freeport and has 118 rooms and suites. The standard rooms have a king or two doubles with a balcony or patio, and suites have a king, a sofa sleeper, a work desk, and a balcony. The on-site restaurant serves breakfast, lunch, and dinner, and a poolside bar serves light food. The fitness center has free weights and aerobic machines. Castaways is walking distance to shops, restaurants, and a movie theater.

★ **Pelican Bay Hotel** (Sea Horse Rd.,

tel. 242/373-9550, www.pelicanbayhotel.com, $148) known as the Happiest Hotel in Grand Bahama. Each room has spectacular views from private balconies, complimentary coffee and Nespresso machines, Wi-Fi, cable TV, and fridges. On-site are Bones Bar and Sabor Restaurant and Bar as well as the Garden Delite salad bar. Pelican Bay features 96 waterside staterooms that include separate living areas with a sofa beds and workspaces, and 90 waterside hotel rooms with large entries, dressing areas, and workspaces. Rooms are colorful, with organic West Indian batik decor, cool tile flooring, eclectic art from around the world, palm-leaf ceiling fans, and plush beds with crisp linens. The resort has three swimming pools, a hot tub, a day spa, a fitness room, self-service laundry, a full-service business center, and the Canal House, a conference and meeting venue. Pelican Bay is on the edge of the Port Lucaya Marketplace and its shopping, dining, and entertainment, and close to Lucaya Beach and the ferry to Taino Beach.

$150-250

Tucked away from the more crowded beaches of Lucaya, **Island Seas Resort** (Silver Point Dr., Williams Town, tel. 242/373-1271, www.islandseas.com, $183) is a time-share condo property that offers fully furnished one- and two-bedroom suites with full kitchens. Amenities include a spa, a swimming pool with a swim-up bar, a hot tub, a fitness center, and a quiet stretch of white-sand beach. Activities for the whole family include a kids' playground and child-care center, tennis and volleyball courts, and water sports. Check the daily schedule for nature walks, dominoes, trivia challenges, bead-making, kids scavenger hunts, shell-finding, and face-painting. The resort is slightly dated, but you won't be bored. There are two restaurants on-site: Seagrape Grille, which features steaks, pasta, and Bahamian fare, and the more casual Coconuts pool-beachside bar and restaurant, with burgers and sandwiches. Next door is Manta Ray Beach Club and a few local bars to keep you entertained throughout your stay. Ocean Motion Watersports is located on-site with plenty of options to get you in and on the water, including parasailing, Wave Runner tours and rentals, snorkeling, paddleboarding, and kayaking.

Viva Wyndham Fortuna Beach (Churchill Dr., Lucaya, tel. 242/373-4000, U.S. tel. 888/774-0040, www.vivafortunaresort.com, $198 d) is an all-inclusive resort that

Pelican Bay Hotel

includes meals, drinks, nonmotorized sports, a daily activities program, and dance lessons. There's an on-site PADI diving center for dive trips and weekly live music. It's off the beaten path, so expect privacy on this stretch of beach. The clean and comfortable rooms are decorated in island style with plenty of rattan. A buffet is available for breakfast, lunch, and dinner, and there are three reservation-only restaurants for guests: Bamboo, with an Asian menu; Viva Café; and Viva la Pizza, with Italian specialties and wood-fired pizzas. Children under 12 stay free and will be entertained at the Viva Kids Club and children's pool. Choose from three different room types, from the standard garden-view rooms to the Vista Rooms overlooking the ocean. You will need to take a taxi to get to town, but since it's all-inclusive, most are happy to stay close to the resort.

Over $250

Stunning stately grounds at the **Grand Lucayan—Lighthouse Point** (Sea Horse Rd., tel. 242/350-5466, U.S. tel. 855/708-6671, www.grandlucayan.com, $265 d, $530 d all-inclusive) provide an opulent feel of spaciousness at one of the largest resorts in Grand Bahama. Situated on the spectacular one-mile stretch of Lucaya Beach, with an expansive and inviting pool deck overlooking the ocean, this resort has all the amenities. Guest-room and suite options include garden, marina, and ocean-view, decorated in subtle, tasteful tropical colors. There are numerous restaurants on-site, including a beach-pool bar, a coffee shop, a pizzeria, and an Italian restaurant. Activities for the whole family include an oversize chess set, bean bag toss, movie nights, and themed entertainment. For sporty guests, the Reef 18-hole championship golf course is part of the Grand Lucayan, and an on-site tennis pro shop with four tennis courts are available day and night. The Senses Spa offers an array of island-inspired signature treatments to infuse you with serenity, and the Fitness Center has a variety of weekly fitness classes. Choose from all-inclusive packages with ferry transportation to and from the United States, golf packages, and bed-and-breakfast; or book à la carte.

INFORMATION AND SERVICES

Visitor Information

Visitor information centers with representatives from the Ministry of Tourism can be found at the Grand Bahama International

the infinity pool matching the colors of the ocean at the Grand Lucayan

Airport, Freeport Cruise Ship Dock, and at the Port Lucaya Marketplace. Pick up maps and brochures and get general island information. **The Grand Bahama Island Tourism Board** (tel. 242/352-8386, www.grandbahamavacations.com) will be happy to assist with specific information regarding your visit to the island. Make sure to pick up the ***What-to-Do*** guide to Grand Bahama upon arrival. They can be found at the airport, hotels, and many retail stores, or visit www.bahamasnet.com.

For the **Chamber of Commerce,** call tel. 242/352-8329. **Directory assistance** is available at tel. 916 or tel. 242/225-5282. **The Ministry of Tourism** (tel. 242/350-8600) can provide visitor information. For **time and temperature** dial 917, and for **weather** dial 915.

If you're interested in connecting with a Bahamian ambassador to learn more about the culture and lifestyle, contact the **People-to-People Program** (tel. 242/367-3067, www.bahamas.com/people-to-people). Advance reservations to pair you with an ambassador are recommended.

Banks

Visitors can withdraw cash daily 24 hours at ATMs. Bank branches are typically open Monday-Thursday 9:30am-3pm and Friday 9:30am-4:30pm. **Scotiabank** ATMs at Grand Lucayan resort provide both U.S. and Bahamian dollars. ATMs dispending Bahamian dollars are at the main Scotiabank branch in Regent Centre, Freeport Harbour, and the Grand Bahama International Airport. **RBC Royal Bank** ATMs are located at the branch at East Mall and Explorers Way and Port Lucaya Marketplace. Funds are dispensed in Bahamian dollars. Extended banking hours (Mon.-Thurs. 9am-4pm, Fri. 9am-4:30pm, Sat. 11am-3pm) are available at the branch at East Mall and Explorer's Way. A **CIBC First Caribbean** ATM that dispenses Bahamian and U.S. dollars is located at Port Lucaya Marketplace. ATMs dispensing Bahamian dollars are located at the First Financial Centre on East Mall Drive, Solomon's Super Center, Seahorse Plaza, Lucaya, and Rand Memorial Hospital. **Bank of the Bahamas** ATMs dispense Bahamian dollars at branches in Freeport on Woodstock Street and Bank Lane, and at the Harbour West Shopping Center in Eight Mile Rock.

Health and Emergencies

Emergency medical facilities are located in downtown Freeport at the **Rand Memorial Hospital** (E. Atlantic Dr. off E. Mall Way, tel. 242/350-6700 or 242/352-2689, www.gbhs.phabahamas.org, 24-hour emergency services). For nonemergency treatment, visit the **Lucayan Medical Centre** (E. Sunrise Hwy., tel. 242/373-7400, www.lucayanmedical.com, Mon.-Fri. 8:30am-5:30pm, Sat. 8:30am-1pm).

For emergency medical services or an ambulance, dial 242/352-2689, 919, or 911. For **fire** emergencies, dial 242/352-8888 or 911. For the **police,** dial 919 or 911, and for **Bahamas Air Sea Rescue Association** (BASRA), if you run into issues at sea, such as breaking down, dial 242/352-2628, 919 or 911.

Media and Communications

Many hotels and establishments in Grand Bahama use both U.S. and Bahamian phone numbers. Once you are in The Bahamas, U.S. toll-free numbers aren't accessible from Bahamian phones, and any area code other than 242 is international, so be sure to use the local 242 phone number to avoid international calling fees. **BTC** (www.btcbahamas.com) is the main cell service provider if you have questions about costs, roaming, and using your phone in The Bahamas. There are four locations in Grand Bahama: two in Freeport, one in Lucaya, and one in Eight Mile Rock. Most hotels allow you to call locally from the house phone.

GETTING THERE

Air

Grand Bahama International Airport (FPO) has direct flights from Miami, Fort Lauderdale, and Nassau. **Bahamasair** (tel.

242/702-4140, U.S. tel. 800/222-4262, www.bahamasair.com), **American Airlines** (U.S. tel. 800/433-7300, www.aa.com), **Delta** (U.S. tel. 800/241-4141, www.delta.com) and **Silver Airlines** (U.S. tel. 844/674-5837, www.silverairways.com) run international flights, and Bahamasair and other local carriers such as **Sky Bahamas** (tel. 242/702 2600, www.skybahamas.net) and **Western Air** (tel. 242/351-3804, www.westernairbahamas.com) run domestic flights from Nassau.

Boat

Travel on the high-speed **Balearia Caribbean** (U.S. tel. 866/699-6988, www.baleariacaribbean.com) from Fort Lauderdale to Grand Bahama. This ferry runs multiple days per week. Check the website for the current sailing schedule. Travel can be combined with special offers at numerous hotels and resorts. Departing from the Port of Palm Beach, the **Bahamas Paradise Cruise Line** (U.S. tel. 800/995-3201, www.bahamasparadisecruise.com) is a cruise ship with nine decks and 750 staterooms with cruises departing every two days. Stay aboard the ship for a short two-night trip, or hop off and pair your package with the Grand Bahama Cruise and Resort Stay partnerships with the Grand Lucayan, Viva Wyndam, or Taino Beach Resort.

MARINAS

The island has several marinas, most of them fully equipped with electricity hubs, waste-disposal units, and fuel stations. Old Bahama Bay in West End and Port Lucaya Marina in Lucaya are official ports of entry.

Old Bahama Bay Marina (Old Bahama Bay, West End, tel. 242/350-6500, U.S. tel. 888/983-6188, www.oldbahamabay.com) is located at Old Bahama Bay on Grand Bahama's West End. This full-service marina is the closest stopping point from Florida, so it's a popular weekend getaway for South Floridians. The marina has 72 slips and dockside dining for breakfast, lunch, and dinner. They can accommodate yachts up to 120 feet. Customs and immigration are on-site for easy clear-in, along with a fuel dock, showers, laundry, and all hookups.

Blue Marlin Cove Marina (Bootle Bay, West End, tel. 242/349-4101, U.S. tel. 772/485-0040, www.bluemarlincove.com) is a privately owned marina with 30 slips, a cleaning station, and a commercial ice house. They also have 30 apartment rental units in a gated community specifically for fishing. **Port Lucaya Marina** (Port Lucaya Marketplace, Lucaya, tel. 242/373-9090, U.S. tel. 561/290-4792, www.portlucayamarina.com) is located within the Port Lucaya Marketplace, and is a great spot to be amid the action, with restaurants, shopping, and amenities. It has 106 slips for boats up to 190 feet, and customs and immigration on-site.

GETTING AROUND

Due to the island's size, it is necessary to get a taxi, rent a car, or take the jitney bus to sightsee extensively. Taxis meet domestic and international arrivals at Grand Bahama International Airport, and rental car centers are located on-site. If you are staying in Port Lucaya, you can easily walk to shops, restaurants, and beaches. Most tour companies offer hotel pickups, and many hotels offer complimentary shuttles to popular tourists' spots upon request. For safety, remember to look right, then left before crossing the street, since traffic runs on the left in The Bahamas.

Taxis

Taxi fares are set by the government. The general rate is $70 per hour for taxis with a seating capacity of more than five passengers, $55 for less than five. There is no charge for up to two pieces of luggage per person in addition to small carried bags. Each additional regular sized luggage is $2. Contact the **Grand Bahama Taxi Union** (tel. 242/352-7101) or **Freeport Taxi** (tel. 242/352-6666) to arrange a pickup.

Rental Cars

Avis (tel. 242/351-2847, www.avis.com) has

locations at Grand Bahama International Airport and at the Freeport Cruise Ship Dock. **Hertz** (tel. 242/352-9250, www.hertz.com) has a location at Grand Bahama International Airport, with pickup service available from the Cruise Ship Dock. **Thrifty** (tel. 242/352-9325, www.thrifty.com) has a location at the Grand Bahama International Airport.

Brad's Car Rental (tel. 242/352-7930, U.S. tel. 954/703-5246, www.bradscarrental.com) is located at Grand Bahama International airport and offers free pickup. **KSR Car Rental** (tel. 242/351-5737, U.S. tel. 954/703-5819, http://ksrrentacar.biz) is located at the Grand Bahama International Airport. **Island Jeep & Car Rental** (tel. 242/373-4001, U.S. tel. 954/237-6660, www.islandjeepcarrental.com) has locations at Grand Bahama International Airport, the Cruise Ship Dock, and Island Seas Resort.

Jitney

Jitney busses are small vans that travel between downtown Freeport and Port Lucaya Marketplace and from downtown to West End and East Grand Bahama. They don't operate on a fixed schedule, but you can ask your hotel for more information. The fare to any area within the city of Freeport is $1; downtown Freeport to East Grand Bahama ranges from $1.25 to $8, and downtown Freeport to West Grand Bahama ranges from $1.25 to $4. Exact change is required.

Greater Grand Bahama

EAST GRAND BAHAMA

Head east from Freeport through endless towering native pine trees and a savanna-like landscape. The road starts to narrow as you pass through sleepy towns and settlements. High Rock is 45 miles east of Lucaya and about 10 minutes past Lucayan National Park. The town is a collection of well-kept concrete houses and a few local restaurants tucked alongside residential homes; it sees little tourism, except for the restaurant at Bishop's Beach Bar and Resort. Locals smile and wave when you pass through, a sign of being removed from the city. Farther east, the landscape turns to mangrove and is prime bonefishing territory. You won't find much until you reach McLean's Town, about 45 miles from Grand Bahama International Airport.

Peterson Cay National Park

A low-lying limestone cay surrounded by coral reefs, **Peterson Cay** (tel. 242/352-5438, www.bnt.bs) is the smallest national park in The Bahamas at 1.5 acres. It is accessible by boat or kayak from Peterson Beach, 15 miles east of Freeport and 1 mile off the south coast of Grand Bahama. A beach on the northern side of the island and several picnic areas are perfect for a picnic lunch. The cay is home to bridled tern nesting colonies and soldier crabs, a healthy turtle population, elkhorn and soft coral formations, sea fans and rays, eels, spiny lobster, and barracuda. Tours to the cay are available with Grand Bahama Nature Tours and Calabash Eco Adventures.

Owl's Hole

Owl's Hole (off Grand Bahama Hwy., before Lucayan National Park) is a popular spot for a cooling dip or a diving adventure. The brave might jump from the 30-foot perimeter cliff, but there is a ladder to access the hole if you'd like to snorkel or swim. The hole is named for owls nesting in the area. To find it, travel about four miles past University of the Bahamas, and take a dirt road before the road bends toward Ol' Freetown Farm. Follow the dirt road 1.5 miles to a small parking lot. The beach is about 1,000 feet past the hole.

Lucayan National Park

Lucayan National Park (Grand Bahama Hwy., tel. 242/352-5438, www.bnt.bs, daily

8am-5:30pm, $5 adults, $3 ages 5-12), 26 miles east of Freeport, features all Bahamian vegetative zones within its 40 acres, including hardwood forests, sand dunes, beach, mangrove wetland, rocky coppice, and an underwater cave system. It was established by the Bahamas National Trust in 1982 to protect fragile cavern ecosystems. The park is also a prominent avian habitat internationally recognized as an Important Bird and Biodiversity Area.

The park stretches on the north and south side of the Grand Bahama Highway. Start on the north side and stroll the loop that leads to the two caves. Along the walk you'll see flowering trees, orchids, and bromeliads. Fish, crustaceans, and migratory birds inhabit Ben's Cave and Burial Mound Cave. The Burial Mound was the site of the 1986 discovery of the skeletons of four indigenous Lucayans as well as a number of artifacts. The first inhabitants used these caves as ceremonial burial sites, and the bones were preserved under a mound of rocks in about six feet of freshwater.

The cave is also home to a newly discovered class of crustacean, *Speleonectes lucayensis,* which resembles a swimming centipede. Ben's Cave is named for legendary UNEXSO diver Ben Rose. A portion of the cave roof collapsed, giving sightseers the opportunity to venture into the cave system by navigating a short flight of stairs. Follow the winding staircase down into the mouth of the cave to a platform just above the calm freshwater surface. The cave is home to a colony of small harmless bats, and there is an intricate network of underwater caves, making the Lucayan cavern system one of the longest surveyed in the world. Other areas of the cave system are accessible by guided scuba tours with UNEXSO.

Across the highway is a loop that leads to Gold Rock Beach, one of the island's most stunning. Go at low tide, when you can walk out in the shallow water onto the sand banks. At high tide there isn't much beach. It was a filming location for the second and third *Pirates of the Caribbean* films. The loop's elevated walkway runs through the mangroves in both directions. The Creek Trail is slightly more elevated and gives you a good view of the creek and mangroves. The Mangrove Swamp Trail winds through deep mangroves and can be wet at high tide. The Swamp Trail is longer than the Creek Trail, and the boardwalk on the Swamp Trail has wide spaces, so it may be cumbersome in sandals or for children with small feet. The mangroves are home to a variety of waterfowl, fish, and plantlife. You can

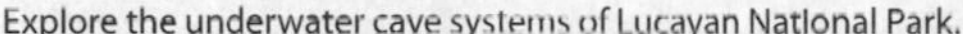
Explore the underwater cave systems of Lucayan National Park.

also explore this wetland system by booking a kayak tour with Grand Bahama Nature Tours.

Ol' Freetown Farm

Ol' Freetown Farm (Grand Bahama Hwy., Freetown, tel. 242/441-8611) is a 20-acre family-owned and operated farm that is home to a variety of rescue animals. In conjunction with the local Humane Society, the owners have taken in multiple horses, pigs, goats, sheep, rabbits, an iguana, and cats and dogs. The farm grows fruits and vegetables and sells local handmade products such as fresh baked bread, jams, jellies, and pepper sauces, which can be purchased at their farm stand or on Saturday at the Rand Nature Centre or Garden of the Groves. The farm is approximately six miles east of University of the Bahamas and about three miles west of Lucayan National Park. Call ahead to find out market schedule and farm visiting hours.

Food and Accommodations

About 10 minutes past Lucayan National Park, you'll feel as though you've stepped into another time zone when you reach **Bishop's Place** (High Rock, East Grand Bahama, tel. 242/353-4515, www.bishopsresort.net, Sun.-Thurs. 10am-6pm, Fri.-Sat. 10am-7pm, food $10-20, rooms $100). There are seven-plus miles of beaches with plenty of opportunity to find a quiet spot, and friendly locals in the community of High Rock who tend to move at a slower pace, keeping the rhythm of the sea. You'll most likely be greeted by Ruben "Bishop" Roberts, the welcoming entrepreneur who runs the establishment.

The bar is situated on the edge of a striking stretch of beach. The restaurant is located inland a few hundred yards, but you can order your food and enjoy it on the open-air deck at the bar overlooking the sea. The menu is simple Bahamian fare, such as whole fried snapper, steamed chicken, and cracked lobster. The restaurant is open for lunch and dinner, but the bar is the preferred hangout spot, and you'll find both tourists and locals on the weekend. The modest rooms have two double beds and are a great option if you just want to escape the crowds for a few nights to enjoy a down-home island hospitality experience.

Adagio Beach Cottage and Art Gallery (35 miles east of Grand Bahama Airport, tel. 242/727-4333, www.adagiobahamas.com, $250) offers a beautiful cottage directly on the beach, home to Del Foxton's papermaking studio. She uses a 2,000-year-old Chinese

the beach bar at Bishop's Place

papermaking technique using recycled materials and local vegetation, and her work is featured in galleries in Nassau and West Palm Beach. Contact her directly to set up an appointment to visit the gallery. **East End Lodge** (McLean's Town, East End, U.S. tel. 561/354-8005, www.eastendlodge.com) is a bonefishing camp that includes lodging, food, and drinks, daily guided fishing, and airport transfers to and from Grand Bahama International Airport. The lodge is on prime bonefishing flats with the opportunity for year-round fishing. Three- to seven-night packages are available.

WEST GRAND BAHAMA

Prior to the development of Freeport in the mid-1950s, the island of Grand Bahama was sparsely populated, with the sleepy town of Eight Mile Rock the main center of commerce. Due to its location only 56 miles off the east coast of Florida, the settlement of West End saw several boom periods as it became a stopping-off point for smuggling supplies during the embargo of the American Civil War and bootlegging during U.S. Prohibition. Today the only thing going on in West End is Old Bahama Bay; the remainder of the town is a sleepy fishing village. Those drawn to this locale are avid boaters, fishing enthusiasts, and water enthusiasts

Sights and Recreation

The Sugar Wreck is a shallow wreck dive off West End, a perennial favorite dive spot because it's only in 15-20 feet of water and teems with a variety of colorful parrot fish, angelfish, wrasse, and the invasive lionfish as well as eels, nurse sharks, grouper, and barracuda. Visibility is impeccable, especially on a sunny day. The four-masted steel sailing ship is over 100 years old and sank in a hurricane while bound for North America from the Caribbean. Book a scuba or snorkel trip with one of the local dive outfits or a private charter with Old Bahama Bay.

Paradise Cove (tel. 242/349-2677, www.deadmansreef.com) gives guests direct access to Deadman's Reef on the island's southwest side. The reef is within swimming distance of the beach and teems with tropical marinelife, such as sea turtles, rays, and coral reefs. Book a snorkel tour through Paradise Cove, which includes transportation, equipment, and flotation belts. The reef is shallow and protected in most weather, so it's a perfect spot for a novice snorkeler. You can also explore the reef in a glass-bottom boat or ocean kayak. **Paradise**

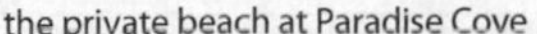

the private beach at Paradise Cove

Cove Beach is a great place to enjoy water activities, or just relax under the shade of an umbrella. You can rent snorkel equipment and kayaks directly from Paradise Cove Resort; the cost is $3 pp to use the beach, chairs, and facilities. Also on the property is the Red Bar, which serves Bahamian food and cold drinks. Parking, restrooms, and showers are available. It's only 20 minutes from Freeport, but it feels like you're in the islands. Bring bug spray as the sand flies from the nearby marsh can eat you alive.

Food and Accommodations

For those who love fishing, boating, diving, and being in and on the water, ★ **Old Bahama Bay Resort & Yacht Harbour** (West End, tel. 242/350-6500, U.S. tel. 888/983-6188, www.oldbahamabay.com, $210) is a popular choice, offering amenities for fly-in and boat-in guests. Located on the western end of the island, this resort is far removed but has a relaxed Out Island feel with contemporary conveniences. There are 73 spacious beachfront suites. Opt for a single room, or for families, book adjoining rooms. The junior suites have a king or two queens and a kitchenette, and the two-bedroom suites have a full kitchen, a patio or balcony, and sleep up to six. Two restaurants on-site are the Dockside Restaurant and Bar, open for breakfast, lunch, and dinner, overlooking the marina, and serving a nice mix of sandwiches, salads, tacos, and elegant dinner entrées such as New Zealand rack of lamb, 12-spice dry-rubbed ribs, and seafood fettucine; and Teasers Tiki Bar, located near the pool and beach, open for breakfast and lunch daily. Be sure to try Eddie's Gully Wash, the local concoction of gin, coconut water, sweetened condensed milk, and nutmeg.

Activities included in the rates range from kayaks, paddleboards, a 4,000-square-foot infinity pool on the edge of the beach, hammocks, lounge chairs, bicycles, snorkel gear, a pool table, ping-pong, tennis and basketball courts, beach volleyball, and lawn games. For additional fees the resort organizes ecology tours, bonefishing and deep-sea fishing, golfing, shopping, and dining trips, and tours of the parks, private boat charters, sunset cruises, spa and massage services, and snorkel trips.

Environmentalist Barry Smith will make you feel right at home at his beloved **Paradise Cove** (west of Holmes Rock, off Queens Hwy., tel. 242/349-2677, www.deadmansreef.com, food $6-12, rooms $175-225), in one of the prime snorkeling locations on the island. The resort has two identical two-bedroom, two-bath cottages with screened-in porches directly on the beach. The units have fully equipped kitchens, air-conditioning, and cable TV. Units can be rented as one-bedroom or two-bedroom units. Rates are $175 for one bedroom and $225 for the two-bedroom option, with discounts for extended stays. Casual dining is available at **Red's Bar.** After you have taken a break from snorkeling or kayaking, enjoy your lunch under one of the two open-air verandas or on a picnic table in the sand. Daily specials include hamburgers, fish, chicken, cracked conch, and lobster, as well as "the best conch fritters on the island."

Getting There

West Grand Bahama stretches from the western edge of Freeport along a skinny arm of land that includes Eight Mile Rock and numerous small settlements and towns. The farther you venture west, the sparser the landscape becomes. It's about a 40-minute drive to West End from Freeport. If you plan on arriving by air, **West End Airport (WTD)** is available for private planes and charters with advance permission. It is a 6,000-foot paved runway for daytime landings only. Contact airport manager Ashley Smith (tel. 242/727-1335, ashleyjamessmith1940@gmail.com).

The Abacos

Look for ★ to find recommended sights, activities, dining, and lodging.

Highlights

★ **Treasure Cay Beach:** Touted as one of the most beautiful beaches in the Caribbean, this treasured beach stretches for 3.5 glorious miles (page 126).

★ **Pelican Cays Land and Sea Park:** A reef system situated in shallow water makes the world's first established marine park a popular place for snorkelers and nature lovers (page 135).

★ **Elbow Cay Reef Lighthouse:** The iconic red-and-white striped lighthouse has looked over the quaint village of Hope Town for 181 years (page 136).

★ **Tahiti Beach:** Aptly named due to its resemblance to the dreamy destination in the South Pacific, this sandbar beach is a picture-perfect spot to while the day away (page 137).

★ **Albert Lowe Museum:** The oldest established museum in The Bahamas houses more than three hundred years of history (page 150).

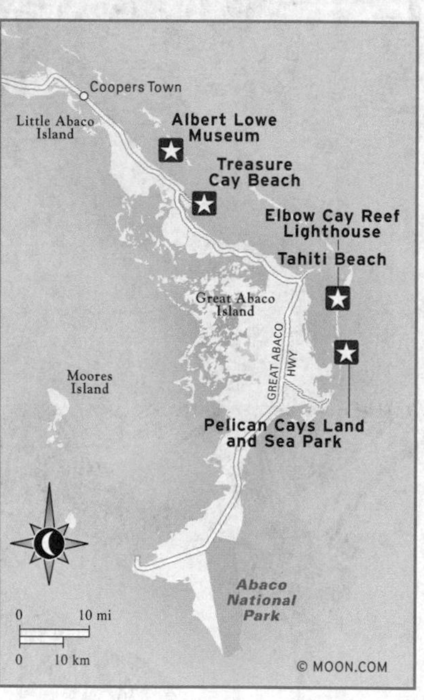

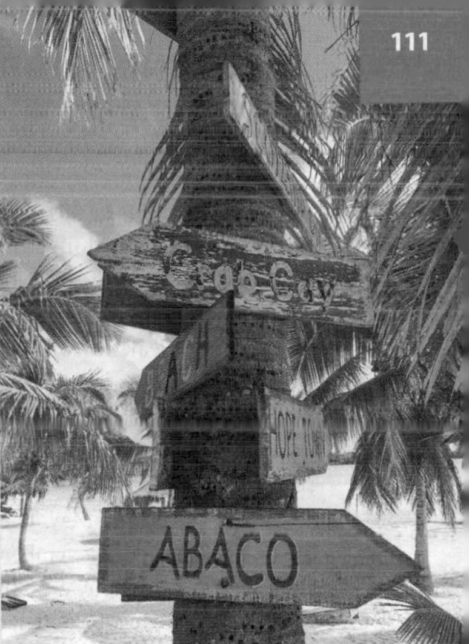

The Abacos islands are close to the doorstep of the United States but truly a world away. East of West Palm Beach by 180 miles, this archipelago consists of more than 100 islands over 120 miles, yet only a handful are populated.

The area attracts sailboats, sportfishing enthusiasts, and yachts that head over from the United States for the weekend or for extended travel in the winter months. The Sea of Abaco can seem like a busy highway with the amount of boat traffic during peak season, but a secluded anchorage can always be found. For a social scene, yachties enjoy drinking with fellow mariners at local watering holes. To sample a taste of the cruising life, try bareboat rentals or captained catamaran charters from The Moorings.

On land, first-class resorts, historic settlements on small cays, uninhabited islands, and expansive wilderness make The Abacos unique. The architecture is colonial, quaint, and colorful, and many settlements utilize golf carts for transportation. There are no casinos or shopping malls in The Abacos, so nature becomes your playground.

The "mainland" of Great Abaco Island will feel like a continent in comparison to its smaller counterparts that stretch along its backbone to the east. Great Abaco Island is one of the largest islands of The Bahamas, with endless miles of mangrove and pine forest, but most of the other inhabited islands are only several square miles and are easily walkable. The Marls, sprawling out along the western side of Great Abaco, is a shallow bank filled with an endless maze of mangroves and creeks. Enjoy world class fishing in an unspoiled and remote setting. Numerous lodges and outfits assist anglers with guided trips. Head out to the surrounding islands and cays and you'll find a casual and unhurried pace lingering among the open-air beach bars and along narrow lanes trimmed with radiant tropical foliage.

With unending opportunities to explore nature, boat, fish, and enjoy the island lifestyle, The Abacos are waiting.

Previous: Elbow Cay Reef Lighthouse overlooking Hope Town Inn & Marina; picnic tables at Coco Beach Bar. **Above:** colorful sign at Bluff House Beach Resort and Marina.

PLANNING YOUR TIME

Due to its northern location in The Bahamas archipelago, well north of the official tropical zone, the winter months can be quite cool, dipping into the 50s at night. The summer months are best for getting in the water, boating, and fishing, and you'll find a domestic crowd mixed with South Floridian weekenders. Peak season is Christmas and New Year's, with a lull in January, and then picking up again for mid-winter break, spring break, and Easter Weekend. You'll find a fairly steady influx of visitors by both land and sea from November until May. The end of August to the beginning of November is peak hurricane season, and many establishments close. The hotels that stay open often offer the lowest rates of the year during this time.

To access the islands of The Abacos, you fly into Marsh Harbour International Airport on Great Abaco. Marsh Harbour is the third-largest populated city in The Bahamas and the hub of travel in this northern island chain. Boaters and land visitors use this opportunity to stock up on supplies and essentials prior to heading out to more remote island settlements, where you will find only modestly stocked food stores and limited services. Plan on spending a night or two at the Abaco Beach Resort in Marsh Harbour and settle into your surroundings before hopping on a boat or catching the ferry to one of the beautiful cays.

The Elbow Cay Reef Lighthouse welcomes visitors to the charming colonial settlement of Hope Town, which has a bustling pedestrian downtown filled with shops and restaurants. The remainder of its home island, Elbow Cay, stretches south to include boutique hotels and vacation cottages with striking views of the Atlantic Ocean and the Sea of Abaco. Plan on spending at least two nights at the Abaco Inn.

A tiny community with a lot of action, Great Guana Cay is a popular destination for beachgoers looking for a quiet stretch of sand and some of the liveliest beach bars in The Bahamas. This is a great day trip for those stationed in Marsh Harbour. Man-O-War Cay is the boatbuilding capital of The Bahamas. It is a dry island (no alcohol) and has two restaurants and a few options for visitors looking for a less-traveled location. Head over for the day and grab lunch at Dock & Dine, and then visit Albury's Sail Shop and watch the women sew canvas creations.

North of Marsh Harbour on the mainland is the Treasure Cay Beach, Marina & Golf Resort, a great place to relax for a few days. If you really want to unplug, catch the ferry over to Green Turtle Cay and explore the sleepy settlement of New Plymouth and the island's many isolated beaches. Head south on Great Abaco and stop for lunch in Little Harbour, home to Pete's Pub and Pete Johnston's Art Gallery and Foundry. For golfing enthusiasts, the Abaco Club on Winding Bay has a Scottish-style links golf course, rated as one of the top courses in The Bahamas, or stay at the Blackfly Lodge at Schooner Bay and take advantage of the bonefishing opportunities right out the back door.

If you want to fit all of this in, you'll need at least a week. Some choose to settle on one island; others take advantage of the opportunity to island-hop.

ORIENTATION

Visitors arrive by boat or by plane. Convenient daily flights run from the United States to Marsh Harbour International Airport. Taxis are available at the airport, but if you plan to stay on the mainland, rent a car for exploring. From Marsh Harbour, the S. C. Bootle Highway runs north toward Treasure Cay and Cooper's Town. One main road runs to Treasure Cay to the Treasure Cay Beach, Marina & Golf Resort, with side roads to the development's residential neighborhoods. S. C. Bootle highway intersects the Great Abaco Highway in Marsh Harbour and heads south. Endless pine forests accompany you on the 30-minute drive south to the turnoff for Little Harbour, Winding Bay, and Cherokee Sound. Ten minutes south of the Cherokee Sound turnoff along the Great Abaco Highway is Schooner Bay. South of Schooner

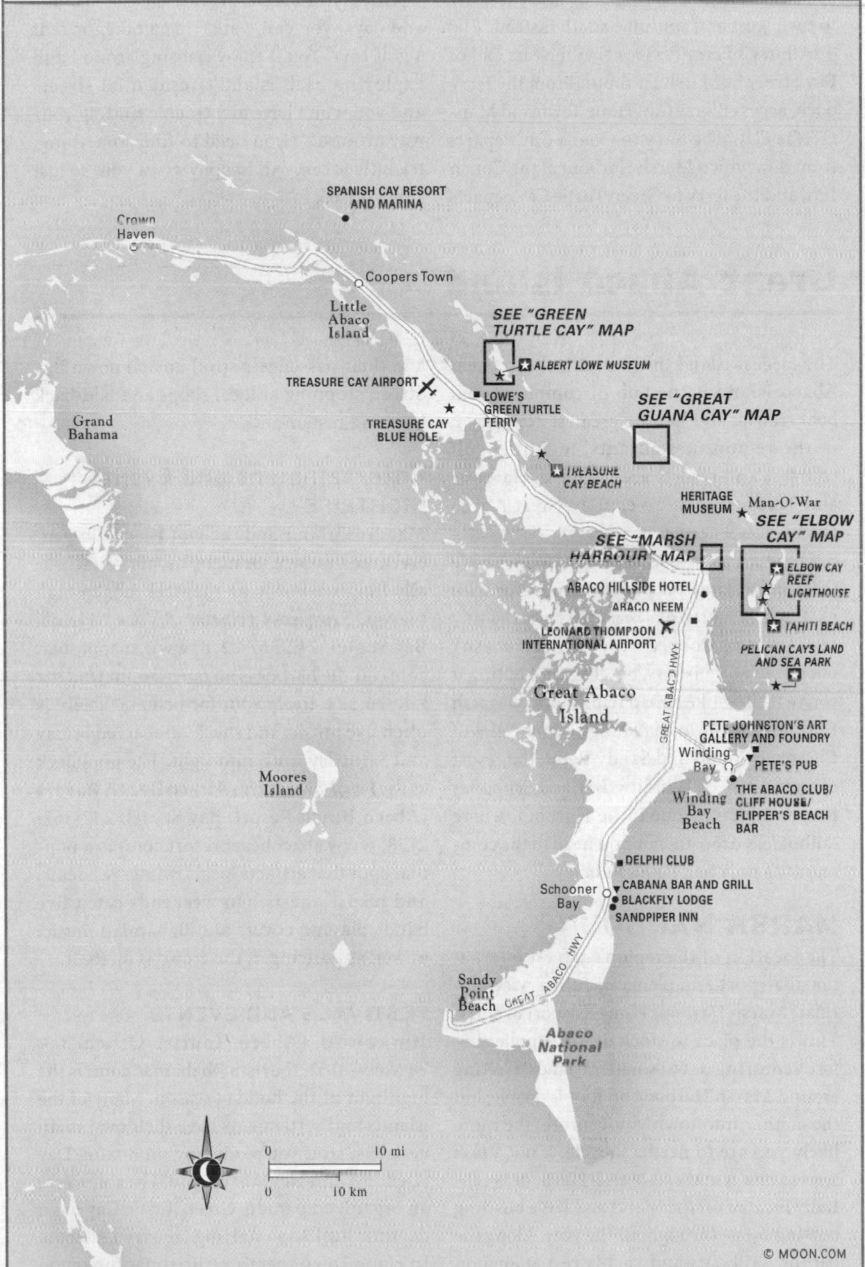
The Abacos
SPANISH CAY RESORT AND MARINA
Crown Haven
Coopers Town
Little Abaco Island
SEE "GREEN TURTLE CAY" MAP
ALBERT LOWE MUSEUM
TREASURE CAY AIRPORT
LOWE'S GREEN TURTLE FERRY
TREASURE CAY BLUE HOLE
Grand Bahama
SEE "GREAT GUANA CAY" MAP
TREASURE CAY BEACH
HERITAGE MUSEUM
Man-O-War
SEE "ELBOW CAY" MAP
SEE "MARSH HARBOUR" MAP
ELBOW CAY REEF LIGHTHOUSE
ABACO HILLSIDE HOTEL
ABACO NEEM
LEONARD THOMPSON INTERNATIONAL AIRPORT
TAHITI BEACH
PELICAN CAYS LAND AND SEA PARK
GREAT ABACO HWY
Great Abaco Island
PETE JOHNSTON'S ART GALLERY AND FOUNDRY
Winding Bay
PETE'S PUB
Moores Island
THE ABACO CLUB/ CLIFF HOUSE/ FLIPPER'S BEACH BAR
Winding Bay Beach
DELPHI CLUB
Schooner Bay
CABANA BAR AND GRILL
BLACKFLY LODGE
SANDPIPER INN
Sandy Point Beach
GREAT ABACO HWY
Abaco National Park
0
10 mi
0
10 km
© MOON.COM

Bay, the highway heads slightly west toward Sandy Point. You can access Abaco National Park by getting off the highway where it starts to turn west and continue south instead.

Albury's Ferry Service is at the east end of Bay Street in Marsh Harbour. From the ferry dock, access Elbow Cay-Hope Town and Man-O-War Cay. The ferry to Guana Cay departs from downtown Marsh Harbour at the Conch Inn, and the ferry to Green Turtle Cay departs from the Treasure Cay Airport Terminal ferry dock.

Once you arrive on the smaller islands and cays, you can walk, ride a bike, or rent a golf cart. You'll enjoy cruising around and exploring each island's residential streets and you won't have any trouble finding your way around. If you need to find something, friendly locals will happily assist you, so just stop and ask.

Great Abaco Island

The largest island in the archipelago, Great Abaco Island is the hub of commerce and boat traffic, and has the greatest population in the region. Restaurants, nightlife, golf courses, and resorts are in Marsh Harbour and Treasure Cay. To explore Great Abaco Island, you'll need a rental car.

Due to its size, Great Abaco doesn't have that small-island feel, but you'll be happy with its beaches. North of Treasure Cay is the tiny settlement of Cooper's Town, which doesn't offer much for visitors, but it's a nice outing if you're feeling like a road trip. South of Marsh Harbour are the local fishing communities of Cherokee Sound and Sandy Point, the resort communities of Winding Bay and Schooner Bay, and picturesque Little Harbour, where sailboaters drop anchor and head to the community's only bar, Pete's Pub.

MARSH HARBOUR

The location of the region's largest international airport and plenty of full-service marinas, Marsh Harbour is an easy port of entry. This is the place to stock up on supplies before venturing out to smaller islands. Getting around Marsh Harbour on foot is doable, but the farther into town you venture, the more likely you are to need a bicycle, if not a taxi service or a rental car. Marsh Harbour is centrally located on the island and has a bustling boating scene throughout the year. Along the harbor, sailboats and yachts rest at anchor, and their passengers stroll up and down Bay Street, stopping at local shops and laid-back bars and restaurants.

Entertainment and Events

NIGHTLIFE

Marsh Harbour and the Out Islands in general aren't known for nightlife, but you'll usually find live music on the weekends in high season. **Snappas** (Harbour View Marina, Bay St., tel. 242/367-2278, www.snappasbar.com) on the harbor is an open-air marina bar known as a lively spot for boaters. There is often live music, and snacks are served Friday and Saturday until midnight. The pool deck at the **Pool Bar at the Abaco Beach Resort** (Abaco Beach Resort, Bay St., tel. 242/367-2158, www.abacobeachresort.com) is a popular spot that attracts locals, winter residents, and resort guests. On weekends catch live bands playing covers and Bahamian music, as well as dancing, if the crowd is up for it.

FESTIVALS AND EVENTS

Junkanoo (Abaco Tourist Office, tel. 242/699-0152, tourism@bahamas.com) is the highlight of the holiday season. Many of the islands and settlements have their own small versions, so if you're visiting on Boxing Day (Dec. 26) and New Year's, you'll be able to see an organized parade. Green Turtle Cay has a daytime Junkanoo starting January 1 at noon. In Hope Town there's a Christmas Junkanoo

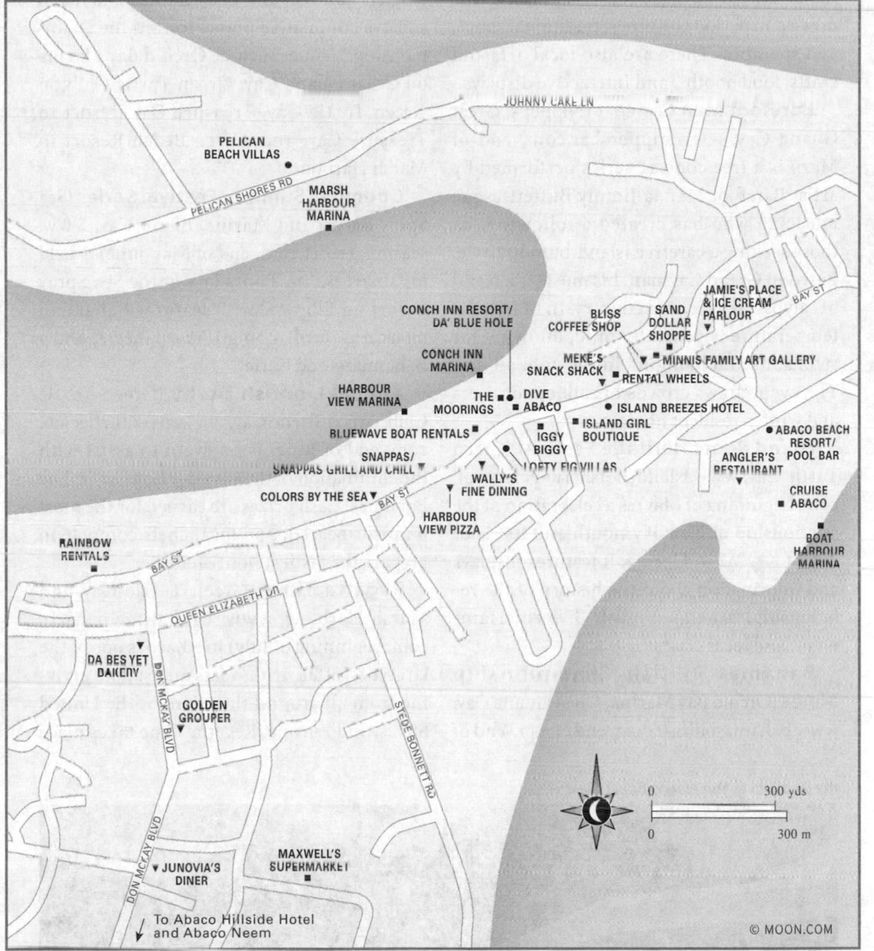

Competition at Sea Spray Resort and a New Year's Eve Children's rush-out (costumed people engaging in choreographed dances and parades). The Abaco Love Rush Junkanoo weekend is held at the end of February in Marsh Harbour. Senior and junior Junkanoo groups compete over two nights. Unlike Nassau, where you sit in bleachers, separated from the action, these parades are small and intimate, so you'll be able to integrate and dance alongside the Junkanoo groups. Some find these events more enjoyable than the larger versions.

Art for the Parks (Abaco Beach Resort, Marsh Harbour, www.bnt.bs, end of Jan.) is a seasonal fund-raiser for the six national parks in Abaco, hosted by the Bahamas National Trust. Local artists showcase their work, and you'll find food, cocktails, live music, and games.

Hope Town Heritage Day (Hope Town, Elbow Cay, www.hopetownmuseum.com, beginning of Mar.) celebrates the history of Loyalist settlement, with reenactments of the arrival of Loyalist settlers, participants dressed in period costumes, traditional songs, and speeches. There are also local arts and crafts, food booths, and interactive displays.

Barefoot Man Concert (Nipper's, Great Guana Cay, www.nippersbar.com, end of Mar.) is a free concert series performed by artist Barefoot Man, a Jimmy Buffett-esque musician who has created a following for those seeking a carefree island-bum lifestyle. Based in Grand Cayman, his music is a blend of calypso, reggae, and country. In March the temperature is generally mild, allowing for swimsuits and lounging in the pool all day. The event draws crowds of sailboat cruisers and winter-resident homeowners.

Island Roots Heritage Festival (Green Turtle Cay, www.islandrootsheritagefestival.com, beginning of May) is a celebration of the relationship of New Plymouth and its sister city of Key West, Florida. It features displays and information about the history of the relationship, Bahamian music, live entertainment, and local crafts.

Bahamas Billfish Championship Series (Orchid Bay Marina, Great Guana Cay, www.bahamasbillfish.com, end of Apr.-end of June) was founded in 1973 and has grown into a huge international event sponsored by Rolex. Anglers can fish any and all tournaments to achieve cumulative points toward the championship. Venues include Orchid Bay Marina on Great Guana Cay, Green Turtle Club on Green Turtle Cay, Treasure Cay Resort in Treasure Cay, and Abaco Beach Resort in Marsh Harbour.

Goombay Summer Festival Series (Sea Spray Resort and Marina, Elbow Cay, www.seasprayresort.com, end of May-June) is held for six weeks on Thursdays at the Sea Spray Resort on Elbow Cay. It features Bahamian musicians, Junkanoo groups, dancers, and a Bahamian food buffet.

Annual Lionfish Derby (Green Turtle Club, Green Turtle Cay, www.greenturtleclub.com, end of June) is an event to assist with the elimination of the invasive lionfish in The Bahamas. Cash prizes are earned for the most lionfish speared, and local chefs compete to prepare the tastiest lionfish dishes.

Regatta Time (Green Turtle Cay and Marsh Harbour, www.regattatimeinabaco.com, beginning of July) in Abaco is one of the largest regattas, with boats and sailors arriving from all around the country, the United States, and Europe. Regatta Time takes place

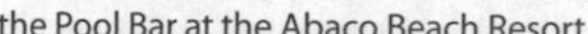

the Pool Bar at the Abaco Beach Resort

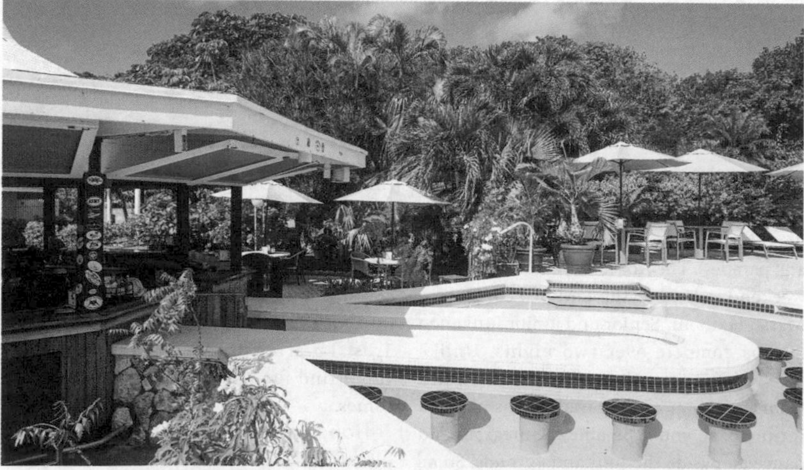

in Green Turtle Cay and includes the famous Fiddle Cay Cheeseburger in Paradise beach party, which is a gathering of boats on a nearby deserted island sandbar with cheese burgers, margaritas, and local sponsors.

Annual Arts & Crafts Festival (Hope Town Harbour Lodge, Hope Town, Elbow Cay, www.hopetownlodge.com, the day after U.S. Thanksgiving in Nov.) invites guests to enjoy a glass of wine, fine cheeses, and hors d'oeuvres while admiring jewelry, paintings, shell crafts, woodcarvings, photography, and Christmas decor.

Hope Town Music Festival (Hope Town, www.combustionmusic.com, beginning of Dec.) is a three-day festival featuring well-known international songwriters raising funds for local charities.

Annual Abaco Christmas Festival (Marsh Harbour, BAIC Park, Abaco Tourist Office, tel. 242/367-3067, 1st Sat. in Dec.) features live performances from choirs, quartets, soloists, and calypso bands; a dog show; an arts and crafts Christmas bazaar; food tents; and an evening Junkanoo performance.

Shopping

After becoming intrigued by the neem tree's ability to control high blood pressure and diabetes, Nick Miaoulis introduced **Abaco Neem** (Don McKay Blvd., tel. 242/367-4117, www.abaconeem.com, Mon.-Sat. 9am-5pm) to The Bahamas in 1993. The operation is now co-run with his wife Daphne, and the couple is passionate about sharing neem's health benefits. The original seeds were imported from India, and the farm is now home to 8,500 neem trees, producing a variety of all-natural healing products, including Neem Cream, with elasticity and skin toning benefits, natural bug repellent, soaps, and pet products. Stop at their retail shop in Marsh Harbour or book a farm tour through the website.

Iggy Biggy (Bay St., across from Conch Inn, tel. 242/367-3596, Mon.-Sat. 9:30am-5pm) is located on the main street of downtown Marsh Harbour in a brightly-colored pink building with charming pineapple accents. Inside you'll find island music, sunglasses, wind chimes, upscale shirts for men, and in-season, locally-made island Christmas decorations. Farther west on Bay Street is **Island Girl Boutique** (Bay St., tel. 242/367-0283, Mon.-Thurs. 10am-6pm, Fri.-Sat. 10am-7pm), featuring swimsuits, gifts, shirts, hats, and flowy light beachwear for women. The **Dive Abaco Gift Shop** (Bay St., tel. 242/367-2787, Mon.-Sat. 9am-5pm) has a

neem trees at the Abaco Neem farm

lovely selection of hand-painted artsy postcards to send home to your friends, and small paintings featuring a variety of mermaid and sea turtle designs.

Sand Dollar Shoppe (Bay St., tel. 242/367-4405, Mon.-Fri. 9am-5pm, Sat. 9am-1pm) has been family-owned and operated for three generations. Although there is a variety of jewelry, the family's talent is in gold jewelry, and everything is produced in-house. Four members of the Minnis family combine their talent toward the **Minnis Family Art Gallery** (Bay St., tel. 242/322-2605, www.eddieminnis.com, by appointment) and individual works in an overall style of photorealism, with absolutely stunning depictions of Bahamian life. One of the largest supermarkets in the Out Islands, **Maxwell's Supermarket** (Stratton Dr., tel. 242/367-7283, Mon.-Thurs. 8am-7pm, Fri.-Sat. 8am-8pm, Sun. 8am-4pm) is the best option for stocking up on groceries and supplies before heading out to the cays.

Sports and Recreation

TOP EXPERIENCE

BONEFISHING THE MARLS

Bonefishing in Abaco is less crowded than in well-known Andros. The Marls, on the western side of Great Abaco, boast 200 square miles of bonefishing flats, also a popular spot for permit and tarpon in the summertime. Several lodges offer packages, including **Blackfly Lodge** (Schooner Bay, tel. 242/577-5577, U.S. tel. 904/540-3184, www.blackflylodge.com). The Blackfly Lodge is a partnership between Blackfly Outfitters in Jacksonville, Florida, Blackfly Restaurant in St. Augustine, Florida, and the location at Schooner Bay. The food is top notch, and the fishing is incredible.

Delphi Club (Rolling Harbour, tel. 242/366-2222, www.delphi-bahamas.com) is a luxury fishing lodge located in remote Rolling Harbour, between Marsh Harbour and Schooner Bay. In a stylish 18th-century plantation-style house, it's a fantastic option for anglers traveling with a nonfishing partner.

Justin Sands Bonefishing (tel. 242/367-3526 or 242/359-6890, U.S. tel. 561/531-5073, www.justfishjs.com) has been a top guide since 1997, and Justin knows the Marls like the back of his hand, having won numerous prestigious awards for fishing. He leads guided fishing expeditions Monday-Friday in his well-equipped 16-foot flats boat. Based in Marsh Harbour, he can pick up guests from hotels, guest houses, marinas, and the ferry dock. Advance reservations are advised.

SAILING AND BOATING

The Moorings (Conch Inn Resort and Marina, Bay St., Marsh Harbour, tel. 242/367-4000, U.S. tel. 800/416-0814, www.moorings.com) is an international charter company specializing in boating expeditions throughout the Caribbean. The convenient location in Marsh Harbour allows you to hop aboard a boat to explore The Abacos on your own agenda. Depending on your experience level, you can rent bareboat mono- and twin-hull sailboats or power catamarans, or opt to book a worry-free getaway with a captain and chef for six to eight people.

Cruise Abaco (Boat Harbour Marina, Marsh Harbour, U.S. tel. 321/473-4223, www.cruiseabaco.com) is a local owner-operated outfit offering bareboat and crewed excursions on overnighting mono- and twin-hull sailboats and powerboats. They also offer the unique concept of "captain by day, bareboat by night," which provides you with the opportunity to have a captain take you to all the best sights during the day, get you safely to your anchorage, and then leave you in peace for the evening. They also offer private charters with sailing lessons for those keen to learn the ropes.

Bluewave Boat Rentals (Harbour View Marina, Marsh Harbour, tel. 242/367-3911, www.bluewaverentals.com) offers a range of sizes of power center consoles with tee-tops, from easily manageable 21-footers to a more

a sailboat at the dock in Marsh Harbour

family friendly 33-footer that seats up to 12 people. Located at Harbour View Marina, facilities are included with the rental, such as the swimming pool, a barbecue area, a laundry room, and shower facilities.

Rainbow Rentals (west of Union Jack Dock, Bay St., Marsh Harbour, tel. 242/367-4602, www.rainbowboatrentals.com) offers 22-26-foot twin-hull boats that are wide and comfortable, with seating for up to eight on the larger boats. Included are ice chests for fishing and picnics, and all the required safety equipment. Boats are rentable by the day, week, or month.

SNORKELING AND DIVING

In operation since 1978, **Dive Abaco** (at the Conch Inn Resort and Marina, Bay St., Marsh Harbour, tel. 242/367-2787, U.S. tel. 386/957-7902, www.diveabaco.com) regularly receives the TripAdvisor certificate of excellence. Take scuba and snorkeling trips to reefs, tunnels, caverns, and wrecks, or specialized night and shark dives. Scuba instruction is available along with equipment sales and rentals. Book a dive and hotel combo package with the Conch Inn.

BIKING

Along with rental cars, **Rental Wheels** (Bay St., Marsh Harbour, tel. 242/367-4643, www.rentalwheels.com) offers single-speed beach cruisers with baskets, a perfect option if you need to get to the grocery store or check out the town. Rent them daily or weekly.

KAYAKING AND ECOTOURS

Lucayan Nature Tours (tel. 242/477-5953 or 242/367-2749, www.abaconaturetours.com) is operated by Reggie, an eighth-generation Bahamian who is an expert in native vegetation and wildlife. Visit the off-the-beaten-path Hole in the Wall Lighthouse on the southern point of the island, only accessible by 4WD vehicle on a dirt road. Also witness a wide variety of native and migratory birds, including the Bahama parrot, and discover blue holes hidden in the bush. Your tour is tailored specifically for you and your interests.

YOGA

At the **Abaco Beach Resort and Marina** (Abaco Beach Resort, Bay St., tel. 242/367-2158, www.abacobeachresort.com), yoga is offered twice weekly for resort and marina guests at the Below Decks Terrace. Check with concierge to make reservations, as space is limited to 10.

Food

Marsh Harbour has a great selection of restaurants, from high-end dining to local digs. There's a lot of crossover on menu items, and you'll likely find fish tacos, hamburgers, and chicken wings almost everywhere. I suggest taking advantage of the bounty of the sea and the many twists on traditional Bahamian cuisine.

BAHAMIAN

Jamie's Place & Ice Cream Parlour (Bay St., tel. 242/367-2880, Mon.-Sat. 7am-9pm,

Cruiser's Net: VHF Radio

Within island communities, often with limited cell phone service, it is not uncommon for residents to communicate primarily via VHF radio. Most boaters use it to communicate with each other and will answer it just as they would a phone. VHF communication has specific etiquette. Channel 16 is a working hailing and emergency channel only. Hail your desired establishment or boat on channel 16, taking care to repeat the name three times, such as "Sea Breeze, Sea Breeze, Sea Breeze," and then state immediately "Come back," or state your own boat name or call sign. If they are listening, they will respond, and decide which channel you will switch to. If you get no answer, wait 10 minutes or so and try again.

Working channels in the United States and Bahamas region include channels 9, 12, 16, 17, 68, 69, 71, and 72. Be aware that many people will eavesdrop on your conversation. Most handheld radios work within five nautical miles at sea level. Those with tall antennas, such as sailboats, work at greater distances. Boaters and landlubbers alike tune in to the daily Cruiser's Net broadcast from Marsh Harbour at 8:15am on VHF channel 68 for announcements, weather, and events. You can also listen to a live streaming online at www.cruisersnet.org.

$12-17) serves a mix of Bahamian and American food. It's slightly different than your average Bahamian fare, with items such as conch wrap, coconut fried crawfish (lobster), stuffed hen, Eleuthera pineapple barbecue chicken wings and Philly cheesesteak. **Golden Grouper** (Don Mckay Blvd., tel. 242/367-2301, Mon.-Fri. 7am-3pm, Sun. 7am-2pm, $10-15) is a great spot for breakfast prior to heading out on the water. Located in an unassuming plaza in the commercial area of downtown Marsh Harbour, Golden Grouper serves hearty Bahamian favorites like chicken or pork souse with a side of grits and johnnycake, and for lunch try fried grouper or a cracked conch burger with a heaping pile of french fries.

Dine in or take out at the simple, tasty local **Junovia's Diner** (Don McKay Blvd., tel. 242/367-1271, Mon.-Fri. 7am-11am, Sat. 7am-10am, $10-15), known for their home-cooked healthy portions of breakfast and some of the best souse around. It's also a good place to find boiled or stewed fish. American breakfast options and omelets are also available.

da' Blue Hole (Conch Inn Resort and Marina, Bay St., Marsh Harbour, tel. 242/801-2583, hwww.dabluehole.com, daily 11:30am-4pm and 6pm-midnight, $20-40), previously Curly Tails, this restaurant re-opened with its new name in early 2018 after major renovations to the building, implementing elegant decor and upscale ambience. Stepping up from the pub food it was known for, da' Blue Hole serves gorgeous presentations of fresh seafood, sushi, and pastas with Caribbean twists overlooking the marinas on the harbor. Gluten free and vegan options are available.

FINE DINING

★ **Angler's Restaurant** (Abaco Beach Resort, Bay St., tel. 242/367-2158, www.abacobeachresort.com, daily lunch 11:30am-2:30pm, dinner 6pm-10pm, $30-50) is nestled among mature palms overlooking the harbor and marina at the Abaco Beach Resort. Both casual and elegant, you'll find some folks dressed up, others dressed down. Enjoy breakfast and lunch on the veranda as you watch the boat traffic. At dinner, crisp white tablecloths, expansive bay windows overlooking the brightly lit yachts in the marina, and subtle warm lighting invite you to linger over an after-dinner drink. For a more casual experience, chat with the friendly bartenders at the bar. Grouper is the specialty; try the macadamia nut-encrusted version. You'll also find lobster, rack of lamb, and various cuts of steak. If you're not in the mood for meat dishes, the ever-changing vegetable stack depends on what's in season. For dessert, try bread pudding with warm coconut rum, fried banana caramel cheesecake, or the famous house-made guava duff. This is one of Abaco's best restaurants.

A brightly colored pink and purple cartoonish sign welcomes you to **Wally's Fine Dining and Boutique** (Bay St., tel. 242/367-2074, 11:30am-3pm and 6pm-9:30pm Mon.-Sat., $25-40) on the main street of Marsh Harbour, just across from Mangoes Marina. The coral-pink wooden building is tucked away from the road and fronted by a robust green garden and white picket fence. The decor is rattan with pink everywhere. When lobster is in season, the specials include lobster in champagne beurre blanc, lobster in mango curry sauce, cracked lobster, and lobster wraps. Dinner favorites include curried shrimp, sashimi, steaks, steamed snapper, grilled lamb, and seafood penne with mushroom cream sauce. Lunch offers robust menu items like bacon cheeseburgers with onion rings, coconut shrimp, chicken tacos, a grilled fish BLT wrap, and a variety of light salad options.

BARS AND PUBS

For a laid-back experience, check out the **Pool Bar** (Abaco Beach Resort, Bay St., tel. 242/367-2158, www.abacobeachresort.com, daily 11am-10pm, $15-20) at the Abaco Beach Resort, a circular open-air bar with a swim-up seating and live music on weekends. It tends to draw a mix of boaters, residents, and vacationers in party mode. Pizzas, sandwiches, and burgers are staple menu items, as well as pub grub like potato skins, fish fingers, and cracked lobster bites.

★ **Snappas Grill & Chill** (tel. 242/367-2278, www.snappasbar.com, daily lunch 11am-4pm, dinner 5pm-9:30pm, $15-30) overhangs the harbor next door to the Harbour View Marina. It's popular for cruisers and boaters and has a true seafaring vibe. Seagulls mill around the docks waiting to share a french fry. A hodgepodge of shark and giant billfish figures, old signs, and custom-made stickers from yacht crews that have patronized the establishment adorn the walls, giving it an organized yet thrown together feel. Pizza, steak, kebabs, sandwiches, and burgers are menu staples, and a Friday-Saturday late-night menu satiates with mozzarella sticks, hot dogs, onion rings, and wings. A dinghy dock is available for boaters. Freeport-produced

Snappas Grill & Chill

Sands beer is served, as this is one of the few places in the islands with draft beer. If you're not a beer fan, try one of their intoxicating Snappa rum drinks. Enjoy sunsets over the harbor, happy hour daily 5pm-7:30pm, and live music on weekends.

Colors by the Sea (Bay St., tel. 242/699-3294, daily 11am-11pm, $15-20) is a small bar on the harbor and a great place to chill out with the locals. Simple home-cooked comfort dishes like minced lobster with garden salad and sweet plantain, meatloaf with mashed potatoes, and stuffed chicken and whole fried snapper are served with a smile. It's a popular place to watch baseball, basketball, football, and boxing, with specialty drinks and buckets of beer.

PIZZA

If you're looking for something other than seafood, **Abaco Pizza** (tel. 242/367-4488, Mon.-Sat. 11am-9pm, $10-20) is a great spot to get your pizza fix. If you still want seafood, try their conch pizza. Abaco Pizza does takeout and delivery only. **Harbour View Pizza** (Bay St., across from Harbour View Marina, tel. 242/375-9550, Sun.-Thurs. 4pm-9:30pm, Fri. 4pm-10:30pm, Sat. 11am-4pm and 6pm-10:30pm, $10-20) serves up made-to-order pizzas, calzones, and wings. They make their own dough and utilize as many local ingredients as possible, including chicken wings from the local free-range Abaco Big Bird farm.

CAFÉS AND LIGHT BITES

In a tiny building on the harbor side of Bay Street downtown is **Meke's Snack Shack** (Bay St., Marsh Harbour, tel. 242/367-4005, $8-12), touted as the home of Abaco's best beef, chicken, fish, or conch burgers. If you have an affinity to heat, choose from a variety of pepper-infused specialties: spicy Swiss, spicy fried chicken, or spicy bacon. Otherwise go for grilled cheese, Philly cheesesteak, or grouper BLT. For the sweet tooth, try the homemade ice cream.

The friendly staff at **Da Bes Yet Bakery** (Don Mckay Blvd., near Queen Elizabeth Dr., tel. 242/367-3616, Mon.-Fri. 7am-6pm) serves fresh baked breads and pastries. Located in a strip mall along the main street, patrons crowd the small space to order curated baked goods from the counter. They offer some of the best cinnamon rolls in the islands, and the coconut pie is exquisite.

The artsy ★ **Bliss Coffee Shop** (Bay St., tel. 242/367-5523, daily 8am-5pm) is the center of the action on the island. Beautiful framed artwork on the wall is for sale, or browse through a collection of matted prints to take home with you. Sit indoors on a comfy couch, or opt for a front-row people-watching vantage point on the sidewalk deck. Fresh ground coffee and espresso are on offer, along with almond and coconut milk creamers. Delectable breakfast items include pumpkin rolls, cream-cheese bars, cinnamon buns, and breakfast sandwiches.

Accommodations

There are numerous lodging options in Marsh Harbour for plush pampering and for a simple place to lay your head after a day of exploring. Vacation rental homes are popular throughout the islands. These listings indicate high-season double-occupancy rates for a standard room, not including tax and resort fees.

$100-150

Abaco Hillside Hotel (Great Abaco Hwy., tel. 242/367-0112, www.abacohillside.com, $120) is outside town, so you will need a car to access amenities, but it's a great spot for budget accommodations to explore the island. Standard rooms are available as well as one- and two-bedroom units with full kitchens, perfect for independent families.

In the heart of Marsh Harbour, **Island Breezes Hotel** (Bay St., tel. 242/367-3776, www.islandbreezeshotel.com, $150) is walking distance to popular bars, restaurants, and shopping. This eight-room hotel is sufficient if you plan on being out during the day; there is no pool, and the accommodations are no-frills, but it's clean and comfortable.

$150-250

Three miles from the Marsh Harbour International Airport in the center of town, **Conch Inn Resort and Marina** (tel. 242/367-4000, www.moorings.com, www.diveabaco.com/conch, $225) is on the same property as the Moorings charter boat rentals and Dive Abaco. Bookings for rooms can be made through either of these businesses. Rooms are nestled between the main street and the quiet harbor, and the Inn is walking distance to restaurants, bars, and shopping. Ten pastel-colored rooms with two double beds, a small kitchenette, and air-conditioning make a comfortable place to settle in. The property has all marina amenities and a freshwater pool. No beaches are nearby, but the Great Guana Cay ferry departs from the dock on-site. To book dive and lodging packages, contact **Dive Abaco** (tel. 242/367-2787, www.diveabaco.com).

Pelican Beach Villas (Pelican Shores Rd., tel. 242/367-3600, U.S. tel. 877/326-3180, www.pelicanbeachvillas.com, $250) is on the peninsula across from downtown Marsh Harbour. Beautiful beachfront cottages front a small sandy beach, one of the few in the area. Nearby is Mermaid Reef, a great spot for snorkeling. Six beachfront villas have two bedrooms, two baths, full kitchens, and brightly colored tropical decor. For couples, plan in advance for the lone one-bedroom, one-bath economy efficiency, located inland from the beach. It books up quickly in season, but it's a budget option with all the great amenities of the beachfront villas. There are few food options nearby, so you'll need a rental car or a boat to get to town.

Lofty Fig Villas (Bay St., tel. 242/367-2681, www.loftyfig.com, $198) are downtown and within walking distance of everything. The single-story rooms have air-conditioning, full kitchens, and private covered patios. Outside are a freshwater swimming pool and a shady gazebo, a communal gathering place for a group. There is no restaurant on-site, but all of the local hangouts are within steps of the villas. Dive Abaco offers dive and hotel packages with Lofty Fig.

OVER $250

Enter the stately grounds of the ★ **Abaco Beach Resort and Boat Harbour** (east of Conch Sound Marina, tel. 242/367-2158, U.S. tel. 877/533-4799, www.abacobeachresort.com, $450) through a canopy of mature palm trees and you'll be welcomed by a bright yellow reception center and warm friendly staff

Abaco Beach Resort and Boat Harbour

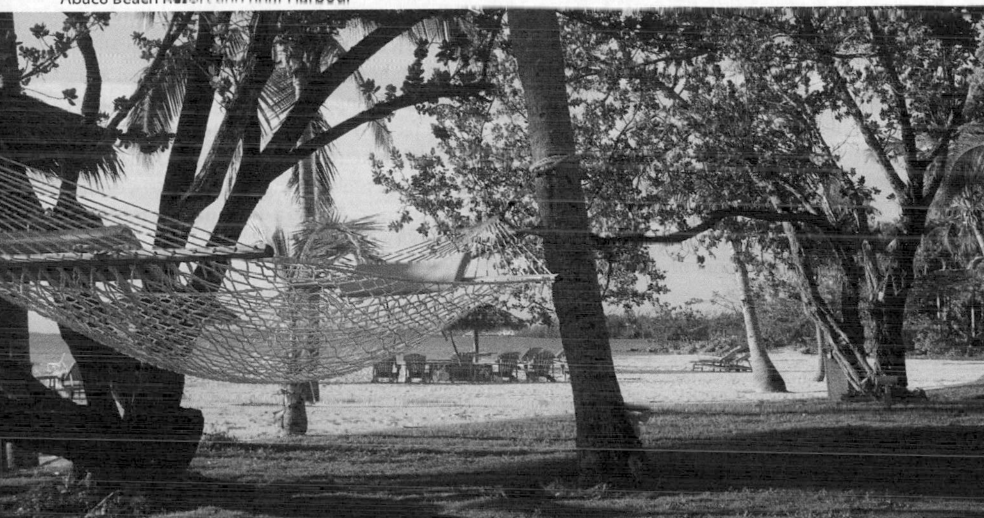

ready to make your stay a memorable one. This is the largest hotel in Marsh Harbour, on 40 acres on the Sea of Abaco, with a beautiful private stretch of white sandy beach and ample spots to sit under the shade of an umbrella in a lounger. A swimming pool, a marina with full amenities, a fitness gym, a health spa, and two restaurants are on-site. Lodging options include expansive rooms overlooking a grassy courtyard, suites with full kitchens, cottages, two-bedroom residences, and penthouses. Wake up in the morning and walk out on your balcony to hear only the rustle of palm fronds and the lapping of the waves on the private white-sand beach. Use of paddleboards and kayaks is complimentary, or head to the pool and grab a cocktail at the swim-up pool bar. It's right downtown, so walking, even to the ferry dock to visit other islands, is possible without a vehicle.

Information and Services

VISITOR INFORMATION

Happy to assist with aspects of your Abaco visit, **Abaco Tourist Office and Information Center** (tel. 242/699-0152, www.bahamas.com, Mon.-Fri. 9am-5pm) has a location at the Government Complex near Tropical Shipping off S. C. Bootle Highway. You can also stop at the **Ministry of Tourism visitors center** (Mon.-Fri. 9am-5pm) in the Harbour Place Building on Queen Elizabeth Drive, just before Bay Street, to pick up brochures.

If you're interested in connecting with a Bahamian ambassador to learn more about the culture and lifestyle, contact the **People-to-People Program** (tel. 242/367-3067, www.bahamas.com/people-to-people). Advance reservations to pair you with an ambassador are recommended.

BANKS

Stock up on cash before going out to the cays, as you not likely to find ATMs or banks on the smaller cays. **RBC Royal Bank** (Don Mackey Blvd., tel. 242/367-2420, Mon.-Thurs. 9am-4pm, Fri. 9am-4:30pm) or **Commonwealth Bank** (Queen Elizabeth Dr., tel. 242/367-2370, Mon.-Fri. 9am-3:30pm) both have 24-hour ATMs. Most resorts, upscale restaurants, rental car and cart companies, and sightseeing operations take credit cards, but more local, casual, and rustic establishments are likely to be cash-only.

HEALTH AND EMERGENCIES

There are several clinics for visitors: **Marsh Harbour Community Clinic** (Great Abaco Hwy., just before S. C. Bootle Hwy., tel. 242/367-2510 or 242/367-4594, Mon.-Fri. 9am-5pm), **Green Turtle Cay Community Clinic** (New Plymouth, tel. 242/365-4028, Mon.-Fri. 9am-5pm), and **Hope Town Community Clinic** (Hope Town, tel. 242/366-0108, Mon.-Fri. 9am-5pm). All clinics offer basic health services for minor outpatient issues and a limited selection of pharmaceuticals. For major medical emergencies, the clinics will assist with arranging transport to Nassau or the United States.

For emergencies or police services, contact **Royal Bahamas Police Force** (tel. 911, 919, or 242/367-2560). Fire services are available through **Marsh Harbour Fire & Rescue** (tel. 242/367-2000), **Treasure Cay Fire Department** (tel. 242/365-8919), **Green Turtle Cay Fire Department** (tel. 242/365-4019), and **Hope Town Fire & Rescue** (tel. 242/475-0144). **Emergency Medical Services** (tel. 242/367-2911) are available throughout The Abacos. If you need assistance getting an airlift to the United States, contact **Air Ambulance** (tel. 242/327-7077) or **Jet Rescue in Florida** (tel. 305/504-1093). For issues concerning marine vessels, contact **Bahamas Air Sea Rescue Association** (BASRA, tel. 242/366-0282).

MEDIA AND COMMUNICATIONS

Internet throughout The Abacos is hit or miss. Don't plan on a working vacation with speedy internet requirements unless you confirm with your accommodations they have high-speed or fiber-optic internet installed. Cell service is good in Marsh Harbour and

Treasure Cay, but the farther you venture from the larger communities, the spottier it becomes. Hope Town's cell service is known to be intermittent, so many people communicate, contact local businesses, and make dinner reservations by using VHF radio on channel 16.

Prior to your trip, you can also check ***The Abaconian*** (www.theabaconian.com), a newspaper and online publication for news, events, and updates specific to The Abacos.

Getting There

AIR

Marsh Harbour has daily flights from Nassau on **Bahamasair** (tel. 242/702-4140, www.bahamasair.com) and **Sky Bahamas** (tel. 242/702-2600, www.skybahamas.net) and direct flights from Fort Lauderdale on **Silver Airways** (U.S. tel. 801/401-9100, www.silverairways.com) and **Bahamasair,** from Miami on **American** (U.S. tel. 800/433-7300, www.aa.com), and from Atlanta on **Delta** (U.S. tel. 800/241-4141, www.delta.com). **Exclusive Aviation** (tel. 242/357-8877, www.flyexclusivebahamas.com) has weekly flights to Marsh Harbour from Odyssey Aviation in Nassau on a small Piper Navajo that seats up to eight.

Flying via Nassau allows you to preclear U.S. immigration and customs on the way out, skipping the hassle when you land in the United States. If you have to make a connecting flight in the United States, Nassau is a good option to shorten your transit time.

BOATING

The Abacos are known as a boating playground and attract many boaters throughout the mild winter and spring months. Call ahead to make reservations at one of the following marinas if you plan on visiting by boat, especially on a holiday weekend or during spring break.

Boat Harbour Marina (Abaco Beach Resort, tel. 242/367-2158, U.S. tel. 877/533-4799, www.abacobeachresort.com) has 198 slips on the protected Sea of Abaco side, with services that include power, water, ice, fuel, laundry, showers, and 24-hour security. It can accommodate boats up to 200 feet and regularly hosts a mix of sportfishing enthusiasts, yachts, and cruising sailboats. Immigration and customs is on site, as are two restaurants, bars, and a pool. **Conch Inn Marina** (tel. 242/367-4000, www.moorings.com) has 80 slips right downtown with easy access to the Sea of Abaco. Showers, laundry, and a pool are available for marina guests.

Located downtown next to Snappas Grill & Chill, **Harbour View Marina** (tel. 242/367-3910, www.harbourviewmarina.com) is a small family-owned full-service marina with 29 slips for boats of all sizes, including catamarans. It has a grilling station, a pool, and showers. **Marsh Harbour Marina** (tel. 242/367-2700, www.jibroom.com) is across from downtown near Pelican Shores. It is far from shopping, restaurants, and amenities, but if you have a dinghy, you can just pop across the harbor. There are 68 slips with fuel, ice, laundry, and showers, and transient and long-term dockage is available, with discounts for BoatUS members.

For those who aren't in a hurry to get to The Abacos, a budget option is **The Sealink** (tel. 242/323-2166, www.bahamasferries.com, $71 one-way). This Mail Boat, which delivers supplies to the islands, travels between Nassau and Marsh Harbour, a 13-hour trip, departing Monday evening and arriving Tuesday morning.

Getting Around

Taxis will be waiting by the airport. Fares to most local Marsh Harbour resorts, hotels, and marinas are $15-30. Fares increase with distance.

Renting a car is the best way to explore Great Abaco Island. Most rentals range $60-70 per day. **Rental Wheels** (Bay St., Marsh Harbour, tel. 242/367-4643, www.rentalwheels.com) is in Marsh Harbour but will deliver a vehicle or pick you up at the airport with advance notice. Customer service is quick and efficient, and they are easy to work with. Other companies are **A&P Auto Rentals** (tel. 242/367-2655, www.aandpautorentals.com) and **Bargain Car Rentals** (tel. 242/367-0500).

Getting out to the islands is easy with **Albury's Ferry Service** (tel. 242/367-0290, www.alburysferry.com). Albury's Ferry Service provides daily scheduled service to Great Guana Cay from the Conch Inn Marina, and to Hope Town and Man-O-War from the ferry dock on the east side of town. Private charter services are available to and from specific locations or for private groups. They also offer a concierge service and will shop for groceries and liquor for a 25 percent ordering fee, and deliver to the island you're staying on.

TREASURE CAY

Originally called Sand Banks Cays before the name was changed to attract foreign investors and visitors, Treasure Cay is now a resort development with a healthy population of seasonal second-home owners. Treasure Cay was once separated from Great Abaco by an inlet, but over time a series of hurricanes and storms connected them with a sandy strip. So even though it's still called a cay, you can drive to it without taking a ferry.

Located 30 minutes north of Marsh Harbour, the community is about four miles long and one mile wide, with a majestic white-sand beach to the north and mangrove and tidal flats to the south. The Treasure Cay Beach, Marina and Golf Resort is the center of commerce. Most other development is privately owned residences. There isn't much in the way of amenities outside the resort area, but within the resort community are several restaurants, a medical clinic, a hardware store, gift shops, golf-cart rentals, a small grocery store, a liquor store, a post office, a police station, and a bank.

★ Treasure Cay Beach

Considered one of the best beaches in the Caribbean, and at 3.5 glorious miles long, **Treasure Cay Beach** has actually won awards for its unabashed allure. The beach resembles a white wind-blown mountain covered in snow, but you'll forget the bite of winter once you gaze at the shimmering shallow expanse of turquoise water and its inviting soft sandy bottom. On a windy day, the powdery sand flies, and kiteboarders rush out to perform. On a windless day, you couldn't imagine a more perfect beach for an afternoon swim.

Along the beach is Coco Beach Bar, part

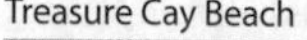

Treasure Cay Beach

of the Treasure Cay Beach, Marina & Golf Resort, along with the Bahama Beach Club and private homes. At the northwest end is Treasure Sands Club. Treasure Cay Beach, Marina & Golf Resort guests can use any of the beach facilities and chairs, but if you're just visiting, Coco is a great place to grab a bite to eat, enjoy a beautiful view, and take a dip. If you've rented a boat, a great way to access the beach is to pull in from the Sea of Abaco. The vantage point from the water is just as breathtaking as looking out to sea.

Treasure Cay Blue Hole

Heading north on S. C. Bootle Highway, about 10 minutes north of Treasure Cay is a small sign marking the **Treasure Cay Blue Hole.** If you hit the Green Turtle Cay ferry terminal, you've gone too far. Follow a dirt road for about 2.5 miles and you'll see another small sign for the blue hole, with a narrow track road to the left. A short drive on the track leads to this impressive blue hole, prominent in the forest and surrounded by tall Abaco pine and native bush. Although there are several blue holes on Great Abaco Island, this is one of the easier ones to locate and access. It's popular as a swimming hole on hot summer days, and with its rocky perimeter only a foot or so above the water level, it's easy to get in and out of. This one is more than 100 feet across and about 200 feet deep. It consists of a mix of salt- and freshwater, but there is no known marinelife within it.

Sports and Recreation

GOLF

Upon entering Treasure Cay, you'll pass the stately **Treasure Cay Golf Course** (tel. 242/365-8045, www.treasurecay.com, $85 hotel and marina guests, $105 nonguests) on the right. The course is a Dick Wilson-designed 18-hole, par 73, and is suitable for all levels but tends to have challenging conditions when the wind picks up. Golf carts are available for rent, and there are a pro shop, a driving range, and a putting green. Booking a tee time is not necessary.

BIKING

Treasure Cay is a great place to explore by bike because the road is wide and people drive fairly slow, with periodic speed bumps along the way. Meander through the endless side streets of the housing community and go all the way to the farthest point on the cay by first heading east on Treasure Cay Road, then winding down to the south and heading west again, following Windward Beach Road. The end is a fairly undeveloped cul-de-sac and the end of the beach. **Wendall's Bicycle Rentals** (tel. 242/365-8687) rents bikes $5 half day, $7 full day, $42 per week.

BOATING AND FISHING

If you are based in Treasure Cay, after a few days of lounging on the beach you might want to get out on the water. **Treasure Cay Boat Rentals** (tel. 242/365-8582, www.treasurecayboatrentals.com) rents by the day and longer, offering 21 to 27-foot center consoles that are easily to maneuver to navigate the Sea of Abaco. They also offer half- and full-day fishing and guided island-hopping adventures.

WATER SPORTS

Rent kayaks, paddleboards, snorkel gear, or a Hobie Cat by the hour or the day through the **Treasure Cay Resort** (tel. 242/365-8801, www.treasurecay.com). Resort and marina guests receive complimentary beach chairs and umbrellas; nonguests can rent them by the day.

TENNIS

Treasure Cay Tennis (tel. 242/365-8045, www.treasurecaytennis.org) is a private club that allows access for guests of Treasure Cay Resort. There is an hourly court fee of $25. Reservations can be made through resort reception.

TOURS

If you want to get out and explore your surroundings while you're on vacation, **Bahamas Adventure Tours** (tel. 242/365-8801, www.

bahamasadventuretours.com) will keep you entertained for the duration of your trip. They are your go-to source to arrange tours in all areas of ecotourism, land tours, and water adventures. Fishing trips include fly-fishing the saltwater flats for bonefish, tarpon, permit, or gray snapper, and deep-sea fishing for wahoo, mahimahi, or tuna. Explore Great Abaco Island in a golf cart or off-road vehicle, or on a bus tour. Book a day trip on the water to visit the swimming pigs, a picnic on a secluded beach, or lunch at Nipper's Beach Bar & Grill on Great Guana Cay. If you prefer just to rent gear and do it yourself, they can provide you with snorkel equipment, fishing gear, boogie boards, kayaks, or paddleboards.

SPA AND YOGA

Island Spirit Spa (tel. 242/525-3047, suzettecolquhoun@yahoo.com) is located next to the Tipsy Seagull and massage, nail care, and facials. Suzette Colquhoun has been a certified massage therapist for 19 years, working at other major resorts throughout The Bahamas. She is trained in deep tissue and sports massage, Thai massage, reflexology, hot stones, facials, aromatherapy, and clinical massage therapy. Contact Suzette to make an appointment.

Yoga is offered throughout the winter season on the beach every Monday and Friday morning, along with periodic holistic wellness classes such as block therapy. Contact the front desk at the Treasure Cay Resort (tel. 242/365-8801, www.treasurecay.com) for a current schedule.

Food and Drink

BAHAMIAN

Café La Florence (Treasure Cay Resort shopping center, tel. 242/365-8185, Mon.-Sat. 7am-7pm, Sun. 7am-noon) is a bakery, coffee shop, and ice cream parlor specializing in homemade bread, pastries, muffins, and cookies. Typical Bahamian fare, such as conch chowder and Jamaican meat patty, is served for lunch. Private catering is available for those staying in the Treasure Cay area, or if you are heading out on the water for the day and would like to pack a lunch, arrange a morning pickup and take it out.

Creative Hands Bakery, Restaurant and Catering (Treasure Cay Rd., near S. C. Bootle Hwy., tel. 242/365-8153, winter Mon.-Sat. 7am-6pm, summer Mon.-Sat. 7am-7pm, $6-12) serves breakfast, lunch, and early dinner, and will cater for weddings and events. Friendly staff are ready to chat, making you feel at home. Filling the menu are Bahamian staples such as fantastic cracked conch, Caribbean-style curry, and fried snapper, but no visit would be complete without trying the fresh baked bread and pastries. The key lime pie alone is worth a visit.

Fish Net Bar & Grill (S. C. Bootle Hwy., just outside the entrance to Treasure Cay, tel. 242/475-7856, Mon.-Fri. 11am-10pm, Sat.-Sun. 7am-10pm, $8-12, cash only) is in a bright lime and pale-pink round yurt-style building just off the highway. The dining room is small but serves tasty Bahamian favorites like coconut hog snapper and cracked lobster bites as well as pizza, spaghetti, and anything else the chef is in the mood to prepare. Everything is made to order, and it's one of the most reasonably priced restaurants in the area.

CONTEMPORARY

Spinnakers Ocean Grill & Wine Bar (Treasure Cay Resort, tel. 242/365-8469, www.treasurecay.com, Wed.-Sun. 6pm-9pm, $15-50) is just steps from the guest rooms at the resort on a quiet corner of the marina. Choose from indoor seating in the lofty air-conditioned dining room or out on the patio under a cozy veranda overlooking the marina. A wide selection of made-to-order pizza, pasta, and entrée salads are available for all types of eaters. Try the Calypso shrimp skewers with Asian citrus slaw or the "fall off the bone" ribs with Bacardi rum barbecue sauce. Visit on Saturday night for the roast prime rib special, served with vegetables, french fries, baked or garlic-roasted potatoes, and a house salad.

On the northern corner of Treasure Cay

Beach is the ★ **Treasure Sands Club** (tel. 242/365-9385, www.treasuresandsclub.com, lunch daily noon-4pm, dinner Mon.-Sat. 6pm-9:30pm, $30-45). The club is open to nonguests, but you'll feel as though you've stumbled into an exclusive members-only establishment, with its chic and subtly tasteful surroundings. Enter to a coral stone-lined pool deck surrounded by inviting chaise lounges trimmed with pastel pink and blue accents as well as private cabanas. The restaurant is perched on the beach, enclosed by a light screen to keep the sandflies and mosquitoes at bay on calm evenings. The restaurant specializes in a farm-to-table experience, sourcing from the local Bahama Woodstar farm, the local Abaco Big Bird free-range chicken ranch, and local fishermen. For lunch try the garlic conch, sautéed with fresh tomatoes, white wine, and lime, or the Treasure Sands snapper cake, with black beans and sweet mustard aioli. For dinner, try the Caribbean bouillabaisse with lobster, shrimp snapper, and conch in a roasted tomato saffron broth. The beach bar is open Monday-Saturday noon-10:30pm, Sunday noon-5pm. Reservations are strongly advised on weekend nights during high season.

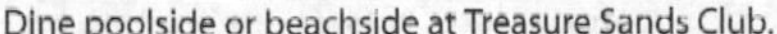

Dine poolside or beachside at Treasure Sands Club.

BARS AND PUBS

Coco Beach Bar (Treasure Cay Resort, tel. 242/365-8470, www.treasurecay.com, breakfast daily 8am-10:30am, lunch daily 11am-4pm, dinner Fri.-Wed. 6pm-9pm, $15-30) is the center of the action to let loose. This laid-back, utterly beachy open-air haunt couldn't be any more quintessentially Caribbean. Locals, homeowners, and vacationers rub shoulders at the bar. On Tuesday nights, enjoy a barbecue and a beach bonfire with live Bahamian music and dancing late into the evening. Wednesday is Steak Night, with various options such as prime rib, filet mignon, and rib-eye, along with an unlimited salad bar and baked potato bar.

On the edge of the Treasure Cay Resort's pool deck, overlooking the marina, is the **Tipsy Seagull Pool Bar** (Treasure Cay Resort, tel. 242/365-8814, www.treasurecay.com, daily 11:30am-9:30pm). This rustic establishment has character and charm, and attracts a drinking crowd. Join them for Taco-Rita, Monday 7pm-9pm, with two-for-one margarita specials. Alongside the Tipsy Seagull is **Junkanoo Javas,** featuring coffee and tea, fruit smoothies, pizza, sandwiches, wings, and Bahamian specialties; order your snacks and enjoy them at the bar.

Accommodations

Treasure Cay is limited to staying at the Treasure Cay Beach, Marina & Golf Resort or the Bahamas Beach Club, unless you book a private home. As with many Out Islands, the best bet is using local real estate companies to assist you with vacation rental bookings; they know the properties well.

A team of professional local agents at **Abaco Estate Services** (S. C. Bootle Hwy., just before Treasure Cay entrance, tel. 242/365-8752, U.S. tel. 866/653-7164, www.abacoestateservices.com) can assist you in finding your perfect holiday getaway. Homes in Treasure Cay range from quaint two-bedroom inland cottages ($1,225 per week) up to a five-bedroom beachfront home with a pool ($6,000 per week). Most homes require a one-week minimum stay and 50 percent deposit at the time of booking.

Bahama Beach Club (Treasure Cay Rd., tel. 242/365-8500, U.S. tel. 800/284-0382, www.bahamabeachclub.com, $300) offers 50 island-inspired condos. You have all of the amenities of a five-star resort, including room service, housekeeping, and custom shampoos and soaps, but the feeling is like staying in a spacious vacation home. Choose from two- to five-bedroom condos on Treasure Cay Beach. The three-bedroom units sleep up to six; four-bedroom units sleep up to eight. A beachfront VIP four-bedroom has a loft. Wi-Fi and long distance calling to the United States and Canada are included, and there are a pool and jetted tub on-site. All units offer fully equipped kitchens and screened-in balconies or ground-floor patios, plus a washer, dryer, and optional housekeeper. The club is located just down from the main shopping center, walking distance to Coco Beach Bar.

All of the rooms at the ★ **Treasure Cay Beach, Marina & Golf Resort** (tel. 242/365-8801, www.treasurecay.com, $169) are alongside the marina, with garden or harbor views. The colorful townhouses are inviting and well-equipped, and if you opt for the Mariner Condo Waterfront Suite, you will be wowed with the sunset views from the private balcony. The first-floor units have a sundeck patio, a breakfast bar with a microwave, a fridge, and a coffeemaker. The second-floor units have a full kitchen, a living room, a dining area, and a balcony. There are one- to three-bedroom units available that have pull-out queen sofas. You are walking distance to Spinnaker Restaurant and Lounge and the Tipsy Seagull Bar and Pool, and it's a five-minute walk to Coco Beach Bar on Treasure Cay Beach. You can opt for a meal plan (from $65 pp per day). Beach chairs, towels, umbrellas, and use of nonmotorized water sports gear are available for all resort guests.

Getting There

AIR

In recent years, international flights to **Treasure Cay Airport** (TCB) are limited, but you can fly from Nassau to Treasure Cay on Bahamasair several days per week. From Treasure Cay Airport, a 10-minute taxi ride to Treasure Cay is $30 per couple, plus $3 per extra person. From **Marsh Harbour International Airport** (MHH), a 40-minute taxi ride is $85 per couple, plus $3 per extra person.

BOAT

With 150 boat slips with three T-docks that can accommodate vessels up to 150 feet in length, the **Treasure Cay Marina** (tel. 242/365-8250, U.S. tel. 800/327-1584, www.treasurecay.com) regularly attracts weekend boaters from the United States due to its proximity—it is one of the closest marinas to Florida outside Grand Bahamas and Green Turtle Cay. Treasure Cay Marina is an Official Port of Entry, with immigration and customs on call, as well as a fuel station, electricity hookups, water, wireless internet, and a fish-cleaning station. Mechanical and vessel cleaning services are available as well as transient and long-term dockage rates.

Getting Around

You can drive cars or golf carts around Treasure Cay. If you don't plan on going anywhere else on Great Abaco Island, a golf cart is a perfectly acceptable means of transportation. For car rentals, contact **Ornald Cornish Car Rentals** (Treasure Cay Airport, tel. 242/365-8623) or **Triple J Car Rental** (Treasure Cay Resort, tel. 242/365-8761). To book a golf cart, contact **Cash's Carts** (Treasure Cay Resort, tel. 242/365-8771).

SOUTH OF MARSH HARBOUR

Beaches

Rivaling Treasure Cay Beach for length, expansiveness, and beauty, **Winding Bay Beach** is at the exclusive Abaco Club. Unlike Treasure Cay Beach, this one is located within the compound and is exclusively for guests, members, and homeowners. Winding Bay Beach is protected by a rocky outcrop, reefs, and the tiny Sugar Cay. At low tide, a small point turns into a sandbar and stretches across the bay, and you can wade out to the rocky Sugar Cay and hang out with the resident sea birds. The colors are vivid and breathtaking, and with two miles of powder-soft sand, you'll likely feel like you'll have the beach to yourself, even on crowded days.

Located 50 miles south of Marsh Harbour on a small peninsula that stretches west is the tiny settlement of Sandy Point and **Sandy Point Beach.** For a road trip, it's a great off-the-beaten-path excursion. It doesn't boast the wow factor that Winding Bay Beach has, but visitors appreciate its raw, natural state, with shady casuarinas and calm water. It's rocky, so it's not great for swimming, but if you have snorkel gear, it's a good place to hop in and look for sealife.

Little Harbour

"I have been told of a place that sounds like the paradise we have been looking for. It is called Little Harbour, and is in the Abaco area," wrote Randolph Johnston in his diary in 1952. He arrived via sailboat with his wife and three children, and in that moment he knew he had found home. The American educator and his family pioneered the community, which was originally isolated from the rest of Great Abaco prior to a road to Cherokee Sound settlement being bulldozed in 1986. Where there was once only a lighthouse and the caretakers, there are now about 40 homes. It is still mostly frequented by sailboat cruisers, a laid-back eclectic crowd, and the occasional road tripper willing to trek 45 minutes from Marsh Harbour and two miles on a dirt road from the main highway. About 25,000 visitors come to Little Harbour per year, but 80 percent of them arrive by boat. That being said, Little Harbour is one of the best places to stumble upon, and is highly recommended if you are looking for an unconventional place to hang out for the day.

Johnston brought his talent in art and bronze, and eventually he became an internationally acclaimed wood and bronze sculptor, passing his knowledge and talent down to his son Pete. To this day, the entire community revolves around the only commerce: the Art Gallery and Foundry, and Pete's Pub. Pete continues to maintain the integrity of what Randolph started so long ago, along with a third generation, his sons Tyler and Greg, and Greg's wife, Heather.

Pete Johnston's Art Gallery and Foundry (Little Harbour, tel. 242/577-5407, www.petespub.com, Thurs.-Sun. 10:30am-5pm) features bronze sculptures made using a 5,000-year-old wax process. The foundry is the only one in The Bahamas, and the works can be found in museums, public buildings, private collections, and most notably, one of Randolph's pieces is housed in the Vatican's museum in Rome. The gallery is a solid concrete building built to withstand hurricanes after Hurricane Floyd destroyed the original structure and half the art pieces housed within. It contains jewelry and clothing as well. There is an evident theme of sealife throughout the gallery, and you can still find original works by Randolph, including his *Nine Ages of Man,* an arch representing the cycle of life. Other works include birds, sharks and rays, turtles, fish, and Pete's *Old Man and the Sea* series.

Next door to the foundry is **Pete's Pub** (Little Harbour, tel. 242/577-5487, www.petespub.com, Thurs.-Sun. lunch 11am-4pm, dinner 6pm-9pm), a funky open-air beach bar touting itself not as a topless bar but a "sideless saloon." The menu serves a small selection of daily specials based on what's in season or what Greg might have caught that day. T-shirts from patrons adorn every inch of the space, and the floor is soft sand. You can follow a pathway to the ocean and have a look at the craggy beach with a cocktail in hand. The harbor is extremely well protected, crater-shaped and only about 2,000 feet at its widest point. If you are coming by boat, don't get there early in the day in season, as you might have a hard time finding an aquatic parking spot to drop anchor.

GETTING THERE

To get to Little Harbour, drive south on the Great Abaco Highway from Marsh Harbour for about 25 minutes until you see flag poles on the right and a sign for Winding Bay and Little Harbour on the left. Follow the winding road for another 15 minutes until you see a small sign on the left indicating the turn-off to Little Harbour. You'll turn onto a dirt road and follow it for about two miles until you reach the town.

Cherokee Sound

The settlement of Cherokee Sound is one of the most isolated communities on Great Abaco Island. There are a few quaint houses, abundant sealife, and underwater blue holes that attract fish and marinelife, and therefore fishing. The community is based on fishing and boatbuilding, and there's not much in the way of commerce or amenities. The community has the longest dock in Abaco, aptly named "Long Dock."

THE ABACO CLUB ON WINDING BAY

On the northern side of Cherokee Sound is the picturesque 534-acre **The Abaco Club on Winding Bay** (Cherokee Rd. on Winding Bay, tel. 242/367-0077, www.theabacoclub.com), built on elevated land with striking views of the ocean. Although it's a private club, visitors can rent accommodations and take advantage of the facilities. The developers did their part to maintain the natural landscape by keeping native trees, giving the community a lush rainforest feel that attracts the Abaco parrot. You'll hear them squawking in the trees above

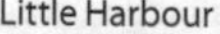
Little Harbour

you, and their bright-green plumage is hard to miss. The club is also home to one of the top-rated golf courses in The Bahamas, a spa and a fitness center, tennis courts, and a two-mile stretch of sandy beach where you may feel as though you are walking on a cloud.

There are two restaurants on the property: The **Cliff House** is what the name implies, a dramatic dining room overlooking the sea with an infinity pool. Head down closer to the beach and you'll find **Flipper's Beach Bar,** serving tropical cocktails and buffet-style food. Rent a cabana ($495-795), a cottage, or a four-bedroom estate home ($2,199-10,000).

GETTING THERE

To get to Winding Bay, drive south on the Great Abaco Highway from Marsh Harbour for about 25 minutes until you see flag poles on the right and a sign for Winding Bay and Little Harbour on the left. Follow the winding road for another 15 minutes. You'll see the turnoff to Little Harbour, and just past it, around the bend, is the Abaco Club gate.

Schooner Bay

From the turnoff to Little Harbour and Winding Bay, head 17 miles south on the Great Abaco Highway until you come to the entrance to Schooner Bay. A marina village, Schooner Bay has been featured in international magazines as a top escape. Canal-front homes welcome boaters, and people cruise around in golf carts. Beaches surround the community on two sides—one protected by a rocky reef, the other side stretching for miles north.

To experience this serene setting, newly opened **Sandpiper Inn** (Schooner Bay, Great Abaco Hwy., tel. 242/699-2056, www.sandpiperabaco.com, $200) offers comfortable chic rooms and cottages and a top restaurant. The bar in the main lobby area is the social hub of the village. On the oceanfront is the **Cabana Bar and Grill,** currently operating part-time with an outdoor kitchen, but there are plans to expand it to include a tiki bar, a swimming pool, and a fire pit. You'll notice the attention to detail that has been influenced by world-renowned Bahamian artist Antonius Roberts. The Cabana was also featured on the cover of *Coastal Living* magazine.

Next door to the Sandpiper Inn is the swanky **Black Fly Lodge** (Schooner Bay, Great Abaco Hwy., U.S. tel. 904/997-2220, www.blackflylodge.com), a top destination escape for bonefishing. Coupled with some of the most fantastic and untouched fishing grounds within a short drive, first-class food is served daily. Fresh seasonal Bahamian seafood, including lobster and stone crab claws, are plated to perfection. The lodge accommodates up to eight. Rates start at $3,075 per person for three nights and two days of fishing, which includes lodging, fishing, and guides as well as food, alcohol, laundry service, and transfers to and from Marsh Harbour airport.

You can also stay in one of the homes at Schooner Bay as part of the rental program. Contact **Schooner Bay** (Great Abaco Hwy., tel. 242/366-2048, U.S. tel. 888/275-1639, www.schoonerbaybahamas.com) directly for rates and information.

Just north of Schooner Bay, in what is technically considered Rolling Bay, a luxury escape to get away from it all is the **Delphi Club** (tel. 242/366-2222, www.delphi-bahamas.com, from $500 d), set in remote wilderness and fronted by an endless stretch of white sandy beach, minutes from prime bonefishing grounds. There is a pool in the gardens, a first-class kitchen serving fantastic fare made with fresh local ingredients, and a wine cellar to pair top-notch wine with your fabulous meal. It is a community lodging setup, so guests have their own rooms and en suite baths, but dining is communal. Although it is touted as a bonefishing lodge, nonfishing partners are welcome, and the consensus is that they have just as wonderful a time as the anglers. Birders will find this place a true haven, as the area has one of the densest bird populations in The Bahamas. It's a fabulous option for groups of up to 16 people. Fishing packages start at $2,300 for three nights and two days of fishing.

Abaco National Park

The Abacos are home to the largest variety of native and migrant birds in The Bahamas, and **Abaco National Park** (tel. 242/393-1317, www.bnt.bs) is the best place to see them. Although the park was established in 1994 on 20,000 acres to protect the breeding area of the endangered Bahama parrot, there are now less than 3,000 left alive, meaning they are near extinction, although their numbers have grown since the creation of the park. The parrots nest in cavities in the rocky limestone forest floor and feed on the seeds of the pine trees. They are the only parrot in the Caribbean to nest in the ground, which makes them vulnerable. Often seen high in treetops squawking loudly, their bright-green plumage and red-and-white heads stand out in the monochromatic environment.

The park is also a breeding ground for the common white-crowned pigeon, and watch for West Indian woodpeckers, Bahama yellow throats, loggerhead kingbirds, swallows, warblers, and mockingbirds. There is about 15 miles of dirt road leading to the Hole in the Wall Lighthouse at the southern tip of the island. After a 1.5-hour drive in a 4WD vehicle, you'll feel like you are at the end of the earth. The lighthouse was built in 1838, along with Hope Town's light, and isn't open to visitors, but you can explore the area or book a tour with **Lucayan Nature Tours** (tel. 242/477-5953 or 242/367-2749, www.abaconaturetours.com). If you venture into the park on your own, don't tramp through the bush unless you know what the poison wood tree looks like. It affects people differently: Some only feel effects if they break the bark and touch the sap, while others break out in a painful rash merely by touching the leaves.

GETTING THERE

If you'd like to venture into the park it is highly suggested that you go on a tour or with a local guide. You can go on your own, but most visitors voice their frustrations about the lack of infrastructure compared to parks in the US or Canada. There is no signage marking the entrance into the park from the main highway, and throughout the park there are no trail heads or informational signs for visitors to learn more about the birds and plants in the area. This is the best way to experience the wonders of the park and hear narrative about the local flora and fauna is to book with a guide, or you may be disappointed. Otherwise if you'd like to go on your own drive 10 miles

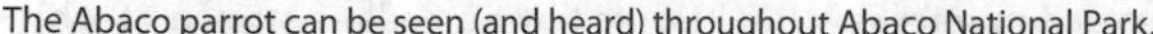

The Abaco parrot can be seen (and heard) throughout Abaco National Park.

past the entrance to Schooner Bay. Where the road bends slightly to the west will be a dirt road heading south. It is a long, dirt road running through the park to the very southern point of the island.

★ Pelican Cays Land and Sea Park

Four small cays and their surrounding waters, totaling 2,000 acres, create the **Pelican Cays Land and Sea Park** (tel. 242/367-6310, www.bnt.bs), eight miles north of Cherokee Sound and managed by the Bahamas National Trust. Established in 1972 by American residents in Abaco to protect the shallow and fragile reef system for future recreation, it became the world's first marine protected area. The reef is in only 25 feet of water, making it ideal for snorkelers. It's a popular dive area because of its accessibility.

You'll see a variety of sealife, including green and loggerhead turtles, rays, and eels. Bottlenose dolphins are often seen. There are underwater caves as well as a variety of vegetation on the cays in the park. Brindled terns nest on High Rock starting in April. Sandy Cay is a fantastic spot for a picnic lunch or a stroll on the white-sand beach. The cay is between two main cuts from the ocean, so even though it's shallow to wade in, the bottom drops off quickly, making for superb snorkeling from the beach. There are ruins of an old house hidden on top of the cay, its elevation making for fantastic views of the surrounding area. You can boat out here with a rental skiff and hook up to a mooring, or book a tour from any outfit in the islands. Fishing, spearfishing, conching, and shelling are not permitted in the park, and this is taken seriously: You will be fined, and your boat could be confiscated. Steer clear of the park if you need to fish.

reef formations just below the surface at Pelican Cays Land and Sea Park

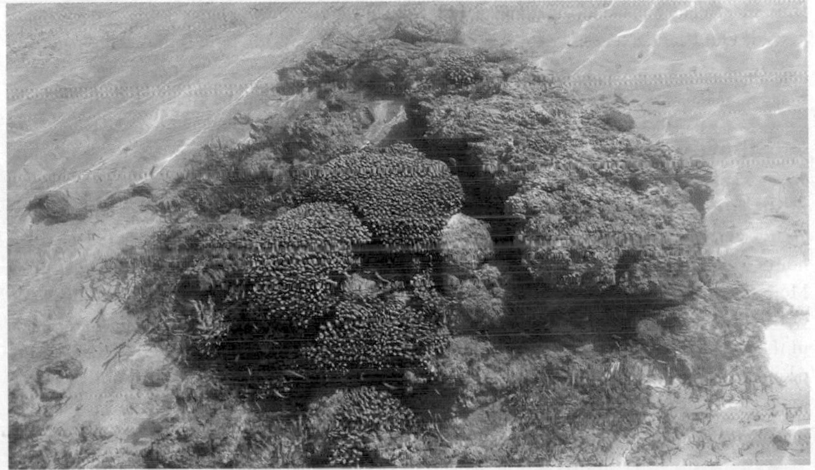

Abaco Cays

ELBOW CAY

Elbow Cay's community of Hope Town surrounds a protected circular harbor, generally filled with boats on moorings or at anchor. The lighthouse towers above the harbor, and colorful New England-style wood cottages surround the quiet lagoon. The town's rich history dates to the late 1700s, and today the full-time population is under 300.

In town there are two 10-foot-wide paved roads. You are not allowed to drive in town without a special permit, but its walkability is what makes the town so quaint and unique. Harbour Street (Front St.) runs along the harbor, and Queens Highway (Ocean St. or Back St.) follows the Atlantic Ocean south. There are small sidewalks and paths connecting the roads.

Heading south on Queen's Highway leads into the more rural area of the island, dotted with colorful vacation homes, boutique lodges, and beautiful beaches on the ocean side, and dramatic harbor views on the sound side.

There is enough going on in this vibrant little community, but the speed is comfortably slow. Elbow Cay is only a 20-minute ferry ride from Marsh Harbour, making it an easily accessible Out Island experience for a day trip.

TOP EXPERIENCE

★ Elbow Cay Reef Lighthouse

The iconic **Elbow Cay Reef Lighthouse** (tel. 242/577-0542, www.elbowreeflighthousesociety.com, visiting hours Mon.-Sat. 9am-6pm, gift shop hours Mon.-Sat. 10am-4pm) was built in 1836, one of three manually operated lighthouses left in the world. At 89 feet, it is one of the most prominent features in an otherwise low-lying region. The lighthouse keeper must wind the weights every two hours throughout the night in order to maintain the sequence of five white flashes every 15 seconds, to be seen 23 nautical miles away. It was built to reduce the number of shipwrecks on the reef, but it was met with objections: As with many communities in The Bahamas at the time, salvaging was an integral part of the local economy. In 1996 there was talk of automating the hand-wound kerosene-burning lighthouse, but the Lighthouse Preservation Society of The Bahamas convinced the government to reconsider, and today residents are fiercely protective of its status and extremely diligent about its upkeep.

Jimmy Buffett's fictional novel *A Salty Piece of Land* follows the character Tully Mars as he attempts to find a rare replacement Fresnel lens for a manual lighthouse. There is a rumor the lighthouse in the novel was inspired by the Fresnel-lens lighthouse in Hope Town, and the cover of the book features a red and white striped lighthouse not unlike this one. An image of the lighthouse is also featured on the Bahamian $10 bill. The 101 steps to the top are not for the faint at heart. The stairs are steep, circular, and open. Once you reach the top, the interior is cramped, but step out onto the platform to witness one of the best views in The Bahamas, with all of Elbow Cay sprawling beneath you, Man-O-War to the north, and Great Abaco and Marsh Harbour to the west.

Elbow Cay Reef Lighthouse has a gift shop on-site and is only accessible by boat, so you'll have to take your own or get dropped off by the ferry at the lighthouse dock on the other side of the harbor from town. More information on the history of the lighthouse can be found in town at the **Wyannie Malone Historical Museum** (Queen's Hwy., tel. 242/366-0293, www.hopetownmuseum.com, Dec.-July Mon.-Sat. 10am-4pm, $5 adults, $2 children).

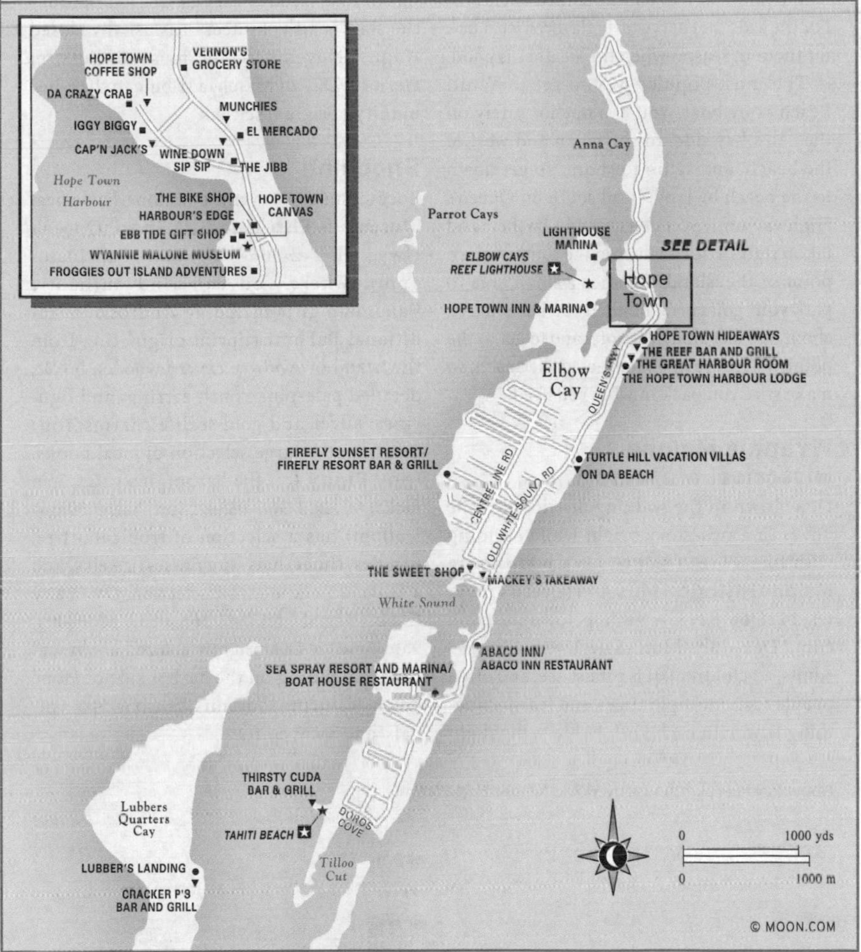

★ Tahiti Beach

The name **Tahiti Beach** instills images of swaying coconut palms in the exotic South Pacific. This particular beach on Elbow Cay, of all the glorious beaches in The Bahamas, is one most resembling a faraway tropical isle. The sand slinks around a curvy point into a protected bay. At its apex it reaches into the protected harbor, giving it a lagoon and castaway-island feel. The beach is beautiful at any time of day, but for a truly mind-blowing backdrop, be here for low tide, when an expansive sandbar is exposed.

The latest addition to this popular beach hangout is the **Thirsty Cuda Bar & Grill** (tel. 242/559-8628, high season daily 11am-dusk, $10-20), a bright blue floating barge that anchors right off Tahiti Beach. This swim-up venue is a new hot spot. Head out by paddleboard, or just swim up with your soggy cash.

They serve light bites like conch fritters and sesame conch bites. The full bar has cold island beers and frozen or blended cocktails. For the kids they serve tasty flavored ice. Look for them in season when the weather is good.

The most popular way to get to Tahiti Beach is by boat. You can anchor safely on the calm bay side, to the north and west of the beach, and swim to shore. To get down to the beach by land, head south on Queen's Highway until you can't go any farther, and take a right. The beach is on the southwestern point of the island. There is a small area to park your golf cart, and then you have to trek about 800 feet along the soft sand to get to the point. There are no amenities at the beach, so make sure you pack in what you need.

Wyannie Malone Historical Museum

Downtown in the walking district of Hope Town in a two-story bright white building with forest green shutters is the **Wyannie Malone Historical Museum** (Queen's Hwy., tel. 242/366-0293, www.hopetownmuseum.com, Dec.-July Mon.-Sat. 10am-4pm, $5 adults, $2 children). It is a must-see, and often people visit multiple times and learn something new with each visit. Exhibits highlight the area's rich history, from the days of the Lucayans to pirates, ship wreckers, and the lighthouse. Hours vary by season because the staff is all volunteer; it is usually closed August-November. The museum puts on Heritage Day in March, a tribute to the community's original settlers.

Shopping

Located in the Wyannie Malone Historical Museum is **Ebb Tide Gift Shop** (Queen's Hwy., tel. 242/366-0088, Mon.-Sat. 10am-4pm), where you can find authentic Bahamian gifts including Androsia, a traditional Bahamian print originating from the island of Andros; carved wooden boxes; detailed pale-pink conch earrings and figurines; silver and gold sealife charms; rope bowls; and a large selection of local books. **Iggy Biggy** (on the harbor, next to Cap'n Jacks, tel. 242/366-0354, Mon.-Sat. 9:30am-5:30pm) has a selection of tropical attire, candles, shoes, hats, sunglasses, jewelry, and a fantastic island music selection. **Da Crazy Crab** (Bay St., tel. 242/366-0537, Mon.-Fri. 9am-5pm) is in a brightly colored green and orange building on the harbor side of Hope Town, featuring souvenirs, beach wraps, sandals, and local crafts.

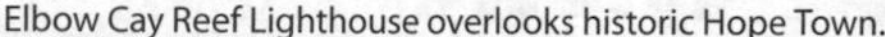
Elbow Cay Reef Lighthouse overlooks historic Hope Town.

At the point where Queens Highway and Harbour Street meet is a green house called **The Jibb** (corner of Bay St. and Queen's Hwy., tel. 242/366-0025, Oct.-Mar., Mon.-Sat. 10am-4pm) where you can see original artwork and crafts by Dr. Hermann Schadt. Schadt served as director at an internationally recognized art school in Germany for many years and has written several books on art history. Since the 1970s he has spent winter in Hope Town and summer in Germany, inspired by the rich colors of The Abacos. His work has been included in exhibitions in The Bahamas and in Europe. Watercolor, acrylic, and oil original and prints are available.

El Mercado (Queens Hwy., tel. 242/366-0661) is across from Wine Down Sip Sip and has affordable finds like T-shirts, dresses, bathing suits, books, and toys. At **Vernon's Grocery Store** (Queens Hwy., tel. 242/366-0037, Mon.-Sat. 8am-6pm), you'll likely meet Vernon himself, who is famous for his pies and bread. He is also the most popular marriage official on the island and is the minister of St. James Methodist Church. **Hope Town Canvas** (Studio One Bldg., Bay St., across from Harbour's Edge Restaurant, www.hopetowncanvas.com, Dec.-Aug. daily 9am-5pm) was established in 2013 as a one-of-a-kind shop featuring artisanal canvas products. All bags and belts are made with used sailcloth. The quality is second to none, and the nautical designs are timeless.

Sports and Recreation

SURFING

Although The Bahamas is not known for surfing, Elbow Cay has some decent beach breaks if the conditions are right, and competitions and surf camps are occasionally held. Learn to surf with **Abaco Paddleboard** (tel. 242/475-0954, www.abacopaddleboard.com) or rent boards by the hour, day, or week.

PADDLEBOARDING AND ECOTOURS

Abaco Paddleboard (tel. 242/475-0954, www.abacopaddleboard.com) provides fitness classes and beginner stand-up paddleboard lessons on the calm harbor side. Tour the mangroves and back creeks, or opt for a day trip with a picnic lunch. For those that would rather remain seated for nonmotorized water sports, try **Abaco Eco Kayak Tours and Rentals** (tel. 242/366-0398 or 242/475-9616, www.abacoeco.com) for tours within White Sound and Hope Town Harbour. Visit Tahiti Beach or paddle near the lighthouse.

Tahiti Beach

You can also rent a kayak for a half day, full day, or long-term and explore on your own.

Froggies Out Island Adventures (tel. 242/366-0431, www.froggiesadventures.com) takes groups of all sizes snorkeling and diving. Weekly trips include Shell Island, swimming with the stingrays and sharks, feeding the swimming pigs, or visiting Pete's Pub. They can customize your trip for island-hopping, sightseeing, or dining on other islands. They have a dive shop that sells and rents equipment for water activities.

BOATING

Island Marine Rentals (tel. 242/366-0282, www.islandmarine.com) rents a fleet of locally manufactured Albury Brothers boats and Boston Whalers. The boats range 17-27 feet and are easily manageable center consoles, rentable daily, for three days, or by the week. They are just off Hope Town on Parrot Cay and will deliver your boat rental to you. **Sea Horse Boat Rentals** (tel. 242/366-0023 or 242/366-0189, www.seahorseboatrentals.com) rents 17- to 27-foot Boston Whalers, Hydra Sports, Albury Brothers, and Paramounts. Their office is located in town but is only accessible by boat, so give them a call and they will pick you up.

FISHING

Most of the charter boat companies will meet you at the docks at Hope Town Harbour, or perhaps at your hotel if you are someplace with a dock. Contact them directly to arrange pickups.

Seagull Charters (tel. 242/366-0266, www.seagullcottages.com) offers half-day and full-day fishing charters that include bait, tackle, and fish cleaning on their new 32-foot Albin Sportfish, which has a salon with air-conditioning. Fish for mahimahi, tuna, and wahoo. The owner of **Wild Pigeon Charters** (tel. 242/366-0234, www.wildpigeoncharters.com), Maitland Lowe, will share with you his years of expertise in fishing the local waters. He specializes in bonefishing, reef fishing, and bottom fishing.

Local Boy Deep Sea Fishing (tel. 242/366-0528 or 242/458-1685, www.hopetownfishing.com) is aptly named for an eighth-generation Hope Town local, captain Justin Russell. His boat is a 34-foot Crusader set up for deep-sea fishing for half-day and full-day charters. **A Salt Weapon** (tel. 242/366-0245 or 242/458-8521, www.asaltweaponcharters.com) is based in downtown Hope Town. A 31-foot Bertram is the vessel of choice, and captain Ira Key II will

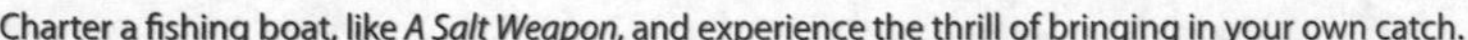

Charter a fishing boat, like *A Salt Weapon*, and experience the thrill of bringing in your own catch.

lead you with a lifetime of experience fishing the local waters.

BIKING

Located in the same building as Hope Town Canvas is **The Bike Shop** (Studio One Bldg., Bay St., across from Harbour's Edge Restaurant, www.hopetowncanvas.com, Dec.-Aug. daily 9am-5pm), offering bike rentals. Elbow Cay is easily bikeable, especially in the cool winter months. Choose from one-speed beach cruisers, fat-tire beach bikes, or electric bikes. Rentals are by the hour or the day

BLOCK THERAPY

Block Therapy (tel. 242/366-0722, www.bahamablocktherapy.com) is a form of fluid isometrics. If you enjoy the calming effects of yoga and massage, Block Therapy integrates the two. Using a therapeutic wood block, participants lay on different pressure points, and the block works to release fascia tissues. A full session entails arms, legs, the mid-section, and finally the head, laying on the temples, forehead, and cheeks. Breathing techniques increase oxygen in the body. Hope Town resident Rachael Aberle is certified in block therapy, massage, and yoga. Contact her to arrange a session; she can come to you or provide service at her home studio.

Food and Drink

There are plenty of dining options on Elbow Cay to keep your palate entertained, but the underlying theme is a laid-back vibe. Don't worry about fine-dining attire; you'll feel overdressed. Instead, kick back, relax, and enjoy a wide range of delicious fresh menu options.

BAHAMIAN

Munchies (Queen's Hwy., tel. 242/366-0423, daily 10am-10pm, $5-20) is a small takeaway that is popular with locals. It's serves some of the best Bahamian cracked conch, tenderized, battered, and fried. They also serve hamburgers, conch burgers, chicken nuggets, conch fritters, and fish sandwiches. Burgers start at $6, and dinner ranges $16-18.

Mackey's Takeaway (tel. 242/366-0396, year-round Tues.-Sat. 7am-3:30pm and 6pm-10pm, high season Mon. 6pm-10pm, Tues.-Sat. 7am-3:30pm and 6pm-10pm, $14-16) is a few minutes south of town, just past T&N Golf Cart Rental on White Sound centerline road, and serves authentic Bahamian dishes like steamed pork chop, baked chicken, and fried fish as well as burgers, wraps, and chicken fingers.

CONTEMPORARY

Harbour's Edge Restaurant & Bar (Bay St., tel. 242/366-0292 or 242/366-0087, www.harbours-edge.com, Wed.-Mon. lunch 11:30am-3pm, dinner 6pm-9pm, bar until late, $20-40) is located in a two-story green building overlooking the harbor and the Hope Town Lighthouse. Lunch is a selection of specialty burgers, sandwiches, and salads, or try Conch in a Bag (battered and fried conch and fries with ketchup and hot sauce served in a paper bag, similar to a traditional English fish-and-chips). For dinner expect a variety of fresh local seafood, steak, and pastas. Those with dietary restrictions or allergies will find they are accommodating. At the bar, sports enthusiasts watch games and enjoy happy hour daily 4pm-6pm. Saturday night is pizza night, and Sunday is a traditional Bahamian souse breakfast. During high season there is live music on Tuesday and Saturday nights. Park near the clinic; it's a short walk along Bay Street.

Sip sip is the Bahamian term for "gossip," which makes **Wine Down Sip Sip** (tel. 242/366-0399, Mon.-Sat. 8:30am-11pm, $15-25) the social house of the island. There is cozy bench seating with colorful throw pillows and air-conditioning. They offer a great wine selection, as well as martinis, specialty margaritas, sipping rums, and port. Menu items include steak, pasta, chicken, and Jamaican patties along with rotating daily specials.

Located toward the south end of the island on White Sound, **Boat House Restaurant**

(Sea Spray Resort, White Sound, tel. 242/366-0065, www.seasprayresort.com, daily 8am-3pm and 6pm-9pm, $20-40) serves breakfast, lunch, and dinner. The dinner menu includes items like flamed T-bone steak, and walnut- and herb-crusted lamb rack, lobster and pumpkin risotto, and a variety of brick oven pizzas. There is an air-conditioned dining room and a large outdoor covered bar area and patio with large flat-screen TVs to watch games. Annual fishing tournaments are held, with Bahamian buffets and Junkanoo bands.

The creators of the famous Firefly Sweet Tea and Moonshine products in South Carolina have their hands in the ★ **Firefly Sunset Resort Bar and Grill** (Centerline Rd., tel. 242/366-0145, www.fireflysunsetresort.com, daily lunch 11:30am-6pm, dinner 6pm-9pm, $15-30). Dine on the deck overlooking the calm harbor and enjoy some of the best sunsets on the island, or enjoy the view in the cozy air-conditioned dining room with picture windows. Even the pickiest of eaters will be hard-pressed not to find something. The menu includes lobster quesadillas, a veggie stack, and burgers done every which way but wrong, as well as pastas, soups, salads, and a variety of light and heavy appetizers.

Perched on an elevated piece of land with views of the ocean on one side and the calm harbor on the other, the ★ **Abaco Inn Restaurant** (tel. 242/366-0133, U.S. tel. 800/468-8799, www.abacoinn.com, 8am-11am, noon-3pm, 6-9pm daily, $20-35) is a charming, welcoming place whether you are a guest of the inn or not. Between the dining room and the bar, you can find a relaxing spot to watch the sunrise over the ocean and watch it set over the harbor. Watch the roar and tumble of the ocean from the intimate dining room, protected from the weather behind large-framed windows. Bright-white wood-paneled walls and ceilings give it a seafaring-lodge atmosphere. Breakfast, lunch, and dinner are served in the dining room, at the bar, or on the open-air porch. Land and sea specialties adorn the menu; be sure to try the crunchy grouper. They also serve a wonderful lobster macaroni. Daphne is a Hope Town native and has been running the lively bar for 22 years, and she can answer questions. Reservations are required for dinner; pickup is complimentary if requested.

The Great Harbour Room (Hope Town Harbour Lodge, Queen St., tel. 242/366-0095, daily 6pm-9pm, $20-40) is a longtime favorite for romantic fine dining. But don't expect tuxedos; this is an island, after all, so there is no formal dress code. Although it's at the top of a fairly steep stair climb, you won't be disappointed with the elevated views from the dining room overlooking Hope Town. For an indulgent feast, try the Reef & Beef, six ounces of Bahamian lobster tail with six-ounce filet mignon. The menu includes a variety of other meat, seafood, and hearty salad options. For a more casual setting, visit **The Reef Bar and Grill** (Hope Town Harbour Lodge, Queen St., tel. 242/366-0095, daily 11:30am-3pm, $12-20) at the pool deck overlooking the ocean. The menu includes a wide selection of sandwiches, wraps, and burgers along with a variety of options for kids.

BARS AND PUBS

★ **On Da Beach** (Turtle Hill, Old White Sound Rd., tel. 242/366-0557, www.turtlehill.com, Tues.-Sun. 11:30am-7pm, $15-20) is located less than a mile south of town, 10-15 minutes on foot. Look for the signs to Turtle Hill at the bend in the road and follow a sandy path down toward the beach, where this colorful open-air bar is elevated above a beautiful stretch of sand. The super casual barefoot vibe makes it one of the top spots for a daytime watering hole. Expect simple and tasty Bahamian dishes like grilled fish sandwiches, shrimp skewers, and lobster salad. Sunday is popular for chicken souse. Kids love the beach. It has one of the longest happy hours, daily 4pm-7pm, and serves draft Sands beer.

Cap'n Jack's (tel. 242/366-0247, http://capnjackshopetown.com, Mon.-Fri. breakfast 8:30am-10am, lunch and dinner 11am-9pm, $15-20) is a bright pink-and-white building overhanging the harbor. Don't come for white-glove service; expect no-frills plastic chairs and tables and a fun casual vibe. The food is tasty and the drinks are cold at one of the most popular bar hangouts in town. Happy hour is Wednesday and Friday 5pm-6:30pm in high season, and there are bingo and trivia nights.

If you feel like you've seen all the sights on Elbow Cay, head over to the tiny neighboring island of Lubber's Quarters and check out **Cracker P's Bar and Grill** (Lubbber's Quarters, tel. 242/577-3139, www.crackerps.com, Wed.-Sun. noon-dusk, $15-20), is owned and operated by Bahamian chef Patrick Stewart and his wife, Linda. Located on a 7.5-acre estate farm that spans from the harbor to the ocean, there are walking trails with native flowers, trees, and a diversity of birds. The restaurant serves up fresh local seafood specialties caught by captain Justin Russell of Local Boy Charters. Bread is baked in-house daily. After dinner enjoy a sipping rum from the large selection and a Cuban cigar. The Full Moon parties are the place to be once a month when the full moon rises. The all-you-can-eat buffet is $25, and there is also a gift shop with T-shirts and artwork by Linda. Get there on your own boat or charter a ferry.

CAFÉS AND LIGHT BITES

Andrew and Heather have created a space to gather around conversation and local art at the **Hope Town Coffee Shop** (Bay St. west of Cap'n Jack's, tel. 242/366-0760, Mon.-Fri. 8:30am-3pm, Sat. 8:30am-noon). There is a living room set up and an outside deck offering beautiful views of the harbor. On the menu are homemade quiche and pastries. They have fruit smoothies and frappés and their own in-house roasted coffee blends. Decorative artwork gives it an urban coffeehouse feel with an island flair.

The Sweet Shop (Centerline Rd., tel. 242/366-0613, Mon.-Sat. 9am-noon, and 1pm-5pm) is tucked away in the native bush in the central part of the island and is great location for a coffee if you are staying central or south and don't feel like heading into town. The fabulous ice cream is brought in from a specialty ice cream producer in the United States. It takes three cargo boats to get to Elbow Cay traveling from West Palm Beach, Florida, to Nassau, then to Marsh Harbour, and finally to Hope Town, so savor each scoop. Most stop in for a morning wake-up espresso, but they also serve delicious pastries, homemade chocolate chip cookies, brownies, and carrot cake.

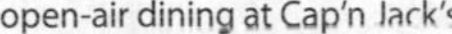
open-air dining at Cap'n Jack's

Accommodations

Most of the resorts and inns in Elbow Cay are located outside town, but if you are interested in staying in town or in an expansive private home right on the beach, consider renting a vacation rental home. **Hope Town Hideaways** (U.S. tel. 561/656-9703, www.hopetown.com) rentals run from $1,200 per week for a two-bedroom cottage on the harbor to $8,000 per week for a four-bedroom beach house. There are plenty of options between the north end and the south end. Just be wary that golf carts can't be driven in town. If you rent on the north side of the island, you may feel isolated, since you can't drive through to the south end. Some visitors rent two golf carts, one for the north and one for the south.

$150-250

★ **Abaco Inn** (tel. 242/366-0133 or 242/366-0333, U.S. tel. 800/468-8799, www.abacoinn.com, $195) comprises 12 bungalows and 8 suites, all with glorious views of the ocean. A renovation is ongoing to add additional rooms on the harbor side. The pool is just above the rocks on the ocean, and on a windy day, the waves will be crashing just below. The suites are cozy, with a balcony and a hammock facing the sea, soft feather bedding, and en suite baths. The inn is located on the central-south end of the island, but you won't feel isolated. Nearby is Sea Spray Resort and Firefly Sunset Resort, both with bars and restaurants, and of course there's the ever-popular on-site Abaco Inn bar and restaurant. Welcoming staff make you feel at home. There is a gift shop in the reception area, where you can find local handmade arts and crafts, chocolates, soaps, and handbags.

On the southern edge of town, just a short walk along the harbor front to bars, restaurants, and shopping, ★ **The Hope Town Harbour Lodge** (Queen St., south end of town, tel. 242/366-0095, www.hopetownlodge.com, $185) is an ideal spot to walk and explore. For beach-lovers, the lodge is on top of a bluff overlooking one of the prettiest two-mile stretches of sand on the island. Directly in front of the hotel is some of the best swimming and snorkeling. The Great Harbour Room and The Reef Bar and Grill are the two restaurants on-site, offering a wide range of casual and fine-dining options. They also have an ice cream bar, and the lodge is a popular spot for destination weddings and private events. The rooms are decorated in comfortable island style, with wood paneling and crisp white linens. Choose from main

the lush entrance to The Hope Town Harbour Lodge

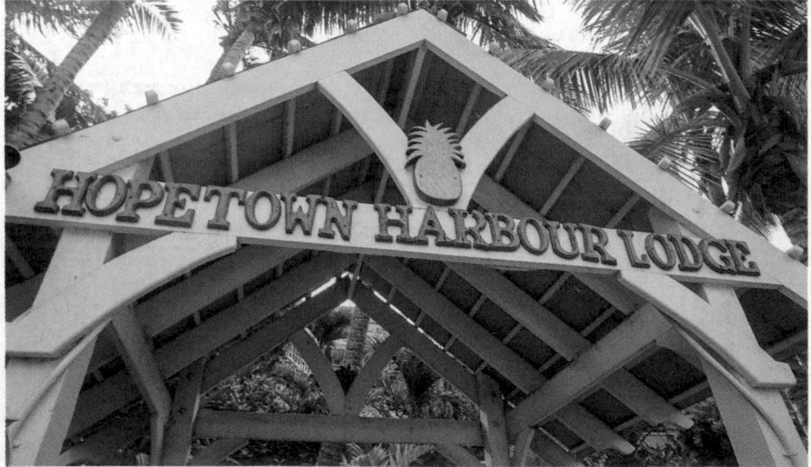

lodge rooms, poolside cabanas, or oceanfront cottages.

Lubber's Landing (Lubbers Quarters Cay, U.S. tel. 772/913-5781, www.lubberslanding.com, $200 one-bedroom cottage, $860 whole compound) is located on the neighboring island of Lubbers Quarters Cay, a five-minute boat ride from Hope Town. Three one-bedroom cottages are connected to a main building by raised wooden walkways. The main building houses the "master bedroom," with views of Tillo Cut and Tahiti Beach, and the main entertaining area with the kitchen, living room, bar, and lounge. To rent the main building, you must rent the full compound; otherwise that building is shared with all guests. There is a beach directly out front that is perfect for swimming, and at night for lighting a bonfire under the stars. The accommodations are quaint and rustic, and it's far from anything else, but it is truly an experience.

The southernmost resort on the island, **Sea Spray Resort and Marina** (White Sound, tel. 242/366-0065, U.S. tel. 717/200-1359, www.seasprayresort.com, $235) is on the southern end of protected White Sound, spanning to the Atlantic side. The restaurant, bar, and marina are on the sound side, with open-air dining, an enclosed dining room, a pool, a lively bar. The cottages are on the ocean side and boast breathtaking views of quiet splendor. Three villas on the ocean side are nestled in the dunes for privacy, and four overlook the green waters of White Sound. The rooms are a bit dated, but you'll find you'll be easily distracted by the expansive views from your private balcony.

OVER $250

★ **Firefly Sunset Resort** (off Centreline Rd., tel. 242/366-0145, www.fireflysunsetresort.com, $395), is located in the central area of the island on the Sea of Abaco side. Drive down a long stately road through native vegetation, reminiscent of a plantation driveway in the U.S. Deep South, as I'm sure the South Carolina owners intended. With the five-star service of an international resort and the hospitality of a local establishment, the resort is family-run by Lorenzo and Hope Town native Patricia, who create an upscale destination featuring colorful cottages on the hillside overlooking the harbor. There are two- to four-bedroom cottages surrounding a pool area. Brazilian wood accents and Caribbean decor with rattan and sisal accents make the rooms inviting and beachy. The on-site Firefly Sunset Resort Bar and Grill is one of the hippest spots on the island for sunsets. The bar serves South Carolina craft-produced Firefly vodkas and bourbons.

Hope Town Inn & Marina (next to Hope Town Lighthouse, tel. 242/366-0003, U.S. tel. 850/588-4855, www.hopetownmarina.com, $430) is across the harbor from the main part of town and is only accessible by boat. The rooms are elegant and uniquely decorated. The grounds feature lush, mature tropical vegetation, and the restaurant and pool deck offer fantastic views of the activity in the harbor. You may feel isolated, since there isn't much within walking distance, but there is a complimentary on demand shuttle to Hope Town.

Turtle Hill Vacation Villas (Old White Sound Rd., tel. 242/366-0557, www.turtlehill.com, $380) are located ocean-side on the outskirts of town. Two- and three-bedroom villas with full kitchens are perfect for families, and you'll have your choice of a dip in the ocean out front or the freshwater pool. The On Da Beach bar and restaurant is on-site and is a popular hangout for locals and visitors from all over the island. Rates include use of a golf cart; there is a two-night minimum stay.

Information and Services

Hope Town Clinic (tel. 242/366-0108, Mon.-Fri. 9am-5pm) is located at the entrance to the downtown walking district. A government doctor comes every two weeks, but there is a nurse on the premises. **Hope Town Fire & Rescue** is always standing by on VHF channel 16 or by dialing 911. On the island there is a **post office** and a **police station** next to the clinic. Cell service is spotty, so if you need to get through to someone, all establishments and most locals have a VHF radio.

Getting There

Albury's Ferry Service (tel. 242/367-0290, www.alburysferry.com, one-way $19 adults, $11 ages 6-11, round-trip $30 adults, $17 ages 6-11, free under age 6) runs to Hope Town from the Marsh Harbour Ferry Dock, located at the east end of Bay Street. It's a 20-minute ride, and they make several stops around Hope Town Harbour, so make sure to ask the best place to disembark for where you need to go.

MARINAS

Lighthouse Marina (tel. 242/366-0154, www.htlighthousemarina.com) offers fuel and ice and has a gift shop and marine hardware store with boating supplies, bait, and fishing tackle. Next to the marina is Hope Town Wine & Spirits, where you can stock up on liquor. **Sea Spray Resort and Marina** (Sea Spray Resort, White Sound, tel. 242/366-0065, www.seasprayresort.com) is one of the most protected marinas in the area, located within White Sound, in a harbor in the Sea of Abaco. The marina offers fuel, electrical hookups, water, ice, showers, and laundry, and has a restaurant and bar on-site.

Hope Town Inn & Marina (tel. 242/366-0003, U.S. tel. 850/588-4855, www.hopetownmarina.com) has 50 boat slips within Hope Town's harbor and can accommodate yachts up to 125 feet at the deep-water dock and has moorings for boats up to 45 feet. It's located across from downtown, an easy dinghy ride to shops and restaurants. The Hope Town Inn has a restaurant and pool for marina guests as well as showers, laundry, lockers, electricity, and water.

Getting Around

There are six cart rental companies on island. Make reservations in advance, especially during peak season. You can walk around town, but if you want to explore the island, you'll need a cart or a bicycle from **Hope Town Cart Rentals** (tel. 242/366-0064, www.hopetowncartrental.com), **T&N Cart Rentals** (tel. 242/366-0069, www.tandncarts.com), **Island Cart Rentals** (tel. 242/366-0048, U.S. tel. 561/208-8160, www.islandcartrentals.com), **JR's Cart Rentals** (tel. 242/699-3799, www.juniorscartrentals.com), **Elbow Cay Cart Rentals** (tel. 242/366-0530, www.elbowcaycartrentals.com), or **Getaway Cart Rentals** (tel. 242/366-0200 or 242/366-0758).

GREAT GUANA CAY

Great Guana Cay, also known as just Guana Cay, is one of the farthest removed islands from the ferry docks, a 35- to 45-minute ferry ride from Marsh Harbour, depending on the weather. With less than 150 full-time residents, the island has a quiet demeanor with which some fall in love. The island is six miles long, with the very northwest end reserved for the private development of Baker's Bay. The remainder of the island is hilly and dotted with vacation cottages.

Town consists of a modest convenience store, a few gift shops, the Dive Guana scuba dive shop, the ferry dock, and Orchid Bay Marina. There are very few places to eat and drink, but the island is home to the famous Nipper's Beach Bar & Grill, one of the hottest beach bars in The Abacos. You can't really get lost on the island, as giant colorful signs at the ferry dock point you in the direction of everything you might, and anything along the lines of commerce is right along Front Street.

Guana Cay Beach

Although The Bahamas has perhaps thousands of beaches, Guana Cay Beach seems to check all the boxes for top beach criteria, including a sense of seclusion, extensive length (it's two miles long), a variety of beachfront vacation rentals where you can rent a home and enjoy tooling around in a golf cart on this extremely low-key island. There's zero high-rise development and a stellar beach bar, Nipper's. At low tide on a calm day, the water at Guana Beach seems to glow, and dark coral heads are evident, allowing you to

Great Guana Cay

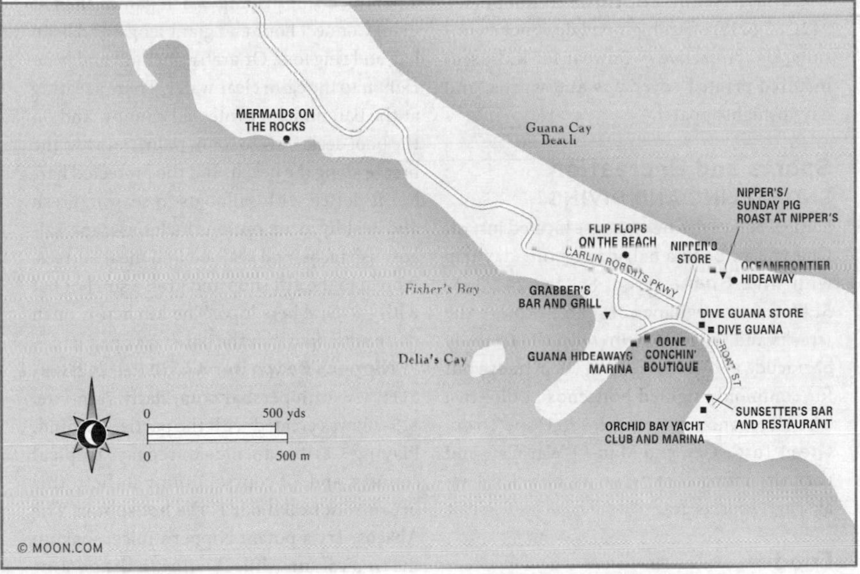

don your snorkel gear and make a beeline toward one. There's usually action in front of Nipper's, but walk in any direction and you'll likely only pass one or two other people. There are no amenities at the beach, such as beach-chair rentals, toilets, and showers. But if you are patronizing Nipper's, there's a shower as you walk up the stairs, and you can purchase a beach towel in their gift shop, as well as toilets, food, and drinks.

Entertainment and Events

On this sleepy island, you will be hard-pressed to find much going on outside the normal beach bar shenanigans, but this one is a little different, with the famous **Sunday Pig Roast at Nipper's.** Every Sunday 12:30pm-4pm, rain or shine, the event draws many die-hard leisure-lifestyle boaters. The ferries are packed all day as families and vacationers from the mainland head over to partake. The menu is roasted pig with hearty Bahamian sides to fill alcohol-saturated bellies. People mill around the pool deck and in the crow's nest, and shake their booties on the dance floor to pop music and reggae beats. As the light of day fades, crowds return to the dock, singing chanteys and swaying with their newfound best friends. It's an event to remember, depending on how many rum punches you had.

Shopping

Nipper's Store (tel. 242/365-5111, www.nippersbar.com) is crammed full of hats, beach towels, and shirts with the Nipper's logo on it, a great conversation piece starter when you are in a faraway city and see someone wearing a Nipper's shirt, too. Sans logo are swimsuits, beach dresses, and beach bags. Be sure to grab a Barefoot Man CD, the epitome of an island soundtrack for hammock lounging and rum drinking.

Dive Guana Store (Front St., tel. 242/365-5178, www.diveguana.com) has a wide selection of all things beachy. You can find sunscreen, straw bags, jewelry, long-sleeve SPF sun tops, ceramic dishes and glasses, dive and snorkel gear, lures and fishing gear, beach clothing for men and women, and Dive Guana logo apparel.

Gone Conchin' Boutique (Front St., tel. 242/365-5215) offers high-end designer swimsuits, UV protective swimwear for kids, sea-inspired printed cover-ups and wraps, and day-to-night apparel.

Sports and Recreation

SNORKELING AND DIVING

Some fabulous diving spots are located just off Guana Cay. Book a half-day or full-day trip with **Dive Guana** (Front St., tel. 242/365-5178, www.diveguana.com) and explore the wrecks and the reef. Swim with the friendly barracuda and groupers, and keep an eye out for commonly sighted bottlenose dolphins. They'll organize custom trips to Hope Town, Green Turtle Cay, and Man-O-War Cay, and they also rent golf carts, boats, bicycles, kayaks, and snorkel gear.

Food

From the ferry dock, head left and you'll quickly stumble upon **Grabbers Bar and Grill** (tel. 242/365-5133, U.S. tel. 386/868-2354, www.grabbersatsunset.com, daily 11:30am-9pm, $20-30), on one of the only slivers of beaches on the Sea of Abaco side. Depending on your energy level, they have the option of a dip in the pool, lounging in a hammock, or playing beach games such as giant Connect Four and giant Jenga, and bean bag and ring toss. Or grab a cocktail and head right into the calm clear water. There's seating at the bar, under a protected canopy, and on the pool deck. Tall coconut palms sway in the breeze along the beach, and the protected harbor is dotted with sailboats in season. Fresh and healthy menu options include wraps, salads, fish tacos, and seafood and meat entrées. Stop in to the gift shop and grab a shirt or hat with the Grabbers logo. The kitchen is open daily until 9pm, but the bar stays open late.

Nipper's Beach Bar & Grill (tel. 242/365-5111, www.nippersbar.com, daily 7am-late, $15-20) was created with the partier in mind. Playing Caribbean music, reggae, tropical country, and, of course, Jimmy Buffett, this oceanfront beach bar is the hot spot in The Abacos. Try a potent Nipper's Juice, soak up the tropical sun while floating in the pool, or wander down to the beach for a cooling dip in the ocean. Food includes tasty Cheeseburgers in Paradise and Bahamian seafood platters. The bar stays open until the last patron departs. Nipper's hosts the annual Barefoot Man concert series (end of Mar.), so if you're in the

Guana Cay Beach

area, see the charismatic performer from Cayman. Many businesses in the Out Islands shut down for slow season (Aug.-Oct.), but Nipper's is open 364 days a year.

Enjoy a view of the boats coming and going in the harbor at **Sunsetters Bar & Restaurant** (Orchid Bay Marina, tel. 242/365-5175, www.orchid-bay-marina.com, Tues.-Sun. lunch noon-3pm, dinner 6pm-9pm, $15-30). Sit outdoors on their deck or inside in the air-conditioning. For lunch they serve quesadillas, wraps, sandwiches, and burgers as well as Bahamian favorites. Dinner has delicious steak and seafood entrées as well as homemade deep-dish pizzas.

Accommodations

There is a limited selection of hotels in Guana Cay, but there are plenty of vacation rental homes. Many homeowners list their properties on websites like VRBO and Airbnb, but using a local company may help you figure out the lay of the land and give you the best options. Try **Everything Guana** (tel. 242/577-0003, www.everythingguana.com). You can find a four bedroom house right on Guana Beach for $2,600-4,200, depending on the season.

Flip Flops on the Beach (tel. 242/365-5215, www.flipflopsonthebeach.com, $300, three-night minimum) has several one- and two-bedroom bungalows and cottages to rent. The bungalows are located just outside town on the beach, walking distance to everything. The bungalows have TV with basic cable, Wi-Fi, fully equipped kitchens, a barbecue grill, and beach chairs and umbrellas. There's a backup generator for power outages, which is a huge bonus as power outages in the islands are common. There is a private shady beach pavilion with chairs, tables, and restrooms. The buildings are a rounded yurt shape, with bedrooms off the main living area. White tile floors and warm island colors will make you feel right at home.

Mermaids on the Rocks Resort, Bar & Restaurant (Sweeting Dr., tel. 242/475-2692, U.S. tel. 844/475-2692, www.mermaidsontherocks.com, Nov.-June, $300) is located on the Sea of Abaco about a mile from town. They will pick you up from the dock, but you may want to rent a golf cart if you want to visit bars and restaurants. On the property is a cliff-side pool, boat dockage, and a gift shop. Kayaks and paddleboards are available for guests. The upscale indoor restaurant serves lunch Friday-Sunday 11:30am-3pm, dinner Wednesday-Sunday 6pm-9:30pm, or

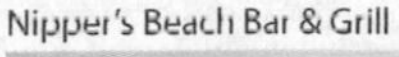
Nipper's Beach Bar & Grill

opt for lighter lunches at the Pool Bar and Café. Guest rooms have en suite baths on the harbor side, and a three-minute golf-cart ride away are the one- and two-bedroom condos on the beach.

Oceanfrontier Hideaway (U.S. tel. 888/541-1616, Canada tel. 519/389-4846, www.oceanfrontier.com, $290) is located on the beach next door to Nipper's. On the property are six two-bedroom beach cottages with private decks and full kitchens, cozily finished with natural wood paneling. Each has a spacious living room and a loft bedroom. Due to its location next door to Nipper's, noise is a concern; request a cottage farther away from the action.

Information and Services

There are no medical services, police, or fire stations on Guana Cay. For emergencies, contact the services in Marsh Harbour. For banking, stock up on cash in Marsh Harbour before you depart for Guana Cay.

Getting There

Albury's Ferry Service (tel. 242/367-0290, www.alburysferry.com, one-way $19 adults, $11 ages 6-11, round-trip $30 adults, $17 ages 6-11, free under age 6) provides transportation to Great Guana Cay departing from the Conch Inn Dock.

MARINAS

Orchid Bay Yacht Club and Marina (tel. 242/365-5175, www.orchid-bay-marina.com) is on the southeast end of the main harbor and is the only full-service public marina on the island. Amenities include fuel, electricity, water and ice, showers, and laundry. There is a pool for marina guests and a restaurant, bar, and gift shop. Short-term and long-term rates are available.

Guana Hideaways Marina (tel. 242/577-0003, www.everythingguana.com) is located between the ferry dock and Grabbers. The marina has 38 slips and offers short-term and long-term rates. Currently the only amenity is water. Rates start at $1 per foot.

Getting Around

If you are staying near town, many people walk, as everything is within close proximity. If you are staying farther from town, rent a golf cart from **Everything Guana** (tel. 242/577-0003, www.everythingguana.com), **Dive Guana** (tel. 242/365-5178, www.diveguana.com), or **Donna Sands Golf Cart Rentals** (tel. 242/365-5195, www.donnasands.com).

GREEN TURTLE CAY

The settlement of New Plymouth on Green Turtle Cay was once the largest in The Abacos, but today the population is around 500 residents. Arriving downtown, you'll get a sense of the town's rich history, established in 1786. The sleepy village is a traditionally Bahamian, with some action in season. Outside the main town are marinas and resorts that attract sailors, divers, and sportfishing enthusiasts.

The island is 3.5 miles long and 1.5 miles wide, with beautiful ocean beaches, just three miles off Great Abaco near Treasure Cay. Snorkeling and scuba sites on the vibrant reefs are just a short boat ride away. Visit the turtles at Coco Bay, and you'll likely be the only person on the beach. Most people drive golf carts on the island, and you'll find enough bars, restaurants, and shopping to keep you entertained.

★ Albert Lowe Museum

Located in New Plymouth in a white clapboard cottage with forest-green trim and gingerbread porches is the **Albert Lowe Museum** (Parliament St., between King St. and Mission St., tel. 242/365-4094, www.albertlowemuseum.com, Mon.-Sat. 9am-4pm, $5 adults, $3 children). The Loyalist cottage was built in 1825 by the Roberts family and once functioned as the public library after a 1932 hurricane destroyed the original structure. In the mid-1970s the building was purchased by Alton Lowe and restored to its original splendor and opened in 1976 as the first and oldest museum in The Bahamas. Alton named the museum after his father,

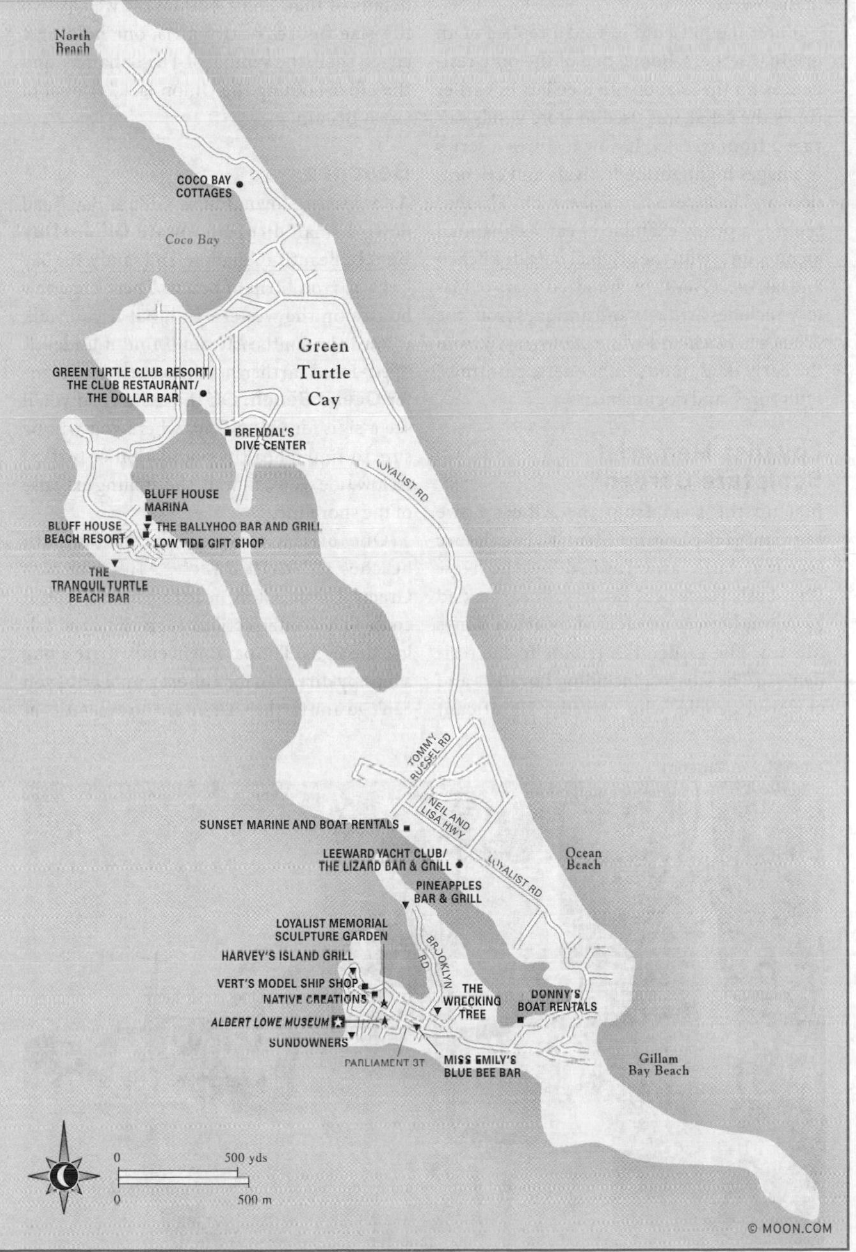
Green Turtle Cay
North Beach
COCO BAY COTTAGES
Coco Bay
Green Turtle Cay
GREEN TURTLE CLUB RESORT/ THE CLUB RESTAURANT/ THE DOLLAR BAR
BRENDAL'S DIVE CENTER
LOYALIST RD
BLUFF HOUSE MARINA
THE BALLYHOO BAR AND GRILL
BLUFF HOUSE BEACH RESORT
LOW TIDE GIFT SHOP
THE TRANQUIL TURTLE BEACH BAR
TOMMY RUSSEL RD
NEIL AND LISA HWY
SUNSET MARINE AND BOAT RENTALS
LEEWARD YACHT CLUB/ THE LIZARD BAR & GRILL
Ocean Beach
LOYALIST RD
PINEAPPLES BAR & GRILL
LOYALIST MEMORIAL SCULPTURE GARDEN
HARVEY'S ISLAND GRILL
BROOKLYN RD
VERT'S MODEL SHIP SHOP
NATIVE CREATIONS
THE WRECKING TREE
DONNY'S BOAT RENTALS
ALBERT LOWE MUSEUM
SUNDOWNERS
PARLIAMENT ST
MISS EMILY'S BLUE BEE BAR
Gillam Bay Beach
0
500 yds
0
500 m
© MOON.COM

Albert, a well-known model ship maker. The cottage has traditional dormers and a spacious porch at the proper angle to take advantage of the breeze.

Enter the museum to find a replica of an original settlers' home, one of the only residences on the island with a cellar. In earlier times the cellar was used to store goods salvaged from wrecks. It now features a series of images highlighting festivals and celebrations and includes a nautical exhibit. The museum is a prime example of early Bahamian architecture, with the original outside kitchen and latrine. Over three hundred years of history includes artifacts and antiques from the 1700s, old black-and-white photographs from the early days, model schooners, paintings, sculptures, and documents.

Loyalist Memorial Sculpture Garden

Just up the road from the Albert Lowe Museum is the Loyalist Memorial Sculpture Garden, built and funded by the New Plymouth Historical Society, spearheaded by Alton Lowe, and created by artist James Mastin. The garden is a tribute to the residents of The Abacos, including Loyalists and enslaved people, who played a significant role in the community during early settlement. The garden contains 24 life-size heads on pedestals representing these residents, with details of their contributions, as well as two life-size figures of two girls, one holding a conch shell, the symbol of The Bahamas, and the other holding the Union Jack, symbol of Great Britain.

Beaches

After leaving town, follow Gillam Bay Road down a small dirt path toward **Gillam Bay Beach.** Beautiful, shallow, and sandy, the bay has a narrow strip of beach. There are a few houses on the western end, but if you walk toward the southeast, you'll find it undeveloped. Head farther north to see access signs for **Ocean Beach.** Off the main road you'll see a sign for **Coco Bay,** where you will be sure to find a healthy population of turtles. At low tide, you can walk the arching expanse of the shoreline.

One of the most off-the-beaten-path beaches is **North Beach.** After you pass Green Turtle Club heading north, you'll come to a T intersection. Turn right and follow the signs. The pavement ends; drive along a bumpy dirt road for almost a mile until you can't go any farther. There are no amenities at

Albert Lowe Museum

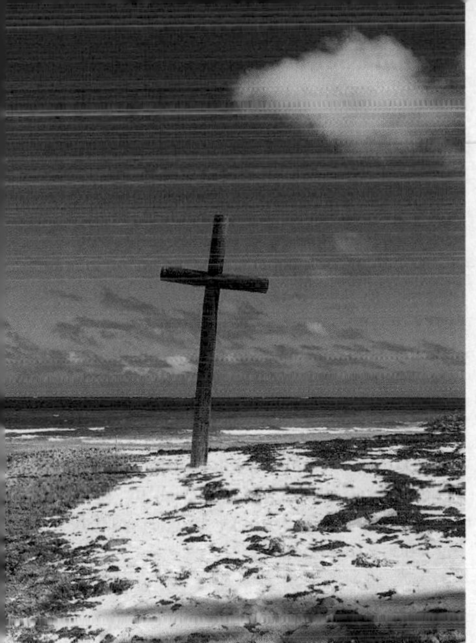
the cross at North Beach

the beach, just a long dock and a sand spit at low tide, but it's a beautiful spot for a picnic and a swim, and you'll likely be the only one on the beach. Walk around the corner to the ocean side to see a giant cross that was erected by local resident Grima Johnson, who had engine trouble off the rocky point in 1981. He swam to shore and with the help of his wife and a neighbor, set off on a rescue mission to save the remaining passengers of the boat. They were brought safely to shore, and after seven years of requests for permits, Johnson was allowed to erect a cross in commemoration of the day his life was saved. It has stood in that place and weathered storms and hurricanes ever since.

Entertainment and Events

MISS EMILY'S BLUE BEE BAR

When visiting the island, make sure you stop by the famous **Miss Emily's Blue Bee Bar** (Victoria St., off Parliament St., New Plymouth, tel. 242/365-4181, Mon.-Sat. 4pm until late), home to the ever-popular Goombay Smash tropical drink. It's a secret recipe, but expect a rummy concoction with orange and pineapple juices. Hundreds of business cards and T-shirts line the walls as this has been an island fixture since the 1960s. Miss Emily died in 1997, but the establishment is run by her daughter Violet. It is *the* place to hang out. Like most places in the islands, it's closed on Sunday.

DOLLAR BAR

An iconic and regularly photographed bar, the **Dollar Bar at the Green Turtle Club** (White Sound, tel. 242/365-4271, www.greenturtleclub.com, 10am-9pm daily, open later for special events) is home to the famous Tipsy Turtle Rum Punch cocktail and is popular among boaters due to its location right on the harbor and marina. The walls are covered floor-to-ceiling with dollars, a tradition that started when the club opened. Many celebrities have visited the Club, and you can look for their signed dollar bills throughout the bar. There is often live music, including the well-known Gully Roosters, who perform their own music as well as reggae hits Wednesday nights in season.

Shopping

Vert's Model Ship Shop (tel. 242/365-4170) sells handcrafted schooners and sloops created by Vert Lowe, who is now retired, so the shop isn't always open, but ask around and you'll most likely be able to track him down. **Native Creations** (Parliament St. northwest of the Albert Lowe Museum, tel. 242/365-4206, Mon.-Sat. 10am-5pm) specializes in woodwork, jewelry, ceramic creations, and Androsia fabric cloth and clothing.

Located at Bluff House in the reception area is the **Low Tide Gift Shop** (Bluff House, White Sound, tel. 242/365-4247, www.bluffhouse.com, daily 9am-5pm), featuring resort wear, sandals, beach bags, and hats, logoed Bluff House apparel, and "Swimming with the Pigs" shirts. Also look for hand painted ceramics by local artist Karen Macintosh of Abaco Ceramics.

Stop by the **Resort Shop at Green Turtle Club** (Black Sound, tel. 242/365-4271, www.greenturtleclub.com, daily 9am-5pm) and you'll find all kinds of treasures: beautiful beachy jewelry featuring sealife charms and designer shirts with the Green Turtle Club logo as well as high-fashion beach cover-ups and sundresses. For men there is a variety of lightweight long-sleeve shirts perfect for fishing and boating.

Sports and Recreation

FISHING AND BOATING

Donny's Boat Rentals and Marina (Loyalist Rd., tel. 242/577-1339, U.S. tel. 407/610-7000, www.donnysboatrentalsgtc.com) offers 17- to 23-foot boats, perfect for getting around the Sea of Abaco. On the property are mooring balls and dockage space. **Reef Boat Rentals** (tel. 242/365-4145, www.reefboatrentals.com) has been family owned and operated company since 1998, offering 17- to 26-foot center consoles for rent. **Sunset Marine and Boat Rentals** (tel. 242/365-4634, www.sunsetmarineandboatrentals.com) offers a wide variety of 17- to 26-foot boats for rent, equipped with GPS, a depth sounder, music systems, and coolers. One-day, three-day, and weekly rates are available.

Ronnie Sawyer (tel. 242/365-4070) is a professional bonefishing and deep-sea fishing guide who has been featured in *Saltwater Fisherman* magazine. Inquire with Donny's Boat Rentals or contact him directly. Captain Rick Sawyer of **Abaco Flyfish and Connection Charters** (tel. 242/365-4261, www.abacoflyfish.com) is a bonefishing and deep-sea guide with over 38 years of experience offering half-day and full-day trips.

Captain Thomas Sawyer was born and raised on Green Turtle Cay and operates **Reel Serious Charters** (tel. 242/365-4019 or 242/577-8195, www.reelseriouscharters242.com). His excursions include visiting the pigs, stingrays and sharks, deep-sea fishing, snorkeling and picnics, bottom fishing, spearfishing, and island-hopping.

SNORKELING AND DIVING

Brendal and his wife, Mary, have been operating **Brendal's Dive Center** (next to Green Turtle Club, White Sound, tel. 242/365-4411, www.brendal.com), ranked one of the top operations in The Abacos, since 1985, offering diving, snorkeling, and island-hoping excursions. They also offer two dives per day from 10 to 100 feet, depending on visitors' abilities; these dives include reefs, shipwrecks,

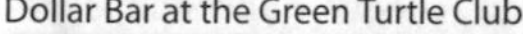

Dollar Bar at the Green Turtle Club

and inland blue holes. If you're inexperienced, you can learn to dive with their certification program.

Lincoln Jones (tel. 242/365-4223) will create an itinerary based on your preferences to include fishing, snorkeling, lobstering, a beach picnic with freshly prepared seafood, and visiting the stingrays at Munjack Cay.

Food

The **Club Restaurant at the Green Turtle Club** (Black Sound, www.greenturtleclub.com, tel. 242/365-4271, U.S. tel. 800/370-4468, $15-30) serves breakfast, lunch, and dinner daily. Breakfast is served daily 7:15am-10:30am on the covered patio overlooking White Sound Harbour, with omelets, french toast with fresh Bahamian bread, and eggs Benedict. Lunch is daily 11:30am-2:45pm on the patio and includes soups, salads, sandwiches, burgers, and seafood entrées. Dinner is an event at the Green Turtle Club, and visitors and homeowners come to this social hub. Dinner starts daily at 6pm with the option of the air-conditioned dining room or the covered screened-in patio. Lobster adorns the menu in season, and the coconut curry chicken, grouper fish-and-chips, and mojito mahimahi are favorites.

Bluff House Beach Resort and Marina (White Sound, tel. 242/365-4247, U.S. tel. 800/745-4911, www.bluffhouse.com) has two options for dining that collaborate to serve breakfast, lunch, and dinner daily. **The Ballyhoo Bar and Grill** ($15-30) is on the harbor side overlooking White Sound and the marina. The open-air bar is adjacent to the pool, and the interior dining room is cozy. Events are often hosted on their spacious deck. They offer Surf-and-Turf every Tuesday with live music by Island Spice, and Pizza and Pasta is every Thursday. The relaxed **Tranquil Turtle Beach Bar** ($10-15) is on the Sea of Abaco side, with a picturesque white-sand beach to lounge under an umbrella or in a hammock. Indoor and outdoor seating is available under a coconut palm or on the deck overlooking the sea. There are delicious burgers, salads, and wraps, and happy hour is daily 4pm-6pm, where you can sample their Tranquil Turtle cocktail.

The Wrecking Tree Restaurant, Bar and Takeaway (Hill St. and Brooklyn Rd., New Plymouth, tel. 242/365-4263, Mon.-Thurs. 11am-6pm, Fri.-Sat. 11am-9pm, $10-20) is popular with both visitors and locals for Bahamian favorites such as conch salad, barbecue ribs, and cracked conch with salad or peas-and-rice. There's a window for easy takeaway and enjoy a cold Kalik while you wait.

Harvey's Island Grill (Bay St. and Charles St., New Plymouth, tel. 242/365-4389, Mon.-Sat. lunch 11am-2pm, dinner 5:30pm-8:30pm, $15-20) is located in town and serves hearty specialties like fried pork chop with creamy chive and onion sauce, and lighter fare like grilled fish wraps with fresh avocado. Every Friday is pizza and wing night.

Pineapples Bar & Grill (tel. 242/365-4039 Mon.-Sat. 11am-8pm, $10-20) is literally off the beaten path: Drive down a short bumpy dirt road and find this local watering hole tucked within the native vegetation on the harbor side, just outside town. Follow Brooklyn Road around from the other side of the harbor. Pineapples has good food, occasional live music, and a glorious sunset.

The Lizard Bar & Grill at the **Leeward Yacht Club** (Loyalist Rd., tel. 242/577-4111 or 242/365-4191, www.leewardyachtclub.com, Mon.-Sat. 11am-8pm, $15-25) is situated on the beautiful pool deck overlooking the harbor, serving lunch and dinner. Try a signature cocktail such as the Swimming Pig (vodka or rum, pineapple juice, lime, ginger, bitters, and mint) or the Dock Master (vodka or gin, grapefruit juice, and a salted rim).

Sundowners (Crown St., New Plymouth, tel. 242/365-4060, daily 5pm-open late) is located on the Sea of Abaco side of town. This owner-operated rustic, eclectic, and funky open-air bar overhangs the water and has a great island vibe going on. Happy hour is 5pm-6pm daily and includes music, dancing, billiards, and darts. They serve up traditional Bahamian lunch and dinner snacks but are best known for cocktails and enjoying the sunset.

Accommodations

Green Turtle Club Resort and Marina (White Sound, tel. 242/365-4271, U.S. tel. 800/370-4468, www.greenturtleclub.com, $229) offers a variety of rooms and villas along White Sound, including the Standard Club Room, close to the pool and resort facilities; Waterfront Rooms; and one- to three-bedroom Waterfront Villas with decks, a short drive around White Sound. The rooms have beautiful hardwood floors and island-inspired linens. Baths are updated and spacious. A freshwater swimming pool and the Dollar Bar and the Club Restaurant are on-site. The ferry will drop you at the club, and golf carts can be rented on-site. They offer stay-and-fly packages with discounts on airfare.

A 12-acre property stretching from White Sound to the Sea of Abaco, with the Tranquil Turtle Beach Bar on a picturesque private white sandy beach, ★ **Bluff House Beach Resort and Marina** (White Sound, tel. 242/365-4247, U.S. tel. 800/745-4911, www.bluffhouse.com, $225) is on the southwest side of White Sound. There is a freshwater swimming pool alongside The Ballyhoo Bar & Grill. Each luxury suite features its own private balcony with an expansive sunset view of the Sea of Abaco, air-conditioning, and newly installed high-speed fiber-optic internet. The rooms are fresh, new, and elegantly decorated in British West Indies style. They also offer three-bedroom cottages that feature full kitchens, TVs, living room areas, and master bedrooms with en suite baths. This is a great choice for weddings and groups.

If you are looking for a quiet, private escape, look no farther than **Coco Bay Cottages** (U.S. tel. 561/202-8149, www.cocobaycottages.com, $250). On the ocean side of the northern part of the island, reach these cottages by traveling a short distance on an unpaved dirt road. Two- to four-bedroom cottages are available. The reef system directly off the beach offers snorkeling opportunities.

In a beautifully landscaped environment, **Leeward Yacht Club** (Loyalist Rd., tel. 242/577-4111 or 242/365-4191, www.leewardyachtclub.com, from $2,800 weekly high season, four-night minimum) offers three- and five-bedroom homes with full kitchens, central air-conditioning and washers and dryers. There is also a restaurant, a bar, and a pool on the property. Contact them for discounted nightly rates during the

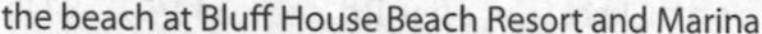

the beach at Bluff House Beach Resort and Marina

summer months. The weekly rental includes a free slip at the marina.

Getting There

From the Treasure Cay Airport Ferry Terminal, Green Turtle Cay is just a five-minute ferry ride. Take the **Lowe's Green Turtle Ferry** (tel. 242/365-4166, www.greenturtleferry.com) to New Plymouth ($14 one-way, $19 same-day round-trip) or White Sound and other points ($15 one-way, $22 same-day round trip).

MARINAS

Green Turtle Club Marina (White Sound, tel. 242/365-4271, U.S. tel. 800/370-4468, www.greenturtleclub.com) offers 40 slips that can accommodate boats up to 130 feet. There are showers, laundry facilities, restrooms, electrical hookups, a fish-cleaning station, and waste removal. The Grog Shoppe is stocked with liquor, wine, beer, and snacks.

Bluff House Beach Resort and Marina (White Sound, tel. 242/365-4247, U.S. tel. 800/745-4911, www.bluffhouse.com) is a full-service marina with 46 slips in protected White Sound. It can accommodate vessels up to 120 feet and has six slips for catamarans. All slips have shore power and water access. There is fuel, bait, ice, restrooms, showers, laundry, and Wi-Fi.

Leeward Yacht Club (Loyalist Rd., tel. 242/365-4191 or 242/577-4111, www.leewardyachtclub.com) offers 24 deep-water slips with free water, laundry facilities, a fish-cleaning station, electrical, and Wi-Fi. The marina store is open daily and sells ice, bait, snacks, and souvenirs. There is a shipyard adjacent to the marina with dry storage and repair services.

Getting Around

If you are on a boat, use it to get around town. If you are staying on land, rent a golf cart in Green Turtle Cay from **T&A Golf Cart Rentals** (tel. 242/365-4259 or 242/375-8055, tnagolfcarts.com), **Brendal's Golf Cart Rentals** (tel. 242/365-4411, www.brendal.com), or **Sea Side Carts** (tel. 242/365-4147 or 242/577-5497, www.seasidecartrentals.com).

SPANISH CAY

Spanish Cay Resort and Marina

Spanish Cay (tel. 242/365-0083, U.S. tel. 954/213-6196, www.spanishcay.com) is a boaters island, only accessible by private boat or plane to truly get away from it all. A private 5,000 foot airstrip is capable of handling turboprops and small jets. Contact Spanish Cay directly for permission to land. An 81-slip marina is able to accommodate yachts up to 250 feet. There is a fuel dock on-site with filtered gas and diesel, and immigration and customs on-site.

For diversions, there is a freshwater pool and a heated spa, four tennis courts, and a games room with ping-pong, darts, shuffleboard, and pool tables. Just off Spanish Cay is a barrier reef that allows for epic diving and deep-sea fishing at the drop-off. A beautiful stretch of beach has a whale's tail-shaped natural rock formation that allows for a beach visit in the lee in almost any weather. The Point House Restaurant overlooks the marina and is open daily for breakfast, lunch, and dinner. On the end of a point is Wrecker's Bar (June-Aug.), only open during the warm summer months. They have beachfront accommodations (from $215 high season) on Barefoot Beach with fridges, coffeemakers, and a wet bar as well as suites and condos near the marina.

Getting There and Around

There is no ferry service to Spanish Cay. Once you are on the island, everything is within walking distance.

MAN-O-WAR CAY

One of the less traveled locations is Man-O-War Cay, with rich history as a boatbuilding community. Less than 300 residents inhabit the island, many of them with heritage dating to the Loyalist period. It is a "dry island,"

Man-O-War Boatbuilding Heritage

Man-O-War Cay has a rich heritage in boatbuilding.

Boatbuilding in Man-O-War Cay dates to the 1800s. Albury is a common Bahamian name from the Loyalist period, but many associate the name with Man-O-War's boatbuilding and maritime heritage. In Man-O-War Cay, the Albury family has built boats, including smacks, sloops, and schooners, for generations. By the mid-1900s Maurice Albury was building Abaco Dinghys, and William Albury began building Albury Brothers boats. Until 1985 the boats were made of wood. Now William's sons Don and Jamie are involved, creating fiberglass outboard runabouts and skiffs from 18.5 to 33 feet. The boats built in Man-O-War Cay today are still made one at a time, but due to heavy demand from Bahamians and Americans, the Albury family partnered with a U.S. manufacturer in 2003 to begin production in the United States. The materials and the construction process is closely monitored by the Albury family to uphold the tradition and family legacy.

meaning no liquor is sold. If you are staying on the island, you're allowed to bring your own libations—alcohol isn't illegal, but sales of it are. The town is well-kept and easily walkable, making it a fantastic place to visit for the day. Residents are intrigued by visitors, and their friendly demeanor will make you feel right at home.

Heritage Museum

The **Heritage Museum** (Queens Hwy. and Pappy Den Hill, tel. 242/365-6599, www.mowmuseum.com, Thurs.-Sat. 10am-noon, free) is in a historical cottage dating back to the 1800s. Artifacts, photographs, and records from the town's boatbuilding history can be found within. Hours are limited, so plan accordingly.

Shopping

ALBURY'S SAIL SHOP

On the north end of Sea Road, right on the harbor, is **Albury's Sail Shop** (Lover's Lane and Sea Rd., tel. 242/365-6014), family-owned and operated for more than three generations, where you can find high-quality sail canvas creations in a variety of colorful nautical and island-inspired prints. Near the back of the shop you can often witness the women sewing bags and hats.

JOE'S STUDIO & EMPORIUM

Specializing in wooden boat models, **Joe's Studio & Emporium** (Sea Rd., tel. 242/365-6082, www.joesstudioabaco.com) is a must-stop on any visit to Man-O-War Cay. Joseph Albury is well known for his creations of half cross-section ships and has won prestigious awards for his handiwork. The models of his 14-foot wooden sailing dinghies are to scale and can be seen around The Abacos. You can also find island gifts and souvenirs, and paintings by local artists.

Food

Dock & Dine (Sea Rd., tel. 242/365-6139, Tues. and Sat. 11:30am-3pm, Mon. and Wed.-Fri. 11:30am-3pm and 5:30pm-8pm, $15-30, cash only) is located on the harbor side, near the ferry dock. Specializing in traditional Bahamian and American food, you can watch the boats come and go at this open-air establishment. Lunch items include crispy calamari, crab cakes, flatbreads, burgers, and sandwiches. Dinner is coconut curry lamb shank, sticky ribs, and island grilled conch.

A newer addition to the limited dining options on Man-O-War Cay is **Hibiscus Café** (Sea Rd., tel. 242/365-6380, Tues.-Wed. 11:30am-1:30pm and 6pm-8pm, Thurs. 11:30am-1:30pm, Fri.-Sat. 11:30am-1:30pm and 6pm-8:30pm, $20-30), which features Bahamian favorites and a mix of pizza, pasta, burgers, and sandwiches. They also have a great selection of ice cream. Across the street from the harbor in a diner-style setting, it's the new popular hangout for locals and is very casual.

Accommodations

Schooner's Landing Ocean Club (Queen's Hwy., tel. 242/367-4469, www.schoonerslanding.com, $275) is on the ocean side of the island and has premium condo rentals. Each two-story unit is fully equipped and has expansive views of the ocean. Three units are suitable for 4-6 people, perfect for group travel. A swimming pool is on-site and out front is an extensive reef system for snorkeling. Although you can walk to town, you might want to rent a golf cart, as it is out of town. Schooner's Landing can help arrange a rental.

Getting There

Albury's Ferry Service (tel. 242/367-0290, www.alburysferry.com, one-way $19 adults, $11 ages 6-11, round-trip $30 adults, $17 ages 6-11, free under age 6) serves Man-O-Way Cay from the Marsh Harbour Ferry Dock at the east end of Bay Street. It's a 20 minute ferry ride.

Man-O-War Marina (Sea Rd., tel. 242/365-6013, www.manowarmarina.com) is full-service and has 28 slips, a freshwater pool, a gazebo with a barbecue grill, Wi-Fi, showers, toilets, and laundry. They offer maintenance and repair services and have a dive and gift shop on-site to purchase or rent snorkel gear and pick up local information and maps.

Getting Around

Although the island is highly walkable at only 2.8 miles long, you may want to rent a golf cart or explore the surrounding area by boat.

Waterways Boat and Golf Cart Rentals (Sea Rd. and Pappy Ben Hill, tel. 242/365-6143 or 242/357-6540, www.waterwaysrentals.com) rents 18- to 23-foot center consoles, including the locally made Albury Brothers boats. Golf cart rentals run $50 per day by credit card, $40 cash.

Eleuthera, Harbour Island, and Spanish Wells

The dynamic landscape of Eleuthera and its surrounding islands comprises rocky headlands reminiscent of the rugged Irish coastline separated by ambling stretches of gentle powdery-sand beaches.

Eleuthera is shaped like a swordfish or a narwhal stretched thin. Cape Eleuthera to the south is situated on the whale's tail, and the north is an anvil-shaped marshy landmass with the "sword" jutting out into Current Island. A smattering of rocks and cays stretches all the way to Nassau, and if there was adequate funding and initiative, a bridge similar to the one connecting the Florida Keys could connect Nassau to Eleuthera. The ocean bears down from all sides on the narrow landmass; to the west is the ever-calm Caribbean, and to the east, the roaring Atlantic Ocean. A narrow strip in North Eleuthera called the Glass Window Bridge showcases the sharp contrast between the shallow turquoise banks and the cerulean blue as the ocean plummets thousands of feet.

The first European settlers arrived on Eleuthera in 1648 and named it with the Greek word *eleutheros,* meaning "free." They traveled from Bermuda seeking religious and political freedom and were shipwrecked on the Devil's Backbone, a treacherous reef well-known for taking many ships and many lives. This area now attracts scuba enthusiasts for the numerous wreck dives. These original settlers eventually established The Bahamas's first settlements in Governor's Harbour, Spanish Wells, and Harbour Island, colorful villages steeped in history and colonial charm.

Today, Eleuthera is a low-key hideaway. Vacation rental homes on pristine beaches seem to make time move more slowly. On the mainland, surfers are drawn to the many breaks around Gregory Town, a funky up-and-coming settlement in an otherwise agricultural community that embraces its pineapple-growing roots. Centrally located Governor's Harbour, the country's oldest settlement, is poised on a protected harbor and stretches along an elevated ridgeline spilling over to the Atlantic side. Farther south,

Previous: colonial homes with painted shutters dot the waterfront on Harbour Island; a signpost in Tarpum Bay. **Above:** fresh made conch salad at Romora Bay.

Look for ★ to find recommended sights, activities, dining, and lodging.

Highlights

★ **Preacher's Cave:** Used as shelter for the first shipwrecked European settlers, this cave was the site of the first Christian religious services in The Bahamas (page 165).

★ **Glass Window Bridge:** This tiny sliver of land divides the deep blue Atlantic Ocean from the calm turquoise Caribbean (page 166).

★ **Leon Levy Nature Preserve:** Explore miles of trails meandering through native vegetation, experience interpretative displays, and scale a lookout tower at this environmental education center (page 176).

★ **Ten Bay Beach:** Pack a picnic and take the family to this shallow sand flat tucked into an often deserted cove (page 178).

★ **Rock Sound Ocean Hole:** Attracting swimmers in the warm summer months, this inland blue hole is believed by locals to have healing powers (page 186).

★ **Pink Sands Beach:** Don your oversize sun hat and relax in luxury on one of The Bahamas' most beautiful beaches (page 193).

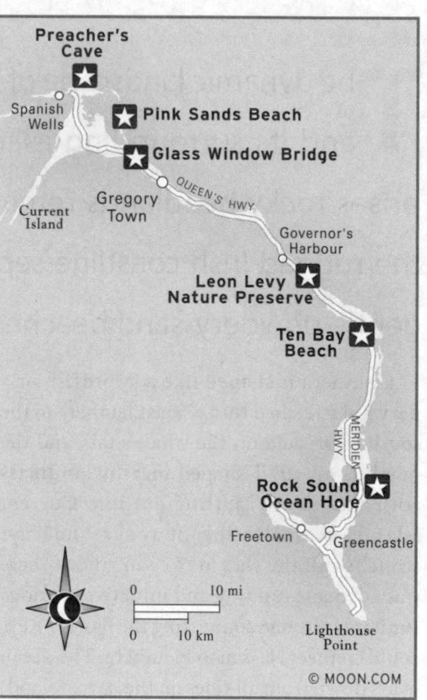

Eleuthera, Harbour Island, and Spanish Wells

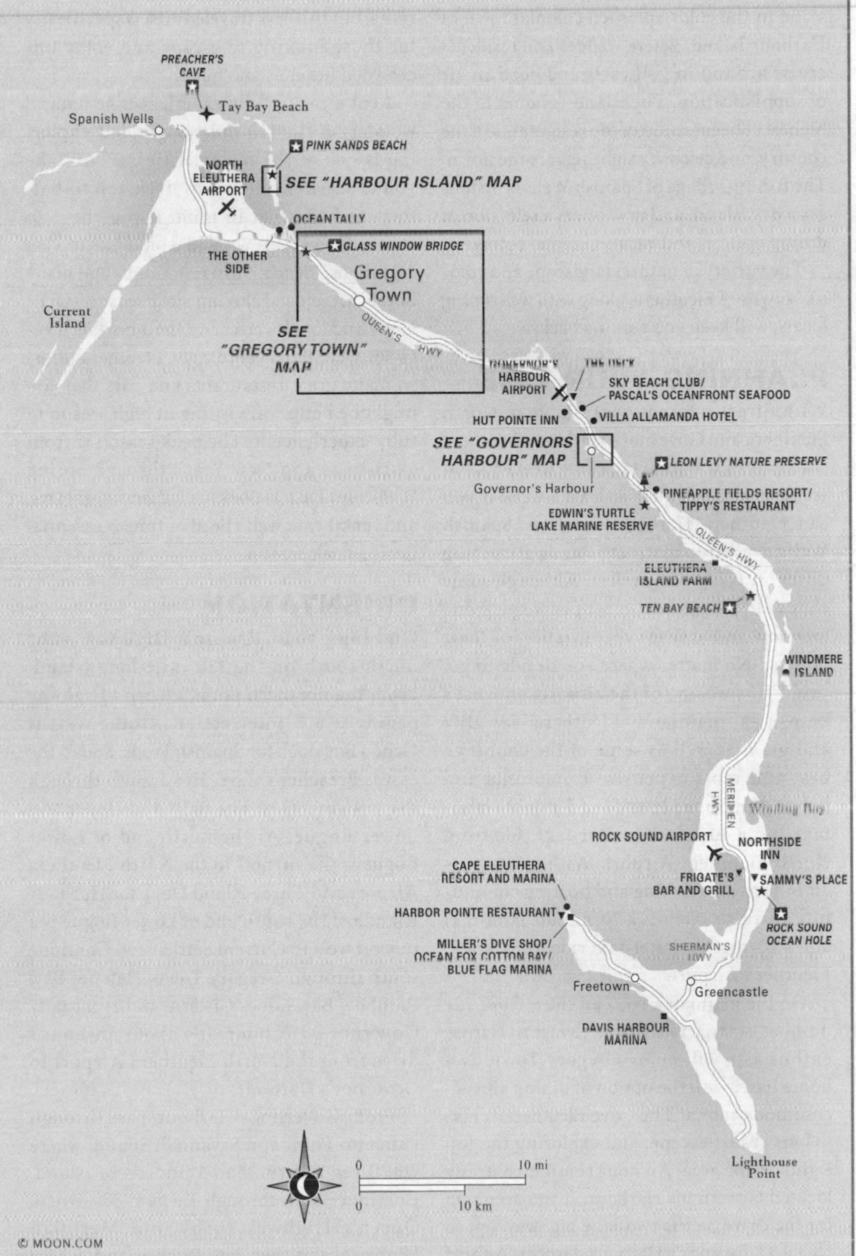
PREACHER'S CAVE
Tay Bay Beach
Spanish Wells
PINK SANDS BEACH
NORTH ELEUTHERA AIRPORT
SEE "HARBOUR ISLAND" MAP
OCEAN TALLY
THE OTHER SIDE
GLASS WINDOW BRIDGE
Gregory Town
Current Island
QUEEN'S HWY
SEE "GREGORY TOWN" MAP
GOVERNOR'S HARBOUR AIRPORT
THE DECK
SKY BEACH CLUB/ PASCAL'S OCEANFRONT SEAFOOD
HUT POINTE INN
VILLA ALLAMANDA HOTEL
SEE "GOVERNORS HARBOUR" MAP
LEON LEVY NATURE PRESERVE
Governor's Harbour
PINEAPPLE FIELDS RESORT/ TIPPY'S RESTAURANT
EDWIN'S TURTLE LAKE MARINE RESERVE
QUEEN'S HWY
ELEUTHERA ISLAND FARM
TEN BAY BEACH
WINDMERE ISLAND
MERIDEN HWY
Winding Bay
ROCK SOUND AIRPORT
NORTHSIDE INN
CAPE ELEUTHERA RESORT AND MARINA
FRIGATE'S BAR AND GRILL
SAMMY'S PLACE
HARBOR POINTE RESTAURANT
ROCK SOUND OCEAN HOLE
MILLER'S DIVE SHOP/ OCEAN FOX COTTON BAY/ BLUE FLAG MARINA
SHERMAN'S HWY
Freetown
Greencastle
DAVIS HARBOUR MARINA
Lighthouse Point
0
10 mi
0
10 km
© MOON.COM

seemingly on the edge of the world, is Cape Eleuthera, an angler's dream.

Step into a scene from *Coastal Living* magazine in the color-splashed colonial town of Harbour Island, where visitors and residents cruise around in golf carts and ooze an air of sophistication. The island is home to the highest concentration of top restaurants in the country, and celebrity sightings are the norm. The fishing village of Spanish Wells is no longer a dry island, and now offers a selection of dining options and vacation rental cottages.

The variety of natural landscape and colonial towns of Eleuthera, along with welcoming locals, will keep you coming back.

PLANNING YOUR TIME

With direct international flights to North Eleuthera and Governor's Harbour, Eleuthera is an easy destination for a long weekend, but settle in and relax for at least a week if you can. Eleuthera, Harbour Island, and Spanish Wells are three distinct islands attracting different types of travelers. Although some choose to island-hop, most people pick one location and stay for the duration of their holiday. No matter where you decide to go, you'll fly into one of the airports on what's known as "mainland" Eleuthera. For glitz and glam as well as some of the country's best and most expensive restaurants and lodging, Harbour Island is a 5-minute land-taxi and a 10-minute water-taxi ride from North Eleuthera Airport. With heritage as an industrious fishing and boating community, Spanish Wells is a 20-minute land-taxi and a 10-minute water-taxi ride from North Eleuthera Airport.

On the mainland, you can chose from any number of large to small settlements. Nature enthusiasts will enjoy Gregory Town as a home base, with the option of dining and accommodations at The Cove Eleuthera, a luxurious resort escape, and exploring the top sights in the area. An hour south is centrally located Governor's Harbour. If you aren't up for the drive on the two-lane highway, opt to fly into Governor's Harbour Airport. A third airport is located farther south in sleepy Rock Sound. There you will find well-stocked grocery stores and a small selection of restaurants, but this less traveled area is specifically for those looking to escape and enjoy uncrowded beaches and quiet.

Rent a car to fully experience the natural wonders of the 110-mile-long island; exploring is one of the top activities. It will take you at least two hours to drive top to bottom, so keep that in mind if you chose to stay in Gregory Town and would like to visit Lighthouse Beach. Most restaurants and many hotels are closed during slow season (Oct.-Nov.) and locals retreat on their northern vacations, so plan accordingly. Eleuthera offers so many great restaurants and bars that you might be better off visiting in high season to fully experience it. The peak season is from Christmas and New Year's through Spring Break and Easter. Booking lodging, golf carts, and rental cars well ahead of time is essential during peak season.

ORIENTATION

One long road, Queen's Highway, runs north-south on the 110-mile-long island. From the northern point, Queen's Highway begins at a T intersection. To the west is Gene's Bay dock for Spanish Wells, and to the east is Preacher's Cave. Head south through the settlements of The Bluff and Upper and Lower Bogue. At the north end of Lower Bogue is the turnoff to the North Eleuthera Airport and Three Island Dock for Harbour Island. At the south end of Lower Bogue is a turnoff west to Current Settlement. Continue south through Gregory Town, Hatchet Bay, Rainbow Bay, James Cistern, and eventually Governor's Harbour. It's about an hour's drive from the North Eleuthera Airport to Governor's Harbour.

From Governor's Harbour, pass through Palmetto Point and Savannah Sound, where you'll see a turnoff to Windemere Island. Continue south through Tarpum Bay, where Queen's Highway turns into Meridian Highway, and then into Rock Sound, where

Meridian Highway turns into Sherman's Highway. Past Greencastle, Sherman's Highway ends at a T intersection. Turning right (north again) leads to Cape Eleuthera. Turning left leads toward Bannerman Town and Lighthouse Point.

Harbour Island is accessible by water taxi from Three Island Dock in North Eleuthera, a five-minute drive east of the North Eleuthera Airport. On Harbour Island, three main roads run north-south. Bay Street runs along the harbor side, where you depart the water taxi at Government Dock. The next street up is Dunmore Street, and the third street is Colebrook Street, which turns into Queen's Highway south of town and runs all the way to South Bar. Numerous other streets run in between these streets.

Spanish Wells is accessible by water taxi from Gene's Bay Dock in North Eleuthera, about 20 minutes' drive north of the North Eleuthera Airport and Lower Bogue. Spanish Wells has two main roads: South Street, which runs along the commercial harbor front, and Main Street (Samuel Guy St.), which runs along the northern side of the island. Both roads intersect and lead to Russel Island at the west end of Spanish Wells.

Gregory Town and North Eleuthera

The region's busiest airport is in North Eleuthera, and many islanders drive from the far south to catch the convenient daily direct flights to Miami, Fort Lauderdale, and Atlanta. North Eleuthera is the connection point for Harbour Island and Spanish Wells, but those looking for a quiet holiday opt to stay on the mainland and explore endless miles of beaches and remote natural beauty. Gregory Town is North Eleuthera's largest settlement, and the smaller communities of Alice Town at Hatchet Bay and Rainbow Bay dot the way toward Central Eleuthera.

The area was home to one of the largest farms, which provided most of the country's produce prior to the 1970s. The farm is no longer in operation, but there are still strong roots in the agricultural community. Small-production family-run organic farms have begun popping up in recent years, providing produce to local restaurants and grocery stores.

Along Queen's Highway, you'll see fields of the famous sweet Eleuthera pineapples surrounding the pineapple capital of Gregory Town, which is also home to the annual Pineapple Festival. For a swankier version of island life, head to The Cove Eleuthera and dine at their sushi bar with breathtaking ocean views.

SIGHTS

★ Preacher's Cave

Located on the northeastern point of the island is **Preacher's Cave,** a place steeped in history. The first European settlers arrived from Bermuda in 1648 seeking religious freedom and were shipwrecked on the nearby shore. With the rugged wind-blown landscape and limited natural resources, the refugees found shelter in this cave, which was eventually used for the first Christian religious services in The Bahamas, leading to its current name. They hand-shaped an altar out of a boulder in the cave, and it can still be seen today. Prior to European settlement, the cave was used as a burial ground for early indigenous Lucayans; charcoal remains from fire pits found in the cave date back to the 8th century AD. Other artifacts excavated by archeologists include pottery, cow and pig bones, pipe fragments, and various Lucayan and colonist burial remains. A petroglyph near the cave entrance resembles similar bull's-eye patterns observed in other parts of the Caribbean as well as Lucayan petroglyphs found on Rum Cay and Crooked Island.

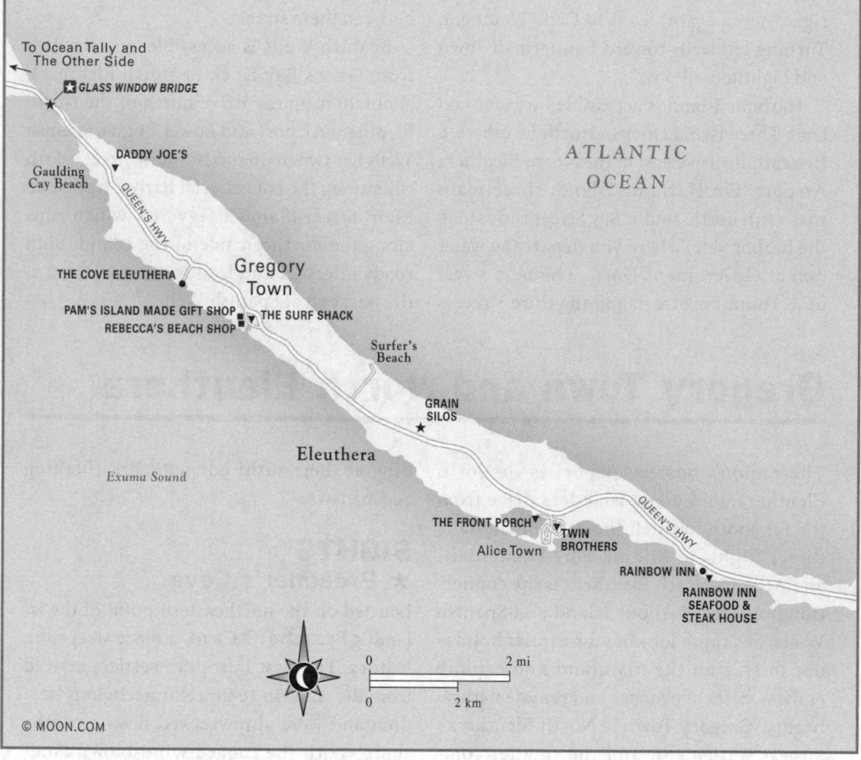

Eleuthera is home to numerous caves due to the limestone composition of its karst, which is cave, sinkhole, and ocean hole topography formed by the limestone dissolving in acidic rainwater. These formations are evident in the jagged shore throughout The Bahamas. The cave itself feels spacious and expansive, with a rounded ceiling 50 feet high and a large skylight in the roof providing light. The cave is only a few yards from Tay Bay Beach, so bring your swimsuit when visiting.

To get to the cave, head north on Queen's Highway until you hit a T intersection. To the left, the road takes you toward Gene's Bay Dock for Spanish Wells, and to the right is a paved road to the cave. It is well marked with signs, parking is available. There is no entrance fee, visitors center, restrooms, or facilities.

TOP EXPERIENCE

★ Glass Window Bridge

The **Glass Window Bridge** seems to divide two opposing worlds. The broad head of Eleuthera tapers down to a tiny strip of limestone, just 65 feet across at its narrowest point, separating the fury of the tumultuous Atlantic Ocean on one side and the shallow tranquil banks on the other side. The locals call the shallow side the "Caribbean" side; technically, however, it's far from the Caribbean Sea. You won't find a name for this water region on charts, but it is part of the Great Bahama Banks. To the east, the rocky headland drops 80 feet to the ocean. Below the surface, the shelf drops off immediately to 1,500 feet, and

Preacher's Cave

several miles offshore plummets even farther to 8,000 feet.

The term *Glass Window* dates to the 19th century and refers to a rock ledge that resembled a natural window. That rock feature has been destroyed by erosion and the fury of the sea, and the window is no longer evident. On a clear day you can navigate up the rocky shoreline for an elevated view of the bridge, which highlights the contrasting ocean colors. Wear proper shoes and be careful, as the limestone is jagged and sharp. The current constructed bridge replaced the natural stone bridge that was washed out in a hurricane. When the bridge was built, it had two lanes, but half of the bridge has since been washed out, so now it is a narrow one-lane bridge on which cars have to take turns crossing.

This area is prone to what Bahamians refer to as "rages," enormous rogue waves that sometimes reach 100 feet high as they are driven upward when they crash into the high, narrow cliffs. These waves can be evident on sunny, clear days, so caution is always to be taken, as they have been known to crash fiercely on the rock cliff and wash both people and vehicles into the ocean. These waves are so powerful that the rocks and the bridge itself have been moved around. On storm days, the bridge is often impassable, prohibiting any transit between North Eleuthera and Gregory Town. The bridge is four miles north of Gregory Town on Queen's Highway. From North Eleuthera Airport it is about 10 miles to the south. There is parking on the side of the road. There are no fees or facilities.

Grain Silos

Along Queen's Highway just before Hatchet Bay are towering ruins of grain silos on land that was once part of the Hatchet Bay Plantation. The nearby town is called Alice Town, but many refer to the area by the name Hatchet Bay. The farm was established in 1937 by an American named Austin Levy and was the base of a thriving agricultural community in North Eleuthera. The farm supplied the country with the majority of its milk, poultry, and eggs, and was one of The Bahamas' greatest successes.

However, upon gaining independence in the 1970s, the government replaced the management of numerous foreign-owned businesses, and many failed. The Hatchet Bay Plantation closed in the 1980s along with countless resorts. The once-booming economy of Eleuthera collapsed, and the island became the quiet rural community it is today. The only signs of its previous greatness are in ruins such as the grain silos. Some are completely covered in vines, but most are bare and make for great photos. The silos are spaced out along Queen's Highway on the three miles between Gregory Town and Hatchet Bay. Use caution when stopping to take photographs, as the road has no shoulder.

BEACHES

Surfer's Beach

With a consistent swell from the Atlantic Ocean, **Surfer's Beach** is one of the few surfing spots in The Bahamas. On the Atlantic

Ocean side just south of Gregory Town, the area has been gaining momentum as a fairly uncrowded spot. The beach itself is glorious for spectators, with white sand gently sloping upward to an elevated hillside. A point juts out and a reef creates a working break during the winter months. The Bone Yard is for experienced surfers only, as the shallow reef below threatens to "break your bones." For swimmers, be cautious of the current and stick within the protected cove at the north end of the beach. To get here, travel two miles south of downtown Gregory Town and look for the sign for Surfer's Manor. Turn east down that road. At the bottom is a T intersection. Turn left and then right onto the sandy road. A 4WD vehicle is recommended but not necessary. Just be cautious about getting stuck in the sand. There are no restrooms or facilities at this beach.

Located at Preacher's Cave on the north end of the island is **Tay Bay Beach.** The beach slopes gently into the ocean, and a constant swell crashes along the shore. During the winter, nor'easters pummel the beach, and there is fairly serious weather from time to time, but during the summer months, it's typically calm and lovely for swimming. Boaters from Harbour Island and Spanish Wells anchor and picnic on the beach. The land along the shoreline is all publicly owned and has remained completely undeveloped. The Devil's Backbone reef system runs just off shore.

Tay Bay Beach is a popular dive and snorkeling spot, but if you are snorkeling from the beach, use a visible dive flag or have a boat anchored nearby, as this area sees heavy boat traffic between Harbour Island and Spanish Wells. There is parking available at Preacher's Cave, but there are no facilities. To get to the beach, head north on Queen's Highway until you hit a T intersection. Turn right and follow the signs to Preacher's Cave.

If there is weather on the east side of the island, hit the beaches on the traditionally calm west side for afternoon sun and shallow-water swimming. **Gaulding Cay Beach** is one mile south of the Glass Window Bridge. Across from Daddy Joe's restaurant is a sandy dirt road marked with a "Beach Access" sign. There are several houses along the beach, but you'll usually find you have the sand to yourself. Casuarina pine trees provide shade, and at low tide the beach expands to sandy tidal flats. The tiny island of Gaulding Cay is located just off the beach and is accessed at low tide by wading through the shallow water. There are rocky features making for

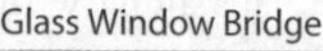

Glass Window Bridge

Gaulding Cay, just off Gaulding Cay Beach

interesting snorkeling. There is limited parking available, and no facilities.

ENTERTAINMENT AND EVENTS

Junkanoo (Eleuthera Tourist Office, tel. 242/332-2142, Harbour Island Tourist Office, tel. 242/333-2621) celebrations abound in Eleuthera during the holidays. In my opinion, the island versions of Junkanoo are the best ones. They are small and energetic and typically happen around 7pm-8pm. Spectators can dance alongside the parade, unlike in Nassau, where they sit in bleachers. Gregory Town and Tarpum Bay host a Junkanoo parade on the evening of Christmas Day, and Harbour Island's parades are on Boxing Day (Dec. 26th) and the evening of New Year's Day.

Harbourside Marine Bahamas Rotary Tuna Classic (Spanish Wells, www.bahamasrotaryfishing.com, Sat.-Sun. early June) is based in Nassau, with a weigh-in station in Spanish Wells. The event attracts local and international fishing enthusiasts who compete over a two-day period for the biggest tuna, wahoo, and mahimahi. The event includes women's and junior categories. An awards ceremony party and pig roast wrap up the weekend.

Spanish Wells Fishermen's Festival (Spanish Wells, www.fishermensfest.com, Fri.-Sat. mid-July) is a celebration of the fishing industry in Spanish Wells and is a send-off for the lobster-fishing boats that head out for the season on August 1. Events include food, dancing, and live music.

North Eleuthera Sailing Regatta (Harbour Island, tel. 242/333-3031, National Heroes Day weekend—Fri.-Mon. early Oct.) is one of the largest sailing regattas in The Bahamas, attracting the top sailing sloops in class A, B, and C categories from around the country.

Started in 1988, **The Eleuthera Pineapple Festival** (Gregory Town, Eleuthera Tourist Office, tel. 242/332-2142, Bahamas Labour Day Weekend—Thurs.-Sun. end of May-early June) celebrates the tradition of pineapple farming in Eleuthera. Events focus on the small sweet Eleuthera pineapples, including cooking contests, pineapple food and drinks, and pineapple-themed activities. There is also a 40-mile cycling race and the Pineappleman sprint triathlon.

SHOPPING

You can find a great selection of souvenirs and shell jewelry at **Rebecca's Beach Shop** (Queen's Hwy., Gregory Town, tel. 242/335-5436, daily 10am-5pm), but it's more of a surf shop. This is also the home of coveted Pirate's Revenge Hot Sauce. The operator, local resident Pete, named the shop after his wife, Rebecca. You can pick up surfboards to rent, and Pete is available to give surf lessons. The shop is tucked in the trees, and you'll be welcomed with beach debris and colorful old surfboards.

Pam's Island Made Shop (Queen's Hwy., Gregory Town, tel. 242/335-5369, Mon.-Sat. 9:30am-4:30pm) offers a great selection of island treasures, such as locally made hot sauces, jams, jellies, and soaps. You're in the pineapple capital of The Bahamas, so pineapple-themed gifts abound, including dish towels and charm jewelry. Eleuthera print shirts are also a popular souvenir, and you'll see both visitors and locals sporting long-sleeve and short-sleeve versions with the silhouette of the island.

SPORTS AND RECREATION

Surfing

Eleuthera has a variety of great surf spots, with beach breaks, point breaks, and reef breaks from Spanish Wells all the way to Rock Sound. October-April is peak surf season. Summertime rarely sees swell unless there's a hurricane. Gregory Town is the surfing hub, with the most popular and aptly named break at Surfer's Beach. Grab drinks and refuel at **The Surf Shack.** Rent surfboards and get surf lessons from **Rebecca's Beach Shop** (Queen's Hwy., Gregory Town, tel. 242/335-5436) or arrange your surf-themed getaway at **Surfer's Haven** (Eleuthera Island Shores, Gregory Town, tel. 242/335-0349, www.bahamasadventures.com), which caters to traveling surfers.

In conjunction with Surfer's Haven, **Bahamas Out Island Adventures** (Gregory Town, tel. 242/335-5436, www.bahamasadventures.com) offers surf lessons and one- to four-night camping surfaris. They also host surf camps for youths and teens in June-July that include surf lessons, yoga, painting and art projects, snorkeling, music, and other outdoor activities.

FOOD AND DRINK

North Eleuthera has limited dining options, but the down-home cooking and high-end dining are top notch. Most restaurants use locally grown produce and fresh seafood. Many places take credit cards, but some do not, so it's best to have cash. Even if an establishment normally takes cards, the electricity regularly fails, preventing them from running a credit card. Beware of the mosquitoes and no-see-ums (sandflies) in Eleuthera. They are apparent throughout the day, but at dawn and dusk can quickly drive people indoors. Most establishments have bug spray, but keep a bottle with you, especially if you make reservations for outdoor dining. Prices listed here reflect entrées and do not include the standard included 15 percent gratuity and 12 percent VAT (sales tax).

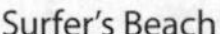

Surfer's Beach

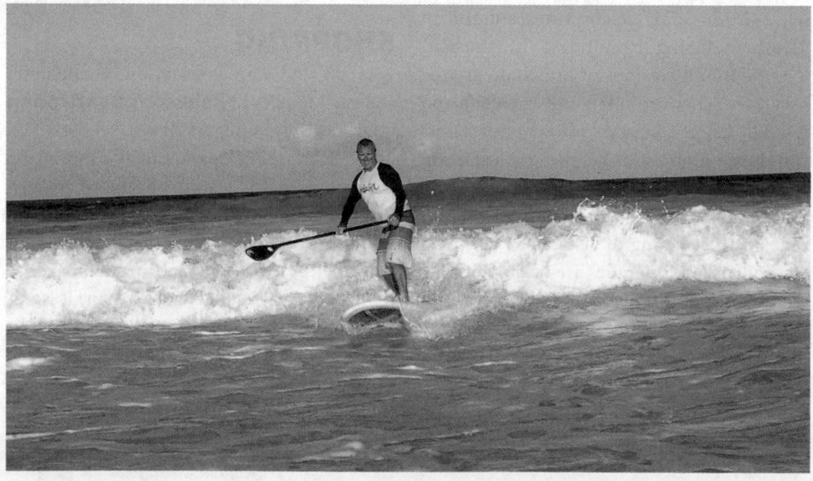

Bahamian

Perched on the protected harbor of Hatchet Bay with sweeping sunset views is **The Front Porch** (Queen's Hwy., Hatchet Bay, tel. 242/335-0727, daily lunch noon-3pm, dinner 5pm-9pm, $25-40). The welcoming wooden building is painted sunset pink with accents of green flash and Caribbean turquoise. Everything is made to order, and the owners are enthusiastic about making sure each patron has an experience to remember. Dine indoors in the air-conditioning or on cheerful teal chairs on the porch overlooking the harbor. Mouth-watering menu items include stone crab claws, jumbo shrimp over local greens with tropical fruit, and in season, grilled Calypso crawfish (Caribbean lobster). The Front Porch is pricey, but the food is consistently good and worth the splurge for a memorable experience. Reservations are advised.

Contemporary

One mile north of Gregory Town on the peaceful bank side, ★ **The Cove Eleuthera** (Queen's Hwy., Gregory Town, tel. 242/335-5141, U.S. tel. 866/644-4452, www.thecoveeleuthera.com, daily breakfast and lunch 7am-4pm, dinner 6pm-10pm, $30-45) serves breakfast, lunch, and dinner daily and offers both an elegant indoor dining room at the Freedom Restaurant and the shady veranda of the Gregory Town Grill, with sweeping views of the protected sandy beach and rugged coastline. This is the chicest dining option in Eleuthera but maintains a casual island feel. For breakfast, try a smoothie or an agua fresca. Lunch is organic beef burgers, grouper fish tacos, and vegetable flatbreads, or opt for the sushi menu, with a delicious selection of poke, nigari, and rolls such as tempura soft shell crab or barbecue eel. In the evening, start off at the Point Bar for a sunset cocktail, then meander indoors for a fusion take on tropical Bahamian dishes. The organic lettuces, herbs, tomatoes and peppers are grown on the property, and the seafood is locally sourced. Gluten-free, vegetarian, and vegan items are highlighted on the menu.

A great hangout to refuel after a surf session, ★ **The Surf Shack** (Queen's Hwy., Gregory Town, tel. 242/470-8369 or 242/556 4467, Thurs.-Mon. 8am-4pm, $15-20) is the new hot spot right in Gregory Town. The vibe is chill and the food fantastic. Breakfast and lunch are staples with surfy names, such as the Goofy Footed Burger, Cowabunga Burger, and Sea-Czar Salad. Daily specials range from

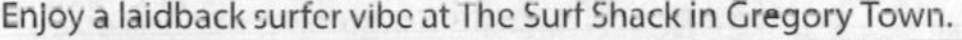
Enjoy a laidback surfer vibe at The Surf Shack in Gregory Town.

smoked fish dip, rice and bean cake, and seared tuna steak with a zingy cream sauce and roasted sliced tomatoes. Their food is fresh and healthy with plenty of options for vegetarians. The Surf Shack also serves cold beer and has a selection of specialty cocktails.

Perched on the hillside in the bedroom community of Rainbow Bay, 2.5 miles south of Hatchet Bay, **The Rainbow Inn Seafood & Steak House** (Queen's Hwy., Rainbow Bay, tel. 242/335-0294, www.rainbowinn.com, Mon. and Wed.-Sat. from 4pm, $15-30), a popular hangout featuring live music and dancing several nights per week in season, along with regularly televised sporting events. The screened-in veranda offers views of the lush surrounding coconut palms and expansive ocean views. Monday is Pizza Night, with thin-crust wood-fired pizza with organic toppings. Saturday is Argentinean Grill Night, with grilled, smoked, and braised meats and poultry. The high-quality steaks are flown in from Chicago twice a week and are never frozen. Order a steak on its own, or split a surf-and-turf platter for two with Bahamian lobster tail, a 14-ounce steak, and fresh fish. Try a delicious salad, featuring greens grown and picked daily from the on-site farm. Call ahead for reservations.

Bars & Pubs

Daddy Joe's (Queen's Hwy., Gregory Town, tel. 242/335-6878, Tues.-Thurs. and Sat. 11:30am-10pm, Fri. and Sun. 3pm-10pm, $20-30) is a popular hangout for live music and tasty Bahamian soul food. One mile south of the Glass Window Bridge, across from Gaulding Cay Beach, it's a big block of a building off Queen's Highway with no ocean views, but come for drinking and dancing. The decor is no-frills, but the colorful hand-painted signs featuring favorite bar quotes and Bahama-isms are charming. Try the Chicken in Da Bag or a conch burger with Bahamian sides like peas-and-rice, baked macaroni, sweet plantain, or cole slaw, and wash it down with a tasty Gregory Town mojito. The popular High Rock Band plays regularly, and specialty nights include Taco and Tequila Tuesday and Winging It Wednesday.

Sleepy Hatchet Bay doesn't have a lot of tourism, but it's home to the internationally famous restaurant and bar **Twin Brothers** (off Queen's Hwy., Hatchet Bay, tel. 242/335-0730, www.twinbrothersbahamas.com). The McCardy twins were born and raised in Eleuthera and eventually migrated to Nassau where they started the successful Twin Brother's World Famous Daiquiris. They continued to open restaurants, the most well-known at the Fish Fry at Arawak Cay, but there are four locations in Nassau and the newest one here in Hatchet Bay. The menu offers plenty of Bahamian favorites as well as burgers, sandwiches, salads, steaks, seafood, and pastas. Try the potent homemade Sky Juice ($6), a mix of gin, coconut water, and Coco Lopez.

ACCOMMODATIONS

Under $100

A budget place to stay with a fun surfer vibe, is **Surfer's Haven** (Eleuthera Island Shores, Gregory Town, tel. 242/335-0349, www.bahamasadventures.com), just south of Gregory Town overlooking Surfer's Beach. They offer private apartments ($80 pp), studios ($60 pp), and tent sites with tent included ($40 pp). The studio rooms have a shared bath and a communal kitchen. The upstairs apartment has a kitchenette, a private bath, and a balcony with spectacular views. The hotel owners run Bahamas Out Island Adventures, so you can organize surfboard rentals, surfing lessons, snorkeling, hiking, and kayaking.

$150-250

The Rainbow Inn (Queen's Hwy., Rainbow Bay, tel. 242/335-0294, www.rainbowinn.com, $135) is a small boutique resort in a grove of tropical palms overlooking the ocean on the peaceful western side of the island. The ocean- and garden-view suites are cozy, colorful, and laid-back. The private beach at the bottom of the hill is a popular spot for destination weddings, with privacy and intimacy for a chic island event. The inn features free in-room Wi-Fi, a saltwater pool, and seaside tennis courts. Amazing reef snorkeling is just off the front, and the inn offers guests complimentary snorkel gear. The on-site restaurant serves breakfast for guests and top-notch steaks and locally grown organic greens. Rainbow Bay is mostly vacation cottages with no services, but within minutes you can be in Hatchet Bay or Gregory Town.

Over $250

Luxurious, dreamy, soothing, and unspoiled, the internationally acclaimed ★ **The Cove Eleuthera** (Queen's Hwy., Gregory Town, tel. 242/335-5141, U.S. tel. 866/644-4452, www.thecoveeleuthera.com, $343) is in a tropical landscape of towering coconut palms interlaced with inviting hammocks. A manicured lawn leads to the private pink-sand beach on the calm western side of Eleuthera. On either side of the beach within the protected cove is rocky bluff coastline. Rooms are whitewashed wood, with crisp white 500 thread-count linens, and each of the cove guest rooms, suites, villas, and cottages offer air-conditioning, 50 inch flat screen TVs, wireless internet, safes, and Nespresso coffeemakers. Rooms are just steps from the restaurant, pool, and beach. Chairs, beach towels, and umbrellas are available for a perfect beach day. Stay active with complimentary paddleboards, kayaks, snorkel gear, and beach cruisers, along with a 24-hour fitness center, a hilltop infinity pool, a games room with billiards tables, and a movie theater where you can arrange private screenings. The resort will also assist you with arranging fishing and boat charters; land tours around Eleuthera, Harbour Island, and Spanish Wells; or a seaplane charter to other islands in The Bahamas.

Ocean Tally (Whale Point Dr., Whale Point, tel. 242/359-7676, $375) is for those looking to truly get away from it all. Three newly built cottages with private balconies overlooking the Atlantic Ocean are breezy and inviting, featuring plush king beds, private baths, flat-screen TVs, and air-conditioning. The restaurant only caters to guests. The coastline below the cottages and restaurant is rugged and rocky, and on calm evenings, guests huddle around a fire pit while the waves crash below. Scale the circular restaurant building and enjoy panoramic views of the ocean, Bottom Harbour, and Harbour Island. On the Bottom Harbour side is a private beach for guests, with a calm shallow protected harbor teeming with turtles and

the tranquil beach at The Cove Eleuthera

starfish. Paddleboards are available to explore the sealife. There is typically a three-night minimum, but they may take one- or two-night bookings during the slow season.

Already internationally recognized by luxe travel magazines, newly opened **The Other Side** (Bottom Harbour, Whale Point, www.ontheos.com, $600) is a boutique collaboration of a visionary young couple. Ben, originally from Harbour Island, and Charlie also run the chic Ocean View Club and specialize in weddings and events. The Other Side is their latest project, an off-the-grid place featuring seven gloriously appointed spacious "tents" with hardwood floors, king beds, air-conditioning, and rain showers, along with three "shacks," with large sundecks and four-poster king beds. The 30-foot skiff will pick you up and deliver you to Harbour Island within minutes for shopping, dining, and socializing, but the evenings are for peace and solitude. The three rate seasons are low, high, and peak. There is a three-night minimum during low and high season, and seven nights during peak. Rates include daily housekeeping, use of vehicles in Harbour Island and Eleuthera, breakfast, snacks, tea, and coffee.

INFORMATION AND SERVICES

Visitor Information

If you're interested in connecting with a Bahamian ambassador to learn more about the culture and lifestyle, contact the **People-to-People Program** (tel. 242/367-3067, www.bahamas.com/people-to-people). Advance reservations to pair you with an ambassador are recommended.

Banks

Larger hotels and resorts take credit cards, but many of the mom-and-pop restaurants do not, so make sure you have cash. Often the ATM is out of cash, and the power fails regularly, making credit card machines go down. There is a bank in Harbour Island and two in Governor's Harbour, but none in North Eleuthera.

Health and Emergencies

Clinics on the island are operated by nurses and typically offer limited services. For major medical emergencies, the clinics will arrange transport to **Princess Margaret Hospital** in Nassau or an airlift to the United States. Try **The Gregory Town Community Clinic** (tel. 242/335-5108, Mon.-Fri. 9am-5pm except public holidays). For emergency services, contact the **Royal Bahamas Police Force Fire and Police** (tel. 919). For directory assistance dial 916, and weather dial 915.

Media and Communications

Internet and cell service in Eleuthera, Harbour Island, and Spanish Wells are some of the best in the country. All resorts and hotels, and most vacation rentals, have reliable internet through Cable Bahamas or Bahamas Telecommunications Corporation (BTC). BTC has many cell towers and limited users, so service rarely drops, and data is quick and reliable. To pick up a cell phone with prepaid minutes while you are visiting, **BTC** has offices in Governor's Harbour (tel. 242/332-2476), Rock Sound (tel. 242/334-2131), Harbour Island (tel. 242/333-2375), and Spanish Wells (tel. 242/333-4053).

You may be able to pick up some radio stations from Nassau, but the local radio station is **Splash FM 89.9,** broadcasting a mix of Bahamian music, reggae, country, and pop from Spanish Wells. Upon arrival, pick up the biannual ***Eleutheran Magazine*** for articles, maps, shopping, and dining guides, and ***The Eleutheran*** (www.eleutheranews.com) newspaper for local news.

GETTING THERE

Air

There are a minimum of seven flights per day from Nassau to North Eleuthera, and more flights are added in high season. Bahamasair is the largest commercial carrier but only offers one flight per day, scheduled at a different time each day. Pineapple Air and Southern Air run smaller twin-propeller planes but are almost always on time and offer more flight times.

FROM NASSAU

Bahamasair (tel. 242/702-4140, www.bahamasair.com) has one flight per day at various times. **Pineapple Air** (ELH tel. 242/335-2081, NAS tel. 242/377-0140, www.pineappleair.com) offers three to five morning and afternoon flights daily from Nassau. **Southern Air** (ELH tel. 242/335-1720, NAS tel. 242/377-2014, www.southernaircharter.com) offers three morning and afternoon flights daily from Nassau. **Bahama Hoppers** (tel. 242/335-1650, www.bahamahoppers.com) offers five daily passenger charter flights from Odyssey Aviation in Nassau to White Crown Aviation in North Eleuthera, next door to the main airport terminal.

FROM THE UNITED STATES

North Eleuthera has a fantastic selection of daily direct flights from the United States. Immigration and customs are a breeze, and many people opt to spend the extra money on tickets to avoid the connecting flight and lay over time traveling through Nassau.

Silver Airways (U.S. tel. 801/401-9100, www.silverairways.com) offers daily direct flights from Fort Lauderdale. **American Airlines** (U.S. tel. 800/433-7300, www.aa.com) offers daily direct flights from Miami. **Delta** (U.S. tel. 800/241-4141, www.delta.com) has daily direct flights from Atlanta in high season. **Aztec Airways** (U.S. tel. 954/601-3742, www.aztecairways.com) offers flights on Monday, Friday, and Saturday from Fort Lauderdale Executive Airport.

Boat

Alice Town, whose motto is "Home to the Country's Safest Harbour," is often referred to as Hatchet Bay, the name of the protected harbor it surrounds. The harbor is not hurricane-proof, as many locals claim, but it offers great protection from winter cold fronts. The harbor was created in the 1940s when a 90-foot opening was dug to access the protected pond. There is no marina, but there are free government mooring balls. For anchoring holding is grassy bottom.

The Bahamas Fast Ferry (tel. 242/323-2166, www.bahamasferries.com) travels from Nassau to Current Settlement ($52 round-trip) on Friday and Sunday on the MV *East Wind* or *Seawind* freight boats, and on Tuesday into Three Island Dock.

GETTING AROUND

A lineup of taxi drivers will be waiting at North Eleuthera airport. Depending on where you are headed, you may want to take a taxi, settle in, and get the lay of the land before renting a car. The taxis are also happy to be your driver and shuttle you around for several hours or for the day.

Taxi

Owner Fred Neely of **Fine Threads** (tel. 242/359-7780 or 242/436-5989) has several large vans in his fleet and can accommodate groups. He can also assist with rental cars. Call or find him at the airport. Amos Johnson of **Amos at Your Service** (tel. 242/422-9130) has a large van.

Rental Car

If you're interested in renting a car and exploring on your own, there are plenty of options. North Eleuthera doesn't have brand-name rental companies, but local companies operate self-drive franchises. Ask around to get a rental car once you get here. Everyone knows everyone, so you could even ask at the airline counter or one of the taxi drivers. The cars are usually well-used and have plenty of dents. Use caution when driving. Queen's Highway is a narrow two-lane road, and people tend to speed and pass. The roads are filled with dangerous potholes, and drivers often swerve to miss them. Drinking and driving accidents at night cause fatalities throughout the year due to the extended distances between bars and lodging. Average rental car prices are $75 per day. Remember to drive on the left, which may add another element of adventure to your Eleuthera experience.

For car rentals, contact **'Lutra Car Rental** (tel. 242/424-8133, www.lutracar.com) or family run **Johnson's Car Rental** (tel. 242/470-8235), who own the service station in Lower Bouge. Michelle has several fuel-efficient vehicles available for island exploration.

Hitchhiking

Hitchhiking is acceptable and common in Eleuthera, where many people don't have cars. You'll often see pickup truck beds filled with hitchhiking passengers. Some visitors, especially the surfer crowd, opt to use this method as a budget means of travel.

Governor's Harbour and Central Eleuthera

Governor's Harbour is the oldest remaining settlement in The Bahamas. Several months after wrecking at Preacher's Cave, some of the settlers migrated south and set up a base at Cupid's Cay, a strip of land that arches around Governor's Harbour. The settlers who stayed in Preacher's Cave established a nearby settlement that was eventually burned by the Spanish, giving Governor's Harbor claim to the oldest settlement. Along a ridge that slopes toward the calm harbor on the west and the Atlantic on the east, historical buildings abound, including Loyalist cottages and ruins of the old jail, dating back 200 years. Governor's Harbour offers a wonderful mix of resorts with fine dining, beautiful stretches of untouched beaches, and the Leon Levy Nature Preserve.

SIGHTS

★ Leon Levy Nature Preserve

Operated by the Bahamas National Trust, the **Leon Levy Nature Preserve** (Banks Rd., Governor's Harbour, tel. 242/332-3831, www.levypreserve.org, year-round daily 9am-5pm, $10 adults, $6 under age 13) protects 25 acres of forest, mangroves, and rocky coppice with the goal of conserving Bahamian native biodiversity and exploring bush medicine. Established by Shelby White in honor of her late husband, Leon Levy, miles of well-kept trails meander through native plants and trees.

At the facility's welcome center, get bird and arthropod guides as well as a trail map and a brief description of the different trails. Head to the elevated Mangrove Boardwalk, which takes you directly into a mix of buttonwood and red, black, and white mangrove forest and swampland. The roots of the red mangrove turn organic matter into peat, giving the water a shocking rusty red color. Next is the Medicinal Trail, which organizes plants based on the ailments they treat, including sunburn, pain, high blood pressure, diabetes, and fever; some blends are claimed to be beneficial in treating cancer. More than 200 plant species are used for medicinal purposes in The Bahamas, including aloe vera, cerasee, fever grass, breadfruit, soursop, and guinep. Bahamian bush medicine has been passed down from the earliest African settlers. Usually the leaves are dried and made into hot tea.

Farther along is the freshwater wetland. A cistern on the property was converted into a pond, and with the help of a landscape architect, the wetland now includes a concrete trail that dissects the pond, passing through clumping waterlilies filled with friendly turtles that will swim right up to you: a fantastic photo opportunity. Continue on Ethan's Tower Loop to scale a wooden tower 75 feet above sea level with panoramic views of the ocean and the surrounding tree canopy. After your trek, head to the gift shop for additional reading on local plants and wildlife, crafts, and Levy Preserve apparel.

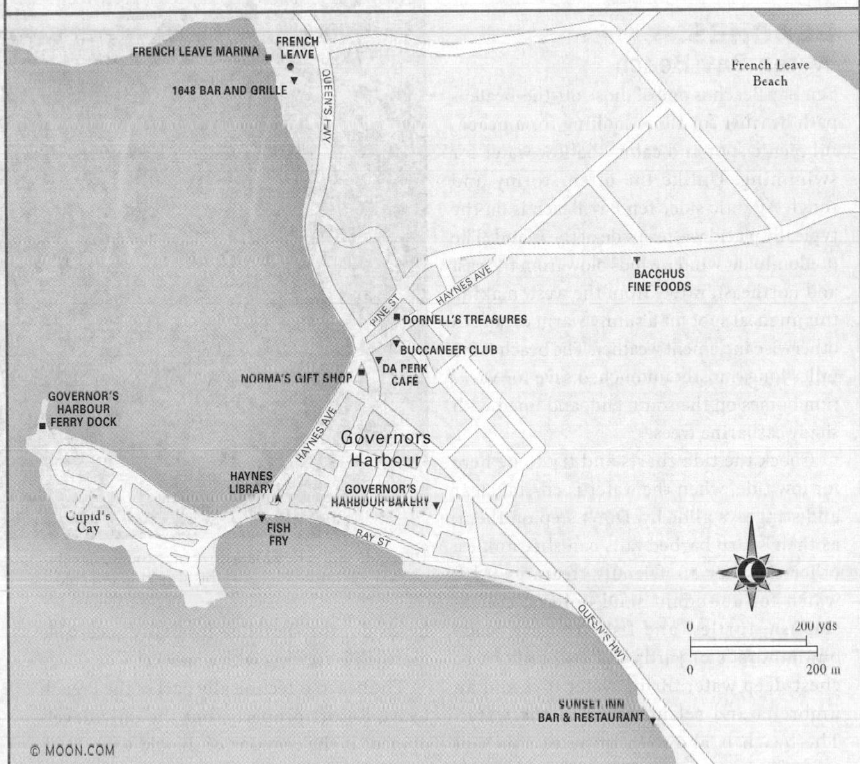

Cupid's Cay

Cupid's Cay is connected to downtown Governor's Harbour by a narrow strip of sandy beach and a one-way loop road. See the oldest buildings in The Bahamas, including the two-cell jail that dates back 200 years, the location of the first Bahamas Parliament from 1746, and the 1897 Haynes Library. Today the cay is a commercial center with a mix of retail stores and a shipping dock. The cay protects the calm, shallow harbor. You'll often see shallow-water skiffs running about across the harbor, but due to the lack of depth and decent holding, it isn't a popular sailboat anchorage.

Haynes Library

The **Haynes Library** (Haynes Ave. and Bay St., Governor's Harbour, tel. 242/332-2877, Mon.-Thurs. 9am-6pm, Fri. 9am-5pm, Sat. 10am-4pm) was built in 1897 and is the oldest government complex on the island. It fell into disrepair until a volunteer organization called Friends of the Library stepped in and restored it to its present status, reopening as a full-time functioning library in 1996. The library is an integral part of the community and is supported by volunteers who include Bahamians, winter residents, and high school students. An extensive selection of books, including a collection of Bahamian history and literature, is here, along with art classes, summer programs, help with homework, computer and internet access, literacy programs, and story hours. Funds are raised through donations and events such as Eleuthera's All That Jazz Festival.

BEACHES

★ Ten Bay Beach

Ten Bay Beach is one of those off-the-beaten-path beaches for those looking for a peaceful picnic spot and calm, shallow water for swimming. Unlike the often stormy and rough Atlantic side, Ten Bay Beach is on the typically placid western side of the island. The predominant winter winds blow from the east and northeast, rarely from the west, making this an ideal spot for a sunny warm escape in otherwise inclement weather. The beach is 0.5 miles long, mostly untouched save for vacation homes on the south end, and lined with shady casuarina trees.

Check the tide charts and try to be here for low tide, when the water is crystal clear and stingrays glide by. Don't step on them, as their sharp barbed tails can slice ankles; otherwise they are friendly creatures. Also watch for abundant sand dollars, conch, starfish, turtles, and fish. You can wade out hundreds of yards and still only be in chest-deep water. Bring water toys and an umbrella and set up camp in the water. The beach is about 15 minutes south of Governor's Harbour, about 0.75 miles past the turnoff for Surfer's Haven. Look for a "Beach Access" sign on the right and follow a bumpy road west. You don't need a 4WD vehicle, but use caution when navigating the sandy, narrow, bumpy road. There are places to park but no facilities. For a peaceful beach getaway, this a great place to look for a vacation rental home.

French Leave Beach

The Atlantic side of the Eleuthera Islands has some of the most beautiful beaches in the world. The pink-sand French Leave Beach is on par with the world-famous Pink Sands Beach in Harbour Island but is must less trafficked. The broad expanse of powdery sand gently slopes into the ocean and stretches for a mile northwest to southeast. Rocky coral heads dot the shoreline for easily accessible marinelife viewing with a snorkel.

The roots of the Red Mangrove give the marsh at Leon Levy Nature Preserve this shocking red color.

The beach is technically part of the French Leave Resort property, but the only development is the remains of the old Club Med, destroyed by Hurricane Floyd in 1999, and a few private homes and vacation rentals at the south end. French Leave guests use the beach, but you will only encounter a few other people, even on a crowded day. Follow the road directly across Queens Highway from French Leave Resort toward the east to find parking and beach access. There are no facilities.

ENTERTAINMENT AND EVENTS

Friday Night Fish Fry

Every week throughout the year, the Governor's Harbour Development Association hosts a **Friday Night Fish Fry** (Bay St. and Haynes Ave., Governor's Harbour, tel. 242/332-2467) at Anchor Bay in Governor's Harbour. Starting at around 6pm, head down for tasty conch salad, fried chicken, fish, peas-and-rice, and traditional Bahamian sides as well as the popular Rum Bubba, a mix of fruit punch, ginger ale, pineapple juice, and rum. The event attracts locals and visitors, and is the social outing of the week for many residents. Later in the evening, music starts pumping and dancing ensues. The proceeds go to the Annual Homecoming and various projects in the community.

Sky Beach Club Sunday Barbecue and Pool Party

Weather permitting, every Sunday 3pm-7pm at **Pascal's** (Queen's Hwy., tel. 242/332-3422, www.skybeachclub.com) is the Barbecue and Pool Party. They serve either barbecue chicken and fish or a whole roast pig. Cost ranges $17-19. This comes with a hearty serving of meat and two sides, which include peas-and-rice, cole slaw, macaroni, potato salad, or green salad. Live music by local bands accompanies this event.

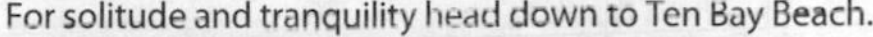

Other Events

Junkanoo (Eleuthera Tourist Office, tel. 242/332-2142, Harbour Island Tourist Office, tel. 242/333-2621) celebrations abound in Eleuthera during the holidays. In my opinion, the island versions of Junkanoo are the best ones. They are small and energetic and typically happen around 7pm-8pm. Spectators can dance alongside the parade, unlike in Nassau, where they sit in bleachers. Governor's Harbour has a Junkanoo festival during Majority Rule holiday weekend (1st weekend in Jan.), which includes concerts, parades, and marching bands, a rush-out, and gospel music over the course of four days.

Ride for Hope (Governor's Harbour, www.rideforhopebahamas.com, beginning of Mar.) is a bicycle-ride fund-raiser for cancer research, care centers, and treatment programs in The Bahamas. The minimum fund-raising donation for all riders is $500, and the event attracts hundreds of participants. The ride starts and ends in Governor's Harbour. There are various lengths, from 10 miles to 100 miles, and an all-day festival for riders and supporters.

Eleuthera All That Jazz Festival (Governor's Harbour, www.eleutheraallthatjazz.com, Thurs.-Mon. end of Mar.-early Apr.) is an annual event featuring Bahamian and international jazz musicians that is used to promote tourism on Eleuthera. All proceeds go to the Haynes Library.

For solitude and tranquility head down to Ten Bay Beach.

SHOPPING

Eleuthera Island Farm (Queen's Hwy., Palmetto Point, tel. 242/332-0141, low season Mon.-Sat. 9am-4pm, high season Mon.-Sat. 9am-4pm, Sat. 9am-6pm) is located on 10 lush acres just south of Governor's Harbour and provides locally grown, organic, non-GMO produce. About 7 acres of land is cultivated at any given time in lettuce, tomatoes, root vegetables, squash, and herbs. They create their own soil by composting. In-house they make sauces, jams, and jellies with repurposed beer bottles, as well as pickles, dips, relish, salad dressing, quinoa salad, soups, hummus, and pesto. Eggs are sourced from a nearby chicken farm. Don't miss bread days, where they bake homemade French baguette and sourdough loaves. Bread baking days are Tuesday and Friday.

Directly across from the Buccaneer Club, **Dornell's Treasures** (Haynes Ave., Governor's Harbour, tel. 242/332-2932, Mon.-Sat. 9am-5pm) is owned and operated by Dorothy Rahming and features her own hand-paintings of island life, along with decorative wreaths, handwoven straw crafts, driftwood and shell art, and Kalik T-shirts. **Norma's Gift Shop** (Queen's Hwy., Governor's Harbour, tel. 242/332-2002, Mon.-Sat. 9am-6pm) is in a bright-yellow building right off Queen's Highway. The variety of items includes duty-free perfumes, jewelry, and handbags as well as clothing and resort wear.

SPORTS AND RECREATION

Kayaking

Tucked between rolling hills and dynamic land features 2.5 miles south of Governor's Harbour is **Edwin's Turtle Lake Marine Reserve** (Queen's Hwy., Governor's Harbour, tel. 242/470-3001, www.edwinsmarinepreserve.com, call for reservations), where three generations of the Burrows family have maintained a sanctuary for turtles, lobsters, and fish. The lake is connected to the ocean by underwater caverns, making it a saltwater hideout for marinelife. Rent kayaks and paddleboards and explore the lake. Paddleboards and kayaks start at $30 per hour.

FOOD

Bahamian

Sunset Inn Bar & Restaurant (Queen's Hwy., Governor's Harbour, tel. 242/332-3487, Fri.-Wed. 9am-3pm and 5pm-9pm, $15-20) is a longtime favorite offering Bahamian

Stop in for seasonal, locally grown organic produce at Eleuthera Island Farm.

downhome cooking with American staples. For breakfast, try the omelets, Bahamian souse, or boiled fish with Johnnycake and corned beef with grits. Lunch is a mix of burgers and sandwiches, and dinner offers hearty meat and seafood entrées served with peas-and-rice, baked or mashed potatoes, and salad or coleslaw. The dining room is open and airy with panoramic views of the ocean. Sit outdoors on the deck if the bugs aren't heavy.

The Deck (Knowles Dr., Governor's Harbour, tel. 242/535-8283, hours vary, $15-25) is open-air, eclectic, serving a mix of Bahamian and American food, including fried conch fritters, fresh caught fish sandwiches, and tasty cheeseburgers. It also has a true beach bar, complete with beach debris and treasures in every corner. It is located on a beautiful stretch of beach five miles north of Governor's Harbour. The owner is a bit of a firecracker, but if you're in the right mood, he can provide entertainment. Be sure to ask for a specialty cocktail; it will be whipped up with every fruit on hand. It may be a little pricier than you expect for this type of venue, but it's worth a stop at least for a cold Kalik.

Contemporary

No trip to Eleuthera is complete without a stop off at ★ **Tippy's Restaurant & Beach Bar** (Banks Rd., Governor's Harbour, tel. 242/332-3331, www.pineapplefields.com, Tues.-Sun. lunch noon-2:30pm, dinner 5:30pm-9pm, bar all day, $15-25). Across the road from Pineapple Fields, this well-known establishment has been drawing the beach bar crowd for years with fresh homemade meals, ocean views, and live entertainment. The open-air restaurant is painted in primary yellow and blue, and the shady dining area overlooks a beautiful stretch of Atlantic beach. Interior whitewashed walls and colorful wood beams accented with string lighting make this a laid back welcoming spot. On Saturday evenings, a crowd of winter residents jams to a local band. The menu changes daily but can include salads with local organic greens, beet salad, homemade pizza pies, homemade conch ravioli, spring rolls, and lasagna.

Buccaneer Club (Haynes Ave., Governor's Harbour, tel. 242/332-2000, daily 7am-9pm, $15-20) is a welcoming country-style diner right in Governor's Harbour on the one-way road heading toward the Atlantic side. The outdoor deck is built around a massive old world lebbeck tree (similar to the poinciana), giving a touch of nature within the bustling town. Try the tasty Bahamian and Caribbean

Tippy's Restaurant & Beach Bar serves a rotating menu of tasty and healthy fare.

fare with fresh ingredients, such as cracked conch with macaroni, a personal favorite, and the lobster salad. Spice it up with house-made hot sauce and wash it down with a cold Goombay Punch (nonalcoholic sweet soda).

A few minutes north of Governor's Harbour, within the expansive Sky Beach property that slopes down the hillside toward the Atlantic, is **Pascal's Oceanfront Seafood Restaurant & Pool Bar** (Sky Beach Club, Queen's Hwy., Governor's Harbour, tel. 242/332-3422, www.skybeachclub.com, Tues., Thurs., and Sat. noon-9pm, Wed., Fri., and Sun. noon-7pm, lunch $15-20, dinner $25-40). The bar and restaurant are next to the pool deck, and you'll often find a crowd of cocktail patrons floating in the pool, occasionally drifting over to the swim-up bar for a refill. The tiki-style decor compliments daytime bar food, including quesadillas, sandwiches, and pizzas. Try the french fries served in a skillet smothered in melted cheese with sliced jalapeños. Dinner is ahi tuna tartare, stone crab pasta, and grilled rack of lamb. Stop by on Sunday for the Barbecue Pool Party.

Named for the arrival date of the original settlers, **1648 An Island Restaurant** (French Leave Resort, Queen's Hwy., Governor's Harbour, tel. 242/332-3777, www.frenchleaveresort.com, daily 7am-10pm, $20-35) is on the French Leave property with unobstructed views of Governor's Harbour and Cupid's Cay. The elegant shaded veranda perched above the harbor and the pool deck are the best spots in town to catch the sunset. Breakfast offers island-inspired lobster benedict and pineapple island pancakes with guava syrup; lunch is healthy burgers, wraps, and pizzas. For dinner, try the conch rangoons, goat-cheese crusted beef tenderloin, or locally caught grouper. Items are available for vegetarian and vegan patrons, and there is a great selection of international wines and Caribbean rum.

Cafés and Light Bites

The organic gourmet market ★ **Bacchus Fine Foods** (Banks Rd., Governor's Harbour, tel. 242/470-6563, Mon.-Wed. and Fri. 9am-6pm, Sat. 9am-4pm, $15-25) is tucked in a quiet courtyard on Banks Road, just before Pineapple Fields, with hand-selected grocery items from around the world as well as local produce, sauces, oils, spreads, coffee, fresh baked bread and pastries, European imported meats, cheeses, and wines. The café serves a beautiful selection of healthy gourmet items such as roasted duck and sautéed chorizo on baguette as well as plenty of vegetarian options, such as curried chickpeas and grilled eggplant stuffed with buffalo mozzarella.

Da Perk Café (Queen's Hwy., Governor's Harbour, tel. 242/332-2620, Mon.-Sat. 8am-4pm) is the local coffee shop that serves up gourmet espresso, fresh squeezed juices and smoothies, and breakfast sandwiches. Right on Queen's Highway in town, it's a great spot to watch the world go by. **Governor's Harbour Bakery** (Tucker Lane, tel. 242/332-2071, Mon.-Fri. 7am-5pm, Sat. 7am-2pm) serves freshly baked doughnuts, muffins, and breads. For something savory, try the chicken or beef patties. It's tricky to find, but look two streets west of RBC bank on Queen's Highway.

ACCOMMODATIONS

$150-250

★ **Pineapple Fields Resort** (Banks Rd., Governor's Harbour, tel. 242/332-3331, www.pineapplefields.com, $249) is one of the most popular destinations, and for good reason. Located on quiet Banks Road, just a few minutes from town, the resort is across from a glorious stretch of beach that provides endless miles of exploration. On five pristine acres, Pineapple Fields is a collection of daffodil-yellow one- and two-bedroom condos with full kitchens and front and back verandas. Adjoining the property on the ocean side is the famous Tippy's Restaurant & Beach Bar, and a short walk down the road is the Leon Levy Nature Preserve. The resort will assist you with organizing land and sea tours, water sports, babysitting services, and grocery delivery.

Atop a ridgeline overlooking the ocean

Peppers and Hot Sauces

Try local Eleuthera specialty hot sauces, such as Pirates' Revenge.

Bahamians are serious about their hot sauces and hot peppers. The most common pepper is the wrinkly orange Bahamian **goat pepper,** which is a cousin to Scotch bonnet, typically found in Jamaican cooking, and habanero. Goat pepper is 12 to 140 times hotter than jalapeño. One-quarter teaspoon of the chopped pepper is enough to set fire to your entire dish. It has great flavor when put whole into stews (without puncturing the skin to release the heat), and its sweet flavor is used in most Bahamian hot sauces. Be extremely cautious when using it. If you touch the inside flesh with your fingers, wash your hands immediately and don't put your fingers near your eyes or other sensitive areas; the burn will spread.

Bird peppers, which are slightly less fiery than goat pepper, are tiny and oblong and come in an assortment of red, orange, yellow, and green. They are known to have numerous health benefits. **Green finger pepper** is an immature red chili pepper and is used along with goat pepper in hot sauces. The lesser utilized **ghost pepper** is known as the hottest pepper in the world.

You will find locally produced hot sauces everywhere in The Bahamas. The Bahamian Pepper Sour, packaged in recycled Kalik bottles, is a fairly mild and flavorful liquid made with goat pepper and lime, to be served over souses. **Crazy Frank's** is one of the hottest hot sauces you can find, sold in repurposed Gerber baby food jars with homemade labels. You can find it in shops in Spanish Wells or Dilly Dally in Harbour Island, or just flag down Crazy Frank when you see him buzz by in his personalized golf cart. Another favorite is the delicious **Pirates' Revenge,** resembling a Jamaican jerk flavor and bottled in a hip flask. It is produced and sold at Rebecca's Beach Shop in Gregory Town, but you can find it at retail establishments throughout the area, including Captain Bob's grocery store in Harbour Island.

is the boutique **Villa Allamanda Hotel** (Jacaranda Dr., Governor's Harbour, tel. 242/332-3934, www.villaallamanda.com, $234). Queen and king studios, suites, and cottages are decorated in bright island colors. Local artwork adorns the walls, painted in sunset oranges, yellows, blues, and greens. It is a 15-minute walk to Twin Coves beach, a beautiful protected whale-tail feature, and a few minutes farther south is French Leave Beach.

Over $250

Eight minutes north of Governor's Harbour, **Hut Pointe Inn** (Queen's Hwy., Governor's Harbour, tel. 242/332-3530, www.hutpointe.com, $255) is a charming family-owned resort with seven suites on lush grounds. The eco-friendly updates include solar hot-water heating, a rainwater collecting cistern, and an on-site organic vegetable garden. The inn was built in 1944 of solid stone and still retains its historical character. The suites have two bedrooms, with kings in the master and two twins in the other. Each unit has large living rooms, a full-service kitchen, a dining area, and balconies on the second-floor suites.

Sky Beach Club (Queen's Hwy., Governor's Harbour, tel. 242/332-3422, www.skybeachclub.com, $395) offers ocean-view bungalows with spacious patios as well as 3,200-square-foot four-bedroom homes with private pools. The buildings are white and modern with geometric lines, but the interiors have relaxed island accents. On-site is Pascal's Restaurant, and a short walk down the hill is a white-sand stretch of Atlantic beach. Room rates fluctuate throughout the year; minimum stay is three to seven nights, depending on the season.

★ **French Leave** (French Leave Resort, Queen's Hwy., Governor's Harbour, tel. 242/332-3777, www.frenchleaveresort.com, $538) offers one and two-bedroom luxury oceanfront and ocean-view villas with nightly rates from $300 to $650, depending on the season and length of stay. The property's thoughtful architecture reflects Bahamian historic style with modern flair, includes limestone rock walls using traditional hand construction, clean white stucco walls, louvered shutters, and cedar-shake roofs. The rooms are decorated in an aesthetically stylish modern design, with tray ceilings, French pane windows, woodblock dining tables, decorative concrete flooring, and natural fiber rugs. Each villa has a golf cart to get to the breathtaking pink-sand beach on the Atlantic side. Concierge service is available for groceries and island activities. On-site is a restaurant serving breakfast, lunch, and dinner, a seven-slip marina, a pool overlooking the harbor with an adjoining hot tub, a fitness center, and complimentary use of kayaks, paddleboards, snorkeling gear, and bikes.

A well-kept secret is 5.5-mile-long **Windermere Island,** attracting celebrity visitors and royalty, including Lady Diana and Prince Charles, who spent their honeymoon on the island, and early homeowners in the 1960s Jacques Cousteau and David Hicks. Today a new wave of celebrities own properties, including India Hicks and Mariah Carey, and many members of the British royalty are regular visitors to the island. Seclusion is guaranteed as the island is only accessible by a small guarded bridge, and only residents and their guests are allowed. There is a stunning four-mile-long pink-sand beach. The Club at Windermere is available for visitors November-May and includes a restaurant, a game room, a TV room, and a library. The pool and two tennis courts are available year-round. The island is about 30 minutes south of Governor's Harbour, near the settlement of Savannah Sound. There are not a lot of activities or amenities, and most visitors arrive looking for privacy. Private homes are rented through websites such as VRBO and Airbnb; a three-bedroom beachfront home starts at $500.

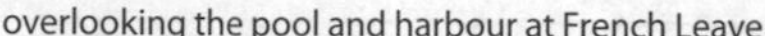

overlooking the pool and harbour at French Leave

GETTING THERE

Air

There are a minimum of seven flights per day from Nassau to Governor's Harbour; more flights are added in high season.

FROM NASSAU

Bahamasair (tel. 242/702-4140, www.bahamasair.com) has one flight per day at varying times. **Pineapple Air** (tel. 242/377-0140, www.pineappleair.com) offers three flights per day: early morning, midday, and afternoon. **Southern Air** (tel. 242/377-2014, www.southernaircharter.com) offers three flights per day: early morning, midday, and afternoon.

FROM THE UNITED STATES

Silver Airways (U.S. tel. 801/401-9100, www.silverairways.com) offers direct flights from Fort Lauderdale. **Aztec Airways** (U.S. tel. 954/601-3742, www.aztecairways.com) offers flights on Monday, Friday, and Saturday from Fort Lauderdale Executive Airport.

Boat

French Leave Marina (Governor's Harbour, tel. 242/332-3616) is a small marina with seven slips for boats up to 180 feet. There is a restaurant-bar, water hookups, Wi-Fi, and electricity. There is no fuel, and it is not a port of entry.

The Bahamas Fast Ferry (tel. 242/323-2166, www.bahamasferries.com, $107 round-trip) travels from Nassau to Governor's Harbour on the Fast Ferry on Monday, Wednesday, and Thursday.

GETTING AROUND

Stanton Cooper Taxi Service and Car Rental (tel. 242/359-7007) is a local minister and has been providing reliable taxi service and car rentals for many years. **Big Daddy's Car Rentals** (tel. 242/332-1592 or 242/470-9003, www.wcbigdaddyrentalcars.com) and **Sabal Palm Car Rental** (tel. 242/470-9951, www.rentalcarseleuthera.com) both offer a variety of compacts, minivans, and SUVs for island exploration.

Visitor Information

At the **Governor's Harbour Tourist Office** (Queen's Hwy., tel. 242/332-2142, www.bahamas.com), you can pick up maps and guides.

Banks

There are two banks in Governor's Harbour: **RBC Royal Bank** (Queen's Hwy., tel. 242/332-2856) and **First Caribbean Bank** (Queen's Hwy., tel. 242/332-2300). Banking hours are Mon.-Thurs. 9:30am-3pm, Fri. 9:30am-4:30pm.

Health and Emergencies

The clinics on the island are operated by nurses and typically offer limited services. For major medical emergencies, the clinics will arrange to transport you to Princess Margaret Hospital in Nassau or airlift you to the United States. Try the **Governor's Harbour Community Clinic** (tel. 242/332-2774, Mon.-Fri. 9am-5pm, except public holidays). Police are at the **Governor's Harbour Police Station** (tel. 242/332-2117) and the **Governor's Harbour Airport Police Station** (tel. 242/332-2323). For emergency services, contact the **Royal Bahamas Police Force Fire/Police** (tel. 919). For **directory assistance,** dial 916. For **Weather,** dial 915.

Rock Sound and South Eleuthera

Although much of Eleuthera is quiet, South Eleuthera is probably the quietest region. Rock Sound, however, is the center of commerce and home to the regional airport. There is a well-stocked grocery store, a hardware store, gas stations, and several restaurants. Just north of Rock Sound is Tarpum Bay, a quaint fishing community to settle in with the locals, hang out on the fishing dock, and find a quiet sunset view. Cape Eleuthera was booming during its heyday in the 1960s, with direct flights from London. The runway was closed and damaged by the DEA in the drug smuggling days of the 1980s and never reopened. The Cape Eleuthera Resort has struggled over the years with changes in ownership, but now with new management and fresh energy, it has gained momentum as a top destination for fishing.

SIGHTS

★ Rock Sound Ocean Hole Park

Located in the southeastern corner of the town, the **Rock Sound Ocean Hole Park** (free) was established by Prime Minister Lynden Pindling in 1970. It is nearly a perfectly round blue hole nestled within native bush, sea grapes, and coconut palms. Although it is 0.25 miles inland, the water is brackish, connected to the ocean through the porous limestone. It is believed to have formed over 300,000 years ago when the island's bedrock eroded. The hole is approximately 600 feet deep and was once explored by Windermere Island winter resident Jacques Cousteau.

The water in the hole has a high mineral and sulfur content, which locals believe have healing powers. On warm, sunny summer afternoons, the hole will be crowded with locals swimming. The rocky wall is about 10 feet off the water level, so there is ample opportunity to make a big splash from an elevated launching spot. Otherwise there are steps going down to a platform at the water's edge.

Within the hole are pretty reef fish—angelfish, parrot fish, and sergeants major—as well as mangrove snappers, schoolmasters, and grunts. These fish were caught in the

Rock Sound Ocean Hole Park within the settlement of Rock Sound

ocean and placed in the hole by local residents. Fishing is not allowed, but it's a great spot to don your snorkel gear and swim with the resident sealife. Bring some bread to attract the fish. To get to the hole, head south on Meridian Highway through Rock Sound. Just past the Lumber Shed is a main road with signs pointing to the Ocean Hole. Follow the road for 1,000 feet and turn right into the parking lot.

BEACHES

Lighthouse Point

For those looking for an adventure, Lighthouse Point has two beautiful beaches, Lighthouse Beach and Lighthouse Bay. About two hours from Governor's Harbour, it is a full-day excursion, so pack food, water, and sunscreen. The beach is on the very southern point of Eleuthera, surrounded by rock formations that provide plenty of shade. To get here, head south on Sherman's Highway. At the T intersection, you can go right to Cape Eleuthera, but go left instead. Drive through the settlement of Wemyss Bight and follow the road south. Where the road veers 90 degrees, go straight, following signs toward Lighthouse Point. The final two-mile stretch to the beaches is unpaved, so using a 4WD vehicle is suggested but not necessary. Following the road, you'll come to Lighthouse Bay, where you can park. Explore the Bay and follow the trails to the old lighthouse and Lighthouse Beach to the east. There are no facilities at this beach.

Winding Bay

Seven miles north of Rock Sound and just southeast of Tarpum Bay is one of Eleuthera's best beaches, even though one could also say Eleuthera's beaches are all great. Make sure you visit on a calm sunny day for the best photo opportunities. It is wider than most other beaches on the Atlantic side, gently sloping into the shallow sandy bay, perfect for swimming. You'll see plenty of starfish and rays. There are a few vacation rental homes in the area for seclusion. From Queen's Highway in Tarpum Bay, head south on Meridian Highway for 0.75 miles. At Kinky's Korner gas station, turn left onto the main road and follow it for 1.3 miles; you'll end up at the beach. There is parking available, but no facilities.

ENTERTAINMENT AND EVENTS

Rock Sound Homecoming (Rock Sound, tel. 242/334-2980, Easter weekend Wed.-Sun.) includes a Junkanoo rush-out (costumed people engaging in choreographed dances and parades), live bands, a beach bash, a wellness walk, a fashion and cultural show, and food tents. Many communities have their own homecomings, which are reunions and an excuse for living away from the island to reconnect with friends and family. There are homecomings in Eleuthera's communities throughout the year, but Rock Sound's attracts domestic and international visitors.

Conch Fest (Deep Creek, tel. 242/557-7701, Wed.-Sun. end of May-early June) is a celebration of cultural heritage and the conch industry that includes Bahamian food, rake-and-scrape, talent shows, arts and crafts, a beach bash, a fashion show, dance contests, and live performances.

SHOPPING

Eleuthera Arts and Cultural Center (Lord St., Tarpum Bay, tel. 242/334-4101, www.oneeleuthera.org) is located in a 250-year-old building formerly known as the Prep School. In 2010 Tarpum Bay's Historical and Heritage Society renovated and restored the building as a center for arts and culture. It is currently used for local artists to display their talent. Monthly programs with artists in residence and ongoing workshops are offered. It will eventually house a museum and art gallery.

SPORTS AND RECREATION

Ocean Fox Cotton Bay (Dive Shop at Cape Eleuthera Resort, tel. 242/332-2291, U.S. tel. 281/201-6198, www.oceanfoxcottonbay.com) is a small outfit based at Cape Eleuthera.

The Island School

In the mid-1990s, Americans Chris and Pam Maxey initiated the Cape Eleuthera Marine Conservation Project, now called the Cape Eleuthera Foundation, and set out to establish a school and research station, now known as **The Island School** (www.islandschool.org). The project received 18 acres of donated land from the Cape Eleuthera Resort, and the school was opened in 1999. The two neighbors are now fairly intertwined on this otherwise undeveloped region of Eleuthera, and today the school offers two 14-week semester programs and a 6-week summer session for both local and international students from high school to college level.

Their goal is to implement, educate, and research means to limit ecological impact to benefit sustainability within the local community and the rest of the world, where many of these students return. The facility uses rainwater-collecting cisterns, solar hot-water heating, photovoltaic solar panels, and local resources wherever possible, including constructing buildings with the invasive casuarina trees. Programs have included creating a biodiesel facility to transform cooking oil and plastic into usable energy, and a bio-digester to transform human waste into energy. Permaculture, aquaculture, and aquaponics on the property seek to reduce the amount of imported food products.

The students undergo a scuba certification program, where oftentimes diving is a part of their coursework, and they complete an eight-day, 30-mile kayak trip with a 48-hour solo experience. A typical day starts with sunrise exercise, training for the end of the semester half marathon or super swim, chores, and maintenance of the campus. Throughout the day, student classes include human ecology, field surveys of local marinelife, the history of The Bahamas, and environmental art. This progressive school changes the lives of students at an impressionable age, creates independence, promotes a sense of adventure, and instills reverence and a connection to our sensitive natural surroundings. It is truly a revolutionary educational facility.

They cater to 8 divers, 6 fishing enthusiasts, or 12 snorkelers. Full-day and half-day deep-sea fishing charters are available, as well as two-tank scuba dives, which include wall and pinnacle dives, shallow reefs, night dives, and shark dives. Inquire about their Shark School, with the intent of bringing humans closer to sharks.

Miller's Dive Shop (Cape Eleuthera, tel. 242/436-3644, www.scubaeleuthera.com) offers scuba excursions of reef, wall diving, or sunken wrecks and planes, and half-day and full-day fishing charters. All excursions meet at Cape Eleuthera Marina.

Eleuthera Adventure Tours (Rock Sound, tel. 242/334-2356, www.eleutheraadventuretours.com) offers boating excursions to Harbour Island, The Exumas, and the Schooner Cays, and dune buggy adventures to Lighthouse Beach. They also offer the specialized Taste of Eleuthera Tour, which takes you through local settlements to learn about the history of these areas.

FOOD

Bahamian

Northside Restaurant and Bar (Northside Inn, tel. 242/334-2573, www.northsideinneleuthera.com, call for hours, $5-15) is a funky ocean-side restaurant with plastic tablecloths and fishnets adorning the ceiling. Rose will welcome you with open arms and make you feel at home as she serves up home-cooked Bahamian food such as whole pan-fried snapper and baked chicken with mac and cheese. It's off the beaten path, about two miles out of town, but it's well worth the trek. From the Rock Sound Ocean Hole, follow signs to the Northside Inn on the Atlantic side.

Sammy's Place (Rock Sound, tel. 242/334-2121, daily 7:30am-9:30pm, $5-15) is a Rock Sound staple restaurant serving Bahamian and American food for breakfast, lunch, and dinner. The restaurant is a comfortable diner with self-serve coffee and tea that attracts both locals and visitors for a quick bite or to catch up on the latest sip sip. Pick up a sandwich to go or dine in one of the booth seats. There aren't really street signs in Rock Sound, so you'll have to look for the signs off Meridian Highway. It's located 1.5 blocks east, behind the Roman Catholic church.

Contemporary

Frigate's Bar and Grill (Meridian Hwy., Rock Sound, tel. 242/334-2778, www.frigatesbarandgrill.com, daily noon-9pm, $10-20) is located in Rock Sound, just one block south of the Market Place shopping center, a fantastic location on the calm western side that offers beautiful sunset views from the porch, the small artificial sandy beach, or the gazebo. The food is a mix of fresh-caught local seafood with locally grown herbs and greens. Lunch is sandwiches and seafood with hand-cut french fries. Dinner offers steaks and pastas, or try the seafood platter with half a lobster tail, shrimp, cracked conch, and fish. For dessert, try the coconut cream pie or the key lime pie.

★ **Harbour Pointe Restaurant** (Cape Eleuthera Resort, Cape Eleuthera Dr., tel. 242/334-8500, U.S. tel. 844/884-1014, www.capeeleuthera.com, Tues.-Sun. 11am-10pm, $15-25) is perched on the edge of Eleuthera surrounded by the marina and sweeping panoramic views of the ocean. Dine indoors in the air-conditioning at Barracuda's Bar, or outdoors on the porch with staggering sunset views. This is casual dining at its finest with friendly service. The menu stays the same for lunch and dinner, offering sandwiches, salads, and pastas. The pan-seared grouper sandwich with dill sauce and a brioche bun is exceptional. Expect a mix of boaters, resort guests, and Island School students, interns, and teachers. Happy hour is daily 4:30pm-6:30pm.

ACCOMMODATIONS

★ **Cape Eleuthera Resort and Marina** (Cape Eleuthera Dr., U.S. tel. 844/884-1014, www.capeeleuthera.com, $250) feels like it's on the edge of the earth. Thirty minutes from Rock Sound, there isn't much of anything in between, making it feel like a hidden oasis. Near the entrance is the world renowned Island School, which attracts young enthusiastic minds from all over the world. Brand-new brightly colored one-bedroom cottages have a kitchenette and a living space and are decorated with island accents and tasteful artwork. Along the marina are the awe-inspiring

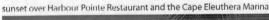

sunset over Harbour Pointe Restaurant and the Cape Eleuthera Marina

two-bedroom villas. The spacious open-layout kitchen and bar area lead to a comfortable living room with a large flat-screen TV. The downstairs balcony looks onto the marina activity. Upstairs you'll find two bedrooms with en suite baths, one with two twins and another with an elevated four-poster king, all with plush pillow-top mattresses. The master suite has its own balcony to watch the sunset. These are fabulous options for families who need space. The marina attracts fishing enthusiasts and is in one of the top fishing grounds in the country, with the bank side for snapper, and just minutes offshore is the Exuma Sound drop-off for deep-sea fishing. There is a swimming pool, a restaurant and bar, a dive shop, and a provisions store.

Northside Inn (Northside Inn, tel. 242/334-2573, www.northsideinneleuthera.com, $120) is a few minutes from Rock Sound on the Atlantic Ocean. The friendly resident Labrador will greet you, and the sea breeze will instill immediate relaxation. Three cottages overlook a beautiful stretch of secluded beach. Rooms have comfortable kings and a kitchenette with a microwave and a mini fridge, with balconies overlooking the ocean. The on-site restaurant serves breakfast, lunch, and dinner for guests. There is a two-night minimum for the $120 rate; for a one-night stay, the rate is $140. Air-conditioning is $5 extra per day.

GETTING THERE

Air

FROM NASSAU

Bahamasair (tel. 242/702-4140, www.bahamasair.com) has two flights per day in the morning and afternoon. **Pineapple Air** (tel. 242/377-0140, www.pineappleair.com) also has two flights per day, morning and afternoon.

Boat

Blue Flag Marina (Cape Eleuthera Resort, U.S. tel. 844/884-1014, www.capeeleuthera.com) has 47 slips serving boats up to 200 feet with full utilities, Wi-Fi, a provisions store, a restaurant, and a pool. It is not a port of entry.

Davis Harbour Marina at Cotton Bay Club (Waterford, tel. 242/334-6303) has 24 slips for boats up to 80 feet, with services that include fuel, water, electricity, ice, showers, groceries, laundry, and a restaurant. It is not a port of entry.

The Bahamas Fast Ferry (tel. 242/323-2166, www.bahamasferries.com, $52 round-trip) travels from Nassau to Rock Sound on Tuesdays on the MV *East Wind* or *Seawind* freight boats.

GETTING AROUND

Taxis will meet you at the airport. For rental cars, contact **Dingle Motor Service** (Rock Sound, tel. 242/334-2031). If you are staying in Cape Eleuthera and have no plans to travel anywhere, you won't need a vehicle, but golf cart rentals are available.

Health and Emergencies

The clinics on the island are operated by nurses and typically offer limited services. For major medical emergencies, the clinics will arrange to transport you to Princess Margaret Hospital in Nassau or airlift you to the United States. Try the **Rock Sound Community Clinic** (tel. 242/334-2226 or 242/334-2139, Mon.-Fri. 9am-5pm, except public holidays). For emergency services, contact the **Royal Bahamas Police Force Fire/Police** (tel. 919), or the **Rock Sound Airport Police Station** (tel. 242/334-2052). For **directory assistance** dial 916. For **weather** dial 915.

Harbour Island

Regularly ranking high as a top island destination, Harbour Island (called "Briland" by the locals) attracts an elite socialite crowd during the winter months to its famous Pink Sand Beach, top restaurants and hotels, and the allure of driving the narrow streets lined with historic cottages in a golf cart. Multimillion-dollar mansions owned by well-known international businesspeople are tucked away on estate properties up a dirt track in what's known as the Narrows. Celebrities are attracted to this 3-mile by 1.5 mile island specifically because locals don't get starstruck, giving them a sense of anonymity.

Dunmore Town is one of the oldest settlements in The Bahamas, named for Governor John Murray, Lord of Dunmore, who resided in Harbour Island when it was the country's capital in the late 1700s. Harbour Island has an intriguing history of shipwrecking, piracy, and boatbuilding. It eventually turned to tourism as a health retreat in the late 1800s. The mascot of the island, the ever-present rooster, will most likely wake you before the sun comes up each morning.

As the most expensive destination in the country, Harbour Island is not for a budget vacation. From accommodations to dining options, you will pay top dollar, but if you decide to visit, your experience will be memorable.

SIGHTS

Lone Tree

Located on what's known as Girl's Bank on the western side of the island is a much photographed tree skeleton. The original **Lone Tree** washed up in Hurricane Andrew in 1992 and landed upright, with its intricate root ball supporting its base. The original tree washed away in another hurricane, but it had become such a landmark that it was eventually replaced by another, much larger tree that was strategically placed in the sand flats.

It has been featured in magazines and is a popular spot for photo shoots. To get here, follow Bay Street north until it curves up to Gusty's Hill. At the curve, you can pull off the road, and on the other side of a few trees is the sand flat with fishing boats lining the shore. Make sure to go at low tide for the best views. At high tide, the water surrounds the tree.

Bay Street

All visitors to Harbour Island arrive by boat, and the main stop is at Government Dock, the center of bustling action with water taxis and domestic and international freight boats several days per week. At the end of the dock is a bright-yellow welcome sign. Perpendicular to the dock is **Bay Street,** the most colorful and picturesque on the island. Turn right to pass by The Landing and Rock House and enter the residential area of the island. Turn left to be awed by the collection of wooden New England-style colonial homes with bright shutters in teal, yellow, and pastel pink. Many of these homes date to the 1800s; look for Beside the Point, Rose Bud, Still Point, and the Little Boarding House for great photo ops. You'll also see the Loyalist Cottage, one of the oldest residences on the island, dating to 1797.

Stop in to the Sugar Mill for boutique resort wear, or meander through the straw market on the edge of the waterfront park, where all the town's festivals and events are held. Farther down is the fishing dock, where local skiffs arrive with the day's catch, and the surrounding restaurants cook up the freshest seafood dishes, including conch salad at Queen Conch. Enjoy a cocktail at the open-air Beyond the Reef bar and watch the sunset over the harbor. Bay Street is also home to Junkanoo on Boxing Day (Dec. 26) and New Year's Day.

St. John's Anglican Church

The oldest religious foundation in The Bahamas, **St. John's Anglican Church**

Harbour Island

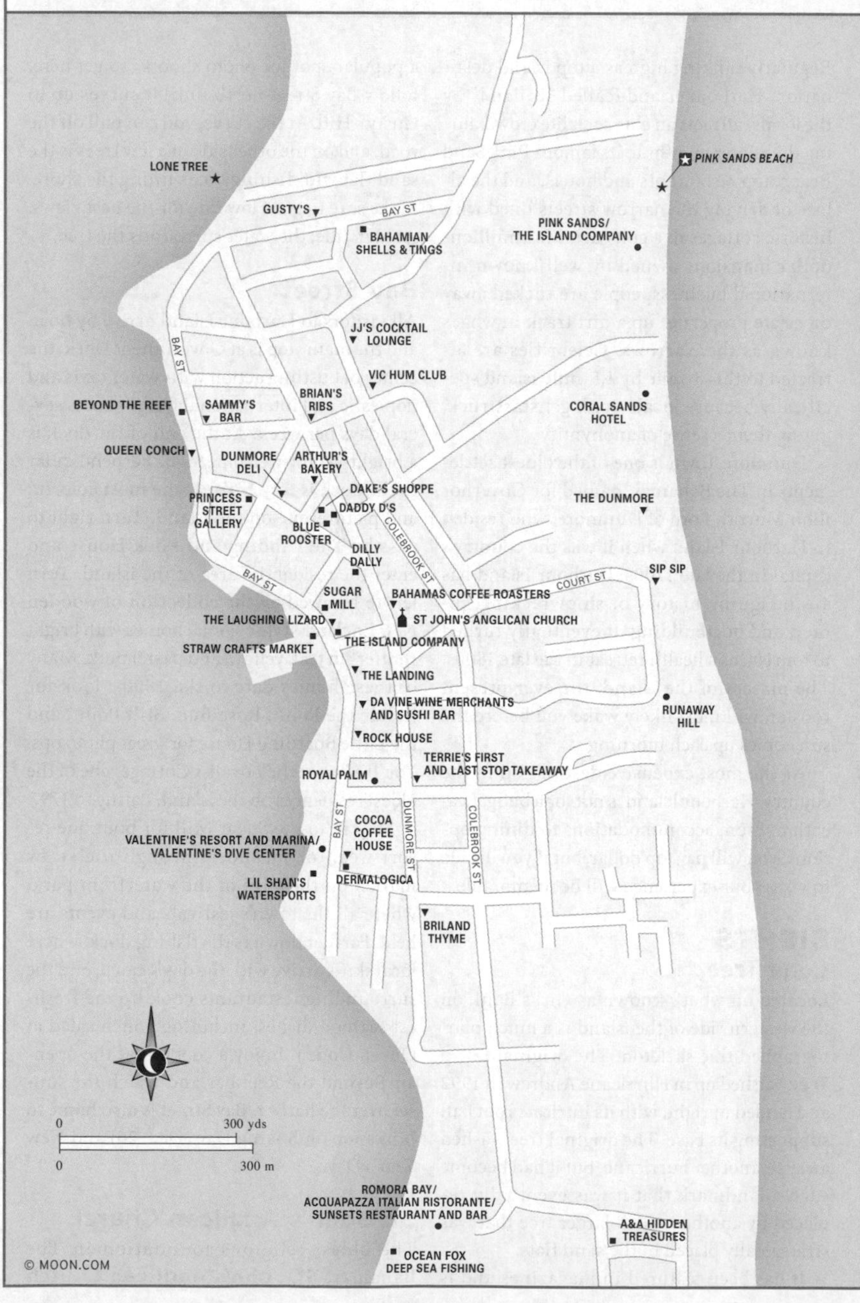
LONE TREE
PINK SANDS BEACH
BAY ST
GUSTY'S
BAHAMIAN SHELLS & TINGS
PINK SANDS/ THE ISLAND COMPANY
JJ'S COCKTAIL LOUNGE
VIC HUM CLUB
BAY ST
BEYOND THE REEF
SAMMY'S BAR
BRIAN'S RIBS
CORAL SANDS HOTEL
QUEEN CONCH
DUNMORE DELI
ARTHUR'S BAKERY
DAKE'S SHOPPE
PRINCESS STREET GALLERY
DADDY D'S
BLUE ROOSTER
THE DUNMORE
COLEBROOK ST
DILLY DALLY
BAY ST
SIP SIP
COURT ST
SUGAR MILL
BAHAMAS COFFEE ROASTERS
THE LAUGHING LIZARD
ST JOHN'S ANGLICAN CHURCH
STRAW CRAFTS MARKET
THE ISLAND COMPANY
THE LANDING
DA VINE WINE MERCHANTS AND SUSHI BAR
RUNAWAY HILL
ROCK HOUSE
TERRIE'S FIRST AND LAST STOP TAKEAWAY
ROYAL PALM
BAY ST
DUNMORE ST
COLEBROOK ST
COCOA COFFEE HOUSE
VALENTINE'S RESORT AND MARINA/ VALENTINE'S DIVE CENTER
LIL SHAN'S WATERSPORTS
DERMALOGICA
BRILAND THYME
0
300 yds
0
300 m
ROMORA BAY/ ACQUAPAZZA ITALIAN RISTORANTE/ SUNSETS RESTAURANT AND BAR
A&A HIDDEN TREASURES
OCEAN FOX DEEP SEA FISHING
© MOON.COM

(Dunmore St., tel. 242/333-2178, service Sun. 8am, 10am, and 7pm, Bible study Wed. 7pm, solemn service Fri. 6am) holds regular services in this building that has been a gathering place for community members for 250 years. The tagline is "Serving God Who Is Great Since 1768." The taffy-pink concrete building's commanding presence on the hill straight up from Government Dock makes it hard to miss. Inside the stained-glass windows and sharply pointed arches give churchgoers a sense of rich history. Harbour Island hosts destination weddings throughout the year, and those not reciting their vows on Pink Sands Beach are likely doing it at St. John's.

BEACHES

★ Pink Sands Beach

Eleuthera is home to a plethora of gorgeous pink sandy beaches, and each offers its own striking beauty. But Pink Sands Beach is slightly different, located among the opulence of Harbour Island. Stretching for three glorious miles with depths of 100-250 feet, depending on the tide, you'll definitely want to take a stroll. Along the beach are resorts, restaurants, and vacation homes. At low tide the sand is firm and level, allowing stable walking. Some of the resorts even have fat-tire beach bicycles for proper beach cruising.

To the north end of the beach are the estate homes of the Narrows, where the elite enjoy a lightly trafficked stretch of beach. Central are the resorts of Coral Sands, Pink Sands, The Dunmore, Ocean View Club, Runaway Hill, and the popular lunch restaurant Sip Sip. Valentines also has beach chairs and umbrellas set up for their harbor-side guests. To the south are vacation rental homes tucked in bright greenish-yellow *Scaevola* and broad-leafed sea grapes, which thrive in the otherwise harsh coastal conditions. Beaches in The Bahamas are public, but lounge chairs are reserved for guests of the corresponding hotels. You can rent beach chairs at the beach access between Coral Sands and Pink Sands from **TeeJay's Beach Chair Rentals** (tel. 242/554-5139). She has chairs and umbrellas, and you can purchase cold drinks, cocktails, and snacks from under her shady hut. She also bartends at Queen Conch, so if she's not at her post, you can likely find her there.

For beach access at Coral Sands, head down Chapel Street from Dunmore Street and park on the side of the road. There are beach accesses all along the island as you head east, or ask a local to point you in the right direction.

Lone Tree on Girl's Bank

ENTERTAINMENT AND EVENTS

Nightlife

The Out Islands are traditionally quiet at night unless you're hitting a fish fry or special event. Many people head to the bars for happy hour and are at home by 9pm. No so on Harbour Island, which has the most hopping nightlife scene after Nassau. To dance late into the night, head to **Daddy D's** (Dunmore St., tel. 242/359-7006). During the holidays and spring break, it is packed with an energy-filled young crowd. Devon "Daddy D" Sawyer spends his days fishing and then heads to the club around 10pm to spin a mix of the latest hit dance songs, often until 4am. The place doesn't pick up until midnight, so take a nap first.

Another popular spot for dancing is **Gusty's** (Bay St., tel. 242/333-2342, daily from 9pm). The floor is covered in sand, and there is a breezy deck overlooking the harbor for fresh air. **Vic Hum Club** (Barracks St. and Colebrook St., tel. 242/333-2161, Mon.-Sat. 8pm-open late) was opened in 1955 by prominent brothers Victor and Humphry Percentie and has been a fixture late-night hangout ever since. The walls are steeped in island history, and it's home to the largest coconut, so be sure to have a look at the 33-inch anomaly when you're here. There's also a basketball court and pool tables.

Just up the road from Vic Hum Club is unassuming **JJ's Cocktail Lounge** (Colebrook St., tel. 242/333-2431, Mon.-Sat. 4pm-open late). This tiny bar is a popular spot for a quick drink when you are bar-hopping. Order a rum and coke and you'll be given a hip flask-size bottle with a can of coke for $5. Along the harbor front is **Beyond the Reef** (Bay St., tel. 242/333-3478, Mon.-Thurs. 11am-midnight, Fri.-Sat. 11am-open late, Sun. 1pm-midnight), is usually a hot spot on Friday and Saturday nights, often with live music or DJs; it's regularly utilized for private events. Across the street from Beyond the Reef is local's hangout **Sammy's Bar** (Bay St.), where you'll often find patrons watching sporting events and slapping dominoes.

SHOPPING

One of the draws of Harbour Island is the variety of boutique shopping options. When you're tired of lounging on the beautiful beach, hop in your golf cart and spend an afternoon perusing a beautiful selection of resort wear. Stores are closed on Sunday.

Princess Street Gallery (Princess St.,

a vibrant scene on Pink Sands Beach

Afrohead Rum

In 2008, Harbour Island resident and Australia native Toby Tyler began handcrafting an artisanal no-name dark rum and serving it at the Landing, which he was involved in at the time. The only image on the label was the graphic he designed for the Landing, the retro-looking silhouette of the first Miss Bahamas from 1963. The rum became so popular that patrons began referring to it as "that rum with the Afro head on it," and so, Afrohead Rum (www.afroheadrums.com) was established. The logo stays true to its original design but has since evolved to include additional West Indian culture, such as a crown, paying tribute to the British Crown; Junkanoo; the rising sun; and seashells.

The sugarcane molasses, sourced mainly from the Dominican Republic, is fermented with Trinidadian yeast and barrel-aged in Trinidad and bottled in Barbados. It is then imported to The Bahamas by the Harbour Island Rum Company. Their flagship dark rum is aged for 7 years in bourbon barrels, and the black-label extra-aged rum sits for 15 years. Once only available in small production at The Landing, Afrohead Rum can now be purchased online through retailers in New York, Florida, Tennessee, and throughout The Bahamas. To pick up a bottle in Harbour Island, look for it at Da Vine Wine Merchants, or ask for it at local fine-dining establishments.

www.harbourislandgallery.com, Mon.-Sat. 10am-1pm and 2pm-5pm) is a beautiful art gallery showcasing the best of Bahamian artists. Much of the artwork is done by local and visiting artists, making most of it specific to Harbour Island. A variety of coffee-table books, black and white historic photographs, and Bahama Handprint bags, towels, and napkins are available.

Dilly Dally (Dunmore St., tel. 242/333-3109, Mon.-Sat. 9:30am-5pm) is the best spot to pick up affordable Harbour Island souvenirs and locally made products, including a selection of books on The Bahamas and the local area, jams, hot sauces, local sea salt, candles, T-shirts, jewelry, and tumblers.

On Bay Street just north of Government Dock is the **Straw Crafts Market,** which features a variety of stalls with locally made straw crafts and T-shirts. For high-quality artisanal straw crafts, however, head south of town on Queen's Highway to **A&A's Hidden Treasures** (Queen's Hwy., tel. 242/448-1556, daily 8am-7:30pm). Alice will be hard at work creating her products, and you can watch her and ask questions about her craft. She makes beautiful handbags, clutches, bowls, and hats. She will even personalize something for you if you'd like. **Bahamian Shells and Tings** (Bay St., on Gusty's Hill, tel. 242/333-2839, Mon. and Thurs.-Fri. 10am-4pm, Tues.-Wed. 9am-1pm) has a wonderful selection of handmade local products, T-shirts, and wraps.

Co-owned by India Hicks and Linda Griffin, the **Sugar Mill** (Bay St., tel. 242/333-3558, Mon.-Sat. 10am-5pm) was actually a functioning sugar mill circa 1925. Opened in November 2005, Linda and India's vision is a boutique filled with global treasures. You'll notice skull and crossbones designs mixed with elegant resort wear, clutches, and jewelry.

With high-end resort wear and beachwear for men and women, **Blue Rooster** (King St., tel. 242/333-2240, Mon.-Sat. 9am-5pm) is located in a historical residence dating back to the mid-1800s. The hardwood floors creak with character, and you'll be welcomed with a smile, likely by the shop's owner, Gabrielle. Nestled behind a white picket fence is **Dake's Shoppe** (Crown St., tel. 242/334-3045, Mon.-Sat. 9am-6pm), a quaint historical cottage with pale pink shutters. Specializing in well-curated men's and women's resort wear, home decor, linens and textiles, Dake brings a worldly blend of style and sophistication. Original rafters, exposed shingle ceilings, and Abaco pine clapboard siding add to the timeless ambience.

Calico Trading Co. (Valentines Resort

& Marina, Bay St., tel. 242/333-3827, daily 10am-6pm) specializes in trendy and eclectic beachwear and swimwear. They also sell Bahamas-specific Briland products, which include a high-quality tailored polo shirt with the signature Lord Dunmore Rooster. **The Island Company** (Bay St. and Pink Sands Hotel, www.theislandcompany.com, Mon.-Sat. 9am-5pm) opened in 2016 on Bay Street, adjacent to Government Dock, and at Pink Sands Resort. Their ever-popular tagline "Quit your job, buy a ticket, get a tan, fall in love, never return" is showcased on shirts, hats, and tumblers.

SPORTS AND RECREATION

Diving

Valentines Dive Center (Valentines Resort and Marina, Bay St., tel. 242/333-2080, www.valentinesdive.com) is a professional operation offering daily dive excursions to the best locations in the area. Dive the many wrecks of the Devil's Backbone, the treacherous reef that spans the length of North Eleuthera, or dive Current Cut, the high-speed drift dive that funnels you between mainland Eleuthera and Current Island, where tidal exchanges flow at speeds of 7-9 knots.

Fishing

Owner Jeff Fox has been operating fishing charters with his self-operated **Ocean Fox Deep Sea Fishing** (tel. 242/333-2323, U.S. tel. 954/727-5743, www.oceanfoxfishingbahamas.com) for nearly 30 years. You'll head out where the shelf drops to 1,500 feet. The underwater shelves make for prime fishing, with spots known as Pinnacle and Shallow Ground, 70-100 feet deep and a gathering spot for all kinds of marinelife. Fish for tuna, wahoo, and mahimahi, depending on the season.

Water Sports

Rent kayaks and powerboats from **Michael's Cycles** (Colebrook St., tel. 242/464-0994 or 242/333-2384, www.michaelscyclesbriland.com), including easily manageable 13- and 17-foot Boston Whalers and 20- and 21-foot Mako center consoles. Michael's also rents golf carts and bicycles. **Lil Shan's Watersports** (Valentines Resort, Bay St., tel. 242/333-3532 or 242/344-9343) offers Jet Ski rentals, boat rentals and charters, snorkel gear, paddleboards, kayaks, and Hobie cats.

Spas and Fitness

Dermalogica (Valentines Resort, Bay St., tel. 242/333-3772) offers massage, body

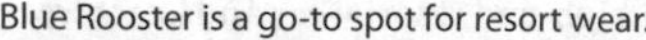
Blue Rooster is a go-to spot for resort wear.

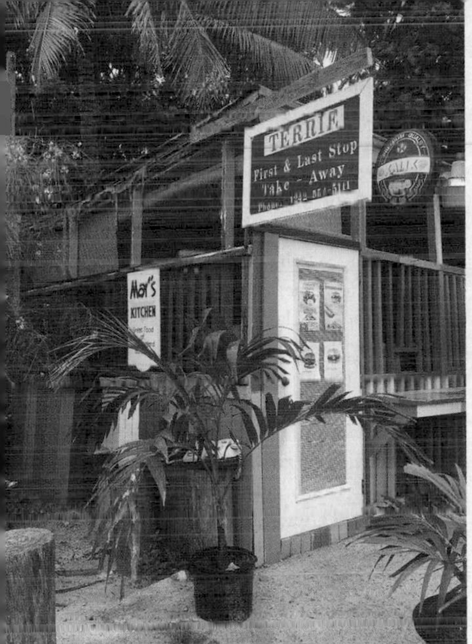

Terrie's First & Last Stop Takeaway offers simple, tasty Bahamian specialties.

treatments, waxing, and tinting. **Fitness with Tamara** (tel. 242/470-1059, www.fitnesswithtamara.com) offers scheduled fitness classes each week, including yoga, circuit training, ball classes, and Zumba. Tamara is also available for private classes. Contact her for the current class schedule.

FOOD

Harbour Island is known for some of the country's best restaurants. Be prepared for swank and putting on your best island resort wear. Most diners get away with collared polos and khakis, and you can show off your finds from the local boutiques. The great thing about Briland is the gamut of food options. From down-home to five-star, you'll find something to elate your taste buds.

Bahamian

For some of the best conch salad in the islands, ★ **Queen Conch** (Bay Street, Harbour Island, tel. 242/333-3811, Mon.-Sat. 11:30am-9pm, $10-20) brings locals and visitors together in a casual open-air establishment on the harbor near the fishing docks. The staff begins taking orders at 11:30am (or as soon as they show up) and stops serving when they run out of fresh conch—usually by 1pm—so don't delay getting your name on the list. Be prepared to settle in, since the salads are made to order. Fantastic entrées include fish wraps with hand-cut french fries and spicy shrimp caesar salad.

Brian's Ribs (Dunmore St., tel. 242/333-3051, Fri.-Sat. from 7pm, $10-15, cash only) is worth an evening out, if only for the experience. This family-run establishment is in Brian Sawyer's home, the porch transformed into an open-air barbecue pit with picnic-table seating. Kids wander in and out of the house, and people mingle around while waiting for food. He serves up delicious jerk and barbecue ribs, chopped pork, chicken, shrimp, and lobster with a choice of sides. Food is served in a to-go box, but you are welcome to enjoy it on the porch. It's BYO alcohol, so grab some beer before you arrive.

For a tasty home-cooked meal that never disappoints, try **Briland Thyme** (South St. and Dunmore St., tel. 242/552-3628, Mon.-Sat. 11:30am-4pm, $10-15, cash only), in a standalone lean-to serving traditional Bahamian cooking such as fried pork chops and cracked conch, as well as some of the best chicken wings on the island.

If you want to try some of the best breakfast souse on the island, as well as traditional Bahamian staples, stop by **Terrie's First & Last Stop Takeaway** (Clarence St. and Dunmore St., tel. 242/554-5111, Mon.-Sat. 7am-3pm, $10-15, cash only). If she isn't busy cooking, Terrie is usually sitting out front in a plastic chair, and she is always happy to have a chat.

Fine Dining

The ever elegant restaurant at **The Dunmore** (Court St., tel. 242/333-2200, www.dunmorebeach.com, lunch daily 11:30am-3pm, dinner Wed.-Mon. 5:30pm-9pm) attracts Harbour Island's elite with its glamourous 1960s resort-style dining room. Comfortable couches invite guests for a pre-dinner cocktail at the mahogany bar, and the Amanda Lindroth-designed orange and white pin-striped booth seats in the dining room are accented with old black-and-white photographs of Harbour Island's heyday. Serving lunch and dinner daily, as well as breakfast for hotel guests, the Caribbean-inspired menu includes crispy tuna nachos, fresh catch fish carpaccio, yuca (cassava) fries, and locally grown greens. Dinner reservations are required.

Rock House (Bay and Hill St., tel. 242/333-2053 U.S. tel. 305/433-2024, www.rockhousebahamas.com, Tues.-Sun. lunch noon-2pm, dinner 6:30pm-9pm, $35-45) offers some of the best harbor-view dining on the island. The restaurant stretches from the terrace balcony, elevated over the harbor, to the pool patio, with a breezy dining room in between. Crisp white tablecloths and upscale Old World ambience allow you to settle in as you enjoy elegant Caribbean fare such as curried New Zealand lamb chops, herb-crusted grouper, or jumbo crab cakes with béarnaise sauce. Dinner reservations with a credit card are required.

The place to see and be seen, **The Landing** (Bay St., tel. 242/333-2707, www.harbourislandlanding.com, breakfast Thurs.-Sat. and Mon.-Tues. 8am-11am, Sun. 8am-noon, $15-20, dinner Thurs.-Tues. 6pm-10pm, $40-50) oozes historic retro allure with solid hardwood floors and Afro-influenced accents. Dine on the veranda overlooking Bay Street and the harbor front or opt for the elegant dining room with cabernet-red walls and ivory wainscoting. One of the best breakfast spots on the island, delicacies include avocado cucumber on sourdough toast with lemon-infused cream cheese and egg. For dinner, try the unique takes on traditional foods with the ABC: avocado, beet, and stone crab, or their beef tenderloin draped in bacon with thin-sliced potato stacks. Dinner reservations are required.

International

A wine shop with sushi is the new hippest spot, as well as the first to introduce Asian-influenced cuisine on the island, **Da Vine Wine Merchants and Sushi Bar** (Bay St., tel. 242/333-2950, wine shop daily 10am-10pm, restaurant daily from noon) is an intimate dining setting, surrounded by racks of wine bottles. Chef Edwin, formally a chef at Nobu, prepares classic sashimi, sushi, and rolls along with soba and ramen noodles, or try lamb chop, black cod miso, and Waygu beef. Wash it down with a fine sake, craft beer, or bottle of wine.

★ **Acquapazza Italian Ristorante** (Romora Bay, Colebrook St., tel. 242/551-1512 or 242/359-7133, www.acquapazzabahamas.net, daily 11am-10pm) is enjoying its new location at Romora Bay. Historically this hard-to-find restaurant was always packed with locals; now perched above Sunsets Bar and Restaurant, closer to town, diners can opt for the air-conditioned dining room, the outdoor piazza under ambient string lighting with beautiful harbor views, or just hit the bar to see who you might meet. Start dinner with lightly battered calamari fritti, served with a spicy marinara sauce. All menu options are superb, but the melanzane parmigiana (crisp cheesy baked eggplant parmesan), fettuccine alla norcina (cream of porcini and white truffle oil), chicken toscano, and snapper livornese are some of the tastiest. Italian owner Manfredi is usually on hand to make sure the guest experience is top-notch, and chef Vernon enjoys cooking in his new spacious and luxurious kitchen. The staff is attentive and unrushed, and the food here is by far the best value on this traditionally expensive island.

Contemporary

★ **Coral Sands** (Chapel St., tel. 242/333-2350, U.S. tel. 888/568-5493, www.coralsands.com, daily lunch 11:30am-3pm, $20-30, dinner daily 6pm-9pm, $25-45) offers two dining options for hotel guests and visitors. For lunch, the Beach Bar's shady deck on top of the sandbank from Pink Sands Beach offers Instagram-worthy views on any given day. Chef Ken serves up simple delicious pizzas and sandwiches such as the shrimp po'boy and lobster salad. Specialty cocktails will convince you to linger into the afternoon. Dinner at Latitude 25 kicks off in the newly renovated dining room above the pool deck, where chef Ludo prepares dishes from his native France with a Caribbean twist, such as coconut-crusted mahi, seared scallops in champagne cream sauce, and lobster mac and cheese.

Follow the shady tree-lined path through the **Pink Sands** (Chapel St., tel. 242/333-2030, U.S. tel. 855/855 9621, www.pinksandsresort.com, daily breakfast 7:30am-11am, $15-20, lunch noon-3pm, $15-30, bar 3:30pm-sunset, dinner 6:30pm-9pm, $35-45) and find yourself at the aptly named **Blue Bar** on the edge of Pink Sands Beach, which serves breakfast and lunch daily and is open for cocktails until sunset. Dinner is served at **Malcolm 51,** near the main entrance and surrounded by lush gardens.

Runaway Hill (off Colebrook St., tel. 242/333-2150, U.S. and Canada tel. 843/278 1724, www.runawayhill.com, breakfast daily 8:30am-10:30am, $10-20, lunch daily noon-2:30pm, $15-25, dinner Tues.-Sun. from 6pm, $30-45) is tucked away on a quiet hillside and provides guests with a more anonymous dining experience than some of the other more social establishments. The bar and dining room exude historic charm, and the wide balcony overlooks the pool and Pink Sands Beach. The chef focuses on locally grown produce and fresh seafood. Happy hour and a tapas menu are Monday 4pm-8pm, Tuesday Sunday 4pm-6pm. Dinner reservations are recommended.

★ **Sip Sip** (Court St., tel. 242/333-3316, www.sipsiprestaurant.com, Wed.-Mon. 11:30am-4pm, $15-25) is the local term for gossip. When you get the "sip sip" on something you're getting insider information. Sip Sip was established as the social house of the community, but word got out, and this lunch-only restaurant is packed daily. The menu changes based on what is in season, but be sure to try the ever-present lobster quesadillas. They are worth the splurge, but it's best to split it with others, since the portion is huge and they are extremely rich. The curried chicken salad with local greens is another staple favorite, and rotating specials can include chilled gazpacho, tuna carpaccio, and grilled wahoo with quinoa. The crafted cocktails are intoxicatingly delightful. Make sure

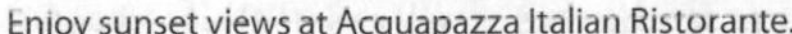

Enjoy sunset views at Acquapazza Italian Ristorante.

you try the passion fruit sangria and the Sip Sip rum punch.

Sunsets Restaurant and Bar (Romora Bay, Colebrook St., tel. 242/333-2325, U.S. tel. 800/688-0425, www.romorabay.com, daily noon-9pm, $20-35) is a gathering place for happy-hour cocktails and sunset viewing. Be sure to stop by Sunday 6pm-9pm for live music by local band the Brilanders, playing Bahamian music and calypso covers. Menu items include classic bar snacks like chips with guacamole, buffalo wings, and conch fritters. Dinner items include sweet potato gnocchi, Abaco chicken, and mango glazed barbecue ribs. They are happy to cater to large groups and events. Happy hour is daily 4pm-6pm.

Valentines Resort & Marina (Bay St., tel. 242/333-2142, U.S. tel. 866/389-6864, www.valentinesresort.com, daily breakfast and lunch 7:30am-10:30am and 11:30am-4pm, $15-20, dinner from 6pm, $30-50) are two open-air dining options offering the same menu at Valentines overlooking the marina. Rooster Tail's Bar & Grill is a casual hangout with cushioned bar table seating, or shady umbrella tables over the water; the Boathouse Restaurant is slightly more formal, but overall maintains a casual and relaxed boater vibe. Both serve tasty burgers, fish tacos, sandwiches, and fresh seafood.

Cafés and Light Bites

★ **Bahamas Coffee Roasters and Bistro** (Dunmore St., tel. 242/470-8015 or 242/359-7106, daily 8am-3pm, $10-15, cash only) is the center of the action in the morning, serving its own blends of hand-roasted coffee. Right in town, people often walk from their vacation rental cottages to this family-run shop. Kirk, Patti, and their son Jake make you feel at home, and by day 3, they will know you by name. Sit inside or on the shaded porch overlooking Dunmore Street for delicious egg-based breakfast burritos, sandwiches, quesadillas, and delectable french toast. For lunch, be sure to try their organic chicken sandwich, with brie cheese, fig spread, and arugula on ciabatta bread.

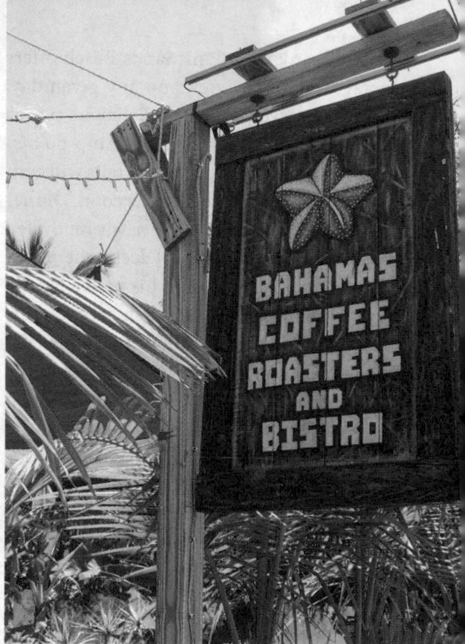

Grab a coffee and catch up on local gossip at Bahamas Coffee Roasters and Bistro.

Cocoa Coffee House (Valentines Resort, Bay St., tel. 242/698-0242, Mon.-Sat. 7am-5:30pm, Sun. 7am-1pm, $10-15) is on the second floor across from the Valentines Marina, serving a healthy selection of breakfast items, including açaí bowls, coconut waffles, and egg sandwiches as well as smoothies, coconut water, and fresh-squeezed juices such as Flu No Mo, with a healthy hit of vitamin C with orange, ginger, and sour orange.

Dunmore Deli (King St., tel. 242/333-2644, Mon.-Sat. 7am-3pm, $10-20) serves breakfast and lunch and offers a selection of delicatessen meats, cheeses, pâtés, and locally grown microgreens and vegetables in their self-serve fridge. Sandwiches are served on fresh baguette and ciabatta and are tasty combinations of jerk beef steak with spicy aioli, roast beef with caramelized onions, and goat cheese and turkey, avocado, and bacon.

Arthur's Bakery (Dunmore St., tel. 242/333-2285, www.myharbourislandbahamas.com, Mon.-Fri. 8am-2pm) has been a Harbour Island staple for many years and is a gathering place for a wide range of patrons. Local real estate agent Robert Arthur and his wife Anna run the establishment and serve fresh-baked breads and pastries.

Serving a mix of Bahamian dishes and healthy paninis and wraps, **The Laughing Lizard** (Bay St., tel. 242/333-3990, daily 7:30am-2:30pm) is located just off Government Dock on Bay Street. The artsy interior and friendly faces will make you a regular.

ACCOMMODATIONS

There are plenty of options for accommodations, but the island is known for regular power outages and salty city water, so you might be happier at a place with a generator and reverse-osmosis water maker (RO) if these issues would cause heartache for you. The options at the lower end of the price scale will not have generators and RO water.

$150-250

Royal Palm (Dunmore St., tel. 242/333-2738, royalpalmhotel.com, $93) is a "native boutique hotel" and the best budget accommodations on the island, with a location that's easily walkable to the town's amenities. Standard rooms and deluxe suites with kitchenettes are available.

Over $250

The historic ★ **Coral Sands Hotel** (Chapel St., tel. 242/333-2350, U.S. tel. 888/568-5493, www.coralsands.com, $395) is a laid-back luxurious destination on Pink Sands Beach. Major renovations in 2015 brought a brand-new lobby and dining room, guest rooms, a gym, a gift shop, and oceanfront guest cottages. Dine in one of two restaurants, lounge by the pool, or order your favorite cocktail from under an umbrella on the beach. An on-site reverse-osmosis water facility provides clean drinking water.

On Bay Street, just off Government Dock, in a historic building dating to the 1800s, **The Landing** (Bay St., tel. 242/333-2707, www.harbourislandlanding.com, $295) has 13 guest rooms designed by international lifestyle specialist, former model, and local homeowner India Hicks to create colonial-influenced plantation-style accommodations for the distinguished guests who frequent the establishment. A top restaurant serving breakfast and dinner is on-site.

Pink Sands Resort (Chapel St., tel.

Sweeping views of the pool and the ocean, intermingled with lush vegetation, make Coral Sands Hotel a relaxing escape.

242/333-2030, U.S. tel. 855/855-9621, www.pinksandsresort.com, $600) is on 20 acres stretching from a protected lush garden environment to Pink Sands Beach. Spacious one- and two-bedroom cottages and ocean-view rooms have mini fridges, flat-screen TVs, and sitting areas. Also on-site are two three-bedroom villa homes with full kitchens. Amenities include a freshwater swimming pool, tennis courts, a gift shop, and two restaurants.

Stripes abound at **The Dunmore** (Court St., tel. 242/333-2200, www.dunmorebeach.com). From the orange and white restaurant dining room, the black and white entrance that tumbles down a palm-lined limestone pathway through quiet guest cottages, and the much photographed teal and white hut on Pink Sands Beach, you'll find no lack of style and fabulousness. A courtyard pool is the perfect spot to retreat when you've had too much pink sand and sun, and the restaurant, serving breakfast, lunch, and dinner, is the social hub of elite winter residents. Garden and ocean view cottages start at $700, and oceanfront and ocean-view villas start at $4,200.

General Manager Joe Dargavage has transformed the look and feel of **Romora Bay** (Colebrook St., tel. 242/333-2325, U.S. tel. 800/688-0425, www.romorabay.com, $400) in recent years. This is now a go-to place for weddings and groups, and Joe is happy to help you plan your event. Relax by the swimming pool in lemon-yellow loungers, enjoy dinner at Sunset's Bar & Grill or at Acquapazza, both on-site, or park your boat in the marina and head out for world-class fishing. Rooms have been recently updated and offer comfortable king beds and harbor views. Reverse-osmosis water is on-site.

Runaway Hill (off Colebrook St., tel. 242/333-2150, U.S. and Canada tel. 843/278-1724, www.runawayhill.com, $400) offers a selection of rooms and cottages in an estate home built in the 1940s. Located on 10 acres between Colebrook Street and Pink Sands Beach, Runaway Hill is a hideaway for those looking for peace, quiet, and privacy.

★ **Valentines Resort and Marina** (Bay St., tel. 242/333-2142, U.S. tel. 866/389-6864, www.valentinesresort.com, $415) is located on the harbor side, within walking distance to bars, restaurants, coffee shops, and shopping. The marina is the busiest on the island and caters to boaters looking for a land base. The studio, one-, and two-bedroom luxury condos are part of a vacation rental pool; fall in love and purchase one for yourself. A pool, a dive shop, a coffee shop, two restaurants, and a gift shop are on the property. Reverse-osmosis water production and backup generators are also used.

GETTING THERE

Fly into North Eleuthera airport and take a land taxi to Three Island Dock ($10 minimum for 1 person, $5 pp for 2 or more). The land taxi takes five minutes to the water taxi dock. Water taxis run throughout the day until around 9pm. It takes 10 minutes to cross the harbor to Government Dock on Harbour Island ($5 pp). The water taxi often makes numerous stops to drop off hotel guests and staff, so make sure you get out at the correct stop. Porters will reach for your bags on arrival, which is beneficial if you need help, but if you plan to carry your own bags, make sure they don't run off with them because they will expect a tip.

The Bahamas Fast Ferry (tel. 242/323-2166, www.bahamasferries.com) travels from Nassau to Harbour Island (Wed.-Mon., $155 round-trip) on the *Bohengy III,* with one stop in Spanish Wells.

Valentines Marina (tel. 242/333-2142, U.S. tel. 866/389-6864, www.valentinesresort.com) has 51 slips for vessels up to 160 feet, offering full services, fuel, a restaurant-bar, a pool, a dive shop, and a marine store. **Romora Bay Marina** (tel. 242/333-2325, U.S. tel. 800/688-0425, www.romorabay.com) has 50 slips for vessels up to 190 feet with full services, including air-conditioned showers,

Chic Rental Cottages

Rent a charming historic cottage in downtown Dunmore Town.

There are a wide range of lodging options on Harbour Island, but return visitors know the coolest spots are the renovated historic cottages of Dunmore Town and the expansive harbor-front new builds that retain Harbour Island charm. These homes are perfect to cook for yourself or hire a personal chef, or for large groups and wedding parties. Most of the homes in town and on the waterfront are for rent, so you'll have a lot of options, but it's also one of the most expensive places in the country to rent a villa. Expect peak rates over Christmas, New Year's, Spring Break, and Easter. Following are a few favorites.

Jewel Box (www.chatterboxbahamas.com, $4,000-4,500 weekly) is on King Street and was featured in *Coastal Living* magazine. Trish Becker took a derelict 1700s residential home in the heart of town and restored it, adding nautical accents and artwork by Bahamian artists. For a fantastic centrally located home with a pool, a main house, a guest cottage, and ample space for outdoor entertaining, **The Hatch** (www.vrbo.com/680481, $6,000 weekly) is ever-popular. On the harbor side, **Buttonwood** ($11,000 per week) is a newly constructed six-bedroom, 6.5-bath home with a pool and a dock. Right next to a beach access at Pink Sands Beach is five-bedroom, five-bath **Stone's Throw** ($9,000 weekly). For more information on rentals, contact local real estate agent Mark Moyle (tel. 242/424-2449, mmoyle@bahamasrealty.com).

water, and ice, a marina office with a gift store, and a pool for guests.

GETTING AROUND

Golf cart companies will pick you up from the dock or drop the cart at your vacation rental. Taxis are available at Government Dock upon arrival. If you are staying in town, it's easy to walk everywhere, but running around in a golf buggy is charming, so most people opt to rent one. Book well in advance in high season and on holidays.

No Limits Rentals (tel. 242/470-8502, nolimitrentals@gmail.com, 24 hours $55 for 4-passenger cart, $80 for 6-passenger cart) offers High Roller carts with big wheels for use in the Narrows ($65 per day). Friendly local **Jack Percentie** (tel. 242/470-8554) rents several carts and will assist with area information. Other reliable cart rental companies are **Daybreak Rentals** (Colebrook St., tel. 242/333-2491), **Dunmore Rentals** (up from Government Dock, off Bay St., tel. 242/333-2373), **Johnson's Rentals** (off King St., tel. 242/333-2122), **Ross Rentals** (Colebrook St., tel. 242/333-2122), and **Briland on the Go** (Colebrook St., tel. 242/333-2573).

Visitor Information

Visit the **Harbour Island Tourist Office** (Bay St., tel. 242/333-2621, www.bahamas.com) for maps and guides.

Banks

The **RBC Royal Bank Harbour Island** (Dunmore St., tel. 242/333-2250, Mon.-Thurs. 9:30am-3pm, Fri. 9:30am-4:30pm) has banking services.

Health and Emergencies

The clinics on the island are operated by nurses and typically offer limited services. For major medical emergencies, the clinics will arrange to transport you to Princess Margaret Hospital in Nassau or airlift you to the United States. Try the **Harbour Island Community Clinic** (tel. 242/333-2227, Mon.-Fri. 9am-5pm, except public holidays). For the **Royal Bahamas Police Force Fire and Police,** dial 919. For the **Harbour Island Police Station,** dial 242/333-2111. For **directory assistance,** dial 916. For **weather,** dial 915.

Spanish Wells

Spanish Wells has recently been added to the tourist map as an affordable location in a vibrant community with a few great dining and bar options. The majority of the island's residents trace their roots to the original European settlers, the Eleutheran Adventurers, and retain the same last names. It's historically a fishing village, so its residents have little interest in tourism. The main industry is crawfish export, so many residents are more reserved fisherfolk than the rest of the West Indian-flavored Bahamas, but it is still a friendly community.

Also a bustling hub for concrete and fill, barge services, dock building, and boat

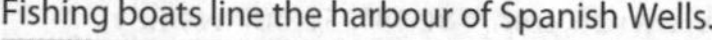

Fishing boats line the harbour of Spanish Wells.

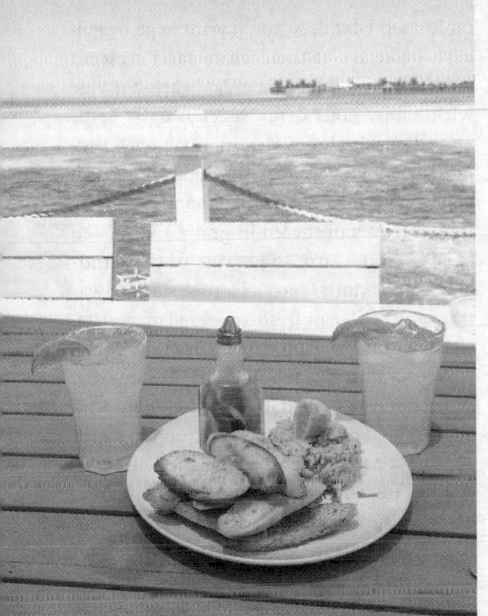

margaritas and smoked fish dip at The Shipyard

haul-out and repair, the island is actually called St. George's Cay, but people only call the island by the town's name, Spanish Wells. It's two miles long and half a mile wide, with a beautiful stretch of white sandy beach reaching out onto shallow sandflats along the entire north edge of the island. Spanish Wells is connected by a bridge to the residential community Russell Island, a three-mile-long island with a community beach and The Sand Bar and Restaurant. The town is clean and well-manicured. Spanish Wells residents take pride in their town.

SHOPPING

Tee's R Us (Samuel Guy St., tel. 242/333-4046) offers a selection of Spanish Wells specific shirts and hats. **Harbourside Rentals** (South St., tel. 242/333-5022), just off the water taxi dock, offers locally made products, gifts, souvenirs, and apparel. **The Islander Shop** (Main St., tel. 242/333-4104) offers "everything under the sun": candy, decorations, stationery, and gifts.

SPORTS AND RECREATION

Fishing and Tours

Spanish Wells Fishing (tel. 242/333-4721, www.spanishwellsfishing.com) offers charter and guided fishing services, including reef fishing, deep-sea fishing, bonefishing, spearfishing, and island tours.

Visit the friendly swimming pigs on a small cay off Spanish Wells with **Da Salty Pig Adventures** (tel. 242/422-9348), which also offers snorkeling, beach picnics, and fishing charters. **Bahamas Ocean Safaris** (tel. 242/470-1930, www.bahamasoceansafari.com) offers beach getaways, reef exploration, and scuba diving.

Kiteboarding

Spanish Wells has become a hot destination for kiteboarders in recent years with the emergence of guest cottages providing easier access than kite spots on the U.S. East Coast. The winds are predominantly from the north and northeast in the winter months, and the beautiful, wide stretch of beach on the north side of the island is a perfect launching spot. Shallow tidal flats and the sandy bottom make it a great place for flat-water riding. Winds typically range 15-25 knots in winter, so conditions are forgiving compared to windier spots like Hawaii, Brazil, and South Africa. There is no kiteboarding school or rentals, so you'll have to bring your own gear. Use caution, as sea rescue isn't always readily available, and the closest major hospital is in Nassau.

FOOD

Spanish Wells only recently developed a restaurant scene, but eateries are flourishing. As a fishing community, there is regular access to some of the country's freshest seafood, and the friendly younger generation provide the best service you'll find. Since the island was historically dry (with no alcohol sales), there were only a few take-out options for food until The Shipyard opened in 2013 as the first sit-down restaurant with a full bar.

Budda's Snack Shack (12th St., tel.

242/333-4111, Mon.-Sat. 11am-10pm, Sun. 5pm-10pm, $5-15) is a quirky open-air establishment on a side street in town, serving simple and tasty bar and Bahamian food, such as chicken wings, jalapeño poppers, a wide selection of burgers and sandwiches (beef, chicken, and fish), as well as chicken, fish, and conch platters. The kitchen operates out of an old school bus, and seating is under an expansive covered porch. The bar is crowded with locals on weekends, and they occasionally host live music and events. One of the island's few liquor stores is also here.

The first establishment to pave the way for Spanish Wells' revival was ★ **The Shipyard** (South St. and Main St., tel. 242/333-5010, Wed.-Sun. 11:30am-9pm, $15-25). Perched on the easternmost tip of the island in a vibrant azure building, the restaurant's deck offers panoramic views of the harbor and calm flats and the bustling sailboats and fishing boats. Try the lobster mac and cheese, and don't pass up the fresh-caught smoked-fish dip with house-made pepper vinegar served on crisp buttery toast. Enjoy top-notch service with a low-key island atmosphere.

The Sand Bar (Vivian Pinder Rd., Russell Island, tel. 242/333-4919 Fri.-Wed. lunch 11am-3pm, dinner 5pm-10pm, $15-20) is out on Russell Island, so you'll want to go by golf cart, or arrive at their white-sand crescent beach by boat. There's a great beach-bar vibe with happy-hour drink specials daily 6pm-8pm. Food includes fish in a bag with veggies and potato wedges, and poutine, a dish you won't typically find on Bahamian menus: french fries smothered in gravy and melted cheese. Make sure to get one of the handcrafted cocktails, such as a rose slushie, watermelon cooler, or fresh-squeezed margarita.

Wrecker's (Spanish Wells Yacht Haven, South St., tel. 242/333-4255, www.swyachthaven.com, daily 8am-10:30pm, $25-30) located on the Yacht Haven property with views over the harbor. Sit on the umbrella-shaded porch or in the covered bar area. The restaurant serves Mediterranean and Bahamian cuisine for breakfast, lunch, and dinner and a full selection of specialty cocktails, beer, and wine.

ACCOMMODATIONS

Check vacation rental websites such as VRBO and Airbnb for vacation rentals in Spanish Wells. Residents have begun snatching up historic cottages, renovating them, and listing them as rentals. Otherwise there are very few places to stay.

Consider renting a cottage for your stay in Spanish Wells.

Vacation Time Inn (South St., tel. 242/333 5022 or 242/359 2954, www.harboursidebahamas.com, $125) is near the bridge to Russell Island. Rent a golf cart if you stay here, since it's a hike to town, but it's operated by Harbourside Rentals, so you'll have no problem arranging a golf cart, paddleboard, bicycle, or snorkeling equipment with them. The suites are on the harbor and within quick walking distance to the island's beautiful beaches. Harbor and road-side rooms have king beds, kitchenettes, and indoor and outdoor sitting areas.

Spanish Wells Yacht Haven and Resort (South St., tel. 242/333-4255, www.swyachthaven.com) has six newly built cottages right in town with two queens and a kitchenette (from $265). The villa has two queens and a sofa sleeper, two baths, a full kitchen, and a lounge area (from $465). All units have terraces that overlook the pool and marina.

GETTING THERE

Fly into North Eleuthera Airport and Pinder's taxi service will take you to Gene's Bay Dock, a 15- to 20-minute ride from the airport. From there, Pinder's ferry service (daily 6am-8pm) runs regularly. For late-night transportation and special runs, contact friendly and reliable **Knight Rider** (tel. 242/557-7299 or 242/333-4291).

Spanish Wells Yacht Haven (tel. 242/333 4255, www.swyachthaven.com) has 30 slips available that can accommodate vessels up to 165 feet. The marina is well protected, so you'll be hard-pressed to find an open slip in foul weather. Fuel, water, electricity, ice, showers, a pool, and a restaurant are on-site.

GETTING AROUND

JJ Golf Cart Rental (tel. 242/333-4575) rents by the hour, day, or week. **Harbourside Golf Cart Rentals** (tel. 242/333-5022, www.harboursidebahamas.com) offers golf carts, water-sports equipment, and suites, apartments, and cottages to rent.

Health and Emergencies

The clinics on the island are operated by nurses and typically offer limited services. For major medical emergencies, the clinics will arrange to transport you to Princess Margaret Hospital in Nassau or airlift you to the United States. Try the **Spanish Wells Community Clinic** (tel. 242/333-4064, Mon.-Fri. 9am-5pm, except public holidays). For emergency services, contact the **Royal Bahamas Police Force Fire and Police** (tel. 919) or the **Spanish Wells Police Station** (tel. 242/333-4030). For **directory assistance,** dial 916. For **weather,** dial 915.

The Exumas

The Exumas have one island for every day of the year. The string of 365 islands and cays runs northwest to southeast, tucked between the Yellow Bank on the west and Exuma Sound on the east.

Eleuthera, Cat Island, and Long Island buffer the Atlantic Ocean swell, leaving the Exumas in tranquil waters most of the year. The islands stretch for 136 miles, from a few craggy rocks and Ship Channel Cay in the north to the "mainland" of Great Exuma, where the largest settlement, George Town, is located. In between you'll find private islands of the rich and famous, small settlements, the Exuma Cays Land and Sea Park, and endless expanses of untouched rugged nature. These islands feel far removed from civilization. You'll know what I'm talking about once you get here.

The Exumas are known for vibrant waters in every shade of blue and green. In recent years the famous swimming pigs have drawn people from around the world. Bahamians are perplexed by their appeal, considering the diversity of sealife, vibrant coral reefs, and the clarity of the water, but I suppose it's not every day you see a pig swimming. In the northern Exumas is a rare species of rock iguana lazing among the rugged limestone of the shoreline.

Farther south, among small settlements of the central chain, there has been an influx of celebrities seeking private island ownership The remoteness, paired with ease of access via private yachts and aircraft, give them the desired privacy, surrounded by lush manicured landscaping edged by picture-perfect glowing white beaches.

George Town on Great Exuma attracts sailboat cruisers and second-home owners during the winter months. The town offers a variety of restaurants and is home to most of the activity operators in the region, but if you're looking for shopping, casinos, and nightlife, The Exumas aren't for you. There are no cruise-ship ports, not much upscale dining, and not even many places to buy souvenirs. It's just local islanders doing their thing—but that's why you'd visit.

Previous: the ocean side beaches of Stocking Island; snorkeling in The Exumas. **Above:** the nurse sharks of Compass Cay.

Look for ★ to find recommended sights, activities, dining, and lodging.

Highlights

★ **Sunday Pig Roast at Chat 'N' Chill:** Head to Stocking Island for the beach party of the year, which just so happens to be every Sunday (page 216).

★ **The Swimming Pigs at Big Major's Cay:** Although The Exumas are a destination for white-sand beaches and breathtaking natural scenery, the famous swimming pigs have stolen the show, making them one of the top attractions of The Bahamas (page 226).

★ **Thunderball Grotto:** Featured in a scene in a James Bond movie of the same name, this grotto is a natural wonder well worth the extra effort it takes to get there (page 228).

★ **Swimming with Nurse Sharks:** Gentle resident nurse sharks are an added attraction to the laid-back Out Island vibes of Compass Cay (page 231).

★ **The Sunken Airplane:** The real story of this supposed crashed drug-running plane may not be as interesting as some of the stories, but snorkeling the site in shallow water is a unique experience (page 234).

★ **Iguanas of Allen's Cay:** The endangered Bahamian rock iguana is only found on a few islands in The Bahamas. With a captive audience, here is your best chance to see them (page 236).

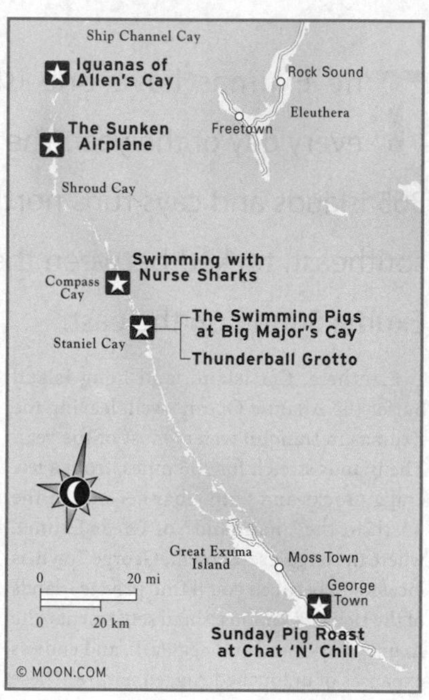

The Exumas

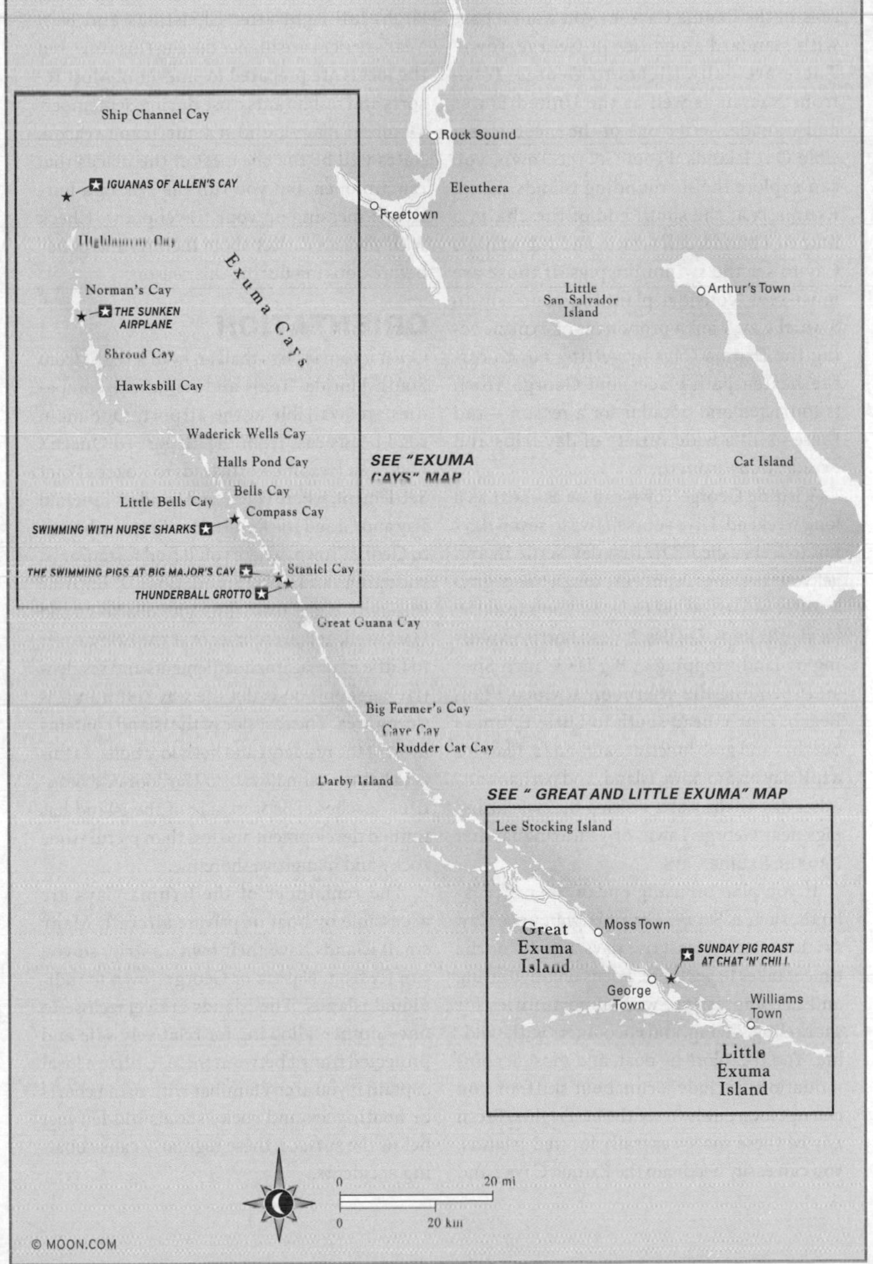

Ship Channel Cay
IGUANAS OF ALLEN'S CAY
Exuma Cays
Norman's Cay
THE SUNKEN AIRPLANE
Shroud Cay
Hawksbill Cay
Waderick Wells Cay
Halls Pond Cay
Bells Cay
Little Bells Cay
Compass Cay
SWIMMING WITH NURSE SHARKS
THE SWIMMING PIGS AT BIG MAJOR'S CAY
Staniel Cay
THUNDERBALL GROTTO
Rock Sound
Eleuthera
Freetown
Little San Salvador Island
Arthur's Town
SEE "EXUMA CAYS" MAP
Cat Island
Great Guana Cay
Big Farmer's Cay
Cave Cay
Rudder Cut Cay
Darby Island
SEE " GREAT AND LITTLE EXUMA" MAP
Lee Stocking Island
Great Exuma Island
Moss Town
SUNDAY PIG ROAST AT CHAT 'N' CHILL
George Town
Williams Town
Little Exuma Island
0
20 mi
0
20 km
© MOON.COM

PLANNING YOUR TIME

First, decide whether you are looking to completely escape in natural surroundings in the Exuma Cays, or you want a base with standard amenities in George Town. There are daily flights to George Town from Nassau as well as the United States and Canada, so it's one of the most accessible Out Islands. From George Town, you can explore the surrounding islands. Great Exuma is at the south end of the chain, a hike to Thunderball Grotto and Big Major's Cay to see the swimming pigs. If those are must-sees, consider planning your trip to Staniel Cay. I am a proponent of experiencing the Exuma Cays by getting out to off-the-beaten-path places, but George Town is touristed and popular for a reason—and there's still a wide variety of day trips and explorations from there.

Visiting George Town can be as short as a long weekend. Give yourself five to seven days not to feel rushed. The first day, settle in and get your bearings, wander through town, grab a coffee at Driftwood Café, and pop into the local gift shops. On day 2, head north, exploring by land, stopping at Big D's Conch Spot and spending the afternoon at Coco Plum Beach. Day 3, head south to Little Exuma's beaches and grab lunch at Santanna's. Plan for a full day on Stocking Island, and perhaps another day on the water visiting the swimming pigs near George Town, or venturing farther into the Exuma Cays.

If you plan on using one of the other islands, such as Staniel Cay or Highbourne Cay, as a base, stay at least five days, if only for the time it takes to get there. Focus on unwinding and decompressing, with opportunities for snorkeling, diving, and encounters with wildlife. You'll explore by boat, and most accommodations include a runabout skiff, or you can opt for a guide to see the best sights. From any of these more centrally located islands, you can easily head into the Exuma Cays Land and Sea Park to hike and experience a varied array of protected sealife underwater.

Peak season is December-April, with a slight lull right after Christmas and New Year's. Prices are higher during this time, but the locals are prepared to entertain. Most resorts and restaurants close during September-October; it's hot and it's hurricane season. Rates will be the cheapest at the places that remain open, but you run the risk of a hurricane messing up your travel plans. Check with your air carrier about their refund policy before booking during this season.

ORIENTATION

Great Exuma is less than an hour's flight from South Florida. Taxis and rental car companies are available at the airport. One main road heads east from the airport to Queen's Highway. Heading north leads to Roker's Point Settlement, where you'll find Sandals Emerald Bay and Grand Isle Resort. Heading south leads to George Town, where you'll find restaurants, shopping, and accommodations. Continue through George Town through Rolle Town and Hartswell, and eventually over the bridge over to Little Exuma. Small settlements and residential neighborhoods dot the way south in this sleepy area. The east side of the island contains most of the residents and hotel locations, as this area has the calm Elizabeth Harbour and beautiful beaches. The west side of the island has limited development and less than picturesque rocky and mangrove shoreline.

The remainder of the Exuma Cays are accessible by boat or private aircraft. Many small islands have their own airstrip, so you can fly from Nassau or George Town to individual islands. The islands are very close to one another, allowing for relatively safe and protected transit between them. Utilize a local captain if you aren't familiar with using charts or boating around rocky shoals hidden just below the surface; these regularly cause boating accidents.

Great Exuma

Great Exuma is the largest of The Exumas and home to George Town, the largest settlement and the center of commerce. Little Exuma is just south of Great Exuma, attached by a short one-way bridge over a saltwater creek. Together these islands span nearly 50 miles. There are endless options for secluded beaches, and this is a great base for jumping off to the cays.

Although George Town is the main center of trade, it's still a quaint close-knit community. One circular road runs through town, past the flamingo-pink Administration Complex and Government Dock. One of the best food stores in the Out Islands, The Exuma Market, sells fresh produce and everything you'd need for your stay, as well as a few artsy souvenir shops and a variety of local restaurants and conch stands.

Throughout winter you'll see sailboaters wandering through town on foot, stocking up on supplies. It's known as Chicken Harbour in the cruiser world because south of George Town there are few supplies and safe harbors until you get to Cuba or Hispaniola. Cruisers congregate here while they consider the long crossing, creating a unique community of transient seasonal foreigners.

SIGHTS

The **Rolle Town Tombs** date to the 1790s. Along with being a landowner, Alexander McKay oversaw 710 acres of land in Rolle Town as part of Square Denny Rolle's extensive land holdings. These properties were inherited by his son Lord John Rolle. Neither father nor son ever visited Exuma, trusting Alexander McKay to oversee it. The land was collectively known as the Commonage Estates, and after the death of Rolle, the land was inherited by the enslaved people who worked it. To this day the town's residents are descendants of Rolle's former enslaved workers, and you'll find a large number of locals with the last name Rolle in Exuma. McKay's wife, Ann, died in childbirth in 1792, along with their infant son, and McKay died in 1794. Tombs were constructed for this family in a cleared field in the middle of town. From Queen's Highway, one main road leads into town. Turn right at the top of the hill and you'll see a weathered "Historical Site" sign marking a well-cleared entrance. Across the street are two derelict homes, bright blue and bright green. Follow the path a short distance and you'll see a stone wall and the three tombs: one for Alexander, one for his wife Ann, and a tiny one for the infant son.

Stromatolites are the oldest living fossils on earth and the first organisms to create oxygen by photosynthesis. They were thought to have been extinct until they were discovered in Shark Bay in Australia in the 1950s. They were recently discovered in The Exumas, the only stromatolites known to exist in the open ocean. You can dive to see them on excursions to remote cays, and some are visible on Stocking Island, if you know what you're looking for. They are single-celled organisms that form flat rocks or coral-like structures and oftentimes create a cloudy glowing turquoise color in the water; imagine dumping milk into Windex. They aren't particularly amazing to look at.

The Exumas are known for gorgeous **sandbars** on the west side of the island chain. At low tide, long white fingers of sand are exposed, creating picturesque swimming and photo ops. The best-known sandbar is near David Copperfield's island, Musha Cay. There is also a collection of sandbars west of Staniel Cay, and another smaller sandbar between Norman's Cay and Highbourne Cay. Check with the local guides to plan your excursion.

BEACHES

Stocking Island Beaches

Stocking Island's gorgeous powdery beaches

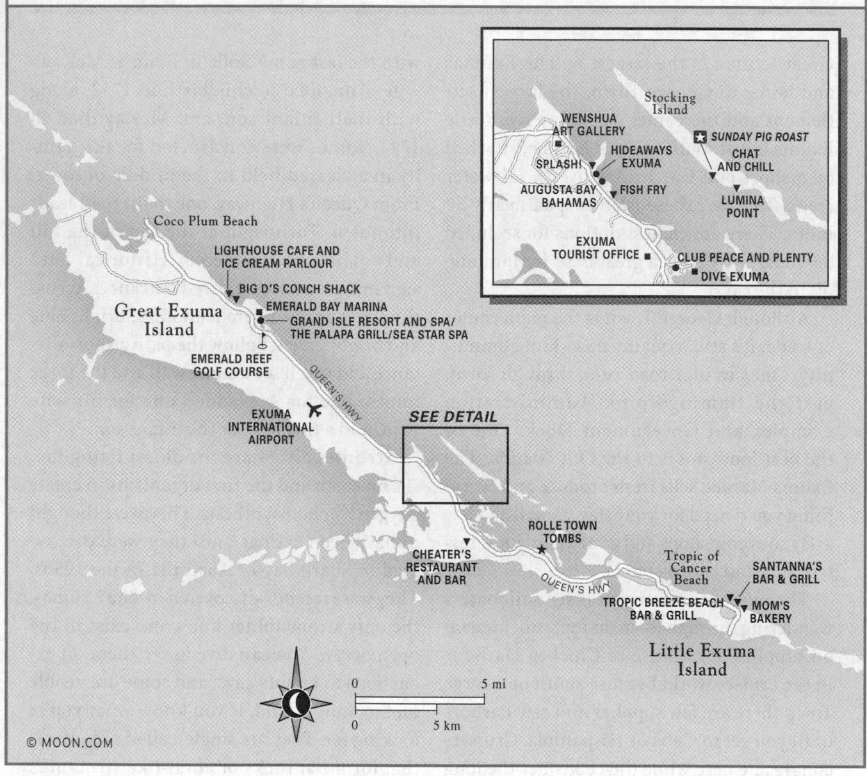

stretch for two miles on the east side of the island. On the north and south ends of the island, dramatic cliffs drop abruptly into Exuma Sound, and along the center of the island, grassy headlands slope gently onto the beaches below. A reef system protects the wild waves from crashing too heavily onto the seashore, and on calm days, you'll find the ocean side just as tranquil as Elizabeth Harbour.

There are plenty of walking trails on the island, leading to the ocean side, including Treasure Trail, traversing the island from just south of Lumina Point and Ocean Beach Path, popping over the hill from Turtle Lagoon. On the west side is **Hamburger Beach,** a small crescent, and farther north is **Starfish Beach,** known for the red starfish, some measuring upward of 12 inches. You'll also find sand dollars and small white crabs. **Chat 'N' Chill Beach** is a gorgeous sandy point along the entrance to the lagoon and seems to have something going on most days of the year.

Great and Little Exuma Beaches

About 1.5 miles north of George Town are two beautiful crescent beaches. **Jolly Hall Beach** is just north of the string of hotels, including Hideaways and Exuma Beach Resort. It's mostly undeveloped, so you can find a patch of sand to yourself. Its protected shape allows for calm spots in most weather conditions as well as shade under the casuarinas. There are no amenities. Park off Queen's Highway, and you'll see a beach access. Just to the north is

Hooper's Bay, marked by a beach access sign. This beach is huddled within homes and small condos, but it is shallow and sandy and a perfect spot for an afternoon swim.

Near the north end of Great Exuma is **Coco Plum Beach.** A dirt road runs 0.5 miles from Queen's Highway to a beach access with ample parking. There are no signs from Queen's Highway, but you can easily spot the road by using a map app on your phone. Otherwise, driving north toward Rolleville, look for the three way junction for Curtus, Stewart Manor, and Rolleville. Continuing toward Rolleville, it's the first road on the right past the junction. There are swings in the water, and sandbars at low tide, making it a great place to find sand dollars. It's a popular spot for locals on sunny warm days in the spring and summer, so be prepared for crowds. There are no facilities.

The Tropic of Cancer is the most northerly circle of latitude on the planet where the sun can be directly overhead. This happens on the June solstice, when the northern hemisphere is maximally tilted toward the sun. The Tropic of Cancer runs directly through the **Tropic of Cancer Beach,** also known as Pelican Beach, in Little Exuma. It's a popular stop for visitors and is a filming location of the first *Pirates of the Caribbean* movie. About five minutes past Forbes Hill in the community of Moore Hill; you'll see a hand-scribbled sign on the side of Queen's Highway. Down a dusty dirt road, it's a quiet community with a few vacation homes, but there's public access to Tropic of Cancer Beach and a small pergola with the Tropic of Cancer coordinates. The beach is wide, with some of the softest sand in the area, and overlooks small rocky cays, giving a dynamic view from the beach. Parking is available, but there are no services.

ENTERTAINMENT AND EVENTS

Just south of Augusta Bay hotel and well north of town are a collection of colorful shacks that make up the **Fish Fry.** This is the center of nightlife action on mainland Exuma. Friday and Sunday are the big nights, but you'll find the restaurants open most days of the week. Porgie's Place is perched on the water with a nice enclosed outdoor area to protect you from the north and easterly winter winds. The ever popular Shirley's Place has air conditioned indoor and outdoor seating and serves a selection of Bahamian food as well as pizza, wraps, sandwiches, and salads. The curried and fried lobster and Cantonese

Jolly Hall Beach

spicy pork chop add an interesting influence to Bahamian cuisine. Friday night, expect late-night crowds, and Sunday often features local rake-and-scrape music.

Junkanoo is held on Boxing Day (Dec. 26) in George Town, ending at Regatta Park. It starts around 3pm, one of the earlier Junkanoos in the country, and includes a traditional Junkanoo parade, and all-day and into the evening barbecue cookouts and music. Contact the Exuma Tourist Office (tel. 242/336-2430).

George Town attracts sailboat cruisers for its safe harbor and because it's the last stopping point before venturing farther into the Caribbean. The **George Town Cruising Regatta** (www.georgetowncruisingregatta.com) is organized by and for the foreign sailboat cruisers and includes sailing races and beach activities such as bocce, beach golf, volleyball, and softball. All proceeds from the event go to local charities and the Junior Sailing Club. The event is one long continuous party, held for two weeks in early and mid-March. Events are at various venues around Great Exuma.

National Family Islands Regatta hosts upward of 60 sloops from all around The Bahamas. Great Exuma is known as the Regatta Capital of The Bahamas, and this event is one of the biggest and longest-running sailing regattas in the country. The races, music, Junkanoo parades, and festivities happen over five days at the end of April. Contact the Exuma Tourist Office (tel. 242/366-2430).

Bahamian Music & Heritage Festival (Regatta Park, tel. 242/366-2430, early Mar. Thurs.-Sat.) is all-encompassing and celebrates Bahamian arts and culture. It includes storytelling, poetry, live music, and demonstrations as well as sugar cane-peeling and conch-cracking competitions. Food tents serve traditional favorites, and Bahamian arts and crafts are showcased for sale.

★ Sunday Pig Roast at Chat 'N' Chill

Each Sunday, rain or shine, the **Sunday Pig Roast at Chat 'N' Chill** attracts visitors and locals from near and far. Chat 'N' Chill is on the west side of Stocking Island, across the harbor from George Town on a beautiful sand spit, with Elizabeth Harbour on one side and a protected anchorage packed with sailboats on the other. A curved sandy beach encompasses three sides, and casuarinas provide shade to picnic tables farther from shore.

The event doesn't officially start until

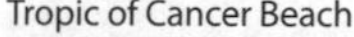
Tropic of Cancer Beach

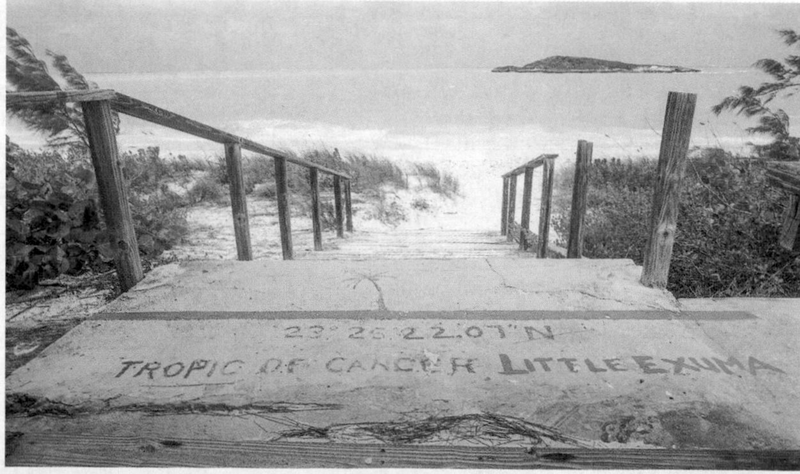

noon, but people start to pull up on the sandbar in dinghies and by water taxi starting around 11am, and the music gets going and drinks start flowing. Chat 'N' Chill starts serving roast pig with mac and cheese, peas-and-rice, coleslaw, and glazed carrots around noon. It's first-come, first-served, and often they run out of pork by 2pm, but the party keeps going until sundown. There's space at the open-air indoor bar, but most people opt to sit outside in the shade, float in the shallow water, or catch some rays on the beach.

A conch stand serves up fresh conch salad, and before you get too sandy or have too many libations, visit the gift shop to pick up your own Chat 'N' Chill apparel or an insulated tumbler. Throughout the winter season, a mix of tourists from nearby hotels and sailboat cruisers from the area use the event as a social gathering to catch up on the latest happenings. These people know how to have fun, so expect plenty of drinking and dancing.

SHOPPING

Sandpiper Arts & Crafts (Queen's Hwy., George Town, tel. 242/336-2084, Mon.-Sat. 8:30am-5pm) is located in downtown George Town across from the pink government Administrator's Office, and features books on the local area, artwork, handmade soaps, a variety of sea-inspired jewelry such as beaded anklets and bracelets with limpet shell clasps, and shirts, hoodies, and tanks designed by local artist Jessica Minns, with sea turtle, dolphin, and ocean-life designs.

Wenshua Art Gallery (Queen's Hwy., Harbour Ridge, tel. 242/336-3023, Tues.-Fri. 10am-5pm, Sat. 10am-4pm) is in a coral-colored building with teal doors, located just past AID auto department store heading north out of George Town. Gorgeous art from talented Exuma artists is on display, as well as rotating exhibits by well-known artists from throughout the Bahamas, including mixed-media, ceramics, oil and acrylic paintings, sculptures, and wood carvings.

Exuma Markets (Queen's Hwy., George Town, tel. 242/226-2033, daily) is a grocery store in George Town, across from Scotiabank. It has the essentials for stocking up, and for an Out Island store, has a fantastic selection of staples as well as a good selection of fresh produce, especially in winter when the tourists and sailboat cruisers rely heavily on it. Parking is available for cars, and for boaters, the Exuma market has a dinghy dock with free tie-up.

dinghies pulled up to the beach for the Sunday Pig Roast at Chat 'N' Chill

SPORTS AND RECREATION

Golf

Emerald Reef Golf Course (Sandals Emerald Bay, Queen's Hwy., Rokers Point, U.S. tel. 888/726-3257, www.sandals.com) is a Greg Norman-designed course and the longest in the Caribbean. It features ocean views and challenging trade winds. If you stay at Sandals, at least two rounds of greens fees are included, and reduced rates are available for guests of Grand Isle Resort. Nonguests can play the course with advance reservations. The front nine wander through seaside dunes, and the back nine are along the rocky peninsula of Emerald Bay. There is a practice range, chipping and putting greens, a golf shop, and a jogging trail along the back nine.

Kiteboarding

Great Exuma is an increasingly popular spot for kiteboarding, but you'll still see few others out on the beautiful flat water and ocean surf. The Exumas are right at the Tropic of Cancer, where the trade winds blow, allowing for more consistent year-round windy conditions than farther north in the Bahamas. Bring your own gear, or contact **Exuma Kitesurfing** (tel. 242/524-7099, www.exumakitesurfing.com) to book a kiting vacation or a lesson. They also offer stand-up paddleboard rentals and tours for days when there's no wind.

Fishing

Bonefish Stevie (Hermitage, Great Exuma, tel. 242/345-0153 or 242/422-7033, www.bonefishstevie.com) is a certified bonefishing guide who also provides deep-sea and reef fishing instruction. Native to the Exumas, Stevie knows the waters well and will ensure you have a great day. For those with kids, he's great about making their experience as enjoyable as for the parents. **Exuma Bonefishing and Fishing Charters** (Great Exuma, tel. 242/551-8443, www.exumafly.com) offers bonefishing charters for all levels, departing from Catch a Fire, just north of George Town in prime bonefishing flats.

setting up for a kiteboarding session

Boating

Out Island Explorers (George Town, tel. 242/524-8246, www.outislandexplorers.com) specializes in sailing excursions and ocean kayak rentals and tours. Ocean kayaking is an incredible way to explore the beautiful islands and cays of The Exumas. Book a three- to five-night guided tour of the cays or into the Exuma Cays Land and Sea Park. Experience one of the small sailboats and find out about the thrill of the Exuma's favorite sport.

Island Boy Adventures (George Town, tel. 242/357-0459 or 242/422-2697, www.islandboyadventures.com) offers private charters for whatever you'd like to do: go to Chat 'N' Chill's Sunday Pig Roast, visit the swimming pigs, snorkel with stingrays, or opt for a fishing charter.

Snorkel Thunderball Grotto; see the swimming pigs, nurse sharks, and iguanas; or book any custom half-day or full-day tour with **Four C's Adventures** (George Town, tel. 242/355-5077, U.S. tel. 954/793-4329, www.exumawatertours.com). For the angler, look into their reef fishing or deep-sea fishing charters.

Spa and Yoga

Sea Star Spa (Grand Isle Resort, Great Exuma, tel. 242/358-5000, ext. 266, www.grandisleresort.com) is open daily at the Grand Isle Resort, or opt for a private treatment in your villa if you're a guest. Numerous massage options include the Exuma Beauty and Lava Shell treatments, as well as facials, body treatments, and even a children's spa, which includes a mini mani or pedi, massage, or hair braiding. Advance reservations are strongly advised.

Island Wellness Exuma (tel. 242/524-8309, www.islandwellnessexuma.com) comes to you, wherever you are in Great Exuma or Little Exuma. A variety of practitioners provide spa and salon services, such as massage, facials, pedicures and manicures, hair color and cuts, and yoga classes.

FOOD

Bahamian

On a sandbar on Stocking Island, ★ **Chat 'N' Chill** (Stocking Island, tel. 242/336-2700, U.S. tel. 954/323-8668, www.chatnchill.com, 11am-7pm daily, $15-25) is a popular spot for cruisers, vacationers, and locals. Only accessible by boat, you'll find the beach crowded with dinghies, but a dock within a small protected harbor allows water taxis and center consoles to pull up so guests can arrive without getting their feet wet. On normal days, the menu serves up burgers and Bahamian food, and on Sunday is the famous pig roast, along with fresh-made conch salad from the conch bar. It's host to numerous events of the George Town Cruising Regatta in April each year. The Chat 'N' Chill's water taxi runs every hour daily 10am-5pm from Government Dock in George Town.

On Queen's Highway near Grand Isle Resort, **Big D's Conch Spot Bar & Grill** (Steventon, Great Exuma, tel. 242/358-0059, noon-11pm daily, $15-20) is on a beautiful stretch of sandy beach. Colorful outdoor picnic tables are for mild days, or sit in the air-conditioned dining room. Although the name may imply that it's a conch stand, there is a full menu of tasty Bahamian food, including whole snapper, cracked conch, hamburgers, and freshly caught fish burgers. **Shirley's at the Fish Fry** (Fish Fry, George Town, Queen's Hwy., tel. 242/336-3737, Tues.-Sat. 5pm-11pm, $15-20) is one of the top fish-fry restaurants, named after the owner's mom. The vibrant

Chat 'N' Chill on Stocking Island

blue and green interior will greet you warmly. Try crispy fried fish wraps, barbecue chicken, and curry fish; or, for something different, a lobster burger, seafood pasta, or conch pizza.

Just south of George Town, **Cheater's Restaurant and Bar** (George Town, Queen's Hwy., tel. 242/336-2535, Tues.-Sat. 7am-4pm, $10-20) is a Bahamian-style highway diner, but instead of high-speed traffic, the passing navigators creep along at a leisurely pace. Cheater's offers simple home-cooked food in a no-frills ambience, a popular option for visitors to pick up take-out or catered food.

★ **Santanna's Bar & Grill** (Queen's Hwy., Little Exuma, tel. 242/345-4102, Mon.-Sat. 11:30am-9pm, $15-20, cash only) regularly sees visitors going out of their way to make the trek to the last settlement on Little Exuma for the food and ambience. Located in an open-air shack on the side of the road overlooking the ocean, the ceiling is cluttered with signed baseball caps from previous visitors adorning exposed beams and plywood. You will be welcomed warmly. Try the lobster in season or lightly battered and fried shrimp with delicious sides. If you're not into fried food, they'll grill it for you. The menu only offers few items, but whatever it is, it's always fresh. Wash it down with a cold Kalik and enjoy the company of other trekkers.

On a picturesque crescent beach among a rocky shoreline, **Tropic Breeze Beach Bar & Grill** (Little Exuma, tel. 242/345-4100, Tues.-Sat. 11:30am-6pm, $12-25) is no-frills, surrounded by latticed railings with plastic chairs and tables, but people come for the views and great food. The signature surf-and-turf burger with a burger patty and cracked conch on a fresh brioche bun will certainly impress. Also available are tasty snacks like Caribbean jerk chicken wings and lobster poppers.

Contemporary

La Fourchette Bahamas (Paradise Bay Resort, Roker's Point, Great Exuma, tel. 242/358-5229, daily breakfast 7:30am-9:30am, lunch noon-3pm, dinner 6pm-9pm, bar 11am-10pm, $15-35, cash only) offers casual dining in a circular cottage on the edge of a gorgeous stretch of beach north of Emerald Bay. Indoor and outdoor dining is available for a mix of French and Bahamian food.

home cooked food and a cold beer at Santanna's Bar & Grill

The Palapa Grill (Grand Isle Resort, Roker's Point, Great Exuma, tel. 242/358-5000, U.S. tel. 844/613-2002, www.grandisleresort.com, daily breakfast 7:30am-11am, lunch noon-5pm, dinner 6pm-10pm, $20-35) is poolside at Grand Isle Resort, edged by the Emerald Reef golf course, and is a relaxed environment where flip-flops and beach cover-ups are acceptable all day. Lunch is healthy light fare like tuna ceviche with homemade chips. Various themed evenings include Bahamian Dinner Night, Island Barbecue with Junkanoo Bonfire on the Beach, and Mexican and Italian nights. Gluten-free, dairy-free, and vegetarian options are labeled on the menu.

Splash! Bar & Grill at Hideaways (Queen's Hwy., George Town, tel. 242/336-2787, www.hideawayspalmbay.com, daily breakfast 7:30am-10:30am, lunch 11am-6pm, dinner 6pm-9pm, $15-20) serves up hearty breakfasts of eggs Benedict and steak and eggs as well as Bahamian favorites such as chicken souse, and tuna and grits. For lunch and dinner you'll find wraps and quesadillas, sandwiches, pizza, and a variety of burgers, such as stuffed mushroom or stuffed cheddar and bacon, as well as pastas and seafood entrées. Special diets can be accommodated, and there are options for kids. Sit in the swinging chairs at the bar, poolside, or along the harbor. This is a popular spot to watch sporting events and for shooting pool and live music on weekends.

Latitudes at Exuma Beach Resort (Queen's Hwy., George Town, tel. 242/336-3100, www.theexumabeachresort.com, Tues.-Sat. noon-8pm, $15-30) offers indoor dining, a mix of 1970s retro chairs and traditional Bahamian architecture alongside a giant stone fireplace, or poolside at the bar, overlooking the harbor. The menu rotates daily, but regular items include burgers, salads, pastas, and steak entrées.

★ **Lumina Point** (Stocking Island, tel. 242/357-0985, www.luminapoint.com, daily lunch noon-5pm, $15-20, dinner 6pm-10pm, $25-40) offers two options for dining: the Lookout for casual outdoor dining throughout the day, and The Beacon for indoor-outdoor dining in the evenings. The Lookout is at the highest point of the property, with 360-degree views of Elizabeth Harbour and Turtle Lagoon. Menu items include decadent lobster pizza with cream sauce, hearty ratatouille, salads, and wraps. The Beacon utilizes fresh, locally grown produce from area farms and the on-site garden. Vegan and vegetarian items are available, along with freshly caught seafood, filet mignon, and lobster tail in season. Dinner reservations must be made no later than 2pm.

Cafés and Light Bites

Driftwood Café (Queen's Hwy., George Town, tel. 242/336-2800, Mon.-Fri. 8am-3pm, Sat. 9am-1pm) is right in town, serving coffee and light breakfast and lunch items like egg sandwiches and pancakes, and for lunch, paninis, burgers, and salads. Be prepared to settle in, as service is on island time.

Lighthouse Café and Ice Cream Parlour (Steventon, Great Exuma, tel. 242/358-0400, Wed.-Mon. 11:30am-9pm) serves delicious home-cooked Bahamian food with a menu that changes daily. Try the ice cream specialties, such as rum raisin or butter pecan. The indoor restaurant is very cozy, but the porch offers breezy seating overlooking the ocean.

Mom's Bakery (Queen's Hwy., William's Town, Little Exuma, tel. 242/345-4062) offers daily baked goods; it's worth the trek to William's Town if you're on Little Exuma. Specialties include rich dark rum cakes, deliciously sweet pineapple cake topped with a rum saturated pineapple slice and a maraschino cherry, and fresh-baked bread. The bakery operates in a rustic shed off the owner's home, but they are friendly and welcoming.

ACCOMMODATIONS

There are a variety of accommodations in Great Exuma, including small guest houses, boutique hotels, and high end resorts. If you're making the effort to get all the way to The Exumas, many prefer the true island experience at the smaller resorts and hotels, where you have the opportunity to settle in to your surroundings.

$150-250

An Exuma staple where guests return year after year, ★ **Club Peace and Plenty** (Queen's Hwy., George Town, tel. 242/336-2551, www.peaceandplenty.com, $169) renovated and reopened in February 2018 with rooms overlooking the pool or with a private balcony overlooking the harbor, with two full beds or one queen. Colors are cool and coastal grays, browns, and whites. Each room has a writing desk, a TV, and a mini fridge. There is a restaurant and bar on-site, where bartender Doc has been slinging drinks for over 50 years. Despite the renovations, they kept the integrity of the originally roughly stuccoed royal-blue walls of the bar, adorned with old photographs and memorabilia. In downtown George Town, it's easy to arrange travel to the cays, and close to the ferry dock to Stocking Island.

A string of hotels and guesthouses line the water's edge north of George Town. The bright-yellow cottages of **The Exuma Beach Resort** (Queen's Hwy., George Town, tel. 242/336-3100, www.theexumabeachresort.com, $189) is nestled among them. Simple but clean, most rooms have glimpses of the harbor, with king beds and mini fridges; a one-bedroom cottage has a living room and a full kitchen. A pool overlooks the harbor, and a restaurant on-site serves breakfast, lunch, and dinner as well as coffee in the morning.

Hideaways Exuma (Queen's Hwy., George Town, tel. 242/336-2787, www.hideawayspalmbay.com, $206) offers studios and one- to three-bedroom layouts. The cottages have kitchenettes, and the villas have full kitchens. All rooms are updated, comfortable, and decorated in bright island colors. On-site is a pool, a game room with billiards and board games, and a fitness room. Kayaks, paddleboards, and paddleboats are for guest use in the harbor, and they are happy to assist with arranging activities and day trips. The Splash Restaurant and Bar is on-site, serving breakfast, lunch, and dinner.

Over $250

Augusta Bay Bahamas (Queen's Hwy., George Town, tel. 242/336-2251, www.augustabaybahamas.com, $260) is located among the hotels just north of the Fish Fry in George Town. Rates for queen and king options include a full continental breakfast. Spacious rooms and baths are great for couples, with double vanity sinks. The dining room is cozy and inviting and is a great mingling spot. The outdoor terrace with the pool overlooks the harbor.

Grand Isle Resort and Spa (Roker's Point, Great Exuma, tel. 242/358-5000, www.grandisleresort.com, $575) offers 78 oceanfront and garden-view villas, elegantly designed with contemporary decor and all the amenities. One- to four-bedroom villas have kings, fully equipped kitchens, en suite baths, and washers and dryers. The villas meander among the Emerald Reef golf course, stretching past the marina onto the point, surrounded by Emerald Bay and the ocean. Golf carts are available for rent, and there are grocery services, a convenience store and gift shop, a restaurant, the SeaStar Spa, a fitness

Club Peace and Plenty

center, championship golf course access, and chef and nanny services. There is a minimum stay on weekends in high season and discounts for longer stays.

Sandals Emerald Bay (Roker's Point, U.S. tel. 888/726-3257, www.sandals.com) is a highly-rated resort for the all-inclusive experience, featuring a mile-long beach, 249 rooms on 500 acres, the Red Lane spa, unlimited dining at 11 restaurants, six bars serving premium spirits, three pools and two hot tubs, and land and water activities that include a Greg Norman-designed golf course. This location regularly receives awards for service and hospitality. All-inclusive rates start at $345 pp per night for ocean-view suites.

Arrive at ★ **Lumina Point** (Stocking Island, U.S. tel. 800/686-5935, www.luminapoint.com, $395) and you'll want to venture no farther. On Stocking Island in protected Turtle Lagoon, with Elizabeth Harbour on one side, it's only accessible by boat. This eco-friendly resort is off the grid, run on solar panels, and 12 cottages are nestled in lush native landscape. The cottages each have a sturdy writing desk with a bench seat and views overlooking the harbor. A breezy screened-in porch allows for doors and windows to be open without the threat of mosquitoes or sandflies. The interior is constructed with contrasting natural wood flooring accented with dark trim, whitewashed paneled walls, and caged lantern lighting, giving the feeling of a yacht. Each room is equipped with a composting toilet and an in-room outdoor shower. A ladder leads to a loft, and the king bed has crisp white linens and dangerously soft pillows, perfect for an extended sleep-in. Continental breakfast of yogurt, granola, and homemade pastries is available at The Beacon or delivered to your room. Onsite is a spa, a fitness center, and two restaurants. The Lookout serves lunch overlooking Elizabeth Harbour, and The Beacon serves dinner overlooking Turtle Lagoon. A private stretch of white-sand beach invites a sunset walk, and just south of the resort is access to hiking trails to the ocean side. Boat pickup and drop-off is available for guests.

INFORMATION AND SERVICES

Visitor Information

In George Town where the circular town road meets at the south end of Lake Victoria, visit the **Exuma Tourist Office** (Turnquest Star Plaza, George Town, tel. 242/336-2430, www.bahamas.com) for maps and area information.

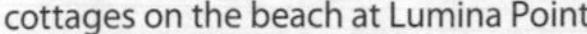

cottages on the beach at Lumina Point

If you're interested in connecting with a Bahamian ambassador to learn more about their culture and lifestyle, contact the **People-to-People Program** (tel. 242/367-3067, www.bahamas.com/people-to-people). Advance reservations to pair you with an ambassador are recommended.

Banks

The larger hotels and resorts take credit cards, but many of the mom-and-pop restaurants do not, so make sure you have cash for your visit. ATMs are at **RBC Royal Bank Harbour Island** (Turnquest Plaza, George Town, tel. 242/336-3251, Mon.-Thurs. 9am-4pm, Fri. 9am-4:30pm), **Scotiabank** (Queen's Hwy., George Town, tel. 242/336-7001, Mon.-Thurs. 9:30am-3pm, Fri. 9:30am-4:30pm).

Health and Emergencies

The clinics on the island are operated by nurses and typically offer limited services. For major medical emergencies, the clinics or your resort will arrange to transport you to Nassau or airlift you to the United States. Try the **George Town Community Clinic** (tel. 242/336-2088), **Forbes Hill Community Clinic** (tel. 242/345-4144), or the **Steventon Community Clinic** (tel. 242/358-0053). Clinic hours are Monday-Friday 9am-5pm, except public holidays.

There are two police stations: the **George Town Police Station** (tel. 242/336-2666) and the **George Town Airport Police Station** (tel. 242/345-0083). For emergency services, contact the **Royal Bahamas Police Force Fire and Police** (tel. 919) or the **George Town Fire Department** (tel. 242/345-0008). For **directory assistance,** dial 916. For **weather,** dial 915.

Media and Communications

Every morning at 8am on VHF channel 72 is the **Cruiser's Net,** with weather, harbor safety and procedures, regatta announcements, thoughts of the day, events, happy-hour schedules, and other community announcements. They also announce beach church, water aerobics, beach yoga, and musical jam sessions. Many establishments have VHF radios, and some resorts have them in-room.

Resorts, hotels, and most vacation rentals have reliable Wi-Fi internet. BTC has numerous cell towers and limited users, so cell service is decent throughout Great Exuma. It gets spotty farther away from civilization in the outer Exuma islands. **Bahamas Telecommunications Corporation** (Queen's Hwy. at the Y-intersection at the south end of town, tel. 242/336-2011, Mon.-Fri. 9:30am-4:30pm) has an office in George Town if you'd like to pick up a cell phone with pre-paid minutes while you are visiting.

GETTING THERE

Air

FROM NASSAU

Bahamasair (tel. 242/702-4140, www.bahamasair.com) has two flights per day to Exuma International Airport on Great Exuma. **Sky Bahamas** (Nassau tel. 242/702-2600, Exuma tel. 242/345-0172, www.skybahamas.net) also has two flights per day. **Bahama Hoppers** (tel. 242/335-1650, www.bahamahoppers.com) has five passenger charter flights from Odyssey Aviation in Nassau to a variety of Out Islands.

FROM THE UNITED STATES AND CANADA

Silver Airways (U.S. tel. 801/401-9100, www.silverairways.com) has daily direct flights from Fort Lauderdale. **American Airlines** (U.S. tel. 800/433-7300, www.aa.com) offers daily direct flights from Miami. **Delta** (U.S. tel. 800/241-4141, www.delta.com) has daily direct flights from Atlanta. **Watermakers Air** (U.S. tel. 954/771-0330, www.watermakersair.com) has flights Thursday-Sunday from Fort Lauderdale Executive. **Air Canada** (Canada tel. 514/393-3333, www.aircanada.com) has flights from Toronto.

Boat

There is plenty of holding and protection

within Elizabeth Harbour in all wind directions. Many cruiser sailboats spend the winter here, some only using the boat as a floating vacation home, and there's a huge social scene among the boaters. Most are content to be on the hook, but if you are looking for marina services, **Emerald Bay Marina** (tel. 242/336-6100, www.marinaemeraldbay.com) offers 150 slips on floating docks in a protected harbor for vessels up to 240 feet. Amenities include a fuel dock, sewage pump out, RO water, electricity, showers, laundry, 24-hour security, immigration and customs, and a convenience and liquor store. Fuel hours are daily 7:30am-5pm. The marina monitors VHF channels 16 and 11.

GETTING AROUND

Taxis are available at the airport. Most rental car centers are also at the airport. Staying in George Town, a car is not necessary, but recommended for stays on mainland Exuma so you can explore by land and visit the many secluded beaches and local eateries.

Taxi

Taxis wait for incoming flights at the airport. Grab your bag and get a taxi to anywhere on Great Exuma. To book in advance, contact **Exuma Travel and Transportation Ltd** (tel. 242/345-0232, www.exumatravelandtransportation.com) for airport transfers as well as sightseeing tours and packages. Limos and vans chauffeur services available for weddings, events, and large groups.

Rental Car

Rental car offices are located at Exuma International Airport. Call ahead or book online in advance, especially during busy season. Rental car companies include **Thompson's Rentals** (airport, tel. 242/336-2442, www.exumacars.com), **Airport Car Rental** (airport, tel. 242/345-0090, www.exumacarrental.com), and **Berlie's Car Rental** (airport, tel. 242/336-3290, www.berliescarrentals.com).

Exuma Cays

If the Exumas are known for anything other than the swimming pigs, it's the endless miles of remote Instagram-worthy islands and cays that skirt the edge of the Exuma Sound. From Great Exuma, the islands run northwest and are only accessible by boat or charter plane.

The private islands of celebrities like David Copperfield, Faith Hill and Tim McGraw, Johnny Depp, and Tyler Perry are interspersed with the local communities of Little Farmer's Cay, Staniel Cay, and Black Point.

North of these communities are 22 miles of relatively undeveloped islands in the Exuma Cays Land and Sea Park. Closest to Nassau and farthest from Great Exuma are the islands of Norman's Cay, Highbourne Cay, and Powerboat Adventure's Ship Channel Cay. These islands are for unconventional and unforgettable getaways. It may seem intimidating to go somewhere so remote, but you likely won't regret it.

GETTING AROUND

If you aren't arriving on your own boat like the hundreds of boaters from the United States do annually, you can book a boat charter from George Town or Staniel Cay. To explore by boat, start with a guided trip to get oriented, as it is easy to get lost and the water can be tricky to read, with many the shoals and rocks.

By air, you can fly a small domestic airline or book charter flights to islands with airstrips, such as Staniel Cay, Black Point, or Farmer's Cay. If you'd like to get to Compass Cay or an island with no air service, look into booking a seaplane with Trans Island Airways, based out of Odyssey Aviation in Nassau. Once you are on one of the islands, you can easily walk, so a rental car or golf cart aren't necessary or perhaps even available.

STANIEL CAY

Staniel Cay is a popular spot among Out Island settlements, with just over 100 residents, but the island sees an influx of visitors by boat, especially in winter. The island has an airstrip but no airport terminal and sees daily flights from Nassau on local Flamingo Air. Food stores feel like walking into someone's living room, complete with opening a household refrigerator to pick your produce. There are limited options for fresh produce and anything other than staple items, so make sure you pack any specialty items with you.

The "town" is three convenience stores, the Staniel Cay Yacht Club marina, bar, and restaurant, and a few other local establishments and take-out places serving Bahamian food. The yacht club has a small market where you can buy phone cards, liquor, apparel, and boating necessities. Using Staniel as a base for boating explorations is the best way to experience the surrounding area. The highlight is the famous swimming pigs on a nearby cay, but many opt to pack a picnic, snorkel the many inlets and reefs, and enjoy the seclusion of one of the many remote beaches and sandbars.

TOP EXPERIENCE

★ The Swimming Pigs at Big Major's Cay

Although there are now pigs all over The Bahamas, the "original" swimming pigs of The Bahamas are on Big Major's Cay, a 10-minute boat ride north of Staniel Cay (inquire about meeting the pigs with the Staniel Cay Yacht Club). Big Major's Cay is a popular anchorage for megayachts and sailboats due to its protected nature and good holding. The pigs are on an uninhabited island, cared for by the local community, who make sure they get food and vet care. If they haven't been fed yet that day, expect them to be restless. If they are happily food-comatose, they may just be lounging in the shade of a coconut tree. You approach the beach by boat, and if they're ready for a snack, they'll come swimming out toward the boat, a spectacle that visitors find delightfully entertaining. Remember they are feral, not domesticated, so they are liable to get pushy and snap for food if they are hungry. Stingrays also frequent the beach, looking for a handout, so tread lightly and make

the rocky limestone shoreline of the Exuma Cays

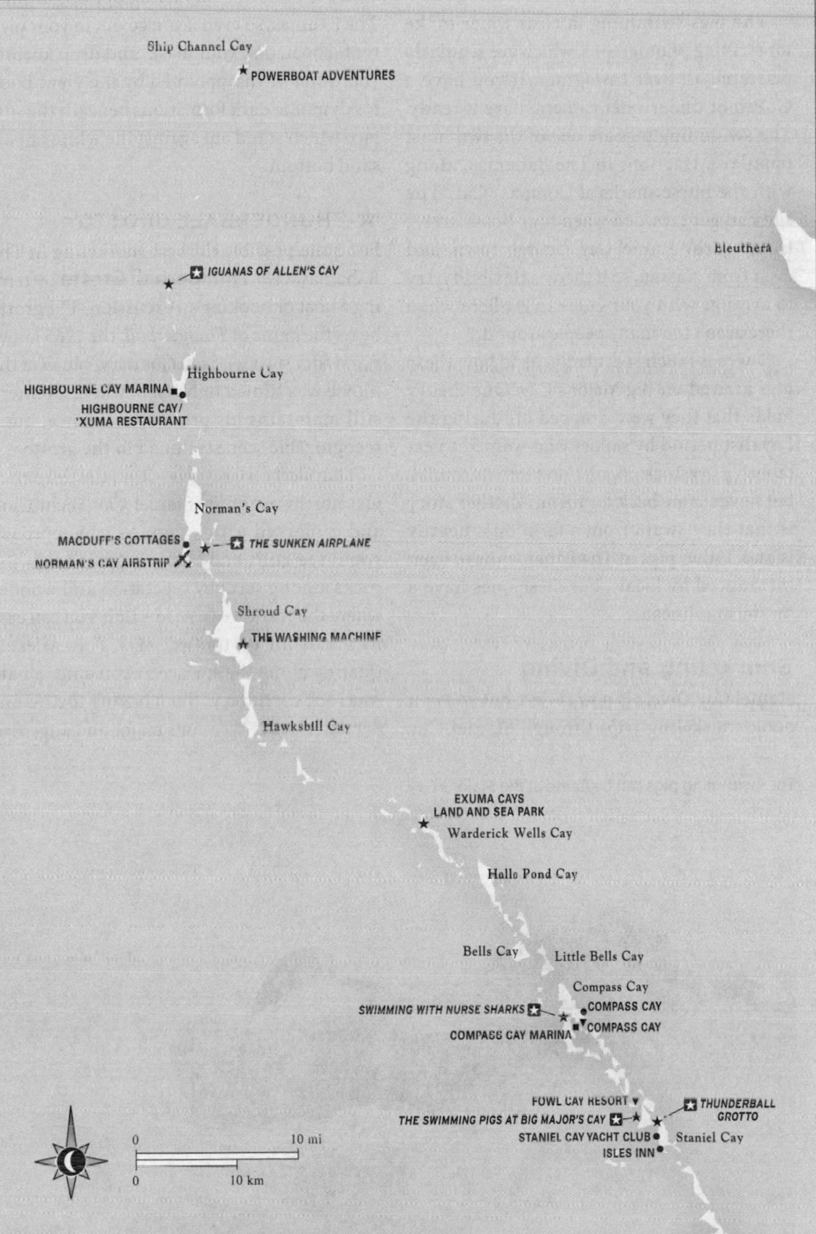
Exuma Cays
Ship Channel Cay
POWERBOAT ADVENTURES
Eleuthera
IGUANAS OF ALLEN'S CAY
Highbourne Cay
HIGHBOURNE CAY MARINA
HIGHBOURNE CAY/ 'XUMA RESTAURANT
Norman's Cay
MACDUFF'S COTTAGES
THE SUNKEN AIRPLANE
NORMAN'S CAY AIRSTRIP
Shroud Cay
THE WASHING MACHINE
Hawksbill Cay
EXUMA CAYS LAND AND SEA PARK
Warderick Wells Cay
Hallo Pond Cay
Bells Cay
Little Bells Cay
Compass Cay
SWIMMING WITH NURSE SHARKS
COMPASS CAY
COMPASS CAY MARINA
COMPASS CAY
FOWL CAY RESORT
THUNDERBALL GROTTO
THE SWIMMING PIGS AT BIG MAJOR'S CAY
STANIEL CAY YACHT CLUB
Staniel Cay
ISLES INN
0
10 mi
0
10 km
© MOON.COM

sure you don't step on one. Although they are docile, their barbs can create deep gashes in human skin.

The pigs swimming in clear water make for striking photographs, which are regularly plastered all over Instagram. If you have a GoPro or underwater camera, have it ready. The swimming pigs are one of the two most popular attractions in The Bahamas, along with the nurse sharks at Compass Cay. The site can get crowded when tour boats arrive from nearby Staniel Cay, George Town, and even from Nassau, so if there is flexibility, try to arrange with your guide to get here when there aren't too many people around.

There is much speculation as to how these pigs arrived on Big Major's Cay. One theory holds that they were dropped off during the Loyalist period by sailors who wanted to establish a livestock population for their return, but never came back for them. Another story is that they swam from a farm on a nearby island. Other pigs in The Bahamas have been introduced by locals, but these ones have a mysterious lineage.

Snorkeling and Diving

Staniel Cay Divers is now closed, but you can book snorkeling trips through Staniel Cay Yacht Club to include Thunderball Grotto and trips into the Exuma Cays Land and Sea Park. There are endless snorkeling options around The Exumas, so even if you go out in your own rental boat, don your mask, and drop anchor, you won't be disappointed by the view. Look for dynamic dark formations beneath the surface which stand out against the white or pale sand bottom.

★ THUNDERBALL GROTTO

For quite possibly the best snorkeling in The Bahamas, visit **Thunderball Grotto** by renting a boat or booking an excursion. The grotto bears the name of *Thunderball,* the 1965 James Bond film starring Sean Connery. Much of the movie was filmed in Nassau, where Connery still maintains his primary residence, but a recognizable scene is filmed in the grotto.

Thunderball Grotto is within the third rock just northwest of the Staniel Cay Yacht Club and is marked with a sign. As you approach you'll see gulls and seabirds perched on the rocks among scrubby vegetation and wonder where the entrance is. At low tide, you can easily access the grotto two ways: The easiest is floating along the surface as you enter a narrow rock corridor, without having to dive underwater. Agile sergeants major and angelfish

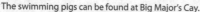

The swimming pigs can be found at Big Major's Cay.

will swarm around, so be sure to bring some bread crumbs for them. A slightly more daring way to enter the grotto is to dive under the surface at a crescent-shaped entrance just south of the main entrance. It's scary, but you won't be disappointed. Below the surface you'll see an eerie blue light glowing through the surrounding dark rocks. Swim toward it, and within seconds you'll come up inside the cave. The cavernous expanse creates an echoing chamber lit by rays of sunlight penetrating a small round opening at the apex. Only the very brave will navigate the exterior sharp limestone rocks and drop through the ceiling into the water below. Inexperienced snorkelers should plan the trip for low tide in to access the grotto more easily. Boat rentals and guided tours are arranged by Staniel Cay Yacht Club (tel. 242/355-2024, www.stanielcay.com).

Food

Serving a contemporary Bahamian mix revolving around fresh seafood, the restaurant at **Staniel Cay Yacht Club** (Staniel Cay, tel. 242/355-2024, U.S. tel. 954/467-6658, VHF channel 16, www.stanielcay.com, daily breakfast 8am-10am, lunch noon-3pm, $15-20, dinner seatings 6:30pm and 8pm or 8:30pm, dinner reservation required by 3:30pm, $25-35) has a bar that has been swinging since the 1950s, said to be one of Jimmy Buffett's favorites. The decor hasn't changed much over the years, a hodgepodge of nautical flags pinned to the ceiling, artifacts from sailing, and life rings from various ships. On any given night you'll likely stumble onto a party or bump into a celebrity who happens to be on a yacht in the area. The yacht club knows how to throw a party for New Years, St. Patrick's Day, U.S. and Bahamian Independence Days, Cinco de Mayo, or Halloween. If you're in the area, don't miss the annual James Bond *Casino Royale*-themed party, held around Easter. Dress up as your favorite Bond character and roll the dice at a pop-up gambling table.

Fowl Cay Resort (Fowl Cay, U.S. tel. 305/284-1300, www.fowlcay.com) offers breakfast, lunch, and dinner for guests. For those staying nearby, call ahead for reservations at the **Hill House Restaurant** (reservations tel. 242/355-2056 or VHF channel 16). Arrive for cocktail hour and the set dining time. You'll mingle with guests inside the bar or enjoy the sunset view from the wraparound porch. Dinner is a four-course meal based on available ingredients and the fresh catch of the day, with a set price per head.

Accommodations

In what could be considered the "town" of Staniel Cay is the ★ **Staniel Cay Yacht Club** (Staniel Cay, tel. 242/355-2024, U.S. tel. 954/467-6658, VHF channel 16, www.stanielcay.com, $270). Don't be fooled by the name; it is anything but pretentious. Colorful bungalows dot the waterfront, so close to the water's edge you feel as though you might fall in. Options include a three-bedroom villa, perfect for families and groups, and cozy waterfront bungalows to watch the sunset from the balcony. Welcoming coastal decor, white washed paneling, and breezy curtains set the mood. Opt for the package rate, which includes a 17-foot skiff, three meals daily, snorkel gear, kayaks, paddleboards, and bicycles. All rooms are updated, and a few are newly built. This is one of the busiest and most popular marinas and restaurants in the Exuma Cays, so you'll never feel far from a vibrant social scene.

Isles Inn (Staniel Cay, tel. 242/355-2007, www.mwpr.com/islesinn.html, $160) is on a small inlet near the airstrip, on a quiet part of the island. From here you can walk to the Staniel Cay Yacht Club, food stores, and restaurants. There are four one- and two-bedroom apartments with full kitchens and a shared balcony overlooking the inlet. This is the best budget option on the island. Vivian and Berkie run the food store downstairs and also offer boat and golf cart rentals.

Just a short boat ride from Staniel Cay is the exclusive getaway **Fowl Cay Resort** (Fowl Cay, U.S. tel. 305/284-1300, www.fowlcay.com, Oct.-Aug.). Rent a villa or the entire island and prepare to be treated like royalty.

The one- and two-bedroom ocean-view villas come stocked with breakfast, lunch, and snack items. Rates include use of your own boat with unlimited gas, a golf cart, all meals and alcoholic beverages, a swimming pool, a fitness center, tennis courts, kayaks and sailboats, and snorkel equipment. The island boasts three natural beaches, so you'll be sure to be able to work on your tan no matter what the wind is doing. Villa rates start at $1,860 in peak season.

Information and Services

There are no police stations, clinics, or banks on the island. The Staniel Cay Yacht Club takes credit cards, but many of the shops and guides do not, so bring cash. BTC has a cell tower on the island, so cell service is good. You can buy prepaid phone cards at the Staniel Cay Yacht Club.

Getting There and Around

AIR

Bahama Hoppers (tel. 242/335-1650, www.bahamahoppers.com) offers five daily charter flights from Odyssey Aviation in Nassau. **Trans Island Airways** (tel. 242/362-4006, www.tia.aero) flies nine-passenger Cessna Caravans, regular and amphibian, for service on both land and water.

Watermakers Air (U.S. tel. 954/771-0330, www.watermakersair.com) flies from Fort Lauderdale Executive on Tuesday and Thursday-Saturday. There are no immigration and customs services on Staniel Cay, so the flight stops briefly on the way to another island, such as Fresh Creek or Andros.

Flamingo Air (tel. 242/377-0345, www.flamingoairbah.com) offers two flights daily from Nassau. The plane is small, and you'll have to step onto the wing and crawl over the cockpit to get into the back, so anyone with physical limitations will not have an easy time. This is an option to get to the island, but recommended is to charter a plane from Nassau or utilize Watermakers Air from Fort Lauderdale.

BOAT

Staniel Cay Yacht Club Marina (tel. 242/355-2024, U.S. tel. 954/467-6658, VHF channel 16, www.stanielcay.com) has 18 slips accommodating yachts up to 185 feet and 12 feet of draft. Fuel dock, electricity, fresh water, ice, and bait are available.

rental cottages on Staniel Cay

GOLF CART RENTAL

Golf cart rentals run $65-75 per day for a four- to six-passenger cart. Although they aren't necessary on Staniel due to the small size of the island, it's a nice option to pack a cooler and head to the beach. Contact **Isles General Store** (tel. 242/355-2007, www.mwpr.com) or **Island Rentals** (tel. 242/524-8191, www.stanielrentals.com) for cart rentals.

BOAT RENTAL

If you plan on staying in Staniel Cay for a few days, consider renting your own boat, since the most amazing aspects of the area are seen by water. Boat rentals for a 17-foot skiff start at $250 per day, depending on size. The yacht club can arrange a guide to book a half-day or full-day excursion. Contact **Staniel Cay Yacht Club** (tel. 242/355-2024, www.stanielcay.com), **Isles General Store** (tel. 242/355-2007, www.mwpr.com/islesinn.html), or **Island Rentals** (tel. 242/524-8191, www.stanielrentals.com) for boat rentals.

COMPASS CAY

You may never have been to an island like Compass Cay. The marina is tucked into a creek sanctuary teeming with birds, fish, and friendly nurse sharks. A gorgeous stretch of white-sand beach stretches for 0.5 miles along the east side of the island. This island takes some effort to get to, but everyone who visits agrees it is a special place.

There are a few bungalows for rent and an open-air bar serving burgers and fish sandwiches. There are no services or community, but you'll be welcomed by Tucker Rolle, who has been running the island for many years along with other members of his family.

★ Swimming with Nurse Sharks

Shark dives abound in The Bahamas, but usually you have to remain still and keep your arms glued to your body to avoid being mistaken for a tasty morsel. On Compass Cay, you'll witness the unique opportunity to swim with and pet the resident nurse sharks, which hang around the cleaning station for leftover fish parts. Nurse sharks don't have the same powerful jaws as other elasmobranchs, so this experience isn't like swimming with a reef shark. They have small mouths at the bottom of their heads to bottom feed, and they are docile, slow-moving, and not aggressive. But don't get your fingers or toes beneath their heads, as their teeth will slice your skin.

At Compass Cay, the ebb and flow of the tide leaves the cleaning station dock underwater at times. At high tide, the sharks belly up onto the dock, allowing those that don't quite feel comfortable getting in the water with them a chance to pat their heads from the safety of the dock. The sharks are such regulars that they have their names like Herman, Mutt, and Scar. Ask Tucker about the sharks and he'll tell you a bit about the characteristics of each one.

Although the nurse shark population in The Bahamas is healthy, their numbers are threatened in other parts of the Caribbean and Central and South America. The nurse sharks of Compass Cay are protected, which is enforced by local residents, and fishing is not allowed in the marina, even though it's not within the park boundaries. This is not a Disneyesque attraction: These sharks are wild animals, and there is no safety waiver or medical reimbursement if you get hurt, so use your best judgment when swimming with and petting the sharks.

Food and Accommodations

Compass Cay (tel. 242/355-2064, VHF channel 16, www.compasscaymarina.com, from $2,400 weekly d) offers four cottages to rent on an otherwise undeveloped island for a true Out Island escape. Two and three-bedroom cottages offer bright island decor and full kitchens on the protected west side of the island with dynamic views of the nearby islands, creek, and native foliage. Bring your own food and supplies. It can be a challenge when flying commercially, but you can stock up on produce and essentials in Staniel Cay.

Ask prior to your arrival to make sure you know what you need to bring for your stay.

The cottages include use of a Boston Whaler skiff. On the dock are picnic tables, where you can grab a beer out of the fridge and enjoy it on the deck, surrounded by painted driftwood plaques covered in boat names. Staff serve a simple but tasty menu of hamburgers, fish burgers, and hot dogs with potato chips. The marina store offers cold drinks, ice, apparel, and a few convenience items.

Getting There and Around

BOAT

All visitors arrive by boat, either by dinghy from a larger vessel, on a local charter, or to stay at **Compass Cay Marina.** Call ahead for marina reservations, especially during peak winter season and on holidays. The marina can accommodate yachts up to 180 feet and offers RO water and electricity. For day visitors, there is a $10 pp landing fee and $2 per foot dockage for boats over 25 feet.

AIR

Fly into Staniel Cay by commercial or charter flight and prearrange with Compass Cay to meet you at the airstrip. They will take you to the cay by boat, a 20-minute ride through shallow flats, sandbars, and low-lying islands and cays. This is a perfect introduction to the Exumas.

EXUMA CAYS LAND AND SEA PARK

The Exuma Cays Land and Sea Park was established in 1958 as a safe environment for native wildlife, with 176 square miles, extending 22 miles from Wax Cut and Shroud Cay in the north to Conch Cut and Bell Island in the south. The park is maintained by the Bahamas National Trust and is home to the only land mammal native to The Bahamas, the endangered Bahamian hutia, a rabbit-size nocturnal rodent and can be found on Little Wax Cay and Warderick Wells. On land you'll also find a number of nesting seabirds and the endangered rock iguana.

Under the water is a variety of coral reefs, fish species, and reefs of stromatolite, the oldest known living creatures. The park sees the majority of its visitors by boat and a few by seaplane. The headquarters is on Warderick Wells Cay, and there are a few private islands within the park. Hawksbill Cay and Shroud Cay, farther north, draw visitors for their natural beauty. The park is a no-take zone for

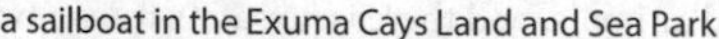
a sailboat in the Exuma Cays Land and Sea Park

fish, conch, shells, or lobster. Nothing living or dead may be removed from the park. For weather and local area information, listen to the announcement on VHF channel 16, and switch to channel 9 at 8am daily.

Warderick Wells Cay

Warderick Wells is the centrally located **Park Headquarters** (tel. 242/225-6402, VHF channel 9, www.exumapark.org, Mon.-Sat. 9am-noon and 1pm-4pm, Sun. 9am-noon). On the island is a visitors center where boaters pay mooring fees and get information on the area. There is a museum of shells and specimens, and on the beach is a full skeleton of 53-foot sperm whale, said to have died after swallowing a plastic bag. The body was recovered and the skeleton placed on the beach to create awareness of the dangers of plastic. On Saturday nights in season, sailboat cruisers gather at the tiki hut for happy hour. The gift shop has books, charts, trail guides, souvenirs, and convenience items.

The Washing Machine at Shroud Cay

At the northern most edge of the park is a tangled bundle of mangroves, dissected by creeks and sandbanks. This island is unique among neighboring rocky islands and their buttonwood and sea grapes. On Shroud Cay is a unique natural feature known as the Washing Machine. Navigate at idle speed through the central creek to get to the east side of the island. The creeks are not quite a cut between islands because at low tide the sand is exposed, but you can boat all the way through at high tide. Hit the Washing Machine on the outgoing tide, and it's a natural lazy river. From a small sandy beach, walk inland on the island and float out, back to the sandy beach. Use inflatable rafts or drift through on your own. There's a bit of turbulence as the tide rushes out, hence the name. To visit the Washing Machine, book a charter out of Staniel Cay or Highbourne Cay.

Kayaking

Kayaking is a great way to see the islands at a leisurely pace and has become a more popular eco-travel option in recent years. **Out Island Explorers** (George Town, tel. 242/524 8346, www.outislandexplorers.com), based in Great Exuma, offers guided trips through the Exuma Cays Land and Sea Park starting from Staniel Cay. Serious adventurers import their own kayaks by barge. Visit the Rocky Dundas caves toward the south end of the park, dramatic caves featuring stalactites and stalagmites, and camp on remote beaches under the stars.

Hiking

There are marked trails throughout the Exuma Cays Land and Sea Park. Over seven miles of trails lace Warderick Wells, including the BooBoo Hill trail to the highest elevation on the island. It has become a popular spot for visitors to bring a painted piece of driftwood with their boat name and date on it and affix it at the top of the hill. Along that hike you'll find blow holes. On some of the other trails toward the south end of the island, you'll pass by ruins from a Loyalist plantation from the 1700s. Hawksbill Cay to the north also has hiking trails, along with ruins of the Russell Plantation. Stay on marked trails when hiking to avoid damaging vegetation and dunes. Make sure you bring water and wear sturdy shoes, as the ground is uneven and rocky.

Getting There and Around

Visitors arrive to the Exuma Cays Land and Sea Park by boat, utilizing the mooring fields of Warderick Wells and anchorages at Hawksbill Cay and Shroud Cay. To book a day trip into the park, arrange it with a charter company on Staniel Cay or Highbourne Cay. By air, **Trans Island Airways** (tel. 242/362-4006, www.tia.aero) offers seaplane charters on their nine-passenger Cessna Caravan and will take you wherever you'd like to go.

NORMAN'S CAY

Located just north of the Exuma Cays Land and Sea Park, this four-mile fish hook-shaped island is everything you imagine the Bahamas to be: ultraviolet waters speckled with deserted islands ringed by beautiful beaches and reefs.

Norman's Cay was originally farmed by a few descendants of the colonial era, then in the 1960s was developed by a wealthy Bahamian family as a weekend getaway for Nassau's rich and famous. The developers installed marina docks, a runway, a clubhouse, roads, and supporting infrastructure, and for a brief period it was a very popular place to be seen. By the late 1970s the development had fallen on hard times and was mostly forgotten.

In the late 1970s, Colombia's Medellin Cartel drug transporter Carlos Lehder ran off homeowners and purchased the majority of the island, and it became infamous as a drug-running hot spot. Lehder was eventually jailed by the U.S. government. Since then an influx of international developers have come and gone. The old yacht club has fallen into disrepair, and the road is a difficult-to-navigate potholed mess. There are currently a restaurant, three villas, and several private homes on the island, but talk of more development has not come to fruition.

★ The Sunken Airplane

A sunken airplane in the shallows just off Norman's Cay is a popular spot to snorkel. There's a lot of speculation about the crash. You might hear all kinds of stories, the most common that it was an overloaded drug-running plane that crashed, or that it was delivering materials to the island and crashed due to mechanical failure. The real story is less exciting: A pilot brought this aircraft from Florida to sell it to drug lord Carlos Lehder, who wasn't interested in buying it. The pilot decided to have a few cocktails and do touch-and-go's, just for fun, and crash-landed the plane just off the southeast dock. Both the pilot and the passenger who was along for the joyride were quickly rescued. Read the full story in Jack Reed and Maycay Beeler's book *Buccaneer.* Reed was Carlos Lehder's first pilot and resident on Norman's Cay during the late 1970s, and the book recounts all the debauchery of the era.

The plane has been called both a C-46 and a DC3, which are very similar, and rests in shallow water just off Norman's Cut.

At low tide the fuselage rises above the water. The plane has deteriorated over time, but it's still impressive to snorkel into the body of the plane among sergeants major and other fish. Bring some bread to feed the fish and your underwater camera to snap a photo

the sunken airplane in Norman's Cay

Norman's Cay's Drug-Smuggling Past

Norman's Cay has a shady past in the drug smuggling era of the late 1970s and early 1980s. The glory days of cash and cocaine were fairly short-lived for Colombian drug transporter Carlos Lehder, but even now stories linger like haze in a smoky bar. In the 1970s transporting marijuana, and eventually cocaine, from Colombia to the United States was an extremely lucrative business. Colombian drug lord Pablo Escobar and his Medellin Cartel had a multitiered international operation, and with the DEA constantly on their tail, Lehder came up with the idea of finding an airstrip halfway between Bogota and New York, where he could transport bulk supply from Columbia and on to the United States in small planes, under the radar, at night.

He found it at Norman's Cay, only 230 miles from the United States, and ran off homeowners, purchasing the island and runway from the Bahamian government in 1978. He then quickly ramped up a wholesale operation. Large cargo planes would fly in by day, the contraband was warehoused, and less conspicuous small planes and boats, under the watch of machine guns and guard dogs, would run the final leg, perhaps to a small private airfield in Louisiana (as seen in recent Tom Cruise movie *American Made*) or to upstate New York. The story goes that so much money passed through the operation on the island that it was weighed, not counted.

Lehder did not take kindly to unwelcome guests, and on the island you'll find remnants of his reign. There's a boat hidden in the bush on top of the hill, just north of the airstrip, on one of the highest points of the island. The story goes that the boat owners refused to get out of the protected pond anchorage, and when they went off for the day, Lehder had the boat lifted out of the water and put on the hill, rendering it useless. Lehder's residence, the Volcano, has been a popular spot for adventurous visitors to attempt to locate. The skeleton structure stood on the north end of the island, but was recently fully destroyed by Hurricane Matthew in 2016. The remains of the old Yacht Club and guest houses can be found on the south end of the island.

To this day, very few people can explain how all of this went on under everyone's noses. By the mid 1980s, the U.S. government put enough pressure on the Bahamian government to shut the operation down, and Lehder was extradited to the United States in 1987, where he is still serving a 135-year jail sentence.

Norman's Cay has been featured in numerous movies and television series, including *Blow* with Johnny Depp and more recently the series *Narcos*. Books about this era include *Turning the Tide* by Sidney D. Kirkpatrick and *Buccaneer* by MayCay Beeler.

of yourself in the cockpit. To get to the sunken plane, you can organize a trip on Highbourne Cay, or with Trans Island Airways to arrive by seaplane.

Food and Accommodations

Norman's Cay has changed ownership several times recently. **MacDuff's** (tel. 242/357-8846, VHF channel 16, www.macduffscottages.com, Fri.-Wed. noon-3pm and 6pm 9pm, $30-50) has a screened-in dining area where you can find hamburgers, fish sandwiches, sushi, and filet mignon. They appear to be targeting a luxury high-end market, and for those looking for a luxe getaway, they offer the perfect private retreat. The oceanfront **MacDuff's Cottages** (from $900), originally built in the 1970s, just prior to Lehder's rein, were recently renovated and are now whitewashed and updated with tasteful contemporary decor and high-end fixtures. Room rates include meals and nonalcoholic beverages, kayaks, and paddleboards. Ask about using the resort's boat.

Getting There and Around

AIR

The island has an airstrip owned and maintained by the Norman's Cay Development. You can only access the island by charter plane. **Bahama Hoppers** (tel. 242/335-1650, www.bahamahoppers.com) offers five-passenger charter flights from Odyssey Aviation in Nassau. **Trans Island Airways** (tel. 242/362-4006, www.tia.aero) flies nine-passenger

Cessna Caravans, regular and amphibian, for services on both land and water. Another option is **Dove Wings Charters** (tel. 242/359-1491, dovewingscharter@gmail.com); contact them for details.

BOAT

Arriving by boat is straightforward. It's only 55 miles from Nassau, and people often visit from Nassau for the day. There are a few good anchorages on the west side of the island, and in calm weather, Norman's Cut is another popular anchorage. A marina is in the works on the south end of the island. As of this writing they have dredged the space but have not started with infrastructure development.

HIGHBOURNE CAY

Owned and operated by the same family as the Island House boutique resort in Nassau, Highbourne Cay has established itself as the headquarters for boaters in the Northern Exumas. The top-notch amenities and luxury villas, coupled with a naturally protected harbor, have evolved over the years to become one of the most popular yachting destinations in The Bahamas.

Highbourne Cay has the only cell tower in the vicinity, so cell service and communications are reliable on the island. Once you get to Norman's Cay and farther south, communications rely on VHF radio. Listen to the Highbourne Cay broadcast with weather and information daily at 8am on VHF channel 71.

★ Iguanas of Allen's Cay

The grouping of islands and cays referred to as "Allen's Cay" includes Leaf Cay, Southwest Allen's Cay, and Allen's Cay. They create a natural shallow anchorage, one of the closest for those coming from Nassau, so it tends to be popular with visitors during the winter months. The iguanas of Allen's Cay are one of seven prehistoric subspecies of Bahamian rock iguanas, simply called the Allen's Cay iguana. Farther south on Warderick Wells you'll find the Exuma Iguana. The subspecies are found on Andros, San Salvador, Acklins, Mayaguana, and several other islands in The Exumas. All iguanas in The Bahamas are protected as very endangered or near extinction. They range from about 2-3 feet long and are pale brown or gold in color. When they are young, they feed on insects and plants, and as they get older, they eat almost exclusively plants. Respect these wild animals in their natural habitat, and don't touch or tease

Allen's Cay iguana

them. If you arrive by boat, don't bring ashore dogs or cats.

To visit the iguanas, you can organize an excursion through Highbourne Cay, or if you are Nassau-based, Powerboat Adventures stops in at Allen's Cay to feed the iguanas on their way to Ship Channel Cay. Pull up to the small stretch of sandy beach on the west side of Allen's Cay, and they'll make their presence known as soon as they see you coming. They are used to human interaction and will run toward you for food, but retreat again as quickly as possible. On Powerboat Adventures, wooden kebab sticks are passed around to safely feed them grapes. They are quick and skittish, but in a rush to grab the food, they snap, so be sure to keep your fingers out of the way. It is advisable not to be wearing red nail polish, as they can mistake it for a tasty treat.

Food and Accommodations

Six cottages and two cabanas at **Highbourne Cay** (tel. 242/355-1008, VHF channel 71, www.highbournecaybahamas.com, from $650) have sweeping views east toward the ocean. Outdoor latticed verandas lead to cool interiors with contemporary decor and neutral tones, highlighted with nautical accents. Crisp white countertops, dark hardwood floors, and oversize dining tables welcome families. The cottages are steps from East Beach, one of the most beautiful and longest in The Exumas, stretching for 1.7 miles. There's another smaller beach on the more protected west side of the island near the marina, conveniently a short distance from the bar. Two-, three-, and four-bedroom cottages and cabanas have an open and airy layout. Included in your stay is a golf cart for navigating the island.

'Xuma's Restaurant and Bar (tel. 242/355-1000, www.highbournecaybahamas.com/xuma, Tues.-Sun. lunch noon-2:30pm, $15-25, dinner from 6pm, $35-40, bar from noon) is elevated and overlooks the entrance to the marina, with sunset views over the rocky cays dotting the horizon. The open-air bar and restaurant serve gourmet takes on Bahamian food, such as a cracked conch burger with calypso sauce and curry conch chowder. For dinner, expect seafood risotto with local lobster (in season), conch, and local caught mahimahi. Dinner reservations are required, and lunch reservations are advised.

Getting There and Around

AIR

A helicopter pad on the island and a seaplane dock welcome arrivals directly. Otherwise, by air, take a charter flight to Norman's Cay. Highbourne Cay will pick you up from the airstrip; it's a 15-minute boat ride to the island.

BOAT

Highbourne Cay Marina (tel. 242/355-1008, VHF channel 71, www.highbournecaybahamas.com) is only 35 miles from Nassau. It can serve boats up to 180 feet with an 8-foot draft. Amenities include a fuel dock, ice, bait, RO water, electricity, showers, and laundry. There is aluminum, glass, and oil recycling as well as mechanical services, and a marina store stocked with produce, dairy products, canned goods, frozen foods, marine parts and supplies, apparel, books, and souvenirs. If you are hailing Highbourne Cay by VHF, make sure you use channel 71. They monitor Channel 16, but they don't always respond on that channel.

Bimini, Andros, and The Berry Islands

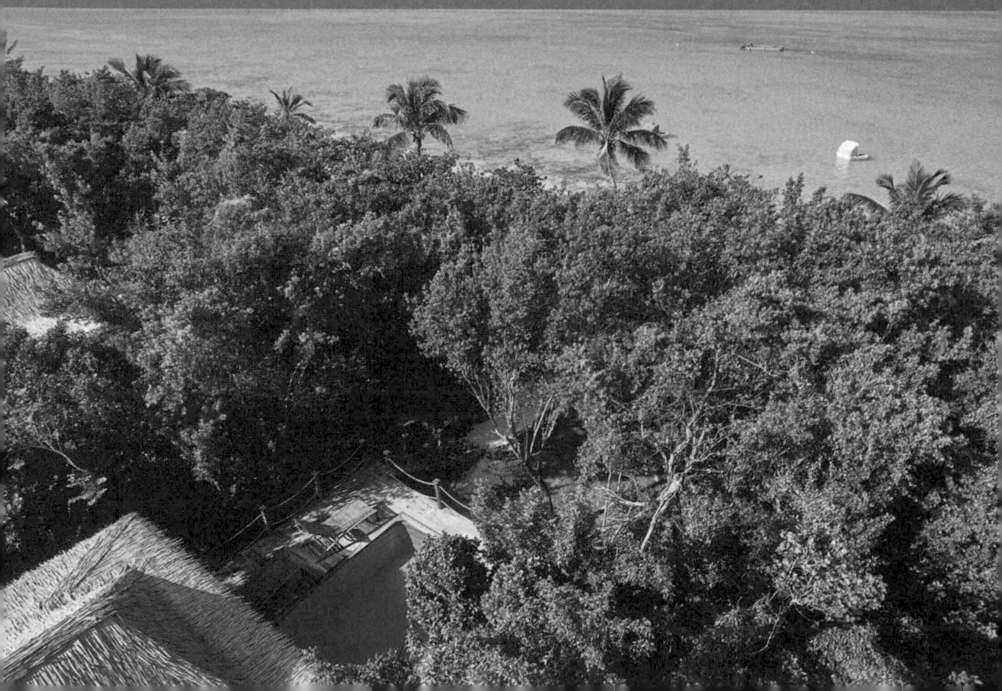

Andros, Bimini, and The Berry Islands are three unique island regions, grouped together only because of the small populations and hotel and restaurant offerings.

But what they lack in numbers, they make up for with natural beauty, peace and quiet, and off the beaten path escapism.

All three of these island regions are within 60-150 miles of Miami, allowing access in under an hour. These islands could be classified as the "underdogs" compared to the more frequented Abacos, Exumas, and Eleuthera islands, but they are certainly no less spectacular. You'll be high-fiving your travel companions for stumbling upon these gems.

All three are known as top destinations for fly-fishing and deep-sea fishing. Ernest Hemingway is famous in the big game fishing capital of Bimini for his record catches in between writing novels. The sparsely populated Berry Islands hug the northern edge of the Tongue of the Ocean, known for deep-sea fishing, and among the shallow banks are prime bonefishing flats. Spread out along the expansive landmass of Andros are a multitude of all-inclusive fishing lodges. Andros is positioned with easy access to deep-water fishing, along with spectacular diving along the Andros Barrier Reef. But what it's truly know for is being the Bonefishing Capital of The Bahamas, boasting endless miles of shallow, protected flats and record-size bonefish, permit, and tarpon.

PLANNING YOUR TIME

Although Andros, Bimini, and The Berry Islands are all located in the Western Bahamas, interisland travel is impossible without chartering your own plane. All three island regions are accessed with direct commercial flights from Nassau, or direct flights from Miami or Fort Lauderdale. Even travel within Andros is difficult, as Mangrove Cay, South Andros, and the landmass of North, Central, and Western Andros are all separated by the bights (expansive mangrove-entangled waterways). There is a ferry service that connects Mangrove Cay and South Andros, but to get from North or Central Andros to Mangrove

Previous: the spa at Kamalame Cay; secluded resorts and fishing lodges abound in Andros. **Above:** partake in some of the best diving in The Bahamas with Neal Watson's Bimini Scuba Center.

Look for ★ to find recommended sights, activities, dining, and lodging.

Highlights

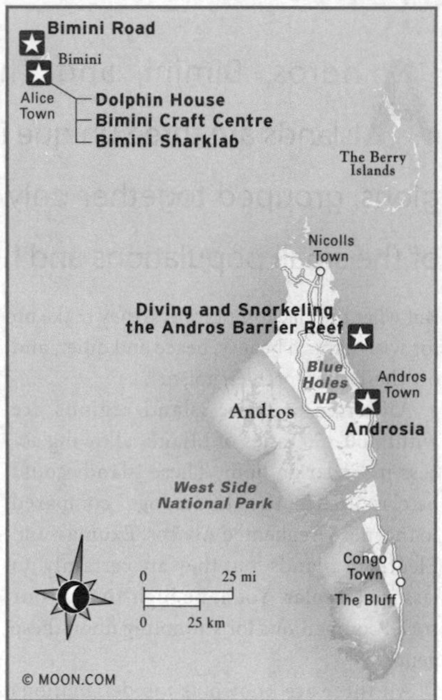

★ **Dolphin House:** A project known as "Poetry in Stone" that has been ongoing for 25 years, Dolphin House is made exclusively from recycled materials and is a tribute to a touching experience with dolphins (page 244).

★ **Bimini Craft Centre:** Shop straw work, shell art, wood carvings, and other locally made crafts in the bustling center of Alice Town (page 246).

★ **Bimini Road:** Believed by some to be the famed Lost City of Atlantis, this underwater rock structure attracts curious snorkelers and divers from all over the world (page 247).

★ **Bimini Sharklab:** Tour this scientific research center to learn about the variety of shark species in the local ecosystem, and see juvenile sharks up close in the transient shark pen (page 253).

★ **Androsia:** Tour the Androsia batik factory and learn about the history and process of this 100-percent Bahamian-made fabric, and create your own fabric as a souvenir (page 259).

★ **Diving and Snorkeling the Andros Barrier Reef:** The third-largest barrier reef in the world, this living organism is home to a variety of sealife and is a destination for avid divers and snorkelers (page 261).

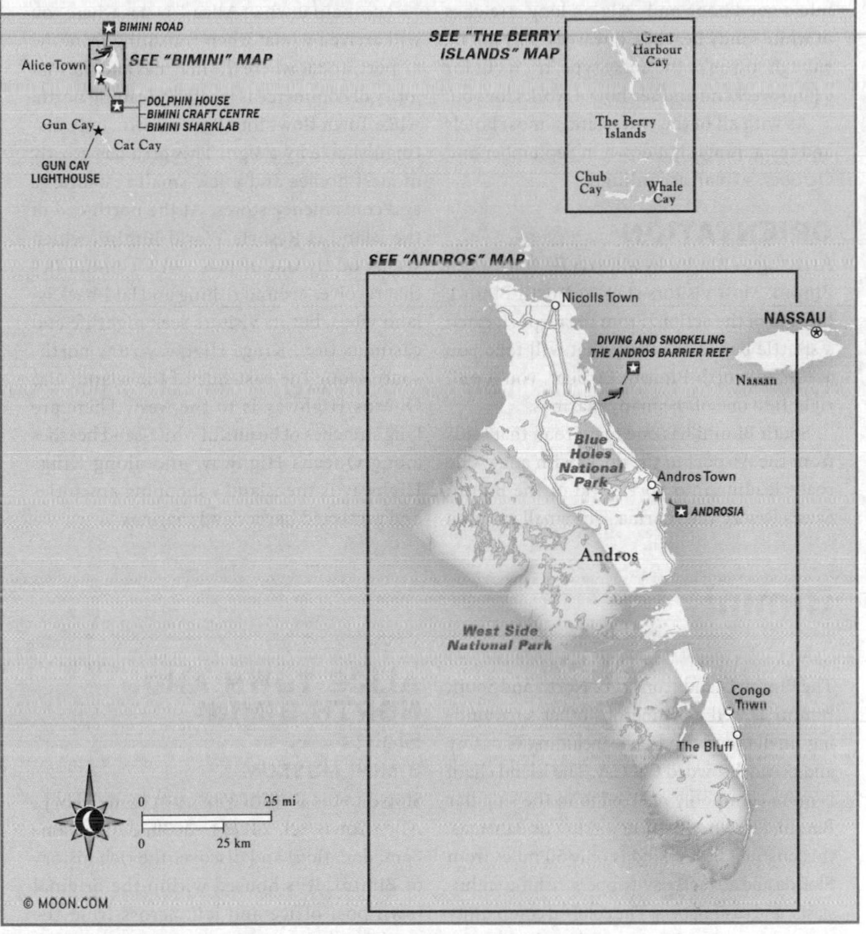

Cay, you must hire a private boat or connect through Nassau.

Unlike the rest of The Bahamas, Bimini's peak season is summertime, attracting visitors mostly from South Florida. Low-season rates can be found in January-February and November-early December. Many visitors come for the weekend on their own boats, by cruise ship, or on a daily flight. Any length of time is suitable for visiting Bimini; the island is small and can be fully explored in one day, so the rest of the time is for settling in and getting into the flow.

You'll want to give yourself a week on Andros. The island is big and there's so much to see, especially for nature enthusiasts. Although you can explore on your own, booking tours and day trips is essential if you want to truly experience all of the ecotourism.

The Berry Islands are for those looking to really get away from it all. Head to Great

Harbour Cay and explore by boat from there. If you are a solitary type who loves to delve into a good book and walk on long stretches of white sandy beaches, one week may not be enough. If you're the antsy type, try it out for a long-weekend and see how it works for you.

As with all of the Out Islands, most hotels and restaurants shut down in September and October, so plan accordingly.

ORIENTATION

Arriving to Bimini by air, you fly into South Bimini. Most visitors stay on North Bimini, the hub of the action. From the airport, catch a shuttle bus to the ferry that will take you across to North Bimini. By boat, you'll pull right into one of the many marinas.

South Bimini has one main road that leads from the Airport to the dock, with a few side roads leading into Port Royal or the Bimini Sands Resort and Marina. The small town on South Bimini is at the very north end of the island.

The main town of Alice Town is where you will arrive by boat when transiting from the airport, and is where the marinas and the majority of commerce is located. Heading north, Alice Town flows into Bailey Town, only distinguishable by a sign. This area has mostly modest homes and a few small restaurants and convenience stores. At the north end of the island is Resorts World Bimini, which seems oddly out of place in a community that revolves around fishing and laid-back island vibes, but its visitors seek nightlife and casino action. Kings Highway runs north-south along the east side of the island, and Queens Highway is to the west. There are long stretches of beautiful white-sand beaches along Queens Highway, and along Kings Highway is the island's shopping amenities and protected harbor and marinas.

Bimini

The Bimini Islands consist of North and South Bimini as well as numerous other surrounding small islands and cays, including Gun Cay and privately owned Cat Cay. The island chain is more commonly referred to in the singular Bimini. Known as the Gateway to The Bahamas, this bustling little island is only 50 miles from Florida and attracts day-trippers, fishing enthusiasts, and casinogoers. The colorful community and stunning beaches attract those looking for a community-oriented getaway with a wide variety of dining options. It is steeped with a rich history of shipwrecking, rum-running, and the haunts of Nobel Peace Prize winners.

Visitor numbers have a larger impact than elsewhere in the Bahamas. Locals are not known to be as friendly as they are deeper in the Out Islands, but they are no less hospitable.

ALICE TOWN AND NORTH BIMINI

Sights

BIMINI MUSEUM

Stop into the **Bimini Museum** (King's Hwy., Alice Town, tel. 242/347-3038, daily 10am-7pm, donation) and discover the rich history of Bimini. It is housed within the original town post office and jail, across from the Straw Market. Read about Martin Luther King Jr.'s visit to the island in 1964, when he worked on his acceptance speech for the Nobel Peace Prize, and you'll also get a chance to see his immigration card. You'll learn about remarkable women of Bimini as well as its sporting heritage. Watch videos of Hemingway dating to the 1920s, and view photos and stories of the prohibition rum-running era, which led to a flourishing economy for Bimini.

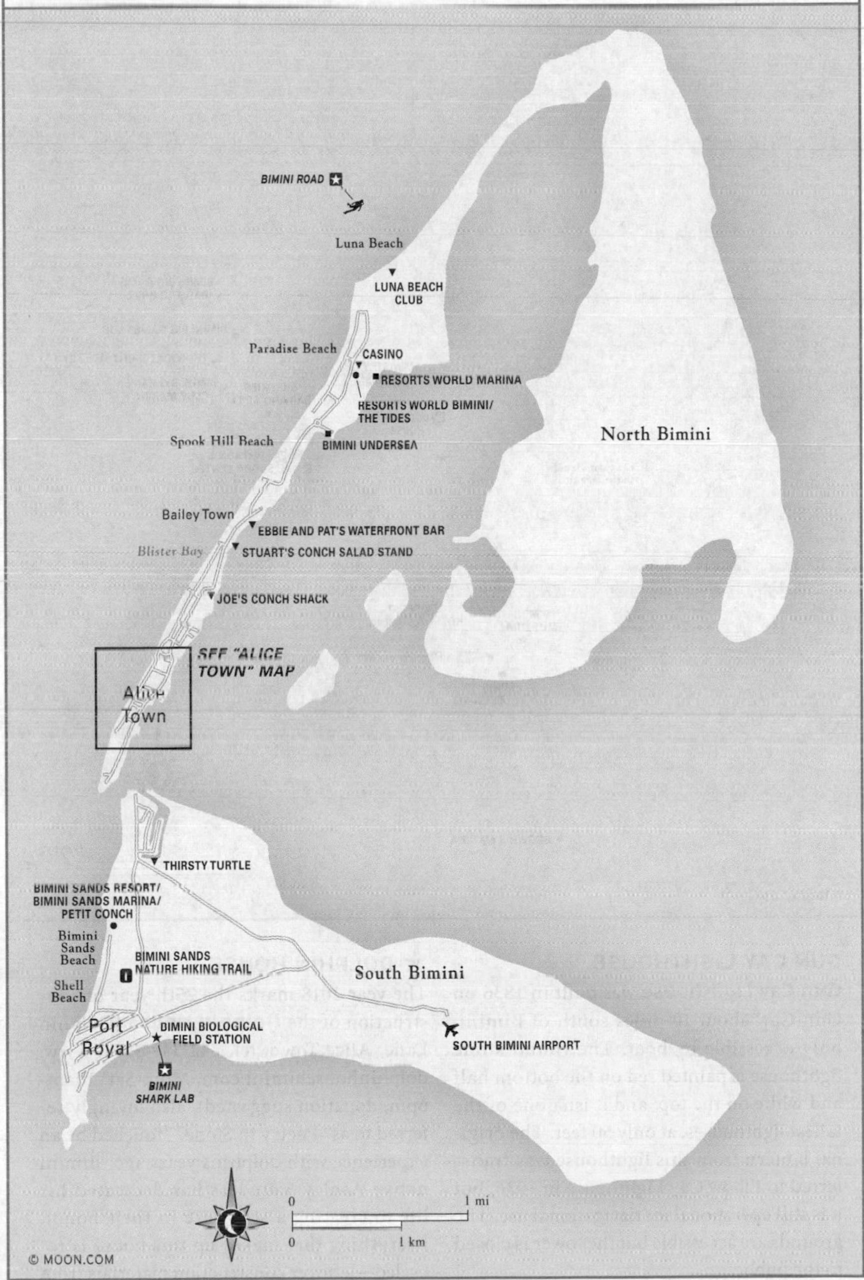
Bimini
BIMINI ROAD
Luna Beach
LUNA BEACH CLUB
Paradise Beach
CASINO
RESORTS WORLD MARINA
RESORTS WORLD BIMINI/ THE TIDES
Spook Hill Beach
BIMINI UNDERSEA
North Bimini
Bailey Town
EBBIE AND PAT'S WATERFRONT BAR
Blister Bay
STUART'S CONCH SALAD STAND
JOE'S CONCH SHACK
SEE "ALICE TOWN" MAP
Alice Town
THIRSTY TURTLE
BIMINI SANDS RESORT/ BIMINI SANDS MARINA/ PETIT CONCH
Bimini Sands Beach
BIMINI SANDS NATURE HIKING TRAIL
South Bimini
Shell Beach
Port Royal
BIMINI BIOLOGICAL FIELD STATION
SOUTH BIMINI AIRPORT
BIMINI SHARK LAB
0
1 mi
0
1 km
© MOON.COM

Alice Town

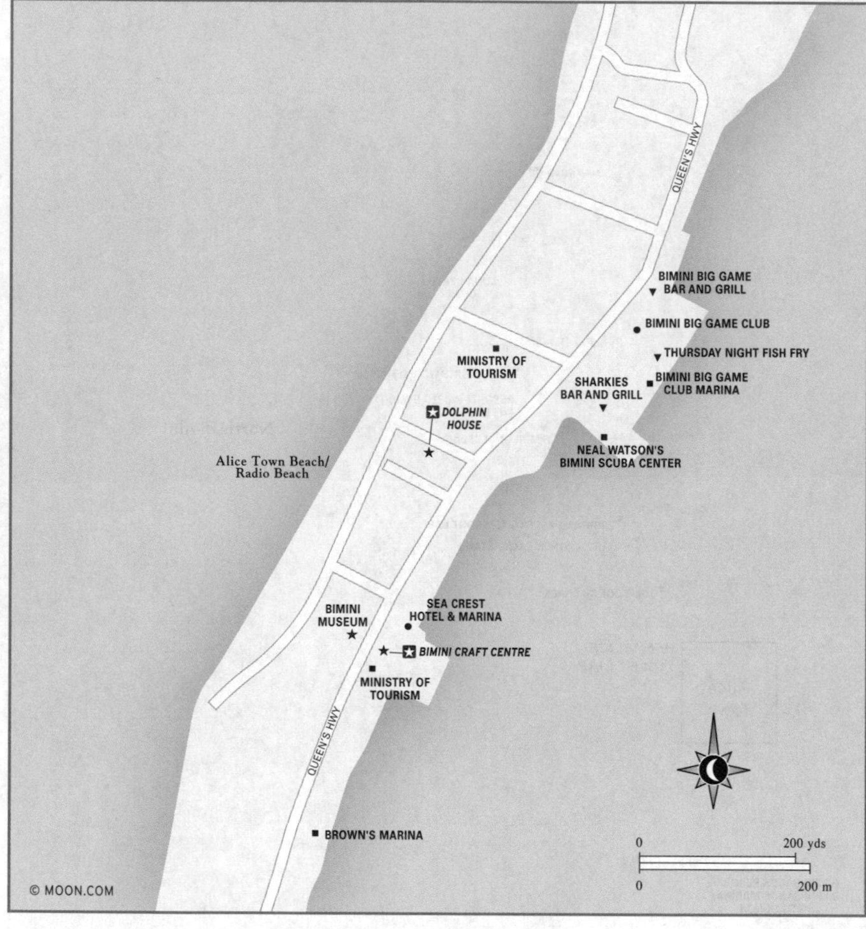

GUN CAY LIGHTHOUSE

Gun Cay Lighthouse was built in 1836 on Gun Cay, about 10 miles south of Bimini, only accessible by boat. The round stone lighthouse is painted red on the bottom half and white on the top, and it isn't one of the tallest lighthouses, at only 50 feet. The original lantern from this lighthouse was transferred to Elbow Cay Lighthouse in 1936, but it is still operational for navigational use. The grounds are accessible but the tower is closed to the public.

★ DOLPHIN HOUSE

The year 2018 marks the 25th year of construction of the **Dolphin House** (Dolphin Lane, Alice Town, tel. 242/347-3201, www.dolphinhousebimini.com, Mon.-Sat. 10am-6pm, donation suggested), also lovingly referred to as "Poetry in Stone." Touched by an experience with dolphins years ago, Bimini native Ashley Saunders has dedicated his life to creating a structure in their honor. Everything that makes up this house is recycled—leftover construction materials from resorts and private homes, debris from the beach, the street, even the dump. Visitors and community members contribute memorabilia. Conch shells, sea glass, and colorful bits of tile are meticulously placed. Everything within the house has a place, and a story.

Mr. Saunders is a fifth-generation Biminite from one of the oldest families of shipwreckers and salvagers. Today his salvage roots are strong as he rounds up materials for his ongoing mosaic. Items that might otherwise be cluttering the earth, have found a meaningful place.

The first floor houses a gift shop and a museum with artifacts, books, coins, and sculptures. View a conch shell dating to the Lucayan era, photographs of Bimini throughout time, book collections of Nobel Peace Prize winners and Hemmingway, coins and currency from around the world donated to the collection, and 50 years of *National Geographic* magazines. Within the gift shop are handmade shell earrings, shark tooth necklaces, music by local artists, and three books written by Saunders. The second floor is a two-bedroom apartment, and he is currently in the process of constructing a third story, another guest apartment, with panoramic views of Bimini.

Stop by and Saunders will give you a walk-through and tour, expressing his genuine views on life, his love for the planet, and his island home. You can feel the energy within this living art.

Beaches

Beaches on Bimini's western side run in an almost continuous straight line, interrupted by a few rock formations that are easily navigated around. The sand slopes gently toward the most brilliant of the electric-blue ocean, glowing vibrantly even on a cloudy day. **Alice Town Beach,** also called **Radio Beach,** is on the southern end of the island and attracts sunbathers from the hotels and resorts in town. Drive along Queen's Highway and find a spot anywhere along the beach to set up camp for the day. The edge is lined with casuarina, coconut palms, and hedging *Scaevola* and sea grape. From the Bank of the Bahamas, head west, and you'll find a few local stands serving Bahamian food and cold beer. Farther north toward Bailey Town's **Blister Bay,** it quiets down into a residential stretch with vacation rental cottages and local's homes.

Across from Spook Hill Cemetery in Bailey town is **Spook Hill Beach. Paradise Beach,** in front of the vacation homes of Resorts World and not technically accessible to the

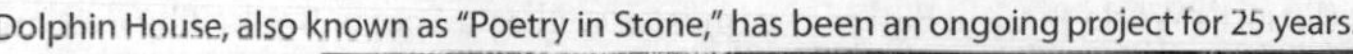

Dolphin House, also known as "Poetry in Stone," has been an ongoing project for 25 years.

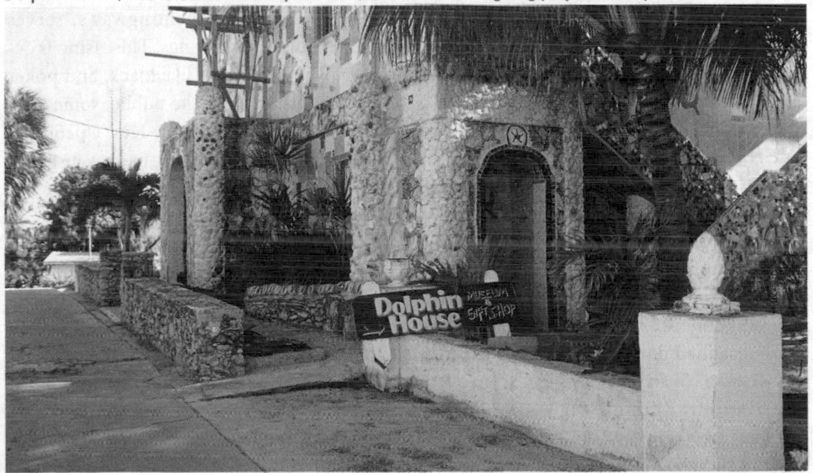

Ernest Hemingway in The Bahamas

Ernest Hemingway arrived in Bimini on his boat, *The Pilar,* in 1935 and returned during the summer of 1936 and 1937. Inspired by the sea and impressive marinelife, he balanced his time between fishing and writing. During his time on the island he completed the novel *To Have and To Have Not.* There are numerous photographs in local establishments and at the Bimini Museum of infamous catches hauled to the docks, which went on to earn Bimini the moniker "Big Game Fishing Capital of the World." One photo depicts Hemingway alongside a gigantic marlin that was bitten in half by a shark, and you can perhaps see his muse for *The Old Man and the Sea*, which he eventually wrote on Bimini in 1951. He also began writing *Islands in the Stream* in 1950, inspired by his time in Bimini, and although the book wasn't published until 1970, after his death, it won a Pulitzer Prize. When Hemingway wasn't living on his boat, he stayed at the Compleat Angler Hotel, which burned down in 2006, and also rented a cottage called the Blue Marlin near Brown's Dock, where he docked his boat.

public from land, unless you are staying in one of the resort's villas. Head all the way to the north end of the island to find **Luna Beach** and the Luna Beach Club.

Entertainment and Events

NIGHTLIFE

You'll find something going any given night of the week in Bimini. Locals and visitors alike love hitting the town. **Thursday Night Fish Fry** (Bimini Big Game Resort & Marina, tel. 242/473-8816, www.biggameclubbimini.com) at the Bimini Big Game Club serves fried fish, conch fritters, and music by a live DJ. **Resorts World Bimini** (Resort's World Bimini, Bailey Town, U.S. tel. 888/930-8688, www.rwbimini.com) often hosts international concerts, so keep an eye out for your favorite artists on the schedule.

EVENTS

The annual **Junkanoo** (Bimini Tourist Office, tel. 242/347-3529) parade is hosted on Boxing Day (Dec. 26) and New Year's Day, and features Bimini's two rival Junkanoo groups, the Tum Tums and the Bimini Stompers, who compete for the title with costumes, choreographed dances, and music. **Bimini Big Game Club Wahoo Smackdown Tournament** (Bimini Big Game Resort & Marina, tel. 242/473-8816, www.biggameclubbimini.com) is hosted annually at the beginning of February. Teams compete over the course of two days for the heaviest wahoo, with a $25,000 payout to the winner.

Casino at Resorts World Bimini

Casinos rarely have windows, but the **Casino at Resorts World Bimini** (Resort's World Bimini, Bailey Town, U.S. tel. 888/930-8688, www.rwbimini.com, Mon.-Thurs. 6pm-2am, Fri.-Sat. 11am-3am, Sun. 9am-midnight) is the only casino in the world to have panoramic water views of the surrounding harbor and marina. The casino has all of your favorite games as well as a Sports Book. The accompanying restaurant, Hemingway's, serves gourmet burgers and wings. The casino is occasionally host to slot, blackjack, and poker tournaments, open to the public, some with high stakes and hefty entry fees. Upcoming casino events can be found on the website.

Shopping

★ BIMINI CRAFT CENTRE

It's hard to miss the **Bimini Craft Centre** (King's Hwy., Alice Town, tel. 242/347-3529, daily 9am-6pm), in the heart of Alice Town on King's Highway near the Government Dock, with a variety of handmade gifts from local artisans. A plethora of pleasantly affordable fluorescent and tie-died shirts with Bahamas and Bimini-inspired designs stands out in wonderful tropical colors. Delve deeper to find straw crafts, wood carvings, and shell work by local artists. The market encircles a courtyard with a lofty white gazebo with bench seating, and is a popular spot to take a few moments out of the sunshine. Plaques throughout the hedge-lined center describe historical rum running, shipwrecking, and Ponce de Léon's search for the Fountain of Youth.

Diving

★ BIMINI ROAD

Bimini Road has long been controversial with historians, archeologists, geologists, and oceanologists but ever-popular with divers looking to get a glimpse of an ancient civilization. Located in only about 20 feet of water 500 yards offshore, this strange limestone rock formation of geometric squares and rectangles has been called an ancient road or wall; some believe it is the lost city of Atlantis. The stones measure up to 13 feet across and stretch for 0.5 miles in a fish-hook shape.

Radiocarbon testing estimates that the beach rock composing Bimini Road formed about 2,800 years ago. Many scientists conclude that the formations are not artificial due to lack of evidence of tool use. However, renowned psychic and clairvoyant Edgar Cayce, who died in 1945, predicted that Atlantis would rise again somewhere off the east coast of North America sometime around 1968-1969. The rock formations of Bimini Road were discovered in September 1968 by three divers. The formations have drawn the curious from around the world. Most opt to snorkel the location due to its shallow depths, and you can book an excursion with **Bimini Undersea** (Bimini Resorts World, U.S. tel. 786/280-6861, www.biminiundersea.net).

The **SS *Sapona*** was a concrete-hull cargo steamer that ran aground in a major hurricane in 1926. It was built in North Carolina and eventually moved to Bimini to serve as a storage facility for alcohol during prohibition. It wrecked in 15 feet of water and is visible above the surface, one of the more popular scuba and snorkel spots because of its accessibility.

Neal Watson's Bimini Scuba Center (Bimini Big Game Resort & Marina, tel. 242/473-8816, U.S. tel. 800/867-4764, www.biminiscubacenter.com) is the top-rated dive center in Bimini and has been in operation since 1975. A featured scuba trip is the Hammerhead Dive, offered every day in season. Another unforgettable experience is swimming with Atlantic spotted dolphins on

Luna Beach

the Wild Dolphin Safari, for snorkelers only. Booking in advance is strongly advised, and dives are weather-dependent.

Bimini Undersea (Bimini Resorts World, U.S. tel. 786/280-6861, www.biminiundersea.net) offers reef, wreck, wall, and drift dives at popular sites such as Tuna Alley, Victory Reef, the Nodules, and the Continental Shelf. They also provide paddleboard and kayak excursions and rentals.

Fishing

Bimini Undersea (Bimini Resorts World, U.S. tel. 786/280-6861, www.biminiundersea.net) offers captained charters with fishing gear and fully equipped boats available for four to six people. Go in search of marlin, tuna and swordfish, wahoo, and mahimahi, or fly-fish for bonefish in the flats. **Bonefish Ebbie** (Bailey Town, tel. 242/359-8273 or 242/347-2053) offers half-day and full-day bonefishing, bottom fishing, and deep-sea guided fishing trips, as well as feeding the stingrays and dolphin snorkel tours.

Food

There are numerous spots to eat in Bimini, with plenty of local establishments to sample home-cooked Bahamian fare, and Resorts World Bimini has a variety of choices, from pub grub to international cuisine. Credit cards are not accepted at local conch stands, so make sure you have cash on hand.

BAHAMIAN

An open-air casual beach bar with sand on the floor and panoramic views of the harbor and marina, **Sharkies Bar & Grill** (Bimini Big Game Club, King's Hwy., tel. 242/347-3391, U.S. tel. 800/867-4764, www.biggameclubbimini.com, Thurs.-Sat. 5pm-late, $15-20) is the place to be on the weekend in season. Thursday kicks off with the weekly fish fry. All meals are grilled at the outdoor barbecue and include ribs, chicken, snapper, pork chops, steak and lobster served with Bahamian mac and cheese, corn on the cob, coleslaw, or potato salad. Sands beer is two for $7 and rum punches are two for $10. There's typically a DJ or live music by local artists, and the party can go late into the night.

Ebbie and Pat's Waterfront Bar (King's Hwy., Bailey Town, tel. 242/359-8273, daily 11am-midnight, $15-20) recently rebuilt and reopened after Hurricane Matthew tore the place apart in 2016. It's located in a welcoming spot on the harbor and is a little more upscale than the other conch stands. They have taken

the Bimini Craft Centre in Alice Town

the extra measures to build covered decks and paint the building and picnic tables in warm tropical colors. Although they serve conch fritters, they are steering away from the fryer and prepare grilled dishes, such as whole snapper, grilled lobster, grouper grill-baked in foil, along with conch salad and lobster salad.

Stuart's Conch Salad Stand (Kings Hwy., Bailey Town, tel. 242/347-2474, Mon.-Sat. 1pm-until late, $5-15) specializes in salads, and not the leafy green type. The standard selection is the traditional conch salad with tomato, bell pepper, onion, and hot pepper. Try Scorch Conch, which in Bahamian terms means "to score." The conch is scored and cut thin and served with onion marinated in sour orange and lime. If you prefer cooked seafood, opt for lobster salad. Located in very simple, rustic plywood structure, there is outdoor seating and a covered bar area overhanging the harbor.

Joe's Conch Shack (Bailey Town, tel. 242/554-6183, $10) serves either conch salad or lobster salad. Watch the owner, Joe, as he expertly cracks the conch shells and pulls out the fresh conch, whipping it into a salad in front of you. Located at a bend in the road in the middle of Bailey Town, the plywood structure is covered in stickers from visiting yachts. There's not much in the way of covered seating, just two picnic tables halfway under an awning, so get your order to go if the weather is inclement.

CONTEMPORARY

Located on the second floor overlooking the marina and the pool deck is the **Bimini Big Game Bar and Grill** (Bimini Big Game Club, King's Hwy., tel. 242/347-3391, U.S. tel. 800/867-4764, www.biggameclubbimini.com, Sun.-Thurs. 7:30am-10pm, Fri.-Sat. 7:30am-11pm, $15-30). Lofty ceilings featuring white-washed shiplap are accented with artwork inspired by *The Old Man and the Sea,* paintings of giant sailfish, and black-and-white photographs of Hemingway's trophy catches. Try the solid breakfast dishes before a day on the water, or request a boxed lunch to bring with you. Lunch is a variety of healthy salads, sandwiches, and gourmet burgers; for dinner, choose from a selection of fresh seafood entrées. The bar serves its own BGBG (Big Game Bar & Grill) Ale on tap. It's a tasty amber-colored beer crafted by Sands Brewery.

The Tides (Resort's World Bimini, Bailey Town, U.S. tel. 888/930-8688, www.rwbimini.com, breakfast Fri.-Sun. 8am-noon, Wed.-Thurs. 8am-11am, $10-20, dinner Fri.-Sun.

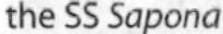
the SS *Sapona*

6pm-11pm, $20-35) is located near the lobby at Resorts World. Dinner is standard resort fare with prices to match. Expect steaks, pasta, and flat-bread pizzas. For a tasty international breakfast, a buffet has fruit, granola, smoked salmon, and cheeses as well as à la carte menu items featuring a wonderful selection of New York strip steak and eggs, eggs Benedict, and the famous Bimini french toast: citrus- and vanilla-infused toast topped with yogurt fruit sauce and mixed berry compote. A bright and sunny view onto the harbor with picture bay windows makes it an inviting breakfast locale.

Luna Beach (Resort's World Bimini, Bailey Town, U.S. tel. 888/930-8688, www.lunabeachbimini.com, Sun.-Thurs. noon-10pm, Fri.-Sat. noon-11pm, $20-30) is touted as Resort World's newest luxury beach club and restaurant. On the most northerly developed point of North Bimini, with a picturesque crescent stretch of sandy beach, guests can lounge under an umbrella for beach service or under the expansive deck. The wraparound bar sits toward the back, and plush pillow-lined seating offers views of the turquoise sea and surrounding palms. Sunset happy hour has half-price drinks; there's live music on Friday-Saturday evenings and a monthly full moon party. Menu items include whole steamed artichoke, beef carpaccio, burgers, steaks, and seafood entrées.

Accommodations

UNDER $150

Sea Crest Hotel & Marina (King's Hwy., Alice Town, tel. 242/347-3071, www.seacrestbimini.com, $120) is located right in Alice Town and features modest accommodations with air-conditioning and a mini fridge with either harbor or ocean views. Two double beds are in the standard rooms, and the suites have a full kitchen. The rooms are slightly dated, but it's a nice option if you plan on fishing or spending the days outdoors. It's a short walk to the beach, and you can walk to most anywhere in town.

$150-250

Resorts World Bimini (Resort's World Bimini, Bailey Town, U.S. tel. 888/930-8688, www.rwbimini.com, $229) is on 750 acres at the northern edge of Bimini and features a mile of white-sand beach stretching toward Bailey Town and Alice Town beaches. There's a rooftop infinity pool, a lagoon-style pool harborside, and a large family-friendly pool with a whirlpool and a swim-up bar. It's

Ebbie and Pat's Waterfront Bar

host to the largest marina complex in The Bahamas, a world-class gaming casino, 10 restaurants, bars and cafés, and the Serenity Spa and Salon. The Hilton resort rooms feature either a king or two queens, or opt a colorful studio to four-bedroom home. Although it's not far from the South Bimini Airport via ferry to North Bimini and a 10-minute drive, many guests opt to arrive on Tropic Ocean Airway's seaplane service directly to the resort.

★ **Bimini Big Game Club Resort and Marina** (King's Hwy., Alice Town, tel. 242/347-3391, U.S. tel. 800/867-4764, www.biggameclubbimini.com, $199) is in the center of the action in Alice Town and hosts nightlife, a bustling marina, two restaurants, and comfortable accommodations. On the property is the popular weekend hangout Sharkies and the more upscale restaurant Big Game Bar and Grill. A welcoming pool deck is surrounded by coconut palms, and there's a full-service marina and the Neal Watson's Scuba Center. A ship's store has liquor, various sundries, and apparel, and a game area has ping-pong and ring-toss. The Hemingway Rum Bar event space is available for groups, meetings, and weddings. Standard rooms are brightly colored in turquoise green and sunbeam yellow. The cottage rooms have kitchenettes, a bar top, and living space, and penthouse suites have full kitchens, a bedroom with a king, a living room with a queen foldout couch, and a balcony overlooking the marina or pool.

Information and Services

Bimini Tourist Office of the Ministry of Tourism (tel. 242/347-3528 or 242/347-3529, Mon.-Fri. 9am-5pm, www.bahamas.com) has two locations; one right next to the Craft Centre, and farther north on King's Highway. Stop in for maps and information.

Bahamas Out Islands Promotions Board (tel. 242/322-1140, www.myoutislands.com) is a separate entity from the Ministry of Tourism, focusing only on the Out Islands. Information can be found on their website, with activities and promotions. Look for the ongoing Fly Free and Air Credit promotions with participating member hotels.

If you're interested in connecting with a Bahamian ambassador to learn more about their culture and lifestyle, contact the **People-to-People Program** (tel. 242/367-3067, www.bahamas.com/people-to-people). Advance reservations to pair you with an ambassador are recommended.

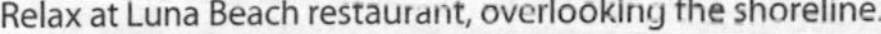

Relax at Luna Beach restaurant, overlooking the shoreline.

BANKS

The only bank on the island is **Bank of The Bahamas** (King's Hwy., Alice Town, tel. 242/347-2106, www.bankbahamas.com, Mon.-Thurs. 9:30am-3pm, Fri. 9:30am-4:30pm). Many local establishments don't take credit cards, so make sure you have cash on hand.

HEALTH AND EMERGENCY

Try the **Alice Town Community Clinic** (tel. 242/347-2210, Mon.-Fri. 9am-5pm, except public holidays). For emergency services, contact the **Royal Bahamas Police Force** (Alice Town tel. 242/347-3144, South Bimini tel. 242/347-3424) by dialing 919, 911, or tel. 242/347-9919. For **directory assistance,** dial 916. For **weather** dial 915.

Getting There

AIR

South Bimini Airport (BIM) has direct daily flights from the United States and Nassau. **Western Air** (tel. 242/351-3804, www.westernairbahamas.com) has two flights daily from Nassau. **Silver Airways** (U.S. tel. 801/401-9100, www.silverairways.com) has one or two flights daily from Fort Lauderdale. **Elite Airways** (U.S. tel. 877/393-2501, www.res.eliteairways.net) has nonstop flights from New York City's Newark airport and Orlando on Thursday and Sunday. **Tropic Ocean Airways** (U.S. tel. 800/767-0897, www.flytropic.com) is a seaplane charter that flies from Fort Lauderdale airport to South Bimini Airport, or the North Bimini Seaplane Base at Resorts World Bimini, offering two or three flights per day in high season.

Upon landing at Bimini Airport, you board the shuttle bus ($5) to go anywhere in South Bimini and to the ferry dock to North Bimini. The fare includes the ferry ride. The ferry trip takes only a few minutes and runs nonstop throughout the day until about 10pm.

BOAT

Bimini sees the majority of its visitors via private boats and ferries from the United States. Many come for the day or the weekend. There are a number of marinas to choose from with full services. Arriving by boat, you must raise your yellow quarantine flag until you have cleared in, and then it is respectful to fly the Bahamas courtesy flag. All crew stays aboard the boat while the captain clears in with immigration and customs. The cost is $150 for boats under 30 feet and $300 for boats over 30 feet and includes a cruising permit that's valid for up to one

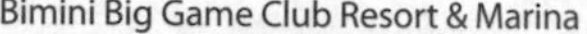
Bimini Big Game Club Resort & Marina

year as well as a fishing permit. Although the cruising permit may be good for a year, people can only be stamped into The Bahamas for a maximum of 90 days. Call in advance for marina reservations, especially in high season or on holiday weekends. All marinas can be hailed on VHF channel 16.

Big Game Club Resort & Marina (Alice Town, tel. 242/347-3391, U.S. tel. 800/867-4764, www.biggameclubbimini.com) has 75 slips for boats up to 160 feet. Water, power, and ice are available. Immigration and customs, fuel, and laundry facilities are located nearby. Two restaurants, a dive shop, an outfitter shop with a liquor store, and a pool are available to marina guests.

Brown's Marina Bimini (Alice Town, tel. 242/347-3116, U.S. tel. 305/423-3213, www.brownsmarinabimini.com) is the first marina you'll come to on entering the harbor. Slips up to 150 feet, showers, electricity, and a bar and restaurant are on-site. **Sea Crest Hotel & Marina** (Alice Town, tel. 242/347-3071, www.seacrestbimini.com) offers water, ice, electricity, and lodging. **Resorts World Bimini Marina** (Bailey Town, U.S. tel. 305/374-6664, ext. 1035, www.rwbimini.com) is a full-service marina that accommodates boats up to 200 feet. Fuel, immigration and customs, water, electricity, and amenities of the resort are available.

FRS Caribbean Ferry (U.S. tel. 877/286-7220, www.frs-caribbean.com) has four trips per week, offering ferry-only and ferry plus hotel packages with Resorts World Bimini.

Getting Around

Once on the island, many opt to rent a golf cart or a scooter ($25 1st hour, $15 each additional hour, $70 85 per day). Taxis are also readily available to take you to your destination. **Sunset Scooter Rental** (King's Hwy., Alice Town, tel. 242/347-3251) is in Robert's Grocery Store. **M&M Golf Cart Rental** (King's Hwy., Alice Town, tel. 242/347-2375 or 242/473-4357) is at Bimini Big Game Club. **Le'Rick's Golf Cart Rental** (King's Hwy., Alice Town, tel. 242/347-4043 or 242/554-4578) is just north of the Bank of the Bahamas, before Bimini Big Game Club.

SOUTH BIMINI

Expansive South Bimini is the quieter and more low-key of the two islands, perfect for those looking to get away from the crowds. The island has more of a focus on conservation and offers a self-guided nature trail as well as the Sharklab, which provides information and encounters with the local shark populations. Bimini Sands Resort is on the eastern side of the island along a beautiful stretch of beach.

Sights

★ BIMINI SHARKLAB

The Bimini Biological Field Station Sharklab (South Bimini tel. 242/347-4538, tours@biminisharklab.com, VHF channel 88A, www.biminisharklab.com, call for visiting hours, $10 pp) was established in 1990 by Dr. Samuel "Doc" Gruber and has been featured on the Discovery Channel, including Shark Week; National Geographic Channel, international news programs; and documentaries. The lab was conceptualized at the University of Miami, and on Bimini lemon shark research trips, it eventually expanded into a research base on the island.

Today, the lab is host to hundreds of volunteers, visiting students and scientists, and 10 staff members. Students typically have ongoing three year thesis projects. Sharklab's mission is "to better understand the elasmobranch (sharks and rays) species around Bimini and the roles they play in their ecosystem." Visiting the lab involves a tour with nine species of juvenile sharks in a pen to see these unique creatures up close. Follow the tour leader into the shallow water as they capture one in a net. Since its inception, the lab has followed the family trees of pupping Bimini lemon sharks, some of the oldest age 40. The lab welcomes visitors and staff is enthusiastic about sharing their wealth of knowledge about conservation and the ecosystem. Tour times vary as they are conducted at low tide.

The Fountain of Youth (Airport Rd., tel. 242/347-3500, www.biminisands.com, free) is one of the oldest historical landmarks in The Bahamas and is maintained by Bimini Sands Resort. The well was supposedly utilized by early Lucayan settlers to restore health, and word got to Spanish explorer Ponce de Léon, who sailed from Puerto Rico to find it in 1513. He never found the fountain in Bimini, but found Florida and the Gulf Stream instead. There is a short path leading to the circular limestone well nestled in native trees. The hole is surrounded by a circular rock wall, topped with an old-fashioned turn-style pulley system with a bucket for retrieving water.

Beaches

Bimini Sands Beach is a gorgeous stretch in front of the Bimini Sands Resort. Breakwater rock walls create a calm environment for swimming. At the resort, a small beach bar serves cocktails and casual food, and you can enjoy volleyball, loungers with umbrellas, and water sports. The beach is for guests of the resort and offers showers and restroom facilities.

Between Bimini Sands Resort and the community of Port Royal to the south is about 0.75 miles of undeveloped land called **Shell Beach.** The Bimini Nature Trail is in the bush just east of the beach. There is fantastic snorkeling just off the beach, and colorful seashells litter this stretch. There is a picnic area but no facilities. A dirt road runs along the shoreline, which can be accessed from the north or south of the undeveloped land.

Sports and Recreation

BIMINI SANDS NATURE HIKING TRAIL

Bimini Sands Nature Hiking Trail (tel. 242/347-3500, www.biminisands.com, free) is a self-guided walking tour just south of Bimini Sands Resort. It is a brief one-mile walk on level ground, with interpretive signs discussing native animals such as the white crowned pigeon and the Bimini boa, as well as signs pointing out native species of silver thatch palms, gumelemi, and poisonwood.

a juvenile nurse shark at the Bimini Sharklab

Food

Petit Conch (Bimini Sands Resort, tel. 242/347-3500, www.biminisands.com, Mon.-Thurs. 7:30am-3pm, Fri.-Sun. 7:30am-9pm, $8-15) is a diner-style restaurant above the main office at Bimini Sands Resort, right at the marina. There's an outdoor deck overlooking the marina and indoor air-conditioned booth and bar seating for hearty American breakfast options such as omlets, pancakes, and egg sandwiches. Lunch and dinner are wings, burgers, pasta, and catch of the day. The bar is a popular hangout for guests of the resort and marina.

Thirsty Turtle (tel. 242/347-4444, Sun.-Thurs. 8:30am-noon, Fri.-Sat. 8:30am-2am, $10-15) is a local hangout in the small settlement of South Bimini, just south of the ferry dock. Open for breakfast and lunch, you'll find it relatively quiet during the day, picking up in the evening with the after-work crowd

the beach at Bimini Sands Resort and Marina

and those looking to let loose on the dance floor on the weekend. Its dark appearance, limited windows, and lack of any sign of interior decorating doesn't attract folks for the ambience, but they do have the best pizza in Bimini and serve daily Bahamian specials. They also offer catering for pickup.

Accommodations

Bimini Sands Resort and Marina (U.S. tel. 888/588-2464, www.thebiminisands.com, $275) offers lovely ocean-inspired one- and two-bedroom marina-view and oceanfront condos with full kitchens, private patios or balconies, and two full baths. Rates range from $185 for a marina view one-bedroom in low season to $289 for a one-bedroom oceanfront condo in high season. The resort has a restaurant and a beach bar and is situated on a beautiful stretch of white sand, used only by guests of the resort. Amenities include an infinity pool that overlooks the ocean, tennis courts, a ship store, and bicycles available for rent.

Getting There

There are direct flights from the United States and Nassau into **South Bimini Airport** (BIM). **Silver Airways** (U.S. tel. 801/401-9100, www.silverairways.com) has one or two flights daily from Fort Lauderdale. **Western Air** (tel. 242/351-3804, www.westernairbahamas.com) has two flights daily from Nassau. **Elite Airways** (U.S. tel. 877/393-2501, www.res.eliteairways.net) has nonstop flights from New York City's Newark airport and Orlando on Thursday and Sunday. **Tropic Ocean Airways** (U.S. tel. 800/767-0897, www.flytropic.com) is a seaplane charter that flies from Fort Lauderdale International to South Bimini Airport on two or three flights per day in high season.

Full-service **Bimini Sands Marina** (U.S. tel. 888/588-2464, VHF channel 68, www.thebiminisands.com) is one of the top-rated marinas in the area, with deep-water access and 66 slips that can accommodate vessels up to 100 feet. Immigration and customs services are available, along with gas and diesel, laundry and shower facilities, fish cleaning stations, power, and water. Making reservations is advised. The marina is host to the Wahoo Fishing Tournament (www.wahootournaments.com) in January.

Getting Around

There are no car or golf cart rental agencies in South Bimini, but you don't need them: A shuttle bus ($3) transports you from the airport to Bimini Sands Resort, and the resort offers complimentary shuttle service for guests of the resort and marina. Otherwise you can walk or hitchhike.

Andros

The largest of the Bahamian islands and the fifth largest island in the Caribbean, Andros is divided into three regions: North and Central Andros, Mangrove Cay, and South Andros. Its 8,000 people are spread over 2,300 square miles. Although the region is sparsely populated, North and Central Andros is the most frequented, offering four national parks, bonefishing lodges, eco-resorts, and luxury accommodations. There are more than 200 registered blue holes on the island, the largest concentration in the world, and many more that have not yet been discovered.

The Andros Barrier Reef hugs the northeastern coastline before it drops thousands of feet into the tongue of the ocean. Serious divers, scientists and environmentalists are attracted to this natural wonder. On land and acres of pine forest, mangrove, and coppice. Over 25 species of orchids, 200 endemic and migrating bird species, wild boars, iguanas, land crabs, and butterflies can be found.

North and Central Andros are separated from Mangrove Cay and South Andros by the North, Middle, and South Bights, where prime bonefishing grounds are located. You'll see dolphins, turtles, and starfish among the flats. Separating the Tongue of the Ocean from Andros is the Andros Barrier Reef, teeming with fish, coral gardens, stingrays, and a variety of other marinelife. On land, legend has it that the island has a gremlin-like mythical creature that resembles an owl, known locally as a chickcharney. If a traveler meets a chickcharney and treats it well, you will be rewarded with good luck, and bad luck if you treat it poorly.

NORTH AND CENTRAL ANDROS

Queen's Highway runs north-south along the eastern perimeter of the island, with very limited access to either side of the highway. The main settlements of North and Central Andros are Fresh Creek (Andros Town) and Nicholl's Creek (San Andros). Red Bays is the only settlement in West Andros and is a full-day trip. The remainder of the West Side of the island is remote, untouched, and inaccessible except by seaplane or by boat.

Sights

NATIONAL PARKS

Blue Holes National Park is home to the critically endangered Bahamian Oriole, endemic to The Bahamas, and the resident specialty, the Great Lizard Cuckoo bird, which is only found on two islands in The Bahamas. The park is roughly 40,000 acres with over 30 registered blue holes. The Sleeper Gobie is the only fish known to live in the Blue Holes. Captain Bill Blue Hole was named after surveyor Bill Souza. The locals called it "Churches" because it was traditionally used as a baptism place.

The park is a bit tricky to find, as there aren't obvious signs off the main road. From Queen's Highway, take Rev. Leory Hanna Road in Love Hill, at the Department of Environmental Services. Travel inland and you'll start to see Bahamas National Trust signs pointing out walking trails. Continue following the paved road until you see the parking area, and you'll find a short trail that will lead you to the Captain Bill's blue hole. Signs along the trails indicate native trees, plants, and birds, and step off onto the side trails to see a variety of orchids growing on trees and on the forest floor.

North Marine Park stretches from Stafford Creek to Staniard Creek. **South Marine Park** is from Love Hill to Fresh Creek. Both were set up to preserve the delicate reef system and are home to spectacular dive sites. To access these marine parks, you can book dive trips through Small Hope Bay Lodge or Kamalame Cay.

Due to the importance of land crabs in

Andros

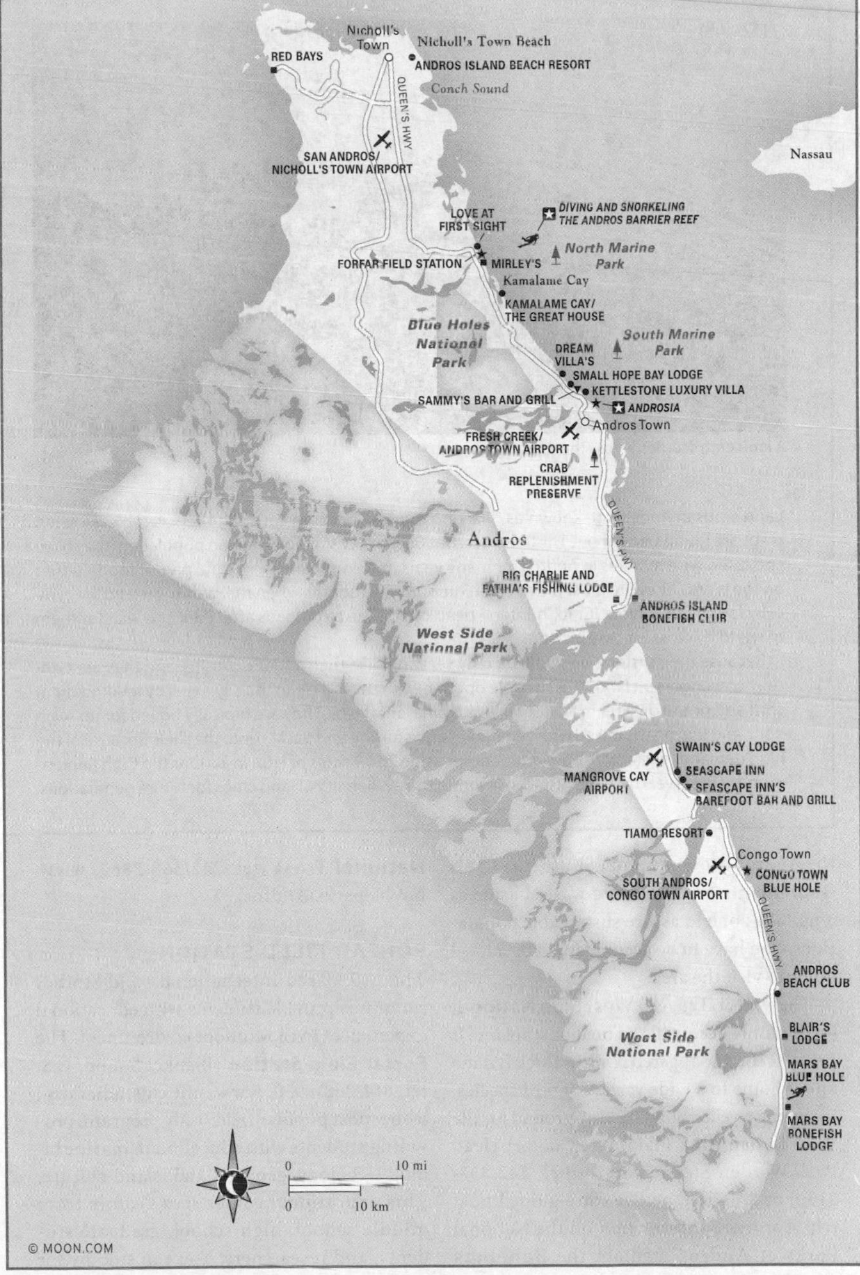
Nicholl's Town
Nicholl's Town Beach
RED BAYS
ANDROS ISLAND BEACH RESORT
Conch Sound
QUEEN'S HWY
SAN ANDROS/
NICHOLL'S TOWN AIRPORT
Nassau
DIVING AND SNORKELING
THE ANDROS BARRIER REEF
LOVE AT
FIRST SIGHT
North Marine
Park
FORFAR FIELD STATION
MIRLEY'S
Kamalame Cay
KAMALAME CAY/
THE GREAT HOUSE
Blue Holes
National
Park
South Marine
Park
DREAM
VILLA'S
SMALL HOPE BAY LODGE
KETTLESTONE LUXURY VILLA
SAMMY'S BAR AND GRILL
ANDROSIA
Andros Town
FRESH CREEK/
ANDROS TOWN AIRPORT
CRAB
REPLENISHMENT
PRESERVE
QUEEN'S HWY
Andros
BIG CHARLIE AND
FATIHA'S FISHING LODGE
ANDROS ISLAND
BONEFISH CLUB
West Side
National Park
SWAIN'S CAY LODGE
SEASCAPE INN
MANGROVE CAY
AIRPORT
SEASCAPE INN'S
BAREFOOT BAR AND GRILL
TIAMO RESORT
Congo Town
CONGO TOWN
BLUE HOLE
SOUTH ANDROS/
CONGO TOWN AIRPORT
QUEEN'S HWY
ANDROS
BEACH CLUB
BLAIR'S
LODGE
West Side
National Park
MARS BAY
BLUE HOLE
MARS BAY
BONEFISH
LODGE
0
10 mi
0
10 km

Land Crabbing and Conservation

A land crab scurries across the road.

Land crabs in Andros are known as "walking money" because catching them is too easy. Land crabs are found throughout The Bahamas, but because of the small human population, they have coexisted with humans in Andros for many years, making them an integral part of food-culture on the island. They are most prevalent in the summer months when the rains come and are typically found out at night. Crab "hunters" head out on the back roads after dark and wait for them to waddle across for easy pickings.

Because their systems aren't flushed by seawater like their aquatic cousins, and they are typically scavengers on land, most people opt to pen them and clean their systems by feeding them corn and rice to give them a sweeter, more pleasant flavor. They are typically boiled for up to an hour, and the meat is mixed with vegetables and stuffing and packed into the shell. Because of the high demand for crabs, the government set aside 2,979 acres of land in 2002 as the Crab Replenishment Reserve. This has assisted in insuring the availability of land crabs for future generations.

the Andros economy and culture, the **Crab Replenishment Preserve** was set aside as a no-take zone to assure sustainable populations. You have to be accompanied by a local guide to visit the area.

The wild and rugged **West Side National Park** is only accessible by boat or seaplane. It protects the endangered Andros Rock Iguana and is home to a wide variety of bird species, including a year-round nesting ground for the West Indian Pink Flamingo. Contact Head Park Warden Stephen Smith (tel. 242/357-2190) or Small Hope Bay for a guided boat trip. For more information on the National Parks of Andros, contact the **Bahamas National Trust** (tel. 242/368-2882, www.bnt.bs/parks/Andros).

FORFAR FIELD STATION

The U.S.-based International Field Studies programs provide students with educational experiences in the outdoor environment. The **Forfar Field Station** (Blanket Sound, U.S. tel. 614/268-9930, www.intlfieldstudies.org) is the most popular field study program, providing students with education in marine biology, ecology, geology, and island culture. This educational center sees visitors from middle school, high school, graduate students, and researchers. You can stop by for

Androsia hand dyes their own batik fabric prints in Fresh Creek.

a visit to learn more about their educational programs.

Beaches

The beaches on mainland Andros aren't as breathtaking as on the Berry Islands, Eleuthera, or The Exumas, but they offer their own beauty. From the North, **Nicholl's Town Beach** is a half-mile stretch and the pride of the community. The Andros Island Beach Resort is located along this stretch, otherwise dotted with homes. **Conch Sound** is a tiny beach but offers a blue-hole diving option right off the beach. There's a picnic table under the shade of casuarinas but no amenities.

Kamalame Cay offers three miles of pristine private beach, and just off Kamalame are government-owned islands and cays that are maintained by Kamalame Cay, with gorgeous beaches and sandbars available for day trips through the resort. **Small Hope Bay Beach** is a soft, arching crescent in front of Small Hope Bay Lodge in Fresh Creek. All beaches are fairly protected from the fury of the depths of the Tongue of the Ocean due to the Andros Barrier Reef.

Entertainment and Events

ALL ANDROS CRAB FEST

The pride and Joy of Andros and a much anticipated annual event is the **All Andros Crab Fest** (Queen's Park, Fresh Creek, tel. 242/368-2286), hosted in Fresh Creek the second weekend in June. It's a true celebration of the land crabbing of Andros and attracts people from all over The Bahamas, featuring Crabs Cook 101 Ways, a crab cultural show, culinary competitions, and educational booths on the habitats, life cycles, and anatomy of land crabs.

Shopping

★ ANDROSIA

Androsia (Fresh Creek, tel. 242/376-9339, www.androsia.com, Mon.-Fri. 9am-4pm) was established by Rosi Birch in the late 1960s. The batik fabric waxing and dying process was done on the beach, and the fabric was sent to local women's homes for sewing. The factory opened in the early 1970s, and the company is now run by Rosi's granddaughter Casey Birch. Their batiks are 100-perecent made in The Bahamas, and you'll find these prints everywhere, in uniforms, banks, nonprofits, and weddings.

Printing starts with a hand carved foam block, which takes about 10 hours to produce. Wax is heated, and the stamp is dipped in the wax and placed on the fabric. The fabric is then hand-dyed in one of their custom colors, then washed in hot water to remove the wax. The fabric is dried in the sun on a clothesline at the back of the factory. Then it's off to the sewing room to turn fabric into dresses, shirts, pants, napkins, or bags. Some of the designs from 40 years ago are still in use today, and all design stencils are preserved. Every yard of Androsia fabric is stamped with their signature, so you'll know when you see the real deal. Although there are imported knock-off versions, Androsia is the only one made in The Bahamas. Call ahead for a tour or a batik lesson where you can create your own colorful fabric to take home with you.

STRAW CRAFTS

Located in Blanket Sound, just south of Forfar Field Station, is **Mirley's** (Blanket Sound, tel. 242/368-6164, Mon.-Sat. 8am-8pm), named after local resident Mirley Conyers. Mirley has been basket weaving for more than 20 years, now well into her 80s and still making straw crafts, most notably beautiful baskets intertwined with Androsia fabric. If the shop doesn't seem to be open during business hours, you can knock on the door at Mirley's home, located right next door.

Head out to **Red Bays,** the only settlement in West Andros, to visit the Seminole community and their thriving basket-weaving and wood-carving heritage. Most residents sell their goods directly out of their homes. It's about 14 miles west of Nicholl's Town on a rough road, so give yourself an entire day to get there and back, especially if you are staying in Central Andros. Small Hope Bay Lodge offers day trips.

Sports and Recreation

TOP EXPERIENCE

FISHING

There are numerous bonefishing lodges and guides around Andros. Stafford, Fresh, and Staniard Creeks are known for bonefishing as well as North Bight, just off the south coast of Central Andros. If you're a die-hard fishing enthusiast, the best bet is to book with a lodge. If you're just learning or would like to do other activities throughout your stay, call one of the many local fishing guides for day trips.

Andros Island Bonefish Club (Cargill Creek, tel. 242/368-5167 or 242/368-5200, www.androsbonefishing.com, starting at $1450, double occupancy for 3 nights/2 days of fishing) offers comfortable rooms with two full-size beds for double occupancy. There's a community kitchen for prepping your own food and a covered outdoor bar and lounge right on the water. Rates include all meals and bonefishing for three to eight nights or longer. Guides are available to take guests to the nearby bonefishing sites or deep-sea fishing in the Tongue of the Ocean.

Big Charlie and Fatiha's Fishing Lodge (Cargill Creek, tel. 242/368-4297 or 242/471-4325, www.bigcharlieandros.com, starting at $1505, double occupancy for 3 nights/2 days of fishing) is right on Cargill Creek and can accommodate eight people at any time. A centralized lounge and dining room is the focal point for storytelling, and Fatiha, originally from Morocco, cooks a mix of Bahamian, Mediterranean, and Moroccan-inspired cuisine for guests. Rates include daily guided fishing and all food and alcoholic and non-alcoholic drinks for two to six days.

Small Hope Bay Lodge (Small Hope Bay, tel. 242/368-2014, U.S. tel. 855/841-6966, www.smallhope.com, $295-315 per person per night) is an all-inclusive lodge for those interested in a variety of activities. It is traditionally well-known as a diving lodge, but if you're specifically into bonefishing, you can opt for their bonefishing package, which includes guided fishing, gear, packed lunches, and all food and alcoholic and nonalcoholic beverages.

For those not staying at a lodge, **Mitchell Thompson** (Behring Point, tel. 242/464-3769) specializes in guided bonefishing expeditions in the North Bight.

NATURE TOURS

Guided nature tours are available to guests of **Small Hope Bay Lodge** by kayak, boat, walking, or biking. **The Bahamas National Trust** (tel. 242/368-2882) to arrange also provides guided tours at their land parks to visit blue holes and learn about native plants and orchids as well as a variety of bird species that call the area home.

TOP EXPERIENCE

Blue Holes of Andros

Although not fully advertised as such, Andros is an ecotourism destination, with the means to be the next Costa Rica in terms of its ecological diversity and untouched land. Along with birding and nature trails, Andros is becoming synonymous with Blue Holes. To the French, touring these *trous bleus* is the newest rage, and The Bahamas has had a lot of coverage in France in recent years as a go-to destination for blue-hole enthusiasts. With **over 200** registered **blue holes,** and many more that have not yet been discovered, Andros has the largest concentration in the world. On a day tour you can hike, jump, and swim your way through **Blue Holes National Park,** and certified divers can dive in the **King Kong Ocean Blue Hole.** With a dive center you can dive deeper into the **Ocean Blue Hole,** an interior blue hole with extensive cave formations.

TOP EXPERIENCE

★ DIVING AND SNORKELING

The **Andros Barrier Reef** is the third longest in the world, stretching 190 miles along the east side of Andros Island. The reef in its entirety is considered a living organism. On the east side of the reef, a sharp underwater cliff drops 6,000 feet into what's known as the Tongue of the Ocean. If you look at a satellite view of The Bahamas, you can see the dark depths of the natural canyon dissecting the shallow Bahama Banks. It runs south from the Berry Islands between Nassau and Andros to the western side of Exuma Sound, resembling a tongue or perhaps a stocking.

The reef is home to a variety of exotic fish, coral gardens, **blue holes,** and, of course, the wrecks of unsuspecting ships that plied these waters before the area was charted. On the outskirts of the reef, on the edge of the drop-off, are hammerhead sharks, marlins, sailfish, turpon, and other large pelagic species. To explore this dynamic ecosystem, organize a dive or a snorkel trip with one of the two operations in Andros. Small Hope Bay Lodge offers stay and dive packages, but nonguests can sign up for the dive trips. Kamalame Cay has a dive center on the island, and you can't get much closer to the reef than this location, as the address is technically in the Andros Barrier Reef. You can sign up for a scuba class or a certification course. Diving is available for students of Forfar Research Station, but sometimes they have spots available to the public, so check with them for additional dive options. Diving is weather-dependent, and unless there's a hurricane, the summer months tend to have calm weather and good lighting.

DIVE OPERATORS

Small Hope Bay Lodge (Small Hope Bay, tel. 242/368-2014, U.S. tel. 855/841-6966, www.smallhope.com) provides three dives per day at coral gardens, blue holes, caverns, and shark dives, and sometimes night dives. Most dive sites are within 15 minutes of the dock, offering dives for all levels and free scuba classes for guests. They cater their diving experiences to in-house guests' interests.

Kamalame Cay (U.S. tel. 876/632-3213, www.kamalame.com) offers one-and two-tank dives, equipment rentals, PADI open-water scuba training courses, and shallow, deep-water, and blue-hole dives.

BIRD-WATCHING

Commonly referred to as "The Big Yard," Andros is home to four endemic bird species (only found on that island), including the endangered Bahamas oriole, and a variety of other species such as the beautiful great lizard cuckoo, greater Antillean bullfinch, Cuban peewee, and egrets, pelicans, herons, flycatchers, and swallows. The West Indian pink flamingo can only be found on certain islands, including West Andros. Many of the birds within The Bahamas are of West Indian descent, dating to prehistoric times when the landmass of Andros was much closer to Cuba, as opposed to being related to North American species.

Grab your binoculars and head out on a guided tour, or if you're already an avid birder, head out and see how many species you can encounter on your own. People come from all over the world to view the beautiful great lizard cuckoo and the Bahamas oriole. Several years ago, the U.S. National Audubon Society worked with the Bahamas National Trust and the Ministry of Tourism to train local residents of top birding locations in Andros and Inagua to become certified bird guides. Nine Bahamians graduated from the Advanced Birding Program, and seven of them are based on Andros. They are ready to lead you into wetlands, rocky coppices, and pine forests to find a variety of birdlife. **Small Hope Bay Lodge** offers tours to four different spots in Blue Holes National Park. **Liz Brace** (lzbrace@gmail.com) can assist you with arranging a guided tour with one of the certified bird guides.

WILD BOAR HUNTING

Wild boars are more prevalent on Andros than any other island because of the amount of land they have for foraging and breeding. Contact **Stephen Smith** (tel. 242/357-2190) if you are interested in a guided hunt. He will show you how he tracks the boar by finding and following their trail. Other guides hunt with dogs, but he uses his own tracking skills.

Food

Food options are few and far between in Andros. Local spots and watering holes are available in each community, but most visitors opt to eat wherever they are staying, as almost all the resorts and lodges offer on-site dining for guests.

★ **Great House Restaurant & Bar** (Kamalame Cay, U.S. tel. 876/632-3213, www.kamalame.com, daily breakfast 7am-10am, lunch noon-3pm, dinner 7pm-10pm, $25-35) is the top choice for world-class dining in Andros. The dining room is a comfortable atmosphere with decor from the owner's worldly travels. A breakfast buffet and cocktail bar are complimented with table service. The food change based on available ingredients, and the focus is on locally sourced produce from local farms on Andros and fresh

Explore a wide diversity of sea life on the Andros Barrier Reef.

seafood. Asian, Bahamian, and Caribbean-inspired food focuses on healthy, wholesome dishes with flavorful sauces and dressings. Vegetarian, vegan, and paleo options are all available. Day passes are available to non-guests depending on the level of occupancy. Call ahead for information.

Brigadier's (Davis Creek, tel. 242/368-2106, www.dreamvillasbahamas.com, daily 10:30am-10pm, $15-20) is at Dream Villas and serves traditional Bahamian food with locally grown ingredients and fresh seafood, as well as pastas, burgers, and sandwiches. They offer a spacious downstairs dining room and outdoor patio overlooking the ocean, and an upstairs event room and balcony.

A brightly colored turquoise, orange, yellow, and blue building is hard to miss as you drive through Calabash Bay, just north of Fresh Creek. **Sammy's Bar and Grill** (Calabash Bay, tel. 242/554-1551, Tues.-Sun. 9am-noon, $10-20) is a family-run establishment serving fresh Bahamian food like conch salad, fritters, grilled fish, and homemade jerk chicken and pork.

Accommodations

★ **Kamalame Cay** (U.S. tel. 876/632-3213, www.kamalame.com, $275) is luxurious and stylish yet decidedly unpretentious. Small and intimate, you can tune into nature in a grove of towering coconut palms along the sandy golf-cart path, or strolling down the pristine three-mile white-sand beach, finding solace at the top of the lookout hill or listening to the waves at the spa on the end of the dock. On the edge of the Andros Barrier Reef, activities include dive trips with the on-site dive shop, lunch on a nearby island or sandbar, bonefishing and deep-sea fishing, or just relaxing on a quiet beach. The narrow island has the calm ocean on one side and mangrove flats on the other. The bungalows and beachfront villa homes are tucked into dense foliage and have ocean views, exuding Old World charm in the rock walls, wood ceilings, and stone tile floors. Kamalame is regularly featured in international magazines, ranked number one in 2016 for *Travel + Leisure*'s best hotels in The Bahamas, Caribbean, and Bermuda, and was on the cover of *Condé Nast Traveler* in January 2018.

Andros Island Beach Resort (Nicholl's Town, tel. 242/329-1009, www.androsislandbeachresorts.com, call for rates) has a laid-back beach vibe in sleepy Nicholl's Town. Four villas and three cottages are cheerfully decorated in island colors and offer full kitchens as well as washers and dryers. The relaxed open-air Tiki Bar is right on beautiful Nicholl's Town Beach and serves Bahamian and American cuisine. Use of bicycles, snorkel gear, and kayaks is included in the rates.

Modest no-frills **Love at First Sight** (Stafford Creek, tel. 242/368-6082 or 242/727-0470, www.loveatfirstsights.com, $150) has been around for 20 years on Stafford Creek, owned and operated by Shelia Blatch, who is on-site 24-7 to make sure you enjoy her warm hospitality and home cooking. Encircling a pool deck are 10 rooms with two double beds each. The restaurant serves typical Bahamian and American dishes and overlooks the saltwater creek, filled with fish and wildlife. Dolphin and manatee sightings are common. Love at First Sight is popular as a base for exploring Andros.

Family-oriented ★ **Small Hope Bay Lodge** (Small Hope Bay, tel. 242/368-2014, U.S. tel. 855/841-6966, www.smallhope.com, $315) was established in 1960 by Dick Birch and is run by his descendants. It was the first dive-oriented resort in The Bahamas, and 70 percent of guests are repeats. The welcoming sense of community is rare today. A large stone fireplace in the great hall is used in the cooler winter months, and homemade meals are enjoyed at communal indoor picnic tables. Seventeen cabins were built in the 1960s of coral rock and pine and are decorated in colorful Androsia prints (also owned by the Birch family) and local art. Standard rates include food, alcoholic and nonalcoholic beverages, bikes, watercraft, and snorkeling. Diving, fishing, and tours can be purchased à la carte, or opt for a dive or fishing package.

Kettlestone Luxury Villa (Fresh Creek, U.S. tel. 800/827-7048, www.kettlestoneluxuryvilla.com, $750) is a three-bedroom private villa in Fresh Creek with dramatic views of the ocean. A gorgeous pool and hot tub have natural rock features, an outdoor kitchen, a grill, and a bar area. Perfect for families or groups, the villa can accommodate up to 12 if the adjacent property is booked. It is newly constructed but maintains the feel of a traditional Bahamian-built home, with organic materials and stone accents. The main house has a large central kitchen and loft rooms; two additional bedrooms are in separate cottages on either side of the main villa.

Information and Services

Central Andros Tourist Office (Mayue Plaza, Fresh Creek, tel. 242/368-2286, Mon.-Fri. 9am-5pm, www.bahamas.com) doesn't offer many brochures, but the staff is helpful. **Bahamas Out Islands Promotions Board** (tel. 242/322-1140, www.myoutislands.com) offers information on the Out Islands. Look for their ongoing Fly Free and Air Credit promotions with participating member hotels.

If you're interested in connecting with a Bahamian ambassador to learn more about their culture and lifestyle, contact the **People-to-People Program** (tel. 242/367-3067, www.bahamas.com/people-to-people). Advance reservations to pair you with an ambassador are recommended.

Banks

Two banks are available in North and Central Andros: **RBC Royal Bank** (Queen's Hwy., Fresh Creek, tel. 242/368-2071, www.rbcroyalbank.com, Mon.-Thurs. 9am-4pm, Fri. 9am-4:30pm) and **Scotiabank** (Nicholl's Town, tel. 242/329-2700, www.scotiabank.com/bs, Mon.-Thurs. 9am-3pm, Fri. 9:30am-4:30pm).

Health and Emergencies

There are several clinics on the island, including the **Nicholl's Town Community Clinic** (tel. 242/329-2055), **Mastic Point Community Clinic** (tel. 242/329-3055), and **Fresh Creek Community Clinic** (tel. 242/368-2038). Clinic hours are Monday-Friday 9am-5pm, except public holidays.

For emergency services, contact the **Royal Bahamas Police Force** in Nicholl's Town (tel. 242/329-2353 or 242/329-2221), Fresh Creek (tel. 242/368-2626), or Cargill Creek

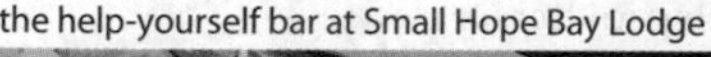
the help-yourself bar at Small Hope Bay Lodge

(tel. 242/368-5090), or by dialing 919 or 911. For **directory assistance**, dial 916. For **weather** dial 915.

Getting There

AIR

San Andros Airport (SAQ) services Nicholl's Town and North Andros and has two daily flights from Nassau on **Western Air** (tel. 242/351-3804, www.westernairbahamas.com). **Andros Town Airport** (ASQ) services Fresh Creek and Central Andros. **LeAir** (reservations tel. 242/377-2356, Fresh Creek tel. 242/368-2919, www.flyleair.com) has two flights daily from Nassau to Andros Town. **Watermakers Air** (U.S. tel. 954/771-0330, www.watermakersair.com) flies from Fort Lauderdale Executive Airport to San Andros (Mon., Wed., Sat.-Sun.). **Tropic Ocean Airways** (U.S. tel. 800/767-0897, www.flytropic.com) is a seaplane charter that flies from Fort Lauderdale International and will land at San Andros, Andros Town-Fresh Creek airport, or at your accommodations.

BOAT

Bahamas Fast Ferries (reservations tel. 242/323-2166, Fresh Creek tel. 242/368-2000, www.bahamasferries.com) has weekly trips on the fast ferry from Potter's Cay in Nassau to Fresh Creek ($107 round-trip). The ferry departs at 7am and arrives in Fresh Creek at 10am.

Getting Around

Taxis are readily available to take you to your accommodations from the airport or the ferry dock. Taxis will also negotiate day and tour rates. For car rentals, contact **Rooney's Auto** (tel. 242/471-0346 or 242/368-2021) in Calabash Bay. Rooney is at the town's gas station but will pick you up from Fresh Creek Airport.

MANGROVE CAY AND SOUTH ANDROS

Mangrove Cay is between Middle and South Bight, surrounded by mangroves and shallow flats. Moxey Town is the main settlement, home to around 800 people in the northeast corner of the landmass. It draws die-hard bonefishing enthusiasts to the epicenter of the sport and is widely known as "the land of giants" for the record fish in the area.

Much like North and Central Andros, both Mangrove Cay and South Andros have one road along the east coast; on Mangrove Cay it runs from Moxey Town to Lisbon Creek, and on South Andros from Driggs Hill to Mars Bay. Small settlements dot the road south along miles of untouched beaches.

Sights

This area is predominantly pine forests, rocky coppices, and miles of mangrove dotted with blue holes and caves. South Andros has miles of untouched beaches along its east coast. Head to any spot and you will likely have it to yourself. Shallow sandflats stretch toward the shore, protected by the reef. As with North and Central Andros, the area is known for its bonefishing grounds, so the island attracts anglers. Your accommodations will offer nearby excursions and guided tours for hiking, birding, kayaking, biking, and snorkeling.

The **Congo Town Blue Hole** is known to local residents as the "Miracle Blue Hole." Sometime in the early 1990s the hole disappeared, covered with sand. In 2015, within a single day, after being covered for 25 years, the hole reopened and has been open since. It is just offshore in the shallow sand flats, its deep turquoise color prominent.

Mars Bay Blue Hole is in the town of Mars Bay. Entering Mars Bay heading south, take the first left to the town's front road on the ocean side. The blue hole sits right on the shoreline. It's most impressive at low tide, when the seawater is on the cusp between the dense sandflat and the drop-off to the blue hole.

Sports and Recreation

There are numerous bonefishing lodges offering lodging and fishing packages. **Mars Bay**

Bonefish Lodge (Mars Bay, tel. 242/357-2106, www.androsbonefish.com, starting at $2900, double occupancy for 4 nights/3 days of fishing) offers four- to seven-night packages that include lodging, meals, boats and guides, and airport transfers for a maximum of eight people at a time. At the south end of South Andros, you'll have the fishing grounds to yourself. **Blair's Lodge** (South Andros, U.S. tel. 800/530-6928, www.blairslodge.com, starting at $2995 per person for 3 nights/2 days of fishing) is an isolated luxury bonefishing lodge in the center of South Andros offering three- to seven-night packages that include lodging, meals, fishing gear, and airport transfers.

Food

The resorts have their own restaurants, often all-inclusive and not open to nonguests. Most visitors end up eating at their accommodations for the duration of their stay, perhaps venturing out to try some local cuisine at the recommendation of a fishing guide.

Located on the edge of a beautiful sandy beach, **Seascape Inn's Barefoot Bar and Grill** (Mangrove Cay, tel. 242/369-0342, www.seascapeinn.com, daily lunch 12:30pm-2pm, dinner 6:30pm-8pm, $15-25) serves breakfasts to guests only, and lunch and dinner to nonguests as well. Reservations for lunch and dinner are required for nonguests. Lunch includes burgers, sandwiches, and salads. Options for dinner may include chicken, pork, steak, fish, or lobster in season, depending on availability.

Accommodations

MANGROVE CAY

Seascape Inn (Mangrove Cay, tel. 242/369-0342, www.seascapeinn.com, $159), on a private stretch of beach just south of Moxey Town on the eastern side of the island, is an adorable owner-operated inn welcoming guests since 1997. Five private cabanas offer queen beds or two twins depending on the cabana. Rates include breakfast and a variety of activities, such as fishing, kayaking, biking, snorkeling, and hiking. Check about the "fly free" program with the Bahamas Out Islands Promotions Board (http://myoutislands.com) for current specials for air credit or free airfare when you book four to six consecutive nights.

★ **Swain's Cay Lodge** (Mangrove Cay, tel. 242/422-5018, www.swainscaylodge.com, $214) offers garden, ocean-view, and

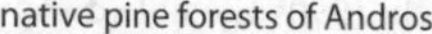
native pine forests of Andros

beachfront suites and three-bedroom apartments. The on-site Reefside Restaurant and Bar serves breakfast, lunch, and dinner for guests and nonguests. Reservations (tel. 242/369-0296) are required for nonguests. Although the lodge attracts fishing enthusiasts and fishing package rates are available, you can also just book a room and arrange activities on your own, making a great option for nonanglers. Kayaking, snorkeling, scuba, biking, and hiking are possible on this seven-mile-long, lightly trafficked island.

★ **Mangrove Cay Club** (Mangrove Cay, tel. 242/369-0731, U.S. tel. 406/222-0624, http://mangrovecayclub.com, $1,700 for 2 nights d, $5,500 weekly d) provides a little taste of everything—the best fishing grounds in The Bahamas, comfortable accommodations, and excellent dining. Four duplex cottages with beautiful views of Middle Bight were designed with privacy in mind, nestled in native foliage. There are a central dining area, a lounge, a bar, and a small beach. Owned and operated by Liz and Alton Bain, the club has the feeling of staying with friends. Bicycles are available to explore, and you'll find a number of caves and old churches in the area.

SOUTH ANDROS

Touted as a luxury eco-chic resort, ★ **Tiamo Resort** (South Andros, tel. 242/225-6871, U.S. tel. 786/374-2442, www.tiamoresorts.com, Nov.-Aug., $850 d) is accessible only by boat or seaplane; although it's on South Andros, no road runs from the airport to the lodge. Fly into Mangrove Cay or Congo Town, both about the same distance, and then take a boat to their dock. Tiamo specializes in keeping guests as active as they chose. Bonefishing is right out the back door, as well as scuba diving on the Andros Barrier Reef, or stay close to the resort with wakeboarding and paddleboarding. There's an air-conditioned gym if you need to get out of the sun. Visit their spa for a massage or body treatment. Ten villas are along a white-sand beach within towering coconut palms with king beds, cool linens, and natural accents. An old-fashioned library has books about the local area, fiction, and classic literature. The Great Room serves up healthy, fresh, local breakfast, lunch, and dinner by the Michelin-starred restaurant-trained chef Keith. Rates include all food and nonalcoholic drinks, airport transfers, and many activities.

All-inclusive **Andros Beach Club** (Deep Creek, South Andros, tel. 242/369-1454, U.S. tel. 954/681-4818, www.androsbeachclub.

the pool overlooking a coconut grove at Tiamo Resort

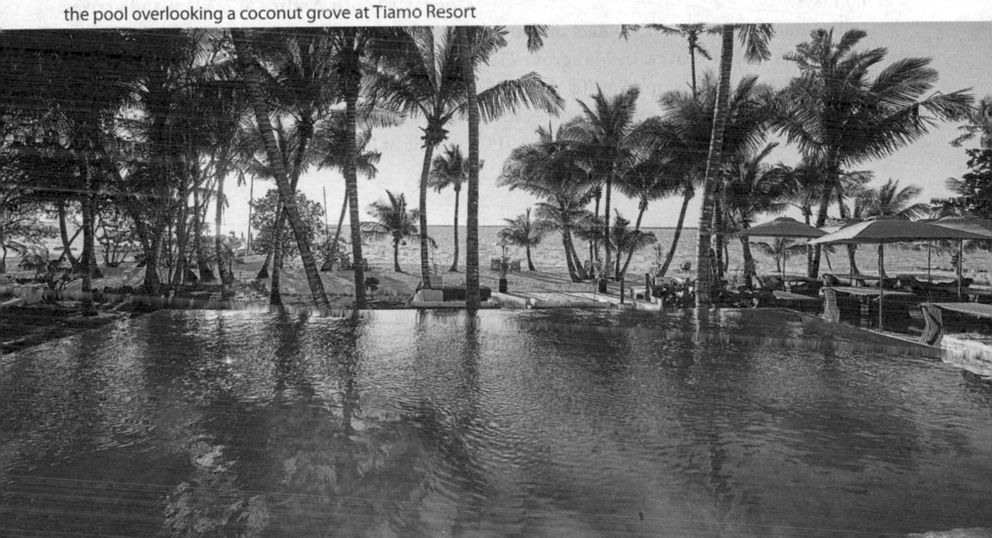

com, $600 d) is on a private beach. Rates include meals, nonalcoholic beverages, bicycles, kayaks, snorkel gear, and airport transfers. Deep-sea fishing, bonefishing, and spearfishing are available. The colorful oceanfront rooms are comfortable and beach-inspired. Dining offers seasonal produce and seafood and is attentive to dietary preferences and allergies.

Information and Services

South Andros Tourist Office (Queen's Hwy., Congo Town, tel. 242/369-1688, www.bahamas.com, Mon.-Fri. 9am-5pm) is located near the Congo Town Airport.

BANKS

Bank of The Bahamas (www.bankbahamas.com) has a branch in Mangrove Cay (Queen's Hwy., tel. 242/369-0502, Mon. and Thurs. 10am-3pm) and one in Deep Creek (Queen's Hwy., tel. 242/369-1787, Tues.-Wed. and Fri. 10am-3pm).

HEALTH AND EMERGENCIES

Clinics are the **Mangrove Cay Community Clinic** (Mangrove Cay tel. 242/369-0089) and the **Green Community Clinic** (Kemp's Bay, South Andros, tel. 242/369-4849). Clinic hours are Monday-Friday 9am-5pm, except holidays.

For emergency services, contact the **Royal Bahamas Police Force** in Mangrove Cay (tel. 242/369-0083), Kemp's Bay (tel. 242/369-4733), or by dialing 919 or 911. For **directory assistance,** dial 916. For **weather,** dial 915.

Getting There

AIR

Mangrove Cay (MAY) has a daily morning and afternoon flight from Nassau on **LeAir** (reservations tel. 242/377-2356, www.flyleair.com) and daily morning and afternoon flights on **Flamingo Air** (tel. 242/351-4963, www.flamingoairbah.com).

Congo Town Airport (TZN) has flights from Nassau on **Western Air** (tel. 242/351-3804, www.westernairbahamas.com) twice daily from Nassau, and **Watermakers Air** (U.S. tel. 954/771-0330, www.watermakersair.com) flies from Fort Lauderdale Executive Airport (Tues. and Thurs.-Sat.).

Getting Around

Most resorts and accommodations pick you up from the airport, but taxis are readily available. For car rentals, contact **PB's Car Rental** (Mangrove Cay, tel. 242/369-0871 or 242/554-0258) or **Lenglo Car Rental** (Congo Town, tel. 242/369-1702 or 242/369-1704).

BOAT

Frederick Major's Ferry Service (tel. 242/376-8533 or 242/322-6111, South Andros tel. 242/554-1880) makes trips between Mangrove Cay (Lisbon Creek) and South Andros (Drigg's Hill) twice daily. The boat departs South Andros at 8:30am and arrives at Mangrove Cay at 8:45am, and departs at 4:30pm, arriving at 4:45pm. From Mangrove Cay to South Andros, the boat departs at 9am and arrives at 9:15am, and departs at 5pm, arriving at 5:20pm.

The Berry Islands

The Berry Islands are a loosely bunched cluster of 30 cays, the majority uninhabited; those that are have limited populations. Known for beautiful vacant beaches, the islands have remained untouched due to the shallow flats, which also makes it relatively inaccessible for sailboat cruising and yachts.

The Berry Islands start at Great Stirrup Cay to the north, owned by Norwegian Cruise Lines as a day center. Neighboring it is Little Stirrup Cay, also known as Coco Cay, a private island used by Royal Caribbean Cruise Lines. Just south of the Stirrups is Great Harbour Cay, the capital of The Berries, with a population of 700 and more millionaires per square mile than any other place in the world, although you'd never guess that, based on its lack of pretentiousness. From Great Harbour Cay, undeveloped islands stretch for 20 miles to Chub Cay, only 35 miles north of Nassau. Chub Cay is known as the Billfish Capital of The Bahamas, as it's right on the northern border of the Tongue of the Ocean.

GREAT HARBOUR CAY

Great Harbour Cay is seven miles long and one mile wide and is the center of commerce in the otherwise undeveloped Berry Islands. The marina at Great Harbour Cay is a great place to check in and get oriented, and then perhaps organize a day trip on a shallow-draft boat. Bullock Harbour is the main town on the island, called "The Village" by local residents. The settlement consists of a few shops, houses, restaurants, and the marina. In terms of Out Island towns, this is one of the sleepi est you'll find. The area attracts bonefishing enthusiasts and deep-sea trollers, but it has become popular for honeymooners, weddings, and family vacations. If you're staying in Nassau and looking for a quick escape, consider a day trip to Great Harbour Cay. LeAir offers daily flights in the morning and afternoon, making it a perfect day-away excursion.

Beaches

Great Harbour Cay is known for its beaches. On the southwest side of the island are protected mangrove bays and waterways, but stretching along the entire northwest side of the island is one continuous beach. North of Bullock Harbour are some stilted homes along the beach, and nearly on the north end of the island is **Sugar Beach.** There's a "Beach Access" sign along a rocky section where you can explore caves and hike the shoreline.

Just east of Bullock's Harbour, **Great Harbour Beach** is a half moon-shaped beach where you'll find Carriearl Boutique Hotel and The Beach Club. Farther south along Great Harbour Drive, you'll eventually hit a dirt road. As long as it hasn't rained, its easily accessible in any vehicle. If it has been raining, be cautious about the huge puddles, threatening to incapacitate your car. The beach access to **Shelling Beach** (also called Sand Dollar Beach by locals because of the large number of sand dollars) is evident in a clearing among the casuarinas. Make sure you head there for low tide to catch the shallow sand flats and amazing photo opportunities. Farther down is **Shark Creek Beach,** a point surrounded by the ocean inlet on one side, protected by rock formations and the creek, which is known to attract sharks.

Shopping

There is limited shopping in Great Harbour Cay. If you need certain dietary items or even fresh produce, pack them with you. There are two liquor stores in Bullock's Harbour and several small grocery and convenience stores. Businesses are open whenever they are open. If you need something, ask around and you'll probably find the shop owner fairly quickly.

A simple variety store with various sundries, clothing, toys, and home goods, **Unique Treasures** (William Dean Hwy., Bullock's Harbour, tel. 242/367-8011) is near

The Berry Islands

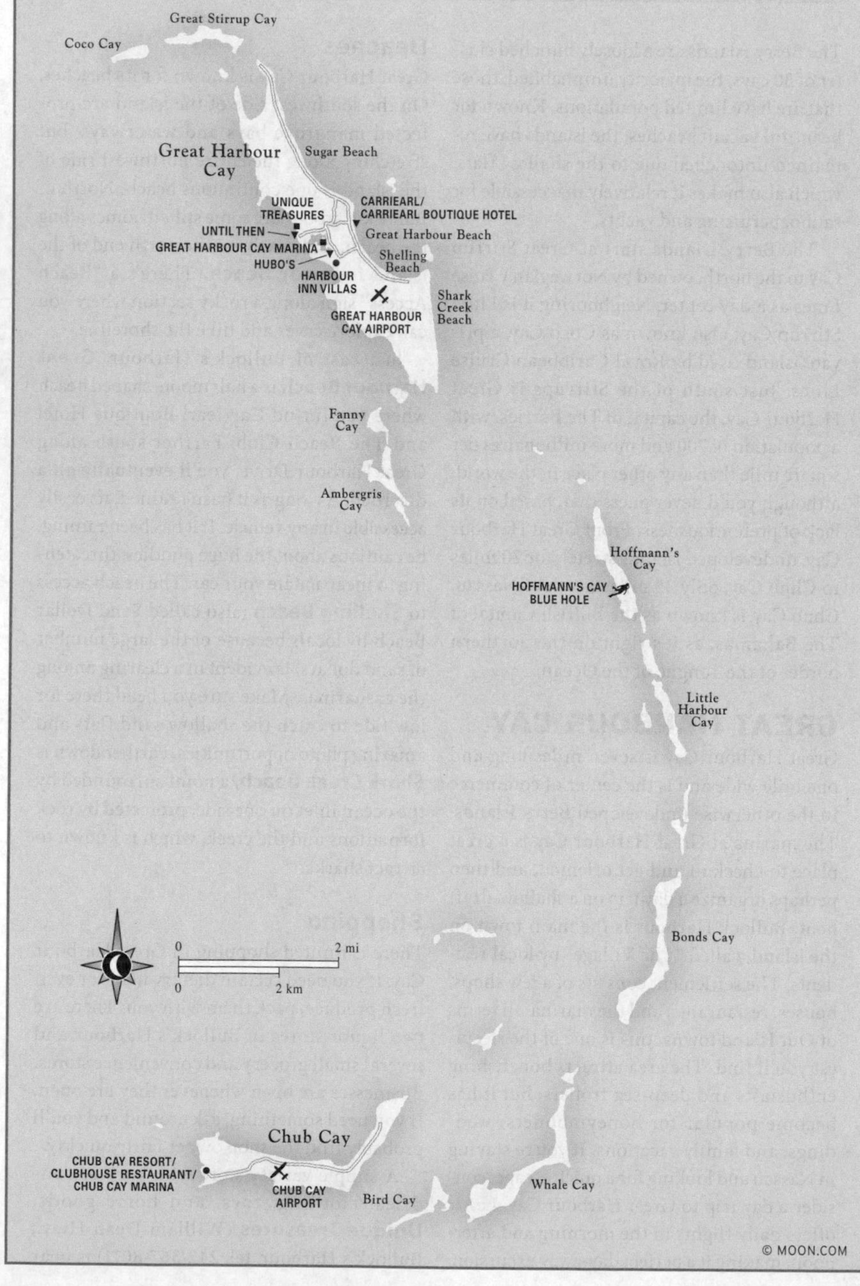
Great Stirrup Cay
Coco Cay
Great Harbour Cay
Sugar Beach
UNIQUE TREASURES
CARRIEARL/ CARRIEARL BOUTIQUE HOTEL
UNTIL THEN
Great Harbour Beach
GREAT HARBOUR CAY MARINA
HUBO'S
Shelling Beach
HARBOUR INN VILLAS
Shark Creek Beach
GREAT HARBOUR CAY AIRPORT
Fanny Cay
Ambergris Cay
Hoffmann's Cay
HOFFMANN'S CAY BLUE HOLE
Little Harbour Cay
Bonds Cay
0
2 mi
0
2 km
Chub Cay
CHUB CAY RESORT/ CLUBHOUSE RESTAURANT/ CHUB CAY MARINA
CHUB CAY AIRPORT
Bird Cay
Whale Cay
© MOON.COM

the government dock. **Tings Necessary** (tel. 242/367-8117, Mon.-Sat. 8am-5pm) is across from the marina and has the same owner as Happy People's convenience store on the dock. If it's not open, go down by the dock to find someone to open the shop, which sells a variety of books, straw crafts, shells, and T-shirts. **Art Shack** (The Beach Club, Great Harbour Dr., tel. 242/367-8018) sells local arts and crafts, and a percentage of profits goes to the local school. They aren't always open; ask at The Beach Club.

Sports and Recreation

FISHING

Captain Percy Darville (tel. 242/464-4149) specializes in bonefishing, deep-sea fishing, and bottom fishing, and he has won awards for his expertise. **Barry North** (tel. 242/116-7161) is an all-around guide, specializing in fishing, but he can also take you to Hoffmann's Cay Blue Hole or on day trips throughout the islands. **Captain Ronnie Brown** (tel. 242/451-1720) is available for boat charters for fishing and excursions.

You can also check in at the **Dockmaster's Office** (Great Harbour Cay Marina, tel. 242/367-8005, daily 7am-6pm) to arrange day trips and fishing charters. Everything is tide-dependent, so make sure you plan your trip in advance.

GOLF

The Great Harbour Cay Golf Course used to be a championship course but has fallen into disrepair. The front nine are somewhat maintained by the homeowner's association on the island, but the back nine are barely evident anymore, unless you ask a local to point them out. Don't bring your own clubs; Carriearl has golf clubs and balls for guests if you are looking for a casual round.

Food

There are very limited restaurant and food options on Great Harbour Cay. A popular form of dining is having your meals catered instead of going out. Catering services can come to your lodgings or are available for pickup.

BAHAMIAN

Shelly Rolle Catering (tel. 242/367-8307) specializes in Bahamian fare, including in-season lobster, fish, ribs, baked chicken, and hearty side dishes like baked macaroni, potato salad, peas-and-rice, and fried plantain. She will cook at your house, or prepare it beforehand for delivery.

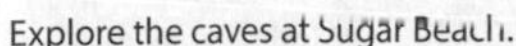
Explore the caves at Sugar Beach.

Honeymooning on Great Harbour Cay

Great Harbour Cay has seen an influx of honeymooners from the United States and Canada in recent years. Endless stretches of pristine beaches beckon you to walk hand-in-hand. Prepare a picnic basket with champagne to watch the sunset, or charter a boat and head out to an uninhabited island and spend the days basking in the rejuvenating Bahamian sunshine in complete isolation. Find a romantic dining experience at Carriearl, or opt for catering services to bring meals to you. Vacation rental homes are available through websites like Airbnb and VRBO if you're looking for a private beach house.

Until Then (Bullock's Harbour, tel. 242/367-8164, daily from 7am, $10-20), is owned and operated by local Ronnie Brown and is located just before the Government Dock, next to the All Ages School. Hours are "until then," meaning whatever time they are done socializing and carrying on. For breakfast they serve authentic souses, boiled fish, and tuna and grits. Lunch and dinner have steak, lamb, pork, chicken, and fresh caught seafood. There is limited seating, and the ambience isn't amazing, but it's welcoming, and the food is tasty. It's located just across the street from the harbor; watch the fresh catch arrive at the cleaning station to be served up Bahamian-style. Catering is available.

Hubo's (tel. 242/451-0264, Mon.-Sat. 7am-4pm) is right on the dock at the marina next to the cleaning station. Find everything from conch salad to pastries and ice cream and home-cooked Bahamian food. There are a few picnic tables on the dock, but most opt for takeout.

CONTEMPORARY

The Beach Club (Great Harbour Dr., tel. 242/367-8108, Tues.-Sun. 8am-3pm, Wed.-Sat. 6pm-10pm) is an open-air bar and restaurant under the shade of a covered patio and mature casuarinas and native trees, directly on the beach across from the airport. Their menu favorites are a simple tasty hamburgers and fresh hogfish. They also serve a variety of sandwiches, salads, and seafood entrées.

★ **Carriearl Restaurant** (Great Harbour Dr., www.carriearl.com, Wed. dinner 6pm-9:30pm, Thurs.-Sat. lunch noon-2pm, dinner 6pm-9:30pm, Sun. brunch 10am-2pm, $20-45) is a wonderful mix of British, Asian, Italian, and Caribbean food and a refreshing option on an island focused on calorie-laden Bahamian cuisine. They offer rack of lamb, filet mignon with peppercorn sauce, fresh seafood specialties, pasta, and a few British favorites such as bangers and mash and English-style fish-and-chips. It's also the only place on the island that serves pizza. The welcoming dining area is a mix of comfortable couches and cushioned chairs intermixed with intimate dining tables. They bake their own French bread and have a beautiful herb garden in the corner overflowing with basil, sage, cilantro, and mint. Nonguests must call ahead for reservations.

Accommodations

Hotels and resorts are limited on Great Harbour Cay, but renting a vacation home is a common way to settle into the relaxed island swing of things. Book directly with homeowners via websites such as Airbnb, VRBO, and HomeAway.

★ **Carriearl Boutique Hotel** (tel. 242/367-8785, www.carriearl.com, Nov.-Aug., $245) owners Angie and Marty will make you feel at home. Four guestrooms are crisp and colorfully decorated with island art. Known as the "Brit's Ritz" by friends, this British couple has been running this establishment for seven years. The restaurant serves breakfast, lunch, and dinner daily for guests. A pool and lounge area is directly on Great Harbour Beach.

a casual lunch at Carriearl Restaurant

Thatched umbrellas at the beach beckon you to spend the afternoon lulled by the waves. The gift shop sells Bahamian gifts, and kayaks, bicycles, and golf clubs are available for guest use. The hotel can assist in arranging activities and day trips such as snorkeling, fishing, and sightseeing.

Krum's Rentals (Bullock's Harbour, tel. 242/367-8321 or 242/367-8370) has two rental options: **Harbour Inn Villas,** ($100-125) across from the marina, offers three modest rooms with two full beds, useful as a crash pad. **The Beach Villas** ($125 plus $60 cleaning fee) are near the airport and have an overhead loft with two beds and a kitchen.

Information and Services

For visitor information, contact the **Berry Islands Tourist Office** (William Dean Hwy., Bullock's Harbour, tel. 242/451-0404 or 242/225-8947, www.bahamas.com or www.myoutislands.com). There is no bank on the island, so be sure you have plenty of cash with you; some places don't take cards.

Getting There and Around

TAXIS

Taxis are readily available to meet incoming flights. For taxi service, contact **Circle** (tel. 242/359-3730). He is known as "Circle" because, as you'll notice after being on the island for a short period of time, he is continuously running in circles, from the airport to town. You can also contact **Milton Rolle** (tel. 242/359-9155).

CAR RENTALS

For car rentals, **Krum's Rent-a-Car** (tel. 242/367-8370 or 242/367-8321), located at the marina, offers vehicles from $70 per day. Another option is **Relly's Rental** (tel. 242/367-8036 or 242/464-4012).

BOAT

Great Harbour Cay Marina (tel. 242/367-8005, VHF channel 16, www.greatharborcaymarina.com) has 65 slips that can accommodate boats up to 135 feet. It is a full-service marina in one of the most protected harbors in The Bahamas. Call ahead for reservations and availability.

AIR

LeAir (tel. 242/377-2356, www.flyleair.com) has two flights daily from Nassau. **Watermakers Air** (U.S. tel. 954/771-0330, www.watermakersair.com) has flights from Fort Lauderdale Executive Airport to Great Harbour Cay (Thurs.-Sun.). **Tropic Ocean Airways** (U.S. tel. 954/210-5569 or 800/767-0897, www.flytropic.com) offers flights from Fort Lauderdale International Airport at Sheltair (Wed.-Fri. and Sun.).

CHUB CAY

Chub Cay is a private island resort and marina at the south end of the Berry Islands. It's traditionally been a through-traffic location for boats clearing in on their way into the Bahamas, and for fuel stop-offs for fishing boats trolling around the Tongue of the Ocean. It has been under construction for many years, but 2017 saw the completion of the impressive Clubhouse and pool area, which has been getting rave reviews from visitors. This island is geared toward boating and fishing, but the new Clubhouse will make even nonanglers feel at home.

There's not much to do on land except stroll the mile-long beach, and there's only one restaurant, so come prepared with your own food if you're looking for variety. Boaters share happy-hour cocktails at the bar.

Beaches

Chub Cay Beach is at the marina and is over a mile long, a great protected spot for swimming and snorkeling. The Clubhouse is just off the beach, so amenities are never far away.

Food

Clubhouse Restaurant (tel. 242/325-1490, U.S. tel. 786/209-0025, www.chubcayresortandmarina.com, daily 8-10am, noon-3pm, 6pm-open late, $20-30) is on the southwest corner of the island, just off a pristine stretch of beach. Enjoy stunning sunset views from the dining room. A gorgeous interior has crisp whites accented with natural wood paneling. Bahamian-inspired dishes such as traditional cracked conch and fried fish are on the menu, but you can also get five-star ahi mango avocado on a bed of fresh greens grown in their own garden, steaks, and pasta dishes. Dinner reservations are strongly recommended.

Accommodations

Chub Cay Resort (tel. 242/325-1490, U.S. tel. 786/209-0025, www.chubcayresortandmarina.com) offers hotel rooms (from $425) and cabanas. Eleven guest rooms and suites offer king beds, wood paneling, and gamefish decor. Most rooms have outdoor balconies. The Villas (from $1,400) are two- to four-bedroom homes with full kitchens, porches, and balconies offering ample space for families. Chub Cay Resort has a beautiful infinity pool with a swim-up bar, a one-mile stretch of white-sand beach, the Clubhouse serving breakfast, lunch, and dinner, and a ship store and gift shop.

Getting There and Around

AIR

Charter flights are available from Odyssey Aviation in Nassau. Five-passenger aircraft are available with **Bahama Hoppers** (Lindy Wells, tel. 242/359-7883, www.bahamahoppers.com). Opt for a nine-passenger aircraft with **Saga Boy** (Raquel Hinds, tel. 242/702-0231, www.sagaboyaircharters.com).

Watermakers Air (U.S. tel. 954/771-0330, www.watermakersair.com) has flights from Fort Lauderdale Executive Airport to Chub Cay (Mon., Wed., and Fri.-Sat.).

BOAT

Most people arrive to Chub Cay by boat and utilize full-service **Chub Cay Marina,** which can accommodate up to 190-foot yachts and offers power, reverse-osmosis water, an air-conditioned fish cleaning house, and barbecue grills. There's also a ship store that offers dry-goods supplies, pharmacy items, cleaning supplies, and sun protection.

HOFFMANN'S CAY BLUE HOLE

Hoffmann's Cay Blue Hole is in the central Berry Islands on Hoffman's Cay. It's about 600 feet wide and has a 20-foot cliff dropping into the water below, where visitors jump into the depths. If you go on your own by boat, study a Google Earth map to locate it. You'll see there is a small crescent-shaped beach on the west side of the island, and a trail will lead you inland to the hole. Tours and day-trip operators can get you there.

Getting There and Around

Contact local tour operators to arrange visiting Hoffmann's Cay and the Blue Hole. On your own boat, navigate to the coordinates 25°37'14.1" N., 77°44'29.5" W., using Visual Piloting Rules to read the water for shoals and sandbars.

The Southern Bahamas

Look for ★ to find recommended sights, activities, dining, and lodging.

Highlights

★ **Dean's Blue Hole:** This deepest known blue hole in the world attracts free divers and nature lovers to its picturesque landscape tucked within a beachside cove (page 280).

★ **Cape Santa Maria Beach:** Nestled on the northwestern corner of Long Island, it rivals the top beaches in the world (page 283).

★ **Long Island Regatta:** Hosted every Labour Day Weekend, this festival highlights the maritime roots of the Out Islands (page 284).

★ **The Hermitage at Mount Alvernia:** Built atop the highest point in The Bahamas, this modest yet architecturally impressive abode was constructed as a spiritual retreat for a monk (page 292).

★ **Watling's Blue Hole Lookout:** Panoramic views of the dynamic landscape of San Salvador, the surrounding ocean, a blue hole, and Watling's Castle make this a beautiful day trip (page 302).

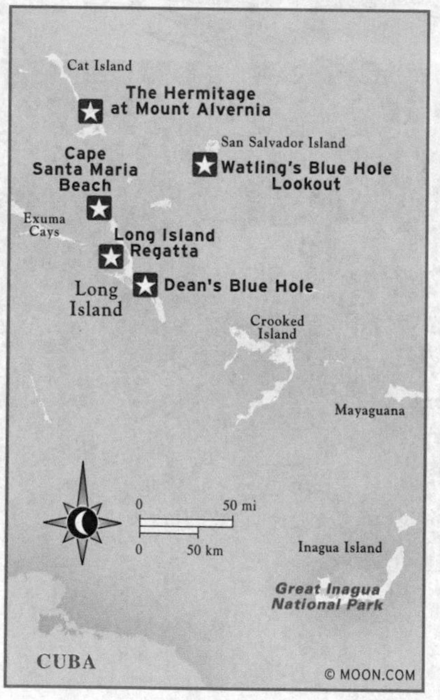

The islands of the Southern Bahamas are much less trafficked than those with closer proximity to the United States, but they are no less picturesque.

Their oceanic waterways teem with vibrant sealife just offshore, and they even offer more for those looking to really get away from it all. The allure is the serenity of island life as it creeps by at a snail's pace, the beaming smiles of local children, and an overabundance of the loveliest beaches you'll ever see.

On any given island, one single road, Queen's Highway, runs the length, perimeter, or leeward side and acts as the lifeline of all commerce. Dirt roads lead from the main highway into small communities. You won't find an island with a population above 2,000. Everyone seems to know everyone, and residents wave and stop to chat, in no hurry to get anywhere. The locals are some of the warmest and friendliest Bahamians you'll meet, and they are proud of their home islands. Given the chance, they will show it to you through their eyes. As the tagline goes, the Out Islands make up 84% of The Bahamas, and they are 100% unspoiled. That's undeniably true.

PLANNING YOUR TIME

Although these islands are grouped together geographically, interisland travel is impossible without traveling by private boat, booking a charter plane, or connecting through Nassau. These islands are completely independent of one another, so when you're planning your trip, you'll want to zero in on one and give yourself time to settle in. Spend a few days in Nassau, and when you tire of the crowds, grab your sun hat and head south. Long Island, Cat Island, and San Salvador all have daily flights from Nassau, but the farther south you go, the more limited the flight options are. Plan for the day of arrival and departure to be full travel days, as most of the flights are at midday and are often delayed. You may even have to arrive into Nassau the night before to catch a connecting domestic flight. Between your arrival and departure day, you'll want at least three or four days to relax and explore, indulge in ecotourism kayaking, snorkeling, fishing, or hiking, or visiting historical sites and ruins.

Previous: bungalows and villas overlook Cape Santa Maria Beach; view from Shanna's Cove, the highest restaurant in The Bahamas. **Above:** the Dixon Hill Lighthouse.

The Southern Bahamas

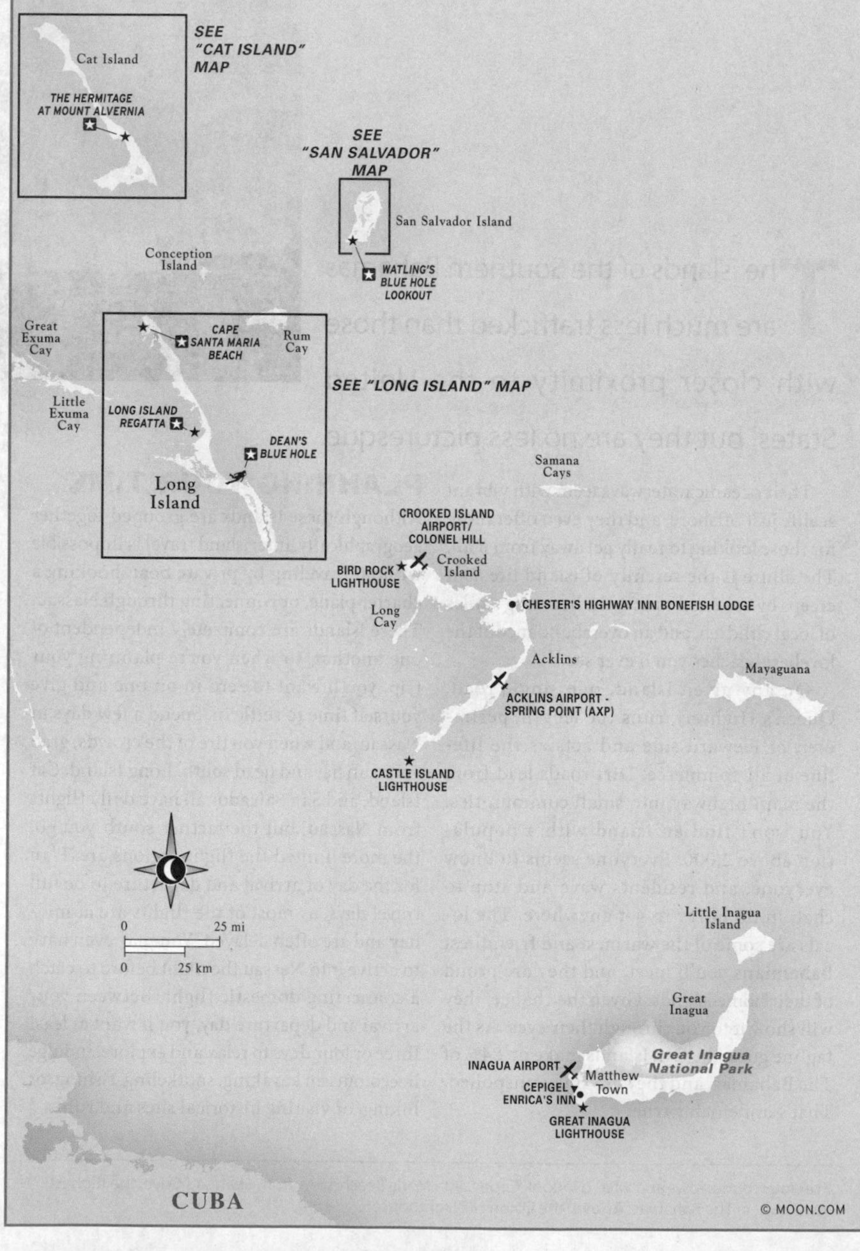

SEE "CAT ISLAND" MAP
Cat Island
THE HERMITAGE AT MOUNT ALVERNIA
SEE "SAN SALVADOR" MAP
San Salvador Island
WATLING'S BLUE HOLE LOOKOUT
Conception Island
Great Exuma Cay
CAPE SANTA MARIA BEACH
Rum Cay
SEE "LONG ISLAND" MAP
Little Exuma Cay
LONG ISLAND REGATTA
DEAN'S BLUE HOLE
Long Island
Samana Cays
CROOKED ISLAND AIRPORT/ COLONEL HILL
BIRD ROCK LIGHTHOUSE
Crooked Island
CHESTER'S HIGHWAY INN BONEFISH LODGE
Long Cay
Acklins
Mayaguana
ACKLINS AIRPORT - SPRING POINT (AXP)
CASTLE ISLAND LIGHTHOUSE
0
25 mi
0
25 km
Little Inagua Island
Great Inagua
Great Inagua National Park
INAGUA AIRPORT
Matthew Town
CEPIGEL
ENRICA'S INN
GREAT INAGUA LIGHTHOUSE
CUBA
© MOON.COM

ORIENTATION

The north end of Long Island is just southeast of George Town in Exuma. Visitors arrive at Stella Maris in the north, or Deadman's Cay in the south. The island is long and skinny, about 65 miles north to south, so you'll want to rent a car once you arrive. Queen's Highway runs the entire length, with small settlements along the highway.

Cat Island, another long skinny island, is southeast of Eleuthera. Visitors fly into Arthur's Town in the north or New Bight in the central part of the island. Queen's Highway runs along the western side of the island. In the north, you'll find the fishing flats of Orange Creek, and at the very southwestern tip of the island is Hawk's Nest.

San Salvador is one of the few islands that is round in shape. It is farther out in the Atlantic than the rest of the islands on the Great Bahama Bank. Visitors fly into Cockburn Town, where most resorts and commerce are. Queen's Highway circles the island, from the inhabited side on the west to the remote and untouched eastern shore.

Farther south is Acklins and Crooked Island. Visitors fly into either Colonel Hill on Crooked Island or Spring Point on Acklins. Visitors come specifically for bonefishing lodges and don't tend to venture outside their guided trips.

Great Inagua's main town is Matthew Town. The town is walkable, but the island itself is one of the larger Bahamian islands. It's not recommended to drive on the island without a guide as visitors regularly get lost.

Long Island

Long Island was originally named Yuma by the indigenous Lucayan people and renamed Fernandina by Christopher Columbus when he arrived in 1492. Eventually it was renamed Long Island by a sailor because it took so long to sail past, and the name stuck. Approximately 65 miles long, it stretches from Gordon's in the south to Seymour's in the north. Its width ranges one to four miles. The second highest point in The Bahamas (after Cat Island) is in Long Island in the settlement of Mortimer's on the southern end, at 178 feet. The Tropic of Cancer crosses the island. On each side are two very different coastlines—east are rocky cliffs and caves that drop into the Atlantic Ocean, and west, what locals call the Caribbean side, are soft gentle beaches, with creeks, mangroves, and prime bonefishing flats.

Long Islanders are known for their hospitality, and you'll have no problem navigating a rental car on the island by stopping and asking for directions. You may get thoroughly confused by locals' use of "down north" and "up south," however, as well as referring to the east side of the island as the north side, and the west side as the south. It's said these terms come from sailing directions. Typically, when heading north, you'd be sailing downwind, hence "down north." You'll hear this occasionally on Eleuthera as well, although it's more prevalent on Long Island.

Clarence Town is home to two churches built by Father Jerome, who built the famous Hermitage in Cat Island, and the island has one of the highest concentrations of churches per capita in The Bahamas. There is plenty of exploring to do on both land and water, including Hamilton's Cave, one of the largest in The Bahamas; world-famous Dean's Blue Hole, the deepest blue hole in the world; the Columbus Monument; plantation ruins; bonefishing; swimming pigs; and world-class diving.

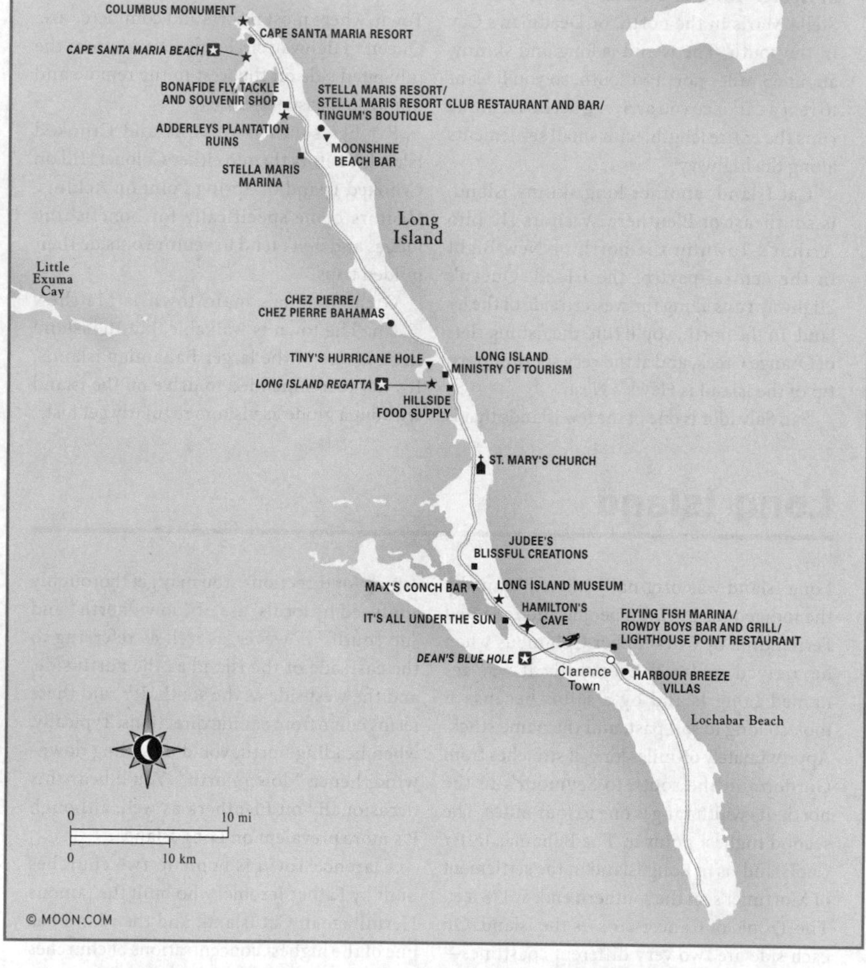

SIGHTS

TOP EXPERIENCE

★ Dean's Blue Hole

Dean's Blue Hole an incredible natural wonder that attracts visitors and professional free divers from all over. It's the world's deepest known blue hole and the second-largest underwater chamber. The hole is 663 feet deep; the first 60 feet ranges 80-120 feet across before it widens into a cavern with a diameter up to 330 feet. Tucked within a protected bay, it's bordered on the east by a vertical curved rock wall. It opens to the west, where it's gently lined with a shallow sandbank and the shoreline of the small bay.

The east side of the island is the side that gets all of the weather, so the natural rock feature allows the hole to be calm in almost any conditions. For an elevated view, scale the rock wall, minding your step on the porous sharp limestone. People often swim in the hole, but use caution if you aren't a strong swimmer, as the drop from the shallow sandbar into the depths of the hole are dramatic.

On Long Island, you'll bump into professional free divers that spend time on the island training in the hole. Several world records have been set in Dean's Blue Hole in numerous categories, including two in 2016 by New Zealand free diver William Trubridge, and by Long Island native Luke Maillis, setting national records for The Bahamas in three categories. Visibility is usually 50-100 feet.

Dean's Blue Hole is 0.25 miles south of Scrub Hill. Look for a Lloyd's Restaurant on the right. There is a sign on the left hand side. You'll arrive via a bumpy dirt road, and there's limited parking for a few cars. A small sandy beach stretches to the west. Unfortunately the beach is prone to garbage piling up from the ocean, but locals periodically clean it up.

Hamilton's Cave

Lucayan artifacts were discovered in Hamilton's Cave in 1935, giving evidence that it was used as shelter for the indigenous people hundreds of years ago. It's one of the largest cave systems in The Bahamas, with 10-foot-high ceilings that are 50 feet across in some places. This spacious cave system is a fabulous opportunity to experience caving for those normally wary of small spaces, and a nice shady option if you've had enough sunshine. It is on the property of Leonard Cartwright (Hamilton's, tel. 242/337-0235 or 242/472-1796). Look for the sign "Hamilton's Cave Tour" on the right on Queen's Highway in Hamilton's. The **cave tour** ($15 pp) takes several hours.

Columbus Monument

On the northern tip of Long Island, the Columbus Monument was constructed by the Long Islanders Association as a tribute to the arrival of Christopher Columbus. After his initial landing on San Salvador, it is said that Long Island was one of the next islands that Columbus visited in the Americas in 1492. The monument reads: "The monument is dedicated to the gentle and peaceful and happy Aboriginal people of Long Island, The Lucayans, and to the arrival of Christopher Columbus on October 17th 1492."

The monument overlooks stunning Columbus Harbour to the west, and the ocean to the north. You'll need a 4WD vehicle to access the monument, or you can arrange a tour

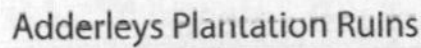

Adderleys Plantation Ruins

through your hotel or resort. Heading north on Queen's Highway, about 0.25 miles past the entrance to Cape Santa Maria, you'll see a sign for the monument. Take a left onto the dirt road and follow it in for almost two miles until you reach the end, with a small parking area and the monument just a short walk away.

Adderleys Plantation Ruins

The Adderleys fled the American Revolution and settled on Long Island, bringing with them a large number of enslaved people. They established a cotton plantation that once occupied all of Stella Maris. The ruins include seven buildings, intact up to the roof. Although locals make an effort to clear the bush periodically, the ruins can be somewhat overgrown.

To reach the ruins, take the first right after Bonafide Tackle Shop as you are heading south, or the first left after you pass the north end of Stella Maris Airport. There is a small sign visible from the south. Follow the dirt road in for 0.5 miles. The road is overgrown with bush on either side and tall grass in the middle. It's passable with a small rental car, but a 4WD would be more comfortable. There is parking at the beach for a few cars. It's a bit of a trek in, so wear decent walking shoes. Follow the signs down the beach, walking directly west. You'll see another sign and a trail heading inland. Follow the well-marked path inland for about 0.25 miles until you reach the first ruin. The others are scattered around in the bush but difficult to get to.

St. Mary's Church

St. Mary's Church is said to have been built by the Spanish in the 17th century, the oldest on the island. In ruins now, and without its roof, it is on the left just south of the Midway Restaurant and Bar in The Bight. The concrete structure is all that remains. Visit in the afternoon for the best lighting for photographs.

Long Island Museum

Since being damaged by Hurricane Joaquin in 2015, the **Long Island Museum** (Buckley's, tel. 242/337-0500, $3) has been closed for repairs, with no reopening date yet set. The Bahamas Historical Society established the museum to showcase a collection of artifacts dating back to the early settlers on the island. The museum curator will lead you on a guided tour explaining the history, culture, and customs of Long Island. In the museum are artifacts from the Lucayan, Taino, and Arawak peoples as well as a complete history of the

St. Mary's Church is the oldest church on the island, said to be built by the Spanish in the 1600s.

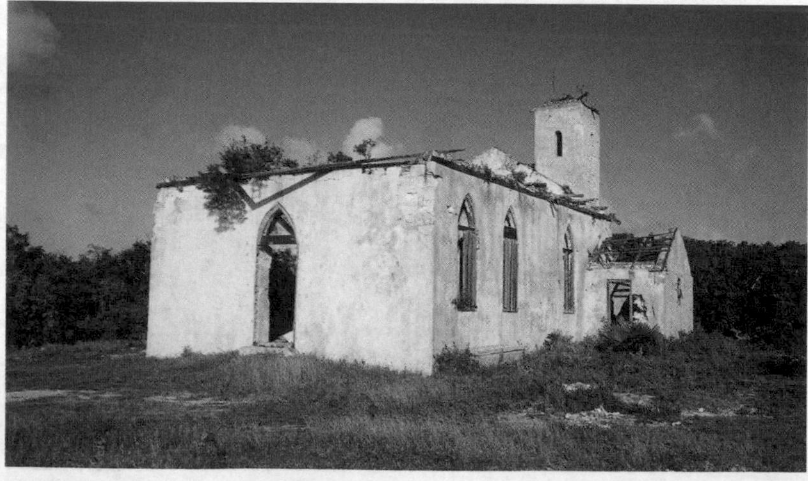

original Loyalist plantation settlers and descendants of today's Long Island residents. Heading south on Queen's Highway, it's a large pink building on your left in Buckley's.

BEACHES

Long Island is filled with gorgeous beaches on both sides, and there are endless opportunities for exploring on the Atlantic side, with its variety of long stretches of exposed beach protected by an exterior reef as well as coves and protected bays. Pick almost any road off Queen's Highway and run into a gorgeous empty stretch of beach. **Lochabar Beach** is on the south end of the island on the Atlantic side and one of the better-known spots. To get here, head south of Clarence Town for about 10 minutes. There are several roads leading east, and none are marked as public beach accesses, but when you start to see consecutive driveways, take the fourth road. It's a popular spot for vacation rental homes.

★ Cape Santa Maria Beach

At the north end on the western side of the island is **Cape Santa Maria Beach,** recognized internationally as one of the best beaches in the world and named for one of Christopher Columbus's ships. Soft, powdery sand stretches for four miles. The Cape Santa Maria Resort borders the northern edge, just before it tucks into inland shallows and protected sandbars and creeks, teeming with bonefish.

To visit the beach, consider dining at Cape Santa Maria Resort, or staying in one of their 40 bungalows and villas just steps from the sand. Beach chairs with shady umbrellas are tucked within palm fronds and edged with bright green *Scaevola*. The water gently laps the shore in most weather conditions, but on a calm day, you'll truly believe you've reached heaven. The white-sand shore gently slopes into pale turquoise. From the resort, you can kayak north into the protected creek and explore endless tidal creeks filled with birds and sealife. Enjoy sunsets with a cocktail at the Beach House, or meander along the wooden walkway.

To get to the beach, head north of the town of Seymour's and take a left onto a dirt road, following signs to Cape Santa Maria. You'll arrive at a T intersection. Heading south leads into a neighborhood of private homes, and to the right is Cape Santa Maria Resort.

Cape Santa Maria Beach is located on the north end of Long Island.

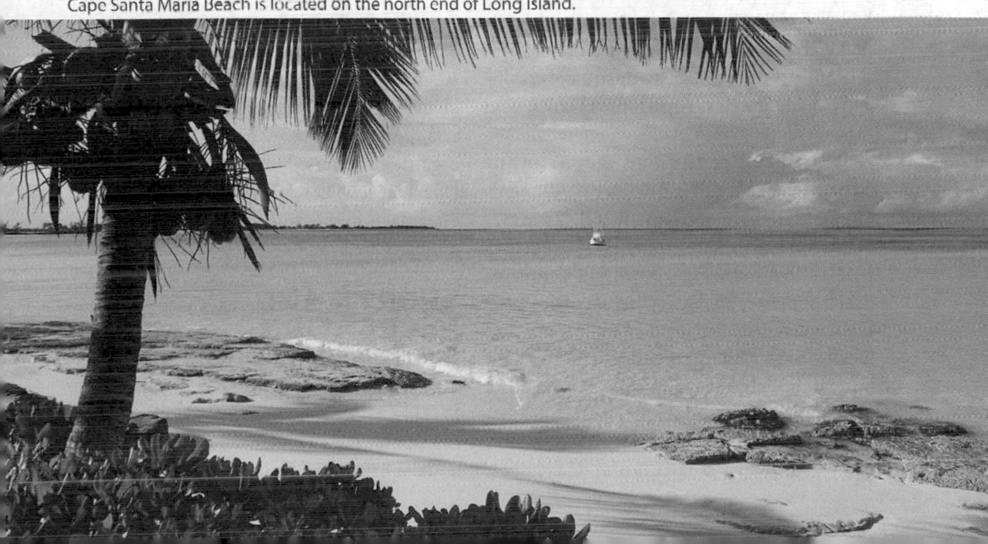

ENTERTAINMENT AND EVENTS

★ Long Island Regatta

The **Long Island Regatta** (tel. 242/338-8668) takes place Thursday-Saturday on Labour Day Weekend (late May-early June). It's one of the biggest regattas in the Out Islands, second only to the Family Islands Regatta in Exuma, and is a major fundraiser. Festivities take place in Salt Pond at the Cultural Site, a collection of colorful plywood structures overlooking a beautiful double bay. Participants come from all over The Bahamas, but some of the participating sloops are built on Long Island in nearby Mangrove Bush. There is live rake-and-scrape music, a variety of Bahamian food, family entertainment, and games. Be aware of planning a visit during this time, as room rates are higher, and reservations should be made well in advance.

Each Saturday you can find locally grown fresh produce, fruits, vegetables, and local crafts at the **Saturday Farmer's Market** (9am-early afternoon) in Salt Pond. Contact Lolita Darville (tel. 242/337-0116) for information.

SHOPPING

Tingum's Boutique (Stella Maris Resort, tel. 242/338-2050, www.stellamarisresort.com, daily 10am-5pm) is an adorable shop in the lobby of Stella Maris Resort. Rustic rock walls make are inviting as you peruse the tasteful selection of resort wear, swimsuit covers, locally made jewelry, flip-flops, bikinis, and other essentials.

It's All Under the Sun Department Store, Coffee Café and Deli (Queen's Hwy., McKenzie Settlement, tel. 242/337-0199, Mon.-Sat. 8am-6pm) is located in a pale-yellow building and offers a mix of beach supplies, pharmacy items, office supplies, souvenirs, shirts and beach wear, and locally made jewelry as well as coffee and light bites at the deli. There's outside patio seating to enjoy your coffee in the fresh air.

Judee's Blissful Creations (Queen's Hwy., Lower Deadman's Cay, tel. 242/357-1081, Mon.-Sat. 9am-4pm) is located in a bright-blue building along Queen's Highway. Once the police station, after a hurricane the structure was deemed unusable, so the police moved next door and Judee took over and turned it into her craft studio. She makes her own jewelry and bush teas. Within the jail cells, she has collections of historic artifacts and will happily talk you through them. Outside the shop are two impressive painted driftwood signs naming all of the settlements on Long Island from down north to up south.

Bonafide Fly, Tackle and Souvenir Shop (Queen's Hwy., Stella Maris, tel. 242/357-1417, www.bonafidebonefishing.com, Mon., Wed., and Fri.-Sat. 8am-3pm) offers rods, reels, and tackle for fly-fishing along with Bonafide logo shirts, hats, and pants. A variety of locally made bracelets, sea glass jewelry, and hand-painted driftwood and glass works by local artists are available.

Cape Santa Maria Resort (Cape Santa Maria, U.S. tel. 800/926-9704, www.capesantamaria.com, daily) has a small gift shop in the lobby with resort wear, drink tumblers, beach bags, flip-flops, and sun hats as well as convenience and pharmacy items, sunscreen products, locally made candles and ceramics, Bahama Handprints products, and locally made hot sauces, jams, and spice rubs.

Hillside Food Supply (Queen's Hwy., Salt Pond, tel. 242/338-0022, Mon.-Fri. 8am-10pm, Sat. 8am-9pm) is the main food store on the island, with a nice selection of produce and specialty items, including dairy-free and organic products. Numerous freezers provide a large selection of meats and seafood. Pharmacy items, toiletries, and household products are available.

SPORTS AND RECREATION

Snorkeling and Diving

Cape Santa Maria Resort (Cape Santa Maria, U.S. tel. 800/926-9704, www.capesantamaria.com) offers two- to three-hour snorkel and scuba trips through the

Fiona Maillis and the Bahamian Calendar

Ask any local about the **Bahamian Calendar** (www.thecalendarfamily.com) and they will know what you are referring to and where to get one. They likely have their own copy at home. Even in this era of digital calendars, there is something comforting about having a paper calendar hanging in your home or office, especially one with such thoughtful and relevant information.

The calendar was started by Long Islander Fiona Maillis in 1987. Her adult children and extended family now help with the creation of the calendar each year, and they have come to be known as the "Calendar Family." Fiona first created the calendar when her fisherman husband, Nick, needed a calendar to track the relationship between the moon phases and fishing seasons. She immediately gained support from friends in the community, and it quickly steamrolled into producing a calendar each year.

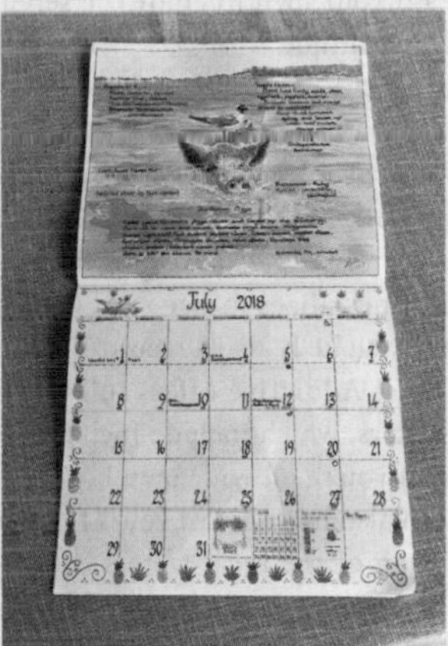

the Bahamian Calendar, established in 1987 and produced annually by the Maillis family of Long Island

The calendar is hand-painted in watercolors and provides moon cycles, fishing guides, gardening tips, recipes, rainfall and average temperatures, and regional island celebrations. Fiona does all the painting, with assistance from her daughter Oceania, who also provides photographs of island destinations for inspiration. Her son Thaddeus provides gardening information, and another son, Luke, an avid fisherman, provides fishing recommendations. Each page is a collection of thoughtful, original works, and the hand-drawn grids vary in size so she can fit in all the information. They are printed on heavy-duty matte paper. Since its inception, Fiona has gained confidence and the frames have become more complex.

The calendar is released the previous year in March or April and is a popular souvenir for visitors, with each month showcasing a different beautiful island scene from throughout The Bahamas. Look for them in grocery stores, pharmacies, and gift shops.

on-site dive shop to wrecks, Conception Island Marine Park for wall diving, and nearby reefs. See hawksbill and green sea turtles, coral reef tunnels, and a variety of colorful reef fish, sharks, and rays.

Stella Maris Resort (Stella Maris, tel. 242/338-2050, www.stellamarisresort.com) offers dive-and-stay packages, instruction, night dives, and overnight dive cruises. Dives are limited to small groups and are personalized based on your interests, including wreck dives, Conception Island trips, and diving with gray reef sharks and hammerheads at local reefs. Accessible by land is Dean's Blue Hole, where you may see turtles, dolphins, and sharks.

Fishing

Bonafide Bonefishing (Queen's Hwy., Stella Maris, tel. 242/357-1417, www.bonafidebonefishing.com) is the only bonefishing outfitter on Long Island. Most of the bonefishing is less than five minutes from Stella Maris, and there's also excellent bonefishing up near Cape Santa Maria. The fly shop has tackle, rods, reels, and flies for a day out on the water. Bonafide is also available for deep-sea and reef fishing.

Long Island Bonefish Lodge (Deadman's Cay, tel. 242/472-2609, www.longislandbonefishinglodge.com) offers assisted DIY bonefishing and lodging packages. There's a communal dining room, a bar and lounge area, and two duplex cottages housing six people. DIY means they will take you out to the flats and be available for guidance, but you're on your own to enjoy the serenity of fishing in solitude.

Reel Addictive Charters (Clarence Town, tel. 242/357-1090, www.charterfishingbahamas.com) is run by Captain Luke Maillis of the Calendar Family. He has years of expertise fishing the local waters and specializes in deep-sea fishing and spearfishing; he is also a record-holding free diver. Reel Addictive offers full- and half-day charters, which include fuel, tackle, and spears. If you're on your own boat, Captain Luke can also hop aboard yours for a guided expedition of the local waters or a fishing charter.

Cameron Knowles (Mangrove Bush, tel. 242/357-1038 or 242/357-1291) offers deep-sea fishing, snorkeling trips, and ecotours based on guest preferences, and can include Long Island's swimming pigs, whom he does his part personally to care for. You can go snorkeling, picnic on a sandbar, or perhaps dive for conch, and he'll make you the freshest conch salad you'll ever eat, washing it down with coconut water from a freshly shucked coconut. The half-day and full-day trips include soft drinks, snacks, and alcohol on request for additional cost. He can accommodate six on one boat, as well as larger groups on multiple boats.

FOOD

Bahamian

★ **Max's Conch Bar** (Queen's Hwy., Deadman's Cay, tel. 242/337-0056, Mon.-Sat. 10am-9pm, $15-25) is on Queen's Highway and adorned with colorful flags, marked with a bright sign. You can't miss it, and you'll quickly be drawn in by the ever-present crowd. Mix with locals under a rustic open-air tiki hut adorned with thatch and shaded by mature sea grapes and coconut palms. A patio in the back has plastic chairs and tables nestled within palm trees and foliage. They are known for conch salad, diced up in front of you, and also serve fish cakes, coconut shrimp, baked chicken, steamed snapper, minced lobster (in season), and a mighty tasty burger. Their tagline, "Fast food is not good, good food is not fast," aptly describes their mentality; don't be in a rush here. Grab a cold drink and enjoy the laid-back island scene.

Rowdy Boys Bar and Grill (Winter Haven Inn, Clarence Town, tel. 242/337-3062, www.winterhavenbahamas.com, daily

Experience the thrill of fly fishing the shallow flats with Bonafide Bonefishing.

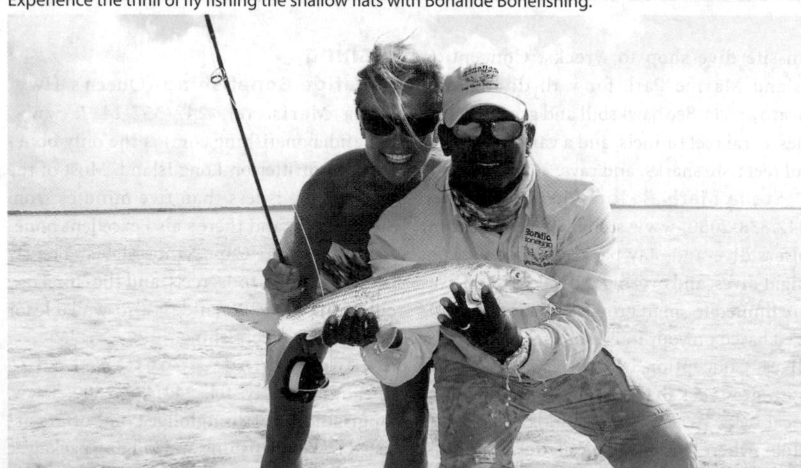

8am-10pm, $12-25) is open for breakfast, lunch, and dinner and serves wings, egg rolls, chili, sandwiches and burgers, and seafood entrées. The decor and ambience is casual and no-frills, but you'll be greeted warmly, and it's a social scene on weekends. Dine indoors with air-conditioning or on the outdoor patio overlooking the pool and ocean.

Contemporary

Cape Santa Maria Beach House Restaurant and Bar (Cape Santa Maria, U.S. tel. 800/926-9704, www.capesantamaria.com, lunch $14-16, dinner $20-30) serves breakfast, lunch, and dinner daily with meal plans available for resort guests, including full, half, and kids plans. They are happy to accommodate allergies and special dietary needs. Divine and indulgent breakfast options include stone crab and fish cake eggs Benedict and lobster scrambled eggs. Dinner has a wonderful selection of pastas, jerk chicken, barbecue ribs, and local seafood. Have a drink at the bar or watch the sunset on the ocean-side patio, and then meander to the upstairs dining area. Dinner reservations are advised.

Stella Maris Resort Club Restaurant and Bar (Stella Maris, tel. 242/338-2050, www.stellamarisresort.com, daily breakfast 7:30am-10am, $12-18, lunch noon-2pm, $12-20, dinner 7:30pm-9pm, $20-35) is located in the main house and lobby of Stella Maris Resort. Breakfast is a selection of omelets, pancakes, french toast, and fresh fruits. For lunch, find deli sandwiches, cracked conch burger, and pizzas. Dinner offers plenty of seafood options and fresh salads. The Moonshine Beach Bar serves light fare, such as paninis, pitas and wraps, burgers, and chicken tenders throughout the day. The Bar Snack menu is offered daily 2pm-9pm at the bar near the lobby, and if you'd like a packed lunch to take with you, opt for sandwiches, salads, and fruit. Meal plans are available for guests.

Chez Pierre Bahamas (Miller's Bay, tel. 242/338-8809 or 242/357-1374, www.chezpierrebahamas.com, $20-30, closed June-Sept.) is down a long dirt road on the edge of a gorgeous stretch of sunset-view beach. French Canadian chef Pierre runs the restaurant and guest cottages and serves European-influenced cuisine, homemade pizza, pastas with homemade sauces, and Italian seafood dishes. Get your own drinks at the honor-system bar and mingle with guests and other visitors in this casual environment. Reservations are required.

Located down a long dirt road, ★ **Tiny's**

Max's Conch Bar

Hurricane Hole (Thompson Bay, Salt Pond, tel. 242/338-0149 or 242/472-8104, www.tinysbahamas.com, Wed.-Sat. noon-9pm, Sun. 2pm-9pm, cash only) is relatively new. Come for mid-afternoon to catch the view during daylight. Try the fantastic cocktails, such as a Tiny's Tonic, Moscow Mule, or homemade margaritas. Food prices range from a $10 burger to $20 seafood and meat entrées and $45 for their handmade seafood pizza. Enjoy sunset on the tiny stretch of white-sand beach overlooking the protected bay while you mingle with sailboat cruisers and local expats. Find a quiet reprieve under the gazebo with hammocks and Adirondack chairs.

Lighthouse Point Restaurant (Flying Fish Marina, Clarence Town, tel. 242/337-3435, www.flyingfishmarina.com, daily 11:30am-9pm, $15-20) is on the second floor, above the main marina office, with panoramic views of the harbor and marina. Windows can be open for the open-air experience, or closed and air-conditioned on hot buggy evenings. The mosaic bar and dark wood ceilings provide a sense of refinement that doesn't take away from the laid-back marina vibe. The food is conch, sandwiches, fish and shrimp tacos, chicken, steak, and seafood entrées veggies, mac and cheese, peas-and-rice, or potatoes.

ACCOMMODATIONS

VRBO and Airbnb rentals are a great way to stay on Long Island for an extended period. Stock up with groceries and cook your own meals. Popular rental areas are Stella Maris, Clarence Town, and Lochbar. There's a large selection in the $100-200 range, depending on the time of year. Resort prices listed here reflect high-season double occupancy and do not include VAT (sales tax) or additional resort fees.

$150-250

Tiny's Hurricane Hole (Thompson Bay, Salt Pond, tel. 242/338-0149 or 242/472-8104, www.tinysbahamas.com, 2-night minimum, $150) has two 400-square-foot studios on the beach with Tiny's Bar and Restaurant. Units have kitchens, and laundry facilities are on-site. There are discounts for weekly and longer stays, and use of kayaks, paddleboards, hammocks, and lounge chairs is included.

Harbour Breeze Villas (Lochbar, Clarence Town, tel. 242/337-3088, www.harborbreezevillas.com, $160) has 15 newly built studio, one-, and two-bedroom villas

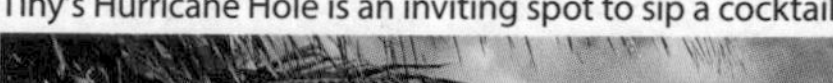

Tiny's Hurricane Hole is an inviting spot to sip a cocktail.

Stella Maris Resort boasts gorgeous views.

just south of Clarence Town, steps from a gorgeous protected sandy beach via a path way under bougainvillea and lined with lush foliage. Each villa has private balconies and full kitchens. Villas are decorated by the individual owners, making each unique.

Rustic ecological **Chez Pierre Bahamas** (Miller's Bay, tel. 242/338-8809 or 242/357-1374, www.chezpierrebahamas.com, Oct.-May, $175) offers six beachfront cottages on a private bay with over half a mile of white-sand beach. Cottages are spaced out for privacy, with screened-in porches. The generator runs during the day to provide power for a few lights and fans in the evenings. There is no air-conditioning, no TV, and the water is fairly salty. Rates include breakfast and dinner for two and use of kayaks and snorkel gear.

★ **Stella Maris Resort** (Stella Maris, tel. 242/338-2050, www.stellamarisresort.com, $220) is just a few minutes from Stella Maris airport on the east side of the island. Towering palms sway as you amble on cobblestone roads toward the ocean. Three swimming pools, a restaurant and bar with a lounge area, and a beach bar on the edge of the ocean accompany a variety of lodgings, including hotel rooms, one- and two-bedroom cottages, and three- and four-bedroom oceanfront houses. For a group, look into four-bedroom Dolphin House, with an expansive patio and pool overlooking the ocean. Rates include snorkeling, beaches, swimming pools, bicycles, kayaks, and paddleboards. Ask about free flights when booking multiple consecutive nights.

Over $250

Beachfront bungalows and villas line one of the most beautiful beaches in The Bahamas at ★ **Cape Santa Maria Beach Resort and Villas** (Cape Santa Maria, U.S. tel. 800/926-9704, www.capesantamaria.com, $350 bungalow, $795 villa). Bungalows are one- and two-bedroom duplex cottages with private verandas at beach level with views of the ocean. Spacious and well-equipped villas sleep six to eight and include central air and washers and dryers. Arrange scuba and snorkel trips, deep sea fishing, bonefishing, and trips to Columbus Point. A restaurant and bar serves meals daily with options for meal plans. It's worth the splurge to stay here.

INFORMATION AND SERVICES

For information, visit the **Long Island Ministry of Tourism** (Queen's Hwy., Salt Pond, tel. 242/338-8668, Mon.-Fri. 9am-5pm, www.bahamas.com). The **Bahamas Out Islands Promotions Board** (tel. 242/322-1140, www.myoutislands.com) offers information specific to the Out Islands. Look for the Fly Free and Air Credit promotions with participating member hotels.

If you're interested in connecting with a Bahamian ambassador to learn more about the culture and lifestyle, contact the **People-to-People Program** (tel. 242/367-3067, www.bahamas.com/people-to-people). Advance reservations to pair you with an ambassador are recommended.

The Mail Boat

Mail Boats in Nassau Harbour

The Out Islands of The Bahamas have always been dependent on interisland freight boats to deliver supplies and transport residents. Even today, boat travel can be the only way to reach some islands. Freight and passenger boats evolved from sailboats to steam engines in the early 19th century, and diesel engines took over in the 20th century. The captains were usually colorful characters, living their lives in constant nomadic flux. You'll still find independent supply boats serving remote and private islands with no less colorful characters captaining them.

The Bahamas Mail Boat was established in the 1960s to provide a scheduled link between Nassau and the Out Islands, carrying cargo, passengers, and, yes, mail. These bright blue and yellow cargo boats regularly leave Nassau Harbour on their way to scheduled island destinations. Sometimes rough weather and hurricanes hinder the schedule, leaving the Out Islands without a delivery that week. If you are on an Out Island in rough weather, head to the food store and stock up.

Looking for the ultimate island adventure, book travel from Potter's Cay in Nassau to any of the main hubs. Bahamians regularly use the Mail Boat for transportation as it's the most economical option. It's a great opportunity to get to know real Bahamians. The service can take up to 30 hours, depending on the destination, and includes a hot meal and a comfortable place to sleep. Additional food and drinks are available for purchase, and expect a lively beer-drinking crowd, especially on Out Island event weekends, such as regattas and homecomings. The Mail Boat has recently been acquired by the **Bahamas Ferries** (tel. 242/323-2166, www.bahamasferries.com), so you can book directly through the ferry office.

Banks

Many Out Island bank branches are closing, leaving some islands without any banks at all, bring cash with you. The RBC Royal Bank in Gray's Settlement recently closed, leaving only **Scotiabank** (Queen's Hwy., Buckley's Settlement, tel. 242/337-1029, www.scotiabank.com/bs, Mon.-Thurs. 9am-3pm, Fri. 9:30am-4:30pm).

Health and Emergencies

Health clinics include **Clarence Town Community Clinic** (tel. 242/337-3333), **Deadman's Cay Community Clinic** (tel. 242/337-1222 or 242/337-1242), and **Simms Community Clinic** (tel. 242/338-8488). Clinic hours are Monday-Friday 9am-5pm, except public holidays.

For emergency services, contact the **Royal**

Bahamas Police Force in Clarence Town (tel. 242/337-3919), in Deadman's Cay (tel 242/337-0999), in Simms (tel. 242/338-8555), in Stella Maris (tel. 242/338-2222), or by dialing 919 or 911. The **Air Ambulance** (tel. 242/323-2186) and **Bahamas Air and Sea Rescue Association** (BASRA, tel. 242/325-8864) are also available. For **directory assistance,** dial 916. **For weather,** dial 915.

GETTING THERE

Air

Flights are subject to leave later or earlier, so make sure to leave two to three hours to catch connecting flights in Nassau. There are two airports on Long Island: Stella Maris in the north and Deadman's Cay in the middle. If you are staying at the north end of the island, fly with **Stella Maris Air Service** (tel. 242/338-2050 or 242/357-1182, www.stellamarisresort.com/air-service) on a charter flight with per-seat pricing. They depart out of Jet Aviation in Nassau, just a short taxi ride from Lynden Pindling International Airport.

Commercial domestic flights to Long Island can be booked on **Southern Air** (Stella Maris tel. 242/338-2095, Deadman's Cay tel. 242/337-1722, Nassau tel. 242/377-2014, www.southernaircharter.com) with one flight per day from Nassau, making stops in both Stella Maris and Deadman's Cay, and on **Bahamasair** (tel. 242/702-4140, www.bahamasair.com) with one flight per day to Deadman's Cay.

Boat

Bahamas Fast Ferries (reservations tel. 242/323-2166, www.bahamasferries.com) has monthly trips on the fast ferry from Potter's Cay in Nassau to Simms ($130 round-trip) The ferry departs at 3pm and arrives in Simms at 10am the next day.

Marinas

Flying Fish Marina (Clarence Town, tel. 242/337-3430, U.S. tel. 954/654-7084, VHF channel 16, www.flyingfishmarina.com) has 21 slips and is the only marina and dockage on the east side of the island. There's a fuel dock, ship store, laundry, showers, Wi-Fi, water and ice, a pool, and the Outer Edge bar and Lighthouse Point restaurant.

Stella Maris Marina (Stella Maris, tel. 242/338-2050, VHF channel 16, www.stellamarisresort.com) is on the west side of Long Island. Approach is 5 feet at low tide and 7 feet at high tide. Sixteen slips are available with dockside electricity and water, short and long term wet and dry storage, and a fuel dock. Repair work is available. For marina guests, showers, Wi-Fi, and access to the swimming pool and resort facilities are included.

GETTING AROUND

Taxis are readily available to take you to your accommodations from the airport. A rental car is recommended for exploring the island. If you are staying at Stella Maris Resort or Cape Santa Maria Resort, let them know when you book, and they will leave a car at the airport for your arrival. You'll fill out all the paperwork when you check in to the hotel.

For car rentals in Stella Maris, contact **KRS Car Rental** (tel. 242/464-2077); in Clarence Town, **Unique Wheels Rentals** (tel. 242/337-3088); in Seymours, **Omar's Rental Cars** (tel. 242/338-5273 or 242/357-1043).

Cat Island

Wedged between Long Island and Eleuthera and of similar shape, Cat Island is long and skinny, running 48 miles northwest to southeast, with an Italy-style boot-shaped landmass at the south end. The island is littered with the ruins of stone cottages from the original settlers of the plantation era. Cat Island was originally called San Salvador (the name that Columbus gave the first place he made landfall), and there is a bit of a controversy as to whether he made initial landfall in today's San Salvador, or on Cat Island, or elsewhere in The Bahamas. When the name San Salvador was transferred to Watling's Island in 1926, Cat Island allegedly took its name from Arthur Catt, a pirate who plied the waters so frequently, hiding his treasure among the caves and hills, that it became known as Catt's Island.

Sleepy Cat Island is not known for nightlife, except for when rake-and-scrape gets going. Very few bars are open long past sunset, as most visitors spend their days in the sun and out on the water, heading in early at night. The area is known for its incredibly gorgeous beaches, scuba diving, fishing, kiteboarding, plantation ruins, and The Hermitage, located at the top of Mount Alvernia, the highest point in The Bahamas.

Cat Island is one of the few that maintains traditional island culture due to its remote location in the archipelago. You may hear whispers and stories of *obeah,* or black magic, used for both healing and cursing, and most residents can trace their ancestry back to the original settlers. The island is enticing, locals are welcoming, and life moves at a slower pace. Some want more development on the island, but most visitors prefer it the way it is.

SIGHTS

TOP EXPERIENCE

★ The Hermitage at Mount Alvernia

The Hermitage is perched atop Mount Alvernia, the highest elevation in The Bahamas at 206 feet. It was built by Father Jerome in the 1930s as his hermit residence

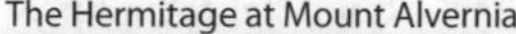
The Hermitage at Mount Alvernia

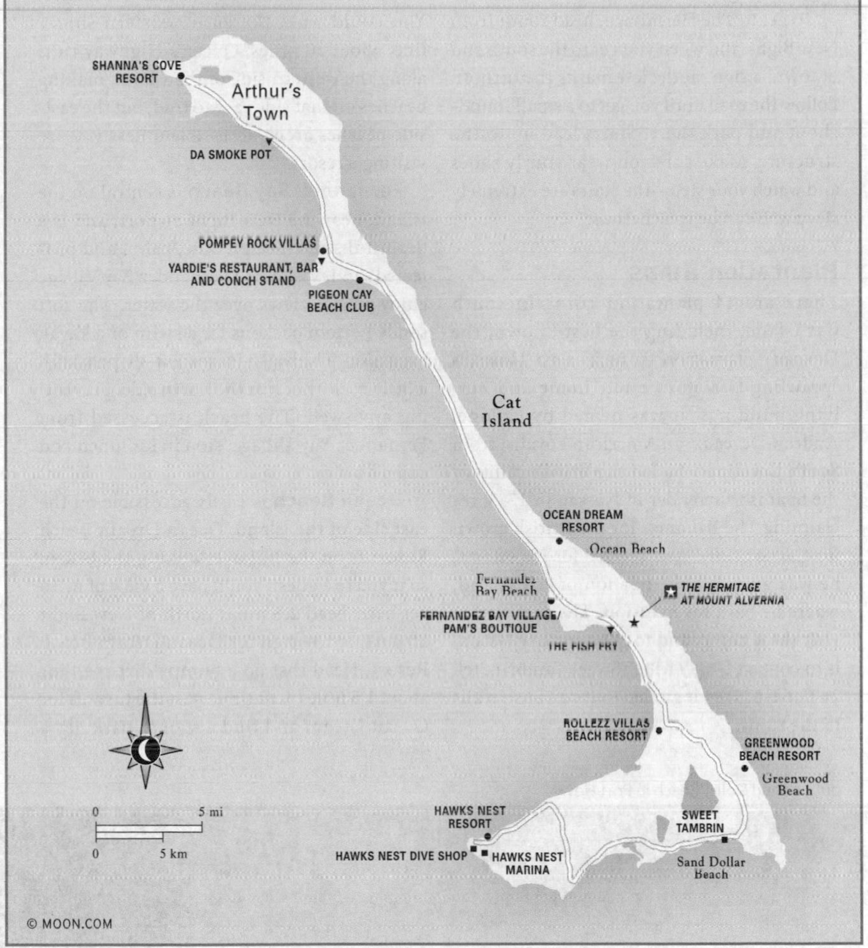

and prayer refuge. An architect and minister from England, Jerome built numerous churches and cathedrals on Cat Island and Long Island during his years in The Bahamas. On a return visit after 27 years, the Mail Boat that Jerome was on ended up stuck at Cat Island due to weather. He saw the tallest hills in The Bahamas and knew he wanted to build a hermitage and live out his final days here.

The Stations of the Cross lead the way up steep stone steps to the top. The views are breathtaking, looking out toward Hawk's Nest in the south, the Exuma Sound to the west, and the Atlantic to the east. As you arrive, there's a small cave where Father Jerome is buried, marked by a cross. Inside the stone hermitage is a "bed" on the stone floor, a writing desk overlooking Exuma Sound, a small kitchen, a shower with a drain, and a rainwater collecting system with a pump handle. Down past the main site is what is thought to have been his bread oven. Even farther down the back side is an overgrown path to a small cave where Father Jerome lived while he was constructing the Hermitage.

To get to The Hermitage, head south from New Bight, and when you get to the south end of town, a sign on the left marks the turnoff. Follow the road until you get to a small roundabout and park there. Stairs lead up to the structure. Make sure you wear sturdy shoes and watch your step—the stairs are extremely steep and can be treacherous.

Plantation Ruins

There are 14 plantation ruins in south Cat Island, including the best-known, the Deveaux plantation ruins in Port Howe, a sprawling two-story estate home and outlying buildings. It was owned by Colonel Andrew Deveaux, an American Loyalist from South Carolina who led the British military the Spanish surrender in Nassau in 1783, reclaiming The Bahamas for the British crown for the last time. As a reward for his efforts, he was given a large portion of Cat Island, where he built his mansion. The best way to visit these ruins, and to get a history lesson, is to contact **Daisy Mae** (Sweet Tambrin, tel. 242/464-6351), for guided tours on bush trails to the ruins.

BEACHES

Cat Island is known for its stunning, untouched, and oftentimes vacant beaches. You could walk the entire eastern shoreline, about 50 miles. Queen's Highway runs along the western side of the island, making beaches on that side easy to find, but the eastside beaches aren't accessible unless you are visiting a resort.

Fernandez Bay Beach is central on the island, near the New Bight airport, and is a beautiful stretch of pristine, calm, and protected sand. Visitors to Fernandez Bay Village enjoy sunset views over the water. The soft sandy bottom beckons for a swim or a kayak excursion. The beach is crescent-shaped, with a little rocky hook at the north side, preventing any swell. The beach is accessed from Fernandez Bay Village; stop in for lunch and enjoy a swim.

Ocean Beach is easily accessible on the east side of the island. Ocean Dream Beach Resort is on the hill overlooking the beach, so if you're a guest, you'll have a view of it. To get here, head 2.5 miles north of New Bight airport, to the sign for Ocean Dream Beach Resort. Head east on a bumpy dirt road for about 1.5 miles. Continue past the turnoff for Ocean Dream and find a spot to park; it's a

public Sand Dollar Beach in Port Howe

Rake-and-Scrape Music

What is rake-and-scrape? A dash of polka, a bit of bluegrass, and the percussion of Africa. Rake-and-scrape music originates in the Turks and Caicos Islands, where it is known as "rip saw," and was brought to Cat Island in the 1920s, eventually spreading to other islands by the 1940s.

The sounds are an original mix of the music of enslaved Africans, blending in European components from the British. The main unique component is the carpenter's saw, on which the tooth side is scraped with a screwdriver or a butter knife. The saw is leveraged and bent to create varying sounds, comparable to instruments such as the Nigerian wood-block *guiro* and the *cabasa,* or to maracas in Latin music. The use of scraping sticks was common in West African music and was adapted in America with the use of the washboard. Harmonizing with the saw is the European accordion, providing the element of polka, and the Goombay drum, also seen in Junkanoo. The drum is made of goatskin, originally stretched over a wooden barrel, now stretched over metal, a transition that changed the sound.

You can find rake-and-scrape throughout the Out Islands. To listen to rake-and-scrape music, keep an eye out for Cat Island's Bo Hog and the Rooters. You'll likely hear spontaneous pickup music at the fish fry or local establishments.

short walk to the beach. This beach is known for decent surfing on the north end near the rocky outcrop. There's not a lot of shade, so bring an umbrella There are no restrooms, food, or amenities.

Greenwood Beach is off the regular tourist path, fronting the Greenwood Beach Resort and a community of vacation rentals. Head south on Queen's Highway to a roundabout where you can head to Hawk's Nest or toward Port Howe. Head west toward Port Howe. At the sign for Greenwood Beach Resort, follow a dirt road for one mile until to a T intersection; access the beach here. Guests of Greenwood Beach Resort can take kiteboarding lessons and rent kiteboards.

Public **Sand Dollar Beach** is in Port Howe, at the very southern end of the island, protected by a rocky reef and shaded by casuarinas. It's not a great spot for swimming, as it's very shallow and prone to seaweed, but makes for a nice stroll. There are no services or amenities. Limited parking is available. Look for the beach access sign from Queen's Highway as you pass through Port Howe.

ENTERTAINMENT AND EVENTS

Cat Island Rake-and-Scrape Festival

Cat Island Rake-and-Scrape Festival is hosted on Bahamas Labour Day Weekend (1st weekend in June) in Arthur's Town. This is known as a signature event for Cat Island, as rake-and scrape music is an integral part of Cat Island culture. The music is performed by local and well-known national artists and includes a battle of the rake-and-scrape bands. Food stands serve Bahamian food, crafts, and straw products, and there's a fish and farmers market. Proceeds go to a selected high school graduate.

Cat Island Regatta

Cat Island Regatta is held over Emancipation Day weekend (1st weekend in Aug.). It is a popular homecoming weekend for Cat Islanders, and visitors and sloops from around The Bahamas come together to celebrate. It is hosted at the Regatta Beach venue in New Bight and features sloop racing, live music and entertainment, food and drinks, games, and culture.

Regatta Beach Fish Fry

The **Fish Fry** is on a bypass road that runs from Queen's Highway to "downtown" New Bight. The only sights you'll find along this bypass are a collection of weathered, brightly colored open-air shacks known as the Fish Fry, and the regatta stage for watching the sloops in the harbor during the regatta. It's along an attractive stretch of sandy beach, shaded by casuarinas. The big nights for Fish Fry are Friday-Saturday, but any day of the week you might find people milling around drinking beer, slapping dominoes, and feasting on Bahamian food such as cracked conch, cracked lobster, and jerk chicken. Hidden Treasures is the favored choice for locals; check out one of their fresh fruit smoothies, such as tamarind, soursop, papaya, or other in-season local fruit.

SHOPPING

Pam's Boutique (Fernandez Bay Village, tel. 242/342-3043, www.fernandezbayvillage.com, daily 10am-5pm) is just off the lobby at Fernandez Bay Village and features locally made soaps, postcards and art prints, Fernandez Bay apparel, swim covers, resort wear, bush teas, and hot sauces.

Sweet Tambrin (Queen's Hwy., Port Howe, tel. 242/464-6351, or tel. 242/342-5016, call ahead for information) is a mix of a restaurant and gift shop selling unique homemade products such as watermelon jam, hot pepper jelly, tomato relish, and tamarind hot sauce. Ask owner Daisy Mae about the health benefits of bush teas, which utilize the leaves of native plants and trees.

SPORTS AND RECREATION

Snorkeling and Diving

Cat Island is a diver's haven, with several fantastic options. It is not uncommon to have visibility of 200 feet when heading out for a dive. There are fantastic reef and wall dives where the shelf drops from 40 to 3,000 feet. Highlights include one of the healthiest populations of oceanic whitetip sharks, as well as blacktip Caribbean reef sharks and hammerheads.

Shanna's Cove Resort (Orange Creek, tel. 242/354-4249, www.shannas-cove.com) will customize your trip depending on your level of experience. Dive sites are 5 to 30 minutes by boat and vary in depth and difficulty. **Hawk's Nest Marina Dive Shop** (Hawk's Nest, tel. 242/342-7050, U.S. tel. 954/376-3865, www.hawks-nest.com) offers dive trips for guests of Hawk's Nest Resort with an experienced dive master. Near Hawk's Nest are dive spots for all levels, including reefs, tunnels, canyons, and walls teeming with hammerhead sharks.

Greenwood Beach Resort (Ocean Dr., Port Howe, tel. 242/342-3053 or 242/376-3004, www.greenwoodbeachresort.biz) is fully focused on water activities. Pauline is the only EFR dive instructor on the island and is a PADI master diver. She offers instruction for beginners and speaks French, English, and Spanish. Within just a few minutes' boat ride are 20 dive sites off the south end of the island.

Fishing

Shanna's Cove Resort (Orange Creek, tel. 242/354-4249, www.shannas-cove.com) provides a 22-foot boat and all equipment for guest use. They will help you arrange your perfect day on the water, bonefishing in nearby Orange Creek or deep-sea fishing around the corner on the Atlantic side.

Hawk's Nest Fishing (Hawk's Nest, tel. 242/342-7050, U.S. tel. 954/376-3865, www.hawks-nest.com) offers charters on their 43-foot center console with Captain Randy for reef or deep-water fishing. Your half-day or full-day trip includes a packed lunch and beverages. Hawk's Nest hosts several large fishing tournaments: the Wahoo Championship (mid-Jan.), the Hang 'Em High Challenge (mid-Mar.), the White Marlin Smackdown (mid-Apr.), and the Blue Marlin Battle (end of May).

Kiteboarding

Greenwood Beach Resort (Ocean Dr., Port Howe, tel. 242/342-3053 or 242/376-3004, www.greenwoodbeachresort.biz) attracts die-hard kiters enthusiastic about gliding through uncrowded, crystal-clear water. Professional kiteboarder, sports coach, and resort manager Antoine instructs all levels. The winds are predominantly onshore, with the ability to cruise the shoreline for eight miles. On the south end of the island is shallow flat-water riding at Port Howe, a great spot for beginners. The best riding is November-April, with summer winds dropping off June-October. A variety of kites available includes Cabrinha and North brands, as well as boards, harnesses, and wetsuits.

FOOD

North Cat Island

BAHAMIAN

Da Smoke Pot (off Queen's Hwy., Arthur's Town, tel. 242/354-2094, Tues.-Sun. noon-open late) is easily found down a short dirt road, marked with a sign. The building is tucked back from a rocky iron shoreline in a brightly colored orange, green, and blue building accented with ocean debris. A laid-back island vibe serves downhome food, such as slow-cooked ribs and fresh seafood. If the party gets rolling, you'll likely hear some rake-and-scrape. Call ahead for reservations.

Yardie's Restaurant, Bar and Conch Stand (Benett's Harbour, daily 7am-8pm, $12-15) serves Jamaican and Bahamian food and the best conch salad, chopped up right in front of you. Jamaican favorites include oxtail, curried mutton (goat), and jerk chicken and pork. Yardie's also serves tasty hot dogs and hamburgers. Settle into a picnic table with a cold beer at the casual outdoor covered patio along the highway.

EUROPEAN

Shanna's Cove Restaurant (Orange Creek, tel. 242/354-4249, www.shannas-cove.com, daily breakfast, lunch, and dinner, lunch $10-20, dinner $45) is the highest restaurant and bar in The Bahamas, overlooking the beautiful protected bay. Sit on the porch and watch the sunset, or inside in the air-conditioning if the bugs are out. The European-influenced menu consists of homemade breads, fresh fruits, and breakfast eggs cooked to order. Lunch serves a variety of gourmet pizzas. Dinner varies daily based on ingredients available, but is usually a three-course meal including a seafood or meat main with an

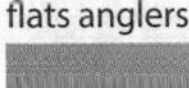

flats anglers

appetizer and dessert. They can accommodate special dietary needs. Reservations are required, as they only prepare for who they are expecting.

South Cat Island

BAHAMIAN

Daisy Mae will welcome you warmly to **Sweet Tambrin** (Queen's Hwy., Port Howe, tel. 242/464-6351 or 242/342-5016, daily) at the south end of the island in Port Howe. Her cozy dining room is located within a bright orange building on the side of the road where she serves up home-cooked Bahamian comfort food. Make sure you call ahead for reservations. She lives right across the road, but isn't cooking unless she knows you're coming.

CONTEMPORARY

Fernandez Bay Village Restaurant (Fernandez Bay Village, New Bight, tel. 242/342-3043, www.fernandezbayvillage.com, daily breakfast, lunch, and dinner, $20-48) serves three buffet-style meals per day at set prices. Breakfast is a wonderful buffet of eggs, bacon, ham and sausage, pancakes, and fresh-baked breads and pastries. Fresh fruit and cereal is available. Lunch and dinner options change daily but often include sandwiches, burgers, and salads for lunch and tender chicken, prime-cut beef, and fresh seafood served with creative vegetable sides. An honor bar is on the outdoor patio, where you can mix up your own cocktail or a glass of wine and mingle with other patrons. If you are a guest, you can always find fresh coffee, cookies, and snacks throughout the day.

Hawk's Nest Resort Restaurant and Bar (Hawk's Nest, tel. 242/342-7050, U.S. tel. 954/376-3865, www.hawks-nest.com, daily breakfast 8am-10:30am, lunch noon-2:30pm, dinner from 7pm, $15-30) has ample space for dining, including an air-conditioned dining room and a shaded outdoor poolside patio. Breakfast is cinnamon toast, eggs your way, or continental. Lunch has a variety of burgers, sandwiches, and salads. At dinner you can expect fresh catch, meat entrées such as marinated pork tenderloin, spicy and sweet Caribbean chicken, and steamed conch. A bar snack menu is served all day with wraps, burgers, wings, and fritters. Guests sometimes fly in to the nearby airstrip for lunch.

Enjoy breakfast, lunch, and dinner in a family-style dining room and bar or on the stone patio overlooking the breezy ocean at **Greenwood Beach Resort** (Ocean Dr., Port Howe, tel. 242/342-3053 or 242/376-3004, www.greenwoodbeachresort.biz, 7pm-open late, $40 per person for buffet and self-serve drinks). Nonguests can come in for dinner and mix with the eclectic crowd of adventure-sports addicts, European retirees, and backpackers. Serve up your own drinks at the honor bar and lounge in the numerous couch seating areas or on the patio on the edge of the beach. Dinner is buffet-style and serves a mix of fresh seafood, chicken, and meat dishes with plenty of vegetable sides. Periodic entertainment includes live music on Friday and open mic and movie nights.

Accommodations

Rates listed reflect double occupancy in high season (Nov.-May) and do not include VAT (sales tax) and any additional resort fees. Rates are typically lower in summer. Most resorts are closed September-October. Most of the accommodations listed are members of the Out Islands Promotions Board. Contact each resort directly about travel and lodging packages that can include free airfare when you book in advance.

$100-150

★ **Greenwood Resort** (Ocean Dr., Port Howe, tel. 242/342-3053 or 242/376-3004, www.greenwoodbeachresort.biz, Nov.-Aug. $135) is a great budget option for a social hostel feel and family environment but with the privacy of your own room. Rooms come with and without air-conditioning, which you'll want April-August. Greenwood is on the beach on the east side of the island, with cool breezes throughout the year. Breakfast, lunch, and dinner are served with meal-plan options. Managers Antione and Pauline specialize in scuba and kiteboarding. After a day on the water, take a dip in the pool. It's located at the southeast end of the island, pretty far removed from anywhere, but if you plan to partake in their water-sports offerings, you can settle in. They can also organize on-shore activities such as hiking.

Seven round yurt-like beachfront bungalows line the shore at **Pompey Rock Villas** (Bennett's Harbour, tel. 242/354-6003, www.pompeyrockvillas.com, $120). Modest rooms with decks overlooking the ocean are a great spot for groups. Single rooms start at $120, an affordable oceanfront option. South of Arthur's Town on the west side, the villas boast sunset views. The restaurant serves breakfast, lunch, and dinner daily, and the bar is usually a happening spot for happy hour.

$150-250

About one-quarter of the way down from the north end of the island, and three miles south of Bennett's Harbour, a sandy tidal spit known as Pigeon Cay is home to the **Pigeon Cay Beach Club** (Roker's, tel. 242/354-5084, www.pigeoncaybahamas.com, $180). A dirt road from Queen's Highway into a vacation home area is marked by colorful hand-painted signs. You'll feel like you're in the islands as you make your way down the dirt road. Breakfast is available daily, and dinner is available Wednesday-Saturday for guests as room service or outdoor dining at Palapa, along with the honor bar. The stone cottages, with dark wood-paneled ceilings, offer garden or ocean views. Studios, suites, and cottages with full kitchens are available.

On 450 acres on the tip of the "boot" of Cat Island and down a long dirt road, **Hawk's Nest Resort and Marina** (Hawk's Nest, tel. 242/342-7050, U.S. tel. 954/376-3865, www.hawks-nest.com, $175) feels like it's on the edge of the earth. With its own airstrip and marina, you can arrive by air or sea; coming by land is possible but time-consuming. During your visit, you may get the opportunity to meet the owners, who live nearby, and hear tales of the drug-running days, which involved the airstrip. A beautiful stretch of beach is located near the marina on the lee and sunset side, and hammocks overlook the ocean. The king and queen rooms overlook the glistening sea, and there are a pool and restaurant on site. Within the development are several multiple-bedroom vacation rental homes. Hawk's Nest hosts several major fishing tournaments each year, attracting anglers

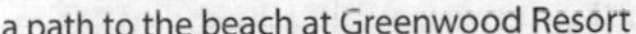

a path to the beach at Greenwood Resort

from all over. Kenny Chesney chose Hawk's Nest as the location for his "Save it for a Rainy Day" music video, which highlights the beauty of the area.

Located down a bumpy dirt road is a welcoming refuge at **Ocean Dream Beach Resort** (New Bight, tel. 242/342-2052, www.oceandreambeachresort.com, $195). You might never want to leave. Colorful hilltop cottages overlook the Atlantic and a stunning stretch of beach that rambles for eight miles. One- and two-bedroom cottages with kitchenettes and dining areas are decorated in cozy island decor, and lovely breezy patios overlook the crashing waves. There is a restaurant for guests, and the property is 100-percent solar-powered. Olga will make you feel at home.

On the northwestern corner of the island is **Shanna's Cove Resort** (Orange Creek, tel. 242/354-4249, www.shannas-cove.com, $220), run by a wonderful European couple who built all five cottages and the restaurant themselves. One of the highest-elevation developed properties in The Bahamas, Shanna's boasts the highest restaurant in the country. The spacious rooms were recently updated and offer comfortable accommodations with beautiful views of the tranquil crescent beach below, just steps away. Walking trails lead through the native vegetation to the north beach.

Rollezz Villas Beach Resort (Joe Sound Creek, Old Bight, tel. 242/557-0005, U.S. tel. 305/280-5719, www.rollezz.com, $230) offer adorably equipped cottages on a gorgeous stretch of private beach. There's not a lot of shade on the beach, so the sun can feel a little intense, but the bungalows and restaurant are cool. Call directly for the best rates, not always shown online.

Over $250

Just a stone's throw from New Bight Airport, ★ **Fernandez Bay Village** (Fernandez Bay Village, New Bight, tel. 242/342-3043, www.fernandezbayvillage.com, Dec.-mid-Aug., $283) offers cottages, villas, and suites in traditional Bahamian stone architecture. Established in the 1970s by Tony Armbrister, who can trace his ancestry back to the first Loyalist settlers in the late 1700s, the Fernandez Bay Village is truly a family operation, run by Tony, his wife Pam, their daughter Tameron, and her husband Jason. The Clubhouse's thatched ceilings and rough stonework feel Old World. This is the center of socialization throughout the day and the meeting place for all meals and happy hour, with an honor bar and comfortable lounge seating. The resort is along a one-mile stretch of private beach that beckons for a swim, a kayak excursion, or gazing out from under a beach umbrella. The suites offer luxuriously comfortable beds overlooking the beach. Request Shane Shack, one of the favored cottages, with a sitting area, fridge, and outdoor private bath and shower. The multiple-room villas have full kitchens. Enjoy complimentary coffee, fruit, and fresh-baked cookies throughout the day.

the clubhouse and dining area at Fernandez Bay Village

INFORMATION AND SERVICES

Bahamas Out Islands Promotions Board (tel. 242/322-1140, www.myoutislands.com) offers information specific to the Out Islands. Look for their ongoing Fly Free and Air Credit promotions with participating member hotels.

If you're interested in connecting with a Bahamian ambassador to learn more about the culture and lifestyle, contact the **People-to-People Program** (tel. 242/367-3067, www.bahamas.com/people-to-people). Advance reservations to pair you with an ambassador are recommended.

Banks

There are no banks on Cat Island, so bring cash. Hotels and resorts will take credit cards, but restaurants and bars often do not.

Health and Emergencies

Try the **Bain Town Community Clinic** (tel. 242/342-5057), **Old Bight Community Clinic** (tel. 242/342-3121), **Bight Community Clinic** (tel. 242/342-4049), or **Orange Creek Community Clinic** (tel. 242/354-4050). All clinics are open Monday-Friday 9am-5pm, except public holidays.

For emergency services, contact the **Royal Bahamas Police Force** in Arthur's Town (tel. 242/354-2046) or New Bight (tel. 242/324-3039), or by dialing 919 or 911. For **directory assistance,** dial 916. For **weather,** dial 915.

GETTING THERE

Air

Flights are subject to leave later or earlier, so make sure to book at least two to three hours between connecting flights in Nassau. There are two airports in Cat Island: Arthur's Town in the north and New Bight in the middle.

Commercial domestic flights to Cat Island can be booked on **Sky Bahamas** (Arthur's Town tel. 242/354-2236, New Bight tel. 242/342-2256, Nassau tel. 242/225-4460, U.S. tel. 954/317-3751, www.skybahamas.net) with two flights per day from Nassau to either Arthur's Town or New Bight. If you book on a day when they only fly to Arthur's Town and you booked to New Bight (and vice versa), they will bus you to your final destination.

Boat

MARINAS

Hawk's Nest Marina (Hawk's Nest, tel. 242/342-7050, U.S. tel. 954/376-3865, www.hawks-nest.com) is on the edge of prime fishing grounds with 28 slips and a seven-foot depth at low tide. The marina has fuel, water, ice, showers, and laundry, two air-conditioned fish-cleaning houses, and visitors can use the resort facilities, swimming pool, and clubhouse, where there is a restaurant and bar.

GETTING AROUND

Taxis are available to take you to your accommodations from the airport, but a rental car is recommended for exploring the island. **Bob's Car Rentals** (tel. 242/354-6120) is located in Arthur's Town. **Gilbert's Car Rentals** (tel. 242/342-3011) is at the New Bight Food Store.

San Salvador

In 1951 the U.S. government built a missile- and submarine-tracking facility and a Coast Guard station in San Salvador. The military left the island in the late 1960s but left an electrical power station, a paved airstrip, and infrastructure that are now being utilized by the Bahamian government.

At 63 square miles, with a population of around 1,000, San Salvador is one of the rare circular-shaped islands, largely undeveloped and with a few resorts and a perimeter of sandy beach and rocky headlands. There is a surprising abundance of hills and natural elevation. Outdoor adventurers thrive here, with ample opportunities for scuba, kiteboarding, and hiking.

SIGHTS

Columbus Monument

There are several tributes to Christopher Columbus's arrival in the New World throughout The Bahamas and on San Salvador. The easiest to visit is the monument on the side of Queen's Highway, about five minutes south of Cockburn Town. A white cross stands prominently on the shore, erected in 1956 by Ruth Durlacher Wolper on Christmas Day. The ocean provides a backdrop for photographs. Parking is available. Also located at this park is the Mexico Olympic Monument.

Mexico Olympic Monument

Located in the same park as the Columbus Monument, the Mexico Olympic Monument was erected by the Mexican Government to signify a stopping point as the Olympic flame was brought from Greece by ship on its way to Mexico City for the opening of the 1968 Olympic Games. This was the only time the Olympic flame passed through The Bahamas. The flame is not currently lit, as it was damaged in a recent hurricane, but there are plans to relight it.

Dixon Hill Lighthouse

One of the last still in operation that is run on kerosene, **Dixon Hill Lighthouse** stands 235 feet above sea level and is visible for 19 miles. On the northeastern part of the island, called United Estates, it was built in 1886 by the British government and built by the Imperial Lighthouse Service, responsible for provisioning and maintaining lighthouses, lightvessels, and buoys in the British Empire. This is one of nine similar lighthouses constructed around The Bahamas in that era. The property was a plantation that belonged to John Dixon. Visitors can come any time and scale the steep 79 steps to the top to enjoy breathtaking views. There is a guest registry and donation box. It is located off Queen's Highway, marked with a sign.

★ Watling's Blue Hole Lookout

If you visit San Salvador, make an effort to get to the **Watling's Blue Hole Lookout.** Within Sandy Point Estates are the ruins of Watling's Castle and Watling's Blue Hole, viewable from a platform on the crest of a hill, accessed by stairs from the main road. Watling's Castle is the ruins of an 18th Century Loyalist plantation house named for pirate John Watling. The ruins include a three-story Great House, a kitchen, slave quarters, barns, and boundary walls. Heading south on Queen's Highway from Cockburn Town the road veers east when it reaches the south end of the island. Turn right and head west into Sandy Point Estates. Take the first right and another quick right, and you'll see the Blue Hole Overlook. Walk to the top of the stone staircase, 85 feet above sea level, and enjoy panoramic views of the ocean and the island, Watling's Castle ruins, and the blue hole.

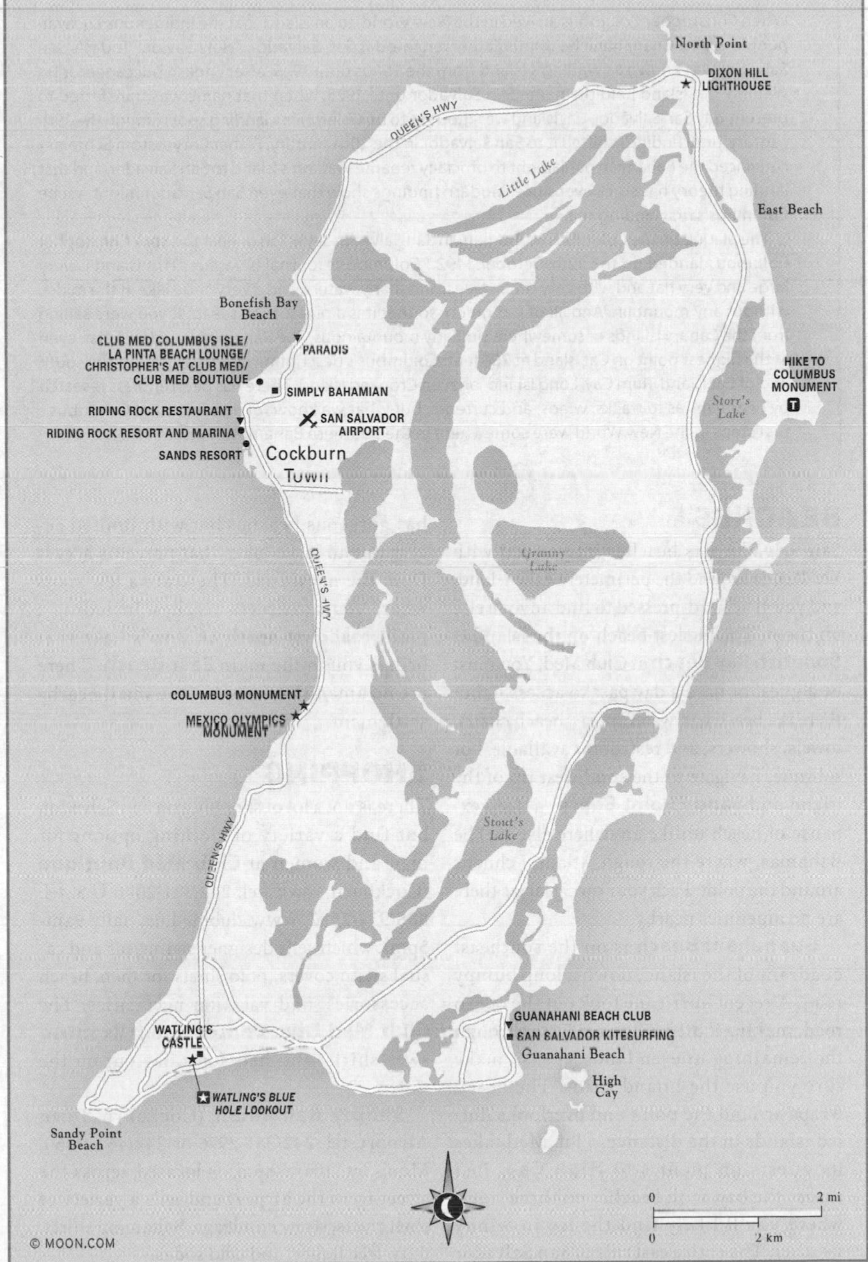
San Salvador
North Point
DIXON HILL LIGHTHOUSE
QUEEN'S HWY
Little Lake
East Beach
Bonefish Bay Beach
CLUB MED COLUMBUS ISLE/ LA PINTA BEACH LOUNGE/ CHRISTOPHER'S AT CLUB MED/ CLUB MED BOUTIQUE
PARADIS
SIMPLY BAHAMIAN
HIKE TO COLUMBUS MONUMENT
Storr's Lake
RIDING ROCK RESTAURANT
RIDING ROCK RESORT AND MARINA
SAN SALVADOR AIRPORT
SANDS RESORT
Cockburn Town
Granny Lake
COLUMBUS MONUMENT
MEXICO OLYMPICS MONUMENT
Stout's Lake
GUANAHANI BEACH CLUB
SAN SALVADOR KITESURFING
Guanahani Beach
WATLING'S CASTLE
High Cay
WATLING'S BLUE HOLE LOOKOUT
Sandy Point Beach
0
2 mi
0
2 km
© MOON.COM

The Columbus Controversy

When Christopher Columbus arrived in the New World, to an island that the indigenous Lucayan people called Guanahani, he immediately renamed it San Salvador, "Holy Savior." Today's San Salvador was known as Watling's Island from the 1680s until 1925, after English buccaneer John Watling. Cat Island held the name San Salvador until 1925, when that name was transferred to present-day San Salvador. Cat Island was thought to be Columbus's landing spot through the 19th century, until findings shifted it to San Salvador in the 20th century. Father Chrysostom Schreiner convinced the Bahamian parliament to officially rename Watling's Island to San Salvador, and that landing theory has stuck ever since. Modern findings show that even San Salvador might not be Columbus's first landing site.

The plaque on the Columbus Monument in San Salvador says, "On or near this spot Christopher Columbus landed on the 12th October 1492." Columbus's journal is vague: "This island is very large and very flat and with very green trees, and many waters, and a very large lake in the midst, without any mountain. And all of it is green, so that it is a pleasure to see it." If you were sailing from the Canary Islands or somewhere similarly mountainous, The Bahamas would look flat, even at the highest point on Cat Island at 206 feet. Columbus's description could easily be of the south end of Cat Island, Rum Cay, Long Island, or even Crooked Island. There has been endless research by historians as to tracks, winds, and currents, but what we know for certain is that Columbus's first steps in the New World were somewhere in the Southern Bahamas.

BEACHES

San Salvador has beaches intermixed with headlands around the perimeter of the island, and you'll be hard-pressed to find anyone else on them. The busiest beach on the island is **Bonefish Bay Beach** at Club Med. You must be a guest or have a day pass to access it, but there is a beach bar, water sports, beach chairs, towels, showers, and restrooms available. For solitude, navigate to the southwest tip of the island and **Sandy Point Beach,** a deep expanse of beach unlike anywhere else in The Bahamas, where the rough Atlantic churns around the point. Pack your own gear, as there are no amenities nearby.

Guanahani Beach is on the southeast quadrant of the island, down a long bumpy road. A recent hurricane took out the ocean road, making it difficult to navigate through the remaining uneven landscape, so make sure you use the inland roads. The beach wraps around the point and overlooks dotted islands in the distance. Club Med takes its guests on picnics to **High Cay,** just across the bay, with beaches on three sides, where you'll likely find the lee in windy weather. The entire east side of San Salvador has gorgeous beaches but with limited access due to large lakes that prevents access from the main road. There are a few spots where you can access beaches, including a main road just north of Storr's Lake that brings you to the main **East Beach.** There are no amenities except in the small nearby settlement.

SHOPPING

There is not a lot of shopping on San Salvador, but find a variety of clothing options for men and women at **Club Med Boutique** (Cockburn Town, tel. 242/331-2000 U.S. tel. 888/932-2582, www.clubmed.us, daily 9am-5pm), which sells designer swimwear and casual swim covers, polo shirts for men, beach accessories, and vacation necessities. The **Club Med Dive Center** also sells shirts, sweatshirts, and hats for a day out on the water.

Simply Bahamian (Cockburn Town Airport, tel. 242/331-2976 or 242/464-9060, Mon.-Sat. 10am-6pm) is located across the street from the airport and sells a variety of shell crafts, straw handbags, Bahamian shirts, duty-free liquor, and cold sodas.

SPORTS AND RECREATION

Hiking

On the very northern end of the island is a rocky headland that juts out into the ocean. A short hike on the **North Point** trail provides a refreshing vantage point. The trail is easy to navigate, taking 10 minutes to reach the point. The waves crash on the rocky shoreline, reminiscent of northern Europe. Parking is available at a community park just past Gerace Research Center, and the trail is well marked.

Once you start heading south on Queen's Highway from the north end of the island, you'll pass through United Estates settlement. In about 1.5 miles is a main road to **East Beach.** You can walk along the shoreline bordered between Storr's Lake and the ocean south for 1.8 miles to reach a rocky headland. Another Columbus monument is located on the headland. Make sure you wear sturdy shoes and carry water.

Snorkeling and Diving

Some of the best diving in The Bahamas is located just minutes off San Salvador, one of the top wall-diving destinations in The Bahamas. Most of the top dive spots are on the lee of the island, so there will likely be calm seas.

Riding Rock Resort and Marina (Cockburn Town, tel. 242/331-2631, U.S. tel. 800/272-1492, www.ridingrock.com) specializes in diving excursions, and you can book dive-stay-meal packages through the resort. Their boats are well-equipped to handle up to 20 divers and offer two dives daily.

For guests of Club Med, utilize the professional **Seafari Dive Center** (Cockburn Town, tel. 242/331-2000, U.S. tel. 888/932-2582, www.clubmed.us), open daily, depending on the weather.

Kiteboarding

San Salvador is one of the last truly untouched locales for kiteboarding, with steady winds throughout the year. **San Salvador Kitesurfing** (tel. 242/452-0927, www.sansalkitesurfing.com) offers professional IKO instruction with Jonathan Knowles in the epic shallow flat waters of the lagoon and within Guanahani Bay.

FOOD

Contemporary

★ **Club Med** (Cockburn Town, tel. 242/331-2000, www.clubmed.us) offers a variety of restaurant options, including Christopher's and La Pinta Beach lounge. Purchase an evening

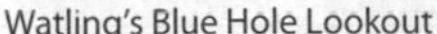
Watling's Blue Hole Lookout

pass ($70 pp) that includes drinks and dinner seating at 7:30pm. Reservations must be made to dine at La Pinta, but you can meander down the boardwalk and have a drink, then head to Christopher's for the open seating, where guests can arrive anytime after the buffet opens. Unless you grab a table for two, expect to be joined by other guests or resort staff, who do their best to make your visit enjoyable. Christopher's buffet is diverse, from healthy to heavy. Weekly themed nights include a White Party and other various color themes, a formal evening, and Mexican, Italian, and other international fare, including fresh vegetables, made-to-order pastas, and a homemade bread bar with anything you could possibly want to slather on a baguette or crusty sourdough, including European style mayonnaise, mini-gherkins, tapenades, olive oil, and creamy butter. Take another lap and hit the fabulous dessert bar.

Guanahani Beach Club Restaurant (Snow Bay, tel. 242/452-0438, www.guanahanibeachclub.com, 8-10am, noon-2pm, 7pm-open late, $20-30) is open for guests of the resort and by reservation for nonguests. Breakfast is homemade cakes and pastries, yogurt, and fresh fruit. Lunch is healthy salads and a delectable pesto baguette with smoked salmon. Dinner is a leisurely three- or four-course dining experience with a fish or meat option paired with fresh in-season ingredients.

Bahamian

Paradis Restaurant and Bar (Cockburn Town, tel. 242/331-2400, Mon.-Sat. 8am-9pm, $10-20) is in a small strip mall just north of Club Med, but don't let its appearance fool you—this is a coveted go-to spot for locals. Beverly has been serving comfort food for 11 years and will welcome you warmly with baked chicken, the popular 8-ounce burger, ribs on the grill, and souse on the weekend. Out Islands typically lack Chinese food, but Paradis serves up Chinese one night per week.

Riding Rock Restaurant (Cockburn Town, tel. 242/331-2631, www.ridingrock.com, daily 7:30am-9am, 12:30pm-2pm, 6:30pm-8:30pm, bar daily 4pm-11pm, $10-20) serves buffet-style meals that include a mix of Bahamian and American food. Dishes range from grouper fingers, baked chicken, pizza, and roast beef to seafood entrées. The bar draws a crowd of locals and divers staying at the resort.

East Beach

ACCOMMODATIONS

Dive-stay packages are available at **Riding Rock Resort** (Cockburn Town, tel. 242/331-2631, www.ridingrock.com, $180). The accommodations are modest yet comfortable, perched over the ocean, each with a covered balcony. A popular spot for divers who just need a place to sleep, the property has a swimming pool, a restaurant, and a bar.

Operated by an enthusiastic team of Bahamians, ★ **Sands Resort** (Cockburn Town, tel. 242/331-2254 or 242/225-3065, www.sansalresortandspa.com, $210) is in lush vegetation on the edge of the ocean, with a small stretch of white-sand beach just outside the recently updated studio and two-bedroom rooms with full kitchens. First-floor units are on the beach; the second floor has elevated views. Spa services include massage on the beach shaded by foliage, and they can assist with booking island tours and snorkeling. The restaurant is for guests, and the Tiki Bar is a chill gathering spot in the afternoon.

Four cottages at the **Guanahani Beach Club** (Snow Bay, tel. 242/452-0438, www.guanahanibeachclub.com, $368) make for an intimate stay on the far reaches of the island at one of San Salvador's most beautiful beaches. Rooms are crisply decorated in modern whites and beiges, bringing the exterior brightness indoors. One- and two-bedroom units have kitchenettes. San Salvador Kitesurfing is on-site to rent gear or take a lesson on the top-notch kite beach in front of the resort. At the far southeast corner of the island, Guanahani is only reachable by a long dirt road, and the cottages are tightly packed on the small property. Rates are for double occupancy, breakfast and dinner, and airport transfers.

All-inclusive **Club Med Columbus Isle** (Cockburn Town, tel. 242/331-2000, U.S. tel. 888/932-2582, www.clubmed.us, from $1,500 weekly d, including airfare) has been welcoming guests since 1992. More than 200 rooms in brightly colored cottages are spaced around the sprawling property, with lush green lawns and towering palm trees. The resort has a European vibe, with a disco, a nightclub-lounge area, and French is spoken prominently. The resort is on a sparkling stretch of white sand at Bonefish Bay, with lounge chairs and umbrellas for guest use. On-site are a L'Occitane spa, a fitness center, a beach, water sports, a dive center, a theater, three bars, two restaurants, and a pool overlooking the ocean.

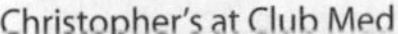
Christopher's at Club Med

INFORMATION AND SERVICES

The San Salvador Tourist Office (tel. 242/331-1928, Mon.-Fri. 9am-5pm) is in Cockburn Town, just south of Riding Rock Marina, for maps and information about the island. **Bahamas Out Islands Promotions Board** (tel. 242/322-1140, www.myoutislands.com) offers information specific to the Out Islands. Look for their ongoing Fly Free and Air Credit promotions with participating member hotels.

If you're interested in connecting with a Bahamian ambassador to learn more about the culture and lifestyle, contact the **People-to-People Program** (tel. 242/367-3067, www.bahamas.com/people-to-people). Advance reservations to pair you with an ambassador are recommended.

Banks

Bank of the Bahamas (tel. 242/331-2237, Mon.-Thurs. 9:30am-3pm, Friday 9:30am-4:30pm) is on Queen's Highway in Cockburn Town.

Health and Emergencies

Try the **Cockburn Town Community Clinic** (tel. 242/331-2105 or 242/331-2106, Mon.-Fri. 9am-5pm except public holidays).

For emergency services, contact the **Royal Bahamas Police Force** in Cockburn Town (tel. 242/331-2919), or by dialing 919 or 911. For **directory assistance,** dial 916. For **weather,** dial 915.

GETTING THERE

Air

Bahamasair (tel. 242/702-4140, www.bahamasair.com) has one flight daily from Nassau to Cockburn Town at varying times of day.

From Miami, **American Airlines** (U.S. tel. 800/433-7300, www.aa.com) has direct flights on Saturday. Charter flights from Montreal and Paris arrive weekly for Club Med. Contact Club Med directly if you plan to fly in from either of those destinations.

Boat

MARINAS

Riding Rock Marina (Cockburn Town, tel. 242/331-2631, VHF channel 16, www.ridingrock.com) offers protected deep-water dockage with electricity, fresh water, diesel and gas, showers and restrooms, laundry facilities,

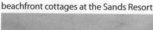

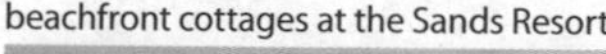
beachfront cottages at the Sands Resort

and satellite TV. There are 25 slips for boats up to 140 feet. Fishing and local guide services are available, and guests can use the resort amenities, swimming pool, restaurant, and bar.

GETTING AROUND

Most resorts include airport transfers and will meet you on arrival. Taxis are also available. A rental car is a recommended way to explore the island.

K's Scooter Rentals (tel. 242/331-2125 or 242/452-0594) is at the Cockburn Town Airport, with hourly and daily rates. Arrange **car rental** through your hotel or resort. Each hotel works with a preferred local company.

Other Islands

The Bahamas has 700 islands, which won't all fit in this guidebook, but I will touch lightly on a few. These smaller islands are ideal to go completely off the beaten path for solitude and tranquility. There's not much nightlife, and often you'll have to make sure the local restaurant knows you're coming for dinner or they might not to open for the evening. Planning a trip to these islands is straightforward once you select your lodging your hotel will assist with everything from flight information to rental cars and airport transfers. Once you settle in, you can venture out to explore the remote landscape and beautiful beaches, and arrange other activities through your lodge.

The less traveled island regions of the Southern Bahamas include Great Inagua, Acklins, and Crooked Island, discussed here, and even less visited Mayaguana, Rum Cay, and Ragged Island. Mayaguana, with a population of around 300, has little infrastructure to support visitors. Rum Cay, with a population of around 50, has a few guest cottages rented through private homeowners but no resorts or hotels. Ragged Island was devastated by Hurricane Irma in 2017, and many residents have not yet returned.

GREAT INAGUA

Inagua is an island for die-hard birders, with over 100 species, including the West Indian pink flamingo. The island's only settlement, Matthew Town, has about 1,000 residents, many employed by Morton's Salt Company, which harvests more than one million tons of salt from the salt pans on the island each year. The prominent salt mounds can be seen from afar in the flat landscape as snowy mountains glisten in the sun. Visitors can tour the salt plant with advance notice.

The Great Inagua Lighthouse

One of the largest of The Bahamas but the least developed, Inagua supposedly experienced the first acts of piracy in The Bahamas in 1713, and ship wrecking subsequently became lucrative income for the island. The Great Inagua Lighthouse was built in 1870, commissioned by the British government to prevent these wrecks. It was built during the same time era as the San Salvador and Hope Town lighthouses. The Great Inagua Lighthouse was originally among the rare kerosene-burning lighthouses, but today it is automated and solar powered. You can climb its 113 feet to enjoy panoramic views of Matthew Town and the island. On a clear day you can see the mountains of Cuba, just 50 miles away.

Inagua National Park

Established in 1965 on 287 square miles, Inagua National Park is one of the most cherished land parks in the Bahamas, protecting the largest nesting population of West Indian pink flamingos in the world. Sighting the flamingos is rare, as they are skittish and tend to hang out in the middle of lakes, but you'll surely see Bahama parrots, roseate spoonbills, brown pelicans, herons, egrets, burrowing owls, and the endemic woodstar hummingbirds up close, along with a variety of other species. The flamingo has made its way back from the verge of extinction, when it was hunted for meat and feathers. Now there are 50,000-60,000 on Inagua. Because of the protection provided here, the population has spread to other islands, including Andros, Crooked, and Acklins, as well as nearby Turks and Caicos, Grand Cayman, and Cuba. There are also wild donkeys throughout the park, and the Pygmy-Bonsai forest, where native trees such as Lignum vitae are stunted and grow close to the ground due to the harsh conditions.

Visitors must contact the **Bahamas National Trust** (tel. 242/393-1317, U.S. tel. 866/978-4838, www.bnt.bs) to arrange for the park warden to take you into the park. Park wardens Henry Nixon and Casper Burrows are both well-known characters in the area, with Henry Nixon's family being instrumental in flamingo conservation. From Matthew Town, it's a 12-mile journey through Morton salt lakes and flats to reach the park entrance, and it can take up to an hour to get into the park.

Food and Accommodations

There are very few options for accommodations and food on Inagua. You can walk across the town in a matter of minutes, and if you are looking for food, you'll have to alert a local restaurant that you will be eating that evening so they make sure to stay open for you. If you have a particular diet, bring your own food; otherwise expect fried seafood, pork chops, peas-and-rice, and canned vegetables. Because the supply boat only comes once or twice per month, locals are accustomed to eating preserved foods.

Highly rated by locals and visitors is **Cepigel Restaurant** (Matthew Town, tel. 242/339-1227). When the owner's son, a properly trained chef, is in town, he will cook up gourmet food, but on any given day, you are sure to have the tastiest Bahamian meal on the island. Always call ahead, well in advance.

Enrica's Inn & Guest House (Matthew Town, tel. 242/339-2127, www.enricasinn.com, $85) offers no-frills but comfortable rooms just a short walk to the beach. The bungalows are brightly colored with covered porches, and some have kitchenettes and fridges. Meals can be arranged on request. They don't take credit cards, so bring cash.

Getting There and Around

Inagua has three flights per week from

West Indian pink flamingos in Inagua National Park with The Great Inagua Lighthouse in the distance

Bahamian Cascarilla Bark and Samana Cay

Samana Cay, north of Crooked Island, is seasonally inhabited by harvesters who collect cascarilla bark, an ingredient in the Italian liqueur Campari, for export. Its natural bitter flavor and spicy aroma are integral to the unique beverage, a bright-red mixture developed by Gaspare Campari in 1860. A secret mixture of herbs is steeped in alcohol. Campari is considered a type of bitters, which were originally used as health tonics and had a low alcohol content, but Campari used the bitters method to make a stronger drink. It's too intense to drink straight, so most people mix it with club soda or orange juice.

Known as sweetwood to locals, cascarilla is native to the Caribbean and is used widely in local herbal remedies for cold, flu, and digestive issues by steeping the leaves in hot water. It is also known to treat diarrhea and vomiting. The bark can used as an inhalant to clear sinuses and in bathwater.

The cascarilla is a small fragrant tree with silver-bronze leaves and pale-yellow bark that thrives on Samana Cay, and also on Acklins and Crooked Island, due to the lack of rain and constant sunshine, which gives it a higher oil content than in damp locations. The bark isn't commercially farmed, so laborers trek through the bush in search of Cascarilla trees and then cut and soak the quills in the sea. The bark is then beaten to soften it, and dried, packaged, and sold for export to Europe. The harvesters earn meager wages, and the bark only gets about $5 per pound, but once the bark is processed and the oil is extracted, it can go for $120 per teaspoon. The concentrated oil can also be used in perfumes, cosmetics, and candles. The oil is not currently processed in The Bahamas, but harvesters are interested in streamlining this system to be able to capitalize on this market in the future.

Nassau (Mon., Wed., and Fri. 9:15am) on **Bahamasair** (tel. 242/702-4140, www.bahamasair.com). Flights sometimes stop in Mayaguana.

Once you arrive, your hotel will pick you up from the airport. You can walk everywhere in town, but to rent a car, check with your hotel when you book to arrange a rental. Rent an SUV, as outside town are only dirt roads. Be cautious driving around, as it is easy to get lost.

ACKLINS AND CROOKED ISLAND

Acklins and Crooked Island, named together, along with Long Cay, are filled with plantation ruins and gorgeous untouched beaches. Avid Bahamian fly-fishing enthusiasts will likely say Acklins has the best fishing in the country. Acklins and Crooked Island are in a U shape, providing extensive shallow flats that attract shallow-water fish. The islands were settled by Loyalists in the late 1780s, and the ruins of plantations and Spanish cannons can be found on Long Cay and throughout the islands. These islands were thought to have the largest populations of indigenous Lucayan people, with numerous historical sites. Today the combined population of both islands is about 800. Acklins is home to a growing population of West Indian pink flamingos, which has become a tourism draw in recent years.

Lighthouses

Bird Rock Lighthouse is on a small cay just off the northwest point of Crooked Island, standing 112 feet and seen from Crooked Island at the nearby settlement of Pittstown Point. Construction started in 1866, and it went into operation in 1876. It was used as a marker for the northern entrance of the Crooked Island Passage, a regular shipping route between Europe and the Caribbean. There is no lighthouse keeper, and it is infrequently visited.

Castle Island Lighthouse is on Castle

Island, 2.5 miles off the southern tip of Acklins and about five miles from the nearest settlement at Salina Point. It was built in 1867 and was said to be a station point for pirates as they attacked ships transiting the nearby passage.

Both lighthouses are only accessible by boat. A visit can be arranged with a local fishing guide or charter company.

FOOD AND ACCOMMODATIONS

There are several inns and lodges on the two islands, mostly catering to fishing. You'll likely eat all your meals at your lodge. **Chester's Highway Inn Bonefish Lodge** (Chester's Bay, Acklins, tel. 242/357-4179, www.chestersbonefishlodge.com, $150, with meals $250) offers comfortable accommodations on the edge of prime bonefishing waters. À la carte and meal-inclusive options are available. Chester's is a perfect escape for fishing, with options for nonfishing partners and family members to explore the islands. Chester's is a member of the Bahamas Out Islands Promotions Board, so ask about free airfare when booking.

Getting There and Around

Bahamasair (tel. 242/702-4140, www.bahamasair.com) services Acklins and Crooked Island twice weekly from Nassau, once on Wednesday morning and once on Saturday at midday. The flight stops at both islands, at Colonel Hill on Crooked Island (CRI) and Spring Point on Acklins (AXP). Charter flights are available from Nassau and Miami or Fort Lauderdale.

Once on the island, your lodging will pick you up from the airport. To rent a car, arrange it in advance with your hotel.

To get between Acklins and Crooked Island, a free pedestrian **ferry service** (Acklins tel. 242/344-3250, Crooked Island tel. 242/344-2197, Mon.-Sat. 8:30am and 4:30pm) runs between Lovely Bay, Acklins, and Cove Point, and Crooked Island.

Background

The Landscape

GEOGRAPHY

In 1864 the Governor of The Bahamas reported that there were 29 islands, 662 cays and 2,387 rocks that made up the colony. Today the general consensus is that The Bahamas consist 700 islands and cays, of which only about 30 are inhabited. The term *Bahamas* is thought to be derived either from the Taino *ba ha ma*, meaning "big upper middle land," or from the Spanish *baja mar*, meaning "shallow sea." "The" is formally part of the name, so it is capitalized; unlike "the United States," it is properly written "The Bahamas."

Although some would argue that The Bahamas is in the Caribbean, it technically isn't. Surrounded by the Gulf Stream and the Bahama Bank on one side and the Atlantic Ocean to the other, the islands are far from the Caribbean Sea. The Lesser Antilles and the Greater Antilles are created by volcanic activity and form the boundary of the Caribbean Sea, but The Bahamas are a shelf of fossil coral and limestone, with no seismic activity. The Bahamas Archipelago, also known as the Lucayan Archipelago, includes Turks and Caicos, and when combined with the Antilles, makes up the West Indies.

The Bahamas Archipelago is as close as 50 miles from Florida and stretches more than 500 miles from Grand Bahama in the north to Great Inagua in the south. Andros is the largest island, and many of the islands are long and skinny, or so small that they are walkable. The islands are dispersed among what is known as the Bahama Bank, which are limestone platforms that have created since the Cretaceous period. The waters among the bank are shallow, averaging 80 feet deep, but drop dramatically to up to 6,000 feet into the Tongue of the Ocean and the Atlantic Ocean. The islands are low-lying, usually no more than an average of 50-65 feet in height, and are mostly home to scrubby native bush. Most of the islands are rocky and flat, with sharp limestone, known as iron shore, some with interior freshwater and saltwater lakes and mangrove marshes. The highest point in the Bahamas is on Cat Island at 206 feet. Native pine forests are found on larger islands in the north, including Grand Bahama, Great Abaco, New Providence, and Andros. There are no rivers or estuaries, which is part of the reason the surrounding ocean water is so clear.

The islands are made up of solid limestone formations, making it difficult for agriculture and lush rainforest environments to flourish without soil. When the limestone is exposed to the atmosphere, it is subjected to chemical weathering, creating the many blue holes, caves, and sinkholes, known as karst topography.

The Bahamas has the clearest waters in the world, with visibility often over 200 feet. It has been scientifically proven that a specific alga that requires light to live is found deeper in The Bahamas than anywhere else on earth. In many areas the waters are very shallow, and generally the Bahama Banks are no deeper than 80 feet.

CLIMATE

The Bahamas is subtropical in the north and tropical in the south, with the Tropic of Cancer running through Long Island and Great Exuma. There are two seasons: wet season (May-Nov.) and dry season (Dec.-Apr.). Wet season is not to be mistaken with monsoon season. The evaporation from the heat of the day on the larger landmasses

Previous: the Lignum Vitae is the national tree of The Bahamas; hawksbill turtle.

creates passing afternoon showers and thunderstorms. They can be intense, with gusty winds, but then pass, and it becomes sunny again. Summer temperatures range from 77°F to 88°F. In the winter, The Bahamas, especially in the northern islands, is affected by cold fronts from the United States, with steady 20-30-mph winds from the northeast, cool water temperatures, and air temperatures that can drop into the 60s. The coolest months are January and February, frost or freeze has never been reported, although temperatures have been known to drop below 50°F.

Hurricane season runs from June to November, with the major hurricanes August through October. Because hurricanes are possible at any time during these months, many hotels in the Out Islands close completely, focusing on repairs and maintenance or giving staff time off. The threat of a hurricane can intensify island life for up to a week in advance, as locals nervously watch the forecasts and tracking reports. Everyone commits their full focus to hurricane preparations, stocking up on water, food, gas, and diesel. Winds up to 140 mph and heavy rainfall can devastate communities. Power outages for extended periods weeks, or even a month—can hinder restoration of normal business.

ENVIRONMENTAL ISSUES

The sea is 95 percent of the geographical area of The Bahamas, and the country is at high risk of being affected by climate change. With the majority of the landmass only a few feet above sea level, sea level rises is a very real concern. The intensity of hurricanes seems to have increased. Hurricane Joaquin devastated parts of the Southern Bahamas, including Long Island, in 2015; Matthew caused widespread damage in New Providence and in Grand Bahama, which saw a direct eyewall hit in 2016; and the effects of Hurricane Irma in 2017 were seen throughout The Bahamas, including devastating Ragged Island and other parts of the Southern Bahamas.

Increasing world populations and demand for specific seafood has led to a decrease in populations of large pelagic fish species, including tuna, swordfish, and marlin, and human activity has resulted in sea habitat destruction, pollution, overfishing, and the introduction of invasive species.

Fishing and Conching: "Conchservation"

The queen conch is an integral part of Bahamian food culture, but overharvesting is leading to degradation of the resource. The conch is a mollusk related to the land snail. As it grows, the shell grows with it, and they move slowly across the ocean floor with a talon-like foot. It takes six years for a conch to grow from an egg to a sexually mature adult. They balance and maintain a healthy marine ecosystem by removing alga buildup on sea grasses and serve as a food source for other sealife, such as nurse sharks, eagle rays, and loggerhead turtles. They are vulnerable to overfishing because they are slow-growing and are easily harvested in the shallow waters of the Bahamas banks. To harvest conch, they should have a flared, well-formed lip that is about a half inch thick. That formation means they have likely had a chance to reproduce. Juvenile conch should not be harvested. Studies comparing conch populations from 20 years ago show up to a 90 percent decline in the population. Conchs are currently being harvested prematurely, preventing reproduction, and exporting them puts additional pressure on the population. The Bahamas National Trust has implemented the Conchservation Campaign, aimed at preserving queen conch populations through building awareness, data collection, and stock assessment.

There are around 5,000 Marine Protected Areas worldwide, but they only account for 1 percent of the oceans. The Bahamas has 17 Marine Protected Areas managed by the Department of Marine Resources and the Bahamas National Trust. The first sea park was established in 1892 off the north coast of New Providence, paving the way for protected areas throughout the world. The 176-acre Exuma Cays Land and Sea Park, established in 1958, was the first protected area in the western hemisphere to include both land and sea environments. Within these zones, human activity is restricted, which includes regulated or prohibited fishing or collecting wildlife, dredging, dumping, or disturbing wildlife.

Locally operated Bahamas Reef Environment Education Foundation (BREEF) is a nongovernmental nonprofit organization that works diligently to promote marine conservation within The Bahamas, hosting charity and fund-raising events, educational forums and programs, and data collection and analysis.

Plants and Animals

TREES

Native

Lignum vitae is the national tree of The Bahamas. Latin for "wood of life," it is one of the densest and strongest hardwoods and was commonly exported to Europe. It was used for shaft bearings in ships, croquet mallets, mortar and pestles, and the British police batons. Modern technology has changed the use of the tree, but it is a potentially endangered species. Bahamians steep the bark to make tea, considering it beneficial for vitality and as an aphrodisiac, as well as a remedy for asthma. The tree is very slow-growing and can grow to 40 feet but is typically seen at 7-15 feet tall. They have small teardrop-shaped light-green leaves and tiny purplish clumping flowers.

The **gumelemi,** also called kamalame and gumbo limbo, are found in all sizes, from shrubs to 50 feet tall with thick reddish trunks. The bark continuously peels, with new green bark coming in as a new layer. They lose their leaves once per year for a short period during dry season (Feb.-Mar.). **Poisonwood** looks very similar to other native trees, and young ones can be mistaken for gumelemi. When it is older, the bark has mottled orange and brown features. The oil from the tree causes painful blistering to human skin. **Buttonwood,** being salt- and drought-tolerant, is commonly found both in coastal areas along the shoreline and inland on small islands and cays with limited rainfall. It is a mangrove shrub, and there are several varietals with darker leaves that blend in with other native bush, but the Silver Buttonwood tends to stand out, with silvery soft leaves and thick scaly bark. **Bahamian pineyards** grow on the larger, more soil-rich island landmasses and consist of forests of towering pines. The pineyards are home to rock iguanas, pygmy boas, and a variety of bird species.

Palms grow well in The Bahamas, but many are introduced. Silver, thatch, buccaneer, and sable palms are native to Florida and the Caribbean, and grow well in the limestone soil. Introduced decorative and ornamental palms are popular for landscaping uses, such as coconut palm, Alexander and *Adonidia,* date palm, Bismarck, royal palm, bamboo palm, fishtails, and *Washingtonia,* among others.

Fruit Trees

In addition to the wider-known tropical fruit trees such as mango, papaya, banana, and citrus, there are numerous lesser-known fruit trees that Bahamians enjoy. You might not see the fruit in food stores, but you'll likely find them in season at roadside produce stands.

Soursop produces medium-size spikey green fruit that have a strawberry-apple sour citrus flavor. The fruit is edible, and the leaves are used in bush remedies and teas. It is widely popular throughout The Bahamas as it is believed to assist with curing cancer. **Sapodilla** can grow into a large tree and produce a sticky white sap and brown kiwi-looking fruit. The fruit's inner flesh is light brown to pale pinkish-yellow and has a sweet malty flavor. It's typically pronounced Sapodilly, and also known as just "dilly."

Guinep produces small, green grape-size fruit with a juicy yellowish flesh and a large seed. They can be either sweet or sour. **Sea grape** grows along the seashore, being a very salt-tolerant plant. It can grow into a large tree size and produces grapes with single seeds. In summer, the green bunches of grapes ripen to a purplish color. Their large round leaves are easily identifiable and unique. Bahamians use the fruit for jams and jellies or to make sea grape wine. **Avocados** in The Bahamas are large with shiny green exteriors. They are commonly referred to as "pear," but don't confuse it with the northern pear, which doesn't grow in The Bahamas.

Introduced and Invasive

The Australian pine, or **casuarina,** is an introduced and invasive species lining the shores of the country. It was introduced to Florida in the late 1800s for shade and wind blockage. In the 1930s it was believed that if it was planted in swampy areas, it would assist in drying the swamp, which it didn't. It was introduced to The Bahamas around the time it was first planted in Florida, and the population has grown wildly. It is not really a pine but a dicotyledonous flowering plant. It grows well in sandy soil, is salt tolerant, and grows and reproduces quickly. When the needles fall, they create dense ground cover, making it difficult for native plants to grow. It is also thought that the roots produce a natural herbicide, known as allelopathic toxins, which further inhibit plant diversity. They can be hedge-like or grow upward of 65 feet. The bark is woody and rough, the needles long and slender. The tiny balled cones are prickly and sharp for bare feet. They are found on almost every island in The Bahamas.

FLOWERS

Vibrantly colored **bougainvillea** spills over fences and walls in all areas of the country. This vine comes in a variety of colors: salmon pink, soft yellow, neon fuchsia, purple, and white. The national flower is the **yellow elder,** a shrub to small tree with bright yellow flowers. Long pods dangle from the branches, and the tree reproduces easily, creating a forest of yellow elders around it.

Orchids grow throughout the native forests and pinelands in the shade of native trees. A variety of species abound, and they are prized for their beautiful flowers. Orchids in the wild are protected and should not be harvested, but you will likely find orchids for sale at local plant sales and nurseries. Andros is home to more than 50 species of wild orchids, many of which are endemic, including three native species of the climbing vanilla orchid.

LAND MAMMALS

Due to the large number of cave formations in The Bahamas, **bats** are fairly common. They are nocturnal and sleep during the day, so when visiting caves, you can often see them clinging to the ceiling, resting peacefully. Fifteen species of bats have been recorded in The Bahamas. The **Bahamian hutia** is a brown rabbit-size mammal in the rodent family and the only land mammal native to The Bahamas. Three islands (Little Wax Cay, Warderick Wells, and East Plana Cay) are home to the only population of this particular species in the world. They were thought to be extinct until they were rediscovered in East Plana Cay. They are protected and listed as vulnerable.

The **Bahamian raccoon** is a subspecies of the common raccoon and can be found in New Providence and other islands with pinelands. It is presumed the raccoon was introduced, and not native, due to its genetic similarity to the common raccoon, but these raccoons are quite small. **Wild pigs** and **boars** are found on islands with limited human populations such as Andros, Great Abaco, Long Island, and Current Island, just off North Eleuthera. They are elusive and are rarely seen unless you have a guide or tracker.

MARINELIFE

Because of the ratio of ocean to landmass in The Bahamas, marinelife is an important part of the ecosystem. Large pelagic fish found in The Bahamas such as **Atlantic bluefin tuna, yellowfin tuna, blackfin tuna, mahimahi** (also called "dolphin" or dolphinfish) and **wahoo** attract avid sportfishing enthusiasts. Billfish include **marlin, sailfish,** and **swordfish** and are fished for, but by law they must be released unharmed. **Nassau grouper** is an important commercial fish, but populations have been declining due to overfishing and reef destruction. They are beautifully striped in brown and white with thick lips. They are considered endangered, and fishing for them is prohibited in the United States.

Dive at a reef and you'll see a variety of colorful reef fish, including bright-blue bluntnosed **parrot fish,** glowing neon **angelfish,** and yellow and black striped **sergeants major.** A variety of **groupers** and **snappers** call the protected reefs home, and you'll often see **octopuses, barracuda, seahorses,** and **eels.**

The **lionfish** is native to the Indo-Pacific and the Red Sea and was recently introduced as an invasive species in The Bahamas. The theory is that they were released from aquarium collections on the East Coast of the United States. The lionfish reproduces quickly and has few natural predators. They are beautiful, with long, spiny venomous quills. Reef dwellers, they eat any species of fish they can fit in their mouths, which includes juvenile Nassau grouper and lobster. Lionfish meat is delicious, and they can be found on menus, which is eradicating their population.

The **West Indian sea star,** also called starfish, can be found in shallow waters and banks. Their bright red or orange coloring pops on the white sandy bottom. The largest sea stars can grow up to 20 inches long. They typically have five arms but can have four, six, or seven. **Caribbean spiny lobsters** live in the reefs and mangroves of The Bahamas. These lobsters are unlike the Maine lobster because they do not have claws. They are also referred to as "crawfish" in The Bahamas.

It was common to kill and eat sea turtles in The Bahamas until laws were introduced to protect them. Hawksbills were protected in 1986, and the complete ban on exploitation of all turtle species was introduced in 2009. The **Loggerhead Turtle** has a large head and a muscular jaw. They are reddish-brown in color and have a thick shell. They are slow to develop, reaching sexual maturity at age 20-30 and can reach up to 400 pounds. **Green Turtles** have a layer of "green" fat under the shell that was used to make turtle soup. The shell color ranges from light to dark brown. They are herbivores subsisting on seagrass and seaweed. **Hawksbills** hang out in coral reefs and feed primarily on sponges. Their shell is brownish in color and has a beautiful pattern. They are critically endangered because historically they have been captured and killed for their shells.

There is a small population of about 15 **West Indian manatees** in the Bahamas that move around and establish territory. They are individually recognizable and have their own names. Local residents pay attention and track their movements. Gina, for example, was first spotted in Andros, and then relocated to Spanish Wells, where she has had four calves. Her son resides in Hope Town, Abaco, and her daughter is in Great Harbour Cay. Her older calf was killed in a boat-motor strike. Gina can be seen in Spanish Wells and on the harbor in Harbour Island. There are two known mature male manatees spotted in Long Island, Cat Island, New Providence, Eleuthera, and the Berry Islands.

Coral

The builders of reefs are billions of tiny animals called polyps. Upward of 100 species of polyps are involved in creating dynamic pinnacles, spires, pillars, and boulder shapes. New coral is built on top of old coral, but coral takes an extremely long time to grow, with staghorn and elkhorn growing about three inches per year. Dredging, filling, and pollution affect the delicate reef system, but so do visitors due to boats and anchors, specimen collecting, or standing on the reef. Coral reefs are extremely important for providing shelter for juvenile fish to grow and develop. They also protect the Bahamas shoreline from storm surges, acting as a breakwater, and, of course, for tourism, attracting thousands of divers and snorkelers each year.

Sharks and Rays

If you go on a diving expedition, you'll likely see some sharks. The most common is the **Caribbean reef shark,** which ranges 6-8 feet long and is dark gray or brownish in color. They are normally shy and steer clear of divers. The second most common species is the **blacktip reef shark,** easily recognizable with the black tip on their fins. The **tiger shark** can grow up to 16 feet and has dark spots and stripes. **Bull sharks** are typically slightly smaller at around 12 feet but can top out at 500 pounds. They have a flat snout and unpredictable behavior. Bull sharks and tiger sharks are the boldest of the shark species and are the species that account for incidents with swimmers and surfers. **Nurse sharks** are commonly found around fish-cleaning stations in shallow waters and are docile creatures. They have flat heads and rounded snouts and are the best bet if you'd like to try to touch a shark. One of the most impressive sharks is the giant spotted **whale shark.** They are gentle giants, on average 30 feet in length as adults and weighing 20,000 pounds. Their lifespan is upward of 70 years.

Manta rays are fairly commonly sighted. Although they are usually small to medium size in shallow waters, they can grow up to 23 feet across. They have a slow reproductive rate and have become vulnerable through harvesting and getting caught in fishing nets. They have a long tail, but do not have a stinging barb. Another common ray you'll see cruising along the shoreline is the beautiful spotted **eagle ray,** dark brown in color, with bright white spots. They have a venomous barb at the end of their long tail. There are several other species of stingrays as well, with barbed stinging tails. Stingrays like to burrow under the sand in shallow waters, so swimmers should always tread lightly so as not to accidently step on one.

Dolphins and Whales

Dolphins are commonly spotted from boats. You'll likely see the **bottlenose dolphin,** of which there are two species in The Bahamas: the smaller coastal version, found in the shallow waters of the Bahamas Bank, and the oceanic version, found in deeper waters. The **Atlantic spotted dolphin** accumulates spots as they age and are commonly seen in groups of 20 or 30. Certain species of whales can be seen in the northern waters around the Abacos, including **pilot whales, orcas,** and **sperm whales.** There are no tour operations specializing in whale-watching due to the rare and sporadic sightings.

Mollusks

The **conch** is an integral part of Bahamian culture, with festivals throughout the island celebrating it. Certain species can produce pearls, and conchs come in a variety of shades, including white, brown, and orange, but pink is the most desirable. A horn-type instrument can be made by cutting off the spiral end of the conch and blowing into it. It is traditional in many parts of the Caribbean, including The Bahamas, to blow a conch horn at sunset to signify the end of the day. There are a variety of species, but the most commonly known and harvested is the **queen conch,** with its pale pinkish-white shell and vibrant polished pink interior. Another stunning shell is that of the **king helmet conch,** with its thick lip and polished finish and mottled brown-and-white coloring. Another member of the mollusk family less commonly utilized in culinary aspects is the **whelk.** They are found along rocky shorelines and in tidal zones. They have a strong flavor that appeals to some Bahamians, but are typically an acquired taste.

BIRDS

There are over 120 species of birds known to live in or migrate to The Bahamas. Some species are rare or have struggling populations and are protected by law and in sanctuary parks. Birds flock to the pinelands, mangrove swamps, and marshy areas of the larger islands of The Bahamas. Along the coastal mangrove regions you'll find **herons, egrets, ibis, ducks, roseate spoonbills,** and **red winged blackbirds,** along with a cacophony of other fluttering singing birds. The rocky coastlines and remote cays are safe breeding zones for **gulls, plovers, terns,** and the seasonal white **tropicbirds** with their recognizable long tail feathers. The shoreline finds **plovers** and **sandpipers** scurrying in the sand and rare sightings of **pelicans.**

Light-colored **mourning doves** are common, and specialty birds found in select locations draw birding enthusiasts in search of sightings. The **great lizard cuckoo** is the largest species of cuckoo, and lives on a diet of lizards, snakes, frogs, and insects. The **Bahama woodstar** is a small hummingbird only 3.5-4 inches in length, and the endangered **Abaco parrot** is a subspecies of the Cuban Amazon parrot. Its scientific name, *Amazona leucocephala bahamensis,* literally means "white headed Amazon parrot from The Bahamas." A common bird in the native bush is the sweet and cheerful yellow and black **bananaquit.** Predatory birds scour the coastline looking for fish. You'll see the **American kestrel,** the smallest in the falcon family, as well as the medium to large **osprey,** in the raptor family, and several species of **hawks.**

The Bahamas is home to the largest population of breeding **West Indian pink flamingos** in the world. They can reach up to five feet tall and prefer to live in remote and lonely places with limited human influence. Breeding grounds are found on the islands of Great Inagua, West Andros, and Acklins and Crooked Island. The flamingos were hunted to near extinction, but populations have been increasing over the last 50 years due to efforts by the Bahamas National Trust in creating laws and setting aside protected land. Their populations are now growing to healthy numbers throughout The Bahamas, Cuba, and the Turks and Caicos.

REPTILES AND AMPHIBIANS

There are three species and seven subspecies of the **Bahamian rock iguana,** differentiated by characteristics individually adapted on each island region. The names of the iguanas take on their location, such as the Exuma Cay iguana, Allen's Cay iguana, Andros iguana, and so on. They are generally brown in color, with lighter underbellies, and are 2.5-3 feet long. They are typically found in dry areas with sandy patches for laying eggs, and also limestone formations to find shade and regulate body heat. They are skittish, but some islands have regular visitors, so they come out if they think there is food available. All Rock Iguanas in The Bahamas are protected.

If you don't see one of the species of iguanas, there is a high probability you'll see one of the common species of lizards. The **brown anole** is very common and shy around humans. They are light brown with dark markings, tend to have a bright-yellow to orange expandable neck (dewlap), and can range 3-8 inches long. The **tropical house gecko** can be found indoors and max out at 5 inches in length. They are almost translucent-looking with large eyes. It is considered good luck to have one in your house, and they eat flies, cockroaches, and other insects, but their large brown feces pellets can be a nuisance. **Curly tails** are the most unique-looking of the Bahamian lizards, with their thick bodies, blunt head, and defining curled tails. They are commonly found around beaches in sandy environments and can get quite big. They are great for photo ops because they are curious and will let you get close to them. **Blue-tailed lizards** sightings are fairly rare, but they are noticeable because of their bright-blue tails.

There are five main snake species in the Bahamas. The largest are the **Bahamian**

boas, which can grow up to 8 feet long. Although they look intimidating, they are completely harmless. **Pygmy boas** are smaller and reach about 1 foot in length. The **brown racer,** plain brown and up to 3 feet in length, are common. **Blind snakes** and **thread snakes** are very small and thin and less than a foot long. Spring and summer are active times for snakes, as temperatures are warmer and food is available. There are no poisonous snakes in The Bahamas, but unfortunately many snakes are unnecessarily killed due to superstition or misinformation. Bahamian snakes are historically docile due to the fact they had few natural predators.

There are several species of both native and introduced frogs in The Bahamas, including the native **greenhouse frog** as well as the native **Cuban tree frog,** the largest frog in the North America, with rough warty skin. They secrete toxic mucus from their skin that can irritate the eyes. They are nocturnal, so it's not likely you'll see one. Several years ago there was an outbreak of the invasive **cane toad** in parts of Western New Providence. These toads are stalky, ranging 4-10 inches. Their skin is brownish-green with dark markings. They have poison glands behind their ears that secrete a white toxin in times of stress, but there are poison glands all over the back of the toad's body. They are known to cause human deaths, but the biggest problem is with domestic pets. Their population seems to be under control, but if you think you have seen one, not mistaking it for a native species, do your best to capture it with a bucket or a crate, or take a photo of it and contact the Bahamas National Trust.

LAND CRABS

Bahamian **land crabs** are known elsewhere as blue land crabs due to their ever so slightly blueish tint, but they can also range from brown to pale gray. They aren't large, topping out at 6 inches, but they have thick shells. Their eyes boggle out from their heads, and they typically eat leaves and insects close to the ground. They are most prevalent during the summer months when the rains come. They are nocturnal, so on islands with limited road traffic, you might seem them scurry across in your headlights at night. They are slow-growing and require 60 molts to reach full size, which is about three times that of other crabs.

INSECTS AND ARACHNIDS

The tropical climate of The Bahamas is a conducive environment for insects. It never gets cold enough to subdue insect populations, so there is year-round potential for insects. **Wasps** are common, but just steer clear of them. If you stay calm, they tend to ignore you and go about their business. Bees are less commonly seen. There is a rather large species of **Bahamian bee** that is black in color. **Centipedes** are found in gardens where rich soil is prevalent, and they can grow up to 12 inches. They are aggressive and have a very painful bite that is generally not life threatening, but reactions can vary in people more sensitive to bites.

The **Caribbean brown recluse** can be found in homes in dark places. They are shy and bites are rare, but it will bite if you get into their space. Their venom is more toxic than a rattlesnake bite, so if you think you have been bitten, seek medical help immediately. The Bahamas also has a very large and rather beautiful spider known as the **banana spider,** also called the golden silk orb weaver. This one is not to be confused with another species of extremely poisonous banana spider found in Central and South America. The banana spider of The Bahamas is only mildly venomous, causing redness and pain in the bite area. Their bodies can be up to 2 inches, not including their legs, and their web is a golden color. You'll find them in the native bush strung between trees in cool dark places. Hairy, thick **tarantulas**, also known as a ground spider, are residents of The Bahamas, but sightings are rare. They have a slight venomous bite, but have never caused a fatality in humans.

The giant bat moth or giant witch is known

in The Bahamas as a **money bat,** large and dark colored with a wingspan up to 7 inches. In some cultures throughout Latin America, it is known as the "death butterfly" and considered a symbol of death or misfortune, but in The Bahamas they are revered and considered harbingers of money or good fortune if you have one come near you or enter your house.

Cockroaches and **mosquitoes** are an unfortunate part of life in The Bahamas. We all know what cockroaches are. Put your food away, don't leave standing water around, and set your cockroach traps. There are a variety of mosquito species, and they tend to lay eggs in standing water, so they are most prevalent during the rainy summer months.

History

EARLY HISTORY

The Lucayan people were the original inhabitants of The Bahamas, prior to the arrival of the Europeans. They were a branch of the Taino people, who inhabited many parts of the Caribbean, and it was estimated there were 30,000 to 40,000 people in the islands at the time of Columbus's arrival.

The Taino crossed to the Bahamas Archipelago, first arriving in present-day Turks and Caicos, in dugout canoes from Cuba and Hispaniola between 500 and 800. They populated the southern Bahamas, including Long Island, San Salvador, Great Inagua, Acklins and Crooked Island, Rum Cay, and Cat Island. Over time they expanded to Eleuthera, New Providence, Andros, and eventually the Abacos and Grand Bahama, but their populations were limited in the northern regions when the Europeans arrived. They lived in round tentlike homes made of poles and thatch. They grew root crops, hunted, and utilized the bounty of the ocean, and were described by the Spanish as peaceful, gentle, and generous people. There are artifacts and sites throughout The Bahamas that give archaeologists an idea of what life was like for the Lucayan.

The Lucayans were the first people that Christopher Columbus met upon his arrival in the New World. He landed on an island the Taino called Guanahani and renamed it San Salvador. It is unclear which island, exactly, that was, based on historical accounts, but it was somewhere in the southern Bahamas.

The Spanish began taking Lucayan people as slaves, and they were eventually removed completely from The Bahamas by 1520. The term *Lucayan* is from the Spanish word *lucayos* and was the Spanish interpretation of the term *lukka cairi,* which is what the Taino called themselves. The Taino word *cairi,* meaning "island," was adapted into Spanish as *cayo,* eventually becoming *cay* in English.

Although there is reference to the Arawak people in The Bahamas, the Arawak were a South American group. The Taino had similar genetics to the Arawak, and they spoke a related Arawakan language, but the indigenous people of the Bahamas were not considered Arawak people.

EXPLORATION AND COLONIALISM

The Spanish arrived in The Bahamas on October 12, 1492, and claimed it for Spain. This has been regarded by Europeans as the discovery of America. The Bahamas didn't have much in the way of natural resources that interested the Spanish—meaning gold—so the islands were utilized solely as a source of slave labor, by capturing the indigenous people and relocating them to Hispaniola. Most died from the harsh conditions and by contracting European diseases. After the final native inhabitants were removed in 1520, the islands were devoid of human population for 130 years, until the first European settlers arrived.

Historical studies show that there were

attempts at colonialization by the French in Abaco in 1565 and again in 1625, but it wasn't until a group from Bermuda called "The Company of Adventurers for the Plantation of the Islands of Eleutheria," otherwise known as the Eleutheran Adventurers, arrived in 1648, with Captain William Sayle, that the islands were officially colonized. Those who left Bermuda were a group of Puritans and republicans who were promised religious and political freedom in this new land. The larger of the two sailing ships wrecked off the northern coast of Eleuthera on what is known as the treacherous Devil's Backbone reef. The passengers took shelter in Preacher's Cave, while the smaller of the two sailboats returned to Bermuda to bring supplies.

New settlers arrived from Bermuda and New England, and the settlements of Governor's Harbour, Harbour Island, and Spanish Wells were established. The new settlers struggled to gain traction due to poor soil and a lack of natural resources, as well as attacks by the Spanish, who raided and burned villages. In 1666 another set of colonists from Bermuda arrived in New Providence, which quickly became the hub of commerce. Between Harbour Island, which held its turn as the capital of the country for a number of years, and New Providence, ship wrecking, farming, and fishing became the staples of the local economy.

The new settlers were of British descent, but The Bahamas bounced back and forth between Spanish and British control. The wrecking of Spanish ships caused many conflicts, and privateers were commissioned to retaliate against efforts by the Spanish. In 1684 the settlements on New Providence and Eleuthera were raided and set on fire by the Spanish. The islands were mostly abandoned until new settlers arrived from Jamaica in 1686. When conflict was settled between the European powers, the privateers who had settled in to protect the colonies turned to piracy, and by the late 1600s Nassau was known as a home base for pirates. Any attempt at governance went by the wayside, and Nassau was known as a wild and lawless place. War broke out among England, France, and Spain, and piracy against ships carrying precious cargo back to Europe increased, earning Nassau the moniker "pirate's republic" at the time. By 1713 it was estimated that at least 1,000 pirates used Nassau as their home port, outnumbering the 200 families who resided there. Many of the settlers retreated to Eleuthera or the Abacos during that time in order to escape the chaos in Nassau.

Britain made The Bahamas a crown colony in 1718 an appointed Woodes Rodgers as governor. This was during the time of peak piracy, and Woodes Rodgers began conceptualizing the intent of putting a stop to the lawlessness. Rodgers came up with a plan and proclaimed a pardon to all pirates who surrendered to the British within one year. Many pirates were interested in retiring, so this seemed to be effective, although there were a few rebels who eventually moved onward. The Spanish were intent on expelling the British from the islands, however, and former pirates were commissioned by the British to become privateers. Continuous conflict remained between the Spanish and the British throughout the 1700s. In 1782 a Spanish fleet appeared off Nassau, and the city surrendered without a fight. The Bahamas was under Spanish rule for one year until British-American Loyalist colonel Andrew Deveaux recaptured The Bahamas for the British crown, establishing The Bahamas as a British colony that would last until Bahamian independence in 1973.

After the American Revolution, the British issued land grants to American Loyalists who wanted to leave the newly independent United States. Many new settlers arrived with their slaves during the late 1700s. The Loyalists developed cotton plantations throughout the islands, and cotton still grows wild in Cat Island, Long Island, and Great Exuma. Enslaved people were brought by the Loyalists to work the land from both America and from Africa. The days of slavery were short lived in The Bahamas, however, after the British abolished the slave trade in 1807. As the Royal

Navy intercepted slave ships, they resettled the liberated people in The Bahamas. In the 1820s, hundreds of enslaved Africans and Seminoles escaped from Florida, where slavery was still prevalent, and settled on Andros. They established the Seminole community of Red Bays, which still exists today.

The plantations were found to have poor soil and insect infestations, and without slave labor to operate them, many Loyalist plantation owners eventually granted their plantation land (and their names) to the newly freed people. For example, wealthy British land owner Denys Rolle owned huge portions of Great Exuma. His son and heir, Lord Rolle, eventually freed the enslaved people working the land and donated the estate to them. The name Rolle died out in England, but Rolle is a common name in The Bahamas, especially in Exuma.

CONTEMPORARY TIMES

In the 19th and early 20th centuries, the Bahamian economy boomed when it became a smuggling base during the embargo of the U.S. Civil War and during U.S. prohibition, when rum-running proved a lucrative business. Communities such as Bimini and West End, Grand Bahama, thrived due to their proximity to Florida. The first airport was built in The Bahamas in Nassau in 1940, and it was used as a base for the Allies during World War II for flight training. The airport became Nassau's International Airport in 1957, which assisted in spurring tourism, and it further benefited when the popular tourist destination of Havana was closed to U.S. visitors in 1961. Freeport was established as a free-trade zone in the 1950s and housed a booming expatriate community of investors, bankers, lawyers, and accountants.

By the late 1970s and early 1980s, The Bahamas was a major stopping point for drug traffickers en route from Columbia to the United States, and bases were set up at airstrips on remote islands. It is estimated that 90 percent of all of the cocaine that entered the United States at that time passed through The Bahamas. There were claims that the government was accepting bribes from the Medellin Cartel in exchange for allowing the smugglers to use The Bahamas as a stopping point. Local communities, churches, and businesses also benefited from the trade, as tourism had slowed at that time. Pressure from the U.S. government led to the Commission of Inquiry in 1983, which heavily investigated the drug trade and the Bahamian involvement, and as smugglers and others involved were eventually imprisoned, the trade tapered off.

Government and Economy

GOVERNMENT

The first political parties were formed in the 1950s. The Progressive Liberal Party (PLP) was formed in 1953 as a social liberal party with the aim of promoting the best interests of the black majority. The United Bahamian Party (UPB) was formed in 1956. They were also known as the Bay Street Boys and represented interests of the white oligarchy. The Bahamas began self-governing as semi-independent from Britain in 1964, with Sir Roland Symonette of the UPB heading as political leader until 1967.

The British House of Lords voted to give The Bahamas full independence as member of the Commonwealth of Nations on July 10, 1973. Sir Lynden Pindling of the PLP became the first black prime minister of the newly independent Bahamas. He maintained his position until 1992, when it was taken over by Hubert Ingraham of the Free National Movement.

The FNM was established in 1971 as a breakaway group of eight MPs from the PLP, initially calling themselves the Free-PLP. The UPB members decided to join forces with the Free-PLP and created a conservative party, which they called the Free National Movement. Hubert Ingham headed the country as prime minister for two terms starting in 1992, until he stepped down for a newly appointed head of the party, Tommy Turnquest. Turnquest was seen as not as strong as Ingham, and Perry Christie of the PLP stepped in in 2002. Christie served two terms and was running for a third, but current prime minister, Dr. Hubert Minnis, won by a landslide in May 2017 with 35 of the 39 seats.

The government of The Bahamas (www.bahamas.gov.bs) is a parliamentary constitutional monarchy, based on the Westminster model, with the executive branch, the legislative branch and the judicial branch. As a member of the Commonwealth of Nations, The Bahamas recognizes Her Majesty Queen Elizabeth II as the head of state. The governor general is a representative of the queen. The Bahamas has a two-party system, with the PLP and the FNM, with several parties that have tried to establish themselves but have been unsuccessful in winning seats in parliament.

ECONOMY

In terms of GDP, The Bahamas is one of the richest countries in the Americas, housing the most offshore entities and companies. Tourism is the most heavily influenced generator of income, accounting for 60 percent of GDP and employing over half the country's workforce. The Bahamas sees approximately 1.5 million visitors and 3.5 million cruise-ship passengers per year. With recent developments with Atlantis Phase III and Baha Mar in New Providence, and growth and development in the Out Islands, as well as foreign real estate investors, The Bahamas is slotted for continued growth. The Ministry of Tourism, along with the Grand Bahama Island Tourism Board and Out Islands Promotions Board, work diligently to promote the diversity of the different islands of The Bahamas.

Banking and international financial services are the second-largest sector of the economy as The Bahamas is still considered a tax haven. This sector accounts for 15 percent of GDP. There are benefits for real estate investors looking to gain residency in The Bahamas. There is no income tax, capital gains tax, or corporate tax, so The Bahamas has become a desirable place for the wealthy elite to establish residence.

Agriculture is the third-largest economic sector, but only accounts for about 5-7 percent. About 80 percent of the nation's food is imported. The Bahamas historically produced its own fruits and vegetables, but with the introduction of the Smoot Hawley Tariff Act in 1930, the United States implemented tariffs on non-U.S. territories, which affected exports from The Bahamas. At the time The Bahamas was exporting pineapples, tomatoes, and citrus. U.S. entities upped production of pineapples in places like Hawaii instead of importing them under the new tariffs. A small dairy and agriculture farming industry remained in Eleuthera from the 1940s through the 1960s, and it was enough to supply The Bahamas without the need for imports, but with independence, the foreign-owned operations struggled with the bureaucracy of the new government, and the farms eventually shut down.

Today there are small privately owned farms throughout the islands. The government established the Agriculture and Marine Sciences Institute on Andros to study agriculture and economics. Andros has Chickcharney Farms, which provides vegetables to Nassau as well as pop-up farmers markets. In Eleuthera, Eleuthera Island Farm and Eleuthera Island Organics (EIO) provide produce to local stores and restaurants. In Nassau, Goodfellow Farms is an aquaponics operation growing lettuce and herbs utilizing feces from tilapia fish, which are also harvested. Lucayan Farms, also in Nassau, provides a variety of lettuce to local food stores.

People and Culture

DEMOGRAPHY AND DIVERSITY

About 90 percent of the population of The Bahamas is of African descent, 4.7 percent are white, and the remainder are Hispanic, Asian, or of other origins. The islands were populated by English Loyalists and the enslaved people they brought with them. The population was more heavily European until the abolition of the slave trade, when people who were freed or escaped from slavery found refuge, and the population of African descendants increased exponentially. Haitians have made their way to The Bahamas, trying to get to the United States, oftentimes stopping in the islands, and if they can find work, they stay.

Foreigners aside, Bahamians categorize themselves as white Bahamian and black Bahamian. Today, the majority of the population is of African descent, and the white Bahamian population—those with a hereditary line dating back to the Loyalist settlers—is limited. These days a growing percentage of Bahamians who were children of Bahamians but lived abroad and married foreigners, maintain two passports. You'll often meet English-Bahamian and Australian-Bahamian residents. There are a few communities throughout the islands that have maintained a strong population of Loyalist-descent residents, such as Spanish Wells, Man-O-War Cay, and Long Island.

There is also a stable expatriate community, especially in Nassau, with British, American, Canadian, South African, and Australian residents, and many work in the financial sector.

RELIGION

The Bahamas is very much influenced by the Christian Council, the major sect being Protestant in groups of Baptists, Anglicans and Pentecostals. The Roman Catholic Church is smaller, with no other sizeable religions outside Christianity. Church is a big deal on Sunday and on religious holidays. Many Bahamians go out to brunch or lunch on Sunday after church, or do their food shopping, so you'll see people out and about in their Sunday best. Easter is taken very seriously. No alcohol is served on Good Friday, and except in Nassau, most stores and shops shut down over the entire weekend, from Good Friday to Easter Monday, except for a few hours on Saturday. Christmas is also an extended period when you can't expect much to get done.

LANGUAGE

The official language of The Bahamas is English. Creole is spoken among Haitian immigrants. Bahamians have an accent that can be difficult to understand along with a variety of slang terms that are used in everyday speech, but they are happy to "translate" for you and tell you the background or story of unfamiliar words. Some of these are quite comical. In proper business environments and among the educated, the language is typically formal, but in poorer areas and in small settlements of the Out Islands, the unending chatter is often indecipherable. You'll also notice regional differences in accents, such as the white Bahamian communities of Spanish Wells or Man-O-War Cay having a completely different accent from, say, black Bahamian communities in Andros.

THE ARTS

Throughout the islands you'll find craft markets selling straw wares that are made from several types of palms that are native to The Bahamas. Weavers make baskets, hats, and handbags, and often the quality and handicraft is second to none. It is an integral part of Bahamian heritage that is still alive and flourishing today. You can find locals selling their wares at stalls in even the smallest settlements throughout The Bahamas.

At the National Art Gallery of The Bahamas, you can see contemporary works by talented Bahamian artists. For the annual Junkanoo festival, intricate costumes are meticulously made using papier-mâché, taking months to create.

The music of The Bahamas is influenced by African and Caribbean roots but is distinctly Bahamian. Many of the songs utilize the European accordion and large goombay drums. Bahamian sacred music, heard in churches, is expressive art in the form of praise. Religious hymns were brought from the United States to The Bahamas by enslaved Creoles and are an integral part of church service today.

Nonreligious Bahamian music has historically been called **goombay,** derived from the Gambian word *gumbay* or large drum, and is integrated with **rake-and-scrape** music, which utilizes a carpenter's saw, a goat-skin drum, and an accordion. **Junkanoo** music accompanies the Junkanoo festival, which is most similar to marching-band music, with goat-skin drums, cow bells, and horns. It is fast-paced, energetic, and lively. **Calypso** music is an Afro-Caribbean style from Trinidad and Tobago that has spread to many parts of the Caribbean, including The Bahamas. Calypso has evolved to another genre called **soca,** which is hip-shaking dance music.

Ronnie Butler is probably the most famous calypso and rake-and-scrape Bahamian artist. A true entertainer, he is considered the "Godfather of Bahamian Music." His career lasted over 50 years and included hits such as "Burma Road" and "Age Ain't Nothing but a Number." Most recently his single "Married Man" was featured in Tyler Perry's Bahamas-filmed movie "Why Did I Get Married Too?" Butler died in November 2017 at age 80, leaving a legacy of songs and memories of his live shows, which he played until his death. Other musicians who focus on traditional Bahamian music are **Phil Stubbs** as well as producer, musician, and songwriter **Fred Ferguson.**

Popular Bahamian songs by various artists include "Stagger Lee," "Shotgun Wedding," "Coo Coo Soup," "Bush Mechanic," and the popular "Just 'Cause She's Fat," which tends to shock visitors whenever it's played in bars, restaurants, and public places.

Contemporary dance and soca fusion is popular with the younger crowd, such as "Boom Pine Apple Wine" by Roachy and music by soca dance music artist **Dyson Knight.** In the 1980s, **The Baha Men** formed as a band called High Voltage, playing disco and funk and self-releasing several albums. In 1991, one of their albums was noticed by Atlantic Records, and they were convinced to change their name to The Baha Men and released their first mainstream album in the genre of modernized Junkanoo music. In 2000, they came out with the Grammy Award-winning single, "Who Let the Dogs Out," for which they are known internationally.

In older music, the funk group from Nassau **The Beginning of the End,** which comprised three brothers, came out with the album *Funky Nassau* in 1971, and the track **"Funky Nassau"** became a hit single in the United States and Britain. Another local hit of the 1970s was the song **"Got a Letter from Miami"** by **Priscilla Rollins,** who is known as the Bahamian Queen of Soul. Popularized by The Beach Boys, the song **"Sloop John B"** is a folk song of The Bahamas about the adventures of sailors in Nassau. It is performed in the a cappella four-part barbershop harmony by the Dicey Doh Singers in The Bahamas. The words were changed by Brian Wilson, but the original lyrics went, "We sail on the sloop *John B.*, my grandpappy and me, round Nassau town we did roam."

Unfortunately, much of Bahamian music is not available online. You'll hear these songs on local radio by listening to Island Classics with Commodore Malcolm McKay on Island FM 102.9, 10am-noon daily.

Chris Blackwell formed **Island Records**

Bahamian Phrases and Sayings

Quite a few sayings and phrases are unique to The Bahamas. You may hear locals chattering and have no idea what they are saying, because these phrases are intertwined with normal conversation. Many phrases are vulgar and describe people and the body, or involve sexual innuendo. You'll likely not understand it unless someone explains it to you. Most Bahamian songs also have explicit meanings, but you wouldn't hear it with the peppy beat. Examples are the lyrics "roach on my bread" and "who put the pepper in the Vaseline"—seemingly innocent sounding songs until you find out what they really mean.

Here are a few common sayings and phrases so you can start to decipher Bahamian talk:

- **bey/bei:** any person, male or female.
- **tingum:** a thing. One of the most useful Bahamian sayings, and a way to express something when you don't know what else to say, as in, *"Put da tingum in da tingum,"* with expressive hand gestures. Usually the point is made somehow. A saying goes, *"Tingum in da bush ain't got no name."*
- **muddasick:** amazement, excitement, exasperation, or other extreme emotion. Usually in the form of *"Well, muddasick."*
- **tief:** to steal, or a thief. "He tiefed that money from her." A saying goes, *"When tief tief from tief, God smile."*
- **God spare life:** I hope I make it until then. You'll hear this often in the context, *"I'll see you next week, God spare life."*
- **I comin' na:** It's supposed to mean "I'm coming now," but it really means "I'll be there in at least a half hour."
- **comin' soon:** I'll be there in 2-4 hours.
- **I comin' later:** I'm probably not coming at all.
- **boongie:** your butt. *"Climbing all those stairs made my boongie ache."*
- **junglas:** a woman with a lack of class, exposing herself in scanty clothing, outrageous hair and nails, with loud and obnoxious behavior.

in 1958 and became one of the most successful independent labels of the 1960s, 1970s, and 1980s. He got Bob Marley and Toots and the Maytals on a roll in Jamaica, establishing a world hit genre of reggae and taking it international, and then in 1977, Blackwell built Compass Point Studios in Nassau, where AC/DC recorded the second-highest-selling album ever, *Back in Black*. Other artists who recorded at Compass Point Studios were The Rolling Stones, the Tragically Hip, Talking Heads, Dire Straits, Lenny Kravitz, James Brown, Eric Clapton, and David Bowie, among many others.

Essentials

Transportation

GETTING THERE

Air

Most visitors arriving to The Bahamas enter through Lynden Pindling International Airport (NAS) in Nassau. Originally known as Windsor Field, after the Duke of Windsor, it became a Royal Air Force station in 1942. After World War II it was turned over for civilian use, and in 1957 it was brought into full operation. The name officially changed in 2006 in honor of Sir Lynden Pindling, the first prime minister of the independent Bahamas. The airport underwent major expansion to keep up with growing traffic starting in 2011. There is now a new terminal servicing only U.S. flights, and a domestic-international terminal for flights to the Out Islands and from Canada, England, and other parts of the Caribbean. At the airport you'll be able to purchase duty free and souvenir items, as well as pick up a bite to eat.

NASSAU

Arrive at **Lynden Pindling International Airport** (NAS) on **American Airlines** (U.S. tel. 800/433-7300, www.aa.com) from Miami, Charlotte, Dallas, or Philadelphia; on **Delta** (U.S. tel. 800/241-4141, www.delta.com) from Atlanta or New York City; on **JetBlue** from Boston, Fort Lauderdale, New York City, or Orlando; on **United Airlines** from Chicago, Houston, or New York City; on **Southwest** from Fort Lauderdale or Washington DC; on **British Airways** from Grand Cayman or London; on **Air Canada** from Toronto; on **West Jet** from Toronto; on **Caribbean Airlines** from Kingston, Jamaica; on **COPA** from Panama City; and on **Bahamasair** (tel. 242/702-4140, U.S. tel. 800/222-4262, www.bahamasair.com) from Havana, Miami, and Orlando.

Also in Nassau are two fixed-base operator (FBO) airports utilizing the same runway as the international airport. **Odyssey Aviation** (www.odysseyaviation.com) and **Jet Aviation** (www.jetaviation.com/Nassau) service private planes and jets, as well as charter flights from the United States and to the Out Islands.

GRAND BAHAMA

Grand Bahama International Airport (FPO) has direct flights from Miami, Fort Lauderdale, Atlanta, and Nassau. **Bahamasair** (tel. 242/702-4140, U.S. tel. 800/222-4262, www.bahamasair.com) flies from Miami and Nassau, **American Airlines** (U.S. tel. 800/433-7300, www.aa.com) from Miami, **Delta** (U.S. tel. 800/241-4141, www.delta.com) from Atlanta, and **Silver Airlines** (U.S. tel. 844/674-5837, www.silverairways.com) from Fort Lauderdale, **Sky Bahamas** (tel. 242/702-2600, www.skybahamas.net) from Nassau, and **Western Air** (tel. 242/351-3804, www.westernairbahamas.com) from Nassau.

THE ABACOS

Marsh Harbour (MHH) has daily flights from Nassau on **Bahamasair** (tel. 242/702-4140, www.bahamasair.com) and **Sky Bahamas** (tel. 242/702-2600, www.skybahamas.net), and direct flights from Fort Lauderdale on **Silver Airways** (U.S. tel. 801/401-9100, www.silverairways.com) and Bahamasair, from Miami on **American Airlines** (U.S. tel. 800/433-7300, www.aa.com), and from Atlanta on **Delta** (U.S. tel. 800/241-4141, www.delta.com).

Previous: the Columbus Monument in San Salvador; a traditional Bahamian meal: cracked conch with peas-and-rice, macaroni, and coleslaw.

Exclusive Aviation (tel. 242/357-8877, www.flyexclusivebahamas.com) has weekly flights to Marsh Harbour from Odyssey Aviation in Nassau on a small Piper Navajo that seats up to eight.

ELEUTHERA, HARBOUR ISLAND, AND SPANISH WELLS

On Eleuthera there are three airports: **North Eleuthera International Airport** (ELH) for Harbour Island and Spanish Wells, **Governor's Harbour International Airport** (GHB); centrally located on the island, and **Rock Sound International Airport** (RSD), on the south end of the island. **Bahamasair** (tel. 242/702-4140, www.bahamasair.com) flies from Nassau to North Eleuthera for Harbour Island and Spanish Wells, Governor's Harbour, and Rock Sound. **Pineapple Air** (ELH tel. 242/335-2081, NAS tel. 242/377-0140, www.pineappleair.com) flies from Nassau to North Eleuthera and Governor's Harbour. **Southern Air** (ELH tel. 242/335-1720, NAS tel. 242/377-2014, www.southernaircharter.com) flies from Nassau to North Eleuthera and Governor's Harbour. **Bahama Hoppers** (tel. 242/335-1650, www.bahamahoppers.com) offers five-passenger charter flights from Odyssey Aviation in Nassau to White Crown Aviation in North Eleuthera, next door to the main airport terminal.

Silver Airways (U.S. tel. 801/401-9100, www.silverairways.com) offers daily direct flights from Fort Lauderdale to North Eleuthera and Governor's Harbour. **American Airlines** (U.S. tel. 800/433-7300, www.aa.com) offers daily direct flights from Miami. **Delta** (U.S. tel. 800/241-4141, www.delta.com) has daily direct flights from Atlanta in season. **Aztec Airways** (U.S. tel. 954/601-3742, www.aztecairways.com) offers flights on Monday and Friday-Saturday from Fort Lauderdale Executive Airport to North Eleuthera and Governor's Harbour.

THE EXUMAS

The Exumas have a variety of airstrips throughout the islands and cays. The main airport is **Exuma International Airport** (GGT), just north of George Town in Great Exuma. **Staniel Cay Airport** (TYM) has domestic and international flights, and Black Point Airport has domestic flights. All other airstrips are privately owned and operated, and pilots must call ahead for landing details. **Bahamasair** (tel. 242/702-4140, www.bahamasair.com) has two flights per day from Nassau to George Town. **Sky Bahamas** (Nassau tel. 242/702-2600, Exuma tel. 242/345-0172, www.skybahamas.net) has two flights per day from Nassau to George Town.

Silver Airways (U.S. tel. 801/401-9100, www.silverairways.com) offers daily direct flights from Fort Lauderdale to George Town. **American Airlines** (U.S. tel. 800/433-7300, www.aa.com) offers daily direct flights from Miami to George Town. **Delta** (U.S. tel. 800/241-4141, www.delta.com) has daily direct flights from Atlanta to George Town. **Watermakers Air** (U.S. tel. 954/771 0330, www.watermakersair.com) has flights Thursday-Sunday from Fort Lauderdale Executive to George Town. **Air Canada** (Canada tel. 514/393-3333, www.aircanada.com) offers flights from Toronto to George Town.

Bahama Hoppers (tel. 242/335-1650, www.bahamahoppers.com) offers five-passenger charter flights from Odyssey Aviation in Nassau to Great Exuma and a variety of islands in the Exuma Cays with operating air strips. **Trans Island Airways** (tel. 242/362-4006, www.tia.aero) flies nine-passenger Cessna Caravans, regular and amphibian, for services on both land and water throughout the Exuma Cays.

Watermakers Air (U.S. tel. 954/771-0330, www.watermakersair.com) has flights from Fort Lauderdale Executive on Tuesday and Thursday-Saturday to Staniel Cay. **Flamingo Air** (tel. 242/377-0345, www.flamingoairbah.

com) offers two flights daily from Nassau to Staniel Cay.

BIMINI

South Bimini Airport (BIM) has direct daily flights from the United States and Nassau. **Western Air** (tel. 242/351-3804, www.westernairbahamas.com) has two flights daily from Nassau. **Silver Airways** (U.S. tel. 801/401-9100, www.silverairways.com) has one to two flights daily from Fort Lauderdale. **Elite Airways** (U.S. tel. 877/393-2501, www.res.eliteairways.net) has nonstop flights from New York City's Newark airport and Orlando on Thursday and Sunday. **Tropic Ocean Airways** (U.S. tel. 800/767-0897, www.flytropic.com) is a seaplane charter that flies from Fort Lauderdale International Airport to South Bimini Airport, or the North Bimini Seaplane Base at Resorts World Bimini, offering two or three flights per day in high season.

ANDROS

In North Andros, **San Andros Airport** (SAQ) serves Nicholl's Town and North Andros and has two daily flights from Nassau on **Western Air** (tel. 242/351-3804, www.westernairbahamas.com). **Andros Town Airport** (ASQ) serves Fresh Creek and Central Andros. **LeAir** (reservations tel. 242/377-2356, Fresh Creek tel. 242/368-2919, www.flyleair.com) has two flights daily from Nassau to Andros Town. **Watermakers Air** (U.S. tel. 954/771-0330, www.watermakersair.com) flies from Fort Lauderdale Executive Airport to San Andros on Monday, Wednesday, and Saturday-Sunday. **Tropic Ocean Airways** (U.S. tel. 800/767-0897, www.flytropic.com) is a seaplane charter that flies from Fort Lauderdale International Airport to San Andros or Andros Town-Fresh Creek airport or at your accommodations.

Mangrove Cay (MAY) has flights from Nassau on **LeAir** (reservations tel. 242/377-2356, www.flyleair.com), offering a daily morning and afternoon flight, and **Flamingo Air** (tel. 242/351-4963, www.flamingoairbah.com), daily in the morning and afternoon.

In South Andros, **Congo Town Airport** (TZN) has flights from Nassau on **Western Air** (tel. 242/351-3804, www.westernairbahamas.com) with two flights daily from Nassau, and **Watermakers Air** (U.S. tel. 954/771-0330, www.watermakersair.com) from Fort Lauderdale Executive Airport to Congo Town on Tuesday and Thursday-Saturday.

THE BERRY ISLANDS

LeAir (tel. 242/377-2356, www.flyleair.com) has two flights daily from Nassau to **Great Harbour Cay Airport** (GHC). **Watermakers Air** (U.S. tel. 954/771-0330, www.watermakersair.com) has flights from Fort Lauderdale Executive Airport to Great Harbour Cay Thursday-Sunday. **Tropic Ocean Airways** (U.S. tel. 954/210-5569 or 800/767-0897, www.flytropic.com) offers flights from Fort Lauderdale International Airport at Sheltair on Wednesday-Friday and Sunday.

Charter flights are available out of Odyssey Aviation in Nassau to Chub Cay. Five-passenger aircraft are available with **Bahama Hoppers** (Lindy Wells, tel. 242/359-7883, www.bahamahoppers.com). Opt for a nine-passenger aircraft with **Saga Boy** (Raquel Hinds, tel. 242/702-0231, www.sagaboyaircharters.com).

Watermakers Air (U.S. tel. 954/771-0330, www.watermakersair.com) has flights from Fort Lauderdale Executive Airport to Chub Cay Monday, Wednesday, and Friday-Saturday.

LONG ISLAND

There are two airports in Long Island: **Stella Maris Airport** (SML) in the north and **Deadman's Cay Airport** (LGI) in the middle of the island. If you are staying on the north end, fly with **Stella Maris Air Service** (tel. 242/338-2050 or 242/357-1182, www.stellamarisresort.com/air-service) on a charter flight with per-seat pricing. They depart Jet Aviation in Nassau, just a short taxi ride from the international airport.

Commercial domestic flights to Long Island can be booked on **Southern Air** (Stella Maris tel. 242/338-2095, Deadman's Cay tel. 242/337-1722, Nassau tel. 242/377-2014, www.southernaircharter.com) with one flight per day from Nassau that stops in both Stella Maris and Deadman's Cay, and on **Bahamasair** (tel. 242/702-4140, www.bahamasair.com) with one flight per day to Deadman's Cay.

CAT ISLAND

Commercial domestic flights into Cat Island can be booked on **Sky Bahamas** (Arthur's Town tel. 242/354-2236, New Bight tel. 242/342-2256, Nassau tel. 242/225-4460, U.S. tel. 954/317-3751, www.skybahamas.net) with two flights per day from Nassau flying into **Arthur's Town Airport** (ATC), on the north end of the island, or **New Bight Airport**, located centrally. If you book on a day when they only fly to Arthur's Town and you had booked to New Bight (and vice versa), they will bus you to your final destination.

SAN SALVADOR

Bahamasair (tel. 242/702-4140, www.bahamasair.com) has one flight daily from Nassau to **San Salvador Airport** (ZSA) in Cockburn Town at varying times of day.

From Miami, **American Airlines** (U.S. tel. 800/433 7300, www.aa.com), has direct flights on Saturday. Charter flights fly from Montreal and Paris weekly in conjunction with Club Med. Contact Club Med directly if you plan to fly from either of those destinations.

GREAT INAGUA

Inagua Airport (IGA) has three flights per week on **Bahamasair** (tel. 242/702-4140, www.bahamasair.com) to Matthew Town. Flights are Monday, Wednesday, and Friday at 9:15am, sometimes stopping in Mayaguana.

ACKLINS AND CROOKED ISLAND

Bahamasair (tel. 242/702-4140, www.bahamasair.com) flies to Acklins and Crooked Island twice weekly from Nassau, once on Wednesday morning and once on Saturday at midday. The flight stops at both islands: **Colonel Hill Airport** (CRI) on Crooked Island and **Spring Point Airport** (AXP) on Acklins. To travel outside those times, charter flights are available from Nassau and the Miami-Fort Lauderdale area.

Sea

Cruise ship passengers make up a large percentage of day visitors to The Bahamas each year. Cruise ships depart from Miami and Fort Lauderdale. Carnival ships arrive at Nassau, Freeport, and Carnival's own private port of Princess Cays on Eleuthera. Norwegian arrives at Nassau, Freeport, and its own private island, Great Stirrup Cay in the Berry Islands. Disney ships arrive at Nassau and Disney's own private island, Castaway Cay, off Great Abaco Island. The ships arrive on a weekly schedule and funnel passengers into downtown Nassau for shopping or tours.

Due to the close proximity to Florida, many private boats and yachts visit the easily accessible Abacos, Bimini, Berry Islands, and Exumas. Sailboats, traveling at a slower pace, typically spend the winter months cruising. If you are planning to arrive by boat, a cruising permit is obtained when you clear in at a port of entry. You'll fly a yellow quarantine flag until you clear in, after which all foreign vessels fly the Bahamian courtesy flag for the duration of the stay. The cost is $150 for vessels up to 35 feet and $300 for vessels over 35 feet. The cost covers the cruising permit, a fishing permit, and the departure tax.

If you arrive by sea, you may want to invest in a set of paper charts. The GPS navigation systems are pretty good but don't have all the shoals and rocks. The Explorer Charts are produced by sailing couple, Monty and Sara Lewis, who have spent over 20 winter seasons cruising in The Bahamas, and they are on the 8th edition. There are three chart books in full color and water-resistant paper, offering area information on individual islands, and regions and ideal anchorage spots. The charts are *Near Bahamas* (including Grand Bahama, Bimini, Abacos, Berrys, Andros, and Nassau), *Exumas and Ragged Islands*, and *Far Bahamas* (including Eleuthera, Cat Island, Long Island, San Salvador, Acklins, and Crooked Island). They cost about $70 each but are well worth it.

GETTING AROUND

On Land

Nassau is easily navigated by catching a taxi or jitney (bus). The jitney is by far the most economical mode of transit, and many locals use these buses for their daily commutes.

Many Out Islands have golf cart rentals, a fun way to explore smaller communities like Harbour Island, Hope Town, and Treasure Cay. For larger islands, organize a car rental prior to your visit if you plan to do any exploring. Many resorts, especially in the Out Islands, will pick you up from the airport and can arrange car rentals. Check with your lodging prior to booking a car rental.

NASSAU

There are international rental car companies in Nassau, but be prepared to drive on the left side of the road. **Avis** (tel. 242/377-7121, www.avis.com.bs), has locations at Lynden Pindling International Airport, Nassau Cruise Ship Dock, downtown, and Paradise Island. **Budget** (tel. 242/325-8154, www.budget-rentacar-nassaubahamas.com) has locations at the international airport and downtown. **Hertz** (tel. 242/377-8684, www.hertz.com) has locations at the international airport, Jet Aviation, and Odyssey Aviation. **Dollar/Thrifty** (tel. 242/377-8300, www.dollar.com) is at the international airport. Local car rental company **Virgo** (tel. 242/793-7900, www.virgocarrental.com), might not have the classiest of vehicles, but they offer great daily rates, with free pickup and drop-off anywhere on the island. Locations are downtown on Kemp Road, on East-West Highway near Marathon, and at the Airport Industrial Park near the airport.

GRAND BAHAMA

Avis (tel. 242/351-2847, www.avis.com) has locations at Grand Bahama International Airport and at the Freeport Cruise Ship Dock. **Hertz** (tel. 242/352-9250, www.hertz.com) has a location at the international airport with pickup service available from the Cruise Ship Dock. **Thrifty** (tel. 242/352-9325, www.thrifty.com) has a location at the international airport. **Brad's Car Rental** (tel. 242/352-7930, U.S. tel. 954/703-5246, www.bradscarrental.com) is at the international airport and offers free pickup. **KSR Car Rental** (tel. 242/351-5737, U.S. tel. 954/703-5819, ksrrentacar.biz) is at the international airport. **Island Jeep & Car Rental** (tel. 242/373-4001, U.S. tel. 954/237-6660, www.islandjeepcarrental.com) has three locations: the international airport, the Cruise Ship Dock, and Island Seas Resort.

THE ABACOS

Rental Wheels (Bay St., Marsh Harbour, tel. 242/367-4643, www.rentalwheels.com) is located in Marsh Harbour, but will deliver a vehicle or pick you up at the airport with advance notice. Other companies are **A&P Auto Rentals** (tel. 242/367-2655, www.aandpautorentals.com) and **Bargain Car Rentals** (tel. 242/367-0500).

ELEUTHERA, HARBOUR ISLAND, AND SPANISH WELLS

'Lutra Car Rental (tel. 242/424-8133, www.lutracar.com) is located in North Eleuthera, and family run **Johnson's Car Rental** (tel. 242/470-8235) is in Lower Bouge, North Eleuthera. **Big Daddy's Car Rentals** (tel. 242/332-1592 or 242/470-9003, www.wcbigdaddyrentalcars.com) and **Sabal Palm Car Rental** (tel. 242/470-9951, www.rentalcarseleuthera.com) are in Governor's Harbour. For rental cars in Rock Sound, contact **Dingle Motor Service** (Rock Sound, tel. 242/334-2031). If you are staying in Cape Eleuthera and have no plans to travel anywhere, you won't need a vehicle, but golf cart rentals are available.

In Harbour Island, **No Limits Rentals** (tel. 242/470-8502, nolimitrentals@gmail.com) offers rates for 24-hour periods. **Jack Percentie** (tel. 242/470-8554) rents several carts and will assist you with area information. Other reliable cart rental companies are: **Daybreak Rentals** (Colebrook St., tel. 242/333-2491), **Dunmore Rentals** (just up from Government Dock, off Bay St., tel. 242/333-2373), **Johnson's Rentals** (off King St., tel. 242/333-2122), **Ross Rentals** (Colebrook St., tel. 242/333-2122), and **Briland on the Go** (Colebrook St., tel. 242/333-2573).

In Spanish Wells, **JJ Golf Cart Rental** (tel. 242/333-4575) rents golf carts by the hour, day, or week. **Harbourside Golf Cart Rentals** (tel. 242/333-5022, www.harboursidebahamas.com) is right in town on the dock and offers golf cart rentals.

THE EXUMAS

Rental car offices are located at Exuma International Airport. Call ahead or book online to reserve a car in advance, especially during busy season. Suggested rental car companies are **Thompson's Rentals** (Exuma International Airport, tel. 242/336-2442, www.exumacars.com), **Airport Car Rental** (Exuma International Airport, tel. 242/345-0090, www.exumacarrental.com), and **Berlie's Car Rental** (Exuma International Airport, tel. 242/336-3290, www.berliescarrentals.com).

For golf cart rentals on Staniel Cay, contact **Isles General Store** (tel. 242/355-2007, www.mwpr.com/islesinn.html) or **Island Rentals** (tel. 242/524-8191, www.stanielrentals.com).

BIMINI

In Alice Town, **Sunset Scooter Rental** (King's Hwy., Alice Town, tel. 242/347-3251) is located in Robert's Grocery Store. **M&M Golf Cart Rental** (King's Hwy., Alice Town, tel. 242/347-2375 or 242/473-4357) is located at Bimini Big Game Club. **Le'Rick's Golf Cart Rental** (King's Hwy., Alice Town, tel. 242/347-4043 or 242/554-4578) is just north of the Bank of the Bahamas, before Bimini Big Game Club.

ANDROS

For car rentals in North Andros, contact **Rooney's Auto** (Calabash Bay, tel. 242/471-0346 or 242/368-2021). He is located at the town's gas station, but he will pick you up from Fresh Creek Airport.

For car rentals in South Andros, contact **PB's Car Rental** (Mangrove Cay, tel. 242/369-0871 or 242/554-0258) or **Lenglo Car Rental** (Congo Town, tel. 242/369-1702 or 242/369-1704).

THE BERRY ISLANDS

For car rentals in Great Harbour Cay, **Krum's Rent-a-Car** (tel. 242/367-8370 or 242/367-8321), located at the marina, offers vehicles starting at $70 per day. Another option is **Relly's Rental** (tel. 242/367-8036 or 242/464-4012).

LONG ISLAND

For car rentals, contact **KRS Car Rental** (Stella Maris, tel. 242/464-2077), **Unique Wheels Rentals** (Clarence Town, tel. 242/337-3088), or **Omar's Rental Cars** (Seymours, tel. 242/338-5273 or 242/357-1043).

CAT ISLAND

Bob's Car Rentals (tel. 242/354-6120) is located in Arthur's Town. **Gilbert's Car Rentals** (tel. 242/342-3011) is at the New Bight Food Store.

SAN SALVADOR

Car rentals can be arranged through your hotel or resort. Each hotel works with a preferred local company. **K's Scooter Rentals** (tel. 242/331-2125 or 242/452-0594) is located at the Cockburn Town Airport and offers hourly and daily rates.

Air

For interisland travel, each island region has its own or several airports with daily commercial flights from Nassau on Bahamasair and other

Driving Tips

When driving, especially in Nassau, traffic can be wild. Fortunately the traffic is slow-paced, and even though the rules of the road are similar to other countries, local driving "etiquette" differs. If you drive in The Bahamas long enough, you'll figure out the nuances, but generally go slow and pay attention.

We drive on the left side of the road, but cars are imported from both the United States and Japan, so you'll find both right- and left-hand drives.

- **Potholes and puddles:** It is common for people veer into the opposite lane to avoid potholes and puddles. When it rains and puddles form, traffic will slow to a snail's pace.
- **Scooters are available but are not recommended.** Tourists drive around in bikinis and shirtless in Nassau, but there is a high rate of accidents and occasional deaths on scooters. Don't ruin your vacation by ending up in the hospital. Rent a car or hire a taxi if you want to get around.
- **Roundabouts:** Learn how to navigate roundabouts (traffic circles), but use extreme caution, because no one else uses them properly. Technically you're only supposed to be in the outside lane if you are turning left or going straight through the intersection. The inside lane is for going straight through or turning right. The easiest way is to make sure no one is next to you while traversing the roundabout.
- **Yielding:** people tend to stop in the middle of the road to yield to other vehicles, thinking they are being polite or helpful, when by law it's not really their place to stop. It gets confusing for anyone used to going by the traffic rules. Be wary of this and proceed with caution.
- **Honking:** Honking is either a way of saying "thank you" or an alert. It's very rarely used in the form of anger or annoyance. If someone gives you right of way, it's custom to give one or two short beeps in thanks. It is also used if someone is not intending on stopping to yield, so they beep in warning to vehicle they might think is going to pull out in front of them.
- **Power outages:** When the power goes out, the traffic lights go out. These are supposed to be treated as a stop sign, but the intersections normally become gridlocked. If you suspect the power is out, get off the roads to save yourself the headache.
- **Signaling:** people don't believe in turn signals, and often a vehicle's brake lights don't work. Leave space between you and the car in front of you—they may suddenly stop or turn with no warning.

On some islands, a golf cart is sufficient transportation. For exploring on other islands, such as Cat Island or Long Island, a 4WD vehicle is recommended.

domestic airlines. A number of the Out Islands can be accessed by direct flights from Miami and Fort Lauderdale. Charter flights to all islands are available from the private airports.

Sea

Locals often travel by Mail Boat (freight boats serving all of the Out Islands) and some islands also have the Bahamas Fast Ferry, based in Downtown Nassau. In The Abacos it is possible to rent a captained or bareboat charter with live-aboard amenities. Throughout most of the other islands, you can rent a small skiff for island-hopping.

Visas and Officialdom

EMBASSIES

The U.S. Embassy (tel. 242/322-1181, http://bs.usembassy.gov) is located in downtown Nassau and has full services for U.S. citizens. Their emergency number is tel. 242/328-2206. Also in downtown Nassau is an embassy for Haiti, Brazil, and China.

IMMIGRATION AND CUSTOMS

A valid passport and a return ticket are required to enter The Bahamas. If you arrive commercially but plan on departing the country via boat or private flight, you may need to provide written documentation, a flight plan, or a cruising permit upon airport check-in or Bahamas immigration, otherwise you may be required to book a return ticket on the spot.

Visas are not required for U.S. and Canadian passport holders. If visiting for any purpose other than tourism, you must contact the Department of Immigration prior to your visit.

Holders of passports from certain countries in Africa and the Middle East require a visa. You will typically be stamped for your length of stay, up to 30 days, upon entry. The Department of Immigration is very strict, so make sure you don't overstay the length stamped in your passport. Working is prohibited without a valid work permit. Visit www.bahamas.gov.bs for more information on visa requirements.

Upon arriving in The Bahamas, nonresidents must fill out and sign a pink and white Immigration form. After clearing immigration, a portion of the card is given to the visitor, and should be returned to the airline agent upon departing. Visitors have to pass through customs and declare items such as cigarettes, alcohol, and gifts.

When leaving, visitors over age six must pay a Departure Tax of $20. It's usually included in the price of your ticket if you arrived on a commercial flight.

There are no vaccination requirements when traveling from the United States or Canada; however, if you are traveling from or have visited a country with a risk of yellow fever, you will need to present a vaccination certificate. This includes a laundry list of countries in Africa and South America. Check with the Department of Immigration or at www.bahamas.gov.bs for an updated list if you are unsure.

Travelers to the United States from Nassau go through U.S. Immigration and Customs at the airport in Nassau before departing. This is a time-saving convenience, especially if you are making a connection at a U.S. airport.

Recreation

TOURS

Each island offers its own unique tour guides. This might include nature tours and eco-adventures, a cultural tour, or fishing and boating guides. On Andros, Great Abaco, and Grand Bahama, you can explore national parks where you'll see a variety of interesting birds and learn about native wildlife. You can visit blue holes, take a kayak tour through the mangroves, or explore hiking trails on your own. Grand Bahama offers bicycle tours, and on Long Island you can tour Hamilton's Cave. In Nassau you can take the Tru Bahamian Food Tour, where you'll visit historical landmarks and sample local cuisine. On almost every island is an option for fishing and dive charters or island-hopping tours with snorkeling, picnicking, visiting swimming pigs, petting sharks, or feeding native iguanas.

These tours are a great way to get to know the uniqueness of an island and are highly recommended. Most of the tours are operated by longtime locals or island natives who will be a wealth of knowledge. Reputable tour operators are listed in this book. There are a variety of other companies, but check them out on TripAdvisor or another website prior to booking; some outfits aren't as professional as others.

BOATING

Due to the close proximity to the United States, sailboat traffic is heavy throughout the winter. The islands are a short hop from Miami and Fort Lauderdale, and many sailboaters spend the entire winter in The Bahamas, and then head back to the safety of U.S. marinas for hurricane season. There are numerous marinas in The Bahamas able to accommodate megayachts, which cruise the waters in winter before relocating north for the summer. The Abacos and The Exumas are both popular destinations for island-hopping enthusiasts.

FISHING

The Bahamas are a dream for fishing enthusiasts. Anglers troll and live-bait for tuna, mahimahi, and wahoo, deep drop for snapper and grouper, and bonefish the shallow flats. The Abacos, Andros, and Bimini are popular destinations because of their close proximity to the United States and fantastic fishing. The Abacos are known for having record catches of marlin, sailfish, and tuna; Bimini is known as the "Big Game Fishing Capital"; and Andros has numerous bonefishing lodges, both rustic and chic.

SNORKELING AND DIVING

Thousands of visitors flock to The Bahamas each year with the sole intent of diving the crystal waters. Dive operations and dive-specific resorts are located throughout the islands. In Nassau, Stuart Cove's will bring you on an exhilarating shark dive. In Grand Bahama, UNEXSO specializes in wreck dives. Experience wall diving at Cat Island with Hawk's Nest or Greenwood Beach Resort. Dive the Andros Barrier Reef in Andros with Small Hope Bay. In San Salvador, Riding Rock and Club Med offer day trips. Neal Watson in Bimini will take you to Bimini Roads and numerous wrecks.

HIKING

The Bahamas is not known for hills and mountains, but there are hiking trails throughout the islands. Opportunities abound to view birds and interesting plants and trees. The best places for hiking are in Andros in Blue Holes National Park, the Rand Nature Centre and Lucayan National Park in Grand Bahama, the Hermitage at Mount Alvernia in Cat Island, and trails in the Exuma Cays Land and Sea Park.

KITEBOARDING

Kiteboarding hasn't quite become mainstream in The Bahamas, making this an uncrowded destination. The winds aren't as consistent farther north in the islands, but near and below the Tropic of Cancer, in Great Exuma, the Exuma Cays, and Long Island, the trade winds provide some fabulous flatwater riding. There are very few kiteboarding outfits, but a few are Exuma Kite and Surf in George Town, Greenwood Beach Resort in Cat Island, and San Salvador Kitesurfing in San Salvador.

PADDLEBOARDING AND KAYAKING

Mangroves and protected shallow waters abound, and on almost every island you'll get the chance to glide through nature on a stand-up paddleboard or kayak. In Nassau, PappaSurf offers paddleboard rentals, tours, and full-moon paddles. Check into Lucayan Nature Tours in Grand Bahama and tuck into the mangroves by kayak to see a variety of birds and sealife.

SURFING

Although reefs run along the edge of most of the islands, there are very few ridable surf breaks in The Bahamas. The only place that has started to capitalize on the surf scene is Gregory Town, North Eleuthera. Surf camps are offered at a few low-budget and low-key surf resorts, and you can rent surfboards at Rebecca's Beach Shop.

YOGA

Yoga has recently caught on in The Bahamas for both locals and visitors. The trend on healthy vacationing has spurred yoga retreats hosted at boutique hotels in the Out Islands. The Sivananda Yoga Retreat and Ashram has been operating since the 1960s on Paradise Island, and Studio Ohana in Nassau has gained momentum since opening its doors in early 2016, offering retreats throughout the islands. Other organizations are working directly with hotels, so inquire as to whether your lodging offers yoga or retreats.

Food

Bahamian food is typically heavy and hearty, and a local Bahamian restaurant or takeout will consist of meat or fish, an option of sides, and a healthy serving of peas-and-rice. Meat choices commonly are steamed chicken on the bone, pork chop, or lamb chop. For seafood you'll find grouper fingers, whole pan-fried snapper (with the bones!), and fried conch.

Vegetarian and vegan travelers historically have had a difficult time finding adequate meals, but in recent years there has been a huge shift in restaurants catering toward specialized diets. You'll find most high-end restaurants have at least one vegetarian dish available, but local mom-and-pop restaurants are still focused on meat and rice. Several local vegans in Nassau have established **Vegan Network Bahamas** (www.vegannetworkbahamas.com), which provides information on restaurants offering vegan choices throughout The Bahamas. Especially in Nassau, you'll have no trouble finding healthy and delicious food for a wide range of diets.

TRADITIONAL BAHAMIAN FARE

With regard to traditional Bahamian fare, the following are a few staple culinary dishes you'll see on most menus throughout The Bahamas.

Conch: Conch is a Bahamian staple, considered the national dish. A common way to serve it is as conch salad. Similar to ceviche, conch salad is made with fresh raw conch, "cooked" in lime juice and mixed with bell peppers, onion, tomatoes, and hot peppers. The tropical version often has mango, papaya, or pineapple, too. There are also conch fritters, cracked conch (battered and fried), conch chowder, stewed conch, steamed conch, and scorched conch.

Peas-and-rice: Peas-and-rice is a side dish that always accompanies fish, chicken, or meat along with potato salad, coleslaw, plantain, or mac and cheese. Pigeon peas are traditionally used for proper Bahamian peas-and-rice, but due to influences from other Caribbean islands, kidney beans are sometimes used instead. Along with beans or peas, ingredients include white rice, onion, tomatoes or tomato paste, fresh thyme, browning sauce (for color), salt pork or bacon, and occasionally hot peppers.

Boiled fish and souse: Traditional boiled fish and souse, a light broth with potatoes and onion seasoned with lime, allspice, and goat pepper (an extremely hot Bahamian pepper), are served at breakfast. The most common souse is made with bone-in chicken wings and drumsticks, but you can be more adventurous and try mutton (goat), sheep's tongue,

Seafood Conservation and Safety

LOBSTER AND GROUPER SEASON

In 2014, a fixed closed season was implemented for Nassau grouper, which runs December-February. The Nassau grouper is an endangered species that is extinct in most of the Caribbean. There is also a closed season for Caribbean spiny lobster, which runs April-July. Don't order grouper or lobster from local menus during these periods: They may say it was captured in season and frozen, but odds are they are obtaining it from illegal harvesters.

TURTLE, SHARK, AND BILLFISH

Turtles are protected by law, and a complete ban on killing, harvesting, or harassing them was implemented in 2009. Turtle soup was commonly found on menus until this law was passed. Over 40 species of sharks are protected in Bahamian waters after long-liners plied the waters and harvesting sharks for their fins to export for shark-fin soup. The Fisheries Resources Act was amended in 2011 to protect sharks, with major support from the public. All billfish are also protected. They can be caught in sportfishing, but they must be returned to the sea unharmed.

CIGUATERA

Be aware that barracuda is prone to ciguatera (a fish toxin that can cause illness) created by toxins that compound in their systems from eating reef fish. Most locals don't eat barracuda, and it's not found on menus, but as it's delicious, some people take the risk and eat it anyway. Ciguatera is less commonly known to occur in larger groupers and snappers. The toxin produces abdominal pain, nausea, vomiting, and diarrhea 1-3 hours after consuming it. In 3-72 hours, neurological symptoms begin to appear, including temperature reversal, tingling sensations, itching, blurred vision, and temporary blindness. The toxin can last for several days to weeks or months and can cause long-term complications.

pig's feet, and chicken's feet souse. Stewed fish uses a similar broth to souse and is typically prepared using grouper, but mahimahi, snapper, and hogfish are substituted when grouper is out of season.

DRINKS

Beer: Kalik is known as the "beer of The Bahamas" and has been producing light island lagers since 1988. Their flagship beer has a nice balance of malt and a slight hoppy flavor, easy to drink along with a plate of cracked conch. They also have Kalik Light, Kalik Gold (extra strong), Kalik Lime, and Kalik Radler, which is a sweet lemon-lime flavored malt beer with about 2 percent alcohol.

Sands products were introduced in 2008 and are known as a "truly Bahamian beer" and are 100-percent Bahamian owned and operated. Sands is a bit lighter in flavor than Kalik, and Sands Light is extremely light. They also produce High Rock lager (similar to Heineken), Strong Back Stout, and Sands Pink Radler, which is a grapefruit-flavored sweet malt beverage with a low alcohol content.

Craft Beer: After years of domination by the mega beer companies of Commonwealth Brewery (producers of Kalik and contract brewers of Guinness and Heineken) and the Bahamian Brewery (Sands products), the craft beer scene has finally made an appearance in The Bahamas. Pirate Republic Brewing Company is the first—and so far the only—craft brewery in The Bahamas, with distribution throughout the islands and a taproom in downtown Nassau featuring regular events. Their flagship beer is the Island Pirate Ale (IPA), along with a kolsch, a stout, and a pilsner. At the brewery, you can sample rotating and seasonal beers.

Rum and signature tropical drinks: John Watlings Rum Distillery on the historic

Liquor Laws

Although you're likely not going to be penalized for riding around with an open container, especially in the Out Islands, there are certain days when liquor can't be sold. Liquor stores are required to be closed on Sunday and holidays, the exception being marinas. You might find a few sneaky liquor stores open. There is on average one holiday per month, so check the calendar to make sure you're not stuck for a Sunday and a holiday Monday without liquor. Liquor stores are also required to close on voting day so that citizens may vote with a sober pen. This includes national elections, held every five years, and referenda. Voting days are announced prior to when they occur.

Buena Vista Estate in Nassau produces several quality rums and vodka and is open for daily tastings and tours. Afrohead Rum is based in Harbour Island and produces premium aged rum that's distributed throughout The Bahamas and the East Coast of the United States. Locally produced rums used in mixed drinks include Nassau Royale Liqueur and Ron Ricardo flavored rums.

No tropical vacation would be complete without an umbrella drink at your favorite beach bar. Each establishment creates their own spin, but you can find a **Bahama Mama, Rum Punch, Goombay Smash** (sweet cocktails made with rum, pineapple juice, orange juice, and a variety of other ingredients, depending on the drink) and **Sky Juice** (gin, coconut water, and sweetened condensed milk) on every drink menu.

Nonalcoholic drinks: Switcha is considered the national drink of The Bahamas and is the perfect way to cool down on a hot summer day. It's a limeade-type drink and can either be found freshly squeezed or in a bottle from retailers. Switcha was said to be brought with Loyalists from the Southern United States in the 1780s. Utilizing key limes, the concoction is simply lime juice, sugar, and water. Some variations use sour orange, or even mint, ginger, or grapefruit. Rum is another addition which gives it a kick. **Vita Malt** is made by Commonwealth Brewery, and **Trible B** is by Bahamian Brewery. Both are nonalcoholic malt beverages, which are popular throughout the Caribbean, and are basically unfermented beer. Malts are combined with water and hops, but the yeast is not added. Yeast typically eats sugar and turns to alcohol, creating carbon dioxide in the process. Because the sugar is still in the beverage, these malt beverages are fairly sweet but have an underlying taste of beer. It's an acquired island taste, but give it a shot; you may find it refreshing. They are said to be high in nutrients and are considered a vitamin and energy supplement.

Accommodations

In The Bahamas there are a variety of options for a wide range of travelers. Price points have historically been on the high end, so budget travelers have found it difficult to visit for extended periods, but with the introduction of private home rentals, inexpensive nightly rates are more common. The only option that isn't available is camping, which is prohibited for tourists. This is widely accepted, as camping in the heat with the mosquitoes and sandflies would be less than pleasant.

RESORTS

The many resort options range from family-friendly to adults-only. Atlantis is probably the best-known family destination, and newly opened Baha Mar is quickly approaching it in reputation. There are all-inclusive resorts along Cable Beach and on Paradise Island. Outside Nassau and Paradise Island, there are limited large international resorts, but Sandals Emerald Bay in Great Exuma is a popular adults-only destination, and Club Med Columbus Isle in San Salvador is a wonderful choice for all ages.

BOUTIQUE HOTELS

Nassau offers a selection of boutique hotels. Harbour Island does not have any high-rises, and all hotels on the island are small and chic. Kamalame Cay and Tiamo in Andros have gained international attention, and Lumina Point in The Exumas is an eco-friendly off-the-grid luxury escape. Cape Santa Maria in Long Island and Fernandez Bay in Cat Island offer guests beautiful accommodations on outstanding beaches.

VACATION RENTALS

Vacation rentals are quickly becoming a hip way to travel that has opened opportunities for a variety of price points. Where hotel prices typically range from $200, you'll be able to find a house or a room on Airbnb or VRBO for $100 or less, depending on the island. On certain islands, such as Great Guana Cay, there are limited hotel options, so you can look into a vacation rental house. On Harbour Island, when the average room rates are some of the highest in the country, you'll enjoy owner-operated rentals. On Long Island, some of the best-priced accommodations in the country are available on online booking sites. They are especially good for families looking for space, or if you intend to cook your own food. Local real estate companies also specialize in assisting visitors with finding vacation rentals. Not all of the options are listed on booking websites, so local companies may be a great way to find what you want.

FISHING AND SPECIALTY LODGES

On islands where bonefishing is a draw, you'll find a variety of options for all-inclusive fishing lodges, ranging from rustic and barebones to luxury with five-star dining or catering to the entire family. You'll find these lodges on Andros, Long Island, and Acklins and Crooked Island. Other lodges cater to diving and ecotourism or kiteboarding and can be found on Andros, San Salvador, and Cat Island.

Conduct and Customs

The pace is slower in The Bahamas and many Bahamians operate on "island time," a leisurely mind-set that things will get done whenever they get done.

Bahamians are conservative for the most part and dress in suit coats and long pants for business. Church, dining, and events not held on the beach are generally fairly formal. Modesty is also taken to the beach as well. Women wear bikinis, but skimpy ones aren't commonly seen except among foreign visitors. Public nudity is frowned upon on beaches, and attempts at topless sunbathing will often be quelled near resorts and hotels. If you are on a secluded beach with no one for miles around, you're probably safe to be as scantily clad as you'd like. You can get away with being barefoot quite often in the Out Islands, but it's not considered appropriate to enter a place of business or a restaurant without a shirt or swimsuit cover-up.

Bahamians are in general friendly, good natured, and genuine people. They are proud of their island nation and are enthusiastic about sharing it with visitors. Many Bahamians take advantage of the hospitality and tourism programs at the University of The Bahamas, setting them up to excel in the nation's largest business sector. Nassau, as the city, is less welcoming in general than the Out Islands, but it is all relative. Many visitors still feel the island kindness in Nassau, but the hospitality is definitely accentuated the farther out you travel.

When passing someone in close proximity, acknowledgement and eye contact are always used. This could be a nod or a casual "yep," or more formally, "Good morning," "Good afternoon," "Good evening," or "Good night." "Good night" is used as a greeting in the evening, so don't be confused or surprised when you hear it. They are not saying "Good-bye" but rather "Hello."

And remember, everything operates at a much slower pace, or sometimes not at all. Be open-minded and flexible. Relax—after all, you're on vacation.

Health and Safety

Traveling to the Out Islands of The Bahamas comes with its risks, namely that there are no hospitals, and if serious injury occurs, you may be looking at an airlift evacuation. Clinics are available in most reasonably sized settlements. If you have special prescription medication, make sure you have an adequate amount for the duration of your trip. The Bahamas imports drugs from Europe and South America, so many of the drugs are different from what you can get in the United States and Canada, or out of stock. Visitors are encouraged to get travel insurance for any medical incidents, and when traveling to remote locations, to have the phone numbers handy for air ambulances, or when boating, the Bahamas Air Sea Rescue Association.

EMERGENCY CONTACTS

Nassau and Grand Bahama have proper hospitals with specialty practitioners. In the Out Islands, the government-run clinics offer basic health services for minor outpatient incidents, and a small selection of pharmaceuticals. For major medical emergencies, the clinics will assist with arranging transport to Nassau or the United States. If you suffer a major accident, get transport directly to the United States. Depending on the severity, you may be sent to the United States when you get to Nassau.

Nassau

Emergency and medical services are located downtown. **Princess Margaret Hospital** (Shirley St., tel. 242/322-2861, www.pmh.phabahamas.org, 24-hour emergency services), **Doctor's Hospital** (Shirley St., tel. 242/302-4600, www.doctorshosp.com, 24-hour emergency services) and the **Walk-In Clinic** (Collins Ave., tel. 242/328-0783, Mon.-Sat. 7am-10pm, Sun. 7am-3pm, holidays 8am-3pm) are recommended.

For **Police** dial 911, 919, or tel. 242/322-4444; for **fire,** dial 919; **ambulance,** tel. 242/322-2861; **air ambulance,** tel. 242/327-7077; **Bahamas Air Sea Rescue Association (BASRA),** tel. 242/646-6395.

Grand Bahama

Emergency medical facilities are located in downtown Freeport at the **Rand Memorial Hospital** (East Atlantic Dr., off E. Mall Way, tel. 242/350-6700 or 242/352-2689, www.gbhs.phabahamas.org, 24 hour emergency services). For nonemergencies, visit the **Lucayan Medical Centre** (E. Sunrise Hwy., tel. 242/373-7400, www.lucayanmedical.com, Mon.-Fri. 8:30am-5:30pm, Sat. 8:30am-1pm).

For **emergency medical services or ambulance,** dial 242/352-2689, 919, or 911. For **Fire** emergencies, dial 242/352-8888 or 911. For **Police,** dial 919 or 911. For **Bahamas Air Sea Rescue Association** (BASRA), dial 242/352-2628, 919, or 911.

The Abacos

There are several clinics for visitors: **Marsh Harbour Community Clinic** (Great Abaco Hwy., just before S. C. Bootle Hwy., tel. 242/367-2510 or 242/367-4594, Mon.-Fri. 9am-5pm), **Green Turtle Cay Community Clinic** (New Plymouth, tel. 242/365-4028, Mon.-Fri. 9am-5pm), and **Hope Town Community Clinic** (Hope Town, tel. 242/366-0108, Mon.-Fri. 9am-5pm).

For emergencies or police services, contact **Royal Bahamas Police Force** (911, 919, or tel. 242/367-2560). Fire services are available through **Marsh Harbour Fire & Rescue** (tel. 242/367-2000), **Treasure Cay Fire Department** (tel. 242/365-8919), **Green Turtle Cay Fire Department** (tel. 242/365-4019), and **Hope Town Fire & Rescue** (tel. 242/475-0144). **Emergency Medical Services** (tel. 242/367-2911) are available throughout The Abacos. If you need assistance with airlift services to the United States, contact **Air Ambulance** (tel. 242/327-7077) or **Jet Rescue in Florida** (tel. 305/504-1093). For issues concerning marine vessels, contact **Bahamas Air Sea Rescue Association** (BASRA, tel. 242/366-0282).

Eleuthera, Harbour Island, and Spanish Wells

Try the **Gregory Town Community Clinic** (tel. 242/335-5108, Mon.-Fri. 9am-5pm, except public holidays). For emergency services, contact the **Royal Bahamas Police Force Fire/Police** (tel. 919). In Governor's Harbour is the **Governor's Harbour Community Clinic** (tel. 242/332-2774, Mon.-Fri. 9am-5pm, except public holidays). There are two police stations: The **Governor's Harbour Police Station** (tel. 242/332-2117) and the **Governor's Harbour Airport Police Station** (tel. 242/332-2323).

Try the **Rock Sound Community Clinic** (tel. 242/334-2226 or 242/334-2139, Mon.-Fri. 9am-5pm, except public holidays). For emergency services, dial 919 or the **Rock Sound Airport Police Station** (tel. 242/334-2052). In Harbour Island is the **Harbour Island Community Clinic** (tel. 242/333-2227, Mon.-Fri. 9am-5pm, except public holidays). Police are at the **Harbour Island Police Station** (tel. 242/333-2111).

The **Spanish Wells Community Clinic** (Mon.-Fri. 9am-5pm, except public holidays) can be reached at tel. 242/333-4064. For emergency services, dial 919 or the **Spanish Wells Police Station** (tel. 242/333-4030).

The Exumas

Try the **George Town Community Clinic** (tel. 242/336-2088), **Forbes Hill Community Clinic** (tel. 242/345-4144), or the **Steventon**

Community Clinic (tel. 242/358-0053). Clinic hours are Monday-Friday 9am-5pm, except public holidays. There are two police stations: the **George Town Police Station** (tel. 242/336-2666) and the **George Town Airport Police Station** (tel. 242/345-0083). For emergency services, contact the **Royal Bahamas Police Force Fire and Police** (tel. 919) or the **George Town Fire Department** (tel. 242/345-0008).

Bimini

Try the **Alice Town Community Clinic** (tel. 242/347-2210, Mon.-Fri. 9am-5pm, except public holidays). For emergency services, contact the **Royal Bahamas Police Force** (Alice Town tel. 242/347-3144, South Bimini tel. 242/347-3424) by dialing 919, 911, or tel. 242/347-9919.

Andros

There are several clinics on the island, including the **Nicholl's Town Community Clinic** (tel. 242/329-2055), **Mastic Point Community Clinic** (tel. 242/329-3055), and **Fresh Creek Community Clinic** (tel. 242/368-2038). Clinic hours are Monday-Friday 9am-5pm, except public holidays. For emergency services, contact the **Royal Bahamas Police Force** in Nicholl's Town (tel. 242/329-2353 or 242/329-2221), Fresh Creek (tel. 242/368-2626), or Cargill Creek (tel. 242/368-5090), or by dialing 919 or 911.

Clinics are the **Mangrove Cay Community Clinic** (Mangrove Cay tel. 242/369-0089) and the **Green Community Clinic** (Kemp's Bay, South Andros, tel. 242/369-4849). Clinic hours are Monday-Friday 9am-5pm, except holidays. For emergency services, contact the **Royal Bahamas Police Force** in Mangrove Cay (tel. 242/369-0083), Kemp's Bay (tel. 242/369-4733), or by dialing 919 or 911.

The Berry Islands

Try the **Bullock's Harbour Community Clinic** (tel. 242/367-8400, Mon.-Fri. 9am-5pm except holidays). **Police** are in **Bullock's Harbour** (tel. 242/367-8344) or at the **Airport Police Station** (tel. 242/367-8096), or dial 919 or 911.

Long Island

Health clinics include **Clarence Town Community Clinic** (tel. 242/337-3333), **Deadman's Cay Community Clinic** (tel. 242/337-1222 or 242/337-1242), and **Simms Community Clinic** (tel. 242/338-8488). Clinic hours are Monday-Friday 9am-5pm, except public holidays. For emergency services, contact the **Royal Bahamas Police Force** in Clarence Town (tel. 242/337-3919), in Deadman's Cay (tel. 242/337-0999), in Simms (tel. 242/338-8555), in Stella Maris (tel. 242/338-2222), or by dialing 919 or 911. The **Air Ambulance** (tel. 242/323-2186) and **Bahamas Air and Sea Rescue Association** (BASRA, tel. 242/325-8864) are also available.

Cat Island

Try the **Bain Town Community Clinic** (tel. 242/342-5057), **Old Bight Community Clinic** (tel. 242/342-3121), **Bight Community Clinic** (tel. 242/342-4049), or **Orange Creek Community Clinic** (tel. 242/354-4050). All clinics are open Monday-Friday 9am-5pm, except public holidays. For emergency services, contact the **Royal Bahamas Police Force** in Arthur's Town (tel. 242/354-2046) or New Bight (tel. 242/324-3039), or by dialing 919 or 911.

San Salvador

Try the **Cockburn Town Community Clinic** (tel. 242/331-2105 or 242/331-2106, Mon.-Fri. 9am-5pm except public holidays). For emergency services, contact the **Royal Bahamas Police Force** in Cockburn Town (tel. 242/331-2919), or by dialing 919 or 911.

CRIME

The Bahamas has gotten a bad rap, especially with the United States setting alerts and travel advisories, marking the Bahamas as "critical" at times. Since 2016 there has been a 26 percent drop in crime. The opening of Baha Mar has provided more jobs, and there is a sense of economic stability. Since most of the crime is due to lack of jobs, income, and economic instability, any upswing in the economy is directly related to a decrease in crime. There have only been a handful of critical incidents involving foreigners and tourists over the past 10 years. A tourist was murdered in 2013 in Nassau, but that person was in a bad part of town in the early hours of the morning and attempted to stop a purse theft. Unfortunately theft is an issue in the more heavily touristed parts of downtown Nassau, and there have been numerous incidents of rape and sexual assault. But when incidents occur, its usually late at night, and alcohol and drugs are involved.

The vast majority of violent crime occurs between gangs in "over the hill" parts of Nassau where tourists normally don't go. Criminals carry knives and firearms, but unless provoked, they will not resort to violence, and are mostly engaging in snatch-and-grab theft. Armed robbers are going after jewelry, cell phones, and cash. If you are confronted, comply with their demands and make the encounter as brief as possible. Report it immediately to the authorities. The water-sports rental industry is loosely regulated, and sexual assaults by motorized watercraft operators have been reported, mostly on Paradise Island. Keep your wits about you, taking the same precautions you would while traveling anywhere. Moderate your alcohol intake, and do your best to stay close to your resort or hotel at night.

SUN SAFETY

The sun's rays are more direct at this latitude than in other parts of the world, and you can easily find yourself with an uncomfortable sunburn or the victim of heat stroke and exhaustion if you don't take necessary precautions. Always wear sunscreen. A hat and a rash top are also recommended.

MOSQUITO-BORNE ILLNESSES

Every few years, dengue fever becomes an issue, and in the past several years there have been alerts about the Zika virus. Both of these diseases are transmitted by mosquitoes. Insect repellent is recommended, especially in the summer months and rainy season, to avoid mosquito bites. If you aren't fond of DEET, look into locally made Abaco Neem products. They offer a mosquito repellent lotion made with the extract of the neem tree.

WATER

In Nassau, the city water is safe to drink from the tap—you won't get sick—but it's not recommended. Locals buy water in one- or five-gallon jugs at food stores and gas stations. On some islands, the water is simply taken from ground reserves without processing, so it's upward of 70 percent salt water. Higher-end resorts on Out Islands have their own reverse osmosis systems, so drinking from the tap is completely safe, and better than any bottled water you could buy. Check with your hotel or resort as to what type of water is coming out of the taps, and what they recommend about purchasing bottled water.

Travel Tips

WHAT TO PACK

The Bahamas is a maritime environment, so any weather condition can be expected, from pouring rain to water spouts and heavy winds. In the winter you'll see locals wearing long pants and even sweaters at night. It is recommended to bring a layering sweater or cover-up for fall, winter, and spring. If you plan to go boating, bring a long-sleeved shirt or an SPF rash top, a hat, and sunglasses. A raincoat is not necessary, as rain showers quickly pass, and you can usually hang out seeking shelter somewhere until it passes. Bring two swimsuits, one you can hang to dry and the other to wear. You'll likely be living in your swimwear. Swimsuit cover-ups are acceptable everywhere. Bring one or two resort-casual outfits to wear to dinner in the evenings. You'll find that people tend to dress up more in Nassau, but attire is very casual in the islands. Bring your own sunscreen, since sunscreen is expensive to purchase on arrival.

WHEN TO GO

High season is December-April, with the peak being Christmas, New Year's, Easter weekend and spring break periods. Slow season is the end of August (when school starts) through November. Expect hotels and restaurants in the Out Islands to be closed during this time. If you're really looking for peace and quiet, and the best rates on hotels, this is a nice time to go, but it's typically windless, hot, and buggy, with the threat of hurricanes. For shoulder season and midrange rates, opt for May-July. Hurricane Season is officially June 1-November 31, but the most active period is August-October. If you are booking during this time, make sure you check with your hotel and airlines about their refund and cancellation policy. If "the big one" is coming, you may not even be allowed into the country.

MONEY

Bahamas banknotes are colorful, featuring the queen and a number of Bahamian specialties, including the Elbow Cay Reef Lighthouse, flamingos, and the yellow elder on the $10, Junkanoo characters on the $5, and a blue marlin on the $100. The Bahamian dollar exchanges at 1:1 with the U.S. dollar, but do your best to exchange your Bahamian cash back into U.S. dollars while you are still in The Bahamas, as you will likely only get 60% from a bank in the United States. U.S. and Bahamian notes are accepted everywhere.

Banks and ATMs are available on many islands, but smaller Out Island may not have a bank, so be sure to check before you travel, and be prepared with cash. Power outages often affect the ability to use credit card as well. Banks are open typically Monday-Thursday 9am-3:30pm and later on Friday, until 4:30pm. Also be sure to notify your bank and credit-card companies of your travel plans, as they are notorious for blocking transactions when purchases are made abroad.

Several years ago, before the VAT (sales tax) was established, many restaurants had an itemized receipt listing "tax." There was no tax in the country, this was actually a 15-percent gratuity for the staff, so many patrons ended up double tipping. Now a 12 percent VAT is added to each bill, and a separate 15-percent gratuity is usually included. Some restaurants don't include the gratuity, so check the bill. The normal rate is 20 percent, so feel free to add an additional gratuity if you enjoyed your service.

The Bahamas is an expensive country, and the farther you venture from Nassau, the more expensive it becomes. Although you can sometimes make your way around inexpensively, don't arrive with the intent of going on a budget vacation.

COMMUNICATIONS

Phones and Cell Phones

Bahamian cell phone carriers have agreements with most U.S. and Canadian cell carriers, and many international phones work in Nassau. In the Out Islands, it may be more limited, depending on which service provider you have. Traditionally, charges for phone calls are $3 per minute for all calls in and out, so it is very pricey to use your phone regularly. If you have an unlocked cell phone or GSM, you can buy a SIM card from BTC or Aliv, the two local carriers. You can get prepaid minutes and data packages. You can also buy a cell phone for under $100 and set up a prepaid plan. For using maps, you can download the Maps.me app for The Bahamas and use it without data or Wi-Fi. Many people use Whatsapp for texting and phone calls because it can be used on Wi-Fi. Most resorts and many restaurants have Wi-Fi, so you'll likely be fine utilizing your device by connecting to Wi-Fi.

Shipping and Postal Service

If you need to receive or ship anything, DHL, FexEx, and UPS have offices in Nassau and Freeport. If you need anything delivered to an Out Island, call the shipping company and confirm arrangements, and they will receive the package in Nassau and take care of forwarding it to you. It is not recommended to use the Bahamian Post Office unless you are just sending a post card. Average sending and receiving time with standard postal services can be several months.

WEIGHTS AND MEASURES

The imperial system, similar to U.S. measures, is used—Fahrenheit is used for temperature, and miles per hour for traffic speeds. The Bahamas is in the eastern time zone, and daylight saving is observed, on the same schedule as in the United States.

OPPORTUNITIES FOR STUDY AND EMPLOYMENT

The Bahamas is one of the more difficult countries to obtain permission to gain employment due to strict policies to provide jobs first to Bahamians. It is possible, with specialty positions, and if your employer is willing to apply for a work permit for you, and after it has been agreed that there are no Bahamians qualified for the position.

There are, however, opportunities for study and for employment with several educational facilities and research stations throughout The Bahamas. **The Island School** at Cape Eleuthera offers fall and spring terms for high school students, six-week summer sessions for high school and college students, and gap-year programs for college students. Students receive scuba certification, work with research scientists, and get hands-on experience in sustainability and conservation, and have an opportunity for cultural immersion at local schools. There are opportunities for employment in the fields of teaching, coordinating, and marketing. Check their website for current job postings.

The **Forfar Field Station** in North Andros offers field study programs in marine biology, geology, and island ecology. Check with them for internships and full-time positions. The **Bimini Sharklab** in South Bimini offers biology and ecology courses for college students, opportunities for visiting and studying scientists, and volunteer programs. **The University of The Bahamas** has a campus in Nassau and in Grand Bahama and offers job opportunities for international professors, and opportunities for international students in all major educational fields, with a heavy focus in business, hospitality, and tourism studies. **The Gerace Research Centre** in San Salvador is an affiliation of the University of The Bahamas with a focus in archeology, biology, geology, and marine science.

ACCESS FOR TRAVELERS WITH DISABILITIES

The Bahamas is not the most disability friendly country, and there is nothing like the Americans with Disability Act. Although the major hotels and resorts have accessible rooms available, getting around can prove a challenge in a wheelchair or if you have mobility difficulties. The sidewalks are uneven and sometimes nonexistent, and most local places will not have an accessible restroom or facilities available. **Cardinal Mobility** (www.cardinalmobility.com) offers wheelchair rentals on Paradise Island.

TRAVELING WITH CHILDREN

Although children are welcome most everywhere in The Bahamas, check with restaurants and hotels about their child policy. Certain restaurants don't allow young children in the evenings, and some tours have age limits. Sandals and a few other resorts are adults-only.

You'll find most everything you need with regard to baby food and diapers. Bahamians call all diapers "Pampers," regardless of the brand. Bahamians love children and usually make an effort to ensure children are enjoying themselves.

A word of warning about dogs: Many visitors assume that all dogs are approachable, but don't let your child pet any dog, unless you have established with the owner that the dog is people-friendly. Street Potcakes and even pets are very different than those in more socialized settings in the United States and Canada, and many of them tend to have low tolerance for children. Keep your child away to prevent potential bites.

TRAVELING WITH PETS

If you plan to travel with a pet, you will need to start your application process with the **Department of Agriculture** (tel. 242/325-7413, www.bahamas.gov.bs) well in advance. Allow 1-2 months for the paperwork to be processed, although you may be able to expedite it by calling and checking on the status often. Politely nagging is the most effective way of getting anything done. Go to the Department of Agriculture section of the government website and download the form. Fill it out and mail in the $10 fee. They will send you a form back to bring to your vet within 48 hours of traveling to sign off on your animal's health and shots. The signed form is presented to customs upon arrival in The Bahamas.

Check with the airline on their pet policy, as some don't fly with pets when it's over a certain temperature. There are limited hotels and vacation rentals that allow pets, and it's not a very pet-friendly country in general. There are no dog parks, and dogs aren't always welcome in public places and in restaurants. Small dogs have been killed by street Potcakes, so keep a close watch on your dog at all times, and don't assume that any dog is friendly, even another domesticated pet.

WOMEN TRAVELING ALONE

Despite the crime warnings, it is relatively safe for women to travel alone. The Bahamas is a patriarchal society, and Bahamian women have fewer rights than men do in certain respects, compared to other first world countries, so there is still a mentality of women being the inferior gender. Traveling alone, you may get queries about where you husband or partner is, because it's not common for any Bahamian woman to travel solo. But Bahamian men are for the most part respectful of women, with a gentlemanly nature, holding the door open or going out of their way to carry a heavy item.

Independent women may have a difficult time with men making dismissive comments, but you're better off laughing it off. Bahamians love to banter, so go ahead and light-heartedly tell them that you're extremely capable, and they will be more impressed than anything. As with anywhere in the world, be wary of your surroundings and limit alcohol intake, as sexual assault and rape do occur. Don't walk around at night on your own.

Weddings and Honeymoons

The Bahamas is a dream destination for a destination wedding and for a romantic honeymoon. The Bahamas enjoys its matrimonial tourism and, therefore, makes marriage a straightforward process. Certain hotels specialize in weddings, so do some research and see if you can get a package deal with a resort or hotel. Harbour Island is a popular place for weddings due to the wedding facilities available, ease of access, and a variety of options for diversions and accommodations for guests. Brides and grooms have the option of getting married in a historic church or on a dreamy white-sand beach. Honeymooners enjoy empty beaches and romantic sunsets throughout the Out Islands.

Couples must be in The Bahamas for 24 hours prior to applying for a marriage license. The marriage license needs to be obtained at least one day prior to the wedding and costs $100. Applicants must be interviewed by the administrator. Birth certificates and a notarized affidavit are required. If appropriate, you'll also need divorce papers, a former spouse's death certificate, or parental consent if under age 18. Same-sex marriages are not legal in The Bahamas.

SENIOR TRAVELERS

If you are an active traveler and can get around easily on your own, The Bahamas is an enjoyable place. The pace is slow, and even scenic drives can be enjoyable, especially in the Out Islands. Medical services aren't as accessible outside of Nassau and Freeport, so consider that if you are concerned about proximity to hospitals and pharmacies.

GAY AND LESBIAN TRAVELERS

Historically, gays and lesbians have been discriminated against, and The Bahamas had strict antigay laws due to the Christian Council's influence on society. Most Bahamians are conservative Christians, and LGBT rights did not fit in with the belief system. But times are changing, and there is more support within the community. LGBT travelers are finding it to be a friendlier place. There are no laws that protect LGBT people, and same sex marriages are illegal, but there are few crimes targeted at LGBT people. For the most part, you will receive the same friendly treatment as anyone else. As with opposite-sex couples, discretion with public displays of affection is advised.

Tourist Information

The **Bahamas Ministry of Tourism** (www.bahamas.com) and the **Out Islands Promotions Board** (www.myoutislands.com) have information on visiting and travel planning. The Grand Bahama Tourist Board separately runs www.grandbahamavacations.com with information specific to Grand Bahama.

TOURIST OFFICES

The Bahamas Ministry of Tourism (tel. 242/356-0435, U.S. tel. 800/224-2627, www.bahamas.com) is an excellent source for information on the island regions, activities, and travel information. Give them a call, and they will be happy to help you plan your time and discover local events. Once you have arrived on the island, pick up the ***What to Do*** guide for up-to-date information. You can find it at the airport and hotels or at www.bahamasnet.com.

Bahamas Out Islands Promotions Board (tel. 242/322-1140, www.myoutislands.com) is a separate entity from the Ministry of Tourism, focusing only on the Out Islands (any islands other than New Providence and Grand Bahama). Information specific to the Out Islands can be found on the website, such as activities, sights, travel stories, and promotions. Look for the ongoing Fly Free and Air Credit promotions with participating BIOPB member hotels.

If you're interested in connecting with a Bahamian ambassador during your visit, in order to learn more about the culture and lifestyle, contact the **People-to-People Program** (tel. 242/367-3067, www.bahamas.com/people-to-people) or sign up online. Advance reservations to pair you with an ambassador are recommended.

Grand Bahama

Visitor information centers with representatives from the Ministry of Tourism can be found at the Grand Bahama International Airport, Freeport Cruise Ship Dock, and at the Port Lucaya Marketplace. Pick up maps and local brochures and get general island information at these centers. **The Grand Bahama Island Tourism Board** (tel. 242/352-8386 or www.grandbahamavacations.com) will be happy to assist you with specific information regarding your visit to the island. Make sure to pick up the ***What to Do*** guide to Grand Bahama upon arrival. They can be found at the airport, hotels, and many retail stores, or at www.bahamasnet.com. **The Ministry of Tourism** (tel. 242/350-8600) can provide visitor information.

The Abacos

Abaco Tourist Office & Information Center (tel. 242/699-0152, www.bahamas.com) has a location at the Government Complex, near Tropical Shipping off S. C. Bootle Highway, to assist you with aspects of your Abaco visit. You can also stop in to the Ministry of Tourism visitor's center (Mon.-Fri. 9am-5pm) in the Harbour Place Building on Queen Elizabeth Drive, just before Bay Street, to pick up brochures.

Eleuthera, Harbour Island, and Spanish Wells

Visit the **Governor's Harbour Tourist Office** (Queen's Hwy., tel. 242/332-2142, www.bahamas.com) or the **Harbour Island Tourist Office** (Bay St., tel. 242/333-2621, www.bahamas.com) as a place to pick up maps and guides.

The Exumas

In George Town where the circular town road meets at the south end of Lake Victoria, visit the **Exuma Tourist Office** (Turnquest Star Plaza, George Town, tel. 242/336-2430, www.bahamas.com) to pick up maps and get local area information.

Bimini

Bimini Tourist Office of the Ministry of Tourism (tel. 242/347-3528 or 242/347-3529, Mon.-Fri. 9am-5pm, www.bahamas.com) has two locations: next to the Craft Centre, and farther north on King's Highway. Stop in for maps and information.

Andros

Central Andros Tourist Office (Mayne Plaza, Fresh Creek, tel. 242/368-2286, Mon.-Fri. 9am-5pm, www.bahamas.com) doesn't offer much in the way of brochures, but the staff is helpful in pointing you in the right direction. **South Andros Tourist Office** (Queen's Hwy., Congo Town, tel. 242/369-1688, www.bahamas.com, Mon.-Fri. 9am-5pm) is located near the Congo Town Airport.

The Berry Islands

For visitor information on The Berry Islands, contact the **Berry Islands Tourist Office** (William Dean Hwy., Bullock's Harbour, tel. 242/451-0404 or 242/225-8947, visit www.bahamas.com, www.myoutislands.com).

Long Island

Long Island Ministry of Tourism (tel. 242/338-8668, Mon.-Fri. 9am-5pm, www.bahamas.com) is located on Queen's Highway in Salt Pond.

San Salvador

Just south of Riding Rock Marina, the **San Salvador Tourist Office** (Cockburn Town, tel. 242/331-1928, Mon.-Fri. 9am-5pm) can provide maps and information about the island.

MAPS

Google Maps (maps.google.com) is a great resource to get a sense of the geographical area. If you use your smart phone while you are in the islands, you can use the Google Maps app, but you will be charged for data roaming. If you'd like to use a map on your phone without using data, get the Maps.me app and download The Bahamas map while you are on Wi-Fi. The app works by using the GPS on your phone and will show you where you are on the map so you can see the surrounding streets. You can't view the satellite version, and you can't get navigation directions, but utilizing a map while you are on the go is helpful nevertheless.

If you arrive by sea, you might want to invest in a set of Explorer Charts. There are three chart books in full color on water-resistant paper covering individual islands and regions with useful information for visiting boaters, including marinas, local food stores, and services. The three chart books are *Near Bahamas* (including Grand Bahama, Bimini, Abacos, Berrys, Andros, and Nassau), *Exumas and Ragged Islands*, and *Far Bahamas* (including Eleuthera, Cat Island, Long Island, San Salvador, and Acklins and Crooked Island).

Resources

Suggested Reading

HISTORY AND MEMOIR

Albury, Kate A. *Life on a Rock,* 2009. A memoir of five years spent managing the island of Highbourne Cay in the Northern Exumas. Albury discusses the challenges and at times life threatening circumstances.

Albury, Paul. *The Story of The Bahamas,* 1976. The history and culture of the people of The Bahamas in the form of a story.

Barratt, Peter. *Bahama Saga: The Epic Story of The Bahama Islands,* 2004. Stories and adventures of the three distinct races of people that have called the Bahama islands home in the past several hundred years. This includes the indigenous people of the islands, the original European settlers, and enslaved Africans. New historical findings make this book fairly dated, with older ideas not currently relevant.

Beeler, MayCay, *Buccaneer: The Provocative Odyssey of Jack Reed, Adventurer, Drug Smuggler and Pilot Extraordinaire,* 2014. Jack Reed was Carlos Lehder's favorite pilot, based on Norman's Cay during the height of the drug smuggling days. Reed was eventually jailed for not ratting out cosmugglers.

Cottman, Evans W. *Out Island Doctor,* 3rd ed., 1999. A biography of a middle-aged man who left a small Midwestern town and moved to The Bahamas to start a new life in the 1940s. The story is based in The Abacos and depicts the often humorous accounts of island life with an inside perspective on the culture and language of islanders.

Kirkpatrick, Sidney D. *Turning the Tide,* 2010. Richard Novak, American professor, was invited by Carlos Lehder to Norman's Cay to study the hammerhead shark population. Novak was quickly immersed in the Medellin Cartel's successful drug-running operation at the time. An entertaining read but not considered a fully factual account of events.

Lawlor, A., and J. Lawlor. *The Harbour Island Story,* 2008. A fantastic and in-depth history of the original European settlers in North Eleuthera, starting with the Eleuthera Adventurers. The book gives detailed accounts of settlers, families, and economic cycles in Harbour Island. More of a history book-type read as opposed to a story.

McCaslin, John. *Weed Man: The Remarkable Journey of Jimmy Divine,* 2011. The memoir of Bahamian Jimmy Moree, who got involved in weed running from Nassau to Florida in the 1970s. Working with the Chief, he was one of the most successful weed runners of the time.

Riley, Sandra. *Homeward Bound: A History of the Bahama Islands to 1850 with a Definitive study of Abaco in the American Loyalist Plantation Period,* 2000. Interesting read relating to family genealogy relevant to the islands of The Abacos.

Van der Water, Fredric F. *The Real McCoy,* 2007. A biography of the rum-running era during U.S. prohibition. Bill McCoy was an American pioneer in rum-running based in Nassau. He was known not to dilute his moonshine whisky, which a lot of rum runners did. Because he was known for his good-quality whisky, the phrase "the real McCoy" was coined, meaning "the real thing."

Wilder, Robert. *Wind from the Carolinas,* 1997. Probably one of the most widely read historical accounts of The Bahamas, in the form of a story that spans multiple generations from the original Loyalists settlers in the Carolinas and their adventures in establishing plantations in The Exumas.

FICTION

Buffett, Jimmy. *A Salty Piece of Land,* 2005. Following the adventures of Tully Mars and his horse, he makes his way from the snowy mountains of Wyoming to a fictional island in Central America. He meets a pirate woman who is intent on finding a replacement Fresnel lens for her red- and white-striped lighthouse. It is thought that the lighthouse is based on the Elbow Cay Reef Lighthouse in Hope Town, and gives readers a bit of background on the importance and rarity of these lenses.

Hiaasen, Carl. *Bad Monkey,* 2015. A cop and detective-fiction novel with plenty of humor, action, and adventure. The story takes place between Florida and The Bahamas.

MUSIC

Bahamas: Islands of Song. A compilation of music from The Bahamas, including goombay, rake-and-scrape, spiritual, and guitar music. All performers participated in the 1994 Festival of American Folklife, an annual event put on by the Smithsonian Institute Center for Folklife and Cultural Heritage in Washington DC.

Suggested Viewing

Bahama Blue by Parallux Film Productions. A six-part documentary TV series delving into geography, wildlife, and sealife. Each episode delves into a unique feature of The Bahamas, including blue holes and caves, mangroves, sandflats, and coral reefs.

Black Sails by Platinum Dunes. A historical adventure TV series that takes place in New Providence and Harbour Island in the early 1700s. It focuses on the new Loyalist settlers, the pirates that used Nassau Harbour as home port, and their threat to maritime trade.

Blow by New Line Cinema. Johnny Depp stars in the story of George Jung and his involvement with the Medellin Cartel and cocaine smuggling from Columbia to the United States in the 1970s. The Bahamas was used as a stopping point, and Norman's Cay appeared in the movie, although it wasn't actually filmed in The Bahamas.

Cargo by Kareem Mortimer. Produced and directed by Bahamian Kareem Mortimer and filmed in The Bahamas, Cargo takes a closer look at the illegal human trafficking of Haitians as they make their way from Haiti to Florida through The Bahamas.

Flipper by the Bubble Factory. Starring Paul Hogan and Elijah Wood, the movie was filmed at Stuart Cove in Nassau and utilized many local residents for all aspects of production.

The Islands of The Bahamas by QCPTV. A short promotional film about the Out Islands of The Bahamas, with interviews from hotel owners and activities operators, about the people, culture, and rich natural beauty. Available on YouTube.

Return to Norman's Cay, produced by May-Cay Beeler, directed by R. J. Gritter. A documentary depicting stories of the colorful history of one of the most notorious drug-running bases of operation in the world.

Thunderball by Elon Productions. A 1965 James Bond spy film featuring Sean Connery, adapted from the Ian Flemming novel. Bond is tasked with finding stolen atomic bombs, which leads him to the islands of The Bahamas. Scenes were filmed in Nassau and at Thunderball Grotto near Staniel Cay in The Exumas.

When Pigs Swim: The Film by GIV Bahamas. A short 15-minute film about the swimming pigs of The Exumas. www.whenpigsswimexuma.com.

Internet Resources

Ministry of Tourism
www.bahamas.com
Responsible for the development and promotion of the islands of The Bahamas.

Out Islands Promotions Board
www.myoutislands.com
An organization focused on the promotion of all islands of The Bahamas, except New Providence and Grand Bahama.

Grand Bahama Tourist Board
www.grandbahamavacations.com
Tourist information for Grand Bahama island.

Out Island Life
www.outislandlifebahamas.com
Information for travelers and potential real estate investors.

Government of The Bahamas
www.bahamas.gov.bs
The official site of the government of The Bahamas.

The Bahamas National Trust
www.bnt.bs
A nonprofit organization that protects and manages the national parks.

United States Embassy in The Bahamas
www.bs.usembassy.gov
The official site of the U.S. Embassy in The Bahamas.

Bahamas Local
www.bahamaslocal.com
The search engine for Bahamas based businesses, with over 15,000 business listings.

The Tribune
www.tribune242.com
Bahamas news, based in Nassau.

The Guardian
www.thenassauguardian.com
Bahamas news, based in Nassau.

Index

A

B

F

G

H

INDEX

T

UVWXYZ

List of Maps

Front Map

Discover The Bahamas

Nassau and New Providence

Freeport and Grand Bahama

The Abacos

Eleuthera, Harbour Island, and Spanish Wells

The Exumas

Bimini, Andros, and The Berry Islands

The Southern Bahamas

Photo Credits

All photos © Mariah Laine Moyle except page 7 © (bottom left) Gina Nelson; page 11 © (top) Imphot | dreamstime.com; (middle) David and Joy Turner; page 13 © (top) allnaturalbeth | dreamstime.com; page 29 © (bottom) Megan Kinnahan; page 45 © Fin Photo - Stuart Cove's Dive Bahamas; page 49 © Gina Jenkins; page 98 © Lyndah Wells; page 101 © Lighthouse Point at Grand Lucayan/Dragonfly Image Partners; page 139 © Megan Kinnahan; page 168 © alexshalamov | dreamstime.com; page 173 © Angela Dovel; page 234 © Out Island Flyers; page 238 © (bottom) Tiamo Resort; page 249 © David and Joy Turner; page 262 © Gina Nelson; page 267 © Tiamo Resort; page 286 © James "Docky" Smith; page 310 © Heather Carey/Bahamas National Trust

MAP SYMBOLS

Expressway	Highlight	Airport	Golf Course
Primary Road	City/Town	Airfield	Parking Area
Secondary Road	State Capital	Mountain	Archaeological Site
Unpaved Road	National Capital	Unique Natural Feature	Church
Trail	Point of Interest	Waterfall	Gas Station
Ferry	Accommodation	Park	Dive Site
Railroad	Restaurant/Bar	Trailhead	Mangrove
Pedestrian Walkway	Other Location	Lighthouse	Reef
Stairs	Campground		Swamp

CONVERSION TABLES

°C = (°F - 32) / 1.8
°F = (°C x 1.8) + 32
1 inch = 2.54 centimeters (cm)
1 foot = 0.304 meters (m)
1 yard = 0.914 meters
1 mile = 1.6093 kilometers (km)
1 km = 0.6214 miles
1 fathom = 1.8288 m
1 chain = 20.1168 m
1 furlong = 201.168 m
1 acre = 0.4047 hectares
1 sq km = 100 hectares
1 sq mile = 2.59 square km
1 ounce = 28.35 grams
1 pound = 0.4536 kilograms
1 short ton = 0.90718 metric ton
1 short ton = 2,000 pounds
1 long ton = 1.016 metric tons
1 long ton = 2,240 pounds
1 metric ton = 1,000 kilograms
1 quart = 0.94635 liters
1 US gallon = 3.7854 liters
1 Imperial gallon = 4.5459 liters
1 nautical mile = 1.852 km

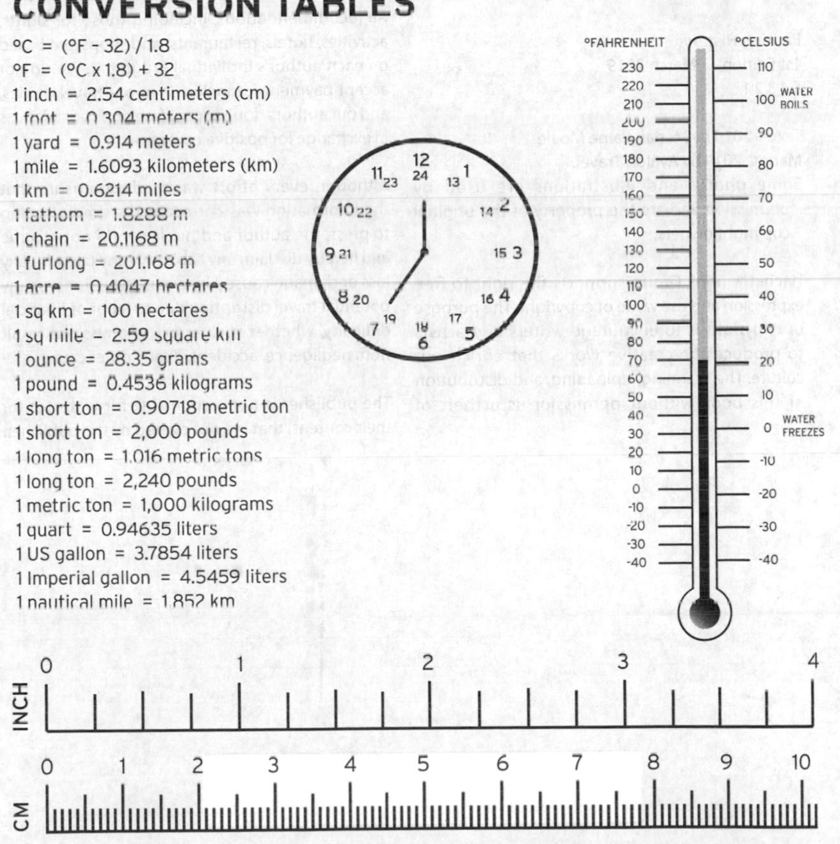

MOON BAHAMAS
Avalon Travel
Hachette Book Group
1700 Fourth Street
Berkeley, CA 94710, USA
www.moon.com

Editor: Kimberly Ehart
Series Manager: Kathryn Ettinger
Copy Editor: Christopher Church
Graphics and Production Coordinator: Darren Alessi
Cover Design: Faceout Studios, Charles Brock
Interior Design: Domini Dragoone
Moon Logo: Tim McGrath
Map Editor: Kat Bennett
Cartographers: Lohnes + Wright and Kat Bennett
Indexer: Greg Jewett

ISBN-13: 978-1-64049-322-3

Printing History
1st Edition — March 2019
5 4 3 2 1

Front cover photo: Beach chairs sit on a beach facing the Caribbean Sea in The Bahamas © Steve Murray / Alamy Stock Photo
Back cover photo: Water sports equipment on Eleuthera © Byvalet | Dreamstime.com

Printed in China by RR Donnelley